Multicultural Education

EIGHTH EDITION

ISSUES AND PERSPECTIVES

Edited by

JAMES A. BANKS

University of Washington, Seattle

CHERRY A. McGEE BANKS

University of Washington, Bothell

D1455416

Vice President & Executive Publisher	Jay O'Callaghan
Acquisitions Editor	Robert Johnston
Assistant Editor	Brittany Cheetham
Content Manager	Lucille Buonocore
Senior Production Editor	Anna Melhorn
Marketing Manager	Margaret Barret
Creative Director	Harry Nolan
Production Management Services	Suzanne Ingrao/Ingrao Associates
Photo Editor	Lisa Gee
Editorial Assistant	Maura Gilligan
Cover Designer	Wendy Lai
Cover Image Credit	Transformation, "Learn and Create. Transform the Future" by T. J. Young, Haida. Copyright © 2010 by Garfinkel Publications, inc., Vancouver, B. C. , Canada. Reprinted with permission. All rights reserved.

This book was set in Times Roman by Wiley Australia and printed and bound by Courier Kendallville. The cover was printed by Courier Kendallville.

Copyright © 2013, 2010, 2006 John Wiley & Sons, Inc. All rights reserved. No part of this publication may be reproduced, stored in a retrieval system or transmitted in any form or by any means, electronic, mechanical, photocopying, recording, scanning or otherwise, except as permitted under Sections 107 or 108 of the 1976 United States Copyright Act, without either the prior written permission of the Publisher, or authorization through payment of the appropriate per-copy fee to the Copyright Clearance Center, Inc. 222 Rosewood Drive, Danvers, MA 01923, website www.copyright.com. Requests to the Publisher for permission should be addressed to the Permissions Department, John Wiley & Sons, Inc., 111 River Street, Hoboken, NJ 07030-5774, (201)748-6011, fax (201)748-6008, website http://www.wiley.com/go/permissions.

Founded in 1807, John Wiley & Sons, Inc. has been a valued source of knowledge and understanding for more than 200 years, helping people around the world meet their needs and fulfill their aspirations. Our company is built on a foundation of principles that include responsibility to the communities we serve and where we live and work. In 2008, we launched a Corporate Citizenship Initiative, a global effort to address the environmental, social, economic, and ethical challenges we face in our business. Among the issues we are addressing are carbon impact, paper specifications and procurement, ethical conduct within our business and among our vendors, and community and charitable support. For more information, please visit our website: www.wiley.com/go/citizenship.

Evaluation copies are provided to qualified academics and professionals for review purposes only, for use in their courses during the next academic year. These copies are licensed and may not be sold or transferred to a third party. Upon completion of the review period, please return the evaluation copy to Wiley. Return instructions and a free of charge return shipping label are available at www.wiley.com/go/returnlabel. Outside of the United States, please contact your local representative.

ISBN 978-1118-36008-8

Printed in the United States of America

10 9 8 7 6 5 4 3 2 1

Preface

Racial, cultural, ethnic, linguistic, and religious diversity in the United States as well as in nations around the world has deepened since the seventh edition of this book was published (Banks, 2009, 2012). The 2010 census reveals that the United States is becoming increasingly non-White because the growth in the population of people of color is greatly outpacing the growth of the non-Hispanic White population. Most of the increase in the population of the United States that occurred between 2000 and 2010 resulted from the rapidly growing Latino population. There were 50 million Latinos living in the United States in 2010, which was approximately one in six of U.S. residents (Mather, Pollard, & Jacobsen, 2011). While the population of people of color increased substantially between 2000 and 2010, the non-Hispanic White population decreased from 69 to 64 percent of the nation's population. Ethnic minorities made up 92 percent of the growth of the U. S. population between 2000 and 2010. While the population of Latinos and Asians increased significantly between 2000 and 2010, the African American population increased only slightly, from 12.3 to 12.6 percent of the U.S. population (Rastogi, Johnson, Hoeffel, & Drewery, 2011).

Students who speak a language other than English at home are the fastest-growing segment of the U.S. student population, making up approximately 19.8 percent of the school-age population in 2010 (U.S. Census Bureau, 2010). A significant percentage of these students have undocumented parents or are themselves undocumented (Peréz, 2011; Yoshikawa, 2011). Yet most of the nation's teachers are White, female, middle class (or aspiring to the middle class), and monolingual. There is thus a wide and growing ethnic, cultural, social-class, and linguistic gap between many of the nation's teachers and their students. Teachers are faced with both the challenges and opportunities of dealing with diversity creatively and constructively in their classrooms and schools.

Multicultural Education: Issues and Perspectives, eighth edition, is designed to help current and future educators acquire the concepts, paradigms, and explanations needed to become effective practitioners in culturally, racially, and linguistically diverse classrooms and schools. An important goal of this book is to help teachers attain a sophisticated understanding of the concept of culture and to view race, class, gender, and exceptionality as interacting concepts rather than as separate and distinct. Consequently, *intersectionality*—or how race, class, gender, and exceptionality are fluid variables that interact in complex ways—is an overarching concept in this book (Caruthers & Carter, 2012; Grant & Zwier, 2012).

Teacher education programs should help teachers attain the knowledge, attitudes, and skills needed to work effectively with students from diverse groups as well as help students from mainstream groups develop cross-cultural knowledge, values, and competencies. The eighth edition of this book—which can help teachers to attain these goals—has been revised to reflect current and emerging research, theories, and practices related to the education of students from both genders and from different cultural, racial, ethnic, and language groups. Exceptionality is part of our concept of diversity because there are exceptional students in each group discussed in this book.

Chapters 2, 4, 8, and 11 are new to this eighth edition. All of the chapters from the previous edition have been revised to reflect new research, theories, census data, statistics, interpretations, and developments. The Multicultural Resources in the Appendix have been substantially revised and updated. We have also added two new sections to the Multicultural Resources: "Special Education and Equity" and "Gifted Education and Equity." The Glossary has been revised to incorporate 2010 census data and new developments in the field.

This book consists of six parts. The chapters in Part I discuss how race, gender, class, and exceptionality interact to influence student behavior. Social class and religion and their effects on education are discussed in Part II. Part III describes how educational opportunity differs for female and male students and how schools can foster gender equity as well as create safe educational environments for lesbian, gay, bisexual, and transgender (LGBT) students. Chapter 8, which is new to this eighth edition, describes how race and gender are interacting rather than separate and discrete variables. The issues, problems, and opportunities for educating students of color and students with language differences are discussed in Part IV. Chapter 11, which focuses on racism in the "backstage" and "frontstage," describes ways in which racism is manifested in the "backstage" in what many commentators are describing as a postracial period in the United States. Part V focuses on exceptionality, describing the issues involved in creating equal educational opportunity for students who have disabilities and for those who are gifted. The final part, Part VI, discusses multicultural education as a process of school reform and ways to increase student academic achievement and to work more effectively with parents. The Appendix consists of a list of books for further reading and a Glossary that defines many of the key concepts and terms used throughout this book.

ACKNOWLEDGMENTS

We are grateful to a number of colleagues who helped with the preparation of this eighth edition. First, we would like to thank the authors, who revised their chapters in a timely and professional way and incorporated our editorial suggestions. We would also like to thank the following authors for taking time from their busy schedules to write new chapters for this eighth edition and for revising them in response to on our editorial comments:

Chapter 2— Christina Convertinto, Bradley A. Levinson, and Norma Gonzáles

Chapter 4— Lois Weis

Chapter 8 —Diane S. Pollard

Chapter 11— Leslie H. Picca and Ruth Thompson-Miller

We would like to thank the following individuals, who helped us revise the list of Multicultural Resources that is included in the Appendix:

Donna Ford, Vanderbilt University

Khyati Joshi, Fairleigh Dickinson University

Charles Lippy, University of Tennessee at Chattanooga

Cris Mayo, University of Illinois at Champaign–Urbana

Diana S. Pollard, University of Wisconsin at Milwaukee

David Sadker, American University and University of Arizona

Sara Schneider Kavanagh, University of Washington, Seattle

Federico R. Waitoller, University of Illinois at Chicago

Lois Weis, University of Buffalo

Karen Zimmerman, American University

We also thank Tao Wang, a research assistant at the Center for Multicultural Education at the University of Washington, for helping to update the statistics in this eighth edition. We wish to acknowledge Kimberly McKaig for her help with the proofreading of this edition.

We hope the contributors to this eighth edition as well as the scholars who helped us bring this edition to fruition in other ways will take pride in it. Reading and editing the chapters for this eighth edition have enriched us.

James A. Banks
Cherry A. McGee Banks

REFERENCES

Banks, J. A. (Ed.). (2009). *The Routledge companion to multicultural education.* New York and London: Routledge.

Banks, J. A. (Ed.). (2012). *The encyclopedia of diversity in education* (4 vols.). Thousand Oaks, CA: Sage.

Caruthers, J., & Carter, P. L. (2012). Intersectionality of race, class, gender, and ethnicity. In J. A. Banks (Ed.), *Encyclopedia of diversity in education* (vol. 2 pp. 1270-1272). Thousand Oaks, CA: Sage.

Grant, C. A., & Zwier, E. (2012). Intersectionality and education. In J. A. Banks (Ed.), *Encyclopedia of diversity in education* (vol. 2, pp. 1262-1270). Thousand Oaks, CA: Sage.

Mather, M., Pollard, K., & Jacobsen, L. A. (2011). *First results from the 2000 Census.* Washington, DC: Population Reference Bureau.

Peréz, W. (2011). *Americans by heart: Undocumented Latino students and the promise of higher education.* New York: Teachers College Press.

Rastogi, S., Johnson, T. D., Hoeffel, E. M., & Drewery, M. P., Jr. (2011). *The Black population: 2010* (2010 census briefs). Washington, DC: United States Census Bureau. Retrieved February 6, 2012, from www.census.gov/prod/cen2010/briefs/c2010br-06.pdf.

U.S. Census Bureau. (2010). *2010 American community survey.* Retrieved November 14, 2011, from http://factfinder2.census.gov/faces/tableservices/jsf/pages/productview.xhtml?pid=ACS_10_1YR_S1603&prodType=table.

Yoshikawa, H. (2011). *Immigrants raising citizens: Undocumented parents and their young children.* New York: Russell Sage Foundation.

Contents

2   Culture, Teaching, and Learning

25

by Christina Convertino, Bradley A. Levinson, and Norma González

3   Race, Class, Gender, and Disability in the Classroom

43

by Carl A. Grant and Christine E. Sleeter

PART II   SOCIAL CLASS AND RELIGION

63

4   Social Class and Education

65

by Lois Weis

PART IV   RACE, ETHNICITY, AND LANGUAGE   177

10   Approaches to Multicultural Curriculum Reform   181

by James A. Banks

11   Backstage Racism: Implications for Teaching   201

by Leslie H. Picca and Ruth Thompson-Miller

12   Language Diversity and Schooling   219

by Manka M. Varghese and Tom T. Stritikus

PART V   EXCEPTIONALITY   241

13   Educational Equality for Students with Disabilities   245

by Sara C. Bicard and William L. Heward

All students should experience educational equity in the schools.

Rob Lewine/Getty Images, Inc.

Ariel Skelley/Blend RF/Glow Images

StockbrokerXtra/Glow Images

Issues and Concepts

The three chapters in Part I define the major concepts and issues in multicultural education, describe the diverse meanings of culture, and describe the ways in which such variables as race, class, gender, and exceptionality influence student behavior. Various aspects and definitions of culture are discussed. Culture is conceptualized as a dynamic and complex process of construction; its invisible and implicit characteristics are emphasized. The problems that result when culture is essentialized are described.

Multicultural education is an idea, an educational reform movement, and a process whose major goal is to change the structure of educational institutions so that male and female students, exceptional students, and students who are members of diverse racial, ethnic, language, and cultural groups will have an equal chance to achieve academically in school. It is necessary to conceptualize the school as a social system in order to implement multicultural education successfully. Each major variable in the school—such as its culture, its power relationships, the curriculum and materials, and the attitudes and beliefs of the staff—must be changed in ways that will allow the school to promote educational equality for students from diverse groups.

To transform the schools, educators must be knowledgeable about the influence of particular groups on student behavior. The chapters in this part of the book describe the nature of culture and groups in the United States as well as the ways in which they interact to influence student behavior.

Rob Lewine/Getty Images, Inc.

Multicultural Education: Characteristics and Goals

CHAPTER 1

James A. Banks

The Nature of Multicultural Education

Multicultural education is at least three things: an idea or concept, an educational reform movement, and a process. Multicultural education incorporates the idea that all students—regardless of their gender; sexual orientation; social class; and ethnic, racial, or cultural characteristics—should have an equal opportunity to learn in school. Another important idea in multicultural education is that some students, because of these characteristics, have a better chance to learn in schools as they are currently structured than do students who belong to other groups or who have different cultural characteristics.

Some institutional characteristics of schools systematically deny some groups of students equal educational opportunities. For example, in the early grades, girls and boys achieve equally in mathematics and science. However, at advanced levels of mathematics, boys score higher on tests such as the SAT college entrance examination (Boaler & Sengupta-Irving, 2012). Girls are less likely than boys to participate in class discussions and to be encouraged by teachers to participate. Girls are more likely than boys to be silent in the classroom. However, not all school practices favor males. As Sadker and Zittleman point out in Chapter 6, boys are more likely to be disciplined than are girls, even when their behavior does not differ from that of girls. They are also more likely than girls to be classified as learning disabled (Donovan & Cross, 2002). Males of color, especially African American males, experience a highly disproportionate rate of disciplinary actions and suspensions in school. Some scholars, such as Noguera (2008), have described the serious problems that African American males experience in school and in the wider society. Women outpace men in graduation rates from both high school and from college and universities. The percentage of bachelor's degrees earned by women increased from 24 percent in 1950 to 57 percent in 2009 (Snyder & Dillow, 2011).

In the early grades, the academic achievement of students of color, such as African Americans, Latinos, and American Indians, is close to parity with the achievement of White mainstream students (Steele, 2003). However, the longer these students of color remain in school, the more their achievement lags behind that of White mainstream students. Social-class status is also strongly related to academic achievement. Weis, in Chapter 4—as well as Knapp and Yoon (2012)—describe the powerful ways in which social class influences students' opportunities to learn.

Exceptional students, whether they are physically or mentally disabled or gifted and talented, often find that they do not experience equal educational opportunities in the schools. The chapters in Part V describe the problems that exceptional students experience in schools and suggest ways that teachers and other educators can increase their chances for educational success.

Multicultural education is also a reform movement that is trying to change the schools and other educational institutions so that students from all social-class, gender, racial, language, and cultural groups will have an equal opportunity to learn. Multicultural education involves changes in the total school or educational environment; it is not limited to curricular changes (Banks, 2009; Banks & Banks, 2004). The variables in the school environment that multicultural education tries to transform are discussed later in this chapter and illustrated in Figure 1.5. Multicultural education is also a process whose goals will never be fully realized.

Educational equality, like liberty and justice, is an ideal toward which human beings work but which they never fully attain. Racism, sexism, heterosexism, and ableism (disability discrimination) will exist to some extent no matter how hard we work to eliminate these problems. When prejudice and discrimination are reduced toward one group, they are usually directed toward another group or take new forms. Whenever groups are identified and labeled, categorization occurs. When categorization occurs, members of in-groups favor in-group members and discriminate against out-groups (Bigler & Hughes, 2009). This process can occur without groups having a history of conflict, animosity, or competition, and without their having physical differences or any other kind of important difference. Social psychologists call this process *social identity theory* or the *minimal group paradigm* (Rothbart & John, 1993). Because the goals of multicultural education can never be fully attained, we should work continuously to increase educational equality for all students. Multicultural education must be viewed as an ongoing process, not as something that we "do" and thereby solve the problems that are the targets of multicultural educational reform.

The Historical Development of Multicultural Education

Multicultural education grew out of the ferment of the Civil Rights Movement of the 1960s. During this decade, African Americans embarked on a quest for their rights that was unprecedented in the United States. A major goal of this movement was to eliminate discrimination in public accommodations, housing, employment, and education. Its consequences had a significant influence on educational institutions as ethnic groups—first African Americans and then other groups—demanded that the schools and other educational institutions reform curricula to reflect their experiences, histories, cultures, and perspectives. Ethnic groups also demanded that the schools hire more Black and Brown teachers and administrators so that their children would have more successful role models. Ethnic groups pushed for community control of schools in their neighborhoods and for the revision of textbooks to make them reflect the diversity of peoples in the United States.

The first responses of schools and educators to the ethnic movements of the 1960s were hurried (Banks, 2006). Courses and programs were developed without the thought and careful planning needed to make them educationally sound or to institutionalize them within the educational system. Holidays and other special days, ethnic celebrations, and courses that focused on one ethnic group were the dominant characteristics of school reforms related to ethnic and cultural diversity during the 1960s and early 1970s. Grant and Sleeter, in Chapter 3, call this approach "single-group studies." The ethnic studies courses developed and implemented during this period were usually electives and were taken primarily by students who were members of the group that was the subject of the course.

The visible success of the Civil Rights Movement, plus growing rage and a liberal national atmosphere, stimulated other marginalized groups to take actions to eliminate discrimination against them and to demand that the educational system respond to their needs, aspirations, cultures, and histories. The women's rights movement emerged as one of the most significant social reform movements of the 20th century (Brewer, 2012). During the 1960s and 1970s, discrimination against women in employment, income, and education was widespread and often blatant. The women's rights movement articulated and publicized how discrimination and institutionalized sexism limited the opportunities of women and adversely affected the nation. The leaders of this movement, such as Betty Friedan and Gloria Steinem, demanded that political, social, economic, and educational institutions act to eliminate sex discrimination and to provide opportunities for women to actualize their talents and realize their ambitions. Major goals of the women's rights movement included offering equal pay for equal work, eliminating laws that discriminated against women and made them second-class citizens, hiring more women in leadership positions, and increasing the participation of men in household work and child rearing.

When *feminists* (people who work for the political, social, and economic equality of the sexes) looked at educational institutions, they noted problems similar to those identified by ethnic groups of color. Textbooks and curricula were dominated by men; women were largely invisible. Feminists pointed out that history textbooks were dominated by political and military history—areas in which men had been the main participants (Trecker, 1973). Social and family history and the history of labor and of ordinary people were largely ignored. Feminists pushed for the revision of textbooks to include more history about the important roles of women in the development of the United States and the world. They also demanded that more women be hired for administrative positions in the schools. Although most teachers in the elementary schools were women, most administrators were men.

Other marginalized groups, stimulated by the social ferment and the quest for human rights during the 1970s, articulated their grievances and demanded that institutions be reformed so they would face less discrimination and acquire more human rights. People with disabilities, senior citizens, and gays and lesbians formed groups that organized politically during this period and made significant inroads in changing institutions and laws. Advocates for citizens with disabilities attained significant legal victories during the 1970s. The Education for All Handicapped Children Act of 1975 (P.L. 94–142)—which required that students with disabilities be educated in the least restricted environment and institutionalized the word *mainstreaming* in education—was perhaps the most significant legal victory of the movement for the rights of students with disabilities in education (see Chapters 13 and 14).

How Multicultural Education Developed

Multicultural education emerged from the diverse courses, programs, and practices that educational institutions devised to respond to the demands, needs, and aspirations of the various groups. Consequently, as Grant and Sleeter point out in Chapter 3, multicultural education in actual practice is not one identifiable course or educational program. Rather, practicing educators use the term *multicultural education* to describe a wide variety of programs and practices related to educational equity, women, ethnic groups, language minorities, low-income groups, LGBT (lesbian, gay, bisexual, and transgender) people, and people with disabilities. In one school district, multicultural education may mean a curriculum that incorporates the experiences of ethnic groups of color; in another, a program may include the experiences of both ethnic groups and women. In a third school district, this term may be used the way it is by me and by other authors, such as Nieto and Bode (2012) and Sleeter and Grant (2009)—that is, to mean a total school reform effort designed to increase educational equity for a range of cultural, ethnic, and income groups. This broader and more comprehensive notion of multicultural education is discussed in the last part of this chapter. It differs from the limited concept of multicultural education in which it is viewed as curriculum reform.

The Nature of Culture in the United States

The United States, like other Western nation-states such as the United Kingdom, Australia, and Canada, is a multicultural society. The United States consists of a shared core culture as well as many subcultures. In this book, we call the larger shared core culture the *macroculture;* the smaller cultures, which are a part of the core culture, are called *microcultures*. It is important to distinguish the macroculture from the various microcultures because the values, norms, and characteristics of the mainstream (macroculture) are frequently mediated by, as well as interpreted and expressed differently within, various microcultures. These differences often lead to cultural misunderstandings, conflicts, and institutionalized discrimination.

Students who are members of certain cultural, religious, and ethnic groups are sometimes socialized to act and think in certain ways at home but differently at school (Au, 2011). In her study of African American students and families in Trackton, a working-class community in the Piedmont Carolinas, Heath (1983) found that the pattern of language use in school was very different from the pattern used at home. At home, most of the children's interaction with adults consisted of imperatives or commands. At school, questions were the dominant form of interactions between teachers and students. A challenge that multicultural education faces is how to help students from diverse groups mediate between their home and community cultures and the school culture. Students should acquire the knowledge, attitudes, and skills needed to function effectively in each cultural setting. They should also be competent to function within and across other microcultures in their society, within the national macroculture, and within the world community (Banks, 2004).

The Meaning of Culture

Bullivant (1993) defines *culture* as a group's program for survival in and adaptation to its environment. The cultural program consists of knowledge, concepts, and values shared by group members through systems of communication. Culture also consists of the shared beliefs, symbols, and interpretations within a human group. Most social scientists today view culture as consisting primarily of the symbolic, ideational, and intangible aspects of human societies. The essence of a culture is not its artifacts, tools, or other tangible cultural elements but how the members of the group interpret, use, and perceive them. It is the values, symbols, interpretations, and perspectives that distinguish one people from another in modernized societies; it is not material objects and other tangible aspects of human societies (Kuper, 1999). People in a culture usually interpret the meanings of symbols, artifacts, and behaviors in the same or in similar ways.

Identification and Description of the U.S. Core Culture

The United States, like other nation-states, has a shared set of values, ideations, and symbols that constitute the core or overarching culture. This culture is shared to some extent by all of the diverse cultural and ethnic groups that make up the nation-state. It is difficult to identify and describe the overarching culture in the United States because it is such a diverse and complex nation. It is easier to identify the core culture within an isolated premodern society, such as the Maoris before the Europeans came to New Zealand, than within highly pluralistic, modernized societies such as the United States, Canada, and Australia (Penetito, 2010).

When trying to identify the distinguishing characteristics of U.S. culture, one should realize that the political institutions in the United States, which reflect some of the nation's core values, were heavily influenced by the British. U.S. political ideals and institutions were also influenced by Native American political institutions and practices, especially those related to making group decisions, such as in the League of the Iroquois (Weatherford, 1988).

Equality

A key component in the U.S. core culture is the idea, expressed in the Declaration of Independence, that "all men are created equal, that they are endowed by their Creator with certain unalienable rights, that among these are life, liberty, and the pursuit of happiness." When this idea was expressed by the nation's founding fathers in 1776, it was considered radical. A common belief in the 18th century was that human beings were not born with equal rights—that some people had few rights and others, such as kings, had divine rights given by God. When considering the idea that "all men are created equal" is a key component of U.S. culture, one should remember to distinguish between a nation's ideals and its actual practices as well as between the meaning of the idea when it was expressed in 1776 and its meaning today. When the nation's founding fathers expressed this idea, their conception of men was limited to White males who owned property (Foner, 1998). White men without property, White women, and all African Americans and Indians were not included in their notion of people who were equal or who had "certain unalienable Rights."

Although the idea of equality expressed by the founding fathers in 1776 had a very limited meaning at that time, it has proven to be a powerful and important idea in the quest for human rights in the United States. Throughout the nation's history since 1776, marginalized and excluded groups such as women, African Americans, Native Americans, and other cultural and ethnic groups have used this idea to justify and defend the extension of human rights to them and to end institutional discrimination, such as sexism, racism, and discrimination against people with disabilities (Branch, 2006). As a result, human rights have gradually been extended to various groups throughout U.S. history. The extension of these rights has been neither constant nor linear. Rather, periods of the extension of rights have often been followed by periods of retrenchment and conservatism. Schlesinger (1986) calls these patterns "cycles of American history." The United States is still a long way from realizing the ideals expressed in the Declaration of Independence. However, these ideals remain an important part of U.S. culture and are still used by marginalized groups to justify their struggles for human rights and equality.

Individualism and Individual Opportunity

Two other important ideas in the common overarching U.S. culture are individualism and individual social mobility (Stewart & Bennett, 1991). Individualism as an ideal is extreme in the U.S. core culture. Individual success is more important than commitment to family, community, and nation-state. An individual is expected to achieve success solely by his or her own efforts. Many people in the United States believe that a person can go from rags to riches within a generation and that every American-born boy can, but not necessarily will, become president. Individuals are expected to achieve success by hard work and to pull themselves up by their bootstraps. This idea was epitomized by fictional characters such as Ragged Dick, one of the heroes created by the popular writer Horatio Alger. Ragged Dick attained success by valiantly overcoming poverty and adversity. A related belief is that if a person does not succeed, it is because of the person's own shortcomings, such as being lazy or unambitious; failure is consequently the person's own fault. These beliefs are taught in the schools with success stories and myths about such U.S. heroes as George Washington, Thomas Jefferson, and Abraham Lincoln.

The beliefs about individualism in U.S. culture are related to the Protestant work ethic. This is the belief that hard work by the individual is morally good and that laziness is sinful. This belief is a legacy of the British Puritan settlers in colonial New England. It has had a powerful and significant influence on U.S. culture.

The belief in individual opportunity has proven tenacious in U.S. society. It remains strong in American culture despite the fact that individuals' chances for upward social, economic, and educational mobility in the United States are highly related to the social-class, ethnic, gender, and other ascribed groups to which they belong (Knapp & Yoon, 2012; Weis, Chapter 4, this book). The findings of social science research, as well as the chapters in this book, document the extent of social-class stratification in the United States and the ways in which people's opportunities in life are strongly influenced by the groups to which they belong (Willis, 1977), yet the belief in individual opportunity remains strong in the United States.

Individualism and Groupism

Although the groups to which people belong have a major influence on their life chances in the United States, Americans—particularly those in the mainstream—are highly *individualistic* in their value orientations and behaviors. The nuclear family reinforces individualism in U.S. culture. One result of this strong individualism is that married children usually expect their older parents to live independently or in homes for senior citizens rather than with them. The strong individualism in U.S. culture contrasts sharply with the groupism and group commitment found in Asian nations, such as China and Japan (Butterfield, 1982; Reischauer, 1981). Individualism is viewed rather negatively in these societies. One is expected to be committed first to the family and group and then to oneself. Some U.S. social scientists, such as Lasch (1978) and Bellah, Madsen, Sullivan, Swidler, and Tipton (1985), lament the extent of individualism in U.S. society. They believe it is harmful to the common national culture. Some observers believe that groupism is too strong in China and Japan and that individualism should be more valued in those nations. Perhaps modernized, pluralistic nation-states can best benefit from a balance between individualism and groupism, with neither characteristic dominating.

Expansionism and Manifest Destiny

Other overarching U.S. values that social scientists have identified include the desire to conquer or exploit the natural environment, the focus on materialism and consumption, and the belief in the nation's inherent superiority. These beliefs justified Manifest Destiny and U.S. expansion to the West and into other nations and the annexation of one-third of Mexico's territory in 1848. These observations, which reveal the less positive side of U.S. national values, have been developed by social scientists interested in understanding the complex nature of U.S. society (Appleby, Hunt, & Jacob, 1994).

In his discussion of the nature of values in U.S. society, Myrdal (1944/1962) contends that a major ethical inconsistency exists in U.S. society. He calls this inconsistency "the American dilemma." He states that American creed values, such as equality and human dignity, exist in U.S. society as ideals. However, they exist alongside the institutionalized discriminatory treatment of African Americans and other ethnic and cultural groups in U.S. society. This variance creates a dilemma in the American mind because Americans try to reconcile their democratic ideals with their treatment of marginalized groups. Myrdal states that this dilemma has been an important factor that has enabled ethnic groups to fight discrimination effectively. In their efforts to resolve their dilemma when the inconsistencies between their ideals and actions are pointed out to them by human rights advocates, Americans, according to Myrdal, often support the elimination of practices that are inconsistent with their democratic ideals or the American creed. Some writers have refuted Myrdal's hypothesis and contend that most individuals in the United States do not experience such a dilemma related to the gap between American ideals and racial discrimination (Ellison, 1995).

Microcultures in the United States

A nation as culturally diverse as the United States consists of a common overarching culture as well as a series of microcultures (see Figure 1.1). These microcultures share most of the core values of the nation-state, but these values are often mediated by the various microcultures and are interpreted differently within them. Microcultures sometimes have values that are somewhat alien to the national core culture. Also, some of the core national values and behaviors may seem somewhat alien in certain microcultures or may take different forms.

The strong belief in individuality and individualism that exists within the national macro-culture is often much less endorsed by some ethnic communities and is somewhat alien within

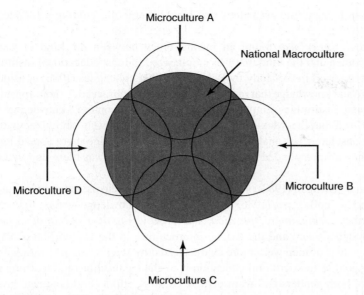

Microculture A

National Macroculture

Microculture D

Microculture B

Microculture C

FIGURE 1.1 Microcultures and the National Macroculture

The shaded area represents the national macroculture. A, B, C, and D represent microcultures that consist of unique institutions, values, and cultural elements that are nonuniversalized and are shared primarily by members of specific cultural groups. A major goal of the school should be to help students acquire the knowledge, skills, and attitudes needed to function effectively within the national macroculture, within their own microcultures, and within and across other microcultures.

Source: James A. Banks. (2006). *Cultural Diversity and Education: Foundations, Curriculum and Teaching,* 5th ed. (Boston: Allyn & Bacon), p. 73. Used with permission of the author.

them. African Americans and Latinos who have not experienced high levels of cultural assimilation into the mainstream culture are much more group oriented than are mainstream Americans. Schools in the United States are highly individualistic in their learning and teaching styles, evaluation procedures, and norms. Many students, particularly African Americans, Latinos, and Native Americans, are group oriented (Irvine & York, 2001; Lee, 2006). These students experience problems in the school's highly individualistic learning environment. Teachers can enhance the learning opportunities of these students, who are also called *field dependent* or *field sensitive,* by using cooperative teaching strategies that have been developed and field-tested by researchers such as Slavin (2012) and Cohen and Lotan (2004).

Some theories and research indicate that female students may have preferred ways of knowing, thinking, and learning that differ to some extent from those most often preferred by males (Belenky, Clinchy, Goldberger, & Tarule, 1986; Halpern, 1986; Taylor, Gilligan, & Sullivan, 1995). Maher (1987) describes the dominant inquiry model used in social science as male constructed and dominated. She contends that the model strives for objectivity: "Personal feelings, biases, and prejudices are considered inevitable limitations" (p. 186). Feminist pedagogy is based on different assumptions about the nature of knowledge and results in a different teaching method. According to Maher and Tetreault (1994), feminist pedagogy enhances the learning of females and deepens the insight of males. In Chapter 7, Tetreault describes feminist pedagogy techniques she uses to motivate students and to enhance their understandings.

After completing a major research study on women's ways of knowing, Belenky and colleagues (1986) concluded that conceptions of knowledge and truth in the core culture and in educational institutions "have been shaped throughout history by the male-dominated majority culture. Drawing on their own perspectives and visions, men have constructed the prevailing theories, written history, and set values that have become the guiding principles for men and women alike" (p. 5).

These researchers also found an inconsistency between the kind of knowledge most appealing to women and the kind that was emphasized in most educational institutions. Most of the women interviewed in the study by Belenky and her colleagues (1986) considered personalized knowledge and knowledge that resulted from firsthand observation most appealing. However, most educational institutions emphasize abstract, "out-of-context" knowledge. Ramírez and Castañeda (1974) found that Mexican American students who were socialized within traditional cultures also considered personalized and humanized knowledge more appealing than abstract knowledge. They also responded positively to knowledge that was presented in a humanized or story format.

Research by Gilligan (1982) provides some clues that help us better understand the findings by Belenky and her colleagues (1986) about the kind of knowledge women find most appealing. Gilligan describes *caring, interconnection,* and *sensitivity to the needs of other people* as dominant values among women and the female microculture in the United States. By contrast, she found that the values of men were more characterized by *separation* and *individualism.*

A major goal of multicultural education is to change teaching and learning approaches so that students of both genders and from diverse cultural, ethnic, and language groups will have equal opportunities to learn in educational institutions. This goal suggests that major changes should be made in the ways that educational programs are conceptualized, organized, and taught. Educational approaches need to be transformed in order to create effective multicultural classrooms and schools.

In her research on identifying and labeling students with mental retardation, Mercer (1973) found that a disproportionate number of African American and Mexican American students were labeled mentally retarded because the testing procedures used in intelligence tests "reflect the abilities and skills valued by the American core culture" (p. 32), which Mercer describes as predominantly White, Anglo-Saxon, and middle and upper class. She also points out that measures of general intelligence consist primarily of items related to verbal skills and knowledge. Most African American and Latino students are socialized within microcultures that differ in significant ways from the U.S. core culture. These students often have not had an equal opportunity to learn the knowledge and skills that are measured in mental ability tests. Consequently, a disproportionate number of African American and Latino students are labeled mentally retarded and are placed in classes for slow learners (Donovan & Cross, 2002). Mental retardation, as Mercer points out, is a socially determined status. When students are placed in classes for the mentally retarded, the self-fulfilling prophecy develops. Students begin to act and think as though they are mentally retarded.

Groups and Group Identification

Thus far, this chapter has discussed the various microcultures that make up U.S. society. Individuals learn the values, symbols, and other components of their culture from their social group. The group is the social system that carries a culture. People belong to and live in social groups (Bullivant, 1993). A group is a collectivity of persons who share an identity, a feeling of unity. A group is also a social system that has a social structure of interrelated roles (Theodorson & Theodorson, 1969). The group's program for survival, values, ideations, and shared symbols constitutes its culture (Kuper, 1999).

The study of groups is the major focus in sociology. Sociologists believe that the group has a strong influence on the behavior of individuals, that behavior is shaped by group norms, and that the group equips individuals with the behavior patterns needed to adapt to their physical, social, and metaphysical environments. Sociologists also assume that groups have independent characteristics; they are more than aggregates of individuals. Groups possess a continuity that transcends the lives of individuals.

Sociologists also assume that knowledge about groups to which an individual belongs provides important clues to and explanations for the individual's behavior. Goodman and Marx (1982) write, "Such factors as shared religion, nationality, age, sex, marital status, and education have proved to be important determinants of what people believe, feel, and do" (p. 7). Although membership in a gender, racial, ethnic, social-class, or religious group can provide us with important clues about individuals' behavior, it cannot enable us to predict behavior. Knowing one's group affiliation can enable us to state that a certain type of behavior is probable. Membership in a particular group does not determine behavior but makes certain types of behavior more probable.

There are several important reasons why knowledge of group characteristics and modalities can enable us to predict the probability of an individual's behavior but not the precise behavior. This is, in part, because each individual belongs to several groups at the same time (see Figure 1.2). An individual may be White, Catholic, female, and middle class, all at the same time. That individual might have a strong identification with one of these groups and a very weak or almost nonexistent identification with another. A person can be a member of a particular group, such as the Catholic Church, and have a weak identification with the group and a weak commitment to the tenets of the Catholic faith. Religious identification might be another individual's strongest group identification. Identification with and attachments to different groups may also conflict. A woman who has a strong Catholic identification but is also a feminist might find it difficult to reconcile her beliefs about equality for women with some positions of the Catholic Church, such as its prohibiting women from being ordained as priests.

The more we know about a student's level of identification with a particular group and the extent to which socialization has taken place within that group, the more accurately we can predict, explain, and understand the student's behavior in the classroom. Knowledge of the importance of a group to a student at a particular time of life and within a particular social context will also help us understand the student's behavior. Ethnic identity may become more important to a person who becomes part of an ethnic minority when he or she previously belonged to the majority. Many Whites who have moved from the U.S. mainland to Hawaii have commented on

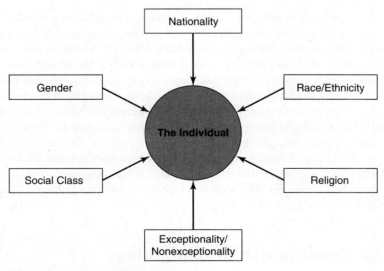

FIGURE 1.2 Multiple Group Memberships

An individual belongs to several different groups at the same time. This figure shows the major groups discussed in this book.

how their sense of ethnic identity increased and they began to feel marginalized. Group identity may also increase when the group feels threatened, when a social movement arises to promote its rights, or when the group attempts to revitalize its culture.

The Teaching Implications of Group Identification

What are the implications of group membership and group identity for teaching? As you read the chapters in this book that describe the characteristics of the two gender groups and of social-class, racial, ethnic, religious, language, LGBT, and exceptional groups, bear in mind that individuals within these groups manifest these behaviors to various degrees. Also remember that individual students are members of several of these groups at the same time. The core U.S. culture was described earlier as having highly individualistic values and beliefs. However, research by Gilligan (1982) indicates that the values of women, as compared with those of men, are more often characterized by caring, interconnection, and sensitivity to the needs of others. This observation indicates how core values within the macroculture are often mediated by microcultures within various gender, ethnic, and cultural groups.

Also as stated previously, researchers have found that some students of color, such as African Americans and Mexican Americans, often have field-sensitive learning styles and therefore prefer more personalized learning approaches (Ramírez & Castañeda, 1974). Think about what this means. This research describes a group characteristic of these students, not the behavior of a particular African American or Mexican American student. It suggests that there is a higher probability that these students will have field-sensitive learning styles than will middle-class Anglo American students. However, students within all ethnic, racial, and social-class groups have different learning styles and characteristics (Irvine & York, 2001). Those groups influence students' behavior, such as their learning style, interactively because they are members of several groups at the same time. Knowledge of the characteristics of groups to which students belong, of the importance of each of these groups to them, and of the extent to which individuals have been socialized within each group will give the teacher important clues to students' behavior.

The Interaction of Race, Class, and Gender

When using our knowledge of groups to understand student behavior, we should also consider the ways in which such variables as class, race, and gender interact and intersect to influence student behavior. Middle-class and highly assimilated Mexican American students tend to be more field-independent than do lower-class and less assimilated Mexican American students. African American students tend to be more field-dependent (group oriented) than White students; females tend to be more field-dependent than male students. Therefore, it can be hypothesized that African American females would be the most field-dependent when compared to African American and White males and White females. This finding was made by Perney (1976).

Figure 1.3 illustrates how the major groupings discussed in this book—gender, race or ethnicity, social class, religion, and exceptionality—influence student behavior, both singly and interactively. The figure also shows that other variables, such as geographic region and age, also influence an individual's behavior. The ways in which these variables influence selected student behaviors are described in Table 1.1.

The Social Construction of Categories

The major variables and categories discussed in this book—such as gender, race or ethnicity, class, and exceptionality—are social categories (Berger & Luckman, 1967; Mannheim, 1936). The criteria for whether an individual belongs to one of these categories are determined by

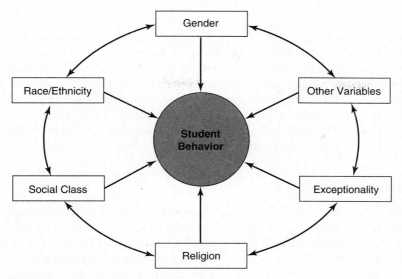

FIGURE 1.3 The Intersection of Variables

The major variables of gender, race or ethnicity, social class, religion, and exceptionality influence student behavior, both singly and interactively. Other variables, such as region and age, also influence student behavior.

human beings and consequently are socially constructed. Religion is also a social category. Religious institutions, symbols, and artifacts are created by human beings to satisfy their metaphysical needs.

These categories are usually related to individuals' physical characteristics. In some cases, as when they are individuals with severe or obvious physical disabilities, the relationship between the labels given to individuals and their physical characteristics is direct and would be made in almost any culture or social system. The relationship between categories that are used to classify individuals and their physical characteristics, however, is usually indirect and complex. Even though one's sex is determined primarily by physical characteristics (genitalia, chromosome patterns, etc.), gender is a social construction created and shaped by the society in which individuals and groups function.

Table 1.1 Singular and Combined Effects of Variables

Student Behavior	Gender Effects	Race/ Ethnicity Effects	Social- Class Effects	Religious Effects	Combined Effects
Learning Styles (Field = Independent/ Field = Dependent)	X[a]	X			X
Internality/Externality			X		
Fear of Success	X	X			?
Self-Esteem	X	X			?
Individual vs. Group Orientation	X	X	X		?

[a]An X indicates that the variable influences the student behavior that is described in the far-left column. An X in the far-right column means that research indicates that two or more variables combine to influence the described behavior. A question mark indicates that the research is unclear about the effects of the variables.

Gender

Gender consists of the socially and psychologically appropriate behavior for males and females sanctioned by and expected within a society. Gender-role expectations vary across cultures and at different times in a society and within microcultures in the same society. Traditionally, normative behavior for males and females has varied among mainstream Americans, African Americans, Native Americans, and Hispanic Americans. Gender-role expectations also vary somewhat across social classes within the same society. In the White mainstream society in the 1940s and 1950s, upper-middle-class women often received negative sanctions when they worked outside the home, whereas women in working-class families were frequently expected to become wage earners.

Sexual Orientation

The discussion of gender roles provides an appropriate context for the examination of issues related to sexual orientation (see Chapter 9). The quest by gays and lesbians for human and civil rights has been an important development within the United States and throughout the Western world in the last several decades. Sexual orientation deserves examination when human rights and social justice are discussed because it is an important identity for some individuals and groups and because many gay youths are victims of discrimination and hate crimes (Lipkin, 1999; Kavanagh, 2012). Sexual orientation is often a difficult issue for classroom discussion for both teachers and students. However, if done sensitively, it can help empower gay and lesbian students and enable them to experience social equality in the classroom. Recognition is one important manifestation of social equality (Gutmann, 2004).

Race

Race is a socially determined category that is related to physical characteristics in a complex way (Jacobson, 1998). Two individuals with nearly identical physical characteristics, or phenotypes, can be classified as members of different races in two different societies (Root, 2004). In the United States, where racial categories are well defined and highly inflexible, an individual with any acknowledged or publicly known African ancestry is considered Black (Davis, 1991). One who looks completely Caucasian but who acknowledges some African ancestry is classified as Black. Such an individual would be considered White in Puerto Rico, where hair texture, social status, and degree of eminence in the community are often as important as—if not more important—than physical characteristics in determining an individual's racial group or category. There is a saying in Puerto Rico that "money lightens," which means that upward social mobility considerably enhances an individual's opportunity to be classified as White. There is a strong relationship between race and social class in Puerto Rico and in most other Caribbean and Latin American nations.

Our discussion of race as a social category indicates that the criteria for determining the characteristics of a particular race vary across cultures, that an individual considered Black in one society may be considered White in another, and that racial categories reflect the social, economic, and political characteristics of a society.

Social Class

Social scientists find it difficult to agree on criteria for determining social class. The problem is complicated by the fact that societies are constantly in the throes of change. During the 1950s, social scientists often attributed characteristics to the lower class that are found in the middle class today, such as single-parent and female-headed households, high divorce rates, and substance abuse. Today, these characteristics are no longer rare among the middle class, even though their frequency is still higher among lower-class families. Variables such as income, education, occupation, lifestyle, and values are among the most frequently used indices to determine social-class status in the United States (Warner, 1949/1960). However, there is considerable disagreement among social scientists about which variables are the most important in determining the social-class status of an individual or family.

Social-class criteria also vary somewhat among various ethnic and racial groups in the United States. Teachers, preachers, and other service professionals were upper class in many rural African American communities in the South in the 1950s and 1960s but were considered middle class by mainstream White society. The systems of social stratification that exist in the mainstream society and in various microcultures are not necessarily identical.

Exceptionality

Exceptionality is also a social category. Whether a person is considered disabled or gifted is determined by criteria developed by society. As Shaver and Curtis (1981) point out, *disabilities* are not necessarily *handicaps*, and the two should be distinguished. They write, "A disability or combination of disabilities becomes a handicap only when the condition limits or impedes the person's ability to function normally" (p. 1). A person with a particular disability, such as having one arm, might have a successful college career, experience no barriers to achievements in college, and graduate with honors. However, this person may find that when trying to enter the job market, the opportunities are severely limited because potential employers view him or her as unable to perform well in some situations in which, in fact, this individual could perform effectively (Shaver & Curtis, 1981). This individual has a disability but is viewed as handicapped in one situation (the job market) but not in another (the university).

Mercer (1973) has extensively studied the social process by which individuals become labeled as persons with mental retardation. She points out that even though their physical characteristics may increase their chance of being labeled persons with mental retardation, the two are not perfectly correlated. Two people with the same biological characteristics may be considered persons with mental retardation in one social system but not in another one. An individual may be considered a person with mental retardation at school but not at home. Mercer writes, "Mental retardation is not a characteristic of the individual, nor a meaning inherent in behavior, but a socially determined status, which [people] may occupy in some social systems and not in others" (p. 31). She states that people can change their role by changing their social group.

The highly disproportionate number of African Americans, Latinos, and particularly males classified as learning disabled by the school indicates the extent to which exceptionality is a social category (Donovan & Cross, 2002). Mercer (1973) found that schools labeled more people mentally retarded than did any other institution. Many African American and Latino students who are labeled mentally retarded function normally and are considered normal in their homes and communities. Boys are more often classified as mentally retarded than are girls. Schools, as Mercer and other researchers have pointed out, use criteria to determine the mental ability of students of color that conflict with their home and community cultures. *Some students in all ethnic and cultural groups are mentally retarded and deserve special instruction, programs, and services, as the authors in Part V of this book suggest.* However, the percentage of students of color in these programs is too high. The percentage of students in each ethnic group labeled mentally retarded should be about the same as the total percentage of that group in school.

Giftedness is also a social category (Sapon-Shevin, 1994, 2007). Important results of the socially constructed nature of giftedness are the considerable disagreement among experts about how the concept should be defined and the often inconsistent views about how to identify gifted students (Ford & Harris, 1999). The highly disproportionate percentage of middle- and upper-middle-class mainstream students categorized as gifted compared to low-income students and students of color, such as African Americans, Latinos, and Native Americans, is also evidence of the social origin of the category.

Many students who are classified as gifted do have special talents and abilities and need special instruction. However, some students who are classified as gifted by school districts merely have parents with the knowledge, political skills, and power to force the school to classify their children as gifted, a classification that will provide them with special instruction and educational enrichment (Sapon-Shevin, 1994).

Schools should try to satisfy the needs of students with special gifts and talents; however, they should also make sure that students from all social-class, cultural, language, and ethnic groups have an equal opportunity to participate in programs for academically and creatively talented students. If schools or districts do not have in their gifted programs a population that represents their various cultural, racial, language, and ethnic groups, steps should be taken to examine the criteria used to identify gifted students and to develop procedures to correct the disproportion. Both excellence and equality should be major goals of education in a pluralistic society.

The Dimensions of Multicultural Education

When many teachers think of multicultural education, they think only or primarily of content related to ethnic, racial, and cultural groups. Conceptualizing multicultural education exclusively as content related to various ethnic and cultural groups is problematic for several reasons. Teachers who cannot easily see how their content is related to cultural issues will easily dismiss multicultural education with the argument that it is not relevant to their disciplines. This is done frequently by secondary math and science teachers.

The irrelevant-of-content argument can become a legitimized form of resistance to multicultural education when it is conceptualized primarily or exclusively as content. Math and science teachers often state that multicultural education is fine for social studies and literature teachers but that it has nothing to do with their subjects. Furthermore, they say, math and science are the same regardless of the culture or the kids. Multicultural education needs to be more broadly defined and understood so that teachers from a wide range of disciplines can respond to it in appropriate ways and resistance to it can be minimized.

Multicultural education is a broad concept with several different and important dimensions (Banks, 2004). Practicing educators can use the dimensions as a guide to school reform when trying to implement multicultural education. The dimensions are (1) content integration, (2) the knowledge construction process, (3) prejudice reduction, (4) an equity pedagogy, and (5) an empowering school culture and social structure. Each dimension is defined and illustrated in the next section.

Content Integration

Content integration deals with the extent to which teachers use examples and content from a variety of cultures and groups to illustrate key concepts, principles, generalizations, and theories in their subject area or discipline. The infusion of ethnic and cultural content into the subject area should be logical, not contrived.

More opportunities exist for the integration of ethnic and cultural content in some subject areas than in others. In the social studies, the language arts, and music, frequent and ample opportunities exist for teachers to use ethnic and cultural content to illustrate concepts, themes, and principles. There are also opportunities to integrate multicultural content into math and science. However, the opportunities are not as ample as they are in the social studies, the language arts, and music.

The Knowledge Construction Process

The knowledge construction process relates to the extent to which teachers help students to understand, investigate, and determine how the implicit cultural assumptions, frames of reference, perspectives, and biases within a discipline influence the ways in which knowledge is constructed within it (Banks, 1996).

Students can analyze the knowledge construction process in science by studying how racism has been perpetuated in science by genetic theories of intelligence, Darwinism, and eugenics. In his important book *The Mismeasure of Man,* Gould (1996) describes how scientific racism developed and was influential in the 19th and 20th centuries. Scientific racism has had and continues to have a significant influence on the interpretations of mental ability tests in the United States.

The publication of *The Bell Curve* (Herrnstein & Murray, 1994), its widespread and enthusiastic public reception, and the social context out of which it emerged provide an excellent case study for discussion and analysis by students who are studying knowledge construction (Kincheloe, Steinberg, & Gresson, 1996). Herrnstein and Murray contend that low-income groups and African Americans have fewer intellectual abilities than do other groups and that these differences are inherited. Students can examine the arguments made by the authors, their major assumptions, and how their conclusions relate to the social and political context.

Gould (1994) contends that Herrnstein and Murray's arguments reflect the social context of the times, "a historical moment of unprecedented ungenerosity, when a mood for slashing social programs can be powerfully abetted by an argument that beneficiaries cannot be helped, owing to inborn cognitive limits expressed as low I.Q. scores" (p. 139). Students should also study counterarguments to *The Bell Curve* made by respected scientists. Two good sources are *The Bell Curve Debate: History, Documents, Opinions,* edited by Jacoby and Glauberman (1995), and *Measured Lies: The Bell Curve Examined,* edited by Kincheloe and colleagues (1996).

Students can examine the knowledge construction process in the social studies when they study such units and topics as the European discovery of America and the westward movement. The teacher can ask the students the latent meanings of concepts such as the "European discovery of America" and the "New World." The students can discuss what these concepts imply or suggest about the Native American cultures that had existed in the Americas for about 40,000 years before the Europeans arrived. When studying the westward movement, the teacher can ask students these questions: Whose point of view or perspective does this concept reflect, that of the European Americans or the Lakota Sioux? Who was moving west? How might a Lakota Sioux historian describe this period in U.S. history? What are other ways of thinking about and describing the westward movement?

Prejudice Reduction

Prejudice reduction describes lessons and activities teachers use to help students develop positive attitudes toward different racial, ethnic, and cultural groups. Research indicates that children come to school with many negative attitudes toward and misconceptions about different racial and ethnic groups (Aboud, 2009; Stephan & Vogt, 2004). Research also indicates that lessons, units, and teaching materials that include content about different racial and ethnic groups can help students to develop more positive intergroup attitudes if certain conditions exist in the teaching situation (Bigler & Hughes, 2009; Stephan & Vogt). These conditions include positive images of the ethnic groups in the materials and the use of multiethnic materials in a consistent and sequential way.

Allport's (1954) contact hypothesis provides several useful guidelines for helping students to develop more positive interracial attitudes and actions in contact situations. He states that contact between groups will improve intergroup relations when the contact is characterized by these four conditions: (1) equal status, (2) common goals, (3) intergroup cooperation, and (4) support of authorities such as teachers and administrators (Pettigrew, 2004).

An Equity Pedagogy

Teachers in each discipline can analyze their teaching procedures and styles to determine the extent to which they reflect multicultural issues and concerns. An equity pedagogy exists when teachers modify their teaching in ways that will facilitate the academic achievement of students from diverse racial, cultural, gender, and social-class groups. This includes using a variety of teaching styles and approaches that are consistent with the wide range of learning styles within various cultural and ethnic groups, being demanding but highly personalized when working with groups such as Native American and Alaskan students, and using cooperative learning techniques in math and science instruction in order to enhance the academic achievement of students of color (Cohen & Lotan, 2004; Slavin, 2012).

Several chapters in this book discuss ways in which teachers can modify their instruction in order to increase the academic achievement of students from different cultural groups and from both gender groups, including the chapters that constitute Parts III and IV.

An Empowering School Culture and Social Structure

Another important dimension of multicultural education is a school culture and organization that promote gender, racial, and social-class equity. The culture and organization of the school must be examined by all members of the school staff. They all must also participate in restructuring it. Grouping and labeling practices, sports participation, disproportionality in achievement, disproportionality in enrollment in gifted and special education programs, and the interaction of the staff and the students across ethnic and racial lines are important variables that need to be examined in order to create a school culture that empowers students from diverse racial, ethnic, and language groups and from both gender groups.

Figure 1.4 summarizes the dimensions of multicultural education. The next section identifies the major variables of the school that must be changed in order to institutionalize a school culture that empowers students from diverse cultural, racial, ethnic, and social-class groups.

The School as a Social System

To implement multicultural education successfully, we must think of the school as a social system in which all of its major variables are closely interrelated. Thinking of the school as a social system suggests that we must formulate and initiate a change strategy that reforms the total school environment to implement multicultural education. The major school variables that must be reformed are presented in Figure 1.5.

Reforming any one of the variables in Figure 1.5, such as the formalized curriculum or curricular materials, is necessary but not sufficient. Multicultural and sensitive teaching materials are ineffective in the hands of teachers who have negative attitudes toward different racial, ethnic, language, and cultural groups. Such teachers are rarely likely to use multicultural materials or are likely to use them detrimentally. Thus, helping teachers and other members of the school staff to gain knowledge about diverse groups and democratic attitudes and values is essential when implementing multicultural programs.

To implement multicultural education in a school, we must reform its power relationships, verbal interaction between teachers and students, culture, curriculum, extracurricular activities, attitudes toward minority languages (Romaine, 2009), testing and assessment practices, and

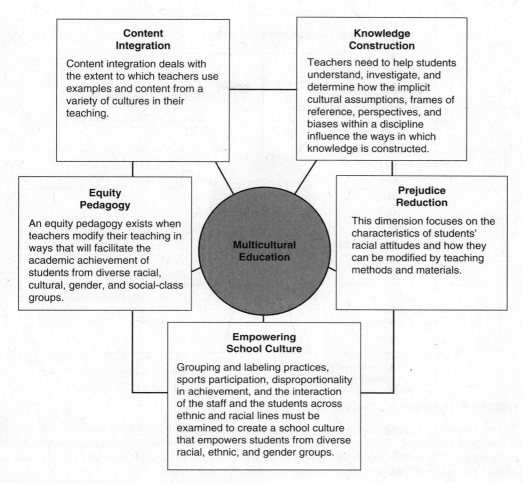

FIGURE 1.4 The Dimensions of Multicultural Education

Source: Copyright © 2009 by James A. Banks.

grouping practices. The school's institutional norms, social structures, cause–belief statements, values, and goals must be transformed and reconstructed.

Major attention should be focused on the school's hidden curriculum and its implicit norms and values. A school has both a manifest and a hidden curriculum. The manifest curriculum consists of such factors as guides, textbooks, bulletin boards, and lesson plans. These aspects of the school environment are important and must be reformed to create a school culture that promotes positive attitudes toward diverse cultural groups and helps students from these groups experience academic success. However, the school's hidden, or latent, curriculum is often more important than is its manifest or overt curriculum. *The latent curriculum* has been defined as the one that no teacher explicitly teaches but that all students learn. It is that powerful part of the school culture that communicates to students the school's attitudes toward a range of issues and problems, including how the school views them as human beings and as males, females, exceptional students, and students from various religious, cultural, racial, and ethnic groups. Jackson (1992) calls the latent curriculum the "untaught lessons."

When formulating plans for multicultural education, educators should conceptualize the school as a microculture that has norms, values, statuses, and goals like other social systems. The school has a dominant culture and a variety of microcultures. Almost all classrooms in the

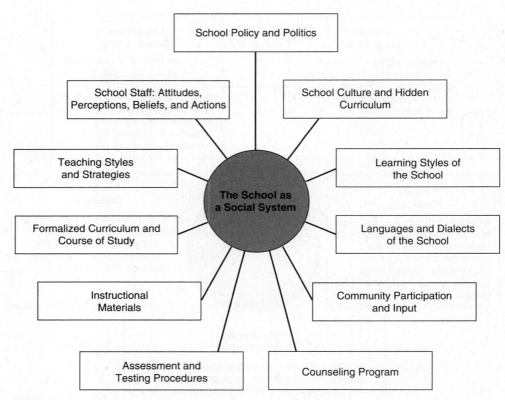

FIGURE 1.5 The School as a Social System

The total school environment is a system consisting of a number of major identifiable variables and factors, such as a school culture, school policy and politics, and the formalized curriculum and course of study. Any of these factors may be the focus of initial school reform, but changes must take place in each of them to create and sustain an effective multicultural school environment.

Source: Copyright © 2012 by James A. Banks.

United States are multicultural because White students as well as Black and Brown students are socialized within diverse cultures. Teachers also come from many different groups. As Erickson (2010) points out, all individuals—including students and teachers—are also *multicultural* because components of more than one culture or group influence their behavior. Each individual belongs to an ethnic or culture group; is gay, straight, or bisexual; and is religious or nonreligious.

Many teachers were socialized in cultures other than the Anglo mainstream, although these may be forgotten and repressed. Teachers can get in touch with their own cultures and use the perspectives and insights they acquired as vehicles for helping them relate to and understand the cultures of their students.

Summary

Multicultural education is an idea stating that all students, regardless of the groups to which they belong, such as those related to gender, ethnicity, race, culture, language, social class, religion, sexual orientation, or exceptionality, should experience educational equality in the schools. Some students, because of their particular characteristics, have a better chance to succeed in school as it is currently structured than students from other groups. Multicultural education is also a reform movement designed to bring about a transformation of the school so that students from both genders and from diverse cultural, language, and ethnic groups will have an equal chance to experience school success. Multicultural education views the school as a social system that consists of highly interrelated parts and variables. Therefore, in order to transform the school to bring about educational equality, all major components of the school must be substantially changed. A focus on any one variable in the school, such as the formalized curriculum, will not implement multicultural education.

Multicultural education is a continuing process because the idealized goals it tries to actualize—such as educational equality and the eradication of all forms of discrimination—can never be fully achieved in human society. Multicultural education, which was born during the social protest of the 1960s and 1970s, is an international movement that exists in nations throughout the world (Banks, 2008). A major goal of multicultural education is to help students to develop the knowledge, attitudes, and skills needed to function within their own microcultures, the U.S. macroculture, other microcultures, and the global community.

QUESTIONS AND ACTIVITIES

1.1 What are the three components or elements of multicultural education?

1.2 How does Banks define *multicultural education?*

1.3 Find other definitions of multicultural education in several books listed under the category "Issues and Concepts" in the Appendix to this book. How are the definitions of multicultural education in these books similar to and different from the one presented in this chapter?

1.4 In what ways did the Civil Rights and Women's Rights Movements of the 1960s and 1970s influence the development of multicultural education?

1.5 Ask several teachers and other practicing educators to give you their views and definitions of multicultural education. What generalizations can you make about their responses?

1.6 Visit a local school and, by observing several classes as well as by interviewing several teachers and the principal, describe what curricular and other practices related to multicultural education have been implemented in the school. Share your report with your classmates or workshop colleagues.

1.7 Define *macroculture* and *microculture.*

1.8 How is *culture* defined? What are the most important components of culture in a modernized society?

1.9 List and define several core or overarching values and characteristics that make up the macroculture in the United States. To what extent are these values and characteristics consistent with practices in U.S. society? To what extent are they ideals that are inconsistent with realities in U.S. society?

1.10 How is individualism viewed differently in the United States and in nations such as China and Japan? Why? What are the behavioral consequences of these varying notions of individualism?

1.11 What is the American dilemma defined by Myrdal? To what extent is this concept an accurate description of values in U.S. society? Explain.

1.12 How do the preferred ways of learning and knowing among women and students of color often influence their experiences in the schools as they are currently structured? In what ways can school reform help make the school environment more consistent with the learning and cognitive styles of women and students of color?

1.13 In what ways does the process of identifying and labeling students with mental retardation discriminate against groups such as African Americans and Latinos?

1.14 In what ways can the characteristics of a group help us understand an individual's behavior? In what ways are group characteristics limited in explaining an individual's behavior?

1.15 How do such variables as race, class, and gender interact to influence the behavior of students? Give examples to support your response.

1.16 What is meant by the "social construction of categories"? In what ways are concepts such as gender, race, social class, and exceptionality social categories?

1.17 List and define the five dimensions of multicultural education. How can these dimensions be used to facilitate school reform?

REFERENCES

Aboud, F. E. (2009). Modifying children's racial attitudes. In J. A. Banks (Ed.), *The Routledge international companion to multicultural education* (pp. 199–209). New York and London: Routledge.

Allport, G. W. (1954). *The nature of prejudice*. Reading, MA: Addison-Wesley.

Appleby, J., Hunt, L., & Jacob, M. (1994). *Telling the truth about history*. New York: Norton.

Au, K. (2011). *Literacy achievement and diversity: Keys to success for students, teachers, and schools*. New York: Teachers College Press.

Banks, J. A. (Ed.). (1996). *Multicultural education, transformative knowledge, and action*. New York: Teachers College Press.

Banks, J. A. (2004). Multicultural education: Historical development, dimensions, and practice. In J. A. Banks & C. A. M. Banks (Eds.), *Handbook of research on multicultural education* (2nd ed., pp. 3–29). San Francisco: Jossey-Bass.

Banks, J. A. (2006). *Race, culture, and education: The selected works of James A. Banks*. London & New York: Routledge.

Banks, J. A. (2008). Diversity, group identity, and citizenship education in a global age. *Educational Researcher, 37*(3), 129–139.

Banks, J. A. (Ed.). (2009). *The Routledge international companion to multicultural education*. New York and London: Routledge.

Banks, J. A., & Banks, C. A. M. (Eds.). (2004). *Handbook of research on multicultural education* (2nd ed.). San Francisco: Jossey-Bass.

Belenky, M. F., Clinchy, B. M., Goldberger, N. R., & Tarule, J. M. (1986). *Women's ways of knowing: The development of self, voice, and mind*. New York: Basic Books.

Bellah, R. N., Madsen, R., Sullivan, W. M., Swidler, A., & Tipton, S. M. (1985). *Habits of the heart: Individualism and commitment in American life*. New York: Harper & Row.

Berger, P. L., & Luckman, T. (1967). *The social construction of reality: A treatise in the sociology of knowledge*. New York: Doubleday.

Bigler, R. S., & Hughes, J. M. (2009). The nature and origins of children's racial attitudes. In J. A. Banks (Ed.), *The Routledge international companion to multicultural education* (pp. 186–198). New York & London: Routledge.

Boaler, J. & Sengupta-Irving, T. (2012). Gender and mathematics education. In J. A. Banks (Ed.), *Encyclopedia of diversity in education*. (vol. 2, pp. 972–975). Thousand Oaks, CA: Sage.

Branch, T. (2006). *At Canaan's edge: America in the King years, 1965–68*. New York: Simon & Schuster.

Brewer, R. M. (2012). Feminist movement. In J. A. Banks (Ed.), *Encyclopedia of diversity in education*. (vol. 2, pp. 896–901). Thousand Oaks, CA: Sage.

Bullivant, B. (1993). Culture: Its nature and meaning for educators. In J. A. Banks & C. A. M. Banks (Eds.), *Multicultural education: Issues and perspectives* (2nd ed., pp. 29–47). Boston: Allyn & Bacon.

Butterfield, F. (1982). *China: Alive in the bitter sea*. New York: Bantam.

Cohen, E. G., & Lotan, R. (2004). Equity in heterogeneous classrooms. In J. A. Banks & C. A. M. Banks (Eds.), *Handbook of research on multicultural education* (2nd ed., pp. 736–750). San Francisco: Jossey-Bass.

Davis, F. J. (1991). *Who is Black? One nation's definition*. University Park: Pennsylvania State University Press.

Donovan, M. S., & Cross, C. T. (Eds.). (2002). *Minority students in special and gifted education*. Washington, DC: National Academy Press.

Ellison, R. (1995). An American dilemma: A review. In J. F. Callahan (Ed.), *The collected essays of Ralph Ellison* (pp. 328–340). New York: Modern Library.

Erickson, F. (2010). Culture in society and in educational practices. In J. A. Banks & C. A. M. Banks (Eds.), *Multicultural education: Issues and perspectives* (7th ed., pp. 33–56). Hoboken, NJ: Wiley.

Foner, E. (1998). *The story of American freedom*. New York: Norton.

Ford, D. Y., & Harris, J. J., III. (1999). *Multicultural gifted education*. New York: Teachers College Press.

Gilligan, C. (1982). *In a different voice: Psychological theory and women's development*. Cambridge, MA: Harvard University Press.

Goodman, N., & Marx, G. T. (1982). *Society today* (4th ed.). New York: Random House.

Gould, S. J. (1994). Curveball. *The New Yorker, 70*(38), 139–149.

Gould, S. J. (1996). *The mismeasure of man* (rev. & exp. ed.). New York: Norton.

Gutmann, A. (2004). Unity and diversity in democratic multicultural education: Creative and destructive tensions. In J. A. Banks (Ed.), *Diversity and citizenship education: Global perspectives* (pp. 71–98). San Francisco: Jossey-Bass.

Halpern, D. F. (1986). *Sex differences in cognitive abilities*. Hillsdale, NJ: Erlbaum.

Heath, S. B. (1983). *Ways with words: Language, life, and work in communities and classrooms*. New York: Oxford University Press.

Herrnstein, R. J., & Murray, C. (1994). *The bell curve: Intelligence and class structure in American life*. New York: Free Press.

Irvine, J. J., & York, E. D. (2001). Learning styles and culturally diverse students: A literature review. In J. A. Banks & C. A. M. Banks (Eds.), *Handbook of research on multicultural education* (2nd ed., pp. 484–497). San Francisco: Jossey-Bass.

Jackson, P. W. (1992). *Untaught lessons*. New York: Teachers College Press.

Jacobson, M. F. (1998). *Whiteness of a different color: European immigrants and the alchemy of race*. Cambridge, MA: Harvard University Press.

Jacoby, R., & Glauberman, N. (Eds.). (1995). *The bell curve debate: History, documents, opinions*. New York: Times Books/Random House.

Kavanagh, S. S. (2012). Lesbian, gay, bisexual, and transgender students: Conceptual approaches in research literature. In J. A. Banks (Ed.), *Encyclopedia of diversity in education* (vol. 3, pp. 1387-1390. Thousand Oaks, CA: Sage.

Kincheloe, J. L., Steinberg, S. R., & Gresson, A. D., III (Eds.). (1996). *Measured lies: The bell curve examined*. New York: St. Martin's Press.

Knapp, M. S., & Yoon, I. (2012). Social class and education. In J. A. Banks (Ed.), *Encyclopedia of diversity in education*. Thousand Oaks, CA: Sage.

Kuper, A. (1999). *Culture: The anthropologists' account*. Cambridge, MA: Harvard University Press.

Lasch, C. (1978). *The culture of narcissism*. New York: Norton.

Lee, C. D. (2006). *Culture, literacy, and learning: Taking bloom in the midst of the whirlwind*. New York: Teachers College Press.

Lipkin, A. (1999). *Understanding homosexuality: Changing schools*. Boulder, CO: Westview.

Maher, F. A. (1987). Inquiry teaching and feminist pedagogy. *Social Education, 51*(3), 186–192.

Maher, F. A., & Tetreault, M. K. (1994). *The feminist classroom*. New York: Basic Books.

Mannheim, K. (1936). *Ideology and utopia: An introduction to the sociology of knowledge*. New York: Harcourt Brace.

Mercer, J. R. (1973). *Labeling the mentally retarded: Clinical and social system perspectives on mental retardation*. Berkeley: University of California Press.

Myrdal, G., with Sterner, R., & Rose, A. (1962). *An American dilemma: The Negro problem and modern democracy* (anniv. ed.). New York: Harper & Row. (Original work published 1944.)

Nieto, S., & Bode, P. (2012). *Affirming diversity: The sociopolitical context of multicultural education* (6th ed.). Boston: Pearson.

Noguera, P. A. (2008). *The trouble with Black boys, and other reflections on race, equity, and the future of public education*. San Francisco: Jossey-Bass/Wiley.

Penetito, W. (2010). *What's Maori about Maori education?: The struggle for a meaningful context*. Wellington, New Zealand: Victoria University Press.

Perney, V. H. (1976). Effects of race and sex on field dependence–independence in children. *Perceptual and Motor Skills, 42*, 975–980.

Pettigrew, T. F. (2004). Intergroup contact: Theory, research, and new perspectives. In J. A. Banks (Ed.), *Handbook of research on multicultural education* (2nd ed., pp. 770-781). San Francisco: Jossey-Bass.

Ramírez, M., & Castañeda, A. (1974). *Cultural democracy, bicognitive development and education*. New York: Academic Press.

Reischauer, E. O. (1981). *The Japanese*. Cambridge, MA: Harvard University Press.

Romaine, S. (2009). Language, culture, and identity across nations. In J. A. Banks (Ed.), *The Routledge international companion to multicultural education* (pp. 373–384). New York and London: Routledge.

Root, M. P. P. (2004). Multiracial families and children: Implications for educational research and practice. In J. A. Banks & C. A. M. Banks (Eds.), *Handbook of research on multicultural education* (2nd ed., pp. 110–124). San Francisco: Jossey-Bass.

Rothbart, M., & John, O. P. (1993). Intergroup relations and stereotype change: A social-cognitive analysis and some longitudinal findings. In P. M. Sniderman, P. E. Telock, & E. G. Carmines (Eds.), *Prejudice, politics, and the American dilemma* (pp. 32–59). Stanford, CA: Stanford University Press.

Sapon-Shevin, M. (1994). *Playing favorites: Gifted education and the disruption of community*. Albany: State University of New York Press.

Sapon-Shevin, M. (2007). *Widening the circle: The power of inclusive classrooms*. Boston: Beacon.

Schlesinger, A. M., Jr. (1986). *The cycles of American history*. Boston: Houghton Mifflin.

Shaver, J. P., & Curtis, C. K. (1981). *Handicapism and equal opportunity: Teaching about the disabled in social studies*. Reston, VA: Foundation for Exceptional Children.

Slavin, R. E. (2012). Cooperative learning. In J. A. Banks (Ed.), *Encyclopedia of diversity in education*. (vol. 2, pp. 451–458). Thousand Oaks, CA: Sage.

Sleeter, C. E., & Grant, C. A. (2009). *Making choices for multicultural education: Five approaches to race, class, and gender* (6th ed.). New York: Wiley.

Snyder, T. D., & Dillow, S. A. (2011). *Digest of education statistics 2010*. Washington, DC: National Center for Education Statistics.

Steele, C. (2003). Stereotype threat and African-American student achievement. In T. Perry, C. Steele, & A. Hilliard III, *Young, gifted and Black: Promoting high achievement among African-American students* (pp. 109–130). Boston: Beacon.

Stephan, W. G., & Vogt, W. P. (Eds.). (2004). *Education programs for improving intergroup relations: Theory, research, and practice*. New York: Teachers College Press.

Stewart, E. C., & Bennett, M. J. (1991). *American cultural patterns: A cross-cultural perspective* (rev. ed.). Yarmouth, ME: Intercultural Press.

Taylor, J. M., Gilligan, C., & Sullivan, A. M. (1995). *Between voice and silence: Women and girls, race and relationships*. Cambridge, MA: Harvard University Press.

Theodorson, G. A., & Theodorson, A. G. (1969). *A modern dictionary of sociology*. New York: Barnes & Noble.

Trecker, J. L. (1973). Teaching the role of women in American history. In J. A. Banks (Ed.), *Teaching ethnic studies: Concepts and strategies* (43rd Yearbook, pp. 279–297). Washington, DC: National Council for the Social Studies.

Warner, W. L., with Meeker, M., & Eells, K. (1960). *Social class in America, a manual of procedure for the measurement of social status*. New York: Harper Torchbooks. (Original work published 1949.)

Weatherford, J. (1988). *Indian givers: How the Indians of the Americas transformed the world*. New York: Fawcett Columbine.

Willis, P. (1977). *Learning to labor*. New York: Columbia University Press.

Ariel Skelley/Blend RF/Glow Images

Culture, Teaching, and Learning

CHAPTER 2

Christina Convertino, Bradley A. Levinson, and Norma González

> *I think the best way to learn about a multicultural society is to study many cultures. If during class we studied one culture a day, we might scratch the surface on what it would be like to be informed of and about numerous cultures.*

The preceding statement represents one pre-service student's ideas about what is meant by a "multicultural society" and about how educators can best prepare themselves to teach in multicultural schools. His understanding of the relationship between culture and society follows the *tossed salad* or *mosaic* theory: the idea that many distinct cultures comprise a multicultural society. From his perspective, *culture* represents a set of characteristics (e.g., language, customs, food, holidays) attributable to clearly identifiable, distinct, and bounded groups of people; therefore, his suggestion to study one culture per day seems like an efficient and logical way for teachers to learn about the overwhelming number of cultures within a multicultural society.

This particular approach to understanding culture, also known as the *tourist-based* or *transmission approach*, is fairly common, especially in teacher training. It typically involves "experts transmit[ting] to practitioners certain traits of Culture 'X' or Culture 'Y'" (González, 1995, p. 237). Yet in spite of the prevalence of a tourist-based understanding of culture in schools, this approach does not offer to educators an accurate or adequate view of culture. In fact, the idea of culture as a set of bounded behaviors and traits attributable to a social group, which can be studied in one day, may actually do significant harm in the context of schools and schooling.

If culture, then, is not a set of identifiable characteristics, what is it, and what significance should it have for educators, students, and learning? If tourist-based understandings of culture are counterproductive, why are they so popular? One of the main goals of this chapter is to answer these questions in order to provide educators with a better understanding of the concept of culture and enable them to put such understanding to work. Specifically, this chapter examines culture as a complex and layered construct rather than a list of traits attributable to different, usually "exotic," social groups; such a complex construct cannot be learned in one day.

What we refer to in this chapter as *getting to know culture* means actually grappling with the complexity that surrounds the different meanings and uses of the culture concept in education. Accordingly, *getting to know culture* means asking questions like: Where does the concept come from? For what purposes has it been used in education? How has the concept changed over time? Why has it changed? What is the usefulness of the concept? What are the limitations of the concept? What other concepts are connected to culture? All of these together represent the multiple layers that make up the concept of culture; all are necessary for educators to understand how culture is implicated and reflected in teaching and learning.

The other overarching goal of this chapter is to provide educators with an understanding of culture that will help them to make more effective connections between their students' social lives and their learning in schools. *Putting culture to work* depends on *knowing culture* in all of the previously mentioned ways so that it can be applied effectively and appropriately in teaching and learning. More specifically, in the latter part of the chapter we discuss how 21st-century educators can *put culture to work* in classrooms by understanding how culture and learning are inextricably connected—in ways that go beyond superficial understandings of culture as a set of traits and characteristics or of learning as a simple matter of transmission and acquisition.

Getting to Know Culture: An Overview of Culture's Meanings and Uses

As in a complex labyrinth, no single or direct pathway leads to a meaningful understanding of culture. In fact, although *culture* is one of those seemingly commonsense words that gets used on a daily basis, few people can clearly define it. Depending on the circumstances, *culture* might refer to the idea of "capital C" Culture: what is often referred to as high culture, invoking associations with certain refined tastes and habits typified by the classical arts, like a Bach overture or the *Mona Lisa*. In this sense, some people have "more" culture, while others have much less. In other circumstances, someone might use *culture* as a catchall term for the beliefs and practices that differentiate groups of people, such as traditional Japanese food, dress, and decorum. In this sense, everyone "has" culture in equal measure, but the *substance* of culture is different. In the context of schools and classrooms, moreover, culture is often something that the "other" has, and it is often viewed as a "problem" to be solved. This trend frequently surfaces in teacher education courses, where White/Anglo pre-service teachers consistently claim that they have no "culture" and are therefore genuinely concerned about how they will teach "culturally diverse" students in their classrooms.

The differences, tensions, and conflicts embedded in the meaning and uses of *culture* are actually not new, but rather reflect the difficulty of defining a seemingly commonsense concept. Anthropologists, for whom culture has been the central focus of their study, have struggled and often failed to reach consensus on a singular definition of *culture* (Kuper, 1999), in large part because of the complexity of the concept as well as the different ways in which the concept gets used to explain human life. Moreover, the concept of culture continues to change according to broader social, economic, and political shifts, such as industrialization and, more recently, globalization. In fact, some contemporary anthropologists question whether the concept of culture is still relevant at all or whether it needs to be replaced.

For educators, the question of what culture is can be particularly challenging, since most teacher training programs increasingly emphasize the importance of culture to learning but rarely provide enough examples or experience to aid teachers in understanding the concept. Moreover, little effort is made to differentiate between the understandings and uses of culture in different academic fields. For example, the majority of educators are introduced to the culture concept through discussion of and coursework on multicultural education, where the primary focus is often on student identity and a representation of ethnic groups across the curriculum. In other words, "*culture,* for multiculturalists, refers primarily to collective social identities engaged in struggles for social equality" (Turner, 1993, p. 412). In contrast, "anthropology and its various concepts of culture are not primarily oriented towards programs of social change, political mobilization, or cultural transformation" (p. 412), and yet anthropological understandings of how cultural practices are produced, and thus mediate learning, are essential to providing a meaningful and effective education to all students.

The fact that these different approaches to understanding the connections between culture and education are not made explicit results in much of the confusion and the superficial applications of culture that characterize most teaching in schools today. This fact also explains why so many teachers automatically link culture to ethnic or racial identity and fail to understand that "every individual participates in *many* cultures" that are not necessarily tied to ethnic or racial group membership (Pollock, 2008, p. 370). In fact, "culture matters because it shapes all aspects of daily living and activity. [And] unfortunately, the manner in which culture manifests itself for students is frequently not understood in schools and is not used effectively to enhance teaching and learning for all students" (Howard, 2010, p. 51).

Thus, teachers must cultivate deeper understandings of how culture is implicated in teaching and learning, moving beyond superficial tourist—or "holiday and hero"— approaches. At the same time, the persistent achievement gap between low-income students and students of color, on the one hand, and middle- to upper-middle-income White/Anglo students, on the other, demands a view of culture aimed toward transforming educational inequities. Educators are in the unique position of being cultural brokers who cross intellectual borders between anthropology, sociology, psychology, cultural studies, and multicultural education, to arrive at understandings of culture that are both theoretically rich and pedagogically effective.

In this chapter, we focus primarily on anthropological approaches to understanding culture through a critical lens that contributes to the multiple dimensions of multicultural education (Banks, 2001). In the following sections, we provide an overview of how anthropologists have developed culture as a set of ideas that have changed throughout history in response to broader socioeconomic and political shifts. We do not provide a comprehensive or "truer disciplinary history of the concept" (Visweswaran, 2010, p. 2) but rather focus on the development of those aspects of the culture concept that pertain most significantly to teaching and learning (see also Erickson, 2011).

Some Early Origins of Culture

Following the Industrial Revolution, the concept of culture went from meaning the growth of something, like horti*culture* or agri*culture*, to signifying the creative aspirations of the human mind. These early notions of culture, as a series of increasingly superior manifestations of human creativity and intellect, were closely tied to other prevalent modes of thought at the time— Eurocentrism and evolutionism in particular. Consequently, the idea of culture was associated with late-19th- and early-20th-century ideas about the progression of evolutionary stages that ranked racial groups in terms of levels of intelligence or development. In this Eurocentric view, there were civilized and primitive peoples. The civilized were those who had developed higher levels of culture, while the primitives had either little or no culture.

In response to the racism embedded in this concept of culture, the German-born American anthropologist Franz Boas set out to disprove the idea of cultural evolutionism by conducting extensive ethnographic fieldwork around the turn of the 20th century among the coastal Indians of British Columbia. Using a historical comparative method, Boas replaced the "theory of progress" with a theory of "cultural relativism" (Visweswaran, 2010, p. 77) by demonstrating that cultures are neither superior nor inferior; they are just different from one another. Accordingly, differences in human development and behavior were based on ways of knowing and traditions specific to the adaptation and reproduction of social groups, rather than on overall levels of progress or development.

For 21st-century educators, there are two central components of this earlier version of culture that remain significant and largely misunderstood. First is the use of culture to replace scientific racism in explaining differences in human behavior. Subsequent sections in the chapter discuss the persistent and insidious conflations of culture and race, which unfortunately reflect the limited success of these earlier efforts by Boas and others to show that cultures are neither inherently superior nor inferior. Second is the centrality of teaching and learning to the very meaning and substance of culture. One cannot conceive of education in the absence of culture; education is the process by which culture is constantly transmitted and produced.

Culture as Transmission and Adaptation

At a fundamental level, the meaning of culture is deeply implicated in education. Moreover, as the 21st century opened, it has become abundantly clear that efforts to improve education cannot ignore culture. The very process of education is one in which cultural knowledge is constantly transmitted, acquired, and produced. Cultural beliefs and values shape what occurs within formal education systems. Economic and political changes are often expressed in cultural terms through value conflicts about what should be taught in schools: for example, conflicts related to curriculum, including creationism versus evolutionism, English-only immersion versus dual-language bilingualism, phonetics versus whole language, and so on. Meanwhile, culture also works as a force to reshape the environment and therefore, in turn, influences economic and political systems.

As stated earlier, the definition of culture remains contested. In current popular discourse, culture often refers to the beliefs, values, and meanings that can bind a group of people together. Culture is often invoked as a group's entire way of life, including patterns of behavior and uses of material artifacts. At this point in the discussion, we will emphasize culture as shared symbol systems as well as the cognitive models that make such symbol systems meaningful and intelligible. In short, *culture refers to the symbolic meanings by which the members of a society communicate with and understand themselves, each other, and the world around them.*

Human beings are, above all, great symbol makers and manipulators. Unlike most other animals, our instinctual repertoire is quite limited. The behavior needed to survive, with which most other animals are genetically hard-wired, we must acquire through learning and knowledge acquisition. We are probably the only species to regularly use symbols in this learning process and the only species to systematically transmit the rules of symbol use to succeeding generations. We certainly seem to be the only species to engage in the self-reflexive manipulation of symbols—what we might call metacognition. In each culture, in each individual, we seemingly re-create the entire evolutionary process through which human beings learn to create, communicate, interpret, and use symbols. In fact, this is a workable definition of education. At heart, education is the transmission and acquisition of symbolic knowledge for understanding, controlling, and transforming the world.

Of course, education is much broader than *schooling*, which is an institution of more recent historical invention. Until the development of agriculture and the rise of city-states, tribal societies likely educated their young through complex and deliberate practices, but not in separate institutions like those we call schools. Rather, education was probably a seamless part of everyday life, taking place through the productive and ritual activities characterizing a society's way of life. A school, on the other hand, is typically an age-graded, hierarchical setting where, as Judith Friedman Hansen (1979) puts it, "learners learn vicariously, in roles and environments defined as distinct from those in which the learning will eventually be applied" (p. 28). Only since the beginnings of the modern period some 200 years ago—a period characterized by the rise of capitalism, large-scale urbanization, the consolidation of the nation-state, and the ubiquity of the printing press—have mass school systems been created and has much of human learning been assigned to schools. Especially since World War II, schools have become the dominant format for learning in most areas of the world. Still, schools are no less influenced by culture than are other informal means of education.

Given the centrality of culture to human life, we might go so far as to call human beings the "symbolizing animal." As animals, we share an important biological legacy and an equally important ecological fate with the rest of the organic world. The anatomical and neurological design of our bodies—evolved through millions of years of highly successful adaptation to multiple environments—provides the most basic parameters for how we can and ought to be educated. Yet along with our biology, we have evolved a deep dependence on the communicative role of symbols. Clever but physically defenseless proto-humans and early *Homo sapiens* required complex forms of social coordination, communication, and tool use to survive. Basic forms of language and culture thus undoubtedly emerged as distinctive adaptive traits of early human social cooperation. Over time, the very structure of the human brain co-evolved with this unique sociocultural adaptation—this way of thinking and talking that relies on creating and manipulating symbols to interpret the world.

In the broadest sense, then, education underwrites every human group's ability to adapt to its environment and thereby reproduce the conditions of its existence. It is, in this sense, a fundamentally conservative social process. As Jules Henry (1963) puts it, if education can "free" our minds, it rather more often "fetters" them (p. 284). Yet amidst this group imperative, individuals may also develop their own educational repertoires from the cultural resources at their disposal. Through their creative agency, both constrained and enabled by culture, individuals may alter the pattern by which social groups reproduce themselves. The dialectic of continuity and change inherent to culture often constitutes a balancing act between group concerns and individual interests. This is why we should never think of individuals as simply "acting out" a cultural script.

From an anthropological perspective, then, the educational process fundamentally oscillates between an emphasis on continuity and an emphasis on change. This is because the challenges of evolution, broadly speaking, require a social group to adapt to novel circumstances through innovation and then to consolidate and perpetuate this adaptation through repeated inculcation. Through the use of culture, human groups have wrested a living from the environment and assured themselves biological and social continuity.

Finally, we must also be cautious about how we conceive of the "group" that educates. As human societies have grown more differentiated, biological and cultural adaptation to the physical environment has become more highly mediated by complex traditions and institutions. Intensive agriculture, urbanization, and industrialization have led to occupational and class stratification as well as large-scale political formations, such as empires or nation-states. The concerns of the nation-state as a large-scale human group, for instance, must not be confused with the concerns of those groups that constitute any given nation-state. While some educational systems and processes may seem adaptive for the nation-state as a whole, they may be highly maladaptive for particular groups, such as the Amish farmers of the United States or the Quechua Indians of Peru, or even for the punk rockers on the outskirts of Lima, the capital of Peru. Moreover, certain kinds of educational processes, such as the teaching of an ethic of competitive individualism, may be adaptive in relation to the economic foundations of a capitalist nation, but not in relation to a self-sufficient community or, ultimately, in relation to the well-being of the Earth's biosphere. All of this explains why we cannot view education as benefiting all individuals and groups in a given society or as providing a means of adaptation in some simple functional sense. Education can just as likely serve as the vehicle for domination of one group over another in the pursuit of its own interests.

Creating Culture: Cultural Transmission and Education

As we have seen, the educational process cannot be separated from the broader human process of cultural adaptation. The following social science concepts represent some of the foundational ideas about the way that culture has been described and portrayed in the educational process.

From the very origins of their academic disciplines in the late 1800s, anthropologists and sociologists wondered how human societies could reproduce themselves from one generation to the next without falling into disarray. What allowed a society to adapt to its environment while retaining some historical cohesion and continuity? How did a society conserve essential features of its cultural and technological repertoire? Social science theories of education largely sought to address these questions through an analysis of the process of *cultural transmission*—the passing on of basic cultural knowledge and values across the generations. Contemporary schools and classrooms are replete with examples of cultural transmission; for example, traditional classroom management teaches dominant cultural communication patterns, like raising hands for turn-taking.

Enculturation refers to the basic process of cultural transmission by which individuals come to acquire the crucial meanings and understandings of their primary culture, usually the local community or kin group (cf. the related sociological term *socialization*). In Western industrial nations, school culture typically reflects the dominant culture. Consequently, students who are enculturated in the dominant culture—White/Anglo, middle to upper-middle class—possess greater *cultural capital*. Cultural capital represents the "views, standards and cultural forms" (Ferguson, 2001 p. 50)—the physical characteristics, gestures, traits, styles of talking, and so on—that are specific to the varied classes in a capitalist society. Since school structures and practices tend to exemplify the cultural capital of the dominant class, those students who possess the cultural capital of the dominant class have a significant advantage in terms of school success over those whose cultural capital does not match that of the schools (Bourdieu & Passeron, 1977).

Schools privilege the cultural capital of students from dominant groups by bestowing on them greater legitimacy. This in turn provides them with superior academic credentials and the necessary symbolic currency to access greater economic opportunities once they finish schooling. Conversely, those students who do not possess sanctioned cultural capital experience "symbolic violence," wherein their cultural and social resources are devalued by schooling (Bourdieu & Passeron, p. 4; see also Fordham, 1996). Since schools typically legitimize only the traits of the dominant group's cultural capital, subordinated groups do not receive the resources, validation, or opportunities needed to alter their social position; thus, schools may often serve to reproduce class structures and inequalities (Levinson, Foley, & Holland, 1996).

Acculturation refers to the processes through which individuals from different cultures come into contact with each other. For example, children frequently make friends with peers from different cultures in the context of the classroom or other learning contexts, such as camp, neighborhood, church, mosque, temple, or after-school programs. As a result of the contact, each individual's cultural ways of being are influenced and to some degree changed. Qin (2006) describes "dissonant acculturation" as the growing gap between the children and parents of recent immigrant families due to the fact that most school-age children from these families learn how to speak English and participate in U.S. culture more quickly than do their parents. Based on her research with Chinese immigrant families, Qin further attributes dissonant acculturation to what she calls *parallel dual frames of reference*, according to which immigrant parents tend to compare their child's behavior with cultural norms of behavior in China; in turn, the child increasingly compares his or her parents to friends' parents in the United States or to mainstream U.S. parents depicted in the media.

Finally, with increasing contact between different societies and cultures, and increasing recognition of the value of cultural diversity, elements of various belief systems may be incorporated into a kind of hybrid personal belief system. This phenomenon of *transculturation* has been receiving increased attention, especially as globalization accelerates new flows of people and ideas and as transnational migration makes new kinds of *hybrid identities* possible and desirable.

Education, Society, and Cultural Continuity

Working in small, face-to-face societies, anthropologists have historically examined informal teaching, often conducted through simple mechanisms of imitation or rote memorization. They have also emphasized the educative role of ritual for binding members of a society to a common cultural vision. Sociologists, on the other hand, have tended to examine the industrial, urbanized, and highly stratified societies that began to emerge in the 1800s. The rise of industrial capitalism and the consolidation of the nation-state as the most widely accepted political framework went hand in hand with the development of modern school systems. In the characteristic view of the great French sociologist Emile Durkheim, such school systems functioned to produce the kinds of persons deemed necessary by the predominant institutions in society to carry out the different work needed to reproduce those very social institutions. Above all, in a highly differentiated, stratified society, Durkheim thought that schools ought to create a "degree of homogeneity; education perpetuates and reinforces this homogeneity by fixing in the child, from the beginning, the essential similarities that collective life demands" (cited in Levinson, 2000, p. 61).

Meanwhile, scholars like Karl Marx, and later the German sociologist Max Weber, drew attention to the potentially pernicious effects of such homogenizing education systems. Though they rarely criticized formal schooling per se, these scholars provided the conceptual foundation for analyzing education as a modern tool of *social domination*. In Durkheim's view, a complex division of labor presided over by a political elite was a precondition of social integration under modern capitalism, and an education system designed to secure consent for such an arrangement was highly desirable. In this formula, society would function smoothly, and all parties would win. Marx and Weber, on the other hand, inaugurated the "conflict" perspective in sociology, which has viewed the goal of consent through schooling as an apology for a highly exploitative social system. In this perspective, homogenization serves only the ruling classes and enables domination to persist.

In the context of multicultural education, a parallel concept that pertains specifically to culture, assimilation, represents the complete "elimination of cultural differences and differentiating group identifications" (Banks, 2001, p. 105) toward the larger goal of creating a homogeneous body of citizens to govern and constitute a nation-state. Elimination of cultural diversity through assimilation likewise ensures the persistence of the dominant culture. Spring (2007) provides a detailed history of the ways in which education has been used to strip major ethnic groups of their cultures in the United States from the earliest years of European settlement to the present day. It is a phenomenon that occurs most strongly under situations of classical colonialism or internal colonialism, as in the case of American Indians sent to boarding schools to be shaped "in the White man's image" (Lomawaima, 1994). A more recent example is the passage of legislation (HB 2281) that bans ethnic studies—Chicano studies in particular—from the academic curriculum of an Arizona school district (Sleeter, 2011).

Culture Change: Cultural Psychology and Cultural Production

After many years of focusing on processes of cultural transmission and the achievement of cultural continuity, anthropologists and sociologists began to examine more closely how education contributed to change. If cultural transmission occurred smoothly, how did societies challenge their own inertia? If education mainly served to mold the young into the cultural patterns of a society, how did innovation ever occur? From cultural transmission and the role of teachers, attention turned to *cultural acquisition* and the role of the learner. How did relatively novice individuals acquire the basic cultural knowledge of a society, and what distinctive interests and traits might they bring to the learning process? This question spawned a tremendously fruitful collaboration between anthropology and psychology, giving rise to the new field of *cultural psychology*. The work of the Soviet psychologist Lev Vygotsky (1978), with its emphasis on the role of symbolic "tools of mediation" in the relation between individual and society, has become central to this field. Cultural psychology has been especially adept at showing how peer-group socialization and good teaching can use such tools of mediation in moving students to higher and more complex forms of cognition.

More recently, Jean Lave and Etienne Wenger (1991) have proposed a powerful theory of "situated learning," in which society is fundamentally composed of overlapping "communities of practice" that serve as the vehicles for cultural acquisition. Such an account places identity at the heart of cultural learning. As one moves from "legitimate peripheral participation" (p. 14) to a more central, expert role in a community of practice, one increasingly develops identities of mastery and their corresponding emotional investments.

An important overarching concept that has emerged to encompass the processes of cultural transmission and acquisition is that of *cultural production*. Education may be seen as a constant process of cultural production. Even if education is oriented primarily toward the achievement of continuity in a relatively closed system, the theoretical possibility of modification and change always exists. In the process of acquiring transmitted cultural knowledge, individuals or subcultures can modify or extend the knowledge, in effect organizing the knowledge for themselves while producing and adding new knowledge to the common stock. For example, as a carpenter teaches an apprentice the techniques of stair-laying, as well as the cultural value of precision, the apprentice may discover a new cut that saves time without sacrificing much precision. The communication of this discovery can become an act of cultural production, even as the apprentice moves from the periphery toward the center of his or her community of practice. Over time, most carpenters in the community may adopt the change, or some may resist and deem it too sloppy a compromise. As Judith Friedman Hansen (1979) summarizes, "the transmission of knowledge is subject both to conservative forces and to tendencies toward continual redefinition" (p. 26).

The capacity for individuals to change culture is referred to as *agency*. Stated in a different way, agency represents how individuals actively appropriate certain elements of cultural practices while discarding others. Due to the persistent reliance on tradition and cultural transmission in modern schools, *student agency* is rarely recognized, valued, and implemented in ways that contribute to innovating school knowledge, curricula, and practices. More frequently and ironically, schools generate and thus legitimize student production of new forms of cultural knowledge that are resistant to schooling. In his book *Learning to Labor* (1977), Paul Willis describes student agency in an ethnographic study of working-class "lads" in England. Within this framework, students were seen as resisting the false bargain of social mobility proffered by their school. Their resistance constitutes a form of agency, but by opposing the middle-class ideologies of the school through cultural practices such as "having a laff," the lads ironically reproduce their working-class status. What Willis's work shows is how individuals need not be portrayed as "cultural dopes" doomed to endlessly reproduce a static and unyielding culture, but rather should be seen as actively manipulating and tinkering with cultural elements, although not always to their educational benefit.

Critiques of Culture

In the world today, globalization and the concomitant rise of technology have accelerated the circulation and flow of peoples, ideas, and goods across the globe. As a result of the growing diversity within and across societies, previous ideas about culture seem to have lost their utility and relevance. And while anthropologists have not agreed on a single definition of culture, the once-preeminent idea of culture as bounded, holistic, and static—a "laundry list of cultural traits" (Spindler, 1996), a set of contending "billiard balls" (Wolf, 1982)—has become even less tenable. Instead, culture is increasingly viewed as *dynamic, interactional, and emergent*. Often, new concepts of culture are tied to examining *borderlands* (Anzaldúa, 1987) that are composed of emergent practices and mixed conventions that do not conform to expectation. Gupta and Ferguson (1992), for example, note that

> *the fiction of cultures as discrete object-like phenomena occupying discrete spaces becomes implausible for those who inhabit the borderlands. Related to border inhabitants are those who live a life of border crossings—migrant workers, nomads, and members of transnational business and professional elite. What is "the culture" of farm workers who spend half a year in Mexico and half a year in the United States? (p. 7)*

Another theorist, Homi Bhabha (1995), in his provocative work *The Location of Culture*, argues for examining "border lives" as exemplars of moments "of transit where space and time cross to produce complex figures of difference and identity, past and present, inside and outside, inclusion and exclusion" (p. 1). It is these "in-between" spaces, he argues, that

> *provide the terrain for elaborating strategies of selfhood—singular or communal—that initiate new signs of identity, and innovative sites of collaboration and contestation in the act of defining the idea of society itself. (p. 1)*

But students don't need to live on or near borders to create new, complex cultural identities. Increasingly, through their participation in cross-cutting youth cultures, students draw from an intercultural and hybrid knowledge base.

Another critical theoretical turn in conceptualizations of culture was the rise of postmodernism and poststructuralism. Postmodernism questioned whether what had become known as the culture of the modern world was still viable in more fragmented and decentered economic and political conditions. Within a postmodern perspective, the idea of general models and grand theories gave way to considering contradiction, ambiguity, and local and contingent ways of positioning knowledge. Michel Foucault (1969), a French social theorist, explored how knowledge was intimately connected with the conveyance of power. An increasing emphasis on textuality and *discourse* came to dominate discussions about the cultural. Discussions of culture gave way to the exploration of discourses that have the capacity to construct, rather than merely reflect, our realities. For example, educational policies and practices frequently represent broader discourses about what it means to be a "good" or "bad" student, or likewise to "fail" or "succeed" in school. As these discourses circulate in schools and within public education, they often serve to constitute subjectivities or certain "types" of students as *different*, *deviant*, *outcasts,* or *misfits* and, thus, constrain the educational opportunities and outcomes of these students who are viewed as in conflict with school norms and practices (Convertino, 2011).

Culture and Educational Achievement

Up to this point, we have focused on varied and changing versions of the culture concept, particularly in terms of its connections with teaching, learning, and schooling. In this section, we explore how earlier understandings of the culture concept—as a set of bounded and static traits attributable to a social group—came to be a major focus in educational scholarship from the 1950s to today. Specifically, we examine both the contributions and drawbacks of major educational theories that posit culture as the preeminent concept for explaining differences in educational achievement.

Cultural Deficit Models

In the late 1950s, the anthropologist Oscar Lewis (1959) argued that membership in a group that has been poor for generations constituted a separate culture, a "culture of poverty." For Lewis, the culture of poverty model was meant to be a counter-discourse to notions of supposed familial instability and disorganization as well as an alternative to racist biological notions of race and poverty. Unfortunately, the concept was taken up as a distortion of the complexity of the lives of the poor, and what emerged was a view that the "culture of poverty" was antithetical to school achievement and thus explained educational failure. This theory led to the development and expansion of *cultural deficit models* in schooling, according to which poor and minority students were viewed through a lens of deficiency and were considered substandard in their socialization practices, language habits, and familial orientation toward scholastic achievement.

Vestiges of the cultural deficit models continue to have a negative and harmful impact, particularly where minority and poor students are concerned. The widespread use of Ruby Payne's (1996) *Framework for Understanding Poverty* in teacher training is just one significant example of cultural deficit models that continue to influence teachers' thinking and understanding of culture. According to Payne's framework, since poverty is as much cultural as it is monetary, middle-class educators cannot relate to their poor students because they don't know the hidden rules of surviving poverty any better than poor students know the hidden rules of middle-class culture. For example, the teacher no more knows how to physically fight and defend him- or herself than the poor student knows how to reserve a table at a restaurant. According to Payne, in order for educators to be effective with poor students, they need to teach them the hidden rules of middle-class culture. Not unlike the tourist-based approach, Payne's framework is popular among educators and school administrators because it provides seemingly simple and quick solutions to very complex problems.

The cultural deficit model in both its original and contemporary renderings illustrates two very important misunderstandings of culture that in turn lead to misuses of the concept of culture in education. First is the misunderstanding that culture is composed of a set of static and bounded traits and values evenly attributable to all members of the group. For example, all students from cultural group X are poor and consequently cannot learn to read, don't want to work, and have parents who don't care about education. Besides blatant stereotyping and eliminating group and individual diversity, this misunderstanding of culture can lead to extremely harmful educational practices that actually create the conditions for educational failure (e.g., disproportionate use of discipline and "deficit talk" with poor and minority students).

The other significant misunderstanding is the fact that the cultural deficit model is actually used to explain the educational failure of poor and/or minority students. In other words, the culture of these students is characterized as deficient in contrast to the culture of middle- and upper-middle-class nonminority students, which explains the latter groups' higher educational achievement. This mode of thought and use of culture blames the individual and fails to account for the *structural* conditions that consistently characterize the schools that poor and minority students attend, including unequal resources, lack of qualified teachers, and greater use of heavy-handed discipline (Ferguson, 2001; Fine, 1992; Kozol, 1992; Oakes, 2005).

Additionally, underlying the cultural deficit model are the old ideas of racial ranking that originally plagued 19th-century anthropologists; simply put, educators following the cultural deficit model are likely using culture as a stand-in concept to represent deep-seated notions about race. Ladson-Billings (2006) refers to the phenomenon in teacher education of tying culture and race together, and then using culture as a catchall term for difference and deviance, as the "poverty of culture"—an intentional play on the concept of the "culture of poverty." She points to educators' reliance on "culture" to explain the misbehavior of students who are ethnically, racially, or linguistically different from themselves. She provides the following example from the field experiences of a teacher education program (Ladson-Billings, 2006):

> *I listened as they described their students' misbehavior in terms of culture. "The black kids just talk so loud and don't listen," said one teacher education student. I asked her why she thought they spoke so loudly. "I don't know; I guess it's cultural." I then asked if she thought they were talking loudly because they were black or because they were kids. She paused a moment and then said, "I guess, I've never thought about that." This is an interesting response since so much of this student's teacher preparation includes a focus on development. Why don't more of our students say things like, "Since my students are eight years old I expect that they will behave in this particular way?" (p. 106)*

In another example, Valenzuela (1999) explores the academic achievement and educational affiliations of Mexican and Mexican American students attending a comprehensive inner-city high school in Texas. Although students in the study reported a positive attitude toward education in general, they expressed decreases in positive affiliations with school due to school-based policies and practices that were dismissive of their cultural and linguistic resources. Valenzuela uses the concept of *subtractive schooling* to describe how educational policies and practices require the loss or subtraction of crucial aspects of students' cultural and linguistic identities in order for them to be academically successful. Mexican American students' cultural backgrounds are seen as *deficient*, and they are encouraged to *assimilate*. English-only legislation in California and Arizona is a current example of the *subtractive schooling* policies that similarly hinder the social and academic achievement of English language learners.

Cultural Difference Model and Mismatch Hypothesis

Approximately a decade after sociologists introduced the cultural deficit model as a means to explain disparities in educational achievement and social mobility, the emphasis on culture took another turn in the fields of anthropology and education. Consistent with academic attention to the educational disparities of minority students, anthropologists during the 1970s and 1980s refuted the deficit-driven approach and posited that the consistent educational failure of certain groups of students was due to a *mismatch* between the culture of home and community and that of schools (Heath, 1983; Levinson et al., 1996). In other words, poor and minority students' cultures were merely *different* from the prevailing beliefs and practices of school culture, not deficient. Here one can see the return of anthropological *relativism* working against a veiled form of evolutionist racism.

Heath's (1983) landmark study *Ways with Words* offers one of the more compelling examples of variance in student experiences and outcomes due to the mismatch between home and school culture. In her study, Heath looked at the home literacy practices of three different communities in a South Carolina town: a working-class African American community, a working-class White/Anglo community, and a middle-class White/Anglo community. Each community demonstrated a distinct approach to literacy; however, only the literacy orientation and practices of the middle-class White/Anglo (mainstream) community matched those of the school. The distinct literacy practices of the two nonmainstream communities constituted a "mismatch" between home and school literacies that had progressively greater negative outcomes for the school-age children of these two communities (see also Valdes, 1996). According to the *cultural difference model* or *mismatch hypothesis* exemplified by Heath's study, since school culture is linguistically and/or materially a different cultural world for underrepresented students, educators should seek to know and appreciate the culture of their students by engaging with the community-based linguistic patterns of their communities and building pedagogically upon them.

Although these were powerful concepts that held sway for almost 30 years, the cultural difference paradigm nonetheless focused primarily on micro-interactional processes—that is, on classroom and language practices—and generally assumed that all members of a particular group share a normative, bounded, and integrated culture. This approach tended to mask the underlying issues of political-economic and power relations between dominant and minority populations, and sought answers instead through "fixing" teachers' interactional patterns.

Educational Achievement: Voluntary versus Involuntary Immigrant Students

To address the broader or macro-level issues of power that contribute to differences in educational achievement between dominant and minority students, John Ogbu (1978) observed that some students (recent Chinese immigrant students, for instance) who are culturally very different tend to do well in school, while long-standing minority populations do not fare as well. He urged educators to look instead at the "cultural frames of reference" toward schooling that implicated historical conditions, echoing in some way Boas's earlier admonition to look carefully at particular histories. Ogbu elaborated his theme to account for the reasons that "caste-like" involuntary minorities (in the United States, mostly African American, Native American, and some Latino groups) often see school in negative terms, while historical circumstances cast a different, more positive light on schooling for immigrant students who are "voluntary" minorities. This formulation shifted the gaze from the micro to the macro and questioned larger structural influences on school achievement. Levinson, Foley, and Holland (1996), in reflecting on the impact of Ogbu's reconfiguration, noted how the cultural difference approach ignored relations of power:

> *Neglecting to emphasize how communication styles, cognitive codes, and so on were the cultural practices of variably empowered groups, historically produced within relations of power, the cultural difference approach tended to essentialize the cultural repertoires of minoritized groups. As Ogbu (1981) pointed out, the absence of such a critical analysis permitted confident reformists to attempt amelioration of school-based conflicts in cultural styles through remedial programs and "culturally responsive" pedagogies. The deeper structural context of cultural production and school failure remained obscure and largely unaddressed. (p.8)*

Although Ogbu's work has been rightfully criticized for repeating the error of essentializing and overly typologizing groups, it does provide an analysis of educational achievement that points to how cultural attitudes toward schooling of minority students are "historically produced within relations of power" (Levinson et al., 1996, p. 8). The trick, as we shall see, is to preserve Ogbu's fundamental insights into the effects of history and domination on certain groups, while allowing for a more fluid, complex, and situationally emergent understanding of culture.

Putting Culture to Work: Culture and Learning in the 21st Century

Earlier in this chapter, we discussed the development of the culture concept and how the concept has changed in response to broader social, economic, and political shifts. Changes brought on by globalization emphasize the hybridity of cultural practices and have served to complexify simplistic notions of culture as a static, bounded, and cohesive tradition used to distinguish groups of people. We also demonstrated how teacher training programs frequently appropriate the latter version of culture to explain the connection between culture and education, thus falling into tourist- and transmission-based approaches.

In addition, we highlighted how static and bounded notions of culture are used to explain differences in educational achievement that have "often viewed nondominant students and communities as the 'other' and have assumed a singular pathway of development based on American middle class norms" (Nasir, Rosebery, Warren, & Lee, 2006, p. 490). In schools, teachers and administrators frequently appropriate these deficit discourses to explain student failure. Similarly, school personnel often perceive culture as a set of traits shared among all members of a (usually nondominant) group. According to this line of thinking, "culturally responsive" teaching is a matter of providing instruction that reflects the traits of a certain cultural group; as a simple example, since Native American students share the cultural trait of preferring cooperation over competition, a teacher using culturally responsive instruction would have Native American students work primarily in groups. Often well intended, this approach, also known as the *cultural styles approach*, depends on the idea that differences in learning styles reflect the traits of cultural groups (Gutiérrez & Rogoff, 2003). Consistent with tourist-based approaches and educational achievement theories, cultural learning style constructs perpetuate shallow cultural analyses of learning and school achievement patterns (Pollock, 2008).

In the next section of this chapter, we explore learning as a cultural process that complexifies earlier anthropological notions of learning as cultural transmission and acquisition. We outline key theoretical approaches that provide for deep cultural analyses in education based on culture as *partial, emergent, fluid,* and *dynamic.* Accordingly, the discussion is focused on how today's educators can *put culture to work* in classrooms by understanding how culture and learning are inextricably connected in ways that go far beyond superficial understandings of culture as a set of traits or characteristics and learning as simply a matter of acquisition and transmission.

To this end, we emphasize the critical idea that culture is not the "name for a thing"; rather, culture is "a placeholder for a set of inquiries—inquiries which may be destined to never be resolved" (Stolzenberg, 2001, p. 444). Consequently, *putting culture to work* depends on educators' willingness and ability to recognize and engage with the fact that *getting to know culture* is never a complete or finished endeavor. Moreover, *getting to know culture* and being able to *put culture to work* represents a holistic orientation towards learning that (1) accounts for learning inside as well as outside of schools; (2) understands that a cultural view of learning recognizes that there are "multiple dimensions to learning, including cognition, discourse, affect, motivation, and identity" (Nasir et al., 2006, p. 490); (3) recognizes diversity within and across cultural groups; (4) understands that all individuals participate in multiple cultures that change across a lifetime; and (5) recognizes and engages with the fact that culture is not just what students bring from home—schools are also cultural sites and teachers are themselves cultural beings (Ladson-Billings, 2006; Pollock, 2008).

Rethinking Learning and Cultural Processes in Education

The concept of culture emphasized in schools has focused on how shared norms shape individual behavior and thus on discovering and implementing standardized rules for behavior. However, when we move away from uniform categorizations of a shared group culture, the realities of ambiguity and contradiction come into focus. Processual approaches to culture take into account multiple perspectives by focusing on the processes of everyday life in the form of daily activities as a frame of reference. Instead of individual representations of an essentialized group, *cultural practices are viewed as dynamic, emergent, and interactional.* By focusing on understanding processes rather than locating characteristics, "learning is conceived of as a process occurring within ongoing activity and not divided into separate characteristics of individuals and contexts" (Gutiérrez & Rogoff, 2003, p. 20). Likewise, cultural differences are "attributed to variations in people's involvement in common practices of particular cultural communities" (p. 21), and these practices cannot be identified strictly with membership in ethnic, racial, or linguistic groups.

Consequently, to understand cultural variations, educators must attend to students' histories of participation in cultural communities that constitute their linguistic and cultural-historical repertoires of practice. According to a cultural-historical approach, cultural repertoires of practice represent the "ways of engaging in activities stemming from observing and otherwise participating in cultural practices" (Gutiérrez & Rogoff, 2003 p. 22). Based on prior experiences, repertoires prepare individuals with a range of competencies that reflect community-based approaches. By understanding their students' repertoires of practices, teachers can facilitate learning based on developing "dexterity in using both familiar and new approaches" (p. 23).

Cultural Modeling (Lee, 2007) is a design framework that organizes tasks and participation structures as mediational tools to facilitate relevant and meaningful learning opportunities for students. Two core components of this framework are a focus on the cultural practices that youth participate in outside of school and a focus on the very specific demands of different disciplinary domains in school. In order for educators to design curriculum and instruction based on the cultural modeling framework, they must understand how to make connections between students' cultural repertoires of practice and school-based knowledge. This requires that teachers have a sophisticated and in-depth understanding of their students' participation in communities of practice outside of schools, derived from the teachers' own long-term observation of and participation in those communities. In the next section, we discuss how teachers can come to know the cultural resources and practices that mediate how their students learn.

Learning in Context: What Teachers Need to Know

In "Getting to Know Students' Communities," Wyman and Kashatok (2008) provide conceptual and concrete suggestions for how teachers can better know their students in order to improve their teaching in culturally relevant, meaningful, and appropriate ways. Wyman, a White/Anglo non-Native female educator and researcher, and Kashatok, a Native Yup'ik male educator and researcher, base their suggestions on 15 years of experience working in and with small Alaskan communities. Although their article focuses on the particular circumstances and communities of practice in the highly isolated contexts of small Alaskan villages, their suggestions have value for all teachers in terms of getting to know their students and their communities. In particular, they posit that the tendency for non-Native teachers to insulate themselves from the communities in which they teach by restricting the hours and community contexts in which the teachers participate often results in teacher and student relationships that are based on stereotypes that undermine student learning. In contrast, teachers who adopt a "triangulating stance" are better able to support their students because they know their students' cultural repertoires of practice as a result of participating in various community contexts and are continuously learning about the students and their community(ies).

The funds-of-knowledge framework (González, 2005) is a similar conceptual and methodological approach to designing curriculum and instruction based on conducting systematic and ethnographic research with students' households to identify the pedagogical resources and strengths embedded in those households and communities. Here, again, the underlying assumption is that teaching and learning are enhanced when teachers have in-depth knowledge of their students' everyday lives. Moreover, because a funds-of-knowledge approach is based on teachers' learning from students' households and communities, it does not assume a static and unchanging notion of "culture." Rather, Moll and González (2004) emphasize engaging life by "living culturally" through situated practices. When teachers draw on household knowledge, student experience is legitimated as valid, and classroom practices can build on familiar knowledge bases that students can manipulate to enhance learning in mathematics, social studies, language arts, and other content areas. As a note of caution, a funds-of-knowledge approach does not represent a linear transference of subject knowledge (e.g., mathematical knowledge from household to classroom). Since knowledge is always mediated through social interaction and particular contexts, it is not possible to disembed knowledge from its social meanings. In other words:

> [H]uman thinking is irreducible to individual properties or traits. Instead, it is always mediated, distributed among persons, artifacts, activities, and settings. . . . How social relationships, ideas, or activities become resources for thinking, then, must be studied in relation to the concrete and varied practices of human beings. (González, Andrade, Civil, & Moll, 2001, p. 122)

To be sure, this is different from the case of a teacher conducting a single home visit to catalogue the different hobbies or activities that students' households engage in. A funds-of-knowledge approach seeks to understand not only what knowledge exists in households but also how that knowledge is socially and collectively constructed. An emphasis on the social and collective construction of knowledge and learning also highlights the significance of examining how individuals who are not group members, like teachers, are intertwined in "consequential interactions" with students that serve to mediate student learning (Pollock, 2008, p. 371). Becoming culturally competent not only includes educators getting to know their students' everyday practices outside of school; it also involves educators becoming aware of their "own consequentially patterned interactions with students inside of classrooms" (p. 373). Accordingly, by examining how they interact with and respond to students in real time, teachers can better understand how they create or prohibit opportunities for learning in individual students' lives. Writes Pollock, "That is, when people [teachers] realize that they too participate in patterned interactions with major consequences for children, they finally are thinking culturally" (pp. 373–374). And engaging in different forms of classroom and community ethnographic research, such as those suggested by Carolyn Frank (1999), can undoubtedly help teachers to see and reflect upon such culturally situated interactions.

Concluding Remarks

In the context of a rapidly changing world, *adaptive knowledge*—"the development of flexible knowledge and dispositions that facilitate effective navigation across varied settings and tasks" (Nasir et al., 2006, p. 490)—is increasingly important and necessary for both educators and students. For youth from nondominant communities who are consistently faced with major societal challenges and obstacles, the importance of adaptive expertise is even greater. Given accelerated changes in what counts as relevant and necessary knowledge, existing normative ideas about learning and thus teaching are inadequate. Furthermore, in the context of a global world characterized by an expanding multiculturalism through the constant circulation of ideas and people, the social relations that mediate learning and the production of knowledge cannot be reduced to a singular or normative reference (e.g., an individual, a nation-state, or a bounded cultural group). Learning, then, is mediated through and with cultural practices and processes that are themselves diverse, partial, and fluid. In other words, learning is inscribed in shifting and multiple practices situated within dynamic and changing contexts.

Consequently, today's educators cannot rely on one-dimensional views of teaching and learning; rather, they must cultivate the capacity to view themselves, their students, and their learning and teaching as multidimensional. We argue that for educators to "know" how to teach in a multicultural society, they must practice a cultural approach to learning and teaching. Beyond tourist- and transmission-based approaches, a cultural approach to teaching and learning examines the "organization of people's everyday interactions in concrete contexts" (Pollock, 2008, p. 369) in order to understand "patterns of people's approaches to given situations" (Gutiérrez & Rogoff, p. 22) and how others make sense of their lives.

QUESTIONS AND ACTIVITIES

2.1 After reading this chapter, what new ideas and understandings do you have about the meaning of culture?

2.2 What is the role of culture in learning and teaching? Why is it essential to implement a complex understanding of culture in the classroom? What does this involve?

2.3 How does the way in which culture is described in this chapter differ from the tourist-based approaches to culture that are common in schools and classrooms?

2.4 How do the ways in which culture is understood and used in schools differ from the ways in which it is understood and applied in anthropology? How can these two ways of understanding culture be blended to improve learning in schools?

2.5 How does a complex understanding of culture help to reduce stereotypes of groups of people? What are the implications of a deep understanding of culture for teaching and learning?

2.6 How can teachers' understanding of their own cultural practices help them to put culture to work in the classroom?

2.7 What problems result when teachers essentialize students according to their culture?

2.8 What does it mean to say that culture is complex, fluid, and hybrid? Why is it important for educators to understand complex cultural ways of being?

REFERENCES

Anzaldúa,G. (1987). *La frontera: The new mestizo.* San Francisco: Spinsters/Aunt Lute.

Banks, J. A. (2001). *Cultural diversity and education: Foundations, curriculum, and teaching* (4th ed.). Needham Heights, MA: Allyn & Bacon.

Bhabha, H. (1995). *The location of culture.* London: Routledge.

Bourdieu, P., & Passeron, J. C. (1977). *Reproduction in education, society, and culture.* Beverly Hills, CA: Sage.

Convertino, C. (2011). *Forced to choose: School choice and the spatial production of youth identities in a post-industrial age* (doctoral dissertation). Retrieved April 12, 2912 from http://sabio.library.arizona.edu.ezproxy2.library.arizona.edu.

Erickson, F. (2011). Culture. In B. A. Levinson & M. Pollock (Eds.), *A companion to the anthropology of education* (pp. 25–33). Walden, MA: Wiley/Blackwell.

Ferguson, A. A. (2001). *Bad boys: Public schooling and the making of Black masculinity.* Ann Arbor: University of Michigan Press.

Fine, M. (1992). *Framing dropouts: Notes on the politics of an urban public high school.* Albany: State University of New York Press.

Fordham, S. (1996). *Blacked out: Dilemmas of race, identity and success at Capitol Hill.* Chicago: University of Chicago Press.

Foucault, M. (1969). *The archaeology of knowledge.* Milton Park, Abingdon, UK: Taylor & Francis.

Frank, C. (1999). *Ethnographic eyes: A teacher's guide to classroom observation.* Portsmouth, NH: Heinemann.

González, N. (1995). Processual approaches to multicultural education. *Journal of Applied Behavorial Science, 31*, 234–244.

González, N. (2004). Disciplining the discipline: Anthropology and the pursuit of quality education. *Educational Researcher, 33*(5), 17–25.

González, N. (2005). Beyond culture: The hybridity of funds of knowledge. In N. González, L. Moll, & C. Amanti (Eds.), *Funds of knowledge: Theorizing practices in households, communities and classrooms* (pp. 29–46). Mahwah, NJ: Erlbaum.

González, N., Andrade, R., Civil, M., & Moll, L. (2001). Bridging funds of distributed knowledge: Creating zones of practices in mathematics. *Journal of Education for Students Placed at Risk, 61*(1 & 2), 115–132.

Gupta, A., & Ferguson, J. (1992). Beyond "culture": Space, identity and politics of difference. *Cultural Anthropology, 7*, 6–23.

Gutiérrez, K., & Rogoff, B. (2003). Cultural ways of learning: Individual traits or repertoires of practice. *Educational Researcher, 32*(5), 19–25.

Hansen, J. F. (1979). *Sociocultural perspectives on human learning: Foundations of educational anthropology.* Prospect Heights, IL: Waveland.

Heath, S. B. (1983). *Ways with words: Language, life, and work in communities and classrooms.* New York: Cambridge University Press.

Henry, J. (1963). *Culture against man.* New York: Random House.

Howard, T. C. (2010). *Why race and culture matter in schools: Closing the achievement gap in America's classrooms.* New York: Teachers College Press.

Kozol, J. (1992). *Savage inequalities: Children in America's schools.* New York: Harper Perennial.

Kuper, A. (1999). *Culture: The anthropologists' account.* Cambridge, MA: Harvard University Press.

Ladson-Billings, G. (2006). It's not the culture of poverty, it's the poverty of culture: The problem with teacher education. *Anthropology & Education Quarterly, 37*(2), 104–109.

Lave, J., & Wenger, E. (1991). *Situated learning: Legitimate peripheral participation.* Cambridge, UK: Cambridge University Press.

Lee, C. D. (2007). *Culture, literacy and learning: Taking bloom in the midst of the whirlwind.* New York: Teachers College Press.

Levinson, B. A. (Ed.). (2000). *Schooling the symbolic animal: Social and cultural dimensions of education.* Lanham, MD: Rowman & Littlefield.

Levinson, B. A., Foley, D. E., & Holland, D. (Eds.). (1996). *The cultural production of the educated person: Critical ethnographies of schooling and local practice.* Albany: State University of New York Press.

Lewis, O. (1959). *Five families: Mexican case studies in the culture of poverty.* New York: Basic Books.

Lomawaima, K. T. (1994). *They called it prairie light: The story of Chilocco Indian School.* Lincoln: University of Nebraska Press.

Moll, L., & González, N. (2004). Engaging life: A funds of knowledge approach to multicultural education. In J. Banks & C. A. M. Banks (Eds.), *Handbook of research on multicultural education* (2nd ed., pp. 699–715). New York: Jossey-Bass.

Nasir, S. N., Rosebery, A. S., Warren, B., & Lee, C. D. (2006). Learning as a cultural process: Achieving equity through diversity. In R. K. Sawyer (Ed.), *The Cambridge handbook of the learning sciences.* (pp. 489–504). Cambridge, UK: Cambridge University Press.

Oakes, J. (2005). *Keeping track: How schools structure inequality* (2nd ed.). New Haven, CT: Yale University Press.

Ogbu, J. (1978). *Minority education and caste: The American system in cross-cultural perspectives.* New York: Academic Press.

Payne, R. (1996). *A framework for understanding poverty* (3rd rev. ed.). Highlands, TX: aha! Processes, Ink.

Pollock, M. (2008). From shallow to deep: Toward a thorough cultural analysis of school achievement patterns. *Anthropology & Education Quarterly, 39*(4), 369–380.

Qin, D. B. (2006). "Our child doesn't talk to us anymore": Alienation in immigrant Chinese families. *Anthropology & Education Quarterly, 37*(2), 162–179.

Sleeter, C. E. (2011). *The academic and social value of ethnic studies: A research review.* Washington, DC: National Education Association.

Spindler, G. (1996). Comments from Exploring Culture Institute, San Francisco, CA. In R. Henze and M. Hauser. *Personalizing culture through anthropological and educational perspectives.* [Educational Practitioner Report #4, Center for Research on Education, Diversity and Excellence (CREDE).] Retrieved April 12, 2012 from http://www.cal.org/crede/pdfs/epr4.pdf.

Spring, J. (2007). *Deculturalization and the struggle for equality: A brief history of the education of dominated cultures in the United States* (5th ed.). Boston: McGraw-Hill.

Stolzenberg, N. M. (2001). What we talk about when we talk about culture. *American Anthropologist, 103*, 432–446.

Turner, T. (1993) Anthropology and multiculturalism: What is anthropology that multiculturalists should be mindful of it? *Cultural Anthropology, 8*(4), 411–429.

Valdes, G. (1996). *Con respeto: Bridging the distance between culturally diverse families and schools: An ethnographic portrait.* New York: Teachers College Press.

Valenzuela, A. (1999). *Subtractive schooling: U.S.-Mexican youth and the politics of caring.* Albany: State University of New York Press.

Visweswaran, K. (2010). *Un/common cultures: Racism and the rearticulation of cultural difference.* Durham, NC: Duke University Press.

Vygostsky, L. (1978). *Mind in society: The development of higher psychological processes.* Cambridge, MA: Harvard University Press.

Willis, P. (1977). *Learning to labor: How working class kids get working class jobs.* New York: Columbia University Press.

Wolf, E. (1982). *Europe and the people without history.* Berkeley: University of California Press.

Wyman, L., & Kashatok, G. (2008). Getting to know students' communities. In M. Pollock (Ed.), *Everyday anti-racism: Getting real about race in school* (pp. 299–305). New York: The New Press.

StockbrokerXtra/Glow Images

Race, Class, Gender, and Disability in the Classroom

Carl A. Grant and Christine E. Sleeter

Schools have always been a focal point of debate. What should be taught? How should students be organized for instruction? How should teachers be prepared? What constitute acceptable standards, and who should set them? Ongoing social issues continuously fuel debate about these questions. We will discuss three such current patterns.

First, the standards and testing movement coupled with a privatization movement currently drives much of schooling. Although many of you might not remember schooling before these movements took hold, they began to affect schooling with the report *A Nation at Risk: The Imperative for Educational Reform* (National Commission on Excellence in Education, 1983), which warned that U.S. preeminence on the world stage was being eroded by the mediocre performance of its educational institutions. A system of setting standards and measuring student performance based on them was cemented by passage of the No Child Left Behind Act in 2001, which requires that by 2014, all students will perform at a proficient level or higher in reading and math. Testing was built into the federal Race to the Top system for allocating federal funds to schools, and curriculum standards into the Common Core Standards that states are adopting. As a vice principal recently remarked to one of us, "Everything in our school is being driven by tests." Effects of these movements vary widely. Schools in which students had already been achieving well have continued to operate much as they had before. In schools that had not been doing well—particularly schools in low-income communities and those with large proportions of students of color and/or English learners—pressure to raise test scores has been found to turn the work of teachers into that of curriculum technicians and test managers (Valli, Croninger, & Chambliss, 2008), often while school district budgets are being slashed. Furthermore, distinctions between public and private schooling are becoming blurred, shifting schools in many areas toward corporate control and away from democratic community participation (Lipman & Haines, 2007). Many advocates of multicultural education quickly found attention to diversity and equity being replaced by attention to standards and student test scores, particularly in schools in which multicultural education had been seen as having to do mainly with getting along rather than with improving academic teaching and learning (Sleeter, 2005, 2007).

Second, at the same time, since the 1970s universities had developed an increasingly rich intellectual foundation supportive of diversity. The amount of multicultural research and curriculum mushroomed (Banks, 2009a; Banks & Banks, 2004), advancing perspectives that differed—in some cases sharply—from those of most political and economic leaders. This intellectual work paralleled the tremendous growth in ethnic and racial diversity the United States has experienced. By 2006, the population was roughly 64 percent non-Latino White, 16 percent Latino, 13 percent African American, 5 percent Asian and Pacific Islander, 1 percent Native American, and 1 percent other (U.S. Census Bureau, 2011). Whites were no longer the majority in many cities. In California, Hawaii, Louisiana, Mississippi, New Mexico, and Texas, no racial or ethnic group was a majority in the public schools. The largest portion of immigrants in the United States—about 53 percent—came from Latin America and the Caribbean (U.S. Census Bureau, 2010a), contributing to a social phenomenon being called "the hispanization of

America" (U.S. Department of Homeland Security, 2003). Although Christianity is by far the largest religion in the United States, one increasingly finds Islamic centers and mosques, Hindu and Buddhist temples, and Jewish temples in addition to more traditional churches (Eck, 2002). Islam is the fastest-growing religion in the United States as well as in several European nations such as the United Kingdom and France (Banks, 2009a). In 2006, the U.S. Census (2010b) reported that in U.S. households, 80 percent spoke only English at home while 20 percent spoke a language other than English.

Third, the United States became increasingly polarized along several dimensions. The September 11, 2001, attacks and then the wars in the Middle East led to a strong wave of patriotism and reluctance on the part of many people to criticize any aspect of U.S. culture or policy. Public sentiment about diversity rapidly became more negative, particularly toward Muslims and people of Arab descent. According to a Washington Post–ABC News poll, "a growing proportion of Americans are expressing unfavorable views of Islam, and a majority now say that Muslims are disproportionately prone to violence" (Deane & Fears, 2006). Politically and socially, Americans find themselves more divided than ever. On the one hand, the election of President Obama suggested the possibility of improved race relations. On the other hand, the construction of a 15-story, $100 million mosque and community center located near New York City's Ground Zero ignited national controversy. How should such a controversy be taught and who should decide? And how should teacher candidates be taught to deal with such issues?

Fourth, by 2001 the United States had grown increasingly segregated by race and class (Orfield & Lee, 2005), with gaps between "haves" and "have-nots" continuing to widen. The gradually rising levels of educational attainment had not been accompanied by a rising quality of life. As transnational corporations exported jobs to Third World nations in order to cut wages, many middle-class and working-class people in the United States experienced an erosion of their lifestyles, and the poverty level rose, especially among women and children (Johnston, 2007; Ulrich, 2004). According to the U.S. Census Bureau (2004), while the wealthiest fifth of the U.S. population's share of income increased from 44 percent of the total in 1973 to 50 percent in 2002, everyone else's share decreased. In 2010, Hacker and Pierson argued that we live in a "winner take all economy" in which, since the mid-1970s, the income of the top 1 percent of households increased by almost 260 percent, while the income of the lower 80 percent barely increased during the same time period. The growing gap between rich and poor in the United States was increasingly discussed in news media (Taylor, 2011).

While education is necessary for upward mobility and community uplift, education does not wipe away racial advantages. For example, African Americans and Latinos earn consistently less than their White counterparts with the same level of education. In 2006, White high school graduates earned a median annual income of $32,931, compared to $26,368 for African Americans and $27,508 for Latinos. White professionals with advanced degrees earned a median annual income of $83,785, while African Americans with the same educational level earned $64,834 and Latinos earned $70,432 (U.S. Census Bureau, 2007).

Poverty and unemployment have hit communities of color harder than White communities (U.S. Census Bureau, 2000). Prisons have become a growth industry. Many leaders of color view the explosion of prison populations as a new form of slavery, a warehousing of unemployed young men of color. Indeed, between 1977 and 1985, "when the prison population almost tripled, 70 percent of new inmates were African American, Latino, or other nonwhite minorities," a fact that had been downplayed by classifying Latinos as White (Chanse, 2002, p. 3).

Most adults with disabilities are either unemployed or underemployed, and their earnings are often below the poverty level. In 2006, only 37 percent of disabled adults aged 16 and over were employed. About 21.5 percent of the population with disabilities was living on an income below the poverty level (U.S. Census Bureau, 2006). Passage of the Americans with Disabilities Act was designed to protect people with disabilities from discrimination, and while it has helped, it cannot solve many issues, such as lack of enough affordable housing.

A major thread running through the debates about schooling is the relative importance of preparing students for jobs versus preparing them for active citizenship. Schools have always done both, but much discussion about what schools should do increasingly has emphasized job preparation; little has been said about citizenship. What kind of a nation do we want for ourselves and our children given the challenges and problems we have been facing? How should limited resources be distributed given our diversity and virtually everyone's desire for a good life? How can tomorrow's citizens who are in the schools now be prepared to build the kinds of institutions that support a diverse democracy in which people are truly equal? Who gets to decide the most effective ways of educating children from diverse backgrounds? Students we teach usually give one of three reasons for wanting to become teachers: (1) They love kids, (2) they want to help students, or (3) they want to make school more exciting than it was when they were students. If one of these is the reason you chose to enter the teaching profession, we hope you will see the demographic and social trends previously described as being challenging and will realize that your love and help are needed not just for some students but for all students.

This chapter discusses the importance of race, class, gender, language, and disability in classroom life and provides alternative approaches to dealing with these issues in the classroom.

Race, Class, Gender, Language, Disability, and Classroom Life

Ask yourself what you know about race, ethnicity, class, gender, language, and disability as they apply to classroom life. Could you write one or two good paragraphs about what these words mean? How similar or different would your meanings be from those of your classmates? How much do these dynamics of social organization influence the way you think about teaching? If you and your classmates organize into small discussion groups (try it) and listen closely to one another, you will probably notice some distinct differences in the ways you see the importance of these dynamics. The point of such an exercise is not to show that you have different ideas and interpretations but to challenge you to think clearly about what your ideas and interpretations mean for working with your students: How will you teach with excellence and equity?

Race, social class, and gender are used to construct categories of people in society. On your college application form, you were probably asked to indicate your race, ethnicity, gender, disability status, and parents' place of employment. Most institutions want to know such information in order to analyze and report data related to any or all of your ascribed characteristics. Social scientists studying school practices often report results according to race, class, home language, and gender. Dynamics of race, class, language, gender, and disability can influence your knowledge and understanding of your students. It is important for you to consider these dynamics collectively, not separately. Each of your students is a member of multiple status groups, and these simultaneous memberships—in interaction with dynamics in the broader society—influence the students' perceptions and actions.

For example, a child in the classroom may be not just Chinese American but also male, middle class, native English speaking, Buddhist, and not disabled. Thus, he is a member of a historically marginalized group—but also of a gender group and a social class that have histori-cally oppressed others. Therefore, his view of reality and his actions based on that view will differ from those of a middle-class Asian American girl whose first language is Korean or a lower-class Asian American boy whose first language is Hmong and who has spina bifida. A teacher's failure to consider the integration of race (including national origin), social class, and gender can lead to an oversimplified or inaccurate understanding of what occurs in schools and, therefore, to an inappropriate or simplistic prescription for educational equity and excellence. You may have noticed, for example, teachers assuming (often mistakenly) that Mexican Amer-ican students identify strongly with one another and that they view issues in much the same way, or that African American male students have the same goals and views as African American female students.

We often begin working with teacher candidates by having them take a self-inventory of the sociocultural groups they have been exposed to in their own schooling and religious or work situations. The more honestly you examine your familiarity with the backgrounds of different children, the more readily you can begin to learn about people to whom you have had little exposure. It will be a much greater limitation on your ability to teach well if you assume you know more about different students than you actually know than if you recognize whose lives are unfamiliar to you so that you can learn.

Approaches to Multicultural Education

Educators often work with students of color, students from low-income backgrounds, and White female students according to one of five approaches to multicultural education. As we briefly explain these approaches, ask yourself which one you are most comfortable using in your teaching. Before we begin this discussion, you should understand two important points. First, space does not allow for a complete discussion of each approach; for a thorough discussion, please refer to *Making Choices for Multicultural Education: Five Approaches to Race, Class, and Gender* (Sleeter & Grant, 2009). Second, it is fine to discover that you are a true eclectic or that none of the approaches satisfies your teaching style as long as you are not straddling the fence. Indecision, dissatisfaction, and frustration in teaching style and technique may confuse your students. Also, to be the dynamic teacher you want to be, you need a teaching philosophy that is well thought out and makes learning exciting for your students. Good teaching requires that you have a comprehensive understanding of what you are doing in the classroom, why, and how you are doing it.

Teaching of the Exceptional and the Culturally Different

If you believe that a teacher's chief responsibility is to prepare all students to fit into and achieve within the existing school and society, this approach may appeal to you. It may be especially appealing if categories of students, such as students of color, special education students, or language-minority students are behind in the main subject areas of the traditional curriculum. The goals of this approach are to equip students with the cognitive skills, concepts, information, language, and values traditionally required by U.S. society and eventually to enable them to hold a job and function within society's institutions and culture. Teachers using this approach often begin by determining the achievement levels of students, comparing their achievement to grade-level norms, and then working diligently to help those who are behind to catch up.

A good deal of research documents learning strengths of students of different sociocultural groups, suggesting that if a teacher learns to identify and build on their strengths, students will learn much more effectively than if a teacher assumes the child cannot learn very well. For example, based on a study of a school that does an exceptionally good job educating low-income Latino students, Casanova (2010) identified five components to the school's success that all stem from what she calls "academic optimism": high expectations, leadership, counseling and guidance, instruction of English learners based on high expectations and flexibility of placement options, and a continuous search for improvement. She emphasizes that these components are tools for students' success and that how the tools are used in this school depends on the conviction of the principal and teachers that the students are capable of high-quality academic learning.

Teachers who understand how to build on the culture and language of students will read the classroom behavior of such children more accurately and adjust their instructional processes accordingly without lowering their expectations for learning. As another example, Moses and

Cobb (2001) taught algebra to inner-city middle school students by building on their experience. Students were having difficulty with numerical directionality—positive and negative numbers. The teachers sent the students to the local subway and had them diagram the subway system in terms of directionality. The teachers then helped the students represent their experience with the subway numerically in the process, helping them to translate the familiar (subway routes) into the unfamiliar (positive and negative numbers).

Starting where the students are and using instructional techniques and content familiar to them are important. For example, one teacher who used this approach helped two African American students who had moved from a large urban area to a much smaller college town to catch up on their writing skills by having them write letters to the friends they had left behind in the city. Another teacher grouped the girls in her ninth-grade class who were having problems in algebra, allowing them to work together, support one another, and not be intimidated by the boys in the class who had received the kind of socialization that produces good math students. One other teacher provided two students with learning disabilities with materials written at their reading level that covered concepts comparable to those the rest of the class was reading about. Another teacher provided intensive English language development to her two limited-English-speaking Latino students. A teacher may believe that only one or two students in the classroom need this approach or that all of them do, especially if the school is located in an inner-city community or barrio.

In sum, the heart of this approach is building bridges for students to help them acquire the cognitive skills and knowledge expected of the so-called average White middle-class student. This approach accepts the concept that there is a body of knowledge all students should learn but proposes that teachers should teach that knowledge in whatever way works so that students understand and learn it.

Human Relations Approach

If you believe that a major purpose of the school is to help students learn to live together harmoniously in a world that is becoming smaller and smaller and if you believe that greater social equality will result if students learn to respect one another regardless of race, class, gender, or disability, then this approach may be of special interest to you. Its goal is to promote a feeling of unity, tolerance, and acceptance among people: "I'm okay and you're okay." The human relations approach engenders positive feelings among diverse students, promotes group identity and pride for students of color, reduces stereotypes, and works to eliminate prejudice and biases. For example, a teacher of a fourth-grade multiracial, mainstreamed classroom spends considerable time during the first two weeks of each year, and some time thereafter, doing activities to promote good human relations in the class. Early in the year, he uses a sociogram to learn student friendship patterns and to make certain that every child has a buddy. He also uses this activity to discover how negative or positive the boy–girl relationships are. He uses sentence-completion activities to discover how students are feeling about themselves and their family members. Using data, he integrates into his curriculum concepts of social acceptance and humanness for all people, the reduction and elimination of stereotypes, and information to help students feel good about themselves and their families, ethnic, and cultural groups. Also, he regularly brings to his classroom speakers who represent the diversity in society to show all students that they, too, can be successful.

The curriculum for the human relations approach addresses individual differences and similarities. It includes contributions of the groups of which the students are members and provides accurate information about various ethnic, racial, disability, gender, or social-class groups about whom the students hold stereotypes. Instructional processes include a good deal of cooperative learning, role-playing, and vicarious or real experiences to help the students develop appreciation of others. Advocates of this approach suggest that it should be comprehensive, integrated into several subject areas, and schoolwide. For example, a school attempting to promote gender equality is working at cross-purposes if lessons in language arts teach students to recognize sex stereotypes while in the science class girls are not expected to perform as well as boys and thus are not pushed to do so. These contradictory practices simply reaffirm sex stereotypes. While the teaching-the-exceptional-and-the-culturally-different approach emphasizes helping students acquire cognitive skills and knowledge in the traditional curriculum, the human relations approach focuses on attitudes and feelings students have about themselves and one another.

Single-Group Studies Approach

We use the phrase *single-group studies* to refer to the study of a particular group of people, for example, disability studies or Native American studies. The single-group studies approach seeks to raise the social status of the target group by helping young people examine how the group has been oppressed historically despite its capabilities and achievements. Unlike the two previous approaches, this one (and the next two) views school knowledge as political rather than neutral and presents alternatives to the existing Eurocentric, male-dominant curriculum. It focuses on one specific group at a time so the history, perspectives, and worldview of that group can be developed coherently rather than piecemeal. It also examines the current social status of the group and actions taken historically as well as contemporarily to further the group's interests. Single-group studies are oriented toward political action and liberation. Advocates of this approach hope that students will develop more respect for the group as well as the knowledge and commitment needed to work to improve the group's status in society.

For example, women's studies was created with a "vision of a world in which all persons can develop to their fullest potential and be free from all ideologies and structures that consciously and unconsciously oppress and exploit some for the advantage of others" (National Women's Studies Association, 2005). Gay and lesbian studies develops "an intellectual community for students and faculty that is ethnically diverse and committed to gender parity" ("A National Survey," 1990–1991, p. 53). Ethnic studies helps "students develop the ability to make reflective decisions on issues related to race, ethnicity, culture, and language and to take personal, social, and civic actions to help solve the racial and ethnic problems in our national and world societies" (Banks, 2009b, p. 26).

Since the late 1960s and early 1970s, scholars have generated an enormous amount of research about various oppressed groups and have mapped out new conceptual frameworks within various disciplines. For example, Afrocentric scholars redefined the starting point of African American history from slavery to ancient Africa, in the process rewriting story lines for African American history. Beginning history with a group other than European males enables one to view historical events very differently. A group's story may begin in Asia and move east, begin in South or Central America and move north, begin in Europe and move west, or begin right here on the North American continent thousands of years ago. Furthermore, the story is different if one views the group as having started from a position of strength (e.g., African civilizations [Gates, 1999]), having then been subjugated, and now attempting to rebuild that strength rather than starting from a position of weakness (such as slavery) and then rising.

A single-group studies curriculum includes units or courses about the history and culture of a group (e.g., African American history, Chicano literature, disability studies). It teaches how the group has been victimized and has struggled to gain respect as well as current social issues facing the group. It is essential that such curricula be based on scholarship by people who have studied the group in depth rather than on your own ideas about what you think might be important. For example, *Pinoy Teach* (http://www.pinoyteach.com/) is a social studies curriculum from a Filipino studies perspective. Halagao (2004), one of its authors, explains that *Pinoy Teach* "is my insider's attempt to write our people's perspective into social studies. It reflects the experiences of brown people who are not passive bystanders, but rather active figures who construct historical and important moments" (p. 464).

Although single-group studies focus mainly on the curriculum, they also give some attention to instructional processes that benefit the target group. Women's studies programs, for example, have developed what is known as "feminist pedagogy" (see Chapter 7), a teaching approach that attempts to empower students. The main idea is that in the traditional classroom, women are socialized to accept other people's ideas. By reading text materials that were written mainly by men and provide a male interpretation of the world, women learn not to interpret the world for themselves. In the feminist classroom, women learn to trust and develop their own insights. The feminist teacher may assign material to read and may encourage students to generate discussion and reflections about it. The discussion and personal reflection are important parts of the process during which "control shifts from me, the teacher, the arbiter of knowing, to the interactions of students and myself with the subject matter" (Tetreault, 1989, p. 137).

A review of the impact of ethnic studies on students of color demonstrates the positive power of single-group studies, when designed and taught well. Of studies of 16 programs that Sleeter (2011) reviewed, studies of 15 found a positive impact on students' academic engagement, academic achievement, sense of personal empowerment, or a combination of these. Since single-group studies curricula that are designed for students who are members of the group being studied center on students' cultural reality, students become classroom "insiders" whose prior knowledge is linked with academic learning. In that context, their thinking and problem-solving abilities shine; they become intellectually engaged and often begin to acquire an academic identity that supports their ethnic identity.

In summary, the single-group studies approach works toward social change. It challenges the knowledge normally taught in schools, arguing that that knowledge reinforces control by wealthy White men over everyone else. This approach offers an in-depth study of oppressed groups for the purpose of empowering group members, developing in them a sense of pride and group consciousness, and helping members of dominant groups understand where others are coming from.

Multicultural Education Approach

Multicultural education has become the most popular term used by educators to describe education for pluralism. We apply this term to a particular approach that multicultural education theorists discuss most often. As you will notice, this approach synthesizes many ideas from the previous three approaches. Its goals are to reduce prejudice and discrimination against oppressed groups, to work toward equal opportunity and social justice for all groups, and to effect an equitable distribution of power among members of different cultural groups. These goals are actualized by attempting to reform the total schooling process for all children, regardless of whether the school is an all-White suburban school or a multiracial urban school. Schools that are reformed around principles of pluralism and equality would then contribute to broader social reform.

Various practices and processes in the school are reconstructed so that the school models equality and pluralism. For example, the curriculum is organized around concepts basic to each discipline, but content elaborating on those concepts is drawn from the experiences and perspectives of several different U.S. groups. If you are teaching literature, you select literature written by members of different groups. This not only teaches students that groups other than Whites have produced literature but also enriches the concept of literature because it enables students to experience different literature forms that are common to all writing. For example, the universal struggle for self-discovery and cultural connection within a White-dominant society can be examined by reading about a Puerto Rican girl in *Felita* (Mohr, 1990), a Chinese girl in *Dragonwings* (Yep, 1975), an African American boy in *Scorpions* (Myers, 1990), a European American girl in *The Great Gilly Hopkins* (Paterson, 1987), and Iranian youth in *Teenage Refugees from Iran Speak Out* (Strazzabosco, 1995).

It is also important that the contributions and perspectives you select depict each group as the group would depict itself and show the group as active and dynamic. This requires that you learn about various groups and become aware of what is important and meaningful to them. For example, Arab peoples are highly diverse; in contrast to popular stereotypes, they have a long history of feminism (Darraj, 2002), and in some Arab countries, women work as well-educated professionals. As another example, teachers wishing to teach about famous Native Americans would ask members of different Native American tribes whom they would like to see celebrated instead of holding up to their students Pocahontas, Kateri Tekakwitha, or Sacajawea. These Native Americans are often thought among their people to have served White interests more than those of Native Americans. Additionally, African Americans are concerned when an African American athlete or entertainer is so often held up as the hero and heroine for the group instead of African Americans who have done well in other areas of life, such as science or literature.

In this approach, instruction starts by assuming that students are capable of learning complex material and performing at a high level of skill. Each student has a personal, unique learning style that teachers discover and build on when teaching. The teacher draws on and uses the conceptual schemes (ways of thinking, knowledge about the world) that students bring to school. Cooperative learning is fostered, and both boys and girls are treated equally in a nonsexist manner. A staff as diverse as possible is hired and assigned responsibilities nonstereotypically. Ideally, more than one language is taught, enabling all students to become bilingual. The multicultural education approach, more than the previous three, advocates total school reform to make the school reflect diversity. It also advocates giving equal attention to a variety of cultural groups regardless of whether specific groups are represented in the school's student population.

Multicultural Social Justice Education

Reflect back on the various forms of social inequality mentioned at the opening of this chapter. Multicultural social justice education deals more directly than the other approaches with oppression and social structural inequality based on race, social class, gender, and disability. Its purpose is to prepare future citizens to take action to make society better serve the interests of all groups of people, especially those who are of color, poor, female, or have disabilities. The approach is rooted in social reconstructionism, which seeks to reconstruct society toward greater equity in race, class, gender, and disability. This approach also questions ethics and power relations embedded in the new global economy. It draws on the penetrating vision of George Bernard Shaw (1921/2004), who exclaimed, "You see things, and you say, 'Why?' But I dream things that never were, and I say, 'Why not?'"

This approach extends the multicultural education approach in that the curriculum and instruction of both are very similar, but four practices are unique to multicultural social justice education. First, democracy is actively practiced in the schools (Banks, 2007; Parker, 2003). Reading the U.S. Constitution and hearing lectures on the three branches of government is a passive way to learn about democracy. For students to understand democracy, they must live it. They must practice politics, debate, social action, and the use of power (Osler & Starkey, 2005). In the classroom, this means that students are given the opportunity to direct a good deal of their learning and to learn how to be responsible for that direction. This does not mean that teachers abdicate the running of their classroom to the students but rather that they guide and direct students so they learn how to learn and develop skills for wise decision making. Shor (1980) describes this as helping students become subjects rather than objects in the classroom, and Freire (1985) says it produces individuals "who organize themselves reflectively for action rather than men [and women] who are organized for passivity" (p. 82).

Second, students learn how to analyze institutional inequality in their own life circumstances. Freire (1973) distinguished among critical consciousness, naïve consciousness, and magical consciousness:

> *Critical consciousness represents things and facts as they exist empirically, in their causal and circumstantial correlations, naïve consciousness considers itself superior to facts, in control of facts, and thus free to understand them as it pleases. Magic consciousness, in contrast, simply apprehends facts and attributes them to a superior power by which it is controlled and to which it must therefore submit. (p. 44)*

To put it another way, a person with *critical consciousness* wants to know how the world actually works and is willing to analyze the world carefully for him- or herself. A person with naive or magic consciousness does not do that. If one sees the world through magic, one assumes that one cannot understand or affect the world; things just happen. If one sees the world naively, one assumes cause–effect relationships that one wants to assume or that one has been told exist without investigating them or thinking critically for oneself. In a stratified society, Freire (1973) argued, most ordinary people see the world naively or magically as the elite would wish them to see it. Ordinary people believe either that they have no power to change the way the world works for them or that their problems have no relationship to their position in the power hierarchy.

For example, students are taught that education is the doorway to success and that if they obey the teacher and do their work, they will succeed. However, in reality, education pays off better for Whites than for people of color because of institutionalized racism that can be challenged—but only when people recognize it and work collectively to dismantle it. Education also pays off better for men than women due to institutional sexism. Average annual earnings of full-time working women are only about 77 percent of the earnings of full-time working men (Institute for Women's Policy Research, 2011), a gap that has remained constant since 2001 and that contributes heavily to the pauperization of women and children in female-headed households. This approach teaches students to question what they hear about how society works from other sources and to analyze experiences of people like themselves in order to understand more fully what the problems actually are.

Third, students learn to engage in social action so they can change unfair social processes. Parker (2003) explained that teaching for democracy should mean preparing young people for enlightened political engagement: "the action or participatory domain of citizenship" (p. 33), such as voting, contacting officials, deliberating, and engaging in boycotts, based on the "knowledge, norms, values, and principles that shape this engagement" (p. 34). In other words, democracy is not a spectator sport. For example, some stories that elementary school children read could deal with issues involving discrimination and oppression and could suggest ways to deal with such problems. Students of all ages can be taught to identify sexist advertising of products sold in their community and how to take action to encourage advertisers to stop these types of practices. Advocates of this approach do not expect children to reconstruct the world, but they do expect the schools to teach students how to do their part in helping the nation achieve excellence and equity in all areas of life.

Fourth, bridges are built between various oppressed groups (e.g., people who are poor, people of color, and White women) so they can work together to advance their common interests. This is important because it can energize and strengthen struggles against oppression. However, getting groups to work together is difficult because members often believe that they would have to place some of their goals second to those of other groups. Furthermore, racial groups find themselves divided along gender and class lines to the extent that middle-class males of all colors fail to take seriously the concerns of women and of lower-class members of their own groups. Childs (1994) describes "transcommunal" organizations, such as the African American/Korean alliance in Los Angeles, that bring different groups together to identify and work on common concerns.

You now have an idea of the approaches used to teach multicultural education. Which one best suits your teaching philosophy and style? An equally important question is: Which approach will best help to bring excellence and equity to education? The next section of this chapter provides an example of how one teacher brings both excellence and equity to her classroom.

Ms. Julie Wilson and Her Approach to Teaching

The following example describes a few days in the teaching life of Ms. Julie Wilson, a first-year teacher in a medium-large city. Which approach to multicultural education do you think Ms. Wilson is using? With which of her teaching actions do you agree or disagree? What would you do if assigned to her class?

May 23

Julie Wilson was both elated and sad that she had just completed her last exam at State U. As she walked back to her apartment, she wondered where she would be at this time next year. She had applied for 10 teaching positions and had been interviewed three times. As Julie entered her apartment building, she checked her e-mail on her phone. The first message she saw was from a school district where she had interviewed earlier in the week. It started: "We are pleased to offer you a teaching position." Julie leaped up the stairs three at a time. She burst into the apartment, yelling at her two roommates. "I've got a job! I got the job at Hoover Elementary. My first teaching job, a fifth-grade class!"

Hoover Elementary had been a part of a desegregation plan that brought together students from several different neighborhoods in the city. Hoover was situated in an urban renewal area to which city officials were giving a lot of time and attention and on which they were spending a considerable amount of money. City officials wanted to bring the Whites back into the city from suburbs and to encourage middle-class people of color to remain in the city. They also wanted to improve the life chances for the poor. Julie had been hired because the principal was looking for teachers who had some record of success in working with diverse students. So far, students were doing well enough on annual testing that the school was not on the list of schools needing improvement.

Julie had a 3.5 grade point average and had worked with a diverse student population in her practicum and student-teaching experience. She had strong letters of recommendation from her cooperating teacher and university supervisor. Julie also had spent her last two summers working as a counselor in a camp that enrolled a wide diversity of students.

August 25

Julie was very pleased with the way her classroom looked. She had spent the last three days getting it ready for the first day of school. Plants, posters, goldfish, and an old rocking chair added to the warmth of an attractive classroom. There was also a big sign across the room that said "Welcome, Fifth Graders." Tomorrow was the big day.

She had also studied the state curriculum standards and textbooks for her grade level and had sketched out some thematic units that addressed the standards creatively. She checked with her principal to make sure he would support her ideas, which he agreed to do as long as she did not stray from the expected curriculum standards and as long as her students performed well on the state and school district tests.

August 26

Twenty-eight students entered Julie's classroom: fifteen girls and thirteen boys. There were ten White students, two Hmong students, six Latino students, nine African American students, and one Bosnian student. Three of the students were learning disabled, and one was in a wheelchair. Eleven of the students were from middle-class homes, nine were from working-class homes, and the remaining eight were from very poor homes. Julie greeted each student with a big smile and a friendly hello as each entered the room. She asked students their names and told them hers. She then asked them to take the seat with their name on the desk.

After the school bell rang, Julie introduced herself to the whole class. She told them that she had spent most of her summer in England and that while she was there, she had often thought about this day—her first day as a teacher. She talked briefly about some of the places she had visited in England as she pointed to them on a map. She concluded her introduction by telling them a few things about her family. Her mother and father owned a dairy farm in Wisconsin, and she had one older brother, Wayne, and two younger sisters, Mary and Patricia.

Julie asked if there were any students new to the school. Lester, an African American male, raised his hand, along with a female Hmong student, Mai-ka, the Bosnian female student, Dijana, and two Latino students, Maria and Jesus. Julie asked Mai-ka if she would like to tell the class her complete name, how she had spent her summer, and one favorite thing she liked to do. Then she asked the same of the other four. After all five had finished introducing themselves, Julie invited the other students to do the same. Julie then asked Lourdes, a returning student, to tell Mai-ka, Maria, Dijana, Jesus, and Lester about Hoover Elementary. As she listened to the students, she realized that Dijana and Jesus were both newcomers to the United States and neither spoke English fluently. To assist them, she asked two other students to buddy with them for the day. She realized that she would need to figure out a good buddy system and that she would also need help in making her teaching accessible to these students while they learned English.

Once the opening greetings were completed, Julie began a discussion about the importance of the fifth grade and how special this grade was. She explained that this was a grade and class where a lot of learning would take place along with a lot of fun. As Julie spoke, the students were listening intently. Julie radiated warmth and authority. Some of the students glanced at each other unsmilingly as she spoke of the hard work; however, when she mentioned "a lot of fun," the entire class perked up and looked at each other with big grins on their faces. Julie had begun working on her educational philosophy in the Introduction to Education course at State U. Although she was continually modifying the way she thought about teaching, her basic philosophical beliefs had remained much the same. One of her major beliefs was that students should actively participate in planning and shaping their own educational experiences. This, she believed, was as important for fifth graders as twelfth graders.

Julie asked the students if they were ready to take care of their classroom governance—deciding on rules, helpers, a discipline code, and time for classroom meetings. The class responded enthusiastically. The first thing the students wanted to do was to decide on the class rules. Several began to volunteer rules:

"No stealing."

"No rock throwing on the playground."

"No sharpening pencils after the bell rings."

"No fighting."

As the students offered suggestions, Julie wrote them on the whiteboard. After giving about 16 suggestions, the class concluded. Julie commented, "All the rules seem very important"; she then asked the class what they should do with the rules. One student, Richard, suggested that they be written on poster board and placed in the upper corner of the room for all to see. Other class members said, "Yes, this is what we did last year in fourth grade."

William, however, said, "Yes, we did do this, but we rarely followed the rules after the first day we made them." Julie assured the class that this would not be the case this year and that they would have a weekly classroom meeting run by an elected official of the class. She then asked if they thought it would be helpful if they wrote their rules using positive statements, instead of "no" or negative statements. The class said yes and began to change statements such as "no stealing" to "always ask before borrowing" and "no rock throwing" to "rock throwing can severely hurt a friend." Once the rules were completed, the class elected its officers.

After the classroom governance was taken care of, Julie asked the students if they would like her to read them a story. An enthusiastic "yes" followed her question. Julie glanced at the clock as she picked up *Friends: Stories about New Friends, Old Friends and Unexpectedly True Friends* (Martin & Levithan, 2005) from the desk. The book is a varied collection of short stories, especially for young readers, written by authors of different cultural backgrounds. It was 11:35. She could hardly believe the morning had gone by so quickly. She read for 20 minutes. All of the students seemed to be enjoying the story except Lester and Ben, two African American male students. Lester and Ben were drawing pictures, communicating nonverbally between themselves, and ignoring the rest of the class members. Julie decided that because they were quiet and not creating a disturbance, she would leave them alone.

After lunch, Julie had the class do two activities designed to help her learn about each student both socially and academically. She had the students do a self-concept activity, in which they did sentence completions that asked them to express how they felt about themselves. Then she had them play math and reading games to informally assess their math and reading skills. These activities took the entire afternoon, and Julie was as pleased as the students when the school day came to an end.

When Julie arrived at her apartment, she felt exhausted. She had a quick dinner and shower and then crawled into bed. She set the alarm for 7:00 p.m. and quickly fell asleep. By 10:30 that night, she had examined the students' self-concept activity and compared the information she had collected from the informal math and reading assessment with the official information from the students' cumulative records. She thought about each student's achievement record, social background, race, gender, and exceptionality. She said aloud, "I need to make plans soon to meet every parent. I need to find out about the students' lives at home, the parents' expectations, and whether I can get some of them to volunteer."

Julie turned off her desk lamp at 11:45 to retire for the evening. She read a few pages from Anne Fadiman's (1997) *The Spirit Catches You and You Fall Down*, which tells the story of a Hmong child and the culture clash she experienced with American doctors. Then she turned out the light. Tonight she was going to sleep with less tension and nervousness than she had the night before. She felt good about the way things had gone today and was looking forward to tomorrow. As Julie slept, she dreamed of her class. Their faces and most of their names and backgrounds floated through her mind.

Eight of the ten White students were from Briar Creek, a middle-class single-unit housing community; these students were performing at grade level or above in all scholastic areas, and each of them was at least a year ahead in some core-area subject. Charles, who had used a wheelchair since being in an automobile accident three years ago, was three years ahead in both reading and math. However, Elaine and Bob had chosen a mixture of positive and negative adjectives when doing the self-concept activity, and this concerned Julie. She would keep her eye on them to try to determine the cause of their problems.

Estelle and Todd, the other two White students, were between six months and a year behind in most academic areas. Estelle had been diagnosed as learning disabled (LD), but the information in her personal cumulative folder seemed ambiguous about the cause of her problem. Julie wondered whether Estelle was classified as LD based on uncertain reasons. She recalled an article that discussed the LD label as being a social construction rather than a medical condition.

Both Mai-ka and Chee, the Hmong students, were at grade level or very close in their subjects but were having some difficulty with oral English. Chee's family owned a restaurant in the neighborhood. The rumor mill reported that they were doing very well financially, so well that they had recently opened a restaurant in the downtown area of the city. Five of the six Latino students were Mexican Americans born in the United States. Maria, José, and Lourdes were bilingual; Richard and Carmen were monolingual with English as their primary language; and Jesus spoke mainly Spanish. Maria, José, and Lourdes were from working-class homes, and Richard, Jesus, and Carmen were from very poor homes. The achievement scores of Lourdes, Carmen, and Richard were at least two years ahead of their grade level. José was working at grade level, and Maria and Jesus were one to two years behind. Jesus had immigrated to the U.S. only a year ago.

Five of the African American students—Lester, Ben, Gloria, Sharon, and Susan—were all performing two years behind grade level in all core-area subjects. All five lived in the Wendell Phillips low-rent projects. Two African American students—Shelly and Ernestine—lived in Briar Creek and were performing above grade level in all academic areas. Dolores and Gerard lived in Chatham, a working-class, predominantly African American neighborhood. Dolores was performing above grade level in all subjects; Gerard was behind in math. Gerard had also chosen several negative words when doing the self-concept activity.

Finally, Dijana, who had immigrated recently from Bosnia, did not know enough English to participate very well in any of the day's activities. Julie was glad that Shelly seemed to be taking an interest in helping her. Julie realized that she would need to think regularly about how to make sure Dijana was following along and would need to make sure both Dijana and Jesus were being tested for the English as a Second Language program. All students in Julie's class were obedient and came from families that encouraged getting a good education.

May 25, 7:30 a.m.

Julie liked arriving early at school. The engineer, Mike, usually had a pot of coffee made when she arrived. This was her time to get everything ready for the day. She had been teaching for almost one school year and was proud and pleased with how everything was going. The school principal, Mr. Griffin, had been in her class three times for formal visits and had told others, "Julie is an excellent teacher." He usually offered her one or two minor suggestions, such as "Don't call the roll every day; learn to take your attendance silently" and "The museum has an excellent exhibit on food and the human body your class may enjoy."

Julie had also been surprised by several things. She was surprised at how well students responded to active learning, group work, and thematic curricula, given the school district's emphasis on teaching all students the same thing, following the pacing guide. Julie had made several changes in the curriculum. She studied the content standards she was expected to follow so that she would be sure to teach material that would be included on tests. But she carefully wove the standards into a project-based curriculum. She had incorporated trade books into reading and language arts, using them along with the language arts package her school had adopted. She made available to the students a wide assortment of books that featured different races, exceptionalities, and socioeconomic classes. In some stories, both males and females were featured doing traditional as well as nontraditional activities. Stories were set in urban and rural settings, and some featured children with disabilities. It had taken Julie several months to acquire such a diverse collection of books for her students, and she had even spent some of her own money to buy the books, but the excitement the students had shown about the materials made the expense worthwhile. She made sure she was teaching the kinds of reading and language arts skills her students would be tested on but refused to sacrifice the richness of a literature-based curriculum for "test prep." The result in her classroom was that students were generally enthusiastic, engaged, and did somewhat better on the tests than average for fifth-grade classrooms in her district. Thankfully, her principal supported her.

Julie also had several computers in her class. A computer lab was down the hall, but she wanted her students to use the computer on a regular basis. When she discovered that Richard's father owned a computer store, she convinced him to lend the class two iMacs, and she convinced Mr. Griffin to purchase six more at cost. Several of the students from Briar Creek had computers at home. Charles and Elaine, Julie discovered, were wizards at the computer. Julie encouraged them to help the other students (and herself—because she had taken only one computer course at State U). The two students enjoyed this assignment and often had a small group of students remain after school to receive their help. Julie was pleased at how well Charles and Elaine handled this responsibility. Lester and Ben were Charles's favorite classmates; they liked the computer, but Julie believed they liked Charles and his electric wheelchair even more. Julie had heard them say on several occasions that Charles was "cool." Lester's and Ben's work was showing a steady improvement, and Charles enjoyed having two good friends. This friendship, Julie believed, had excellent mutual benefits for all concerned, including herself.

Julie's mathematics pedagogy was built on two principles. First, she built on the thinking and life experiences of the students. Second, she sought to provide students with insights into the role of mathematics in the various contexts of society. These two principles of mathematics pedagogy guided her daily teaching. Julie often took her class to the supermarket, to the bank, and to engineering firms—usually by way of online "field trips." She made certain that she selected firms that employed men and women of color and White women in positions of leadership. During face-to-face field trips, she requested that a representative from these groups spend a few minutes with the students, explaining their roles and duties. On one occasion, Julie's students questioned a federal government official about the purpose and intent of the U.S. Census. Shelly, who was actually biracial, asked, "How are racial categories constructed?"

Julie took the students on a field trip to supermarkets in different areas of town so the students could compare the prices and quality of products (e.g., fruit, meat, and vegetables) between the suburban area and the inner-city area. This led to a letter-writing campaign to the owner of the food chain to explain their findings. The students also wondered why the cost of gas was cheaper in the suburban areas than in the inner-city area. This became a math, social studies, and language arts lesson. Students wrote letters and conducted interviews to ascertain the cost of delivering the gas to the inner city as compared to the suburban areas of the city and to ascertain the rental fee for service station property in the inner city in comparison to the suburban areas. Math skills were used to determine whether there needed to be a difference in gas prices between the areas after rental fees and delivery charges were taken into consideration.

Julie used advertisements and editorials from newspapers and magazines to help students see the real-life use of such concepts as sexism, justice, and equity. She supplemented her social studies curriculum on a regular basis. She found the text biased in several areas. She integrated into the assigned curriculum information from the history and culture of different racial and ethnic groups. For example, when teaching about the settling of the local community years ago, Julie invited a Native American historian and a White historian to give views on how the settling took place and on problems and issues associated with it. She invited an African American historian and a Latino historian to discuss what was presently happening in the area. She had her students identify toys that had been made in Third World countries, and she explored with them the child labor and low-wage work that many transnational corporations had put in place in order to maximize corporate profits. Students were usually encouraged to undertake different projects in an effort to provide a comprehensive perspective on the social studies unit under study. Choices were up to the student, but Julie maintained high expectations and insisted that excellence in every phase of the work was always necessary for each student. She made certain that during the semester each student was a project leader. She also made certain that boys and girls worked together. For example, Julie knew that Ben, Lester, and Charles usually stayed close together and did not have a girl as a member of their project team. She also knew that Carmen was assertive and had useful knowledge about the project on which they were working, so she put Carmen on the project team.

Julie made sure that class projects were connected with the curriculum standards, and she closely her monitored students' learning regularly. By the end of the year, Julie's students were scoring well on the district-mandated achievement tests; on average, they compared well with other fifth-grade students. She was especially pleased to see how well her new immigrant students, Jesus and Dijana, had learned to work with the curriculum and the rest of the class. Although they had been quiet and timid at the beginning of the semester, they were now talkative and inquisitive.

Julie did have two problems with her class that she could not figure out. Shelly and Ernestine did not get along well with any of the other African American students, especially Ben and Lester. George and Hank, two White boys from Briar Creek, had considerable difficulty getting along with José and went out of their way to be mean to Lourdes and Maria. Julie was puzzled by George's and Hank's behavior; she did not think it was racially motivated because both of the boys got along pretty well with Shelly. She labored over this problem and discussed it with the school counselor. She wondered whether she had a problem related to a combination of race, class, and gender in George's and Hank's relationship with José, Lourdes, and Maria. She also concluded that she might have a social-class problem among the African American students.

Julie decided to discuss her concerns with the students individually. After some discussion, she discovered that the problem Shelly and Ernestine had with Ben and Lester was related to social class and color. Both Shelly and Ernestine had very fair skin color. They had grown up in a predominantly White middle-class community and had spent very little time around other African American students. Ben and Lester were dark-skinned male students who lived in a very poor neighborhood. Julie felt that if her assumptions were true, she would need help with this problem. She was successful in getting an African American child psychiatrist to talk to her class. She did this in relationship to an art unit that examined "color, attitude, and feelings." His discussion enabled Julie to continue her discussion with Shelly and Ernestine and get them to examine their prejudice.

George and Hank admitted to Julie, after several discussions, that they did not care too much for any girls. But Hispanic girls who wore funny clothes and ate non-American foods were a big bore. It took Julie several months of talking with George and Hank, using different reading materials and having them all work on a group project under her direction, to get George and Hank to reduce some of their prejudices. At the end of the semester, Julie still believed this problem had not been completely resolved. Thus, she shared it with the sixth-grade teacher.

At the end of the school year, Julie felt very good about her first year. She knew she had grown as a teacher. She believed her professors at State U, her cooperating teacher, and her university supervisor would give her very high marks. They had encouraged her to become a reflective teacher—committed, responsible, and wholehearted in her teaching effort. Julie believed she was well on her way to becoming a reflective teacher, and she looked forward to her second year with enthusiasm.

She also realized that her sensitivity to things she did not know had grown, and she planned to engage in some learning over the summer. As she had become aware of resentments that students from low-income families felt toward students from upper-income families, she began to wonder what the city was doing to address poverty. She heard that the National Association for the Advancement of Colored People (NAACP), some Latino community leaders, and heads of homeless shelters were trying to work with the city council, and she wanted to find out more about how these groups viewed poverty in the city. She decided to join the NAACP so she could become more familiar with its activities. She also wanted to spend time with some Latino families because before her teaching experience, she had never talked directly with Latino adults; her principal suggested she should meet Luis Reyes, who directed a local community center and could help her do this. In addition, Julie felt somewhat overwhelmed by the amount of back-ground information she had never learned about different groups in the United States and decided to start reading; because she enjoyed novels, she would start with some by Toni Morrison, Louise Erdrich, James Baldwin, and Maxine Hong Kingston. She would also read the novel *Reading Lolita in Tehran* by Azar Nafisi (2003).

From what you know of Julie, what is her approach to multicultural education? Would you be comfortable doing as Julie did? Discuss Julie's teaching with your classmates. How would you change it?

Conclusion

In Julie's classroom, as in yours, race, class, gender, and disability are ascribed characteristics students bring to school that cannot be ignored. To teach with excellence, Julie had to affirm her students' diversity. Why do we say this?

For one thing, Julie needed to pay attention to her students' identities in order to help them achieve. She needed to acknowledge the importance of African American males to American life to hold the interest of Lester and Ben; she needed to acknowledge the prior learning of Mai-ka, Chee, Jesus, and Dijana to help them learn English and school material; she needed to become familiar with her students' learning styles so her teaching would be most effective.

For another thing, Julie needed to pay attention to her students' personal and social needs to help them perceive school as a positive experience. Some of her students disliked other students because of prejudices and stereotypes. Some of her students did not know how to relate to people in wheelchairs or to people who looked or talked differently. Some of her students felt negative about their own abilities. Such attitudes interfere not only with achievement but also with quality of life both today as students and later as adults in a pluralistic society.

Julie realized over the year the extent to which schools are connected with their social context. She remembered having to take a course called School and Society and had not under-stood why it was required. She remembered reading about societal pressures on schools; during the year, she had come to see how societal pressures translated into funding, programs, and local debates that directly affected resources and guidelines in her classroom. Furthermore, she realized the extent to which students are connected with their own cultural context. The African American students, for example, emphasized their African American identity and did not want to be regarded as White; teachers who tried to be color-blind regarded this as a problem, but teachers who found the community's diversity to be interesting saw it as a strength. On the other hand, immigrant students tried hard to fit in; Julie would not have understood why without considering why their families had immigrated and the pressures the children experienced.

Julie also knew that the future of the United States depends on its diverse children. Her students will all be U.S. adults one day regardless of the quality of their education. But what kind of adults will they become? Julie wanted them all to be skilled in a variety of areas, to be clear and critical thinkers, and to have a sense of social justice and caring for others. Julie had some personal selfish motives for this: She knew her own well-being in old age would depend directly on the ability of today's children to care for older people when they become adults. She also knew her students of today would be shaping the society in which her own children would one day grow up. She wanted to make sure they were as well prepared as possible to be productive citizens who had a vision of a better society. She drew from all of the approaches at one time or another to address specific problems and needs she saw in the classroom. But the approach she emphasized—the one that guided her planning—was multicultural social justice education.

How will you approach excellence and equity in your own classroom? We can guarantee that all of your students will have their identities shaped partly by their race, social class, and gender; all of them will notice and respond in one way or another to people who differ from themselves; and all of them will grow up in a society that is still in many ways racist, sexist, and classist. You are the only one who can decide what you will do about that.

QUESTIONS AND ACTIVITIES

3.1   Why is it important for teachers to strive to attain both excellence and equity for their students? What can you do to try to achieve both goals in your teaching?

3.2   What does each of these terms mean to you in relationship to classroom life: *race, ethnicity, language, class, gender,* and *disability?* How are your notions of these concepts similar to and different from those of your classmates?

3.3   Give an example of how such variables as race, language, class, and gender interact to influence the behavior of a particular student.

3.4   Name the five approaches to multicultural education identified by Grant and Sleeter. What are the assumptions and instructional goals of each approach?

3.5   In what significant ways does the multicultural social justice education approach differ from the other four approaches? What problems might a teacher experience when trying to implement this approach in the classroom? How might these problems be reduced or solved?

3.6   Visit a school in your community and interview several teachers and the principal about how the school has responded to diversity and equity both within the school and in the larger society. Using the typology of multicultural education described by the authors, determine what approach or combination of approaches to multicultural education are being used within the school. Share your findings with your classmates or fellow workshop participants.

3.7   Which approach to multicultural education is Julie using? Which aspects of her teaching do you especially like? Which aspects would you change?

3.8   Which approach to multicultural education described by the authors would you be the most comfortable using? Why?

REFERENCES

Banks, J. A. (2007). *Educating citizens in a multicultural society* (2nd ed.). New York: Teachers College Press.

Banks, J. A. (Ed.) (2009a). *The Routledge international companion to multicultural education.* New York & London: Routledge.

Banks, J. A. (2009b). *Teaching strategies for ethnic studies* (8th ed.). Boston: Allyn & Bacon.

Banks, J. A., & Banks, C. A. M. (Eds.). (2004). *Handbook of research on multicultural education* (2nd ed.). San Francisco: Jossey-Bass.

Casanova, U. (2010). *¡Sí, se puede! Learning from a high school that beats the odds.* New York: Teachers College Press.

Chanse, S. (2002). Racefile. *Colorlines, 5*(1), 3.

Childs, J. B. (1994). The value of transcommunal identity politics. *Z Magazine, 7*(7/8), 48–51.

Darraj, S. M. (2002, March). Understanding the other sister: The case of Arab feminism. *Monthly Review*, pp. 15–25.

Deane, C., & Fears, D. (2006, March 9). Negative perceptions of Islam increasing. *The Washington Post.* Retrieved August 28, 2011, from www.washingtonpost.com/wp-dyn/content/article/2006/03/08/AR2006030802221.html.

Eck, D. L. (2002). *A new religious America: How a "Christian country" has become the world's most religiously diverse nation.* San Francisco: HarperCollins.

Fadiman, A. (1997). *The spirit catches you and you fall down.* New York: Noonday.

Freire, P. (1973). *Education for critical consciousness.* New York: Seaburg.

Freire, P. (1985). *The politics of education: Culture, power, and liberation* (D. Macedo, Trans.). Boston: Bergin & Garvey.

Gates, H. L., Jr. (1999). *Wonders of the African world.* New York: Knopf.

Hacker, J. S., & Pierson, P. (2010). *Winner-take-all politics.* New York: Simon & Schuster.

Halagao, P. S. (2004). Holding up the mirror: The complexity of seeing your ethnic self in history. *Theory and Research in Social Education, 32*(4), 459–483.

Institute for Women's Policy Research. (2011). The gender wage gap: 2010. Retrieved August 29, 2011, from http://www.iwpr.org/publications/pubs/the-gender-wage-gap-2010-updated-march-2011.

Johnston, D. C. (2007, March 29). Income gap is widening, data shows. *New York Times.* Retrieved August 4, 2008, from http://www.nytimes.com/2007/03/29/business/29tax.html?ref=business.

Lipman, P., & Haines, N. (2007). From accountability to privatization and African American exclusion: Chicago's "Renaissance 2010." *Educational Policy, 21*(3), 471–502.

Martin, A. M., & Levithan, D. (Eds.) (2005). *Friends: Stories about New Friends, Old Friends and Unexpectedly True Friends.* New York: Scholastic.

Mohr, N. (1990). *Felita.* New York: Bantam.

Moses, R. P., & Cobb, C. E., Jr. (2001). *Radical equations: Civil rights from Mississippi to the Algebra Project.* Boston: Beacon.

Myers, W. D. (1990). *Scorpions.* New York: Harper Trophy.

Nafisi, A. (2003). *Reading Lolita in Tehran.* New York: Random House.

National Commission on Excellence in Education. (1983). *A nation at risk: The imperative for educational reform*. Washington, DC: U.S. Department of Education.

A national survey of lesbian and gay college programs. (1990–1991). *Empathy, 2*(2), 53–56.

National Women's Studies Association. (2005). *NWSA mission*. Retrieved May 11, 2005, from http://www.nwsa.org/about.html.

Orfield, G., & Lee, C. (2005). *Why segregation matters: Poverty and educational inequality*. Cambridge, MA: Harvard University Civil Rights Project.

Osler, A., & Starkey, H. (2005). *Changing citizenship: Democracy and inclusion in education*. New York: McGraw-Hill Education.

Parker, W. C. (2003). *Teaching democracy: Unity and diversity in public life*. New York: Teachers College Press.

Paterson, K. (1987). *The great Gilly Hopkins*. New York: Harper Trophy.

Shaw, G. B. (2004). *Back to Methuselah* [eBook]. Salt Lake City, UT: Project Gutenberg Literary Archive Foundation. Retrieved November 3, 2008, from http://www.gutenberg.org/etext/13084 (Original work published 1921).

Shor, I. (1980). *Critical teaching and everyday life*. Boston: South End Press.

Sleeter, C. E. (2005). *Un-standardizing curriculum: Multicultural teaching in the standards-based curriculum*. New York: Teachers College Press.

Sleeter, C. E. (Ed.). (2007). *Facing accountability in education: Democracy and equity at risk*. New York: Teachers College Press.

Sleeter, C. E. (2011). *The academic and social value of ethnic studies: A research review*. Washington, DC: National Education Association.

Sleeter, C. E., & Grant, C. A. (2009). *Making choices for multicultural education: Five approaches to race, class, and gender* (6th ed.). New York: Wiley.

Strazzabosco, G. (1995). *Teenage refugees from Iran speak out*. New York: Rosen.

Taylor, C. (2011). WJBC forum: The widening gap between rich and poor. *WJBC – The voice of central Illinois*. Retrieved August 28, 2011, from wjbc.com/wjbc-forum-the-widening-gap-between-rich-and-poor/.

Tetreault, M. K. T. (1989). Integrating content about women and gender into the curriculum. In J. A. Banks & C. A. M. Banks (Eds.), *Multicultural education: Issues and perspectives* (pp. 124–144). Boston: Allyn & Bacon.

Ulrich, R. (2004). Taxing proposals. *TomPaine.commonsense*. Retrieved June 3, 2005, from http://www.tompaine.com/articles.

U.S. Census Bureau (2000). *Statistical abstract of the United States, 2000*. Washington, DC: U.S. Government Printing Office.

U.S. Census Bureau (2004). *Statistical abstract of the United States, 2004–2005*. Washington, DC: U.S. Government Printing Office.

U.S. Census Bureau (2006). *2006 American community survey*. Retrieved August 5, 2008, from http://www.census.gov/hhes/www/disability/2006acs.html.

U.S. Census Bureau (2007). *Current population survey*. Retrieved August 5, 2008, from http://www.census.gov/hhes/www/income/incomestats.html#cps

U.S. Census Bureau (2010a). Place of birth of the foreign-born population: 2009. Retrieved August 28, 2011, from www.census.gov/prod/2010pubs/acsbr09-15.pdf.

U.S. Census Bureau (2010b). Language use in the United States: 2007. Retrieved August 28, 2011, from http://www.census.gov/prod/2010pubs/acs-12.pdf.

U.S. Census Bureau (2011). Overview of race and Hispanic origin: 2010. Retrieved August 28, 2011 from www.census.gov/prod/cen2010/briefs/c2010br-02.pdf.

U.S. Department of Homeland Security (2003). Yearbook of immigration statistics 2003. Retrieved June 2, 2005, from http://uscis.gov/graphics/shared/statistics/yearbook/YrBk03Im.htm.

Valli, L., Croninger, R. G., & Chambliss, M. J. (2008). *Test driven: High-stakes accountability in elementary schools*. New York: Teachers College Press.

Yep, L. (1975). *Dragonwings*. New York: Harper & Row.

Religion and social class are two powerful variables that influence student behavior, beliefs, and achievement.

Masterfile Royalty-Free

© Juanmonino/iStockphoto

Stockbroker/Purestock/SuperStock

Social Class and Religion

The two chapters in Part II discuss the effects of two powerful variables on student behavior, beliefs, and achievement: social class and religion. Social class is a powerful variable in U.S. society despite entrenched beliefs about individual opportunity in the United States. As Lois Weis points out in Chapter 4 and as Jonathon Kozol (2005) notes in his disturbing book *The Shame of the Nation: The Restoration of Apartheid Schooling in America*, students who attend affluent middle- and upper-class schools have more resources, better teachers, and better educational opportunities than do students who attend low-income, inner-city schools. Students from the lower, middle, and upper classes usually attend different kinds of schools and have teachers who have different beliefs and expectations about their academic achievement. The structure of educational institutions also favors middle- and upper-class students. Structures such as tracking, IQ tests, and programs for gifted and mentally retarded students are highly biased in favor of middle- and upper-class students.

Students who are socialized within religious families and communities often have beliefs and behaviors that conflict with those of the school. Religious fundamentalists often challenge the scientific theories taught by schools about the origin of human beings. The controversy that occurred over intelligent design during the 2005–2006 school year epitomizes this phenomenon. Religious fundamentalists also attack textbooks and fictional books assigned by teachers that they believe violate or contradict their doctrines. Conflicts about the right to pray in the school sometimes divide communities. The school should help students mediate between their home culture and the school culture. Lippy, in Chapter 5, describes the religious diversity within the United States and some of its educational implications.

REFERENCE

Kozol, J. (2005). *The shame of the nation: The restoration of apartheid schooling in America*. New York: Random House.

Masterfile Royalty-Free

Social Class and Education

CHAPTER 4

Lois Weis

Section 402 of the 1964 Civil Rights Act ordered a survey to determine the relationship between student achievement and the kinds of schools students attend. This was done with the expressed intent of determining the extent to which U.S. schools provide opportunities for minority children, with an eye toward finding out whether schools can reduce racially linked inequalities in academic achievement. It was widely expected that massive inequities would be revealed between the characteristics of schools that Black and White children attend (although other racial groups were included in the survey, the primary goal of the survey was to pinpoint reasons for Black/White differences in achievement) and that specific school characteristics could be identified that serve to produce academic outcomes. It was thought that if such variables could be teased out in the analysis, monetary intervention could be justified, and that "lacking" schools could work to build up the pinpointed characteristics through an infusion of federal dollars, thereby equalizing academic outcomes by race.

Unfortunately, it proved not to be so simple, as the research did not yield the expected results. In 1966 James Coleman and his team reported, in what is popularly known as "The Coleman Report," that differences in achievement across race and socioeconomic status are not easily explained by differences in school-based resources. Their research suggests that individual achievement is, in fact, much more highly correlated with family socioeconomic status (hereafter referred to as social class) than with school characteristics. When standardized test score averages (academic achievement) are compared across sampled schools, more variation exists *within* schools than between them. The general conclusion of this congressionally mandated report is that the quality of school facilities and programs minimally affects academic achievement when compared with the effect of social class. This set in motion the long-standing mantra "schools make no difference." Put another way, after family background is held constant in the analysis, differences in school facilities and/or programs barely alter academic achievement at all. Academic achievement, argue Coleman and his colleagues, is almost wholly dependent on family background rather than on what goes on in schools.

The Coleman Report jump-started a multidecade research program on the relationship between family background and school-related outcomes, most specifically, academic achievement and attainment (how far one goes in school). Christopher Jencks and colleagues (1972) affirmed and extended Coleman's findings in the somewhat later, and highly controversial, volume *Inequality: A Reassessment of the Effect of Family and Schooling in America*. By reanalyzing the Coleman data, Jencks and colleagues furthered the intellectual project regarding the production of inequality through schools. Employing new data as well as that collected by Coleman, the authors concluded that inequality in the United States can be reduced only by 1 percent through balancing the quality of high schools. Additional expenditures on schools, they argued, are unlikely to boost achievement, and any redistribution of school-based resources is not likely to reduce the racially related test score gap. In a widely discussed statement (cited in Karabel & Halsey, 1977), Jencks and colleagues argued that a more fundamental change in society is required before equalizing educational opportunity can make a difference in achievement outcomes. In a highly controversial and contested move, they suggested that "socialism" is the only way to affect the existing distribution of wealth and power in the United States, thereby suggesting that schools can and, in fact do, little. More pointedly, they argue that we must stop tinkering with "marginal" institutions such as schools and get down to the "real" business of equalizing opportunities through equalizing access to jobs and flattening earnings.

The conclusions of both Coleman and Jencks (although Coleman has received more sustained attention over the years) are often used to support the argument that equalizing school funding will have little direct effect on student achievement. Since the release of the Coleman Report (and, later, the Jencks volume), issues regarding the validity of the test measures employed have emerged. The use of a general intellectual measure (verbal ability)—instead of a test targeted more specifically to what is taught in school—may have led to an underestimation of the importance of schooling (Rutter, Maughan, Mortimore, Ouston, & Smith, 1979). Carver (1975) similarly argues that the results of the Coleman Report are not a surprise, since psycho-metric tests are designed to maximize individual differences and are, therefore, poor measures of achievement. He recommends either the use of criterion-referenced tests, which measure whether a standard has been achieved, or edumetric tests, which reflect gain due to a treatment. Additionally, if student learning is the concern, argues Carver, students should be tested at the beginning and end of a specified period of time in school rather than being compared according to school-level test scores. This, he argues, renders Coleman's cross-sectional design inappropriate as a way of assessing the "effects" of school.

Consolidating the critique, Bowles and Levin (1968) raised questions about the specification of school-based variables such as per-pupil expenditure and student–teacher ratio, which they argue most likely led to an underestimation of the effects of schooling as opposed to student family background.

Rutter and colleagues' (1979) later work in England offers a more optimistic appraisal of the role of schooling with regard to decoupling the linkage between class and achievement, thereby equalizing academic outcomes. Although suggesting that student achievement differs across secondary schools and that initial variation between schools holds nearly constant over five years, the authors nevertheless upend Coleman's "schools make no difference" mantra. Unlike Coleman and Jencks, Rutter's team concludes that it matters *which* school a student attends because particular characteristics of schools (those associated with the academic and social ethos of the school) lead to student success.

Although Rutter and colleagues challenge the notion that schools exert scant effect on student outcomes as compared to family background, a large corpus of evidence since Coleman points toward the role that schools play in the reproduction of social-class inequalities both at the individual and collective societal level. Even though individuals can, of course, transcend their class background through schooling (and there are many examples of such class transcendence), *it is arguably the case that schools work largely to reproduce and maintain class inequalities rather than fundamentally challenge them.* The critical question is, of course: How does this happen? More specifically: What is it about families and schools that serve to reproduce the relatively tight relationship between social class and educational outcomes?

Keeping in mind both the vastness of the research in this area and the fact that one chapter can offer only a partial answer to this broad-based question, my goal in this chapter is twofold: (1) to review select scholarly work on the ways in which elementary, secondary, and postsecondary schools in the United States are specifically linked to the production and maintenance of social-class inequalities, and (2) to articulate key areas where important research remains to be done. In the latter regard, I address the following: (1) the necessity of intensifying research efforts on those already privileged, and (2) the importance of globalizing our research imagination as we probe the relationship between class and education in the massively shifting global context.

Education and the Production of Social and Economic Inequalities

As noted above, researchers argue that school outcomes, whether achievement or attainment, are linked in large part to student social-class background (Coleman et al., 1966; Gamoran, 2001, 2008; Gamoran & Long, 2007; Jencks et al., 1972). Ironically, in spite of the massification of the U.S. system of education during the 20th century (Arum, Gamoran, & Shavit, 2007), differences by social class have persisted at largely consistent levels.

Beginning with Coleman, social scientists have long argued that school outcomes, whether achievement or attainment, are linked in large part to student social-class background, that is, student socioeconomic background, often measured by parents' level of education, occupation, and income (Coleman et al., 1966; Gamoran, 1987, 2001, 2008; Gamoran & Long, 2007; Jencks et al., 1972). What is most stunning, perhaps, is that in spite of the massification of the U.S. system of education during the 20th century, differences by social class have persisted at largely consistent levels. Campbell, Hombo, and Mazzeo (2000), for example, suggest persistent relative class differences in achievement-related outcomes (as linked to National Assessment of Educational Progress [NAEP] test score data over three decades), while Hout, Raftery, and Bell (1993) indicate that class differences in attainment (how far one goes in school) have remained relatively constant.

In the "millennium" issue of *Sociology of Education*, Gamoran (2001) offers a forecast for the future of inequality. His prediction that the next hundred years would see a substantial decline in race-based inequality in the United States received enough criticism from other social scientists to cast doubt on this prediction. However, he later confirmed his conclusion regarding continued social-class inequality with new evidence that became available after 2001, the year his original paper was published (Gamoran, 2008). As Gamoran notes in this 2008 follow-up piece: "To foreshadow my current findings, the updated evidence and new policies do not provide a basis for overturning the earlier conclusion that the outcomes of US education will continue to be stratified by social class" (p. 169).

Although my focus in this chapter is education and social class, there is a strong correlation between race and class in the United States, as high proportions of African Americans and Latinos/Hispanics who are from nonprivileged backgrounds suffer under the weight of exclusion and marginalization. In highlighting social class, then, I do not mean to deny the ongoing and independent effects of race in the production of inequalities through school, a point that is particularly salient in the United States and increasingly important in the United Kingdom, Germany, and France, where immigrant populations of color have significantly altered the social and economic landscape since World War II. Rather, it is to suggest that class is a fundamental organizer of social experience, both objective and subjective, and that it additionally constitutes an organizer that is at times ignored in our discussions of race and ethnicity. As work by Banks and Banks (2010), Ladson-Billings (2006), Ogbu (1988), McCarthy (1988), and others remind us, however, the experiences of racially subordinated groups cannot be understood entirely by looking at social class because race has its own independent trajectory with regard to the production of subjectivities and lived-out inequalities (Massey & Denton, 1993; Oliver & Shapiro, 1995).

There is a rich literature spanning the ways that class stratification in families and K–12 educational institutions affect three sets of educationally related outcomes: academic achievement and attainment, college-going patterns (postsecondary attendance, destinations, and graduation rates), and short- and long-term employment opportunities and income. Such class-related stratification through schools serves to privilege those already privileged, while simultaneously denying opportunities to poor, working-class, and, increasingly, lower-middle-class students. These include, among others:

- Social and cultural capital embedded within families and the extent to which such varying forms of capital are differentially valued by schools (Horvat & Antonio, 1999; Ladson-Billings, 1995, 2006; Lareau, 2000, 2003)

- Academic tracking (Gamoran & Mare, 1989; Kelly, 2008; Lee & Bryk, 1988; Lucas, 2001; Oakes, 1985)

- High-stakes testing (Haney, 1993; McNeil, 2000; Nichols & Berliner, 2007)

- Differential access to academic knowledge in elementary school (Anyon, 1981)

- Differential access to rigorous math and science courses in secondary school (Aaronson, Barrow, & Sander, 2007; Alexander & Cook, 1982; Burkam & Lee, 2003; Ma & McIntyre, 2005; Oakes, Joseph, & Muir, 2003; Riegle-Crumb, 2006; Wimberly & Noeth, 2005) that are directly linked to college attendance patterns

- Dropout and push-out patterns (Fine, 1991) that contribute to pipeline constriction, particularly in secondary schools (Haney et al., 2005)

- Increased segregation and hyper-segregation resulting from the repeal of desegregation court orders (Orfield & Lee, 2005)

Although all the above mechanisms of exclusion are important in producing and sustaining class inequalities, space prevents discussion of all of those noted. Here I highlight two such mechanisms, as they are key to the role of K–12 institutions in class production and reproduction: (1) ability grouping and tracking, and (2) "official" knowledge and its distribution.

Ability Grouping and Tracking

Ray Rist (1970) conducted groundbreaking work by observing a group of African American children through their kindergarten, first-grade, and second-grade years. Based on careful ethnographic data gathering, he notes that the kindergarten teacher divides students into separate reading groups in the classroom according not to measured ability but to characteristics typically associated with differential social-class backgrounds, such as appearance, behavior, and language use. After the eighth day of kindergarten, students are placed at three tables, with students at the highest-ability reading table more closely approximating children of middle-class background in their dress and grooming (for example, hair is carefully brushed and tied or braided) as well as in their use of standard American English. The remaining two tables of medium and low reading ability are composed of students who are poorly dressed and speak in a neighborhood-based dialect.

Throughout the three years of observation, Rist chronicles a class-based "self-fulfilling prophecy," one accompanied by the teacher spending relatively less time instructing the lower-ability groups (students at table 3 could not even see the board due to the placement of the table). Over time, students themselves begin to refer to one another as "smart" or "dumb" based on table placement. Rist argues that this self-fulfilling prophecy creates an immovable class-linked "caste system," wherein students placed at table 1 on day 8 of kindergarten are the only ones who both learn to read at grade level and have a chance at success. Most interestingly in light of the argument in this chapter, the kindergarten teacher in Rist's study is Black, thereby affirming the power of class in relation to race in this particular instance.

By second grade, students at table 3 are referred to as "the clowns." This is in spite of the fact that student IQ test scores in kindergarten reveal no significant differences across the three tables. Over time, however, vast differences emerge with regard to academic achievement—differences that Rist and others attribute to subjective judgment and subsequent teacher behavior as related to assumed class differences in academic ability.

What begins with Rist as a blistering critique of the effects of ability-group assignment as related to class production and reproduction begins to temper somewhat over time. Key research since Rist expands into math ability groups (Hallinan & Sorensen, 1987; Useem, 1992) as well as into later elementary school grades and the relatively long-term effects of ability grouping. The gender of students (Hallinan & Sorensen, 1987) joins social class and race as variables considered in conjunction with sorting, and the effects of social class per se are seen as less robust. No studies, however, use the longitudinal approach pioneered by Rist as a way of assessing the effects of ability grouping over time, suggesting that ability-group placement in the early elementary years may have long-standing class-linked effects. Studies of older students or those studies that do not employ a longitudinal design (that is, studying the same children over time from a young age) may miss the full impact of initial group placement on high school track placement and academic achievement.

Findings—quantitative (those that are statistical in nature) and qualitative (those that are ethnographically driven)—related to social class and the high school track structure are more compelling with respect to the creation and/or maintenance of social inequalities. Rosenbaum's (1975) highly quantitative assessment of the internal workings of the track structure in a homogeneous White working-class school challenges the notion that track placement is accomplished meritocratically (that is, solely through factors such as test scores). A high proportion of variance in track placement cannot be explained by any of the variables ostensibly used to sort students into tracks, and measured IQ (the most valid and stable of the variables by virtue of Rosenbaum's statistical analysis) accounts for the smallest amount of variance in track placement when compared with all other competing variables. Fifty percent of college attendance, on the other hand, can be explained by track placement, suggesting that track placement takes on a life of its own once students are tracked into specific locations in the track structure. Rosenbaum argues that since track placement cannot be explained by a set of valid and stable criteria, and since such placement is so powerful in terms of predicting college attendance, tracking should be eliminated.

Oakes (1985) explores qualitatively the tracking experiences of students at 25 junior high and high schools, which, unlike the work of Rosenbaum, includes students from varying social-class and racial backgrounds. Her work extends that of Rosenbaum in that she looks closely at the tracking experience of students who are not White as well as those of varying class background. Oakes finds that college tracks (as opposed to noncollege tracks) foster independence in students, involve more time spent on instruction, and are composed of a more White and middle- to upper-middle-class student population. Lower or noncollege tracks, on the other hand, enforce conformity, spend less time on classroom instruction, and include higher levels of non-White and working-class students.

Vanfossen, Jones, and Spade (1987) explore tracking through the use of 1982 follow-up data from the 14,825 sophomore and senior students in the High School and Beyond (HSB) study, concluding that key individual, school-level, and social-psychological variables affect track placement. They argue that academic or college track students are more committed to academic goals, exhibit better classroom discipline, and receive better treatment from teachers than students in noncollege tracks. These findings support the work of Rosenbaum (1975) and Oakes (1985) as well as expand on the variables involved, broadening the scope of existing tracking research in terms of social-class and racial groups. Gamoran (1987) uses the sophomore data from both the original (1980) and follow-up (1982) High School and Beyond studies to determine between- and within-school differences with respect to learning opportunities, concluding that variation in student experiences in school exerts important effects on student achievement, with patterns in course-taking being the most significant within-school factor.

Research is quite clear then that track placement has consequences in terms of the type of knowledge students are exposed to and the college options available to such students when they leave high school (Oakes, 1985; Rosenbaum, 1976). Unfortunately, recent research suggests that track structures are difficult to alter because of the social, political, and economic forces that work to maintain them (Fine, Weis, Powell, & Wong, 1997; Oakes & Wells, 1996). Yonezawa and Wells (2005), for instance, argue that classes continue to be segregated by race and class, maintaining low-income and minority student populations in the lowest levels in spite of attempts by select schools to break down such race/class links to tracking. Predominantly African American and Latino/Latina students, who form the low and middle tracks, resist entering high-track classes even when given a "choice" because of the ways in which these classes are both presented to them (as "not for them") and perceived by them.

Official Knowledge and Its Distribution

Spurred by early calls from Black scholars such as W. E. B. DuBois (1935, 1975) with regard to what is (and is not) taught about African history and culture in U.S. schools, as well as later calls in England for a "new" sociology of education that focuses on the nature of school knowledge, scholars address what constitutes "official" knowledge as well as the ways in which such knowledge is differentially distributed through schools (Banks, 1993; Gordon, 1990; Page & Valli, 1990). Both the nature of school knowledge and its distribution are key mechanisms through which schools serve to produce and reproduce class-based inequalities. It is important to note that although the focus on legitimate knowledge is often seen as having originated among White British scholars, Black scholars were thinking, theorizing, actively pursuing change, and producing scholarship about the issues related to power, ideology, and development of school knowledge prior to the work of White scholars within and outside the United States and Britain. Banks (1992, 1993) and Gordon (1990) have made important points about the contributions of these early Black scholars and the attribution of "newness" to much later scholars who make largely the same theoretical points.

The theoretical starting point for most of these analyses is articulated by Michael F. D. Young (1971), who argues that there is a "dialectical relationship between access to power and the opportunity to legitimate dominant categories, and the processes by which the availability of such categories to some groups enable them to assert power and control over others" (p. 31). Stated more simply, what counts as school (or "legitimate") knowledge tends to embody the interests and culture of the group or groups who have the power to distribute and legitimate their worldview through educational institutions. Young (1971), Apple (1979, 1982), Bernstein (1977), Bourdieu (1977), Cornbleth (1990), and other scholars argue that the organization of knowledge, the form of its transmission, and the assessment of its acquisition are factors in the production and reproduction of class.

In the United States, Apple (1979, 1982) exhibits the most sustained focus on the ways in which curricular knowledge (both the form and content of the "commodified" culture in school) is part of a selective tradition that serves to ideologically buttress, while simultaneously naturalizing, structurally based social and economic inequalities. Apple's investigation into what he later calls "official" knowledge (Apple, 1993) is one of the most enduring contributions in this area, serving to highlight the ways in which school knowledge works to marginalize working-class and poor students in school.

Looking more specifically at the distribution of knowledge—or, to put it another way, "who gets what kind of knowledge"—Anyon (1980, 1981) focuses on the ways in which "official" knowledge in a range of U.S. elementary schools is differentially distributed to students. Working-class students, for example, are offered knowledge as rote memorization and a series of structured tasks, while knowledge distributed to students in what she calls "executive elite" public schools is far more challenging. Students in these latter schools are socialized into an academic culture of excellence while working-class students are socialized into a culture of rote memorization, a finding confirmed in later studies by both McNeil (1986) and Weis (1990) as well as in studies of the track structure of U. S. high schools (Oakes, 1985). The notion that knowledge is differentially distributed extends Bowles and Gintis's (1976) focus on what they call the "correspondence principle," wherein they argue that the everyday actions/activities of schools serve to socialize students into their future (and highly differentiated) place in the labor force.

This corpus of research on the workings of K–12 institutions suggests that schools largely ensure that poor and working-class students, if they graduate from secondary school at all, are less well positioned than their more privileged counterparts for college and university entrance/persistence/graduation. Because postsecondary education is a key sorting ground for well-paying and stable employment in our increasingly competitive global economy, it must be taken into account in any serious analysis of education and social class.

Access and Outcomes in the Postsecondary Sector

Arum and colleagues (2007) argue that the most important question with regard to the expansion of education is "whether it reduces inequality by providing more opportunities for persons from disadvantaged strata, or magnifies inequality by expanding opportunities disproportionately for those who are already privileged" (p. 1). In Shavit, Arum, and Gamoran's (2007) path-breaking edited volume *Stratification in Higher Education: A Comparative Study*, the contributors stress the centrality of this broad question for research on higher education.

Higher education has expanded rapidly in response to intensified demands for democratization of access at the same time as the worldwide knowledge economy renders higher education a key point of access for an increasing number of jobs. The authors in the Shavit and colleagues (2007) volume draw data from 15 nations, mostly in Western Europe (France, Italy, Germany, the Netherlands, Sweden, Switzerland, Great Britain) but also in Eastern Europe (Russia, the Czech Republic,) and East Asia (Japan, Korea, Taiwan), as well as Israel, the United States, and Australia. Data indicate that the pinpointed systems of higher education vary in rate of expansion (massification), extent of differentiation (type of institution within the tertiary sector—two year, four year, etc.), and the market structure within which they sit (highly marketized in the sense of depending on a higher proportion of private relative to public funds rather than vice versa). However, worldwide evidence suggests that although expansion is pervasive, with only a few national exceptions, inequality rates in the transition from secondary school to higher education are either stable or actually increased under conditions of massification. This means that as the postsecondary system numerically expands, there is greater class-linked inequality rather than the reverse.

Research on U.S. postsecondary education underscores this point. In the United States, working-class and poor students are entering colleges and universities in greater numbers than ever before (Ellwood & Kane, 2000). While research on linkages between the type and selectivity of postsecondary institution attended is certainly not new (Karabel, 1972), evidence suggests that the social-class-related gap in type of institution attended is widening under conditions of massification. Thomas and Bell (2008) demonstrate that while less privileged students increasingly attend institutions of higher education, attendance at the most selective ones is increasingly composed of more privileged students. Using Pell Grants (a federal grant in the United States that demands a high literacy level even to fill out applications) as a proxy for low income/poverty, Thomas and Bell note that "it is not just the most selective institutions which are seeing lower numbers of low-income students. Low-income students are less likely to be in four-year institutions in general than they were a decade ago" (p. 281). Looking across years 1992–1993 and 2000–2001, "there was a 2.9 percent drop in the enrollment share of Pell Grant recipients at four-year institutions across all states, with 48 of the states seeing a decline in their Pell enrollment shares" (Mortenson, 2003, quoted in Thomas & Bell, 2008, p. 281). Conversely, during the same time, Pell enrollment at two-year public colleges increased by 1.2 percent (Mortenson, 2003), continuing a longer-term trend that began in the 1970s (Mortenson, 2006). Although the net gain or loss in percentage points may appear small, this represents a very large number of low-income students who are increasingly locked out of higher-prestige institutions.

More recently, Bowen, Chingos, and McPherson (2009) argue that the state "flagship" universities (for example, University of Wisconsin–Madison and University of California–Berkeley) have become much more selective over time and that such selectivity has been accompanied by changes in the social-class background of admitted students (Cook & Frank, 1993; Hearn, 1990; Kingston & Lewis, 1990). In the less selective institutions detailed by Bowen and colleagues, "more than 40 percent of undergraduates come from families in the top-quartile of the income distribution" (p. 17). While eventual movement from the two-year to four-year college sector should be possible, research by Clark (1960), Weis (1985), Brint and Karabel (1989), and Dougherty and Kienzl (2006) suggest difficulties associated with such movement.

Factors specifically linked to colleges and universities increasingly point toward the production of social-class inequalities and arrangements. Recent changes in financial aid policies and processes that reduce grants to low-income students (in favor of loans) make it more and more difficult for poor, working-class, and lower-middle-income students to attend and persist in postsecondary institutions (Avery & Kane, 2004; Heller, 2001; Hoxby, 1997; National Center for Public Policy and Higher Education, 2001; St. John, 2003). Because family incomes have not kept pace with college costs, students shoulder a larger financial burden, making financial aid that much more critical for this group at the same time as middle- and upper-middle-class students have more sustained access to family funds, thereby attending and completing college in record numbers.

Concurrently, the emergence of a nationally integrated market for elite and selective colleges (Bowen et al., 2009; Hoxby, 1997) intensifies pressure for admittance to elite and highly selective postsecondary institutions, encouraging greater numbers of privileged students to seek entrance to the somewhat less selective four-year sector (relative to the elite and highly selective sector) than was the case in prior decades (Ellwood & Kane, 2000; Mortenson, 2003, 2006; Thomas & Bell, 2008). This means that poor and working-class students are increasingly "locked out" of state flagship universities, institutions that offered a key mechanism for social mobility for past generations of working-class students (Bowen et al., 2009; Thomas & Bell, 2008). Recent studies make clear that poor, working-class, and lower-income students are attending flagship state institutions less and less often, as these institutions are becoming increasingly the purview of the children of the privileged (Bowen et al., 2009; Shavit et al., 2007; Thomas & Bell, 2008).

Additionally, McPherson and Schapiro (1998), Gumport (2007), and Slaughter and Rhodes (2004) point to specific economic and organizational changes that have encouraged colleges and universities to shift from selecting students as a "charitable" function to balancing full-paying students or high-merit students with low-income and first-generation college students. This makes it less and less possible for low-income students to attend a wide range of colleges. An important force here, of course, is intensified state disinvestment in public higher education. This contributes both to a marked increase in tuition bills and to a decreased amount of money available for scholarships tagged for low-income students.

Decades of research, then, point to an array of K–16+ "mechanisms of exclusion" that serve, by and large, to relegate poor and working-class students to less valued positions in the economy while increasingly "propping up" those who are already privileged. While perhaps unintended, this means that the K–16+ educational system in the United States works predominantly to ensure the reproduction of social-class inequalities both at the individual and collective levels. It is important to note, however, that while the "logic" of the system functions as described here, there are always individuals who come from very humble backgrounds and effectively use the educational system to reposition themselves in class terms. Although noteworthy to be sure, the success of these outstanding individuals does not empirically describe (nor can it be used to serve as a proxy for) the overall shape of the educational opportunity structure, a structure that largely serves to maintain class inequalities.

Research on Class Privilege

Much scholarly work takes as its starting point the exclusionary processes through which poor, working-class, and lower-middle-class students end up in the same relative class position as their parents. By turning our scholarly attention disproportionately toward the ways in which educational institutions work (or do not work) to marginalize and/or open up opportunities for those historically disenfranchised, we ignore the ways in which educational institutions work explicitly on behalf of the relatively privileged as well as the ways in which privileged groups themselves work to maintain what Bourdieu (1984) calls "distinction." Given that we now recognize that the production of class must be understood relationally (that is, the production of those who *lack* privilege and the processes through which this occurs must be understood in relation to the production of those who *have* privilege and the processes through which this occurs), scholars take this line of research increasingly seriously.

For example, although the poor and the working class have objectively made great strides with regard to generalized academic achievement and attainment in the United States, such improvement pales in comparison to that of the privileged, who seemingly naturalized exhibit a capacity to run harder and faster. Rather than reflecting naturally occurring patterns toward increasing inequality, however, research indicates that those involved in the production of privilege (parents, children, schools, colleges and universities) work exceptionally hard on a day-to-day and year-to-year basis to ensure that their own privileged position and that of their children is maintained.

Lareau (2003), for example, turns her attention to class-linked child-rearing practices, arguing that middle- and upper-middle-class child-rearing practices across race position already advantaged children for both greater academic success in school and the ability to advocate for themselves in relation to adult authority. Weininger and Lareau (2009) indicate that middle- and upper-middle-class child-rearing practices of "concerted cultivation"—in contrast to working-class child-rearing practices that emphasize "natural growth"—remain evident throughout the college search and application process, substantially advantaging middle- and upper-middle-class students relative to their working-class and poor counterparts. This advantage occurs irrespective of measured "intelligence" and works across race.

Scholars also focus on the ways in which elite secondary schools advantage students in the college application/admissions process. Cookson and Persell (1985) offer early work on private school advantage, focusing on the ways in which private boarding schools prepare students for power. More current work by Proweller (1998), Howard (2008), Howard and Gatzambide-Fernández (2010), Gatzambide-Fernández (2009), Kahn (2011), and Demerath (2009) pinpoints specific school-based mechanisms that confer advantage in relatively privileged secondary schools. These include a sustained and intense focus on high-status knowledge, specific attention to tutoring and preparation for college entrance tests, and the editing of college essays/applications, all of which serve to confer specific and targeted advantage to those already privileged. Weis, Cipollone, and Jenkins (in press) also tackle this set of issues in their ethnographic investigation of students in three privileged secondary schools: two elite independent day schools and one affluent public suburban school. They similarly conclude that the maintenance of privilege is anything but "natural."

In an important qualitative study, McDonough (1997) documents a range of class/race-related opportunities for college counseling in secondary schools as linked to differential postsecondary destinations, paying particular attention to the role of counselors in the college search and application process. In more recent quantitative work, Hill (2008) finds that organizational practices tied to what she calls the "college linking process" vary considerably by secondary school and make a difference for postsecondary attendance patterns, with some schools better able to position their students for college admission.

Beyond differential preparation for, and admission to a range of colleges and universities, selectivity of college takes on a life of its own with regard to persistence and graduation rates. Recent work by Bowen and colleagues (2009) indicates that there are a large number of students whose secondary school preparation appears to qualify them to attend more highly selective four-year institutions than they end up attending. The authors note that such "under matching" has grave consequences for persistence and graduation rates from postsecondary institutions, as students are more likely to persist and graduate if they attend more highly ranked institutions to begin with.

Research by Stephan, Rosenbaum, and Person (2009) similarly concludes that *where* one goes to postsecondary school predicts persistence and graduation rates above and beyond the entering characteristics of admitted students. The authors argue that "academic preparation is an important mechanism of stratification at college entry, but even comparable students (similar on many characteristics, including preparation) have different degree completion chances at different types of colleges" (p. 585). The selection of an institution *in and of itself* matters, then, with regard to outcomes, as students in more selective postsecondary institutions exhibit much higher persistence and graduation rates than those in less selective institutions. As noted above, this is also the case when researchers hold the social class of admitted students constant in the analysis.

Beyond having higher rates of student persistence and graduation, we also know that selective institutions have better resources than less selective institutions (increasingly so, and the private research universities are now rising head and shoulders above even the state flagship universities) and confer on their graduates both special entrée to the best graduate and professional programs in the country (Eide, Brewer, & Ehrenberg, 1998) and well-documented labor-market advantages (Bowen & Bok, 1998; Rumberger & Thomas, 1993; Thomas, 2000; Thomas & Zhang, 2005). Again, this relationship holds even when characteristics of entering students are held constant in the analysis.

A focus on privileged students and privileged secondary and postsecondary schools (as represented in this critically important yet understudied area) points toward two conclusions. (1) Despite their class advantages at birth, those who are privileged still work very hard on a daily basis to maintain "distinction." More specifically, elite and affluent secondary schools, *as institutions*, work tirelessly to maintain the advantage that children bring with them to school, as do privileged parents and children. (2) At least at the postsecondary level, the selection of the institution to attend in and of itself matters with regard to persistence and graduation rates, linkages to valued graduate and professional programs, and labor-market outcomes. This suggests an increasingly segmented educational system in which it is exceedingly difficult to "jump tracks," so to speak, as institutional privilege enables entrance to the next highly valued sector, making it very difficult for those who attend less privileged institutions to scale the class structure by virtue of education.

To wrap up, then, class counts but must be worked at, and the structure of institutional arrangements also counts, as privileged institutions enable moves to the next level to a greater extent than do less privileged ones. It must be noted, however, that in spite of these empirically documented deepening inequalities in educational achievement and attainment, important research has directed our attention toward marked progress in educational opportunities for previously excluded groups in the population (Hurtado, Inkelas, Briggs, & Rhee, 1997; Perna, 2000; St. John, Musoba, & Simmons, 2003). However, leaving aside the historically based yet lessening class/race inequalities in elite private institutions like Harvard, Yale, and Princeton (Bowen & Bok, 1998; Bowen, Kurzweil, & Tobin, 2005; Karabel, 2005), it is arguably the case that there has been marked reorganization in the opportunity structure of postsecondary education, with the middle and upper-middle classes now solidifying their grasp on elite public institutions—institutions that were established by virtue of the Morrill Act of 1862 to "promote the liberal and practice education of the industrial classes in the several pursuits and professions in life" (Morrill Act of 1861, sec. 4, cited in Thomas and Bell, 2008, p. 274). Despite notable progress for select racial and ethnic groups, evidence clearly suggests that the widespread expansion of educational opportunities has, by and large, worked best for those already privileged (Gamoran, 2008; Shavit et al., 2007) and that the relationship between social class and education is perhaps stronger than ever. As I suggest here, this is accomplished both by what the poor and working classes do not get by virtue of schooling, as well as what the children of the privileged do get, and their families are able to demand, by virtue of their privilege.

Globalizing Our Imagination

In light of our rapidly globalizing world, it is important to broaden our research and thinking to encompass the ways in which what happens in the rest of the world is related to what goes on in the United States (Weis & Dolby, 2012). Although a number of volumes call for increased research into the role that education plays in the production of class and social structure more generally, relatively little serious scholarly attention is devoted to the relationship between education and social class in the global context.

In this regard, "globalizing the research imagination," in the phrasing of Kenway and Fahey (2008), has two meanings. First, it means that we must situate our analyses of education and social structure within a broadened range of countries, including first-wave industrialized nations, such as the United States, the United Kingdom, and Germany, as well as new players in the global arena, such as Singapore, China, Mexico, and India. Second, it means that we must take into account the ways in which what goes on within one nation is both similar to and increasingly linked to what goes on in the rest of the world. In other words, we must sustain a clear focus on education and class in varying national contexts while simultaneously acknowledging intensified global movement in the form of the transnational migration of commerce, information, capital, and peoples as it impacts class construction in any given national context. We must, then, invoke a "defiant" rather than "compliant" territorial imagination, seeking to pry open questions related to education and social class in a global context in new ways.

The increasingly globalized and knowledge-based economy creates a reality in which movement affects the fundamental structures of our lives, whether or not we ourselves are mobile. Since the 1970s, we have witnessed a massive realignment of the global economy. In the first wave of this realignment, working-class jobs—primarily in manufacturing—were increasingly exported from highly industrialized countries, such as the United States, the United Kingdom, and Japan, to poor countries, where the truly desperate take jobs that pay starvation wages and offer no job protection or benefits. In the current second wave, middle-class jobs are also being exported, as members of a new middle class in countries such as India and China are increasingly educated as architects, accountants, medical technicians, and doctors. They are willing to work for American, British, Canadian, and Australian companies at a fraction of the salary they would be paid for the same work at corporate headquarters in Western nations. Such movement has implications for the production of social structure and associated class processes in a wide variety of nations.

For example, as Brown, Lauder, and Ashton (2011) note, the American middle class is being ripped apart by the global forces of knowledge capitalism. With the rise of all-consuming processes of globalization, the competition for jobs no longer exists within national boundaries. Rather, the job market increasingly constitutes a "global auction" wherein bidders work across national contexts to obtain the highest-quality work at the lowest cost. Although not new in the sense that owners of capital historically sought to minimize the costs of labor (and workers, of course, fought back to gain a "living wage"), companies now have myriad options as they traverse the now-global marketplace to lower the cost of doing business. The nation-state, then, no longer constrains the "bidding wars" or the construction of job sites in the way that it once did, setting in motion entirely different processes of class construction and a new relationship between education and social structure worldwide (Reich, 2001, 2007).

In this regard, the globalization of the economy creates markedly altered economic opportunities for people worldwide, as companies seek the cheapest locale in which to situate manufacturing plants, call centers, and so forth. Tied to this is the fact that the shifting macro-structure of the global economy interacts with the movement of people across the globe. Such intensifying transnational migration patterns have implications worldwide for education and the forms of social structure, as social-class formations and positionalities in a wide range of countries are now being produced and realigned in relation to large numbers of recent immigrants/migrants in nations that are differentially positioned in relation to globalizing capital and culture. This includes those who possess "flexible citizenship" (Ong, 1999)—those who can take their inherited or cultural capital and/or academic credentials and relocate to other nations to take up professional and high-level technical positions—and those who enter both rich and poor nations as immigrants or refugees with little more than the clothes on their back. In point of fact, a relatively high proportion of such migrants/immigrants do relatively well in school in nations such as the United States and Canada, in stark contrast to their predicted educational achievement and attainment based on current class position in their adopted land (Li, 2005, 2007; Rumbaut & Portes, 2001).

What I am suggesting here is that it is no longer the case that the linkage between education and social class can be bounded by national context, as movement (of cultures, information, capital, and peoples) is the hallmark of the new global reality. In this sense, then, future research must go well beyond understandings offered in this chapter. Such broadening of our own research frame will enable empirically informed and increasingly productive discussion about class and education in the 21st century.

QUESTIONS AND ACTIVITIES

4.1 What was the significance of the Coleman Report? In what ways did the work of Jencks and Rutter challenge and/or extend this work? To what extent do the debates opened by this work continue to influence discussions on school equity and funding today?

4.2 In what ways does social class shape schooling? In what ways does schooling shape social class? How do the upper classes (the educated middle class, the affluent, and the wealthy) maintain the social structure? To what benefit? To what detriment?

4.3 Is all school knowledge equally valued by society? Is tracking compatible with equal opportunity and meritocracy? Explain. If students receive fundamentally different types of education based on their academic track/ability group, what are the long-term implications beyond school? Can schools be detracked? Should they be detracked? Explain.

4.4 How has the expansion of higher education, and access to such education, increased social and economic inequality? Current trends in higher education highlight the need to create online opportunities as a mechanism for increasing access. To what extent, based on your previous discussion of expansion and access, do you believe online education will increase access? What are some of the other potential consequences?

4.5 What conclusions can be drawn regarding the construction of class privilege from studying privileged students and privileged school settings (secondary and postsecondary)? What does such study reveal about class practices and social class more broadly?

4.6 What have been the major impacts of a globalizing economy? In what ways has globalization both opened and constrained opportunities? How does the move away from a manufacturing-based economy toward a knowledge-based economy affect schooling and the construction of social class more broadly?

4.7 A phrase heard often in the United States is "pull yourself up by your bootstraps," meaning that one is responsible for one's own station in life. In other words, through hard work, one is capable of determining one's place in society. Based on what you read in this chapter, what evidence can you provide to challenge this sentiment? Provide a counter-argument informed by this chapter and your own life experiences. How have your experiences at home, in school, and elsewhere influenced who you are today and the path you are currently pursuing?

REFERENCES

Aaronson, D., Barrow, L., & Sander, W. (2007). Teachers and student achievement in the Chicago public schools. *Journal of Labor Economics, 25*, 95–135.

Alexander, K., & Cook, M. (1982). Curriculum and coursework: A surprise ending to a familiar story. *American Sociological Review, 47*(5), 626–640.

Anyon, J. (1980). Social class and the hidden curriculum of work. *Journal of Education, 162*(1), 67–92.

Anyon, J. (1981). Social class and school knowledge. *Curriculum Inquiry, 11*(1), 3–42.

Apple, M. (1979). *Ideology and curriculum*. Boston: Routledge & Kegan Paul.

Apple, M. (1982). *Education and power*. Boston: Routledge & Kegan Paul.

Apple, M. (1993). Official knowledge: Democratic education in a conservative age. New York: Routledge.

Arum, R., Gamoran, A., & Shavit, Y. (2007). More inclusion than diversion: Expansion, differentiation, and market structure in higher education. In Y. Shavit, R. Arum, & A. Gamoran (Eds.), *Stratification in higher education: A comparative study* (pp. 1–38). Stanford, CA: Stanford University Press.

Avery C., & Kane, T. J. (2004). Student perceptions of college opportunities: The Boston, COACH program. In C. M. Hoxby (Ed.), *College choices: The economics of where to go, when to go, and how to pay for it* (pp. 355–394). Chicago: University of Chicago Press.

Banks, J. A. (1992). African American scholars and the evolution of multicultural education. *Journal of Negro Education, 61*(3), 273–276.

Banks, J. A. (1993). The canon debate, knowledge construction, and multicultural education. *Educational Researcher, 2*, 4–14.

Banks, J. A., & Banks, C. A. M. (Eds.). (2010). *Multicultural education: Issues and perspectives* (7th ed.). Hoboken, NJ: Wiley.

Bernstein, B. (1977). Social class, language, and socialization. In J. Karabel & A. H. Halsey (Eds.), *Power and ideology in education* (pp. 473–486). New York: Oxford University Press.

Bourdieu, P. (1977). Symbolic power. In D. Gleeson (Ed.), *Identity and structure: Issues in the sociology of education*. Driffield, UK: Nafferton Books.

Bourdieu, P. (1984). *Distinction: A social critique of the judgment of taste* (R. Nice, Trans.). Cambridge, MA: Harvard University Press.

Bowen, W. G., & Bok, D. (1998). The shape of the river: Long-term consequences of considering race in college and university admissions. Princeton, NJ: Princeton University Press.

Bowen, W. G., Chingos, M. M., & McPherson M. S. (2009). *Crossing the finish line: Completing college at America's public universities*. Princeton, NJ: Princeton University Press.

Bowen, W. G., Kurzweil, M. A., & Tobin, E. M. (2005). *Equity and excellence in American higher education*. Charlottesville: University of Virginia Press.

Bowles, S., & Gintis, H. (1976). Schooling in capitalist America: Educational reform and the contradictions of economic life. New York: Basic Books.

Bowles, S., & Levin, H. M. (1968). The determinants of scholastic achievement—an appraisal of some recent evidence. *The Journal of Human Resources, 3*(1), 3–24.

Brint, S., & Karabel, J. (1989). The diverted dream: Community colleges and the promise of educational opportunity, 1900–1985. Oxford, UK: Oxford University Press.

Brown, P., Lauder, H., & Ashton, D. (2011). *The global auction: The promise of education, jobs, and income*. New York: Oxford University Press.

Burkam, D. T., & Lee, V. E. (2003). *Mathematics, foreign language, and science course taking and the NELS: 88 transcript data* (NCES document no. 2003–01). Washington, DC: U.S. Department of Education, National Center for Education Statistics.

Campbell, J. R., Hombo, C. M., & Mazzeo, J. (2000). *NAEP trends in academic progress: Three decades of school performance* (NCES document no. 2000-2469). Washington, DC: US Government Printing Office.

Carver, R. (1975). The Coleman Report: Using inappropriately designed achievement tests. *American Educational Research Journal, 12*(1), 77–86.

Clark, B. (1960). The cooling out function in higher education. *American Journal of Sociology, 65,* 569–576.

Coleman, J., Campbell, E., Hobson, C., McPartland, J., Weinfeld, F., & York, R. (1966). *Equality of educational opportunity*. Washington, DC: U.S. Government Printing Office.

Cook, P. J., & Frank, R. H. (1993). The growing concentration of top students in elite schools. In C. T. Clotfelter & M. Rothschild (Eds.), *Studies of supply and demand in higher education* (pp. 121–140). Chicago: University of Chicago Press.

Cookson, P., & Persell, C. (1985). *Preparing for power: America's elite boarding schools*. New York: Basic Books.

Cornbleth, C. (1990). *Curriculum in context*. London and New York: Falmer.

Demerath, P. (2009). Producing success: The culture of personal advancement in an American high school. Chicago: University of Chicago Press.

Dougherty, K. J., & Kienzl, G. S. (2006). It's not enough to get through the open door: Inequalities by social background in transfer from community colleges to four-year colleges. *Teachers College Record, 108*(3), 452–487.

DuBois, W. E. B. (1935). Does the Negro need separate schools? *The Journal of Negro Education, 4,* 328–335.

DuBois, W. E. B. (1975). *Gift of Black folk: The Negroes in the making of America*. Millwood, NY: Kraus International Publications.

Eide, E., Brewer, D., & Ehrenberg, R. (1998). Does it pay to attend an elite private college? Evidence of the effect of undergraduate college quality on graduate school attendance. *Economics of Education Review, 17,* 71–376.

Ellwood, D., & Kane, T. J. (2000). Who is getting a college education?: Family background and the growing gaps in enrollment. In S. Danziger & J. Waldfogel (Eds.), *Securing the future* (pp. 283–324). New York: Russell Sage Foundation.

Fine, M. (1991). Framing dropouts: Notes on the politics in an urban public high school. Albany: State University of New York Press.

Fine, M., Weis, L., Powell, A., & Wong (Eds.) (1997). *Off White: Readings on race, power, and society*. New York & London: Routledge.

Gamoran, A. (1987). The stratification of high school learning opportunities. *Sociology of Education, 60*, 135–155.

Gamoran, A. (2001). American schooling and educational inequality: A forecast for the 21st century. *Sociology of Education, 74*, 135–153.

Gamoran, A. (2008). Persisting social class inequality in U.S. education. In L. Weis (Ed), *The way class works: Readings on school, family and the economy* (pp. 169–179). New York and London: Routledge.

Gamoran, A., & Long, D. A. (2007). Equality of educational opportunity: A forty-year retrospective. In R. Teese, S. Lamb, & Duru-Bellat (Eds.), *International studies in educational inequality: Theory and policy* (pp. 23–47). New York; Springer.

Gamoran, A., & Mare, R. (1989). Secondary school tracking and educational equality: Compensation, reinforcement, or neutrality? *American Journal of Sociology, 94*, 1146–1183.

Gatzambide-Fernández, R. (2009). *The best of the best: Becoming elite at an American boarding school*. Cambridge, MA: Harvard University Press.

Gordon, B. (1990). The necessity of African American epistemology. *Journal of Education, 172*(3), 88–106.

Gumport, P. (2007). *Sociology of higher education: Contributions and their contexts*. Baltimore, MD: Johns Hopkins University Press.

Hallinan, M., & Sorensen, A. (1987). Ability grouping and sex differences in mathematics achievement. *Sociology of Education, 60*(2), 63–72.

Haney, W. (1993). Testing and minorities. In L. Weis & M. Fine (Eds.), *Beyond silenced voices: Class, race and gender in United States schools* (pp. 45–73). Albany: State University of New York Press.

Haney, W., Abrams, L., Madaus, G., Wheelock, A., Miao, J., & Gruia, I. (2005). The education pipeline in the United States, 1970–2000: Trends in attrition, retention, and graduation rates. In L. Weis & M. Fine (Eds.), *Beyond silenced voices: Class, race, and gender in United States schools* (2nd ed., pp. 21–45). Albany: State University of New York Press.

Hearn, J. C. (1990). A pathway to attendance at elite colleges. In P. W. Kingston & L. S. Lewis (Eds.), *The high-status track: Studies of elite schools and stratification* (pp. 121–145). Albany: State University of New York Press.

Heller, D. (Ed.). (2001). The states and public higher education policy: Affordability, access, and accountability. Baltimore, MD: Johns Hopkins University Press.

Hill, L. (2008). School strategies and the college-linking process: Reconsidering the effects of high schools on college enrollment. *Sociology of Education, 81*, 53–76.

Horvat, E., & Antonio, A. (1999). "Hey, those shoes are out of uniform": African American girls in an elite high school and the importance of habitus. *Anthropology & Education Quarterly, 30*(3): 317–342.

Hout, M., Raftery, A., & Bell, E. O. (1993). Making the grade: Educational stratification in the United States, 1925–89. In Y. Shavit & H. P. Blossfeld (Eds.), *Persistent inequality: Changing educational attainment in thirteen countries* (pp. 25–49). Boulder, CO: Westview.

Howard, A. (2008). Learning privilege: Lessons of power and identity in affluent schooling. New York and London: Routledge.

Howard, A., & Gatzambide-Fernández, R. (2010). *Education elites: Class privilege and educational advantage*. Lanham, MD: Rowan & Littlefield.

Hoxby, C. (1997). *How the changing market structure of U.S. higher education explains college tuition* (Working paper no. 6323). Cambridge, MA: National Bureau of Economic Research.

Hurtado, S., Inkelas, K. K., Briggs, C., & Rhee, B. (1997). Differences in college access and choice among racial/ethnic groups: Identifying continuing barriers. *Research in Higher Education, 38*(1), 43–75.

Jencks, C., Smith, M., Acland, H., Bane, M. J., Cohen, D., Gintis, H., Heyns, B., & Michelson, S. (1972). *Inequality: A reassessment of the effect of family and schooling in America*. New York: Harper Colophon.

Kahn, S. R (2011). Privilege: The making of an adolescent elite at St. Paul's School. Princeton, NJ: Princeton University Press.

Karabel, J. (1972). Community colleges and social stratification. *Harvard Educational Review, 42*, 521–562.

Karabel, J. (2005). The chosen: The hidden history of admission and exclusion at Harvard, Yale, and Princeton. New York: Houghton Mifflin.

Karabel, J., & Halsey, A. (1977). Educational research: A review and an interpretation. In J. Karabel & A. H. Halsey (Eds.), *Power and ideology in education* (pp. 1–85). New York: Oxford University Press.

Kelly, S. P. (2008). Social class and tracking within schools. In L. Weis (Ed.), *The way class works: Readings on school, family, and the economy* (pp. 210–224). New York and London: Routledge.

Kenway, J., & Fahey, J. (2008). *Globalizing the research imagination*. New York and Boston: Routledge.

Kingston, P. W., & Lewis, L. S. (Eds.). (1990). *The high-status track: Studies of elite schools and stratification*. Albany: State University of New York Press.

Ladson-Billings, G. (1995). Toward a theory of culturally relevant pedagogy. *American Educational Research Journal, 32*, 465–491.

Ladson-Billings, G. (2006). From the achievement gap to the education debt: Understanding achievement in U.S. schools. *Educational Researcher, 35*, 3–12.

Lareau, A. (2000). Home advantage: Social class and parental intervention in elementary education. Lanham, MD: Rowman & Littlefield.

Lareau, A. (2003). *Unequal childhoods: Class, race and family life*. Berkeley: University of California Press.

Lee, V., & Bryk, A. (1988). Curriculum tracking as mediating the social distribution of high school achievement. *Sociology of Education, 61*(2), 78–94.

Li, G. (2005). Culturally contested pedagogy: Battles of literacy and schooling between mainstream teachers and Asian immigrant parents. Albany: State University of New York Press.

Li, G. (2007). Culturally contested literacies: America's "rainbow underclass" and urban schools. New York and London: Routledge.

Lucas, S. (2001). Effectively maintained inequality: Education transitions, track mobility, and social background effects. *American Journal of Sociology, 106*, 1642-1690.

Ma, X., & McIntyre, L. J. (2005). Exploring differential effects of mathematics courses on mathematics achievement. *Canadian Journal of Education, 28*, 827–852.

Massey, D., & Denton, N. (1993). *American apartheid: Segregation and the making of the underclass.* Cambridge, MA: Harvard University Press.

McCarthy, C. (1988). Marxist theories of education and the challenge of a cultural politics of non-synchrony. In L. G. Roman, L. K. Christian-Smith, & E. A. Ellsworth (Eds.), *Becoming feminine: The politics of popular culture* (pp. 185–203). London: Falmer.

McDonough, P. (1997). Choosing colleges: How social class and schools structure opportunity. Albany: State University of New York Press.

McNeil, L. (1986). Contradictions of control: School structure and school knowledge. New York: Routledge & Kegan Paul.

McNeil, L. (2000). Contradictions of school reform: Educational costs of standardized testing. New York and London: Routledge.

McPherson, M. S., & Schapiro, M. O. (1988). *The student aid game: Meeting need and rewarding talent in American higher education.* Princeton, NJ: Princeton University Press.

Mortenson, T. (2003, March). Pell Grant students in undergraduate enrollments by institution type and control, 1992–93 to 2000–2001. *Postsecondary Education Opportunity, 141.*

Mortenson, T. (2006, February). Access to what? *Postsecondary Education Opportunity, 164.*

National Center for Public Policy and Higher Education. (2001). *Losing ground: A national status report on the affordability of American higher education.* Washington, DC: Author. Retrieved from www.highereducation.org

Nichols, S. L., & Berliner, D. C. (2007). *Collateral damage: How high-stakes testing undermine education.* Cambridge, MA: Harvard University Press.

Oakes, J. (1985). *Keeping track: How schools structure inequality.* New Haven, CT: Yale University Press.

Oakes, J., Joseph, R., & Muir, K. (2003). Access and achievement in mathematics and science. In J. A. Banks & C. A. M. Banks (Eds.), *Handbook of research on multicultural education* (2nd ed., pp. 69–90). San Francisco: Jossey-Bass.

Oakes, J., & Wells, A. (1996). *Beyond the technicalities of school reform: Policy lessons from detracking schools.* Los Angeles: Research for Democratic School Communities, University of California, Los Angeles Graduate School of Education and Information Studies.

Ogbu, J. (1988). Class stratification, racial stratification, and schooling. In L. Weis (Ed.), *Class, race and gender in American schools* (pp. 163–182). Albany: State University of New York Press.

Oliver, M., & Shapiro, T. (1995). Black wealth/White wealth: A new perspective on racial inequality. New York and London: Routledge.

Ong, A. (1999). Flexible citizenship: The cultural logics of transnationality. Durham, NC: Duke University Press.

Orfield, G., & Lee, C. (2005). Segregation 50 years after *Brown*: A metropolitan challenge. In L. Weis & M. Fine (Eds.), *Beyond silenced voices: Class, race, and gender in United States schools* (rev. ed., pp. 3–20). Albany: State University of New York Press.

Page, R., & Valli, L. (1990). *Curriculum differentiation: Interpretive studies in U.S. secondary schools.* Albany: State University of New York Press.

Perna, L. (2000). Differences in the decision to attend college among African Americans, Hispanics, and Whites. *Journal of Higher Education, 71*, 117–141.

Proweller, A. (1998). Constructing female identities: Meaning making in an upper middle class youth culture. Albany: State University of New York Press.

Reich, R. (2001). *The future of success.* New York: Knopf.

Reich, R. (2007). Supercapitalism: The transformation of business, democracy, and everyday life. New York: Knopf.

Riegle-Crumb, C. (2006). The path through math: Course sequences and academic performance at the intersection of race-ethnicity and gender. *American Journal of Education, 113*, 101–122.

Rist, R. (1970). Student social class and teacher expectations: The self-fulfilling prophecy in ghetto education. *Harvard Educational Review, 40*, 411–451.

Rosenbaum, J. (1975). The stratification of socialization processes. *American Sociological Review, 40*(1), 48–54.

Rosenbaum, J. (1976). Making inequality: The hidden curriculum of high school tracking. New York: Wiley.

Rumbaut, R., & Portes, A. (2001). *Immigrant America: A portrait* (3rd ed.). Berkeley: University of California Press.

Rumberger, R.W., & Thomas, S. L. (1993). The economic returns to college major, quality and performance: A multilevel analysis of recent graduates. *Economics of Education Review, 12*, 1–19.

Rutter, M., Maughan, B., Mortimore, P., Ouston, J., & Smith, A. (1979). *Fifteen thousand hours: Secondary schools and their effects on children.* Cambridge, MA: Harvard University Press.

Shavit, Y., Arum, R., & Gamoran, A. (Eds.). (2007). *Stratification in higher education: A comparative study.* Stanford, CA: Stanford University Press.

Slaughter, S., & Rhodes, G. (2004). *Academic capitalism and the new economy: Markets, state, and higher education.* Baltimore, MD: Johns Hopkins University Press.

St. John, E. P. (2003). Refinancing the college dream: Access, equal opportunity, and justice for taxpayers. Baltimore, MD: Johns Hopkins University Press.

St. John, E. P., Musoba, G. D., & Simmons, A. B. (2003). Keeping the promise: The impact of Indiana's Twenty-first Century Scholars program. *The Review of Higher Education, 27*(1), 103–123.

Stephan, J., Rosenbaum. J, & Person, A. (2009). Stratification in college entry and completion. *Social Science Research, 38*(3): 572–593.

Thomas, S. (2000). Deferred costs and economic returns to college quality, major and academic performance: An analysis of recent graduates in baccalaureate and beyond. *Research in Higher Education, 44*(3), 263–299.

Thomas, S. L., & Bell, A. (2008). Social class and higher education: A reorganization of opportunities. In L. Weis (Ed.), *The way class works: Readings on school, family, and the economy* (pp. 273–287). New York and London: Routledge.

Thomas, S. L., & Zhang, L. (2005). Changing rates of return to college quality and academic rigor in the United States. Who gets good jobs in America? *Research in Higher Education, 46,* 437–459.

Useem, E. (1992). Middle schools and math groups: Parents' involvement in children's placement. *Sociology of Education*, 65(4), 263–279.

Vanfossen, B., Jones, J., & Spade, J. (1987). Curriculum tracking and status maintenance. *Sociology of Education*, 60(2), 104–122.

Weininger, E., & Lareau, A. (2009). Class and child rearing: An ethnographic extension of Kohn. *Journal of Marriage and Family, 71,* 680–695.

Weis, L. (1985). Between two worlds: Black students at an urban community college. Boston: Routledge, Kegan and Paul.

Weis, L. (1990). Working class without work: High school students in a de-industrializing economy. New York: Routledge.

Weis, L. & Dolby, N. (Eds.) (2012) *Social class and education: Global perspectives*. New York: Routledge.

Weis, L., Cipollone, K., & Jenkins, H. (in press.). *Class warfare: Class and race in affluent and elite secondary schools.* Chicago: University of Chicago Press.

Wimberly, G. L., & Noeth, R. J. (2005). *College readiness begins in middle school.* Iowa City, IA: American College Testing.

Yonezawa, S., & Wells, A. (2005). Reform as redefining the spaces of schools: An examination of detracking by choice. In L. Weis & M. Fine (Eds.), *Beyond silenced voices: Class, race, and gender in United States schools* (2nd ed., pp. 47–61). Albany: State University of New York Press.

Young, M. (Ed.). (1971). Knowledge and control: New directions for the sociology of education. London: Collier-Macmillan.

Photo Credit: © Juanmonino/iStockphoto

Christian Nation or Pluralistic Culture: Religion in American Life

Charles H. Lippy

Two seemingly paradoxical themes mark American religious history:

1. The United States is a Christian nation founded on biblical principles. Other religious communities are tolerated, but the many forms of Christianity remain dominant in common life.

2. Religious diversity flourishes in the United States. No one group or belief system dominates, but because of separation of church and state, religious pluralism prevails, with Americans free to believe and worship as they choose—or not believe.

Both perceptions have long histories; both are vital to understanding American religion and culture in the 21st century.

Europeans Plant Christianity in North America

European settlement in the British colonies that became the United States in 1776 had a history of less than 175 years. Most settlers coming from England shared a religious consciousness shaped by Protestant Christianity (Lippy, Choquette, & Poole, 1992). In southern areas such as Virginia, although some variety existed, colonial arrangements included legal establishment of the Church of England, meaning that public tax money supported its parishes and clergy and that all living there were theoretically part of a parish.

To Massachusetts in the North came settlers with deep ties to the Church of England but dissatisfied with presumed compromises it had made with Roman Catholic ways in order to craft a religious establishment with broad appeal. These dissenters set up churches reflecting their own understanding of religious truth. Generally, we label them all Puritans; all sought a purer form of Protestantism than they found in the Church of England. But they exhibited differences. The Pilgrims who settled Plymouth in 1620 believed such religious falsehood engulfed the Church of England that only by separating from it, relocating, and forming their own religious institutions could they ensure their salvation. Puritans who settled other areas of New England still saw themselves as Anglicans but thought that abandoning a structure headed by bishops and simplifying worship rendered their churches purer.

Both thought that settling in North America gave them religious freedom, generating the idea that the United States was founded on the principle of religious freedom. But none believed that those who disagreed with them should have religious freedom; they thought alternative views dangerous. For example, Massachusetts authorities banished Roger Williams in the 1630s because he was too much a religious seeker. Later acclaimed a beacon of religious liberty who influenced Baptist developments, Williams was regarded as a dangerous heretic. So he moved a few miles to what is now Rhode Island, where Massachusetts authorities lacked power, and set up a church reflecting his own views.

By the end of the 17th century, British policy required a broader toleration of variant forms of Protestantism if they did not disrupt public order. Roman Catholics, however, lacked formal recognition but had a legal haven in Maryland. They flourished especially in Pennsylvania, where the Quaker-dominated government supported the "holy experiment" of the colony's founder, William Penn, which welcomed settlers of all religious persuasions if they supported the commonweal.

Early Signs of Diversity

Immigration brought more diversity than English policy recognized. The arrival of the first slave ships, in 1619, added an African tribal substratum to southern religions; many congregations in time became biracial. White Christians were at first reluctant to proselytize among the slaves, fearing that conversion would require their freedom. More sustained efforts to convert African Americans after the middle of the 18th century brought a vibrant fusion of African ways with evangelical Protestantism. The chant, song, and dance central to tribal religiosity joined with the enthusiastic, often emotional style of evangelicalism to give African American Christianity a distinctive aura. Africans whose forced migration brought them first to the Caribbean added other twists, including practices associated with voodoo. Both Europeans and African Americans were drawn to slaves with a gift for preaching. However, few Whites recognized how the power of slave preachers echoed that of tribal conjurers, a blending that endured after the abolition of slavery and the emergence of independent African American denominations. Also, some of the first slaves were Muslims, although the conditions of slavery made it impossible to sustain Muslim practice.

Ethnicity reflected other manifestations of diversity. The Dutch who settled New York (New Netherlands) generally espoused a Calvinistic Reformed faith; even under English control, they remained a strong presence there. In what became New Jersey, Scandinavian immigrants brought strands of the Lutheran tradition. German immigrants coming to Pennsylvania carried many religious labels, usually variants of Protestant Christianity. Almost from the inception of the colonies came Jewish immigrants; they remained on the religious margins but established synagogues and communities in places such as Charleston, South Carolina; Savannah, Georgia; New York; and Newport, Rhode Island. Often ignored because Christian colonists rarely understood them as religious were practices of Native American tribes. They, too, added to the growing diversity.

By the middle of the 18th century, Scots-Irish immigrants had planted their brand of Presbyterianism, especially in the middle colonies and then farther south along the eastern slopes of the Appalachian Mountains. By mid-century, too, Methodism, then a "new religion" in England, had made its way to North America. Even so, the first national census in 1790 showed that only around 10 percent of the population held formal religious membership. That figure underestimates the influence of the churches in common life and ignores the popular conviction that joining a church (actually becoming a member) was a serious step. Many regularly attended worship and tried to live by religious moral codes but never took that step.

Spanish settlements in areas from Florida through Texas and the Southwest to California brought other layers of diversity. The last of the Spanish missions (San Francisco) was founded in 1776, the year that the English colonies proclaimed their independence from Britain. In addition, a French expression of Catholicism reflecting the French experience flourished along the Gulf of Mexico from Mobile to New Orleans and along the southern Mississippi River. When these areas joined the United States, they added both Spanish and French Catholicism to American religious diversity.

Common Themes

Presbyterians, Methodists, Lutherans, Dutch Reformed, Congregationalist Puritans, and Baptists all had roots in the European Protestant heritage grounded in the Reformation of the 16th century. Although they had differences, common features became more evident in the decades after independence as the nation struggled to define what it meant to be a republic, a representative democracy. Widely shared was some sense that personal experience informed vital religion, but people disagreed about whether one freely chose to experience salvation or whether God alone determined who received salvation. Congregationalists, Presbyterians, and Dutch Reformed, whose belief reflected the theological ideas of John Calvin, tended to attribute all to the work of God; Methodists believed that people accepted God's gift of salvation of their own free will. Some Baptists emphasized free will, and some believed that God alone determined who would be saved. Anglicans (those who were part of the Church of England) and Lutherans also showed diversity, but for many, the work of God in salvation remained a mystery, gradually becoming apparent to those who faithfully attended worship and accepted church doctrine.

In the middle of the 18th century, emphasis on personal religious experience received a boost when waves of revivals called the Great Awakening swept through the colonies, although there is some debate about whether historians invented both the phenomenon and the label. For about a decade after 1740, folks seemed to exhibit intensified interest in religion. Many talked about being converted, some convinced that God gave them signs that they were chosen for salvation and some believing they had freely accepted God's offer of salvation. The revival enriched the biracial character of Christianity in the southern colonies; several evangelical preachers, as mentioned, actively sought converts among enslaved African Americans.

Although church members remained a minority of the population, the influence of Protestant denominations emphasizing personal decision and free will grew immensely in the first half of the 19th century. Those stressing election by God slowly shed that idea. Free will and choice resonated with the democratic ideas informing American political life. In this approach, all persons were equal, whether as sinners or as those who chose salvation. Just as wealth and rank supposedly did not matter in a democracy, they likewise had no clout in evangelical denominations, such as the Methodists and Baptists, that offered salvation to all. These groups (along with Presbyterians, who gradually jettisoned the idea that God predestined some to salvation) aggressively presented their message to ordinary folk.

As the growing American population moved westward, evangelicals became proponents of camp meetings, which brought together frontier people living far apart for times of preaching and fellowship. As factory towns developed along the rivers and canals in the North (the Erie Canal in New York is a prime example), urban evangelists transformed camp meeting techniques to make revivalism a major device for spreading the influence of Protestant Christianity. Revivalists and itinerant evangelists built their reputations on preaching that moved the minds and emotions of audiences, not on the erudite theological discourse once favored by New England Puritans. Denominations requiring clergy to have formal training saw their influence dwindle; few had the time or the money to prepare for ministry this way. Table 5.1 shows the relative growth of Christian groups from 1650 to 1996.

The Spread of Evangelical Protestantism

These currents helped a broad evangelical Protestantism dominate Christianity in the United States by the time of the Civil War. The arrival of thousands of Roman Catholics from Ireland in the 1830s and 1840s did not diminish that influence, for Protestants continued to control business, industry, and political life. This Protestant Christian character became more deeply etched into American culture as public education began to develop in the 1830s. The *McGuffey Readers*

Table 5.1 Number of Places of Worship

	1650	1750	1850	1950	1996
Baptist	2	132	9,375	77,000	98,228
Congregationalist	62	465	1,706	5,679	6,748
Episcopal	31	289	1,459	7,784	7,517
Presbyterian	4	233	4,824	13,200	14,214
Methodist	0	0	13,328	54,000	51,311
Roman Catholic	6	30	1,221	15,533	22,728
Jewish	0	5	30	2,000	3,975
Holiness/Pentecostal	0	0	0	21,705	52,868

Source: Adapted from *New Historical Atlas of Religion in America*, by E. S. Gaustad and P. L. Barlow, 2001. San Francisco: Harper, p. 390.

(Westerhoff, 1978; Williams, 1980), standard fare in primary education for generations, exhibited an evangelical Protestant tone in their lessons, fusing Protestant beliefs and moral values with sound learning. Although other groups (Irish Catholics, German Catholics, Jews, and more) were growing, this broad evangelical Protestantism pervaded common life, reinforcing the image of the United States as a Christian nation.

As European immigration peaked between the Civil War and World War I, challenges came to that hegemony. Most of those millions of immigrants came not from Protestant or even Catholic areas of Northern and Western Europe but from Southern, Central, and Eastern Europe. The majority were Roman Catholics, Eastern Orthodox Christians, and Jews. Many Catholic parishes established parochial (parish) schools, in part because Protestant assumptions informed public school curricula. Some in positions of social, economic, and political power recoiled at both the religious orientation of these immigrants and their cultural and ethnic folkways. Calls to Americanize the immigrants were often ill-disguised calls to Protestantize them, to force conformity to the dominant religious style in order to buttress the idea that the nation was a (Protestant) Christian country.

The Congregationalist Josiah Strong, who worked for the interdenominational Evangelical Alliance, claimed, in his *Our Country* (1886/1964), that the religions of the immigrants, along with their concentration in the nation's cities and the rapid industrialization spurred by their swelling of the workforce, threatened American identity. But they were threats only if one wedded American identity to evangelical Protestant Christianity.

The steady growth of African American Protestant denominations, most of them Methodist or Baptist, added another layer of diversity. Never mirror images of their White counterparts, these groups became crucibles in forging an indigenous leadership that later propelled the civil rights movement of the 20th century. In much of the South, where legal discrimination replaced slavery, churches were frequently the only property owned by African Americans, and the preachers serving them were often the only ones with advanced educations. Especially in the rural South, churches became broad social institutions, centers of community life offering essential social welfare programs as long as legal racism penetrated the larger society.

Nonetheless, mainline Protestants exerted an influence in business and political affairs increasingly out of proportion to their numbers in the whole population. After World War I, Congress enacted the first laws limiting immigration overall as well as expanding earlier restrictions on Asian immigration, which primarily affected areas of the West. Quotas ensured that the bulk of those allowed to enter the United States would have at least nominal Protestant associations, sustaining the image that the United States was a Christian nation. Table 5.2 presents data on religious affiliation from 1830 to 2007. Trends since 1990 suggest a gradual decline in the proportion of Christians in the population, thanks largely to changes in immigration policy made in 1965.

Religious Freedom and the Separation of Church and State

Countervailing forces always challenged the reality of the image of the United States as a Christian nation, reinforcing the conviction that religious diversity and pluralism prevailed. In this view, the United States was never a Christian nation per se but one where religious freedom meant no one religious group or tradition had special privilege. This perspective has roots in the First Amendment to the Constitution, with its declaration that "Congress shall make no law respecting an establishment of religion, or prohibiting the free exercise thereof." Ever since the adoption of the Bill of Rights, courts and pundits have debated precisely what those words mean.

In the early U.S. Republic, one reason not to have a nationally established religion was pragmatic. If most citizens identified with one of the numerous Christian bodies, primarily Protestant ones, no one denomination or sect counted a majority as adherents, much less as members. Baptists, Methodists, Presbyterians, Quakers, Lutherans of many ethnic varieties, Episcopalians, and a host of others lived together in relative peace and harmony. This diversity, celebrated by some as leading to pluralism, made it unfair (undemocratic) to grant one group governmental support. Another reason stemmed from the conviction that all religious groups inculcated the moral values that made their followers good citizens. Common morals taught by all religions trumped theological differences.

In addition, leading political thinkers embraced the ideas of rationalism and freedom of thought associated with the Enlightenment. The Age of the Revolution was also the Age of Reason. Thomas Jefferson, Benjamin Franklin, George Washington, and a host of others subscribed to Enlightenment ideas. Contrary to later lore, they were not 21st-century fundamentalists disguised as 18th-century politicians, nor were they what a later age labeled secular

Table 5.2   Percentage of Americans Claiming Religious Affiliation

	1830	1890	1990	2007
Baptist	25.0%	18.0%	20.0%	17.2%
Congregationalist	12.3	2.5	1.5	0.8
Episcopal	5.0	2.6	1.8	1.5
Presbyterian	17.0	6.2	2.7	2.7
Methodist	23.4	22.3	11.8	6.2
Roman Catholic	4.2	30.2	38.9	23.9
Jewish	*	*	4.4	1.7
Holiness/Pentecostal	*	*	4.4	4.4
Lutheran	3.4	6.0	6.0	4.6
Muslim	N/A	N/A	N/A	0.6

Sources: Adapted from *New Historical Atlas of Religion in America*, by E. S. Gaustad and P. L. Barlow, 2001. San Francisco: Harper, p. 389; and U.S. Religious Landscape Survey, by The Pew Forum on Religion and Public Life, 2008. Retrieved January 20, 2009, from http://www.census.gov/compendia/statab/tables/09s0074.pdf

humanists. Most believed that an overarching Providence, whom the more orthodox called God, worked through human affairs. All thought that religious doctrines, even those they rejected, molded people into moral citizens and therefore supported peace and social order. All were suspicious of anything not demonstrated through logic. Logic and reason also decreed that one had a right to think as one wished, to follow the truth given by one's own mind.

This rationalist emphasis on what the 18th-century Boston pastor Jonathan Mayhew (1749) called the "right of private judgment" and the evangelical Protestant emphasis on a personal experience of conversion or election were actually complementary. Both made the individual (not churches, ministers, priests, or even Scripture) the final authority in matters of belief and practice. No one could have an experience of conversion for another; only the individual could determine what the mind deemed right and true. Most rationalists were confident (if not naively optimistic) that truth would look pretty much the same to everyone. Because there was no guarantee, a democracy had to allow for latitude of belief among citizens. If different minds arrived at different truths, so be it, so long as difference did not disrupt civil order.

For advocates of reason, the danger of government's endorsing any belief system, no matter how worthy, or giving official status to any one religious group or tradition, no matter how influential, was the potential to exert tyranny over others. If a religious community could call on the coercive power of the state to force conformity to its beliefs and practices, the state lost legitimacy. The religious community no longer had to persuade people of its truth rationally or move people to experience for themselves the reality of salvation.

Before ratification of the Bill of Rights, Virginia had adopted a statute providing for nearly total religious freedom. Inspired by Thomas Jefferson, the Virginia statute became a model for many states because the Constitution restricted only the Congress from establishing a religion. A few New England states continued to pay the salaries of teachers of religion and morals from public funds. The last to end such provision was Massachusetts in 1833.

The phrase *separation of church and state* never appears in the Constitution. It comes from a letter written in 1802 by President Thomas Jefferson in which he referred to a "wall of separation between church and state." Jefferson noted that, like the Connecticut Baptists who had written to him, he believed that "religion is a matter which lies solely between man and his God, that he owes account to none other for his faith or his worship" and "that the legislative powers of government reach actions only, and not opinions" (cited in Wilson, 1965, pp. 75–76). Jefferson acknowledged the reality of God, but wanted to avoid government involvement in determining what individuals believed and how they worshiped and lived their faith.

Legal provision for religious freedom did not mean, however, that all sorts of fanatics suddenly came to the United States, although numerous individuals tried to gain a following for their own points of view. One result paralleled Enlightenment-era shifts in Europe, namely, ensuring that there were no political disabilities attached to Jewish identity. For centuries, many European Jews were forced into ghettos, prohibited from practicing certain occupations in the larger community, denied access to political life, and restricted in their educational opportunities. Separation of church and state, although using a Christian term (*church*) to refer to all religions, would make that impossible in the United States but did not eradicate either overt or covert anti-Semitism in American culture.

This legal arrangement also meant that the United States became a nation where extraordinary religious experimentation flourished, even if a broad evangelical Protestantism dominated public life. In the 1830s in upstate New York, for example, Joseph Smith reported having a vision that led to the founding of the Church of Jesus Christ of Latter-day Saints, popularly called the Mormons. Because their teachings seemed to undermine orthodox Protestant doctrine, Mormons encountered hostility that forced them to relocate several times. Garnering more followers as they moved, they finally settled around the Great Salt Lake, just before Mexico transferred the Utah area to the United States. The Saints represent what some historians regard as the first genuinely "new" religion to emerge in the American context.

Around the same time, John Humphrey Noyes came from Vermont to Oneida in upstate New York, preaching a gospel that drew scores to his communitarian enterprise with its practice of complex marriage. The Shakers, although planted on American soil by Ann Lee and a handful of adherents just before the American Revolution, also reached their peak in the 1830s. About 6,000 men and women followed the simple, celibate life in nearly two dozen different communities, several of them in upstate New York and in New England. Countless other groups gathered around inspired teachers who carved a niche for themselves because government would not interfere in matters of personal belief and practice. Many experimented with communal living. As in a marketplace, each group competed to gain a following; those adept at convincing men and women of their truth reaped the most adherents.

Immigration in the early 19th century ensured that the United States would be home to a significant Jewish population. Although several small Jewish communities existed in the English colonies—with the earliest synagogues organized in places such as Newport, Rhode Island, and Charleston, South Carolina—the immigration of Jews from German cultures brought diversity to the Hebrew tradition itself. Eager to seize opportunities for fuller participation in public life that came after the Enlightenment and the end of forced exclusion from society, many Jews were drawn to Reform Judaism. The Reform movement sought to modernize Judaism by abandoning nonessential features of Jewish practice thought to be inextricably wedded to ancient Near Eastern culture.

Later Jewish immigrants found Reform too radical, yielding too much. Those resisting most strongly became known as Orthodox Jews, although in time the largest body became known as Conservative Jews. Conservative Jews modified some traditional practice to accommodate life in a religiously pluralistic culture but believed the Reform movement jettisoned too much. Despite the Christian domination of American religious life, by the middle of the 19th century, a vibrant Jewish community represented a dynamic alternative.

In the first half of the 19th century, other religious teachers regularly preached at camp meetings or worked the lecture circuit, a form of popular entertainment, in the larger cities. Along the frontier, several sought to restore what they regarded as the actual practice of first-century New Testament Christianity. That meant shedding denominational structure and sometimes even religious professionals such as clergy. This restorationist impulse gave birth to groups that later coalesced into the Disciples of Christ and the Churches of Christ.

In northern cities, individuals such as William Miller drew crowds to their presentations on biblical prophecy. Miller, eagerly expecting the imminent return of Christ to usher in the millennial age, fixed a date when the second advent would transpire, more than once revising his calculations when Christ did not return on schedule. Most of his followers scattered because of the "great disappointment" that ensued, but this teaching found new life in the Seventh-Day Adventists and the doctrines advocated by their early leader, Ellen G. Harmon White.

By the end of the 19th century, many other groups had emerged, some reflecting the diverse religious styles of new immigrants and others the ideas offered by dynamic speakers and writers. Among the better known are the Amish and their religious cousins, the Mennonites, who sought to live their version of a simple life without involvement in a larger society hopelessly corrupted by modernity. Their major immigration to the United States and Canada came shortly after the Civil War. During that epoch, interest in science and the application of scientific techniques to religious expression also increased. Mary Baker Eddy, for example, named her use of mental power to effect healing Christian Science. Her influence grew rapidly as she published her views and as practitioners fanned out across the country, promoting her ideas.

These examples illustrate the diversity and pluralism shaping American religious life, made possible in part because of the First Amendment. Other factors aided this religious experimentation. The seemingly vast expanse of land in the nation provided room for various religious teachers and groups to go about their business without really interrupting or interfering with the lives of those around them. Consequently, the American experience demolished a myth that had buttressed Western civilization since the days of the Roman Empire, namely, that religious uniformity (or at least tacit conformity to one religious tradition) was a necessary precondition for political stability and social harmony.

Diversity, Religious Freedom, and the Courts

At the same time, some religious groups seemed to many Americans, primarily those who were Protestants, to overstep the limits of freedom. After all, they were minority groups on the margins of the larger religious culture. If their beliefs and practices diverged too much from those of the majority, should they be restrained or curtailed lest they undermine the dominant religious style? When would diversity in the free exercise of religion become dangerous? How could government protect the majority without becoming tyrannical?

One example emerged when the Latter-day Saints founder Joseph Smith advocated plural marriage. A revelation he believed divine convinced him that his followers should adopt the ancient biblical practice of men having more than one wife. Most Americans were aghast at the idea of polygamy, and most states forbade the practice when the Utah Territory sought admission to the Union. The situation was convoluted, and historians differ about how subsequent Mormon teaching came to prohibit polygamy. Although the Saints once insisted polygamy was part of their free exercise of religion, abandoning it became a condition for Utah's admission as a state. In the process, the U.S. Supreme Court heard two cases dealing with plural marriage, *Reynolds v. United States* in 1878 and *Davis v. Beason* in 1890 (Miller & Flowers, 1987). Although the official position changed and Utah's state constitution prohibited plural marriage, some individuals claiming Mormon identity continued the practice. In 2008, one such example in Texas attracted wide attention in the media and the courts, but most instances are ignored because practitioners tend to live in remote areas where residents often overlook what does not upset public order.

Laws protecting Sabbath observance began in the colonial period. Among the earliest were provisions in Virginia, part of "Dale's Laws" in 1610, that required attendance at Christian worship and also prohibited "any gaming" in public or private on Sunday. As the American Jewish population grew, Orthodox Jews, who strictly observed the Sabbath from sundown Friday until sundown Saturday, found laws favoring Sunday as the Sabbath discriminatory. However, because the number of Jews was small and the Jewish population fairly scattered, few challenged the status quo.

Sunday laws also affected Seventh-Day Adventists, who, as their name indicates, hold the Hebrew Sabbath—the seventh day, or Saturday—as sacred. Most Christian groups, whether Protestant, Catholic, or Orthodox, believed that their practice of keeping Sunday, the first day, as sacred superseded seventh-day Sabbath observance. Well into the 20th century, many states and local communities legally restricted Sunday labor, sale of certain products, and access to some recreational activities. Popularly known as *blue laws*, such regulations aroused little concern when Christians constituted the overwhelming majority of citizens in a town or area. They tended to keep Sunday sacred even without legal restraints. But what about those for whom the seventh day was holy?

Most legal challenges involving Seventh-Day Adventists and Orthodox Jews came in local and state courts. Early challenges to blue laws reaching the U.S. Supreme Court did not directly involve religious groups, although the issues at stake did. For example, the arrest of discount store employees for selling restricted products on Sunday propelled *McGowan v. Maryland* (1961); *Two Guys from Harrison-Allentown, Inc. v. McGinley* (1961) was similar, but different enough to require a separate decision. In both, the Court upheld Sunday blue laws using an "argument from history" and insisted that even if blue laws indirectly supported Christian observance, they promoted the general welfare by mandating one day of rest in seven. Bringing such cases to the Supreme Court resulted in moves to repeal most blue laws.

In times of war, most court cases dealing with religion have concerned those who refused to engage in combat and sometimes in activities that supported combat. Although hundreds have been imprisoned, generally the courts concluded that members of religious groups, such as the Quakers, the Mennonites, the Church of the Brethren, and other historic "peace churches," could refuse military service, but most performed alternative service. One consequence of protest against the U.S. military presence in Vietnam was extending conscientious objector classification to those morally opposed to war even if they were not members of a religious body.

Over the years, free exercise issues have also involved groups that reject certain medical procedures (e.g., blood transfusions), such as the Jehovah's Witnesses and the Church of Christ, Scientist. Generally, the courts have upheld the right of persons of legal age to refuse medical treatment on religious grounds. More complex situations arise when parents refuse to authorize medical procedures for their minor children on religious grounds. Here the issue has been whether government's responsibility to promote the welfare of minors could mandate protocols rejected by parents' faith communities.

Apparent conflict between promoting the general welfare and upholding free exercise also informed many of the cases, mostly on a state level, that concerned ritual serpent handling and ingesting of poisonous liquids such as strychnine. Serpent handlers claimed a biblical basis for the practice in the Gospel of Mark, Chapter 16, insisting they did only what Scripture required. Did possible death from snake bite make serpent handling a practice that undermined the general welfare, allowing the government to prohibit it? Because serpent-handling groups are concentrated in the mountains of central Appalachia, most laws making serpent handling illegal were passed by states in that region. Few were regularly enforced, and most had been rescinded by the end of the 20th century.

Numerous cases wrestled with whether sanctioning particular practices resulted in a de facto establishment of religion. Many involved public school education. Some of the earliest concerned children affiliated with the Jehovah's Witnesses. Witnesses refuse to salute the flag, insisting that reciting the Pledge of Allegiance elevates the state above God. Before the rights of the Witnesses received legal protection, several episodes resulted in children who were Witnesses being expelled from school and their parents being prosecuted. At first, the Supreme Court rejected refusal to recite the Pledge of Allegiance as an exercise of religious freedom. In *Minersville School District v. Gobitis* (1940), the Court decreed that the social cohesion resulting from requiring students to recite the pledge superseded free exercise. But in *West Virginia State Board of Education v. Barnette* three years later, the Court reversed its position, setting a precedent that has prevailed since.

More recent debates center on the words *under God* inserted into the Pledge of Allegiance by Congress in 1954. In June 2004, the Supreme Court dismissed one such case from California, where a lower court had found the phrase unconstitutional; the Court ruled that the parent who had initiated the case, an avowed atheist, lacked standing because he did not have legal custody of his daughter, the one required to recite the pledge. Subsequent cases brought by different parties resulted in a federal appeals court in 2010 allowing the phrase to stand because no law actually required anyone to say the challenged words or even to recite the pledge at all.

As noted earlier, when public education began to become the norm in the United States in the 19th century, curriculum materials often reflected the beliefs and practices of mainline Protestant denominations. Christian holidays, such as Christmas and Holy Week before Easter, saw classes suspended; Jewish holy days did not as a rule receive such preferential treatment, although Jewish children incurred no penalties for absences on religious holidays. In some school districts, religious groups—usually Protestants—used educational facilities for religious instruction, sometimes during the regular class day. In *McCollum v. Board of Education* (1948), the Supreme Court prohibited using school facilities and class time for instruction in a particular faith tradition, even when participation was voluntary.

Some accommodation came in 1952 in *Zorach v. Clauson*, when the Court sanctioned dismissing children early from regular classes to attend voluntary off-site religious instruction. For several decades, children could be dismissed from public school early one day a week to attend religious programs conducted by both Protestant and Roman Catholic churches. By the end of the 20th century, when recruiting volunteers to staff such programs became difficult and other extracurricular options expanded, most such endeavors were dismantled.

The greatest controversy has revolved around Bible reading and prayer in the public schools and whether such activities create a tacit establishment of religion or favor a particular religious tradition. In some communities, questions arose about prayers preceding athletic events or during commencement exercises. In 1962, the Supreme Court in *Engel v. Vitale* struck down a New York State Board of Regents requirement that public school students begin each school day by reciting a presumably nonsectarian prayer. As furor over that judgment mounted, the Court in *Abington v. Schempp* (1963) declared unconstitutional any devotional Bible reading and recitation of the Lord's Prayer, even if those for whom such were not acts of worship were excused.

Five decades later, school districts and state legislatures are wrangling with ways to get around these decisions. Subsequent cases, mostly in lower courts, have whittled away at the absolute prohibitions, allowing some student-initiated prayers and the use of school facilities by voluntary student religious groups outside class hours if they are available for other extracurricular programs. Frequently overlooked in the heat of controversy is the Supreme Court's insistence that prohibiting devotional practices did not ban the academic study of religion in public schools, which is different from teaching that any belief system contains ultimate truth. Nor have courts banned study of sacred texts such as the Bible from literary and historical perspectives since literary and historical study does not necessarily promote personal belief and commitment. Yet public school systems have been reluctant to offer the academic study of religion lest it be misconstrued as endorsing one religion over another. Appropriate curriculum materials for religion courses continue to increase, but few have the training to teach religion as an academic subject.

In the early 21st century, debates continued over what separation of church and state involves and how to ensure the free exercise of religion. Some, such as a case involving whether Santeria is a religion and its ritual of sacrifice of chickens a protected religious practice, echoed earlier themes. Other cases concerned ways to link religion and education legally, such as whether states or communities could provide citizens with vouchers to defray the cost of religiously sponsored education. Several focused on whether biology textbooks should include creationism as a scientific perspective alongside theories of evolution. Because many saw creation science as introducing a single religious viewpoint into public education, courts consistently rejected claims to include it in school curricula.

When others advocated intelligent design as an explanation for the origins of the universe, new court battles ensued. Intelligent design seemed merely a new name for creation science. Moves to introduce intelligent design challenged the traditional teaching of science and appeared poised to open doors to introduce other matters of faith into public school curricula. In the first cases making their way through the judicial system, the courts generally refused to require teaching theories of intelligent design because they were construed as promoting religion; in some instances, however, they mandated presenting evolution as speculative theory, not as accepted scientific fact. A critical case arose in Dover, Pennsylvania, in 2005. The local school board required teaching intelligent design in its biology curriculum as well as discussing evolution as a theory, not as universally accepted scientific fact. Judge John E. Jones III overturned the board's policy, declaring that intelligent design was not science (Raffaele, 2005). Although this ruling seemed likely to become a precedent, efforts to promulgate supernatural explanations of cosmic and human origins did not disappear.

In retrospect, some believe that early legal cases concerned how to protect the rights of religious minorities but that later cases imposed minority rule on the majority. Regardless, legal cases concerning religion reveal that a deep and abiding diversity marks American life, even if a broadly based evangelical Protestantism once exercised dominant influence.

Pluralism Becomes the Norm

The court cases of the 1960s concerning prayer and Bible reading came as the image of the United States as a Christian nation was unraveling. As early as 1955, Will Herberg, one-time labor union organizer and Jewish professor of the sociology of religion at a Methodist seminary, in his *Protestant, Catholic, Jew* (1960) argued that most Americans regarded the many forms of Protestantism, Roman Catholicism, and Judaism as equivalent in molding adherents into responsible citizens. Any religious label was a badge of social worth. For Herberg, equally important, although disturbing, was the emergence of a cultural religion, the "religion of the American Way of Life." It emphasized materialism and conspicuous consumption, not the commitment and discipleship permeating biblical faith. That unconscious push to a common ground minimizing denominational particularities and distinctions among faith traditions echoes in the statement attributed to President Eisenhower: The government of the United States "makes no sense unless it is founded on a deeply felt religious faith—and I don't care what it is" (cited in Herberg, p. 95).

Military service during World War II introduced thousands of Americans to persons of other religious persuasions; shared experiences in battle minimized faith differences. As veterans reentered civilian life after the war, employment opportunities frequently entailed relocation. The model of Americans living from birth until death in the same community or area disappeared. Relocation for many meant finding a new church with which to affiliate, often chosen for reasons other than denominational label. If the denomination of one's birth had no congregation nearby, it was easy to affiliate with another one.

The suburban sprawl accompanying mobility also eroded denominational loyalty. Mainline Protestant denominations raced to build new churches in mushrooming suburban communities, often cooperating with each other so as not to "overchurch" an area. Church bureaucrats knew that families likely identified with congregations, regardless of denomination, with programs oriented toward young families. Denominational switching became the norm. Denominations could no longer assume that those raised within the fold would retain a lifelong identification with a particular tradition. Bonding to a particular heritage disappeared; people related only to the specific local congregation they attended. Those not deeply steeped in their tradition rarely reared their children with a firm commitment to that heritage.

The rush to the nation's colleges and universities in the postwar years, spurred by the G.I. Bill, undermined denominational loyalty in a different way. The collegiate environment, like military experience, introduced many to varieties of ways of being religious. It was not, as some feared, that college education destroyed religious faith, but it brought exposure to persons from many faiths, removing much of the apprehension surrounding alternative religions. Consequently, higher education led people to see faith communities as functionally equivalent, with none having an exclusive claim to truth. Some Protestants demurred, believing this exposure dangerous, resulting in compromise with falsehood and contamination of authentic faith.

Mobility, military service, and collegiate experience were catalysts stimulating a sharp increase in interreligious marriage. Marriage across Protestant denominational lines had long been common. Now there came a dramatic increase in marriages between Protestants and Roman Catholics and between Christians and Jews; the boundaries separating these larger faith traditions had previously proved more unyielding than those between Protestant denominations. Then, too, hundreds of Americans who had served in the Pacific during the war brought home spouses from various Asian or Pacific cultures who, like other immigrants, sought to retain their religions of origin. Individual families carved out their own religious identities from those brought together in a single household. Some compromised, identifying with yet another religious group;

sometimes husbands and wives maintained separate religious affiliation, perhaps exposing their children to both, perhaps just to one, often to none. Many dropped out of organized religion.

No matter how families resolved such issues, new dimensions of pluralism took on increasing importance. The ecumenical movement, primarily among Protestants, contributed to this diversity. Cooperative endeavors through councils of churches, mergers of denominations within the same religious family such as the reunion of northern and southern Presbyterians in 1983, and talks of church union spearheaded by the Consultation on Church Union formed in the early 1960s created the impression that all Protestant bodies were much alike and that denominations really made little difference and had no distinctive ways of expressing what Christian faith was. If labels made no difference, then loyalty to a particular denomination made no difference. In promoting unity among Protestants, the ecumenical movement unwittingly undermined denominational loyalty.

In addition, social forces unleashed by the civil rights movement and the antiwar efforts associated with U.S. engagement in Vietnam challenged all forms of authority within American life, including the authority of religious groups and their leaders. The baby boom generation, reaching adulthood during that turbulent epoch, more than earlier generations shunned commitment to all social institutions, including religious ones. Reared when denominational loyalty was eroding, they had no abiding identification with organized religion. Earlier generations had drifted away from religious communities in late adolescence and early young adulthood but generally returned when they had children, if only to provide some moral anchor for them. Boomers did not return in the same proportion. Many, however, identified themselves as spiritual even as they resisted being called religious.

Robert Wuthnow (1998) has argued that in the second half of the 20th century, Americans exchanged a religious "home" or center, usually fixed around a tradition or group, for a "quest," something more individualistic and idiosyncratic. The subtitle of an article in a popular journal captured the mood: "Design Your Own God" (Creedon, 1998). Women from the boomer generation, for example, probed beliefs well beyond those of standard denominations to forge a spirituality grounded in female experience. Some looked to pagan and pre-Christian forms of expression, sparking panic among some Christians that feminist spirituality threatened the integrity of the churches. The following point to a dynamic spirituality that exists alongside and frequently outside organized religion:

1. Gathering in forest groves to celebrate rituals marking experiences unique to women, from childbirth to menopause

2. Rarely attending worship but claiming to be spiritual because they occasionally read the Bible along with practicing Zen meditation techniques

3. Fashioning home altars that juxtapose a cross with New Age crystals

4. Sporting What Would Jesus Do? (WWJD) bracelets or other religious objects in ways previous generations had made the cross a piece of jewelry

5. Silently walking the universal mandala, the labyrinth, because organized religion had become too noisy

At the same time, Christian groups experiencing growth resisted this privatization of spirituality. At the peak of the civil rights and antiwar movements, analysts recognized that, among Protestants, denominations and independent congregations with more orthodox religious teaching, those inclined to variations of fundamentalist and Pentecostal expression, were growing (Kelley, 1977). For generations, scholars had consigned such forms of Christianity to the periphery, mistakenly assuming that fundamentalism and Pentecostalism attracted only the economically disadvantaged and politically powerless.

Fundamentalists, Pentecostals, and other evangelicals had developed strong networks, cementing bonds and providing resources to sustain their institutions during their time on the margins (Carpenter, 1997). They gathered strength from their conviction that they possessed unquestioned truth, protected from the cultural attacks on authority of the later 20th century. If mainline Protestants and Catholics confronted internal turmoil over civil rights, Vietnam, and feminism, fundamentalism and Pentecostalism offered a refuge, a secure way of looking at the world not battered by social controversy but buttressed by certainty that they still had absolute truth. The presence of fundamentalists and Pentecostals also complicates efforts to find a single religious base for American culture, and their leaders often propel debates about public education, such as teaching intelligent design.

Some talk about the "Judeo-Christian tradition," an artificial construct, as reflecting the dominant religious mood in the United States. At the beginning of the 21st century, particularly after the terrorist attacks of September 2001, many who called for posting the Ten Commandments in schools and other public buildings hoped that this amorphous amalgamation of biblical traditions could still provide social cohesion. Undercutting those efforts was another facet of religious pluralism, namely, the dramatic increase in the number of Americans identifying with religious traditions such as Islam, Buddhism, and Hinduism.

New Faces of Pluralism

Changes in immigration laws in 1965 spurred a rise in immigration from Latin America, Africa, and Asia. With them has come fresh interest in religions indigenous to those areas and a new appreciation of the links between ethnicity and religion. The Sun Belt experienced the greatest proportional growth in immigration from Latin America, the Near East, and Asia. From 1990 to 2000, the percentage of those who were foreign born in North Carolina and Georgia (as well as in Nevada) increased by more than 200 percent; in 2000, more than one-quarter of the population of California was foreign born (Malone, Baluja, Costanzo, & Davis, 2003). In Whitfield County, Georgia, the heart of the state's carpet industry, Hispanic Americans now constitute almost 50 percent of the population, and more than 50 percent of students in the public schools are Hispanic (Mahoney, 2002). Figures reported in the 2000 census indicate that 4.2 percent of the U.S. population was born in Asia (Reeves & Bennett, 2004), a figure that is increasing steadily. Even before the 2010 census, estimates indicated that those of Hispanic stock (38.8 million) outnumbered African Americans (38.3 million) to constitute the largest single ethnic minority in the nation (U.S. Census Bureau, 2003). Indeed, more than 10 million persons of Hispanic origin have entered the United States legally or illegally since 2000 (Camarota, 2007).

Preliminary analysis of data from the 2010 census suggests that these trends have continued and will shape American life for decades to come. According to the U.S. Census, Americans of Hispanic/Latino background increased by 43 percent between 2000 and 2010, and represented approximately 16.3 percent of the population in 2010. That proportion may well reach 22.5 percent by mid-century. Those of Asian background, accounting for 4.8 percent of the population in 2010, will represent 10.3 percent by 2050. These estimates do not include persons whose background may include more than one ethnic or racial component (Day, 2011; U.S. Census Bureau, 2011).

In most urban areas, Roman Catholic parishes have added services in Spanish, recognizing that Hispanic Catholicism brings to religious life a rich blend of traditions reflecting the cultures of Central and South America. Cuban immigrants in the Miami area, for example, have erected a shrine to Our Lady of Charity that signals both a particular religious sensibility and a Cuban nationalism (Tweed, 1997). These immigrants are replicating what Italian and Irish Catholics and others did more than a century ago by bringing with them the festivals, patron saints, and fusion of religious and ethnic ways that give them a sense of identity and cultural cohesion.

Some Protestant denominations have launched special ministries to Spanish-speaking Americans. Many, especially those in the Pentecostal fold, provide services and programs designed to reflect the spiritual style of Hispanic followers. Theologically, Hispanic Americans (both Protestant and Catholic) tend to be more traditional and conservative in their thinking even as their practice reveals considerable syncretism in its expression. Even within the Christian tradition, it has become impossible to look at Anglo American styles as normative.

Immigration from Asia swelled the ranks of Hindus, Buddhists, and Muslims in the United States. American interest in Asian religious cultures has a long history. In the 19th century, transcendentalist writers such as Ralph Waldo Emerson found Asian religious philosophy appealing, and thousands devoured reports of seemingly exotic religious practices in Asia through letters from missionaries published in popular religious magazines. But, except for a small number of immigrants from China and Japan on the West Coast, few Americans had firsthand experience with these religions; even fewer practiced them.

More direct exposure came with the World's Parliament of Religions, held in Chicago in 1893 in conjunction with the Columbian Exposition marking the 400th anniversary of Columbus's first voyage to America. Representatives from a number of religions, including Hindus and Buddhists, came to Chicago; some, like the Hindu philosopher Vivekananda, remained in the United States for an extended period, speaking in larger cities and attracting some interest, primarily among intellectuals, in Asian thought. American military involvement during Asia in World War II, the Korean War, and the Vietnam War introduced thousands to Asian ways of being religious. Some brought spouses back to the United States who sought to continue the religious ways that had nurtured them.

The 1960s witnessed the arrival of several Asian religious figures seeking American converts, particularly from among those disenchanted with traditional American religious life because it seemed mired in racism and torn apart over government policy in Vietnam. The International Society of Krishna Consciousness, popularly known as Hare Krishna, became a familiar presence in cities and college towns; thousands were drawn to practices such as transcendental meditation, promoted by the Maharishi Mahesh Yogi and made fashionable by celebrities such as the Beatles. A generation later, the Dalai Lama became a symbol of American interest in Tibetan Buddhism, aided by the devotion of celebrities such as Richard Gere.

While some forms of Buddhism, such as that promoted by the Dalai Lama, and some popular forms of Hinduism, such as Krishna Consciousness, have primarily attracted American devotees of non-Asian background, the majority of American Buddhists, Hindus, and Muslims come from families who are doing what Americans have done for centuries—practicing the religion that the first generation of immigrants brought with them, albeit adapting it to the American context. The increase in the number of immigrants for whom these traditions represent the heritages they bring with them when they come to the United States is changing the face of pluralism. Table 5.3 illustrates their relative growth.

Estimates suggest that the United States was home to only 30,000 Buddhists in 1900 but to between 2 million and 4 million in 2010; to a mere 1,000 Hindus in 1900 but to more than a

Table 5.3   Estimates of Adherents of Asian Religions

	1900	1970	2000
Buddhists	30,000	200,000	2,000,000
Hindus	1,000	100,000	950,000
Muslims*	10,000	800,000	3,950,000

*Not including the Nation of Islam.

Source: Figures based on data from the U.S. Census Bureau.

million in 2010; to just 10,000 Muslims in 1900 but perhaps (and the estimates vary widely here) to between 4 million and 6 million just over a century later, not counting those affiliated with the Nation of Islam (Lippy, 2009; Pluralism Project, 2011; U.S. Census Bureau, 2000). Some believe that by 2010 the Muslim population actually exceeded 6 million, although estimates are plagued by problems ranging from the relatively small proportion of U.S. Muslims affiliated with mosques, fears of prejudice in the wake of the 9/11 terrorist attacks, and the willingness of some Muslims to abandon religious practice in the American context.

The Hindu tradition has never actively proselytized; in other cultural contexts, Buddhists and Muslims have more aggressively sought converts. In the United States, there is relatively little association between the various immigrant Buddhist communities and centers catering primarily to American-born converts. American Muslims are reluctant to proselytize because of popular negative perceptions of Islam and assumptions that all Muslims advocate international terrorism. American converts to Islam are more likely to be persons of African descent; they join a small but growing number of African immigrants who are also Muslim.

A closer look at American Hindus, Buddhists, and Muslims suggests that these traditions will grow much more rapidly from internal propagation than any Christian or Jewish group will. In 2008, the Pew Forum on Religion and Public Life released a detailed study profiling adherents of all major religious communities in the nation. That survey found that around three-quarters of all American Muslims, Buddhists, and Hindus were under 50 years of age, an indication that many were in their peak childbearing years and that a much larger proportion were children and adolescents than was true for the general population. By contrast, just half of mainline Protestants were under age 50. This internal growth combined with immigration to make Islam one of the fastest-growing religions in the nation. There is little wonder, then, that the historian of religion Diana Eck (1997) titled her study of these trends *A New Religious America: How a "Christian Country" Has Become the World's Most Religiously Diverse Nation*. With practices and holy days that diverge from those prevalent in a "Judeo-Christian" culture, schools and other public institutions face fresh challenges in accommodating diversity in order to protect the free exercise of religion.

Two examples must suffice. First, traditional Muslim practice calls for the devout to pray five times daily facing in the direction of Mecca. Stated times for prayer clash with the standard workday and school day in the United States. Accommodating them poses challenges. Second, controversy erupted over the building of mosques and Islamic centers in various communities in 2010 and 2011. The most widely publicized concerned plans to erect such a center in New York City, near the former World Trade Center demolished in terrorist attacks in 2001. But other communities also faced turmoil. In Murfreesboro, Tennessee, for example, residents sought to block construction of a mosque and educational center on the grounds that the Muslim imperative to convert and/or subdue non-Muslims represented a threat to the free exercise of religion by non-Muslims. However, courts dismissed the claim and allowed construction to continue.

Given the increasing globalization that marks contemporary life, trends in the United States need to be seen in a larger framework. Internal migration within Europe and immigration from nations once part of Europe's colonial empires have transformed the religious landscape there. Pluralism, sometimes called multiconfessionalism in Europe, has brought not only the same challenges to European society as to U.S. society but also some that reflect the distinctive character of European cultures. For example, France, once the colonial power controlling much of Muslim North Africa, will likely see Muslims accounting for 10.3 percent of its population by 2030 (Pew Forum on Religion and Public Life, 2011). Since the French Revolution, France has more thoroughly kept overt religious influence out of public life than has the United States, despite the American separation of church and state. Consequently, controversy over whether to allow Muslim females to wear traditional garb not only in schools but also in most public venues has highlighted the limits of toleration and the depth of residual prejudice. As the

Muslim population of Europe grows at a rate surpassing that expected in the United States, similar tensions will erupt elsewhere, spilling over into the schools.

Additional challenges come when schools attempt to offer academic study of world religions. Teachers and school boards look askance at materials written by practitioners, regarding them as uncritical and self-serving. Adherents often find presentations by scholars skewed, relying heavily on Christian terms to explain ideas that are very different from any Christian notions. For example, although most Buddhists reject calling the Buddha a deity or God, some curricular materials make it appear as if the Buddha is the equivalent of God as understood in Christianity.

Nonetheless, the new pluralism and the prospects for the growth of the religions it represents not only have become a hallmark of American spiritual life but also illustrate the impossibility of regarding a single tradition as normative or perhaps even culturally dominant. Alongside the mushrooming pluralism linked to immigration is the slow but steady increase in the number of Americans who eschew formal religious identity altogether and do not identify themselves as members of any religious body. Recent studies suggest that the proportion of those who are unaffiliated grew from one of five Americans in 1991 to at least one of every three by 2004 ("Ratio of 'Unchurched,'" 2004). Add to that cluster the millions who called themselves "spiritual but not religious" (Fuller, 2001), and it is clear that the very character of pluralism has expanded in such a way as to undermine any assumption that the United States now shares a common religious base.

Summary and Educational Implications

From the colonial period to the 21st century, the American landscape became ever more religiously diverse. If the early European invaders brought with them a range of Christian sensibilities, their efforts to plant a Christian culture in America always faced challenges. These challenges came from the Native Americans whose tribal religions once flourished in the same places where Europeans settled as well as from enslaved Africans who sustained an African religious consciousness despite the horrors of slavery. They also came from a variety of other groups who promoted alternative ways of being religious. Diversity was part of the American religious experience from the outset.

That diversity received acknowledgment when the Bill of Rights added an amendment to the U.S. Constitution guaranteeing the free exercise of religion. But the questions of what free exercise means and how to balance the religious sensibilities of the majority with those of many minorities have challenged the courts ever since. In the 20th century, many of those challenges concerned the role of religion in public education.

Immigration has been a major force enhancing religious diversity over the centuries. Immigration helped cement a Roman Catholic and Jewish presence in American life in the 19th century. By the 21st century, immigration was swelling the ranks of Buddhists, Hindus, Muslims, and a variety of others who called the United States home. At the same time, the number of Americans claiming no religious identity or formal affiliation was rising slowly but steadily.

If public education in its early years in the middle third of the 19th century could assume that the bulk of students shared a broadly based evangelical Protestant background, by the end of that century those assumptions were no longer viable, although they had by no means vanished. By 2010, religious pluralism rendered it impossible for education or any other dimension of the public sector to presume that a majority shared common beliefs and values—or even a common religious sensibility. As federal policy moved more and more in the direction of funding "faith-based initiatives" on a local level to deal with ongoing social problems, it was increasingly difficult to determine how to distribute such funds without favoring any one group, how to ensure that recipients were not using funds to coerce those being helped into aligning with the religious group, and even how to ascertain which groups represented legitimate "faith-based" entities.

Even more challenging is deciding how to study the religious mosaic that is the United States without either presuming allegiance to a particular faith tradition or granting any one faith community a privileged position.

Resources

Jon Butler and Harry S. Stout (1998) have edited a seventeen-volume series of texts on religion in American life suitable for classroom use at the secondary level. Published by Oxford University Press, some are chronological in focus (colonial America, the 19th century, the 20th century), some treat particular groups (Catholics, Jews, Mormons, Protestants, Muslims, Buddhists, Hindus, Sikhs), and others deal with specific topics (African American religion, church and state, immigration, women, Native American religion, alternative religions). The concluding volume is a biographical supplement and index. All are by leading scholars. The URL for this series is http://www.oup.com/us/catalog/general/series/ReligioninAmericanLife/?view=usa&sf=all.

Also helpful is the nine-volume *Religion by Region* series (2004–2006) produced under the auspices of the Greenberg Center for the Study of Religion in Public Life at Trinity College, Hartford, Connecticut, and edited by Mark Silk and Andrew Walsh. All are published by AltaMira Press. Eight focus on distinctive geographic regions of the country, examining how the particular religious cultures and history of a region have implications for the public policy, including education. The final volume examines the role of region more generally in determining the interplay of religion and public policy. The URL for this series is https://rowman.com/Action/Search/RLA/religion%20by%20reg.

Numerous materials appropriate for classroom use are identified in the several sections of the Web site for the Religion and Public Education Resource Center based at the California State University at Chico (www.csuchico.edu/rs/rperc).

Also specializing in teaching resources about American religious culture is the Wabash Center (www.wabashcenter.wabash.edu).

The Pluralism Project at Harvard University has focused primarily on the new diversity represented by the growth of Buddhism, Hinduism, and Islam in the last half-century. Its Web site includes not only state-by-state maps but also a directory of religious centers, news summaries, profiles of groups, and teaching resources (www.pluralism.org).

The most recent demographic profiles appear in the U.S. Religious Landscape Survey conducted by the Pew Forum on Religion and Public Life. See http://religions.pewforum.org for a wealth of data on the texture of American religious life released in 2008. Other Pew Forum studies augment this endeavor. In a similar vein, researchers at Hartford Theological Seminary produced the study *Faith Communities Today* that provides helpful information. The results are accessible at www.fact.hartsem.edu.

Several initiatives of the Social Science Research Council (SSRC) look at the impact of immigration on American religion from historical and comparative persectives, the role of religion in public life, and various aspects if Islam in the United States and elsewhere. Especially helpful is *Immigration and Religion in American History: Comparative and Historical Perspectives,* edited by Richard Alba, Albert J. Raboteau, and Josh DeWine (2009), a collection of essays resulting from a consultation on immigration. See www.ssrc.org.

There are also helpful Web sites on particular groups or topics that illustrate the diversity within American religious life. On African American religious history, for example, see http://northstar.vassar.edu.

The Cushwa Center at Notre Dame University offers many resources on facets of U.S. Roman Catholic life and history (www.nd.edu/~cushwa).

Similarly, the American Jewish Historical Society identifies much that is useful to tracking the American Jewish experience (www.ajhs.org).

QUESTIONS AND ACTIVITIES

5.1 The principle of separation of church and state is a keystone of religious freedom in the United States. Investigate how closely church and state are tied together in the United States today. For example, can churches receive federal funding? If so, under what conditions? Can parochial and other religious schools receive support from public school districts? If so, what kind of support can they receive, and what conditions do they need to meet in order to qualify for support?

5.2 Large numbers of African Americans and European Americans are members of Protestant churches and share religious traditions. However, services in African American and European American churches can be very different. Visit a Methodist church service and an African Methodist Episcopal (AME) church service. Compare the services at the two churches by identifying factors such as the length of service, the music, and the enthusiasm of the minister. Discuss your findings with your classmates. An informative reference for this activity is *The Black Church in the African American Experience* (Lincoln & Mamiya, 1990).

5.3 Arrange to visit a local Hindu temple, Muslim mosque, or Buddhist center. Describe what you see there. How is it different from what you have seen in other religious settings? How does the space reflect a cultural heritage as well as a religious identity?

5.4 The media have become a powerful force for disseminating religious messages that are tied to political positions. Form a group of approximately five students and identify five different religious television programs to watch over a one-month period. Record key themes that are embedded in the programs. Analyze the themes and ideas to determine whether they include political messages. Discuss the extent to which the paradox discussed at the beginning of the chapter is being exacerbated by the media.

5.5 Most racial and ethnic groups in the United States are members of the major faith communities. However, most faith communities in the United States are segregated. Investigate churches, mosques, and temples in your community to find out the extent to which faith communities are segregated. Interview heads of religious communities. Ask them why they think faith communities tend to be made up predominately of one racial or ethnic group. Also ask them whether they have made efforts to desegregate their faith communities.

5.6 Revivals continue to play an important role in evangelical Protestant churches. Go to the Internet and investigate the types of revivals that are being held today, where they are being held, their goals, and their intended audience. To what extent do modern revivals reflect the chapter's discussion of the new faces of pluralism?

5.7 Religion in the United States is frequently associated with the roles that men have played in formulating religious ideas and institutions. However, women have made significant contributions to religious life in the United States. Read the biographies of women religious leaders, such as Mary Baker Eddy and Ellen G. Harmon White. Also read *Righteous Discontent: The Women's Movement in the Black Church, 1880–1920* (Higginbotham, 1993). Discuss how gender has influenced the lives of women in the church.

5.8 How does social class intersect with religion? Are religious congregations primarily composed of people from the same social-class background? How do different religious organizations respond to low-income people? How do low-income people in your community feel about religious organizations? Study these questions by dividing the class into groups.

REFERENCES

Alba, R., Raboteau, A. J., & DeWine, J. (Eds.). (2009). *Immigration and religion in American history: Comparative and historical perspectives.* New York: New York University Press.

Butler, J., & Stout, H. S. (Eds.). (1998). *Religion in America: A reader.* New York: Oxford University Press.

Camarota, S. A. (2007). Immigration to the United States, 2007. Retrieved September 11, 2008, from www.cis.org/articles/2007/back1007/html/.

Carpenter, J. A. (1997). *Revive us again: The reawakening of American fundamentalism.* New York: Oxford University Press.

Creedon, J. (1998, July/August). God with a million faces: Design your own god. *Utne Reader*, pp. 42–48.

Day, J. C. (2011). Population profile of the United States. Retrieved May 17, 2011, from www.census.gov/population/www/pop-profile/natproj.html

Eck, D. (1997). *A new religious America: How a "Christian country" has become the world's most religiously diverse nation.* San Francisco: Harper.

Fuller, R. C. (2001). *Spiritual but not religious: Understanding unchurched America.* New York: Oxford University Press.

Herberg, W. (1960). *Protestant, Catholic, Jew: An essay in American religious sociology* (rev. ed.). Garden City, NY: Doubleday.

Higginbotham, E. B. (1993). *Righteous discontent: The women's movement in the Black church, 1880–1920.* Cambridge, MA: Harvard University Press.

Kelley, D. M. (1977). *Why conservative churches are growing* (2nd ed.). New York: Harper.

Lincoln, C. E., & Mamiya, L. M. (1990). *The Black church in the African American experience.* Durham, NC: Duke University Press.

Lippy, C. H. (2009). *Introducing American religion.* London and New York: Routledge.

Lippy, C. H., Choquette, R., & Poole, S. (1992). *Christianity comes to the Americas, 1492–1776.* New York: Paragon House.

Mahoney, P. (2002, July 26). Study says Hispanic buying power rising. *Chattanooga Times Free Press.* Retrieved May 16, 2003, from www.timesfreepress.com/2002/july/26jul/disposableincomehispanic.html.

Malone, N., Baluja, K. F., Costanzo, J. M., & Davis, C. J. (2003). *The foreign-born population: 2000* (Census 2000 Brief C2KBR-34). Washington, DC: U.S. Department of Commerce, Economics and Statistics Administration, U.S. Census Bureau.

Mayhew, J. (1749). *Seven sermons.* Boston: Rogers & Fowle.

Miller, R. T., & Flowers, R. B. (Eds.). (1987). *Toward benevolent neutrality: Church, state, and the Supreme Court* (3rd ed.). Waco, TX: Baylor University Press.

Pew Forum on Religion and Public Life. (2008). U.S. religious landscape survey. Retrieved January 20, 2009, from http://religions.pewforum.org/.

Pew Forum on Religion and Public Life. (2011). The future of the global Muslim population. Retrieved May 20, 2011, from http://pewresearch.org/pubs/1872/Muslim-population-projections-fast-growth.

Pluralism Project. (2011). Statistics by tradition. Retrieved May 17, 2011, from www.pluralism.org/resources/statistics/tradition.php.

Raffaele, M. (2005, December 21). Judge rules "intelligent design" can't be taught in schools. *Chattanooga Times Free Press.* Retrieved May 19, 2011, from http://eedition.timesfreepress.com.

Ratio of "unchurched" up sharply since 1991. (2004, June 1). *Christian Century,* p. 15.

Reeves, T. J., & Bennett, C. E. (2004). *We the people: Asians in the United States* (Census 2000 Special Reports CENSR-17). Washington, DC: U.S. Department of Commerce, Economics and Statistics Administration, U.S. Census Bureau.

Strong, J. (1964). *Our country* (J. Herbst, Ed.). Cambridge, MA: Harvard University Press. (Original work published 1886)

Tweed, T. A. (1997). *Our lady of the exile: Diasporic religion at a Cuban Catholic shrine in Miami.* New York: Oxford University Press.

U.S. Census Bureau. (2000). Statistical abstract of the United States. Retrieved May 1, 2003, from www.census.gov/statab/www/.

U.S. Census Bureau. (2003). U.S. Census Bureau guidance on the presentation and comparison of race and Hispanic origin data. Retrieved September 11, 2008, from www.census/gov/population/www/socdemo/compraceho.html/.

U.S. Census Bureau. (2006). Population estimates. Retrieved September 11, 2008, from www.census/gov/popest/National/.

U.S. Census Bureau. (2011). 2010 census data. Retrieved May 17, 2011, from http://2010.census/gov/2010census/data/index.php.

Westerhoff, J. H. (1978). *McGuffey and his readers: Piety, morality, and education in nineteenth-century America.* Nashville, TN: Abingdon.

Williams, P. W. (1980). *Popular religion in America: Symbolic change and the modernization process in historical perspective.* Englewood Cliffs, NJ: Prentice Hall.

Wilson, J. F. (Ed.). (1965). *Church and state in American history.* Boston: Heath.

Wuthnow, R. (1998). *After heaven: Spirituality in America since the 1950s.* Berkeley: University of California Press.

Student-teacher interaction and the curriculum are two important factors in creating equal educational opportunities for female, male, and LGBTQ students.

© Fancy Collection/SuperStock

Christopher Futcher/Getty Images, Inc.

Stockbroker/Glow Images

Gender

Social, economic, and political conditions for women have improved substantially since the women's rights movement emerged as part of the civil rights movement of the 1960s and 1970s. However, gender discrimination and inequality still exist in schools and in society at large. In 2010, the ratio of women's to men's earnings, for all occupations, was 81.2 percent (U.S. Department of Labor, 2010). The status of women in the United States in the last three decades has changed substantially. More women are now working outside the home than ever before, and more women are heads of households. In 2010, 58.6 percent of women worked outside the home (U.S. Department of Labor, 2010). In 2010, 30.7 percent of U.S. households were headed by women (U.S. Census Bureau, 2010). An increasing percentage of women and their dependents constitute the nation's poor. Some writers use the term *feminization of poverty* to describe this development. In 2010, 56 percent of families below the poverty level in the United States were headed by women (U.S. Census Bureau, 2010).

The first three chapters in Part III describe the status of women in the United States, the ways in which schools perpetuate gender discrimination, and strategies that educators can use to create equal educational opportunities for both female and male students. As Sadker and Zittleman point out in Chapter 6, both males and females are harmed by sex stereotypes and gender discrimination. Tetreault, in Chapter 7, describes how male perspectives dominate school knowledge and how teachers can infuse their curricula with perspectives from both genders and thereby expand their students' thinking and insights. Pollard, in Chapter 8, describes how race, gender, class, and disability are interlocking variables that need to be understood together rather than as separate and discrete categories. She argues that it is essential for teachers to comprehend the ways in which these variables interact in order to create gender-equitable classrooms and schools.

Mayo, in Chapter 9, examines the role of queer studies and sexual and gender minorities in multicultural education. She asks classroom teachers to grapple with issues such as the privileging of heterosexism within schools and society, the invisibility of gay students and their families in the curriculum, and the reason it is essential for students to study the positive aspects of lesbian, gay, bisexual, and transgender/transsexual (LGBTQ) communities and cultures. Mayo believes that to fully implement multicultural education, LGBTQ students must experience civic equality, social justice, and recognition (Gutmann, 2004) in the classroom and on the schoolyard.

REFERENCES

Gutmann, A. (2004). Unity and diversity in democratic multicultural education: Creative and destructive tensions. In J. A. Banks (Ed.), *Diversity and citizenship education: Global perspectives* (pp. 71–98). San Francisco: Jossey-Bass/Wiley.

U.S. Census Bureau. (2010). Poverty status in the past 12 months by household type by age of householder universe: Households. Retrieved November 17, 2011, from http://factfinder2.census.gov/faces/tableservices/jsf/pages/productview.xhtml?pid=ACS_10_3YR_B17017&prodType=table.

U.S. Department of Labor. (2011). *Labor force characteristics by race and ethnicity, 2010.* Retrieved November 17, 2011, from http://www.bls.gov/cps/cpsrace2010.pdf.

U.S. Department of Labor. (2010). Women at work. Retrieved November 17, 2011, from http://www.bls.gov/spotlight/2011/women/.

Stockbroker/Purestock/SuperStock

Gender Bias: From Colonial America to Today's Classroom

CHAPTER 6

*David Sadker and Karen Zittleman**

A sage once remarked that if fish were anthropologists, the last thing they would discover would be the water. We are all like those fish, swimming in a sea of sexism, but few of us see the water, the gender bias that engulfs us. Sexism in schools is a major influence on children in urban, suburban, and rural America, in wealthy and poor communities, and in communities that are diverse as well as those that are homogeneous. In short, gender is a demographic that binds all schools and challenges all educators. Yet a cultural shortsightedness, coined "gender blindness," makes it difficult for educators to see how sexism influences virtually every aspect of how we teach and learn (Bailey, Scantlebury, & Letts, 1997; Glasser & Smith, 2008). As a result, they lack the perspective and tools necessary to challenge sexism in school.

Many teachers, parents, and students are confused about gender equity in schools. They are not alone. We recently received a call from a young reporter who wanted to speak about our work "in making women superior to men." The reporter viewed gender bias in school as males versus females. We do not. Gender bias short-circuits both boys and girls, and *both* move forward when gender restrictions are removed.

This chapter provides a context for understanding gender bias in school. It includes (1) a brief historical overview of women's struggle for educational opportunity, (2) an update of the progress made and yet to be made in ensuring gender equity in schools, (3) an analysis of gender bias in curricula, (4) insights into gender bias in instruction, (5) a view of today's trends and challenges concerning gender issues in school, and (6) some practical suggestions for creating gender-equitable classrooms.

The Hidden Civil Rights Struggle

For centuries, women fought to open the schoolhouse door. The education of America's girls was so limited that less than one-third of the women in colonial America could even sign their names. Although a woman gave the first plot of ground for a free school in New England, female children were not allowed to attend the school. In fact, women were commonly viewed as being mentally and morally inferior to men, relegated to learning only domestic skills. Not until the 1970s and 1980s did they win the right to be admitted to previously all-male Ivy League colleges and universities, and not until the 1990s did they breach the walls of the Citadel and the Virginia Military Institute. It is rare indeed that such a monumental civil rights struggle—so long, so recent, and influencing so many—has remained so invisible. Let's take a brief look at this hidden civil rights struggle.

---

* Myra Sadker co-authored earlier versions of this chapter. Myra died in 1995 while undergoing treatment for breast cancer. To learn more about her work, visit www.sadker.org.

During the colonial period, dame schools educated very young boys and girls (with few exceptions, *White* boys and girls) in the homes of women who had the time and desire to teach. Girls lucky enough to attend such schools would learn domestic skills along with reading (so that they could one day read the Bible to their children). Such schools also taught the boys how to write and prepared them for more formal education. Girls graduated to the kitchen and the sewing area, focusing on their futures as wives and mothers.

With a new democracy came new ideas and the promise of more educational opportunities for females. Elementary schools gradually opened their doors to females, and for the families financially able, secondary schools in the form of female seminaries became possible. Seminaries provided a protected and supervised climate melding religious and academic lessons. In New York, Emma Hart Willard battled to establish the Troy Female Seminary, and in Massachusetts, Mary Lyon created Mount Holyoke, a seminary that eventually became a noted women's college. Seminaries often emphasized self-denial and strict discipline, considered important elements in molding devout wives and Christian mothers. By the 1850s, with help from Quakers such as Harriet Beecher Stowe, Myrtilla Miner established the Miner Normal School for Colored Girls in the nation's capital, providing new educational opportunities for African American women. While these seminaries sometimes offered a superior education, they were also trapped in a paradox they could never fully resolve: They were educating girls for a world not ready to accept educated women. Seminaries sometimes went to extraordinary lengths to reconcile this conflict. Emma Willard's Troy Female Seminary was devoted to "professionalizing motherhood." (Who could not support motherhood?) But en route to reshaping motherhood, seminaries reshaped teaching.

For the teaching profession, seminaries became the source of new ideas and new recruits. Seminary leaders such as Emma Hart Willard and Catherine Beecher wrote textbooks on how to teach and how to teach more humanely than was the practice at the time. They denounced corporal punishment and promoted more cooperative educational practices. Because school was seen as an extension of the home and another arena for raising children, seminary graduates were allowed to become teachers—at least until they decided to marry. More than 80 percent of the graduates of Troy Female Seminary and Mount Holyoke became teachers. Female teachers were particularly attractive to school districts—not only because of their teaching effectiveness but also because they were typically paid one-third to one-half the salary of male teachers. By the end of the Civil War, a number of colleges and universities, especially tax-supported ones, were desperate for dollars. Institutions of higher learning experienced a serious student shortage due to Civil War casualties, and women became the source of much-needed tuition dollars. But female wallets did not buy on-campus equality. Women often faced separate courses and hostility from male students and professors. At state universities, such as the University of Michigan, male students would stamp their feet in protest when a woman entered a classroom, a gesture some professors appreciated.

While an economic necessity for many colleges, educating women was not a popular idea, and some people even considered it dangerous. In *Sex in Education,* Dr. Edward Clarke (1873), a member of Harvard's medical faculty, argued that women attending high school and college were at medical risk. According to Dr. Clarke, the blood destined for the development and health of their ovaries would be redirected to their brains by the stress of study. Too much education would leave women with "monstrous brains and puny bodies . . . flowing thought and constipated bowels" (pp. 120–128). Clarke recommended that females be provided with a less demanding education, easier courses, no competition, and rest periods so that their reproductive organs could develop. The female brain was too small and the female body too vulnerable for such mental challenges. He maintained that allowing girls to attend places such as Harvard would pose a serious health threat to the women themselves, with sterility and hysteria potential outcomes. It would take another century before Harvard and other prestigious men's colleges would finally admit women.

Clarke's ideas constructed some powerful fears in women. M. Carey Thomas, future president of Bryn Mawr and one of the first women to earn a PhD in the United States, wrote of the fears created by writers like Clarke. "I remember often praying about it, and begging God that if it were true that because I was a girl, I could not successfully master Greek and go to college, and understand things, to kill me for it" (cited in Sadker & Zittleman, 2012, p. 169). In 1895, the faculty of the University of Virginia concluded that "women were often physically unsexed by the strains of study" (cited in Sadker & Zittleman, 2012, p. 169). Parents, fearing for the health of their daughters, would often place them in less demanding programs reserved for females or would keep them out of advanced education entirely. Even today, the echoes of Clarke's warnings resonate—some people still see well-educated women as less attractive, view advanced education as "too stressful" for females, or believe that education is more important for males than for females.

There were clear racist overtones in Clarke's writing. The women attending college were overwhelmingly White, and education delayed marriage and decreased childbearing. As a result, while women of color were reproducing at "alarming" rates, wealthy White women were choosing college rather than motherhood. The dangers to the White establishment were clear.

By the 20th century, women were winning more access to educational programs at all levels, although well into the 1970s, gender-segregated programs were still the rule. Although they attended the same schools as males, females often received a segregated and less valuable education. Commercial courses prepared girls to become secretaries, and vocational programs channeled them into cosmetology and other low-paying occupations. With the passage of Title IX of the Education Amendments of 1972, females saw significant progress toward gaining access to educational programs, but not equality.

While Title IX became law as the women's movement gained momentum, it applies to males as well as females. The opening section of Title IX states:

> No person in the United States shall, on the basis of sex, be excluded from participation in, be denied the benefits of, or be subjected to discrimination under any education program or activity receiving federal financial assistance.

While most people have heard of Title IX in relation to sports, it reaches far beyond the athletic field. Every public school and most of the nation's colleges and universities are covered under Title IX, which prohibits discrimination in school admissions, in counseling and guidance, in competitive athletics, in student rules and regulations, and in access to programs and courses, including vocational education and physical education. Title IX also applies to sex discrimination in employment practices, including interviewing and recruitment, hiring and promotion, compensation, job assignments, and fringe benefits.

In recent years, Title IX enforcement has been sporadic, and the future and strength of this critical law is by no means ensured. For example, in 2007 the federal government changed Title IX to allow for gender segregation through the creation of single-sex schools and classes, a move that may well limit learning opportunities for girls and boys. Some even believe that Title IX is no longer needed and that gender bias has been eradicated (Thomas, 2011). Statistics tell us otherwise.

Report Card: The Cost of Sexism in Schools

The following is a report card you will not find in any school, yet these statistics document how gender inequities continue to permeate schools and society and shortchange students.

- *Boys and schools.* Poor school achievement, especially in the language arts and writing, overdiagnosis and referral to special educational services, bullying, disciplinary problems, and violence remain common school problems plaguing boys. While many lump all boys into a single category, this is misleading. White, Asian, and wealthy and middle-class boys are performing relatively well, but low-income students and Black, Hispanic, and Native American boys are not. Many believe that the socialization of boys into tough and competitive roles sets the stage for such school clashes and that class and race can exacerbate academic problems (Kimmel, 2008; Pollack 2009/2010; Rivers & Barnett, 2011).

- *Girls and schools.* Girls receive higher report-card grades, have fewer disciplinary problems, and are more likely than boys to become valedictorians and go on to college. Gender socialization may explain in part why girls appear to do so well in school. Girls are expected to please others, and working hard at school is part of that. Teachers appreciate students who follow directions and do not cause problems, and this is one reason girls receive better report-card grades than boys. But these higher grades carry a large, hidden cost as docile and compliant children may grow into adults with lower self-esteem and less independence. More than a third of students in grades 3–12 hold the view that "people think that the most important thing for girls is to get married and have children" (Girls, Inc., 2006; Sadker, Sadker, & Zittleman, 2009).

- *Academic courses.* Girls are the majority in biology, chemistry, algebra, and precalculus courses, while far more males enroll in calculus, physics, and computer science.
Males take fewer English, sociology, psychology, foreign language, and fine arts courses than do females (National Center for Education Statistics [NCES], 2011).

- *Academic attitudes.* Boys often view reading and writing as "feminine" subjects that threaten their masculinity. Many boys, especially minority and low-income boys, view school as irrelevant to their futures. College men have fewer intellectual interests and poorer study habits than college women. They enjoy reading books less, take fewer notes, study less, and play more. Despite their lower effort, lower grades, and lower likelihood of completing a college degree, men evaluate their academic abilities higher than those of women (Lederman, 2006; Zittleman, 2007).

- *Dropouts.* More than a million students drop out each year. In fact, one in three boys—often African American, Hispanic, and Native American—will fail to graduate from high school in four years. While media attention focuses on such boys, almost half of all dropouts are girls. Girls of color are most at risk; half of Native American girls and about 40 percent of African American and Hispanic girls fail to graduate each year. When girls leave, they are less likely than boys to return to earn their high school diploma or general education degree (Swanson, 2010).

- *Athletics.* Participation in school athletics is at record levels for boys and girls. More than 4.3 million boys engage in a high school sport. Before Title IX, fewer than 300,000 high school girls played competitive sports; today, 3 million girls compete, but they are only about 40 percent of all high school athletes. Girls' teams typically have less visibility and status than male teams and are often denied the same benefits, like adequate facilities and financial support (National Federation of State High School Associations, 2010-2011).

- *Sexual harassment.* You may be surprised to learn that boys are the targets of sexual harassment almost as frequently as girls: Nearly four out of five students of both genders have been harassed. Nine in 10 students (85 percent) report that students sexually harass other students at their school, and almost 40 percent of students report that school employees sexually harass as well. The most common sexual harassment against boys takes the form of "gay-bashing" or questioning their sexuality, while girls experience verbal and physical harassment, including unwanted touching. (AAUW, 2004; Sadker & Zittleman, 2012).

- *Bullying.* One-third to a half of America's children report being victims of bullying, and 60 percent of students witness bullying at school every day. In a typical classroom of 20 students, 2 or 3 come to school every day fearing being bullied, harassed, or worse. The most likely targets are gay students or students perceived as gay. Males are more likely to bully others and be victims of physical bullying, while females frequently experience verbal and psychological bullying (through sexual comments or rumors) (Aarons, 2010; Maxwell, 2010).

- *Self-esteem.* As girls go through school, their self-esteem often plummets, and the danger of depression increases. In middle school, girls rate popularity as more important than academic competence or independence. Eating disorders among females in schools and colleges are rampant and increasing. Some boys are now also displaying body-image issues, resorting to dieting and steroid abuse. Interestingly, female and male African American students report a stronger sense of self and do not suffer as much from depression, eating disorders, and body-image issues as do other groups (National Eating Disorders Coalition, 2011; Sadker et al., 2009).

- *College enrollments.* Men had been the majority of college students from the colonial period to the early 1980s. Today, women are the majority. Yet it is not White men who are missing from the college ranks, but minority and low-income men. In fact, more women and men attend college today than ever before (NCES, 2011).

- *College majors.* Women earn the majority of degrees in education, psychology, biological sciences, and accounting. Women earn more degrees in pharmacy and veterinary medicine than do males. And in law, women and men have reached parity in degree attainment. Males dominate areas such as business, computer science, and engineering. Women lag behind men in attaining medical and dental degrees (NCES, 2011).

- *Earnings.* Women earn less at every level of education. The median annual earnings of a female high school graduate are at least one-third less than that of her male counterpart. One year after college graduation, a female of any racial, ethnic, or socioeconomic group earns less than a White male with the same college degree. For example, female physicians and surgeons earn 35 percent less per year than their male counterparts, and female lawyers earn 25 percent less than male lawyers; female teachers earn 20 percent less than men, and female computer engineers earn 15 percent less than their male peers. (Hegewisch & Liepmann, 2010).

While female enrollment in many math and science courses has dramatically increased, the connection between girls and science and math remains tenuous. A survey by the Society of Women Engineers found that 75 percent of American girls have no interest in pursuing a career in science, math, or technology. Why? They perceive these subjects as cold, impersonal, and with little clear application to their lives or to society (American Association of University Women [AAUW], 2010).

In the past decades, great progress has been made by males and females in battling sexism. Women are now the majority of college students, the presidents of several prestigious Ivy League colleges, and successful athletes. Today, more boys are scoring higher on standardized tests, enrolling in college more than ever before, and entering prestigious, well-paying careers. (Although for poorer and minority boys and girls, the situation is less encouraging.) But as the preceding statistics remind us, progress can be slow, and gender inequities are still a very real part of school life.

For the typical classroom teacher, gender equity emerges as a continuing challenge on at least two levels. To help you tease out the subtle biases that persist in classrooms, we focus on two central areas of classroom life: the curriculum and student–teacher interaction.

Gender Bias in Today's Classroom: The Curriculum

Few things stir up more controversy than the content of the curriculum. Teachers, parents, and students seem to be intuitively aware that schoolbooks shape what the next generation knows and how it behaves. In this case, research supports intuition. Students spend as much as 80 to 95 percent of classroom time using textbooks, and teachers make a majority of their instructional decisions based on these texts (Fan & Kaeley, 2000; Flinders & Thornton, 2009; Starnes, 2004). When children read about people in nontraditional gender roles, they are less likely to limit themselves to stereotypes. When children read about women and minorities in history, they are more likely to believe that these groups have made important contributions to the country. As one sixth grader told us, "I love to read biographies about women. When I learn about what they've done, I feel like a door is opening. If they can do great things, maybe I can, too." But what if your identity is misrepresented, misremembered, or just plain missing from the school curriculum?

In the 1970s and 1980s, textbook companies and professional associations, such as the American Psychological Association and the National Council of Teachers of English, issued guidelines for nonracist and nonsexist books, suggesting how to include and fairly portray different groups in the curriculum. As a result, textbooks became more balanced in their description of underrepresented groups. While yesterday's stark sexist texts are thankfully gone, subtle bias persists. No matter the subject, the names and experiences of males continue to dominate the pages of schoolbooks. Men are seen as the movers and shakers of history, scientists of achievement, and political leaders. Studies on curriculum from around the world also find that both males and females are depicted in gender-stereotyped ways.

Studying history is a journey through time, but a journey with few women. In telling the story of our national history, current social studies texts include five times more males than females (Chick, 2006). For example, curricula rarely mention female soldiers who also fought in the Revolution, or those women who made their contributions on the home front. During war, women were left to care for their families and manage businesses and farms on their own. In fact, women from Abigail Adams in the Revolutionary War to Rosie the Riveter in World War II were a disposable labor force, hired when the nation needed them and fired when the war was over. Little if anything is said in textbooks about the second-class treatment women faced.

A review of 13 current elementary basal readers found that male characters outnumbered females two to one. But this male dominance comes with a price: Males are still strikingly bound by traditional standards. For example, in a story from a fifth-grade book, the display of male aggressiveness is noteworthy: A boy wants to be in charge of the fair project; he is the biggest and looks at his raised fist while glancing at the other children to signify that no one is to argue. No one does. In other stories, the adult males are shaking their fists and shouting at other males, often chasing them (Evans & Davies, 2000). Unfortunately, it is often little boys causing the trouble, a double impact of out-of-control youths and angry men.

These lessons in gender bias extend beyond the pages of academic texts; they are reinforced by popular, award-winning children's books read daily in classrooms and nightly at home. A study of 200 distinguished children's books—American Library Association award winners, Caldecott selections, and top-selling children's picture books—revealed that these children's tales tell twice as many male-centered tales as female, and illustrations depict 50 percent more males. (Hamilton, Anderson, Braoddus, & Young, 2006).

Females are not the only ones often missing from the pages of children's literature—so are fathers, appearing in less than half of the 200 books. When present, fathers are presented as stoic, hands-off parents, rarely seen hugging or feeding their children. Mothers are shown more often as affectionate caregivers capable of expressing a range of emotions from happiness to sadness.

Although female characters appear in roles such as doctors, lawyers, and scientists, these researchers also discovered that occupational stereotyping is still common. In the 200 books reviewed, women were given traditional jobs ten times as often as nontraditional ones. For example, the lead adult female character in one book is a flight attendant, a maid in another, and a librarian in yet another. Males in children's books remain in traditional roles as well. Boys are presented as fighters, adventurers, and rescuers. They are also shown to be aggressive, argumentative, and competitive. A passage in *Johnny and Susie's Mountain Quest* highlights the rigid roles of a brave boy and a helpless girl: "'Oh, please help me, Johnny!' cried Susie. 'We're up so high! I'm afraid I'm going to fall'" (Hamilton et al., 2006).

How can teachers and students detect gender bias in books? The following are descriptions of seven forms of bias that emerge in today's texts. These forms of bias can also help identify prejudice related to gender as well as to race, ethnicity, the elderly, people with disabilities, non-English speakers, gays and lesbians, and limited-English speakers. Learning these forms of bias develops a useful critical reading skill.

Invisibility: What You Don't See Makes a Lasting Impression

When groups or events are not taught in schools, they become part of the *null curriculum*. Textbooks published prior to the 1960s largely omitted African Americans, Hispanics, and Asian Americans. Many of today's textbooks continue to give minimal treatment to women, depriving students of information about half of the nation's population. When we ask students to name ten famous women from American history, most cannot do it (Sadker et al., 2009). A similar case of invisibility can be made for those with disabilities, gays and lesbians, and males in parenting and other roles nontraditional to their gender.

Stereotyping: Glib Shortcuts

When rigid roles or traits are assigned to all members of a group, a stereotype that denies individual attributes and differences is born. Examples include portraying all African Americans as athletes, Mexican Americans as laborers, and women only in terms of their family roles.

Imbalance and Selectivity: A Tale Half Told

Curricula sometimes present only one interpretation of an issue, situation, or group of people, simplifying and distorting complex issues by omitting different perspectives. A description of suffragettes being *given* the vote omits the work, sacrifices, and physical abuse suffered by women who *won* the right to vote.

Unreality: Rose-Colored Glasses

Curricular materials often paint an illusionary picture of the nation. Our history texts often ignore class differences, continuing racial discrimination, and ongoing sexism. For example, when the nuclear family is described only as a father, mother, and two children, students are being treated to romanticized and sanitized narratives. In fact, this family structure is in the minority today, as many families have one parent, same-gender parents, or no children.

Fragmentation: An Interesting Sideshow

A textbook may place information about women in a special box or insert, separating the discussion from the main narrative. For example, many of today's texts include special inserts highlighting certain gender topics, such as "Famous Women Scientists" or "Ten Women in History to Remember." Such isolation presents women and gender issues as interesting diversions, but not part of the mainstream of history, literature, or the sciences.

Linguistic Bias: Words Count

Language can be a powerful conveyor of bias in both blatant and subtle forms. The exclusive use of masculine terms and pronouns, ranging from *our forefathers, mankind*, and *businessman* to the generic *he*, denies the full participation and recognition of women. More subtle examples include word orders and choices that place males in a primary role, such as "men and their wives" or separate the world into two genders, like "boys and girls."

Cosmetic Bias: Pretty Wrapping

Cosmetic bias offers an "illusion of equity." Beyond the attractive covers, photos, or posters that prominently feature diversity, bias persists. For example, a science textbook might feature a glossy pull-out of female scientists or a cover with photos of scientists from different races. But these attractive features mislead the reader, who will encounter little content in the text about the scientific contributions of women or people of color.

Until publishers and authors eliminate gender bias, it will be up to the creativity and commitment of teachers and parents to fill in the missing pages. Children enjoy exciting, well-written books, and such books can include characters from different races, ethnic groups, religions, social classes, and both genders. But equitable materials are not enough to create a nonsexist educational environment. Attention must also be given to instruction.

Gender Bias in Today's Classrooms: Student–Teacher Interaction

You probably remember an unspoken rule from your own school days. If you wanted to speak, you knew just what to do to get called on. Raising a hand might be your first move, but waving your hand would signal that you *really* wanted to talk. Eye contact with the teacher was always a good idea, but a few strategically placed grunts could work miracles in getting attention. Once called on, you got to speak, your needs were met, and the teacher's needs were met as well. By calling on the eager and willing students, the teacher moves the lesson along at a good pace. Most teachers call on students who want to talk, leave the others alone, and everybody is comfortable. So what's the problem?

Although it *sounds* awfully good, the purpose of school is not to make everyone comfortable. Schools are for education, for learning new and sometimes uncomfortable skills. Talented teachers know that if they select only students who quickly volunteer, reticent students will be relegated to the sidelines. In this topsy-turvy world, the students who need a little more time to think—because they are by nature thoughtful, because English is a new language, because their cultural background encourages a slower response, or because they are shy—become spectators to rapid classroom exchanges. Females lose out, children of color lose out, English language learners are left behind, and shy boys are silenced.

The gendered nature of classroom interactions can be subtle and is often ignored. Watch how boys dominate the discussion in this upper elementary class about presidents.

The fifth-grade class is almost out of control. "Just a minute," the teacher admonishes. "There are too many of us here to all shout out at once. I want you to raise your hands, and then I'll call on you. If you shout out, I'll pick somebody else."

Order is restored. Then Stephen, enthusiastic to make his point, calls out.

Stephen: I think Lincoln was the best president. He held the country together during the war.

Teacher: A lot of historians would agree with you.

Kelvin *[seeing that nothing happened to Stephen, calls out]*: I don't. Lincoln was okay, but my Dad liked Reagan. He always said Reagan was a great president.

Jack *[calling out]*: Reagan? Are you kidding?

Teacher: Who do you think our best president was, Jack?

Jack: FDR. He saved us from the Depression.

Max *[calling out]*: I don't think it's right to pick one best president. There were a lot of good ones.

Teacher: That's a terrific insight.

Rebecca *[calling out]*: I don't think the presidents today are as good as the ones we used to have.

Teacher: Okay, Rebecca. But you forgot the rule. You're supposed to raise your hand.

Teachers are involved in as many as a thousand interactions with students a day, and they are often unaware of inequities in these exchanges. It is not unusual for a few students to monopolize classroom interaction. The fast pace of classroom exchanges leads many teachers to call on the first person to raise a hand. When this happens, it is an open invitation for male dominance.

Studies show that male students frequently control classroom conversation. Males receive more teacher attention—both positive and negative—than do females. Teachers ask males both more factual (lower-order) and thoughtful (higher-order) questions. They give males more precise directions on how to accomplish tasks for themselves or when they are confused. Boys call out and answer more questions more often than girls. They receive more praise for the intellectual quality of their ideas. They are also criticized more publicly and harshly. They are the heart and center of interaction. Some researchers emphasize that low-achieving males get most of the negative attention while high-achieving boys get more positive and constructive academic contacts. However, no matter whether they are high or low achievers, female students are more likely to receive less instructional time, less help, and less positive and negative attention (Beaman, Whel-dall, & Kemp, 2006; Duffy, Warren, & Walsh, 2001; Good & Brophy, 2007; Sadker, Sadker, & Zittleman, 2010; Spencer, Porche, & Tolman, 2003).

In the social studies class about presidents, we saw boys as a group grabbing attention while girls as a group were left out of the action. Not being allowed to call out like her male classmates during the brief conversation about presidents will not psychologically scar Rebecca; however, the system of silencing operates covertly and repeatedly. It occurs several times a day during each school week for 12 years and even longer if Rebecca goes to college; most insidious of all, it happens subliminally. This micro-inequity eventually has a powerful cumulative impact. Researchers observed hundreds of classes and watched as girls typically raised their hands, often at a right angle, arms bent at the elbow—a cautious, tentative, almost passive gesture. At other times, they raised their arms straight and high, but they signaled silently. The educator Diana Meehan (2007) calls this phenomenon the "girl pause": If a teacher asks a question, a girl likely pauses, doubting her knowledge or, worse, her right to speak out loud. She wonders, *"Do I know this?"*

Moreover, gender and race intersect to create inequitable interaction patterns. A three-year study of elementary and secondary schools found that White males were most likely to be involved in classroom discussions, followed by males of color and White females. Students least likely to receive teacher time and attention were females of color. Researchers have correlated the treatment girls experience in school with social and psychological difficulties. As girls go through school, for example, their self-esteem plummets, and the danger of depression increases. Furthermore, in middle and secondary school, girls rate popularity as more important than academic competence or independence (Sadker et al., 2009).

Classroom management issues have been shown to be steeped in gendered expectations, contributing to these inequitable teacher–student interaction patterns. Studies show a strong link between male aggression and the male stereotype, the role boys are expected to play in society (Kimmel, 2008; Pollack, 1998). Since boys are stereotyped as more physically aggressive than girls and more difficult to control, researchers have observed that teachers more closely monitor males in the classroom and often overreact to even the potential of male misbehavior. Males are disciplined more harshly, more publicly, and more frequently than females, even when they violate the same rules. Such disparities are readily detected by students, who report that even innocent boys are often targeted unfairly by teachers and that girls are able "to get away with" inappropriate and hurtful behavior. Females very often become "invisible members of our classrooms" (Zittleman, 2007).

An important factor contributing to male dominance of teacher–student interactions and classroom management issues is the widespread gender segregation that characterizes classrooms. Occasionally teachers divide their classrooms along gender-segregated lines in groups, work and play areas, and seating; more frequently, students gender-segregate themselves. Drawn to the sections of the classroom where the more assertive boys are clustered, the teacher is physically positioned to keep interacting with male students and to be geographically farther away from female students. Such inequities detract from learning and a sense of security for all students. Differences in teacher–student interactions are more than a counting game of who gets the teacher's attention and who does not. Teacher attention is a vote of high expectations and commitment to a student.

Trends and Challenges

The Boy Crisis

Remember when your elementary school teacher would announce the teams for the weekly spelling bee? "The boys against the girls!" There was nothing like a gender showdown to liven things up. A spate of recent books and articles takes us back to the "boys versus girls" fray, but this time with much higher stakes.

The "boy crisis" has become a major media event, with frightening tales of boys falling behind girls in academic achievement and at risk for failure. In "The Genius Gap," a *New York Magazine* article asks if boys are now the second sex and "no longer have what it takes to succeed in school?" (Rosin, 2010). An article in *The New Republic* attacked schools for their "verbally drenched curriculum" that leaves "boys in the dust" (Rivers & Barnett, 2011), and an essay title in the *New York Times* laments: "Boys and reading: Is there any hope?" (Lipsyte, 2011).

The media picture of boys that has emerged is as familiar as it is one-dimensional: antsy and unable to sit for long; often learning disabled; hardwired differently than girls; unable to read and disliking books; unhappy taking orders from women in school; able to focus on sports, computers, and video games but not on academics; a constant source of discipline problems in class; a potential grade repeater; perhaps one day a dropout; certainly someone less and less likely to enter a college classroom. Other boys—quiet boys, unathletic boys, thoughtful boys, caring boys, gay boys, and middle- and upper-class boys acing their schoolwork and going on to the Ivy Leagues—all disappeared overnight.

Is the reality as grim as this picture suggests? Not really. If you look at studies carefully, you will see that we are in the midst of a crisis that is affecting some boys, but not *all* boys. Overall, among nonpoor, suburban, White, Asian, and academically elite students, boys are doing well. In fact, most boys are doing better today than they were a decade or two ago (AAUW, 2008; Rivers & Barnett, 2011).

Boys overall do quite well on most tests. They outperform girls on the SATs and GREs, and their performance on other tests such as the National Assessment of Educational Progress (NAEP)—the nation's "report card"—has improved in recent years. Girls do test better in NAEP reading and writing, and boys often test better in NAEP math and science, but many of these gaps are narrowing. More boys take advanced high school classes in calculus, chemistry, and physics. Crime and substance-abuse rates are down among boys (AAUW, 2008; Rivers & Barnett, 2011).

While females are now the majority in college, more men are attending than ever before. One statistic often missed in the "boy crisis" stories is that men still constitute the majority of students at a number of celebrated colleges and in prestigious academic programs, while women are the majority at the less prestigious two-year community colleges. These female college students are typically older, have children, and are enrolled in programs intended to increase their income. When men and women graduate with the same credential (high school diploma, college degree, or graduate degree), men continue to earn significantly higher incomes. A woman with a college degree earns about the same as a man without a college degree. For women, education has more economic consequences than it does for men. Some have interpreted girls' progress in school to mean that boys are in crisis, as though life is a zero-sum game and if one group advances, another must topple (Rivers & Barnett, 2011).

While the "boy crisis" is a myth, there are legitimate concerns about some boys' achievement. Perhaps the worst thing about the "boy crisis" is that it has distracted us from boys (and girls) who are really in need. Let us take a moment to focus on the differences between males in general and at-risk males.

White and Asian males in suburban schools are not struggling on tests or lagging behind in reading; they are scoring much higher than other males. In fact, the scoring gap between Asian and White males versus males of color is several times higher than the scoring gap between males and females in general. Black, Hispanic, Native American, and poor boys of all races are the ones at risk and are far more likely to be grade repeaters than White or Asian boys (or than girls from any group). More than three-quarters of middle- to higher-income males typically graduate from high school, while only about half of low-income boys do. Although more boys than girls drop out of high school, more African American, Hispanic, and American Indian girls drop out than either White or Asian boys. When girls drop out, they are more likely to be unemployed, earn lower wages, and be on public support than male dropouts (Rivers & Barnett, 2011; Swanson, 2010).

Equally troubling, African American and Hispanic students are suspended at much higher rates than their peers (Gregory, 2011). Does African American and Hispanic school behavior warrant such punishments? Not according to Russell Skiba, a professor of educational psychology at Indiana University (Witt, 2007). His research on school discipline shows that minority students from the same social and economic class are no more likely to misbehave than other students, and he concludes that such inequity reflects institutional racism. While most school districts are acutely aware of these racial disparities in discipline, they continue unabated.

There are no data to suggest that boys are destined to fail in school. But those decrying the "boy crisis" are persistent and offer a reason for the boy problem: feminized schools. Unsympathetic women teachers are promoting a "biologically disrespectful model of education" that is harming boys (Mead, 2006; Rivers & Barnett, 2011). To fix this problem, these critics say, we need to abandon coeducation and reestablish all-boy classes and schools. In fact, many public school educators have heeded their call and done just that.

The Rebirth of Single-Sex Education

At the beginning of both the 20th and 21st centuries, gender in school was center stage (Sadker & Zittleman, 2012). In the early 1900s, doctors argued that girls' fragile anatomy was endangered by too much education and that too much learning could lead to insanity and sterility. Today biology is once again an issue. This time voices proclaim that biology created two different learners, girls and boys, and that trying to educate the two sexes in the same classroom is a disservice to both. By 2011, more than 500 single-sex classrooms had been created in public schools across the nation (National Association for Single Sex Education, 2011). Coeducation, once seen as a beacon of democracy and equality, is now accused of being a barrier to effective teaching and learning.

Is single-sex education a good idea? If you look to research for your answer, you will be disappointed. A decade or two ago, there was some excitement when studies suggested that females in single-sex schools demonstrated strong academic achievement and self-esteem, high career goals, and less sex-role stereotyping (AAUW, 1998; Tyack & Hansot, 1990). But the excitement proved premature. Many believe that single-sex schools did not create these results but simply attracted girls with high academic goals and strong self-esteem. Others interpreted the studies to mean that these schools are excellent schools that just happened to be single-sex. Perhaps it is less likely that single-sex schooling is responsible for this strong female performance and more likely that the small class sizes, skilled teachers, strong academics, involved parents, and a selective admission process are the real reasons for success (Arms, 2007; Datnow & Hubbard, 2002; Rivers & Barnett, 2011).

The research on boys' performance in single-sex education is even less supportive. Fewer studies on boys have been done, and the results conflict. On the positive side, some studies indicate that in single-sex environments, more boys enroll in nontraditional courses such as poetry or art and that poorer boys may develop better work habits (Riordan, 2002). But studies also report that all-male educational environments fan the flames of misogyny and sexism, producing boys and men who look down on girls and women. Moreover, the research does not offer any strong evidence that academic learning is any better in all-male schools and may, in fact, harm boys' success (Campbell & Sanders, 2002; Moller, Forbes-Jones, Hightower, & Friedman, 2008; Rivers & Barnett, 2011).

A Washington, D.C., middle school teacher shares his firsthand experience with single-sex education:

> At first, I felt there were some real advantages to separating the girls and boys. There was certainly less teasing, which had gotten out of hand the year before. So I saw the separation as having marginal advantages. But over time, each gender developed other discipline issues. Cliques of girls began teasing each other. They replaced the boys as the discipline problem. Boys really began acting out. They actually got goofier. Then there was a second problem: boys struggling with their sexual identity really lost out. Some of these boys had girls as their best friends, and when the separate classes began, they literally lost their best friends. They were now isolated in an alpha male environment. They were treated harshly and ridiculed. The third problem was sheer numbers: there were more girls in these classes than boys. The girls' classes got much bigger. The girls got less individualized attention. So what I thought at first would be a help for girls really failed them. It was not a good idea.

> I pride myself in not being an ideologue. I do not like it when people get stuck in one camp or the other. Show me something that works, and I want to find out why and how we can use it. But this did not work.

(Sadker et al., 2009, pp. 253–288)

So how different are boys and girls? Do they have different ways of learning? That's what Janet Hyde at the University of Wisconsin–Madison wanted to find out. Using a sophisticated meta-analytic statistical procedure, she reviewed studies on how boys and girls are similar and different. Are boys more aggressive than girls? Are they better at math and science? Do girls have stronger verbal and fine motor skills? Are girls more nurturing than boys?

What she found surprised many: There are precious few educationally relevant gender differences. So Hyde (2005) settled on a *gender similarities hypothesis*: Rather than demonstrating separate learning styles and needs, males and females are actually more alike than different. In short, more educational differences exist *within* the genders than *between* the genders. Other studies confirm Hyde's finding and show that the greatest challenges in educational achievement have less to do with gender and more to do with race, ethnicity, and economic status (AAUW, 2008; Eliot, 2010; Rivers & Barnett, 2011).

Hyde's work did reveal a few exceptions to the gender similarities hypothesis. In some cases, her findings were counterintuitive: Males exhibited slightly more helping behaviors than females, while self-esteem levels for adult men and women were quite similar. Hyde also found a couple of educationally relevant differences: Boys are more aggressive and have a better ability to rotate objects mentally. But the reason for these few differences is not clear. Are they due to nature or nurture, or a combination of the two? After all, socialization plays a big role in our culture.

For example, researchers at the University of Michigan followed more than 800 children and their parents for 13 years and found that traditional gender stereotypes greatly influence parental attitudes and behaviors related to children's interest in math. Parents provided more math-supportive environments for their sons than for their daughters, including buying more math and science toys. Parents, especially fathers, held more positive perceptions of their sons' math abilities than of their daughters' (Davis-Keen, 2007).

Lise Eliot (2010), a neuroscientist at the Chicago Medical School, believes that such early socialization contributes to gender differences in learning. She describes how the many hours boys clock with Legos, baseball, and video games help develop spatial skills, such as targeting and mental rotation, skills not taught in school. Such spatial skills figure prominently in subjects like physics, trigonometry, calculus, and engineering, subjects in which many boys excel. Girls, by contrast, are encouraged more than boys to read for pleasure outside school. Eliot contends that it is this practice, rather than any genetic or hormonal difference, that best predicts gender differences in reading achievement. Clearly, socialization can be a powerful influence on academic success.

Yet many U.S. public schools continue to create single-sex classrooms and even single-sex schools. Why? Some schools do it to raise test scores because they believe that boys and girls learn differently. Others argue that dividing the genders removes sexual distractions and is a good behavior management strategy. Another reason is the persistent gap between research and popular culture. As we have previously explored, trendy books and media pundits pronounce that boys and girls have different brains and different hard-wiring and need to be taught differently and separately. This feeds into society's conventional view that "men are from Mars and women are from Venus." Parents and educators are told that boys learn best through physical games, tough competition, harsh discipline, and shorter lessons. On the other hand, girls, they are told, are genetically more placid and conforming, relational, and collaborative in nature and prefer a calmer learning atmosphere. Such notions fit easily into traditional belief systems but are not supported by research, which shows there are no important intellectual or psychological differences between females and males that require unique teaching approaches (Eliot, 2010; Hyde, 2005; Rivers & Barnett, 2011).

Importantly, our understanding of how nature and nurture influence gender roles is changing. We typically view genetics and learning styles as pretty much fixed from birth, but recent research shows that it is more complicated than that. The brain, for example, rather than being fixed, is like a muscle that can be developed and changed by our experiences. The ability of our brain to change itself and create new neural pathways is called *neuroplasticity* (Doidge, 2007). We are reminded of this whenever we see quiet boys who love reading or music, or girls who soar in math or on the athletic field. For teachers, this is exciting news. It means that if we offer a variety of challenging and involving activities in our classes, we can not only maintain student interest but also help students grow and cultivate their brains. On the other hand, if we teach to a single learning style or use stereotypes in our teaching, we limit the brain's possibilities. So teachers are wise to encourage all their students, girls and boys, to develop their brains by exploring different learning styles, incorporating both competitive and cooperative activities, integrating both personal connections and active learning, and focusing on the arts as well as traditional subjects.

Generalizing a pedagogy based on a student's gender will surely miss many students who do not fit neatly into a fixed gender mold. The same thing can be said of sexuality. Basing pedagogy on the assumption that all students are heterosexual is bound to miss students who do not fit into that mold either.

Supporting Lesbian, Gay, Bisexual, and Transgender Students (LGBT)

Lesbian, gay, bisexual, or *straight* refers to a person's sexual orientation, an innate characteristic that determines whom one is attracted to sexually. *Transgender* refers to a person's gender identity—a person's innate sense of being male, female, or somewhere in between. Many school practices assume that all people are heterosexual and either male or female. A typical curriculum reflects this assumption in subtle and not-so-subtle ways. Literature such as *Romeo and Juliet,* math word problems such as "David bought Karen one dozen roses . . .", and electing a homecoming king and queen are obvious examples of assumed heterosexuality for all. However, some schools are altering these practices: inviting same-sex couples to the prom, providing gender-neutral or individual bathrooms and locker rooms for transgender students, and including LGBT people and perspectives in the curriculum (McCollum, 2010).

More and more gay students are coming out of the closet earlier, often in middle school, and finding support among peers and teachers. Others find no support and liken school to a war zone (Denzet-Lewis, 2009). These different responses to LGBT students reflect our national cultural division. A number of states have laws preventing teachers from even mentioning the word *homosexual* or mandating that homosexuality be presented in exclusively negative terms in the classroom. Other school districts recognize LGBT people in their nondiscrimination policies, sending a clear message that no student, parent, or school employee will be discriminated against because of their sexual orientation or gender identity. There are more than 3,500 Gay–Straight Alliances (GSAs), student clubs that provide a safe space for LGBT students and their allies. GSAs sometimes engender controversy, but the 1984 Federal Equal Access Act states that if schools allow any noncurricular clubs, then they have to allow them all (McCollum, 2010).

Depending on where you teach, you may or may not be able to include LGBT issues in your teaching. But wherever you teach, you can ensure that democratic norms of equality are followed and that all students are respected regardless of individual differences. Students do not have to agree that "it's okay to be gay," but they should understand that "it's not okay to discriminate against those who are gay." By providing a safe place for all students, teachers can create nurturing classrooms where every child can learn and every family is welcome.

Strategies for Creating Gender-Fair Classrooms

Teachers have the power to make an enormous difference in the lives of students. The following suggestions consist of ways to make your own classroom nonsexist.

1. If the textbooks and software that you are given are biased, you may wish to confront this bias rather than ignore it. Discuss the issue directly with your students. It is entirely appropriate to acknowledge that instructional materials are not always perfect. Teach them about the forms bias take from stereotyping to cosmetic bias. By engaging your students in the issue, you help them to develop critical literacy skills.

2. Ask your students to list famous men and women. Do they have an equal number of women and men? More women? More men? Does the list include individuals of diverse racial and ethnic backgrounds? Individuals with diverse sexual orientations? Discuss with them what their lists teach us. What groups are missing from their lists? How can we learn more about those "missing" Americans?

3. Analyze your seating chart to determine whether there are pockets of racial, ethnic, class, or gender segregation in your classroom. Make certain that you do not teach from one area of the room, focusing your time and attention on one group of students while ignoring another group sitting in another part of the room. When your students work in groups,

create groups that reflect diversity. Monitor these student groups to ensure equitable participation and decision making.

4. Do not tolerate the use of harmful words, bullying, or harassment in your classroom. Do not say "boys will be boys" to excuse sexist comments or behaviors. Nor are racist or antigay comments to be ignored, laughed at, or tolerated. As a teacher, you are the model and the norm setter: If you do not tolerate hurtful prejudice, your students will learn to honor and respect one another.

5. Continue your reading and professional development in gender equity. Be discerning and remember that research publications are less susceptible to political agendas than the popular media or politically funded "think tanks." And be careful that your rights or those of your colleagues are not violated by gender discrimination.

QUESTIONS AND ACTIVITIES

6.1 The chapter lists seven forms of gender bias that you can use when evaluating instructional materials: (a) invisibility, (b) stereotyping, (c) linguistic bias, (d) imbalance, (e) unreality, (f) fragmentation, and (g) cosmetic bias. In your own words, define each form of bias. Examine a sample K–12 textbook or software program in your teaching area and determine whether it contains any of these forms of gender bias. Are there forms of bias reflected against any other groups? Give three examples of how teachers can supplement instructional materials to eliminate the seven forms of gender bias.

6.2 Observe lessons being taught in several classrooms that include boys and girls and students from different racial and ethnic groups. Create a seating chart and count the interactions between the teacher and each student. Did the ways in which the teachers interacted with males and

female students differ? If so, how? Did the teachers interact with students from various ethnic groups differently? If so, how? Did you notice any way in which gender, race, and socioeconomic status combined to influence how teachers interacted with particular students? If so, explain.

6.3 Why do you think single-sex schools are making a comeback? Do you think this trend toward single-sex schooling should be halted or supported?
Check out the requirements of Title IX. Prepare a brief list to remind yourself of some of the ways in which the law is designed to ensure gender equity. (A good place to start is "I Exercise My Rights" at http://www.titleix.info/.)

6.4 After reading this chapter, do you think there are some ways in which you can change your behavior to make it more gender-fair? If yes, in what ways? If no, why not?

REFERENCES

Aarons, D. I. (2010, May 12). Efforts to end bullying, a challenge to leaders, gain new momentum. *Education Week*, 1-3.

American Association of University Women (AAUW). (1998). *Separated by sex: A critical look at single-sex education for girls*. Washington, DC: Author.

American Association of University Women (AAUW). (2004). *Harassment-free hallways: How to stop harassment in school*. Washington, DC: Author.

American Association of University Women (AAUW). (2008). *Where the girls are: The facts about gender equity in education*. Washington, DC: Author.

American Association of University Women (AAUW). (2010). *Why so few? Women in science, technology, engineering, and mathematics*. Washington, DC: Author.

Arms, E. (2007). Gender equity in coeducational and single-sex environments. In S. Klein (Ed.), *Handbook for achieving gender equity through education* (pp. 171–190). Mahwah, NJ: Erlbaum.

Bailey, B., Scantlebury, K., & Letts, W. (1997). It's not my style: Using disclaimers to ignore issues in science. *Journal of Teacher Education, 48*(1), 29–35.

Beaman, R., Wheldall, K., & Kemp, C. (2006). Differential teacher attention to boys and girls in the classroom. *Educational Review, 58*(3), 339–366.

Campbell, P. B., & Sanders, J. (2002). Challenging the system: Assumptions and data behind the push for single-sex schools. In A. Datnow & L. Hubbard (Eds.), *Gender in policy and practice: Perspectives on single-sex and coeducational schooling* (pp. 31–46). New York: Routledge/Falmer.

Chick, K. (2006). Gender balance in K–12 American history textbooks. *Social Studies Research and Practice, 1*(3), 2006. Available online at www.socstrp.org.

Clarke, E. H. (1873). *Sex in education; or, a fair chance for the girls*. Boston: J. R. Osgood and Company.

Datnow, A., & Hubbard, L. (Eds.). (2002). *Gender in policy and practice: Perspectives on single-sex and coeducational schooling*. New York: Routledge/Falmer.

Davis-Keen, P. (2007). *Dads influence daughters' interest in mathematics*. Paper presented at Educating a STEM Workforce: New Strategies for U-M and the State of Michigan, Ann Arbor, MI.

Denzet-Lewis, B. (2009, September 27). Coming out in junior high school. *New York Times Magazine*, pp. 36–41, 52, 54–55.

Doidge, N. (2007). *The brain that changes itself*. New York: Penguin.

Duffy, J., Warren, K., & Walsh, M. (2001). Classroom interactions: Gender of teacher, gender of student, and classroom subject. *Sex Roles, 45*(9/10), 579–593.

Eliot, L. (2010). *Pink brain, blue brain: How small differences grow into troublesome gaps—and what we can do about it*. Boston: Houghton Mifflin.

Evans, L., & Davies, K. (2000). No sissy boys here: A content analysis of the representation of masculinity in elementary school reading textbooks. *Sex Roles, 42*, 255–270.

Fan, L., & Kaeley, G. (2000). The influence of textbooks on teaching strategies. *Mid-Western Educational Researcher, 13*(4), 2–9.

Flinders, D., & Thornton, S. (Eds.), (2009). *Curriculum studies reader* (3rd ed.). New York: Routledge.

Girls, Inc. (2006). *The supergirl dilemma: Girls feel the pressure to be perfect, accomplished, thin, and accommodating*. New York: Author.

Glasser, H., & Smith, J. (2008) On the meaning of gender in educational research: The problem, its sources, and recommendations for practice. *Educational Researcher, 37*(6), 343–350.

Good, T., & Brophy, J. (2007). *Looking into classrooms* (10th ed.). Boston: Allyn & Bacon.

Gregory, A. (2011). The relationship of school structure and support to suspension rates for Black and White high school students. *American Educational Research Journal, 48*, 904–934.

Hamilton, M., Anderson, D., Braoddus, M., & Young, K. (2006). Gender stereotyping and under-representation of female characters in 200 popular children's picture books: A twenty-first century update. *Sex Roles, 55*, 757–765.

Hegewisch, A., & Liepmann, H. (2010). *The gender wage gap by occupation*. Washington, DC: Institute for Women's Policy Research.

Hyde, J. (2005). The gender similarities hypothesis. *American Psychologist, 60*(6), 581–592.

Kimmel, M. (2008). *Guyland: The perilous world where boys become men*. New York: Harper.

Lederman, D. (2006). Clues about the gender gap. *Inside Higher Ed*. Retrieved March 30, 2008, from http://insidehighered.com/news/2007/01/15/freshmen

Lipsyte, R. (2011, August 19). Boys and reading: Is there any hope? *New York Times*, p. BR39.

Maxwell, L. (2008). Principals' views on bullying, *Education Week*, vol. 27, issue 38, p. 5.

McCollum, S. (2010, Fall). Country outposts. *Teaching tolerance*, pp. 32–35.

Mead, S. (2006). *The evidence suggests otherwise: The truth about boys and girls*. Washington, DC: The Education Sector. Retrieved September 30, 2007, from http://www.educationsector.org.

Meehan, D. (2007). *Learning like a girl: Educating our daughters in schools of their own*. New York: Public Affairs.

Moller, A. C., Forbes-Jones, E., Hightower, A. D., & Friedman, R. (2008). The developmental influence of sex composition in preschool classrooms: Boys fare worse in preschool classrooms with more boys. *Early Childhood Research Quarterly, 23*, 409–418.

National Association for Single Sex Education. (2011). Single-sex schools/Schools with single-sex classrooms/What's the difference? Retrieved August 22, 2011, from http://www.singlesexschools.org/schools-schools.htm.

National Center for Education Statistics (NCES). (2011). *Digest of education statistics, 2010*. Washington, DC: U.S. Department of Education.

National Eating Disorders Coalition. (2011, August 26). *Stats about eating disorders: What the research shows*. Retrieved from http://www.eatingdisorderscoalition.org.

National Federation of State High School Associations. (2010-2011). *2010-2011 high school athletics participation survey*. 201011 sportsparticipation-blog-1.pdf.

Pollack, W. S. (1998). *Real boys: Rescuing our sons from the myths of boyhood*. New York: Holt.

Pollack, W. S. (2009/2010, December/January). Cracking the boy code. *PTA Magazine*. Retrieved from http://www.pta.org/3735.htm.

Riordan, C. (2002). What do we know about the effects of single-sex schools in the private sector? Implications for public schools. In A. Datnow & L. Hubbard (Eds.), *Doing gender in policy and practice: Perspectives on single-sex and coeducational schooling* (pp. 10–30). New York: Routledge/Falmer.

Rivers, C., & Barnett, R.C. (2011). *The truth about girls and boys: Challenging toxic stereotypes about our children*. New York: Columbia University Press.

Rosin, H. (June 4, 2010). The genius gap: Are boys the second sex? *New York Magazine*. Retrieved from http://nymag.com/news/intelligencer/66482/.

Sadker, D., Sadker, M., & Zittleman, K. (2009). *Still failing at fairness: How gender bias cheats boys and girls in school and what we can do about it*. New York: Scribner.

Sadker, D., Sadker, M., & Zittleman, K. (2010). Questioning skills. In J. Cooper (Ed.), *Classroom teaching skills* (9th ed., pp. 107–152). Belmont, CA: Wadsworth/Cengage.

Sadker, D., & Zittleman, K. (2012). *Teachers, schools, and society: A brief introduction to education* (3rd ed.). New York: McGraw-Hill.

Spencer, R., Porche, M., & Tolman, D. (2003). We've come a long way—maybe: New challenges for gender equity education. *Teachers College Record, 105*(9), 1774–1807.

Starnes, B. A. (2004). Textbooks, school reform, and the silver lining. *Phi Delta Kappan, 86*(2), 170–171.

Swanson, C. (2010). Diplomas count: Graduation by the numbers. *Education Week, 29*(34), 4–5.

Thomas, K. (2011, July 29). Long fights for sports equity, even with a law. *New York Times,* pp. A1, B13.

Tyack, D., & Hansot, E. (1990). *Learning together: A history of coeducation in American schools.* New Haven, CT: Yale University Press.

Witt, H. (2007). School discipline tougher on African Americans. *Chicago Tribune*. Retrieved October 5, 2007, from http://www.chicagotribune.com/news/nationworld/chi-070924discipline,1,6597576.story?ctrack=1&cset=true.

Zittleman, K. (2007). Gender perceptions of middle schoolers: The good and the bad. *Middle Grades Research Journal, 2*(2), 65–97.

© Fancy Collection/SuperStock

Classrooms for Diversity: Rethinking Curriculum and Pedagogy

Mary Kay Thompson Tetreault

> It's time to start learning about things they told you you didn't need to know . . .
> learning about me, instead of learning about them, starting to learn about her instead
> of learning about him. It's a connection that makes education education.
> (a student of European and African American ancestry)

This student's reflection on her education signals a twin transformation that is pushing us to rethink our traditional ways of teaching. The first is that students in our classrooms are increasingly more diverse; the second is that traditional course content has been enriched by the new scholarship in women's studies, cultural studies, and multicultural studies. It is in the classroom that these transformations intersect, and it rests on the teacher to make education "education" for this student and for the majority who believe their education was not made for them—women of all backgrounds, people of color, and men who lack privilege because of their social class—by bringing the two aspects of the transformation together. The current challenges to classroom teachers are not only to incorporate multiple perspectives into the curriculum but also to engage in pedagogical practices that bring in the voices of students as a source for learning rather than managing or controlling them.

Feminist Phase Theory

One of the most effective ways I have found to set a frame for envisioning a gender-balanced, multicultural curriculum while capturing the reforms that have occurred over the past 40 years is *feminist phase theory*. Conceptually rooted in the scholarship on women, feminist phase theory is a classification system of the evolution in thought about the incorporation of women's traditions, history, and experiences into selected disciplines. The model I have developed identifies five common phases of thinking about women: *male-defined curriculum, contribution curriculum, bifocal curriculum, women's curriculum*, and *gender-balanced curriculum*. A gender-balanced perspective—one that is rooted in feminist scholarship—takes into account the experiences, perspectives, and voices of women as well as men. It examines the similarities and differences between women and men and considers how gender interacts with such factors as ethnicity, race, culture, and class.

The language of this system or schema, particularly the word *phase*, and the description of one phase and then another suggest a sequential hierarchy in which one phase supplants another.

Before reviewing the schema, please refrain from thinking of these phases in a linear fashion; envision them as a series of intersecting circles, or patches on a quilt, or threads in a tapestry that interact and undergo changes in response to one another. It is more accurate to view the phases as different emphases that coexist in feminist research. The important thing is that teachers, scholars, and curriculum developers ask and answer certain questions at each phase.

The following section identifies key concepts and questions articulated initially at each phase, using examples from history, literature, and science; it then discusses how the phases interact and undergo changes in response to one another. The final part of this chapter shows teachers grappling with the intersection of changes in the disciplines and changes in the student population and presents four themes of analysis: *mastery, voice, authority*, and *positionality*. The chapter concludes with specific objectives, practices, and teaching suggestions for incorporating content about women into the K–12 curriculum in social studies, language arts, and science.

Male-Defined Curriculum

Male-defined curriculum rests on the assumption that the male experience is universal, is representative of humanity, and constitutes a basis for generalizing about all human beings. The knowledge that is researched and taught, the substance of learning, is knowledge articulated by and about men. There is little or no consciousness that the existence of women as a group is an anomaly calling for a broader definition of knowledge. The female experience is subsumed under the male experience. For example, feminist scientists have cited methodological problems in some research about sex differences that draws conclusions about females based on experiments done only on males or that uses limited (usually White and middle-class) experimental populations from which scientists draw conclusions about all males and females.

The incorporation of women into the curriculum has not only taught us about women's lives but has also led to questions about our lopsided rendition of men's lives in which we pay attention primarily to men in the public world and conceal their lives in the private world. Historians, for example, are posing a series of interesting questions about men's history: What do we need to unlearn about men's history? What are the taken-for-granted truths about men's history that we need to rethink? How do we get at the significant masculine truths? Is man's primary sense of self defined in relation to the public sphere only? How does this sense relate to boyhood, adolescence, family life, recreation, and love? What do the answers to these questions imply about the teaching of history?

Feminist scholarship—like African American, Native American, Chicano/Latino, and Asian American scholarship—reveals the systematic and contestable exclusions in the male-defined curriculum. When we examine curriculum through the lens of this scholarship, we are forced to reconsider our understanding of the most fundamental conceptualization of knowledge and social relations in our society. We understand in a new way that knowledge is a social construction created by individual human beings who live and think at a particular time and within a particular social framework. All works in literature, science, and history, for example, have an author, male or female, White or ethnic or racial minority, elite or middle class or occasionally poor, with motivations and beliefs. The scientist's questions and activities, for instance, are shaped, often unconsciously, by the great social issues of the day (see Table 7.1). Different perspectives on the same subject will change the patterns discerned.

Contribution Curriculum

Early efforts to reclaim women's rightful place in the curriculum involved searching for missing women within a male framework. Although it was recognized that women were missing, men continued to serve as the norm, the representative, the universal human being. Outstanding women emerged who fit this male norm of excellence or greatness or conformed to implicit

Table 7.1　Male-Defined Curriculum

Characteristics of Phase	Questions Commonly Asked about Women in History*	Questions Commonly Asked about Women in Literature*	Questions Commonly Asked about Women in Science*
The absence of women is not noted. There is no consciousness that the male experience is a "particular knowledge" selected from a wider universe of possible knowledge and experience. It is valued, emphasized, and viewed as the knowledge most worth having.	Who is the author of a particular history? What is her or his race, ethnicity, religion, ideological orientation, social class, place of origin, and historical period? How does incorporating women's experiences lead to new understandings of the most fundamental ordering of social relations, institutions, and power arrangements? How can we define the content and methodology of history so it will be a history of us all?	How is traditional humanism, with an integrated self at its center and an authentic view of life, in effect part of patriarchal ideology? How can the objectivist illusion be dismantled? How can the idea of a literary canon of "great literature" be challenged? How are writing and reading political acts? How do race, class, and gender relate to the conflict, sufferings, and passions that attend these realities? How can we study language as specific *discourse*, that is, specific linguistic strategies in specific situations, rather than as universal language?	How do scientific studies reveal cultural values? What cultural, historical, and gender values are projected onto the physical and natural world? How might gender be a bias that influences choice of questions, hypotheses, subjects, experimental design, or theory formation in science? What is the underlying philosophy of an androcentric science that values objectivity, rationality, and dominance? How can the distance between the subject and the scientific observer be shortened so that the scientist has some feeling for or empathy with the organism? How can gender play a crucial role in transforming science?

*New questions generated by feminist scholars.

assumptions about appropriate roles for women outside the home. In literature, female authors were added who performed well within the masculine tradition, internalizing its standards of art and its views on social roles. Great women of science who made it in the male scientific world, most frequently Marie Curie, for example, were added.

Examples of contribution history can be seen in U.S. history textbooks. They now include the contributions of notable American women who were outstanding in the public sphere as rulers or as contributors to wars or reform movements to a remarkable degree. Queen Liliuo-kalani, Hawaii's first reigning queen and a nationalist, is included in the story of the kingdom's annexation. Molly Pitcher and Deborah Sampson are depicted as contributors to the Revolutionary War, as is Clara Barton to the Civil War effort. Some authors have also included women who conform to the assumption that it is acceptable for women to engage in activities outside the home if they are an extension of women's nurturing role within the family. Examples of this are Dorothea Dix, Jane Addams, Eleanor Roosevelt, and Mary McLeod Bethune (Tetreault, 1986).

The lesson to be learned from understanding these limitations of early contribution history is not to disregard the study of notable women but to include those who worked to reshape the world according to a feminist reordering of values. This includes efforts to increase women's self-determination through a feminist transformation of the home; to increase education, political rights, and women's rights to control their bodies; and to improve their economic status.

A history with women at the center moves beyond paying attention to caring for the unfortunate in the public sphere to examining how exceptional women influenced the lives of women in general (see Table 7.2). Just as Mary McLeod Bethune's role in the New Deal is worth teaching to our students, so is her aggressive work to project a positive image of African American women to the nation through her work in African American women's clubs and the launching of the *Afro-American Woman's Journal* (Smith, 2003).

Table 7.2　Contribution Curriculum

Characteristics of Phase	Questions Commonly Asked about Women in History	Questions Commonly Asked about Women in Literature	Questions Commonly Asked about Women in Science
The absence of women is noted. There is a search for missing women according to a male norm of greatness, excellence, or humanness. Women are considered exceptional, deviant, or other. Women are added into history, but the content and notions of historical significance are not challenged.	Who are the notable women missing from history and what did they and ordinary women contribute in areas or movements traditionally dominated by men, for example, during major wars or during reform movements, such as abolitionism or the labor movement? What did notable and ordinary women contribute in areas that are an extension of women's traditional roles, for example, caring for the poor and the sick? How have major economic and political changes such as industrialization or extension of the franchise affected women in the public sphere? How did notable and ordinary women respond to their oppression, particularly through women's rights organizations? *Who were outstanding women who advocated a feminist transformation of the home, who contributed to women's greater self-determination through increased education, the right to control their bodies, an increase in their political rights, and the improvement of their economic status? *What did women contribute through the settlement house and labor movements?	Who are the missing female authors whose subject matter and use of language and form meet the male norm of "masterpiece"? What primary biological facts and interpretations are missing about major female authors?	Who are the notable women scientists who have made contributions to mainstream science? How is women's different (and supposedly inferior) nature related to hormones, brain lateralization, and sociobiology? Where are the missing females in scientific experiments? What is the current status of women within the scientific profession? *How does adding minority women to the history of science reveal patterns of exclusion and recast definitions of what it means to practice science and to be a scientist? *How is the exclusion of women from science related to the way science is done and thought about? *What is the usual pattern of women working in science? How is it the same as or different from the pattern of notable women? *How do our definitions of science need to be broadened to evaluate women's contributions to science? Do institutions of science need to be reshaped to accommodate women? If so, how?

*New questions generated by feminist scholars.

Bifocal Curriculum

In bifocal curriculum, feminist scholars have made an important shift from a perspective that views men as the norm to one that opens up the possibility of seeing the world through women's eyes (Gornick & Moran, 1971; Millett, 1970). This dual vision, or bifocal perspective, generated global questions about women and about the differences between women and men. Historians investigated the separation between the public and the private sphere and asked, for example, how the division between them explains women's lives. Some elaborated on the construct by identifying arenas of female power in the domestic sphere. Literary critics tried to provide a new understanding of a distinctively female literary tradition and a theory of women's literary creativity. These critics sought to provide models for understanding the dynamics of female literary response to male literary assertion and coercion (Showalter, 1977). Scientists grappled with definitions of women's and men's nature by asking how the public and private, biology and culture, and personal and impersonal inform each other and affect men and women, science, and nature.

Scholars have pointed out some of the problems with bifocal knowledge. Thinking about women and men is dualistic and dichotomized. Women and men are thought of as having different spheres, different notions of what is of value in life, different ways of imagining the human condition, and different associations with nature and culture. But both views are valued. In short, women are thought of as a group that is complementary but equal to men; there are some truths for men and there are some truths for women. General analyses of men's and women's experiences often come dangerously close to reiterating the sexual stereotypes scholars are trying to overcome. Because many people believe that the public sphere is more valuable than the private sphere, there is a tendency to slip back into thinking of women as inferior and subordinate (Christian, 1980; Lerner, 1979; Rosaldo & Lamphere, 1974).

The generalized view of women and men that predominates in the bifocal curriculum often does not allow for distinctions within groups as large and as complex as women and men. Important factors such as historical period, geographic location, structural barriers, race, paternity, sexual orientation, and social class, to name a few, clearly make a difference. Other common emphases in the bifocal curriculum are the oppression of women and the exploration of that oppression. Exposés of woman hating in history and literature are common. The emphasis is on the *misogyny* (the hatred of women) of the human experience, particularly the means men have used to advance their authority and to assert or imply female inferiority. The paradoxes of women's existence are sometimes overlooked with this emphasis on oppression. For example, although women have been excluded from positions of power, a few of them as wives and daughters in powerful families were often closer to actual power than were men. If some women were dissatisfied with their status and role, most adjusted and did not join efforts to improve women's status. Too much emphasis on women's oppression perpetuates a patriarchal framework presenting women as primarily passive, reacting only to the pressures of a sexist society. In the main, it emphasizes men thinking and women being thought about.

Women's scholarship from the 1970s through the present (Collins, 2000; Goldberger, Tarule, Clinchy, & Belenky, 1996; Schmitz, Butler, Guy-Sheftall, & Rosenfelt, 2004) has helped us see that understanding women's oppression is more complex than we initially thought. We do not yet have adequate concepts to explain gender systems founded on a division of labor and sexual asymmetry. To understand gender systems, it is necessary to take a structural and experiential perspective that asks from a woman's point of view where we are agents and where we are not, where our relations with men are egalitarian and where they are not. This questioning may lead to explanations of why women's experiences and interpretations of their world can differ significantly from those of men.

Furthermore, the concepts with which we approach our analysis need to be questioned. Anthropologists have pointed out that our way of seeing the world—for instance, the idea of complementary spheres for women (the private sphere) and men (the public sphere)—is a product of our experience in a Western, modern, industrial, capitalistic state with a specific history. We distort our understanding of other social systems by imposing our worldview on them (Atkinson, 1982). Feminist critics are calling for rethinking not only categories such as the domestic versus the public sphere and production and reproduction but also gender itself (Butler, 1993).

One of the most important things we have learned about a bifocal perspective is the danger of generalizing too much, of longing for women's history instead of writing histories about women. We must guard against establishing a feminist version of great literature and then resisting any modifications or additions to it. We have also learned that the traditional disciplines are limited in their ability to shed light on gender complexities, and it becomes apparent that there is a need for an interdisciplinary perspective (see Table 7.3).

Table 7.3   Bifocal Curriculum

Characteristics of Phase	Questions Commonly Asked about Women in History	Questions Commonly Asked about Women in Literature	Questions Commonly Asked about Women in Science
Human experience is conceptualized primarily in dualist categories: male and female, private and public, agency and communion. Emphasis is on a complementary but equal conceptualization of men's and women's spheres and personal qualities. There is a focus on women's oppression and on misogyny. Women's efforts to overcome the oppression are presented. Efforts to include women lead to the insight that the traditional content, structure, and methodology of the disciplines are more appropriate to the male experience.	How does the division between the public and the private sphere explain women's lives? Who oppressed women, and how were they oppressed? *What are forms of power and value in women's world? *How have women been excluded from and deprived of power and value in men's sphere? *How do gender systems create divisions between the sexes such that experience and interpretations of their world can differ significantly from men's? *How can we rethink categories like public and private, productive and reproductive, sex and gender?	Who are the missing minor female authors whose books are unobtainable, whose lives have never been written, and whose works have been studied casually, if at all? How is literature a record of the collective consciousness of patriarchy? What myths and stereotypes about women are present in male literature? How can we critique the meritocratic pretensions of traditional literary history? How can we pair opposite-sex texts in literature as a way of understanding the differences between women's and men's experiences? How is literature one of the expressive modes of a female subculture that developed with the distinction of separate spheres for women and men? *How can feminist literary critics resist establishing their own great canon of literature and any additions to it?	How have the sciences defined (and misdefined) the nature of women? Why are there so few women scientists? What social and psychological forces have kept women in the lower ranks or out of science entirely? How do women fit into the study of the history of science and health care? How do scientific findings, originally carried out on males of a species, change when carried out on the females of the same species? How do the theories and interpretations of sociobiology require constant testing and change to fit the theory for males and females with regard to competition, sexual selection, and infanticide? How do the networks of associations and disjunctions of the science/gender system—between public and private, personal and impersonal, and masculine and feminine—inform each other and affect men and women, science and nature? *What are the structural barriers to women in science?

*New questions generated by feminist scholars.

Women's Curriculum

The most important idea to emerge in women's scholarship is that women's activities, not men's, are the measure of significance. What was formerly devalued—the content of women's everyday lives—assumes new value as scholars investigate female rituals, housework, childbearing, child rearing, sexuality, friendship, and studies of the life cycle. For instance, scientists investigate how research on areas of interest primarily to women—menstruation, childbirth, and menopause—challenge existing scientific theories.

Historians document women's efforts to break out of their traditional sphere of the home in a way that uses women's activities, not men's, as the measure of historical significance. These activities include women's education, paid work, and volunteer work outside the home, particularly in women's clubs and associations. Of equal importance is the development of a collective feminist consciousness, that is, of women's consciousness of their own distinct role in society. Analyses begun in the bifocal phase continue to explore what sex and gender have meant for the majority of women.

As scholars look more closely at the complex patterns of women's lives, they see the need for a pluralistic conceptualization of women. Although thinking of women as a monolithic group provides valuable information about patterns of continuity and change in the areas most central to women's lives, generalizing about a group as vast and diverse as women leads to inaccuracies. The subtle interactions among gender and other variables are investigated. Historians ask how the particulars of race, ethnicity, social class, marital status, and sexual orientation challenge the homogeneity of women's experiences. Third World feminists critique hegemonic "Western" feminisms and formulate autonomous geographically, historically, and culturally grounded feminist concerns and strategies (Mohanty, 2003).

Feminist scholars have helped us see the urgency of probing and analyzing the interactive nature of the oppressions of race, ethnicity, class, and gender (Collins, 2000; Hune & Nomura, 2003; Kesselman, McNair, & Schniedewind, 2002; Ruiz & DuBois, 2000; Saldivar-Hull, 2000). We are reminded that we can no longer take a liberal reformist approach that does not probe the needs of the system that are being satisfied by oppression (Acuña, 2004; Louie & Omatsu, 2001; Shorris, 2001; Weatherford, 1992). We have to take seriously the model of feminist scholarship that analyzes women's status within the social, cultural, historical, political, and economic contexts. Only then will issues of gender be understood in relation to the economic needs of male dominance and capitalism, both of which undergird such oppressions.

Questions about sex and gender are set within historical, ideological, and cultural contexts, including the culture's definition of the facts of biological development and what they mean for individuals. Researchers ask, for example, why these attitudes toward sexuality are prevalent at this time in history. What are the ways in which sexual words, categories, and ideology mirror the organization of society as a whole? What are the socioeconomic factors contributing to them? How do current conceptions of the body reflect social experiences and professional needs?

Life histories and autobiographies shed light on societies' perceptions of women and their perceptions of themselves. Women's individual experiences are revealed through these stories and contribute to the fashioning of the human experience from the perspective of women. Scholars find it necessary to draw on other disciplines for a clearer vision of the social structure and culture of societies as individuals encounter them in their daily life. Likewise, there are calls for new unifying frameworks and different ways to think of periods in history and literature in order to identify concepts that accommodate women's history and traditions. There is also a more complex conceptualization of historical time. The emphasis in much history is on events, units of time too brief to afford a sense of structural change. Structural changes are changes in the way people think about their own reality and the possibilities for other realities. L'Ecole des Annales (1982) in France (a group of historians who pioneered the use of such public records as birth, marriage, and death certificates in historical analysis) has distinguished between events and what they call the *longue durée*. By this, they mean the slow, glacial changes, requiring hundreds of years to complete, that represent significant shifts in the way people think.

Examples of areas of women's history that lend themselves to this concept are the structural change from a male-dominated to an egalitarian perspective and the transformation of women's traditional role in the family to their present roles as wives, mothers, and paid workers outside the home. Also important is the demographic change between 1800 and 1990 in the average number of children per woman of childbearing age from seven to fewer than two (see Table 7.4).

Table 7.4　Women's Curriculum

Characteristics of Phase	Questions Commonly Asked about Women in History	Questions Commonly Asked about Women in Literature	Questions Commonly Asked about Women in Science
Scholarly inquiry pursues new questions, new categories, and new notions of significance that illuminate women's traditions, history, culture, values, visions, and perspectives. A pluralistic conception of women emerges that acknowledges diversity and recognizes that variables besides gender shape women's lives—for example, race, ethnicity, and social class. Women's experience is allowed to speak for itself. Feminist history is rooted in the personal and the specific; it builds from that to the general. The public and the private are seen as a continuum in women's experiences. Women's experience is analyzed within the social, cultural, historical, political, and economic contexts. Efforts are made to reconceptualize knowledge to encompass the female experience. The conceptualization of knowledge is not characterized by disciplinary thinking but becomes multidisciplinary.	What were the majority of women doing at a particular time in history? What was the significance of these activities? How can female friendships between kin, mothers, daughters, and friends be analyzed as one aspect of women's overall relations with others? What kind of productive work, paid and unpaid, did women do and under what conditions? What were the reproductive activities of women? How did they reproduce the American family? How did the variables of race, ethnicity, social class, marital status, and sexual preference affect women's experience? What new categories need to be added to the study of history, for instance, romance, housework, childbearing, and child rearing? How have women of different races and classes interacted throughout history? What are appropriate ways of organizing or periodizing women's history? For example, how will examining women's experiences at each stage of the life span help us to understand women's experiences on their own terms?	What does the concept of a women's sphere—for example, domesticity and family, education, marriage, sexuality, and love—reveal about our culture? How can we contrast the fictional image of women in literature with the complexity and variety of the roles of individual women in real life as workers, housewives, revolutionaries, mothers, lovers, and so on? How do the particulars of race, ethnicity, social class, marital status, and sexual orientation, as revealed in literature, challenge the thematic homogeneity of women's experiences? How does literature portray what binds women together and what separates them because of race, ethnicity, social class, marital status, and sexual orientation? How does the social and historical context of a work of literature shed light on it?	How do the cultural dualisms associated with masculinity and femininity permeate scientific thought and discourse? How do women's actual experiences, as compared to the physician's analysis or scientific theory, challenge the traditional paradigms of science and of health care systems? How does research on areas of primary interest to women, for instance, menopause, childbirth, and menstruation/estrus, challenge existing scientific theories? How do variables other than sex and gender, such as age, species, and individual variation, challenge current theories? How do the experiences of female primates and the variation among species of primates—for example, competition among females, female agency in sexuality, and infanticide—test the traditional paradigms?

Gender-Balanced Curriculum

This phase continues many of the inquiries begun in the women's curriculum phase, but it also articulates questions about how women and men relate to and complement one another. Conscious of the limitations of seeing women in isolation and aware of the relational character of gender, researchers search for the nodal points at which women's and men's experiences intersect. Historians and literary critics ask whether the private, as well as the public, aspects of life are presented as a continuum in women's and men's experience.

The pluralistic and multifocal conception of women that emerged in the women's curriculum phase is extended to human beings. A central idea in this phase is *positionality* (Alcoff, 2003; Haraway, 1997; Harding, 2004), which means that important aspects of our identity (for example, our gender, race, class, and age) are markers of relational positions rather than essential qualities. Their effects and implications change according to context. Recently, feminist thinkers have seen knowledge as valid when it comes from an acknowledgment that the knower's specific position in any context is always defined by gender, race, class, and other variables (Code, 1991). Drawing on the latest science and scholarship, some scholars argue that race and ethnicity are not things that people or groups have or are, but rather sets of actions that people do (Moya & Marcus, 2010).

Scientists ask explicit questions about the invention and reinvention of nature. For example, they ask questions about the meanings of the behavior and social lives of monkeys and apes and male–female relations in animals and inquire about how such variables as age, species, and individual variation challenge current theories. They also explore contemporary technoscience—its stories and dreams, its facts and delusions, its institutions and politics, and its scientific advances (Haraway, 1991, 1997).

Accompanying this particularistic perspective is attention to the larger context, for example, the interplay among situation, meaning, economic systems, family organization, and political systems. Thus, historians ask how gender inequities are linked to economics, family organization, marriage, ritual, and politics. Research scientists probe how differences between the male and female body have been used to justify a social agenda that privileges men economically, socially, and politically. In this phase, a revolutionary relationship comes to exist between those things traditionally treated as serious, primarily the activities of men in the public sphere, and those things formerly perceived as trivial, namely, the activities of women in the private sphere.

This new relationship leads to a recentering of knowledge in the disciplines, a shift from a male-centered perspective to one that includes both females and males. Studying the dynamics of gender sheds light on masculinity and the implications of gender studies for men. The new field of men's studies investigates the origins, structures, and dynamics of masculinity (Kimmel, Hearn, & Connell, 2005). Men's studies investigates how men can participate in feminism as full and equal partners, respecting gender differences while sharing a common vision with women for an oppression-free future (Schacht & Ewing, 2007). This reconceptualization of knowledge from a feminist perspective works toward a more holistic view of the human experience.

Feminist scholars have cautioned against moving too quickly from a women's curriculum to a gender-balanced curriculum. As the historian Gerda Lerner (1979) observed, our decade-and-a-half-old investigation of women's history is only a speck on the horizon compared to the centuries-old tradition of male-defined history. By turning too quickly to studies of gender, we risk short-circuiting important directions in women's studies and again having women's history and experiences subsumed under those of men. It remains politically important for feminists to defend women as women in order to counteract the male domination that continues to exist. The French philosopher Kristeva (cited in Moi, 1985) and, more recently, Butler (2004) push us to new considerations when they urge women (and men) to recognize the falsifying nature of masculinity and femininity, to explore how the fact of being born male or female determines one's position in relation to power, and to envision more fluid gender identities that have the potential to liberate both women and men to a fuller personhood (see Table 7.5). Of particular interest to teachers is the work of Thorne (1993), who draws on her daily observations in the classroom and on the playground to show how children construct gender and experience gender in the school.

Table 7.5   Gender-Balanced Curriculum

Characteristics of Phase	Questions Commonly Asked about Women in History	Questions Commonly Asked about Women in Literature	Questions Commonly Asked about Women in Science
A multifocal, gender-balanced perspective is sought that weaves together women's and men's experiences into multilayered composites of human experience. At this stage, scholars are conscious of positionality.	What is the knower's specific position in this historical context?	How does the author's specific position, as defined by gender, race, and class, affect this literary work?	What explicit questions need to be raised about the invention and reinvention of nature? What is the meaning of male–female relations in animals?
Positionality represents the insight that all women and men are located in historical contexts—contexts defined in terms of race, class, culture, and age as well as gender—and that they gain their knowledge and their power from the specifics of their situations.	How is gender asymmetry linked to economic systems, family organizations, marriage, ritual, and political systems?	How can we validate the full range of human expression by selecting literature according to its insight into any aspect of human experience rather than according to how it measures up to a predetermined canon?	How do variables such as age, species, and individual variation challenge current theories?
Scholars begin to define what binds together and what separates the various segments of humanity.	How can we compare women and men in all aspects of their lives to reveal gender as a crucial historical determinant?	Is the private as well as the public sphere presented as a continuum in women's and men's experiences?	What are the limits to generalizing beyond the data collected on limited samples to other genders, species, and conditions not sampled in the experimental protocol?
Scholars have a deepened understanding of how both the private and the public form a continuum in individual experience. They search for the nodal points at which comparative treatment of men's and women's experience is possible.	Are the private as well as the public aspects of history presented as a continuum in women's and men's experiences?	How can we pair opposite-sex texts in literature as a way of understanding how female and male characters experience "maleness" and "femaleness" as a continuum of "humanness"?	How have sex differences been used to assign men and women to particular roles in the social hierarchy?
Efforts are made to reconceptualize knowledge to reflect this multilayered composite of women's and men's experience. The conceptualization of knowledge is not characterized by disciplinary thinking but becomes multidisciplinary.	How is gender a social construction? What does the particular construction of gender in a society tell us about the society that so constructed gender?	How do the variables of race, ethnicity, social class, marital status, and sexual orientation affect the experience of female and male literary characters?	How have differences between the male and female body been used to justify a social agenda that privileges men economically, socially, and politically?
	What is the intricate relation between the construction of gender and the structure of power?	How can we rethink the concept of periodicity to accentuate the continuity of life and to contain the multitude of previously ignored literary works, for example, instead of Puritanism, the contexts for and consequences of sexuality?	
	How can we expand our conceptualization of historical time to a pluralistic one that conceives of three levels of history: structures, trends, and events?	How can we deconstruct the opposition between masculinity and femininity?	
	How can we unify approaches and types of knowledge of all social sciences and history as a means of investigating specific problems in relational history?		

Changes in Traditional Ways of Teaching

Feminist scholarship has helped us understand that all knowledge, and therefore all classroom knowledge, is a social construction. This insight affirms the evolving nature of knowledge and the role of teachers and students in its ongoing construction. For me, the term *pedagogy* applies not just to teaching techniques but also to the whole classroom production of knowledge; it encompasses the full range of relationships among course materials, teachers, and students. Such broadened conceptualizations of pedagogy challenge the commonly held assumptions of the professor as a disinterested expert, the content as inherently "objective," and the method of delivery as irrelevant to the message (hooks, 1994). To educate students for a complex, multicultural, multiracial world, we need to include the perspectives and voices of those who have not been traditionally included—women of all backgrounds, people of color, and females and males who perceive their education as not made for them. The anthropologist Renato Rosaldo (1994) has captured well how diverse classrooms contribute to new constructions of knowledge and change relationships among teachers and students:

> The question before us now is . . . how to teach more effectively in changed classroom environments. The new classrooms are not like the old ones. . . . In diverse classrooms, the question of "The Other" begins to dissolve. Who gets to be the we and who gets to be the other rotates from one day to the next, depending on the topic of discussion. And before long the stable us/them dividing line evaporates into a larger mix of differences and solidarity. (p. 405)

Feminist teachers are demonstrating how they transform courses through their attention to cultural, ethnic, and gender diversity and give concrete form to the complexity of the struggles over knowledge, access, and power (hooks, 1994; Maher & Tetreault, 1994, 2001; Weiler, 1988). In *The Feminist Classroom*, Maher and I (Maher & Tetreault, 2001) show how all students may benefit from, and how some are even inspired by, college courses transformed by their professor's attention to cultural, ethnic, and gender diversity. We have found that the themes we used to analyze teaching and learning in 17 classrooms on six campuses across the country apply to elementary and secondary classrooms as well. The four themes—*mastery, authority, voice*, and *positionality*— all relate to issues present in today's classroom. Although all four deal with reconstituted relationships between new students and new disciplinary frameworks, the themes of mastery and authority focus on knowledge and its sources as well as on the voice and positionality of the students themselves.

Mastery has traditionally meant the goal of an individual student's rational comprehension of the material on the teacher's and expert's terms. Women (and other marginalized groups) must often give up their voices when they seek mastery on the terms of the dominant culture. We found classrooms undergoing a shift away from unidimensional sources of expertise to a multiplicity of new information and insights. Students were no longer mastering a specific body of material, nor were they emphasizing subjective experiences that risk excluding students from a wealth of knowledge. Rather, they were struggling through or integrating often widely various interpretations of texts, scientific research, and social problems. These teachers redefined mastery as interpretation, as increasingly sophisticated handling of the topics at hand, informed by but not limited to the students' links to the material from their own experience. For example, a Japanese American student reread an Emily Dickinson poem about silences and invisibilities to comment on her gender and ethnic marginality:

> I couldn't help thinking of the idea of a mute culture within a dominant culture. A "nobody" knowing she's different from the dominant culture keeps silent. . . . But to be somebody! How dreary! How public! So when you become a somebody and buy into the dominant culture, you have to live in their roles. A silly example: It's like watching a Walt Disney movie as a child where Hayley Mills and these other girls dance and primp before a party singing "Femininity," how being a woman is all about looking pretty and smiling pretty and acting stupid to attract men. As a child I ate it up, at

least it seemed benign. But once your eye gets put out and you realize how this vision has warped you, it would split your heart to try and believe that again, it would strike you dead.

(Maher & Tetreault, 1994, pp. 104–105)

Students were stretched by such broadenings of interpretative frameworks and indeed became authorities for one another. A White male student in the same class said:

I could read Dickinson a thousand times and probably never try to relate to that because it just would never make an impression on me, but having the girls in that class interested in that particular topic, "How does that relate to me as a woman?" then I sit back and I think that's a really good question. Although I'm male I can learn how women react to women's texts as opposed to maybe the way I react to it or the teacher reacts to it.

(Maher & Tetreault, 1994, p. 108)

The teachers in our study consciously used their *authority* to give students responsibility for their own learning (Finke, 1993). Students and professors became authorities for one another to the extent that they were explicit about themselves as social and political actors with respect to a text or an issue (Tetreault, 1991). The teachers also struggled with reconceptualizing the grounds for their own authority, both over the subject matter and with students, because their traditional positions as the sole representatives of expertise were called into question by these multiple new sources of knowledge. These professors shared a sense of their authority as being grounded in their own experiences and in their intellectual engagement with feminist scholarship and other relevant fields.

As important as the rethinking of the disciplines is the power of expression that these new forms of knowledge, coming from the students' questions as well as from new topics, give to women and to other previously silenced groups. We explored the effects on students through our theme of *voice*, which is frequently defined as the awakening of the students' own responses. However, we came to think of these classrooms as arenas where teachers and students fashion their voices rather than "find" them as they produce relevant experiences to shape a narrative of an emerging self.

Our fourth theme is *positionality*, which is defined in the section on gender-balanced curriculum. Positionality helps us to see the multiple ways in which the complex dynamics of difference and inequality, which come from outside society, also operate powerfully inside the classroom itself. Much of our emphasis in the past three decades has been on the consequences of sexism and racism on females and on students of color. We have learned much about how universalizing the position of maleness leads to intellectual domination.

Some educators and theorists argue that we need to become conscious in similar ways about the effects of universalizing the position of Whiteness (Frankenberg, 1993, 1997; McIntosh, 1990; Morrison, 1993; Tatum, 1997). For example, how does the norm of Whiteness or maleness shape the construction of knowledge in classrooms? How do those assumptions contribute to the intellectual domination of groups? Why is it that when we think of the development of racial identity in our students, we think primarily of students of color rather than of White students? What happens in classrooms where Whiteness is marked, revealed as a position? In our culture, the presumptions of Whiteness or maleness act to constrict voice by universalizing the dominant positions, by letting them float free of "position."

Maher and I revisited data presented in *The Feminist Classroom* to examine how assumptions of Whiteness shape the construction of knowledge as it is produced and resisted in the classroom (Maher & Tetreault, 1997). We saw how the dominant voices continue to call the tune—that is, to maintain the conceptual and ideological frameworks through which suppressed voices are distorted or not fully heard. We saw more clearly the ways in which a thorough pedagogy of positionality must entail an excavation of Whiteness in its many dimensions and complexities. Understanding all of the ways in which positionality shapes learning is a long, interactive process.

The lessons that follow attempt to model teaching that is constructed to reveal the particular and the common denominators of human experience. These sample lessons are organized by the subject areas of language arts, science, and social studies, but they can be adapted to other subject areas as well.

Sample Lessons

Language Arts

Analyzing Children's Literature

Suggested Activities

Ask students to locate five of their favorite children's books, to reread them, and to keep a written record of their reactions to the books. On a sheet of newsprint, keep a record of the students' (and your) book choices. Divide the class into small groups according to the same or similar favorite books and have students share their written reactions to the books. Ask the groups to keep a record of the most noteworthy ideas that emerge from their small-group discussions. When you bring the small groups together, ask each group to present its noteworthy ideas. Ideas that emerge may be how differently they read the book now than at the time of their first reading, the differences and similarities in so-called girls' books and boys' books, the importance of multicultural or international perspectives, and what the stories reveal about the culture in which the stories are set. A follow-up activity could be to interview grandparents, parents, teachers, and other adults about characters and stories they remember from childhood. Questions to ask include these: How do they recall feeling about those stories? Have images of female and male behavior or expectations in children's stories changed? Is race or ethnicity treated similarly or differently?

Pairing Female and Male Autobiographies

Suggested Activities

Pairings of autobiographies and fiction by male and female authors can contribute greatly to students' multifocal, relational understanding of the human experience. Two pairings I have found to be particularly illuminating are *Black Boy,* by Richard Wright (1945/2000), and *Woman Warrior,* by Maxine Hong Kingston (1976). Other interesting pairings are Maya Angelou's (1969) *I Know Why the Caged Bird Sings* and Mark Twain's (1912/1985) *The Adventures of Huckleberry Finn*; *The Autobiography of Frederick Douglass* (Douglass, 1855/1994) and *Incidents in the Life of a Slave Girl* (Jacobs, 1861/1988); *The Adventures of Tom Sawyer* (Twain, 1910/1996) and *Little Women* (Alcott, 1880/1995).

Dorothy Berkson, a professor we observed at Lewis and Clark College, used teaching logs to demystify the process of interpretation by linking the students' emotional connections to texts with their intellectual analysis. She asked her students to select a passage that puzzled or engaged them or triggered a strong emotional reaction. Believing that some of the best criticism starts with such reactions, she asked the students next to paraphrase the passage they had chosen in order to understand what it means, or, in a sense, to master it (Maher & Tetreault, 1994, p. 249–250).

Students were then asked to look at the passage again to become conscious of what cannot be captured by paraphrase as well as any concerns or questions that escaped them before. Finally, they placed the passage in the context of the entire text, using the following questions: Where does it happen? Are there other passages that relate to it? That contradict it? That confirm it? That raise more questions about it? After students wrote a summary of where this procedure had taken them, they turned in these logs at the end of each class. Returned to the students with Berkson's comments, the logs then became the basis for the students' formal paper. This process forces students to reengage with the text over and over and to engage in continuous reinterpretation of the text rather than to think they have arrived at some final mastery.

Science

Fear of Science: Fact or Fantasy?

Suggested Activities

Fear of science and math and the stereotyping of scientists contribute to the limited participation of some students, most often female, in math and science classes. Their inadequate participation precludes their choosing most undergraduate majors that depend on a minimum of three years of high school mathematics. In *Aptitude Revisited: Rethinking Math and Science Education for America's Next Century*, Drew (1996) argues that the people least encouraged to study mathematics and science in our society are those who have the least power—especially students from poverty, minority students, and young women. Policy makers, teachers, and even parents often steer certain students away from math and science for completely erroneous reasons. The result, Drew contends, is not simply an inadequately trained workforce; this educational discrepancy is widening the gap between the haves and the have-nots in our society. He challenges the conventional view that science and math are too boring or too hard for many students, arguing that virtually all students are capable of mastering these subjects.

The following exercise was designed by the Math and Science Education for Women Project at the Lawrence Hall of Science, University of California at Berkeley (Fraser, 1982). The purpose of the exercise is to decrease female and male students' fear of science by enabling them to function as researchers who define the problem and generate solutions to it.

Ask students to complete the following sentence by writing for about 15 minutes: "When I think about science, I . . ." When they have finished, divide students into groups of five or six to discuss their responses to the cue. Ask each group to state the most important things it has learned. Discuss fear of science with the class and whether there is a difference in how girls and boys feel about science. What could be some reasons for these differences or similarities? When the findings from this exercise are clear, suggest to students that they broaden their research to include other students and teachers in the school. Have each group brainstorm questions that might appear on a questionnaire about attitudes toward science. Put the questions on a sheet of newsprint. Analyze the questions and decide on the ten best.

Decide with the class what group of students and teachers you will research and how you will do it (for example, other science classes, all ninth-grade science classes, or the entire school during second period). Obtain permission to conduct the survey from the administration and other teachers or classes involved in your research project. Have the class complete the survey or questionnaire as a pilot activity. Analyze the questions for gender differences and make minor revisions before giving the survey and questionnaire to your research group.

Distribute the survey or conduct interviews. Have the students decide how to analyze the information. Let each group decide how it will display findings and information. Current statistics about male and female scientists in biology, chemistry, physics, and other sciences can be found via the National Science Foundation (n.d.). Other valuable resources are *Re-Engineering Female Friendly Science* (Rosser, 1997) and *Women, Gender and Technology* (Fox, Johnson, & Rosser, 2006).

Have each group give (1) a report to the class on what it found, using graph displays to convey the information, and (2) recommendations for decreasing science anxiety in the school. Place the entire student research project in the school library, main office, or gymnasium, where the rest of the school population can see the results. Have a student summarize the project and write an article for the school paper.

Doing Science

Suggested Activities

Keller's (1983) biography of Barbara McClintoch, *A Feeling for the Organism*, allows students to explore the conditions under which dissent in science arises, the function it serves, and the plurality of values and goals it reflects. Questions her story prompts include these: What role do interests—individual and collective—play in the evolution of scientific knowledge? Do all scientists seek the same kinds of explanations? Are the kinds of questions they ask the same? Do differences in methodology between different subdisciplines ever permit the same kinds of answers? Do female and male scientists approach their research differently? This book is difficult reading for high school and college students, but it is manageable if they read carefully and thoroughly. The best way I have found to help them manage is to ask them to read a chapter or section and to come to class with their questions about the reading and to propose some answers.

Social Studies

My Family's Work History

Suggested Activities

Women and men of different social classes, ethnic groups, and geographic locations have done various kinds of work inside and outside their homes in agricultural, industrial, and postindustrial economies. Before introducing students to the history of work, I pique their interest by asking them to complete a Family Work Chart (see Table 7.6). When their charts are complete, the students and I build a work chronology from 1890 to the present. Our work chronology contains information gleaned from the textbook and library sources about important inventions, laws, demographics, and labor history.

I then reproduce the work chronology on a chart so they can compare their family's history with key historical events. By seeing their families' histories alongside major events in our collective work history, students can see how their family was related to society. A sample of items from our chart includes: in 1890, women are 17 percent of the paid labor force; in 1915, the telephone connects New York and San Francisco; and in 1924, immigration was restricted (Chapman, 1979). Students conclude this unit by writing about a major theme in their family's work history. They might focus on how the lives of the women in the family differed from the lives of the men. They might focus on how their family's race or ethnicity shaped their work history.

Integrating the Public and Private Spheres

Suggested Activities

Human life is lived in both the public and the private spheres in wartime as well as in peacetime. By asking students to consciously examine individuals' lives as citizens, workers, family members, friends, members of social groups, and individuals, they learn more about the interaction of these roles in both spheres. Wartime is an extraordinary period, when the nation's underlying assumptions about these roles are often put to the test. By having students examine the interaction of these roles in wartime, they can see some of our underlying assumptions about the roles and how they are manipulated for the purposes of war. Through researching the histories of their families and by reading primary source accounts, viewing films, and reading their textbook, they will see the complexity and variety of human experiences in the United States during World War II.

Students research their family's history during World War II by gathering family documents and artifacts. They may also interview relatives about family stories that have passed down through the generations about what life was life for their family during World War II. Students determine questions beforehand to find out how the war affected members of their family. During the two weeks they are researching their family's history, they spend two class

Table 7.6 Family Work Chart

	Work Experience			
			AFTER MARRIAGE	
	YEAR OF BIRTH	BEFORE MARRIAGE	WHILE CHILDREN WERE YOUNG	WHEN CHILDREN WERE GROWN
Your maternal side				
Mother				
Grandmother				
Grandfather				
Great-grandmother				
Great-grandfather				
Great-great-grandmother				
Great-great-grandfather				
Your paternal side				
Father				
Grandmother				
Grandfather				
Great-grandmother				
Great-grandfather				
Great-great-grandmother				
Great-great-grandfather				

Source: This activity was developed by Carol Frenier. Reprinted with permission from the Education Development Center from Adeline Naiman, Project Director, *Sally Garcia and Family Resource Guide*, Unit 3 of *The Role of Women in American Society* (Newton, MA: Education Development Center, Inc., 1978), p. 62.

Historical Events		Your Family History
1890	Women are 17 percent of the paid labor force	
1915	Telephone connects New York and San Francisco	
1924	Restriction of immigration	

periods on this project. During the first period, students give oral reports to a small group of fellow students in read-around groups.

Appropriate readings and films on World War II are widely available. Terkel's (1984) *The Good War* is particularly useful because of the variety of people the author interviewed. For instance, students can read about the internment of Japanese Americans and can role-play an account they read. Their textbook may provide good background information. A moving personal account of internment is *Desert Exile: The Uprooting of a Japanese-American Family*

(Uchida, 1982). My students answer two questions in this unit: World War II has been described as a "good war." From the materials you have examined, was it a good war for the lives of individuals as citizens, workers, family members, friends, and members of social groups? How were their experiences similar to or different from those of your relatives?

Summary

This chapter has illustrated how women's studies is challenging male domination of curricular content. The evolution of that challenge is illuminated by understanding the different emphases that coexist in male-defined, contribution, bifocal, women's, and gender-balanced curricula. We now have a conceptual framework for a curriculum that interweaves issues of gender with ethnicity, culture, and class. This framework acknowledges and celebrates a multifocal, relational view of the human experience.

The idea of the phases of feminist scholarship as a series of intersecting circles, or patches on a quilt, or threads on a tapestry suggests parallel ways to think about a class of students. Each student brings to your classroom a particular positionality that shapes his or her way of knowing. Your challenge as a teacher is to interweave the individual truths with course content into complex understandings that legitimize students' voices.

With the authority of the school behind it, this relational knowledge has the potential to help students analyze their own social, cultural, historical, political, and economic contexts. The goal of relational knowledge is to build a world in which the oppressions of race, gender, and class—on which capitalism and patriarchy depend—are challenged by critical citizens in a democratic society.

QUESTIONS AND ACTIVITIES

7.1   What is a gender-balanced, multicultural curriculum?

7.2   What is feminist phase theory?

7.3.   Define and give an example of each of the following phases of the feminist phase theory developed and described in the chapter: (a) male-defined curriculum, (b) contribution curriculum, (c) bifocal curriculum, (d) women's curriculum, and (e) gender-balanced curriculum.

7.4   What problems do the contribution and bifocal phases have? How do the women's curriculum and gender-balanced curriculum phases help solve these problems?

7.5   The chapter states that "knowledge is a social construction." What does this mean? In what ways is the new scholarship on women and on ethnic groups alike? In what ways does the new scholarship on women and on ethnic groups challenge the dominant knowledge established in society and presented in textbooks? Give examples.

7.6   Examine the treatment of women in a sample of social studies, language arts, mathematics, or science textbooks (or a combination of two types of textbooks). Which phases or phase of the feminist phase theory presented in the chapter best describe(s) the treatment of women in the textbooks you examined?

7.7   What is the *longue durée?* Why is it important in the study of social history, particularly women's history?

7.8   Research your family history, paying particular attention to the roles, careers, and influence of women in your family's saga. Also describe your ethnic heritage and its influence on your family's past and present. Share your family history with a group of your classmates or workshop participants.

REFERENCES

Acuña, R. (2004). *Occupied America: A history of Chicanos* (5th ed.). Upper Saddle River, NJ: Pearson Education.

Alcoff, L. (2003). *Identities: Race, class, gender and nationality*. London: Blackwell.

Alcott, L. M. (1995). *Little women*. New York: Scholastic. (Original work published 1880)

Angelou, M. (1969). *I know why the caged bird sings*. New York: Bantam.

Atkinson, J. M. (1982). Review essay, anthropology. *Signs, 8,* 250–251.

Butler, J. (1993). *Bodies that matter: On the discursive limits of "sex."* New York: Routledge.

Butler, J. (2004). *Undoing gender.* New York: Routledge.

Chapman, A. E. (Ed.). (1979). *Approaches to women's history: A resource book and teaching guide.* Washington, DC: American Historical Association.

Christian, B. (1980). *Black women novelists: The development of a tradition, 1892–1976.* Westport, CT: Greenwood.

Code, L. (1991). *What can she know? Feminist theory and the construction of knowledge.* Ithaca, NY: Cornell University Press.

Collins, P. H. (2000). *Black feminist thought: Knowledge, consciousness, and the politics of empowerment.* New York: Routledge.

Douglass, F. (1994). *The autobiography of Frederick Douglass.* New York: Penguin. (Original work published 1855)

Drew, D. E. (1996). *Aptitude revisited: Rethinking math and science education for America's next century.* Baltimore, MD: John Hopkins University Press.

Finke, L. (1993). Knowledge as bait: Feminism, voice, and the pedagogical unconscious. *College English, 55*(1), 7–27.

Fox, M. F., Johnson, D., & Rosser, S. (Eds.). (2006). *Women, gender and technology.* Champaign–Urbana: University of Illinois Press.

Frankenberg, R. (1993). *White women, race matters: The social construction of Whiteness.* Minneapolis: University of Minnesota Press.

Frankenberg, R. (Ed.). (1997). *Displacing Whiteness: Essays in social and cultural criticism.* Durham, NC: Duke University Press.

Fraser, S. (1982). *Spaces: Solving problems of access to careers in engineering and science.* Berkeley: University of California Press.

Goldberger, N., Tarule, J., Clinchy, B., & Belenky, M. (Eds.). (1996). *Knowledge, difference, and power: Essays inspired by women's ways of knowing.* New York: Basic Books.

Gornick, V., & Moran, B. (Eds.). (1971). *Woman in sexist society.* New York: Basic Books.

Haraway, D. J. (1991). *Simians, cyborgs, and women: The reinvention of nature.* New York: Routledge.

Haraway, D. J. (1997). *Modest-witness@second-millennium. FemaleMan_meets_oncoMouse: Feminism and technoscience.* New York: Routledge.

Harding, S. G. (Ed.). (2004). *The feminist standpoint theory reader: Intellectual and political controversies.* New York: Routledge.

hooks, b. (1994). *Teaching to transgress: Education as the practice of freedom.* New York: Routledge.

Hune, S., & Nomura, G. (2003). *Asian/Pacific Islander American women: A historical anthology.* New York: New York University Press.

Jacobs, H. (1988). *Incidents in the life of a slave girl.* New York: Oxford University Press. (Original work published 1861)

Keller, E. (1983). *A feeling for the organism.* San Francisco: Freeman.

Kesselman, A., McNair, L., & Schniedewind, N. (2002). *Women: Images and realities, a multicultural anthology* (3rd ed.). New York: McGraw-Hill.

Kimmel, M., Hearn, J., & Connell, R. W. (2005). *Handbook of studies on men and masculinities.* Thousand Oaks, CA: Rowman & Littlefield.

Kingston, M. H. (1976). *Woman warrior.* New York: Knopf.

Lerner, G. (1979). *The majority finds its past.* New York: Oxford University Press.

L'Ecole des Annales. (1982). Letters to the editor. *Social Education, 46*(6), 378–380.

Louie, S., & Omatsu, G. (2001). *Asian Americans: The movement and the moment.* Los Angeles: Asian American Studies Center.

Maher, F., & Tetreault, M. K. (1994). *The feminist classroom.* New York: Basic Books.

Maher, F., & Tetreault, M. K. (1997). Learning in the dark: How assumptions of Whiteness shape classroom knowledge. *Harvard Educational Review, 67*(2), 321–349.

Maher, F., & Tetreault, M. K. (2001). *The feminist classroom* (2nd ed.). New York: Rowman & Littlefield.

McIntosh, P. (1990). White privilege and male privilege: A personal account of coming to see correspondences through work in women's studies. In M. L. Andersen & P. J. Collins (Eds.), *Race, class, and gender: An anthology* (pp. 70–81). Boston: Wadsworth.

Millett, K. (1970). *Sexual politics.* Garden City, NY: Doubleday.

Mohanty, C. (2003). *Feminism without borders: Decolonizing theory, practicing solidarity.* Durham, NC: Duke University Press.

Moi, T. (1985). *Sexual/textual politics: Feminist literary theory.* New York: Methuen.

Morrison, T. (1993). *Playing in the dark: Whiteness and the literary imagination.* New York: Vintage.

Moya, P., & Marcus, H. R. (2010). *Doing race: 21 essays for the 21st century.* New York: Norton.

National Science Foundation. (n.d.). Science and engineering statistics Web site. Retrieved on October 27, 2006, from www.nsf.gov/sbe/srs/seind98/start.htm.

Rosaldo, R. (1994). Cultural citizenship and educational democracy. *Cultural Anthropology, 9*(3), 402–411.

Rosaldo, S., & Lamphere, L. (1974). *Woman, culture, and society.* Stanford, CA: Stanford University Press.

Rosser, S. V. (1997). *Re-engineering female friendly science.* New York: Teachers College Press.

Ruiz, V. L., & DuBois, E. (Eds.). (2000). *Unequal sisters: A multicultural reader in U.S. women's history* (3rd ed.). New York: Routledge.

Saldivar-Hull, S. (2000). *Feminism on the border: Chicana gender politics and literature.* Berkeley: University of California Press.

Schacht, S., & Ewing, D. (2007). *Feminism with men: Bridging the gender gap.* New York: Rowman & Littlefield.

Schmitz, B., Butler, J. E., Guy-Sheftall, B., & Rosenfelt, D. (2004). Women's studies and curriculum transformation in the United States. In J. A. Banks & C. A. M. Banks (Eds.), *Handbook of research on multicultural education* (2nd ed., pp. 882–905). San Francisco: Jossey-Bass.

Shorris, E. (2001). *Latinos: A biography of the people.* New York: Norton.

Showalter, E. (1977). *A literature of their own*. Princeton, NJ: Princeton University Press.

Smith, E. (2003). *Mary McLeod Bethune and the National Council of Negro Women: Pursuing a true and unfettered democracy*. Montgomery: Alabama State University.

Tatum, B. (1997). *"Why are all the Black kids sitting together in the cafeteria?" and other conversations about race*. New York: Basic Books.

Terkel, S. (1984). *The good war: An oral history of World War II*. New York: Pantheon.

Tetreault, C. (1991). *Metacommunication in a women's studies classroom*. Unpublished senior honors thesis, Vassar College, Poughkeepsie, NY.

Tetreault, M. K. T. (1986). Integrating women's history: The case of United States history textbooks. *History Teacher, 19*(2), 211–262.

Thorne, B. (1993). *Gender play: Girls and boys in school*. New Brunswick, NJ: Rutgers University Press.

Twain, M. (1985). *The adventures of Huckleberry Finn*. New York: Collier. (Original work published 1912)

Twain, M. (1996). *The adventures of Tom Sawyer*. New York: Oxford University Press. (Original work published 1910)

Uchida, Y. (1982). *Desert exile: The uprooting of a Japanese-American family*. Seattle: University of Washington Press.

Weatherford, J. M. (1992). *Native roots: How the Indians enriched America*. New York: Fawcett Columbine.

Weiler, K. (1988). *Women teaching for change: Gender, class, and power*. South Hadley, MA: Bergin & Garvey.

Wright, R. (2000). *Black boy*. New York: Harper & Brothers. (Original work published 1945)

Christopher Futcher/Getty Images, Inc.

Understanding and Supporting Gender Equity in Schools

Diane S. Pollard

Equity is usually defined as fair and equal treatment among groups. Gender equity is often assumed to be fair and equal treatment between girls and boys and men and women. However, gender equity can also mean the attainment of equal outcomes for females and males even if the treatment required to obtain those outcomes is different. In homogeneous societies, it may be possible to discuss gender equity as a single issue. However, in heterogeneous, multicultural societies, inequities often exist around race and ethnicity as well as gender. In the past, researchers and practitioners often treated equity issues as either–or situations; that is, as if one could be discriminated against on the basis of either gender or race/ethnicity. Furthermore, efforts to overcome or compensate for past or present discrimination or inequalities were often treated in the same manner. For example, in the 1970s and 1980s, it was not unusual to see attempts to increase diversity in education or workplaces described as outreach to women *or* minorities, as if these two groups were mutually exclusive. The categorization of women and minorities as separate and distinct groups ignores the reality that many of us are members of both categories, not to mention others, such as those related to our disabilities, sexualities, and socioeconomic statuses. Furthermore, the ways in which others treat us as well as the ways in which we perceive and cope with our realities are related not only to our gender but also to the positions we occupy with respect to race or ethnicity, disability status, sexuality, and other statuses.

Discussions of gender equity have undergone major changes during the past 30 years. Some perspectives viewed the relationship between gender and other statuses such as race as additive. That is, if a person was both female and African American, it was assumed she was subject to twice as much discrimination as a White woman. Following this logic, a woman who was Latina and disabled might expect triple jeopardy. However, it has become evident that this additive perspective is simplistic. Instead, the experiences of an African American woman might be different from those of a White or Latina woman. Furthermore, an African American woman with a disability might, in turn, have her own unique experiences. This view focuses on ways in which various statuses intersect to shape experience.

This focus reflects changes in conceptions of gender and gender equity that are related to a greater understanding of the complexities of gender as it intersects with other statuses such as race, ethnicity, disability, and sexuality. This more complex perspective on gender equity is particularly relevant to multicultural societies where individuals from various sociocultural groups interact. All cultures organize their members by gender, and there are some commonalities around gender that can be found across cultures. However, some of the ways in which gender is conceptualized and implemented vary not only from one cultural group to another but also within groups. This chapter focuses on issues of gender equity as it is conceptualized and implemented among diverse populations, particularly in the United States. In addition, this chapter discusses the implications of these various conceptualizations of gender equity for education and suggests strategies educators can use to support gender equity among diverse student populations.

Evolution of Thinking about Gender Equity

In the past, discussions about gender equity focused on obtaining equality in treatment and outcomes for women and girls. During the 1970s and 1980s as well as into the 1990s, there was considerable discussion of gender equity, especially in education. Much of this work was characterized as women's equity because it concerned obtaining equal access and treatment for women and girls in schools as well as in the workplace. In addition, much—although not all—of the impetus for this push for women's equity came from White women. During this time, major accomplishments were made in obtaining access to educational and work opportunities for women. However, it was often assumed that the issues and arguments raised were of similar concern to all women and girls regardless of their racial or ethnic background or other status indicators such as disability and sexuality. It is true that there are some issues around gender equity that transcend sociocultural and other background status characteristics—such as having equality in access to schooling and work opportunities and demanding equal resources in classrooms and work sites. However, individuals from non-White groups began to question the assumption that all of the issues raised by White women were equally relevant across diverse populations. In addition, differential treatment between women of color and White women persisted. Furthermore, the focus on women did not take into account the idea that some men, particularly men of color, were also the victims of inequities related to gender.

One early line of questioning came from African American women. For example, the sociologist Patricia Hill Collins (1990) argued that Black women's unique history of subjugation and marginalization in the United States as a result of slavery and continuing racial discrimination led them to hold a different perspective on gender and gender equity than did White women. For example, according to Collins, because Black women had to contend with both male domination and White domination, they were subject to oppression from White women as well as both White and African American men and had to constantly struggle against both. In addition, it has been argued that African American women have had to fight against negative stereotypes and denigrating images that continue to be perpetrated in American society (Oesterreich, 2007).

In addition to African Americans, women of other ethnic groups also began to question the assumption that gender equity had the same meanings and emphases across cultures. Latina, Asian and Pacific Islander, and Native American women wrote about the ways in which their perspectives on gender and gender equity were shaped by their cultural origins. Furthermore, as these cultural differences were explored in greater depth, it became evident that in some cases, gender equity issues applied to men and boys as well as women and girls. For example, Isom (2007) argued that African American males as well as females have been subjected to gender stereotyping and inequitable treatment. Similarly, male members of other marginalized ethnic groups are also perceived and treated negatively within the large societal context.

Other examples of the complexities related to understanding gender and gender equity in multicultural societies can be identified. For instance, Kosciw, Byard, Fischer, and Joslin (2007) asserted that among lesbian, gay, bisexual, and transgendered (LGBT) people, gender equity involves struggles against both sexism and homophobia. Furthermore, among these groups gender-equity issues are related not only to sexual orientation (e.g., LGBT/straight) but also to gender identity (e.g., male/female) and gender expression (e.g., masculine/feminine).

Still another example of intersections of gender with other statuses is evident in writings by American Muslim women (Haddad, Smith, & Moore, 2006; Karim, 2009). These writers indicated that for Muslim women, particularly in the United States, gender intersects not only with race and religion but also with native-born versus immigrant status. Furthermore, these writers argued that Muslim women, like those of other marginalized groups, must often contend with strong negative stereotypes about Muslims in general along with the role and status of Muslim women.

In summary, during the past 25 to 30 years, thinking about gender equity has evolved. Rather than conceptualizing gender equity in terms of a specific set of issues germane to all women, writers, educators, and activists have come to understand that in addition to gender, we are all affected by our statuses with respect to race, ethnicity, sexuality, religion, disability, and other variables. Furthermore, all of these statuses *intersect,* resulting in variations in the meanings of gender and gender equity among and within different groups, including both women and men. These variations, in turn, have implications for supporting gender equity among diverse groups.

Intersections of Gender and other Statuses

Concepts of Gender

Webster's New World Dictionary defines gender as "the fact or condition of being a male or a female human being, especially with regard to how this affects or determines a person's self image, social status, goals, etc." (Neufeldt & Guralnik, 1994, p. 561). This definition indicates that gender is related not only to biological sex but also to how one's sex is perceived by self and others as well as to how females and males are socialized in a society or cultural group.

Since gender has a sociocultural component, it should not be surprising to learn that it has been defined differently by various groups. For example, Calhoun, Goeman, and Tsethlikai (2007) noted that different Native American nations had their own definitions of appropriate male and female roles and that they taught these roles to their children. Furthermore, these authors noted that in many Native American nations, gender roles were defined in ways that might be considered non-normative by contemporary American standards. For example, Calhoun and her colleagues noted that historically in many Native American nations women held powerful societal roles—in some cases more powerful than men. However, these writers noted that these perceptions of gender were undermined by colonization and by the imposition of an educational system that negated these Native perspectives and imposed a norm of male domination over women.

On a slightly different note, several writers have argued that definitions of gender were imposed on African Americans through the system of slavery. For example, Isom (2007) argued that initial perceptions of Africans as "savages" by Europeans were carried over into the American slave system that defined African American men as brutal, aggressive, incompetent, and hypersexual. Many of these stereotypes continue to be perpetrated today through popular media. Similarly, Ladson-Billings (2009) argued that African American women had gender identities imposed on them in slavery that have continued into the present. Some of these gender stereotypes include "Mammy," the stereotype of a women who takes care of others' children while neglecting her own; "Sapphire," the projection of African American women as evil and contentious; and "Jezebel," the perception of Black women as sexually amoral.

A third example of imposed perspectives on gender is described by Haddad and colleagues (2006). These writers argued that Muslim women have been portrayed either as oppressed or as prostitutes and that these images have been perpetuated by colonialism, Christian missionaries, and popular culture. These same sources paint a picture of Muslim men as generally violent and misogynist.

Despite these concepts of gender imposed on women and men from marginalized groups by those with power and privilege, there have been attempts to oppose these stereotypes and recognize how gender is implemented in diverse groups. For example, in *Black Feminist Thought,* Patricia Hill Collins (1990) argued that many Black women resisted stereotypes and defined themselves rather than allow others to define them. Examples of this resistance can be found in the biography of Sojourner Truth; the fiction of Toni Morrison; and the political activism of African American women such as Eleanor Holmes Norton, the current congressional representative from Washington, D.C.

Similarly, Karim (2009) and Haddad and colleagues (2006) rejected stereotyped portrayals of Muslim women. Instead they introduced the concept of Islamic feminism, which Karim (2009) defined as ". . . ideas of gender justice and activism within a framework of faith . . . and acknowledging multiple structures . . . [that] frame Muslim womens' lives" (p. 18). They also noted that Muslim women have served as activists and scholars making a case for gender equity.

Calhoun and colleagues (2007) described two myths that are commonly voiced regarding gender among Native Americans. The first is that gender issues do not exist because these societies are idealistically egalitarian, while the second portrays women as the passive victims of overbearing, dominating men. These authors indicated that while neither is valid, the second myth is belied by the fact that Native American women have held activist roles both within their groups and in efforts to fight colonization from without.

These examples demonstrate efforts by women in diverse groups to resist stereotypes and define concepts of gender in ways that make sense within their particular cultural milieu.

Gender and Diversity

I have already provided some examples of how gender identity intersects with racial or ethnic identity. In particular, I have discussed how the historical and contemporary treatment of particular racial, ethnic, or religious groups in American society has affected how they are perceived as males and females by outsiders as well as their attempts to develop their own concepts of gender and gender equity relevant to their particular groups. However, there are additional factors that have an impact on gender and perceptions of gender equity.

For example, Asher (2008) and Crosnoe and Turley (2011) suggested that not only ethnicity but also immigrant status can intersect with gender roles. Asher noted that there is a tendency to discuss immigrants monolithically when, in fact, they represent multiple cultural orientations. Furthermore, these orientations are somewhat fluid as immigrants strive to take on the identity of hyphenated Americans. Crosnoe and Turley (2011) identified gender differences in what is termed an "immigrant paradox" (p. 129), which is a tendency for immigrant children to outperform their native peers in school even when faced with high levels of economic and social disadvantage. However, these authors noted that this paradox is stronger for boys than for girls but that they do not have an explanation for this sex difference among immigrant populations. However, it could have implications in future research on gender-equity issues.

Gender also intersects with disability. For example, Mertens, Wilson, and Mounty (2007) reported that some issues around gender equity are quite different for women with disabilities as compared to their peers without disabilities. For example, while women without disabilities may be fighting to obtain equal access to educational or work opportunities, women with disabilities may be fighting to obtain equity in these areas along with equity around rights of childbearing and parenting. In addition, these authors noted that girls with disabilities have less access to resources, fewer educational opportunities, and poorer employment outcomes than boys. On the other hand, boys, especially African American boys, tend to be overidentified for special education, while girls tend to be underidentified.

There are other *intersections* between gender, disability, and race that have implications for gender equity. For example, Petersen (2009) conducted a study of African American women with disabilities who had successfully completed high school. These women reported that they had to develop strategies to resist multiple stereotypes, including those of African Americans, women in general, and people with disabilities, in order to move on with their education. Marginalized by these stereotypes, these women had to work hard to get their teachers to view them as individuals rather than as representatives of a generalized category.

The intersection of gender with other statuses has important implications for the assumptions we make about individuals. For example, one often finds debates, particularly in the popular media, about whether girls have lower self-esteem than boys. However, a study by Adams, Kuhn, and Rhodes (2006) indicated that ethnicity may interact with gender in this area. These researchers found that among Hispanics and European Americans, girls evidenced lower self-esteem than boys; however, this was not demonstrated among African Americans.

Within-Group Heterogeneity

In the United States, racial and ethnic groups are very broadly defined. These broad definitions tend to overlook or blur differences that may exist within particular racial or ethnic groups. In addition, groups such as individuals with disabilities and people who identify as LGBT are often categorized without regard to the racial and/or ethnic differences among them. Furthermore, this lack of attention to *within-group differences* may have implications for how gender equity is implemented. For example, as Calhoun and colleagues (2007) noted, there were more than 100 Native nations prior to colonization in America. In some, gender roles were equal, in others women had more power than men, and in still others men had more power than women. Thus, one cannot make overall generalizations about gender and gender equity among Native Americans.

Similarly, Spencer, Inoue, and McField (2007) noted that Asian Americans are often viewed as a monolithic group. Furthermore, Asian Americans/Pacific Islanders are often referred to as the "model minority," particularly with respect to education and achievement. This characterization of Asian Americans/Pacific Islanders can be viewed as an attempt to account for evidence that some Asian American students outperform all other groups, including Whites, on some measures of achievement. Thus, Asian Americans were categorized as distinct from other groups of color who appeared to demonstrate lower measures of performance on the same measures. However, Spencer and her colleagues (2007) identified 15 different specific Asian groups and 8 different Pacific Islander groups. Furthermore, these authors found wide variations among these groups as well as between girls and boys within these groups in achievement performance and outcomes. While some groups of Asian Americans/Pacific Islanders do attain high levels of achievement, others struggle academically. Ignoring these within-group differences will have negative effects for some students and a negative impact on gender equity for others.

Similarly, Ngo (2006) argued that much of the research on Asian Americans has ignored Southeast and South Asian American students, including, for example, those from Vietnam, Laos, and Cambodia. Ngo argued that in part because of their relatively recent immigrant status, these students are marginalized. Furthermore, Ngo suggested that gender issues among these students have also been ignored and need to be studied more extensively.

Recently, some researchers have begun to study *within-group differences* among African Americans, particularly differences between American-born African Americans and immigrants from the Caribbean and Africa. For example, Seaton, Caldwell, Sellers, and Jackson (2008) found differences between African American and African Caribbean youth in perceptions of discrimination. They found that both African American and African Caribbean males reported discrimination more often than did both groups of females. However, they also found that perceptions of high levels of discrimination seemed to have a more negative psychological effect on the Caribbean youth.

Research on intragroup heterogeneity is relatively recent. However, preliminary findings suggest that as more information becomes available in this area, a greater understanding will emerge of how gender equity can be implemented among and within diverse groups.

This section has provided some examples of intersections between gender and other statuses that individuals inhabit, including race, ethnicity, disability, sexuality, and immigrant status. It is important to note that these examples are not intended to be exhaustive. For example, I have not included socioeconomic status—or what some call social class—in this discussion because of space constraints. In addition, religious and other ethnic statuses not mentioned here may have implications for the ways in which we view gender and gender equity. Research on gender across diverse populations is relatively recent. I expect increased knowledge in the future will help educators to better understand the nuances of gender in multicultural societies.

Gender Equity and Diversity: Implications for Education

Researchers have indicated that gender equity is an important aspect of schooling in at least two ways. First, educators need to work to make sure that schools and classrooms are operating in ways that promote equity between females and males. Second, it is important to help students learn to behave in ways that support gender equity in society. Over the years, not only has the United States become more clearly multicultural, we have also begun to realize that we are part of a diverse global community. Schools need to prepare students to function effectively in such communities. As indicated earlier, there is increasing recognition that considerations of gender equity must include cultural diversity. In this section I focus on gender equity among diverse populations within the context of schools. First, I discuss teacher perceptions of gender as it relates to diverse groups. Next, I provide some information on the gender-related experiences of students from diverse populations. The chapter concludes with some suggestions for supporting and promoting gender equity among students from different cultural backgrounds.

Teacher Perceptions and Expectations

Because the teacher is the organizer and leader of the classroom, the teacher's perceptions and expectations of various students are of utmost importance. Several studies have demonstrated that a teacher's expectations can have an impact on students' behavior and performance, particularly with respect to attitudes toward gender as well as race and ethnicity (Irvine, 1990; Sadker & Zittleman, 2009). In addition, other students observe and learn from the teacher's behavior. This can, in turn, shape their attitudes and behavior toward diverse groups. Unfortunately, sometimes teachers are not aware of the messages they convey through their attitudes, comments, or behaviors toward various groups of students. These attitudes, comments, and behaviors are particularly important because while student populations have become increasingly multicultural, the teacher population is predominately White and increasingly female. A number of examples of skewed attitudes held by pre-service and in-service teachers with regard to gender and diversity have been documented.

Asher (2008), a teacher educator, noted that many of her pre-service college students viewed their own culture as more advanced than others. She further noted that many of her students tended to view other cultures monolithically. For example, she reported that many of her pre-service teachers assumed that Asian American students were docile and expected to excel in math and science.

Several studies have shown that teachers hold negative perceptions of both African American girls and boys. For example, in their chapter in the *Handbook for Achieving Gender Equity Through Education,* Welch, Patterson, Scott, and Pollard (2007) noted that African American males are often viewed as "criminals in the making" and "inherently evil" by their teachers (p. 473). On the other hand, these authors noted that many teachers view African American girls as "hypersexual" (p. 473). Furthermore, teachers focus more on African American girls' social behavior rather than their academic work. African American girls and boys are both viewed negatively; however, the particular dimensions vary by gender. In either case, these perceptions tend to focus on these particular students as less educable and more problematic in the classroom. In a study of a low-performing school district that was populated predominately by African American students, Lynn, Bacon, Totten, Bridges, and Jennings (2010) found evidence that negative perceptions of African American males were held by both African American and White teachers. These students were perceived as unmotivated and unwilling to engage in school. The teachers tended to blame the students and their parents for poor academic performance and behavior.

There is also some evidence that teachers' gender may play a role in their perceptions of African American students. Taylor, Gunter, and Slate (2001) reported that more male teachers perceived African American girls as behavioral problems in the classroom than did female teachers.

Wyatt, Oswalt, White, and Peterson (2008) investigated pre-service teachers' attitudes toward gay men and lesbians. Over 300 students completed an attitude questionnaire. The results indicated that overall the students held moderate attitudes toward gay males and lesbians. However, lesbians were viewed more positively than gay males. Furthermore, the attitudes toward lesbians and gay males were more positive among student who felt they were more "well informed and educated on sexuality issues" (p. 178). The authors concluded that more attention needs to be given to educating pre-service teachers on issues related to sexuality and sexual orientation.

Differential perceptions also extend to teachers themselves. For example, Ladson-Billings (2009) noted that the popular media consistently portray Black women teachers negatively, while White women teachers are portrayed positively, often as saviors of unruly African American students. Furthermore, African American women teachers are often viewed as less competent than White women teachers. Ladson-Billings found that these perspectives were exhibited by some of her education students.

These studies indicate that teachers can enter classrooms with deep-seated negative predispositions toward students from cultures other than their own and in some cases even toward students from backgrounds similar to theirs. Some teachers may not even be aware of their attitudes and beliefs or may assume that their perceptions are normative. It should not be surprising to find that these attitudes are often displayed in teacher behaviors toward different groups of students. These teacher behaviors significantly influence the classroom experiences of their students.

Classroom Experiences of Females and Males from Diverse Populations

In classrooms, the intersections of gender with race and/or ethnicity are highly evident in students' depictions of their experiences. In many cases, these reflect attempts not only to resist stereotyping and discriminatory behaviors directed toward them but also to manage and assert their own gendered and cultured identities as they attempt to achieve the academic goals of schooling.

One issue concerns whether or not students even remain in schools that they may perceive as nonsupportive or even hostile to them. Gender intersects with other statuses here. For example, Greene and Winters (2006) studied high school graduation rates in the 100 largest school districts in the United States. These authors found overall gender and racial differences in graduation rates that were not unusual. Specifically, they reported that high school graduation rates were higher for White students than for students of color and higher for females than for males. However, when looking at the intersections of gender and race or ethnicity, these authors found different patterns among different groups. Among African Americans in 2003, 59 percent of females and 48 percent of males graduated; among Hispanics, the rates were 58 percent for females and 49 percent for males. Among Asian American high school graduates, 73 percent were female and 70 percent were male; similarly, among White students, 79 percent of females and 74 percent of males graduated from high school. These data indicate not only that African American and Hispanic students had lower graduation rates but also that the gender gap in high school graduation was greater for these groups. Greene and Winters did not provide explanations for these differences. However, research reporting students' experiences may suggest some indications of factors underlying these statistics.

Gardenhire-Crooks and colleagues (2010) interviewed African American, Latino, and Native American men who were attending community colleges. They found both similarities and differences across these three groups in their descriptions of their high school and college experiences. For example, all three groups of men reported experiencing low expectations, stereotyping, and discriminatory behavior in high school. Their aspirations for higher education were discouraged, and they were denied access to information and counseling related to preparation for college. However, while African American men felt they were judged negatively on the basis of race and gender, Latino men reported they were judged on the basis of ethnicity and socioeconomic status. Native American men were more concerned with the issues of balancing their identities in tribal and mainstream cultures. These issues continued to follow these men when they enrolled in community colleges. Furthermore, individuals from all three groups reported receiving little support from faculty or peers on their college campuses. Despite these problems, the men in this study indicated that they refused to allow these stereotypes and experiences to have a negative impact on their self-esteem or their behavior.

An analysis of enrollment and achievement in math courses among high school students also found differential patterns related to intersections of gender and race/ethnicity (Riegle-Crumb, 2006). Using national data, this author found that African American and Latino males benefited less from taking Algebra I in their freshman year than did White males. Even though all three groups of males began with the same freshman course, African American and Latino males ended up taking fewer higher-level math courses than did White males. Furthermore, this difference in course sequencing could not be explained by academic performance. In fact, the author reported that African Americans with high grades in math received less benefit than might be expected. This pattern was not found for females.

The previous two studies provide examples of gender inequities that differentiate the school experiences among males from different racial and ethnic groups. They point out that more attention needs to be directed toward understanding these experiences and their impact on students' educational attainment.

Additional studies indicate that the intersections of gender and race and/or ethnicity are associated with differential school experiences. Ginorio, Lapayese, and Vasquez (2007) reported that the intersection of gender and ethnicity led to differential tracking for Latino/a students. These researchers reported that Latinos/as generally tended to be underrepresented in college preparatory and gifted programs and overrepresented in remedial and vocational tracks. This pattern has also been found for African American students. However, these researchers noted sex differences in tracking within the Latino/a group. For example, Latinas were more often recommended for gendered occupations that did not require a college degree, such as cosmetology, while Latinos were directed toward fields such as automobile mechanics. Rarely were these students encouraged to consider nontraditional occupations. These authors also noted that often Latino/a students internalized these low expectations, accepting them as their own aspirations.

Overall, gender and race intersect in ways that have implications for the educational experiences and outcomes of girls and boys of color. For example, Wakiroo and Carter (2010) noted that, like Whites, girls of color tend to demonstrate higher academic achievement than boys of color. These authors suggested that minority girls coped with the negative experiences they encountered in schools in ways that allowed them to achieve academically in spite of these experiences. On the other hand, minority boys' encounters with these negative experiences led to less positive outcomes. In part, Wakiroo and Carter attributed these gender differences to the interactions between these students' attempts to develop and express their sex-role identities and the negative reactions that educators and other adults have toward minority males' sex-role expressions. Specifically, Wakiroo and Carter noted, as others have mentioned in this chapter, that the behaviors exhibited by minority males are often perceived as dangerous. As a result, the tendency is to remove them from the classroom or school through suspending them or making them "push-outs." While not viewed positively, minority females are less likely to be viewed as threats.

Gender also intersects with disability to affect students' school experiences. Mertens and colleagues (2007) reported that girls with disabilities tend to be tracked into life skills and home economics curricula, while boys with disabilities are more likely to be tracked into vocational education curricula. As a result, girls with disabilities have fewer successful employment outcomes after high school than boys with similar disabilities. Furthermore, Mertens and her colleagues reported that while boys tend to be overidentified for special education classes, girls are often underidentified. Thus, while some boys are misplaced in special education classes, some girls who may need the resources provided in such classes are denied access to them.

Mertens and her colleagues also noted that gender intersects with race and ethnicity in the school experiences of students who have disabilities. They reported that African American males were labeled mentally retarded three times more often than were White males and that they were labeled emotionally disturbed twice as often as were White males. Furthermore, they pointed out that once labeled, African Americans—especially males—along with Latinos were more likely to be placed in restrictive, segregated educational environments than were White males.

In addition to intersections of gender with race and/or ethnicity and with disability, there is evidence that gender intersects with sexuality in ways that influence students' experiences in school. In their review of research related to gender equity and sexuality, Kosciw and colleagues (2007) noted that LGBT youth are faced with prejudice and discrimination related to hetero-sexism and homophobia. These authors reported that these negative attitudes toward LGBT youth are evident even in the early grades. Furthermore, children and adolescents tend to show more hostile attitudes toward gay males than toward lesbians. Kosciw and his colleagues argued that this may be attributed to students' tendencies to support traditional and restricted gender roles. For students who take on those attitudes, gay males may appear more threatening than lesbians. However, these authors noted that both LGBT males and females are particularly at risk for being victims of bullying and other negative school experiences, especially from their heterosexual peers. However, the specific types of experiences vary by gender. Male students reported being victims of more physical threats and attacks than females because of their sexuality. However, females reported more psychological trauma.

Up to this point, the chapter has focused on the implications of diversity for gender equity in education. Several important trends appear to be evident from studies in this area.

First, data indicate that gender intersects with race, ethnicity, disability, and sexuality in ways that have an impact on individuals' experiences as well as others' perceptions of them. The specific ways in which these intersections are implemented vary from group to group. In some cases, gender roles have been defined historically by members of particular cultural groups. In many others, however, gender roles have been imposed on groups as they were marginalized by slavery, other forms of discrimination, and colonialism. These imposed gender roles have often served to maintain the cultural status quo in American society, which marginalizes individuals on the basis of race, ethnicity, disability, and sexuality.

Second, evidence is continuing to emerge that demonstrates that the intersections of gender with other statuses is very complex. It is clear that one cannot make assumptions about individuals based on gender, race, or any other status alone. Furthermore, there is evidence that the broad racial and ethnic definitions used to categorize people in the United States are not fully adequate for understanding how categorization by gender is implemented. In addition to race and ethnicity, additional inter- and intragroup factors, such as ethnicity, immigrant status, disability status, sexuality, and religion, seem to have implications both for how gender is conceptualized and expressed and for the types of inequities experienced.

Third, it is clear that the intersections of gender with other statuses have implications for students' school experiences and outcomes. Unfortunately, for students who occupy statuses outside of the dominant mainstream, these experiences and outcomes are often negative. It has long been evident that schools in the United States have failed to educate students of color, those with disabilities, and LGBT youth, among other groups, effectively. However, recent research indicates that gender inequities also exist in terms of how these students are perceived and treated in school.

Finally, demographic changes in the characteristics of both students and educators have implications for understanding the intersections of gender with other statuses. Specifically, while both the general and student populations in the United States have become increasingly diverse in the latter part of the 20th century and the beginning of the 21st century, the demographic characteristics of educators have not kept pace. On the contrary, the teaching force remains predominantly White, female, and monolingual.

Given these demographic patterns, if equity is to be advanced in U.S. schools, more information is needed that will help teachers and other school staff members support gender equity among diverse student populations. The final section of this chapter suggests some strategies educators can use to work effectively to promote equity in a way that recognizes the intersections of gender with race, ethnicity, disability, sexuality, and other important inter- and intragroup statuses.

Supporting Gender Equity among Diverse Populations

As adult role models in schools, educators often provide information about the value of equity with their overt and covert actions. Unfortunately, in many situations, these adults may actually promote inequities among groups. In some cases, this may be evident by openly inequitable treatment of individuals because of their gender, race, disability, sexuality, or a combination of these variables. In other cases, the adult educator may unintentionally display inequitable attitudes. A more subtle pattern that promotes inequity may occur when behaviors exhibited by students or other adults, reflecting prejudice and discrimination, are ignored by the adults at school.

As indicated earlier, issues around gender are intertwined with issues around other statuses, particularly among groups that have been marginalized. Thus, it is an oversimplification to focus on one aspect of equity (e.g., gender) without also considering other dimensions that may cause individuals to be mistreated, such as race, ethnicity, immigrant status, religion, sexuality, and disability.

In this section, four strategies aimed at addressing gender inequities among diverse populations are suggested for educators. These strategies are not exhaustive or complete. Rather, they are starting points for teachers and other educators to consider if they want to create classroom and school environments that not only address gender inequities but also promote equity that supports differences in gender, race, ethnicity, sexuality, disability, and other statuses that are associated with discrimination and exclusion.

Strategy 1: Confronting and Addressing Stereotyping and Discrimination

As suggested earlier, discussions of topics related to status differences, inequality, and discrimination are often avoided because they are difficult and uncomfortable to address. In some cases, this discomfort is related to the teacher's inability or unwillingness to examine his or her attitudes toward members of gender, racial, ethnic, or sexual groups different from his or her own. In order to confront and address stereotyping and discrimination by others, a teacher or other educator needs to be clear about his or her own perspectives. For example, Zaman (2008), noting that teachers tend to view African American boys as troublemakers, advocated that they be encouraged to be self-reflective about their attitudes toward boys, especially boys of color, during their pre-service training. Similarly, Asher (2007) suggested that teacher education courses should include opportunities for pre-service students to address issues where gender, race, ethnicity, culture, and sexuality intersect. Noting that issues such as these often invite silence, Asher argued that courses that openly address these intersections can serve as models that pre-service teachers can then implement in their classrooms.

Kosciw and colleagues (2007) noted that issues around sexuality are often repressed or avoided in pre-service teacher education. These authors argued that there is a strong need for teacher training about homophobia and its expression. In addition, teachers need to obtain information about ways to protect LGBT students from physical and psychological assault. In addition, schools need to develop clear and unambiguous policies that promote safety for LGBT students and staff.

In addition to reflecting on their own perspectives with respect to gender, diversity, and equity, teachers also have numerous opportunities to use actual situations as stimuli to help their students understand how inequities are expressed in society and how equity can be promoted. For example, Coltrane and Messineo (2000) analyzed how race and gender intersected to promote stereotyping in television commercials in the 1990s. They found that these commercials tended to portray "white men as powerful, white women as sex objects, African American men as aggressive and African American women as inconsequential" (p. 363). Information such as this could be incorporated into classroom curricula.

Gersti-Pepin and Liang (2010) also examined mass media in an analysis of its coverage of a high school's use of a Native American mascot. They noted that the media coverage reflected both racism and sexism because Native American women were often erased by these mascots and men were reduced to objects. They also argued that school personnel need to address how mascots and other denigrating portrayals of groups became part of school policy. Haddad and colleagues (2006) suggested that another area where schools need to confront issues around gender equity among diverse populations has to do with dress codes, particularly when students' cultures may require dress that is distinct from that of other students. This issue may become quite complex. For example, some Muslim women and girls are required by their religion to wear a certain mode of dress. However, some public schools may prohibit attire associated with a specific religion, arguing that they are required to enforce separation of religion and state.

Examples such as these can provide interesting stimuli for classroom discussions about cultural differences (and similarities) that intersect with gender as well as attitudes that are often accepted as normative but that, in fact, can be quite discriminatory. By addressing these and other instances of difference and stereotyping, teachers can help students understand that equity or inequity is part of the practice of everyday life. Discussions of these and similar situations can also help students begin to reflect on their own perspectives with respect to gender and equity among diverse populations.

Strategy 2: Obtaining Knowledge about Cultures, Statuses, and Intersections

Several researchers have questioned whether teachers are adequately prepared to work with diverse populations of students (Douglas, Lewis, Douglas, Scott, & Garrison-Wade, 2008; Kohli, 2009). In addition to confronting and addressing evidence of stereotyping, prejudice, and discrimination, teachers and other educators need to obtain knowledge about how gender is conceptualized among diverse groups. For example, Calhoun and colleagues (2007) argued that educators need to read works written by Native American women scholars in order to understand the historical and contemporary roles of gender among these groups in the United States. Similarly, Oesterreich (2007) noted the tendency of educators to classify African American girls as "at risk" or "in crisis." Oesterreich suggested that if teachers familiarized themselves with some of the writings of African American feminists, they might be able to understand African American girls' behavior within the context of African American history, racism, and resilience. Similarly, Kosciw and colleagues (2007) called for the inclusion of more writings by LGBT individuals in curricula.

In addition to increasing their own knowledge about the intersections of gender with race, ethnicity, sexuality, disability, and other statuses, teachers can also incorporate literature illustrating these issues into their curricula. For example, Endo (2009) identified books that address gender and youth identity among Asian American youth. These books could be incorporated into adolescents' reading materials. Similar materials by African American, Latino/a, and Native American writers could be included among the readings assigned to students.

Strategy 3: Building on Students' Assets and Strengths

All too often, discussions of gender among students of color and other marginalized groups are characterized by the use of terms such as *plight*, *crisis*, and *victim*. In addition, often research on gender as well as race, ethnicity, disability, and sexuality begins with an assumption that White heterosexual, and abled individuals represent the norm against which all others are to be compared. Sanders and Bradley (2005) argue that reliance on this comparison model tends to focus educators' attention on deficits rather than on strengths and assets these students might bring to bear on their situations. Rather than compare girls and women as well as boys and men from various cultural groups with a so-called normative group, or even with each other, educators may be better served by attempting to understand the social and cultural capital they have learned within their families and communities and how they attempt to use that capital to cope with schools and other societal institutions.

Oesterreich (2007) provided an illustration of this asset-based approach in a case study of an African American high school senior. This student's life was framed by some observers as anchored in poverty and a struggling family situation. Yet an alternative analysis found that this individual actually used African American women's history, contemporary hip-hop, styles of dress, and her mother's activism to define herself as a leader fighting for freedom for herself and her community.

Similarly, Petersen's (2009) study of African American women with disabilities who had successfully completed high school found that an important element of their success included interactions with educators who were able to recognize and support their efforts to resist stereotyping and marginalization. Some of the ways the educators built on these students' strengths included getting to know them individually and personally rather than as members of a particular group, encouraging them to become actively engaged in instruction, and providing them with culturally responsive curricula.

Ginorio and colleagues (2007) called for educators to familiarize themselves with Latino/a culture so that they can recognize the cultural capital that Latino/a families provide for their children. These authors indicated that some of the strengths these students bring to school include a strong sense of altruism and a collective rather than individualistic orientation. As a result, they contended, educators can build on these strengths by means of cooperative rather than competitive educational strategies.

Evidence of assets and strengths related to gender as it intersects with other statuses can be found among all groups. These strengths can become the foundation on which educational skills can be scaffolded.

Strategy 4: Increasing the Number of Female and Male Teachers Who Represent Diversity in Race, Ethnicity, Disability, Sexuality, and Other Statuses

Welch and colleagues (2007) pointed out a steady disappearance of African American teachers since the Supreme Court's *Brown* decision in 1954. Different factors appear to have contributed to this phenomenon. On one hand, Marbley, Bonner, McKisick, Henfield, and Watts (2007) suggested that the decline in the number of African American teachers was a consequence of the 1954 *Brown* decision. African American teachers lost their jobs as African American students entered predominately White schools. In addition, Ramirez (2009) noted that students of color have not been choosing to enter the field of education as often as in the past. Welch and colleagues (2007) noted that in the 2005–2006 school year, although African Americans constituted 20 percent of the student population, they were only 8 percent of the teaching population. African American males were conspicuously absent, accounting for only 1 percent of teachers.

Ginorio and her colleagues (2007) also noted a lack of Latino/a teachers. These authors estimated that Latinos/as constituted only about 5 percent of the teaching population. Furthermore, in California, a state with a large population from this group, 47 percent of students but only 15 percent of teachers were Latino/a. As with African Americans, male Latino teachers are noticeably absent (Gomez, Rodriguez, & Agosto, 2008).

Increasing the numbers of male and female teachers who represent diversity in race, ethnicity, disability, and sexuality has a number of benefits. These teachers can serve as positive role models not only for students whose groups they represent but also for White students, who can learn about the existence of multiple perspectives from them. Furthermore, interactions with teachers from diverse populations may help all students function more effectively in multicultural societies. In addition, these teachers can often bridge cultural gaps between diverse students' communities and schools because of their knowledge of their own communities. These teachers also can help White teachers learn about the intersections of gender and culture, particularly the gendered cultural strengths that diverse populations have to offer schools and society (Ginorio et al., 2007; Gomez et al., 2008; Welch et al., 2007).

Conclusions

For many educators, supporting gender equity in education once meant providing equal access and outcomes for all boys and girls or women and men. However, research over the past 20 to 30 years has indicated that gender-equity issues are considerably more nuanced. Gender is not a status that stands alone. Nor is it a status that can be added on to or prioritized with respect to other statuses. Rather, gender intersects with our other statuses, such as race, ethnicity, sexuality, disability, and religion, to produce unique conceptualizations and implementations of female and male roles. To make matters more complex, these conceptualizations and implementations can emanate from groups representing broadly defined statuses (e.g., African Americans or LGBT groups), from smaller subgroups within a broadly defined group (e.g., specific Native American nations), or from individuals. These conceptualizations and implementations can be group-oriented, such as when members of a particular ethnic group socialize their young girls and boys to take on perspectives that the group deems important. However, these conceptualizations and implementations may also be individually determined as one attempts to establish an identity and cope with the external world.

This more complex perspective means that teachers and other educators no longer have the misplaced luxury of considering gender equity apart from other aspects of equity. Furthermore, an understanding of gender equity as it intersects with equity regarding other statuses will require educators to become more knowledgeable about the historical and contemporary experiences of all the groups that enrich our multicultural society. However, by opening themselves up to new experiences and perspectives, teachers and educators can enrich themselves as well as their students and will become much more competent at creating truly equitable learning environments.

QUESTIONS AND ACTIVITIES

8.1   Think about your development as a male or female in your family and school. Identify some instances in which your gender intersected with other statuses, such as your race, ethnicity, disability status, or sexuality.

8.2   Interview females and males from groups other than your own about their experiences in elementary and high school.

What are some similarities and differences around gender and gender equity?

8.3   Identify a particular form of television programming, for example, situation comedies, crime shows, or reality shows. Review several episodes and analyze how gender is portrayed in diverse populations.

8.4   Read literature written by females and males from diverse cultural groups. What are their perspectives on gender and gender equity?

8.5   Join with some of your peers to identify age-appropriate curricula, literature, and activities that represent how lessons related to gender and diverse population groups are conceptualized and implemented in schools.

8.6   Think of some strategies you could use to confront instances of gender inequity among diverse populations in your classroom or school.

REFERENCES

Adams, S. K., Kuhn, J., & Rhodes, J. (2006). Self-esteem changes in the middle school years: A study of ethnic and gender groups. *RMLE Online: Research in Middle Level Education, 29*(6), 1–9.

Asher, N. (2007). Made in the (multicultural) U.S.A.: Unpacking tensions of race, culture, gender and sexuality in education, *Educational Researcher, 36*(2), 65–73.

Asher, N. (2008). Listening to hyphenated Americans: Hybrid identities of youth from immigrant families, *Theory into Practice, 47*, 12–19.

Calhoun, A., Goeman, M., & Tsethlikai, M. (2007). Achieving gender equity for American Indians. In S. S. Klein, B. Richardson, D. A. Grayson, L. H. Fox, C. Kramarae, D. S. Pollard, & C. Dwyer (Eds.), *Handbook for achieving gender equity through education* (pp. 525–551). Mahwah, NJ: Erlbaum.

Collins, P. H. (1990). *Black feminist thought: Knowledge, consciousness, and the politics of empowerment.* Boston: Unwin Hyman.

Coltrane, S., & Messineo, M. (2000). The perpetuation of subtle prejudice: Race and gender imagery in 1990s television advertising. *Sex Roles, a Journal of Research, 42*, 363–389.

Crosnoe, R., & Turley, R. N. L. (2011). K–12 educational outcomes of immigrant youth. *Future of Children, 21*(1), 129–152.

Douglas, B., Lewis, C. W., Douglas, A., Scott, M. E., & Garrison-Wade, D. (2008). The impact of White teachers on the academic achievement of Black students: An exploratory qualitative analysis. *Educational Foundations, 22*, 47–62.

Endo, R. (2009). Complicating culture and difference: Situating Asian American youth identities in Lisa Yee's "Millicent Min," "Girl Genius" and "Stanford Wong Flunks Big-Time." *Children's Literature in Education, 40*(3), 235–249.

Gardenhire-Crooks, A., Collado, H., Martin, K., & Castro, A. with Brock, T., & Orr, G. (2010). *Terms of engagement: Men of color discuss their experiences in community college.* MDRC (Building Knowledge to Improve Social Policy). Retrieved January 23, 2012, from http://archive.careerladdersproject.org/docs/Terms%20of%20Engagement.pdf.

Gersti-Pepin, C., & Liang, G. (2010). Media misrepresentations of a mascot controversy: Contested constructions of race and gender. *Journal of School Public Relations, 31*(3), 251–269.

Ginorio, A. B., Lapayese, Y., & Vasquez, M. J. T. (2007). Gender equity for Latina/os. In S. S. Klein, B. Richardson, D. A. Grayson, L. H. Fox, C. Kramarae, D. S. Pollard, & C. Dwyer (Eds.), *Handbook for achieving gender equity through education* (pp. 485–499). Mahwah, NJ: Erlbaum.

Gomez, M. L., Rodiguez, T. L., & Agosto, V. (2008). Who are Latino prospective teachers and what do they bring to US schools? *Race, Ethnicity and Education, 11*(3), 267–283.

Greene, J. P., & Winters, M. A. (2006). *Leaving boys behind: Public high school graduation rates.* New York: Center for Civic Innovation at the Manhattan Institute.

Haddad, Y. Y., Smith, J. I., & Moore, K. M. (2006). *Muslim women in America: The challenge of Islamic identity today.* New York: Oxford University Press.

Irvine, J. J. (1990). *Black students and school failure: Policies, practices, and prescriptions.* Westport, CT: Greenwood.

Isom, D. A. (2007). Performance, resistance, caring: Racialized gender identity in African American boys. *The Urban Review, 39*(4), 405–423.

Karim, J. (2009). *American Muslim women: Negotiating race, class, and gender within the Ummah.* New York: New York University Press.

Kohli, R. (2009). Critical race reflections: Valuing the experiences of teachers of color in teacher education. *Race, Ethnicity and Education, 12*(2), 235–251.

Kosciw, J., Byard, E., Fischer, S., & Joslin, C. (2007). Gender equity and lesbian, gay, bisexual, and transgender issues in education. In S. S. Klein, B. Richardson, D. A. Grayson, L. H. Fox, C. Kramarae, D. S. Pollard, & C. Dwyer (Eds.), *Handbook for achieving gender equity through education* (pp. 553–571). Mahwah, NJ: Erlbaum.

Ladson-Billings, G. (2009). "Who you callin' nappy-headed?" A critical race theory look at the construction of Black women. *Race, Ethnicity and Education, 12*(1), 87–99.

Lynn, M., Bacon, J. N., Totten, T. L., Bridges, T. L., & Jennings, M. E. (2010). Examining teachers' beliefs about African American male students in a low-performing high school in an African American school district. *Teachers College Record, 112*(1), 289–330. Retrieved October 10, 2011, from http://www.tcrecord.org (ID Number: 15835).

Marbley, A. F., Bonner, F. A., McKisick, S., Henfield, M. S., & Watts, L. M. (2007). Interfacing culture specific pedagogy with counseling: A proposed diversity training model for preparing preservice teachers for diverse learners. *Multicultural Education, 14*(3), 8–16.

Mertens, D. M., Wilson, A., & Mounty, J. (2007). Gender equity for people with disabilities. In S. S. Klein, B. Richardson, D. A. Grayson, L. H. Fox, C. Kramarae, D. S. Pollard, & C. Dwyer (Eds.), *Handbook for achieving gender equity through education* (pp. 583–604). Mahwah, NJ: Erlbaum.

Neufeldt, V. (Ed. in Chief) & Guralnik, D. B. (Ed. in Chief, Emeritus). (1994). *Webster's New World Dictionary of American English* (3rd college ed.). New York: Macmillan.

Ngo, B. (2006). Learning from the margins: The education of Southeast and South Asian Americans in context. *Race, Ethnicity and Education, 9*(1), 51–65.

Oesterreich, H. A. (2007). From "crisis" to "activist": The everyday freedom legacy of Black feminisms. *Race, Ethnicity and Education, 10*(1), 1–20.

Petersen, A. J. (2009). "Ain't nobody gonna get me down": An examination of the educational experiences of four African American women labeled with disabilities. *Equity and Excellence in Education, 42*(4), 428–442.

Ramirez, A. Y. (2009). Ethnic minorities and teaching: An examination of the low numbers in the teaching profession. *Multicultural Education, 16*(4), 19–24.

Riegle-Crumb, C. (2006). The path through math: Course sequences and academic performance at the intersection of race-ethnicity and gender. *American Journal of Education, 113*(1), 101–123.

Sadker, D., & Zittleman, K. (2009). *Still failing at fairness: How gender bias cheats boys and girls in school and what we can do about it* (8th ed.). New York: Scribners.

Sanders, J.-A. L., & Bradley, C. (2005). Multiple-lens paradigm evaluating African American girls and their development. *Journal of Counseling & Development, 83*(3), 299.

Seaton, E. K., Caldwell, C. H., Sellers, R. M., & Jackson, J. S. (2008). The prevalence of perceived discrimination among African American and Caribbean Black youth. *Developmental Psychology, 44*(5), 1288–1297.

Spencer, M. L., Inoue, Y., & McField, G. P. (2007). Achieving gender equity for Asian and Pacific Islander Americans. In S. S. Klein, B. Richardson, D. A. Grayson, L. H. Fox, C. Kramarae, D. S. Pollard, & C. Dwyer (Eds.), *Handbook for achieving gender equity through education* (pp. 501–524). Mahwah, NJ: Erlbaum.

Taylor, P. B., Gunter, P. L., & Slate, J. R. (2001). Teacher's perceptions of inappropriate student behavior as a function of teachers' and students' gender and ethnic background. *Behavioral Disorders, 26*(2), 146–151.

Wakiroo, N., & Carter, P. (2010). Cultural explanations for racial and ethnic stratification in academic achievement: A call for a new and improved theory. *Review of Educational Research, 79*(1), 366–394.

Welch, O. M., Patterson, F. E., Scott, K. A., & Pollard, D. S. (2007). Gender equity for African Americans. In S. S. Klein, B. Richardson, D. A. Grayson, L. H. Fox, C. Kramarae, D. S. Pollard, & C. Dwyer (Eds.), *Handbook for achieving gender equity through education* (pp. 469–483). Mahwah, NJ: Erlbaum.

Wyatt, T. J., Oswalt, S. B., White, C., & Peterson, F. L. (2008, Spring). Are tomorrow's teachers ready to deal with diverse students? Teacher candidates' attitudes toward gay men and lesbians. *Teacher Education Quarterly,* 171–185.

Zaman, A. (2008). Gender sensitive teaching: A reflective approach for early childhood education teacher training programs. *Education, 129*(1), 110–118.

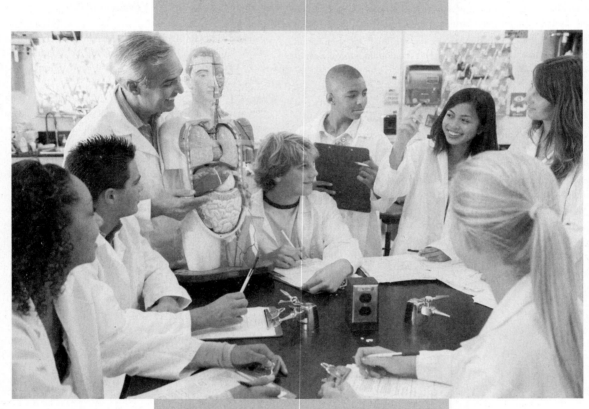

Stockbroker/Glow Images

Queer Lessons: Sexual and Gender Minorities in Multicultural Education

Cris Mayo

Part of the project of critical multiculturalism involves examining the political and social construction of the identities that structure social, political, and educational relations. It may seem relatively unremarkable that school practices and policies are now increasingly interested in addressing some categories of difference. However, other categories of identity such as minority sexuality are often not part of the official school curriculum or multicultural education. The excluded categories often include lesbian, gay, and bisexual identity or gender identity, including students who are gender nonconforming, transgender, or intersex. LGBTQ is an abbreviation for these identities. Recent media coverage of violence against LGBTQ youth, as well as the increase in the number of states that allow gay marriage, underscores both increasing hostility toward nonconforming sexual orientation and gender identity as well as significant gains in rights for some LGBTQ people.

LGBTQ, queer, and gender-identity issues are not always considered part of multicultural education, whether because schools have long seen sexuality as controversial or because there is still acceptance of homophobia in schools and communities. In multicultural education, the reluctance to address LGBTQ issues may be waning, but there may also be conceptual barriers to including sexuality. Perhaps the assumption that *culture* refers to a group of people who have overwhelmingly complete similarities to one another or the concern that something such as sexuality is too controversial to easily fit into a "culture" provides an obstacle to thinking about the relationship between multiculturalism and seemingly noncultural forms of bias. Or there may be the mistaken assumption that because movements for the rights of LGBTQ people are historically relatively young, sexuality is a new form of difference and has not yet reached a point of development into a distinct culture. Or it may be that sexuality challenges some common assumptions about what constitutes a culture or that in order for a group to exist and be recognized as deserving respect, it has to first be a unified culture.

Rather than arguing that sexuality creates a distinct culture—though there has been ample work making similar arguments—it may be better to posit that minority sexuality and gender expression form multiple kinds of cultures, subcultures, counterpublics, and communities. As a result of the globalization of capital and representation—and the transnational movement of people—those cultures, subcultures, counterpublics, and communities are sometimes locally distinct and sometimes globally similar to one another. These same complications regarding the concept of culture have been discussed by many multicultural theorists (for example, Covertino, Levinson, and González in Chapter 2 of this book) and, thus, including the categories of sexual and gender identity when thinking about diversity and difference makes sense.

Sexuality and Gender Identity

Sexuality and gender identity are themselves complicated concepts, including both diversity of sexual partners, gendered bodies and identities, and other related categories of difference increasingly organized under the general term *queer* and in their own distinct communities. Lesbian, gay, and bisexual may seem like relatively easy concepts to understand, but even within those categories there may be cultural and regional differences, different relationships to normative gender identity, and differing degrees of politicization of sexual orientation. Despite histories of a common struggle for rights, different groups that may organize with the LGBTQ movement have different targets for their political action or different emphases on personal and community needs. For instance, transgender people—people for whom gender categories are insufficient to express their identities or people for whom their birth sex does not conform with their gender identity—may find some common cause with lesbian, gay, and bisexual (LGB) people but centralize gender identity above sexual orientation. Gender transgression—that is, activities meant to critique "normal" gender roles and expectations, including drag performances and political activities—have long been part of LGBTQ and queer culture.

All sexual minorities may be very aware and critical of how gender norms constrain their lives, but for transgender people gender identity is a central site of political struggle. Some transpeople may use medical or other interventions in order to bring their bodies into conformity with their gender identity, while other gender-queer transgender people may work to have their bodies and identities reflect gender complexity that moves beyond the normative binary of female or male. Transgender young people are making their gender identity known earlier and finding more support from school districts and parents, but social disapproval remains and attempts to protect the rights of transgender students have not yet found broad support. Other people also concerned with the relationship between gender and normative bodies include intersex people. For intersex people—that is, people with bodies that are not easily categorized by dominant categories of male and female—medical intervention to "normalize" their bodies without their consent is a key political issue. Intersex activism reminds the medical establishment, parents, and the broader community that even young people deserve to be able to give informed consent about an issue so crucial to self-identity as gender.

Queer is a concept and identity that works against problematic forms of normalization, troubling the exclusions that any category of identity may enact. Because the processes of normalization and the pressure to conform to dominant understandings of gender and sexuality affect people of all sexual and gender identities—including heterosexual and conventionally gendered people—examining the processes of normalization provides all people with a way to critically engage cultural, political, and educational messages about gender and sexuality.

LGBTQ Issues and the School Curriculum

Increasingly, sexual and gender minorities are working to see that their issues are represented in school curricula and extracurricular groups largely because they remember the isolation of growing up in some way queer. There has been success in some states, with gender identity and social orientation being included in nondiscrimination laws and school policies. In California, textbooks will now include LGBTQ history. In contrast, some state laws or bills under consideration forbid discussion of minority sexuality in curricula, including a recent law passed by the Tennessee State Senate to outlaw the use of the word *gay* in curricula. In Minnesota, the Anoka-Hennepin school district requires that staff remain neutral on questions about sexual orientation, including situations where students raise questions. Policy and cultural barriers to addressing minority sexuality and gender identity remain even when legal prohibitions against representing LGBTQ issues are lifted. Still, many teachers who know that they are teaching students who are LGBTQ or who are being raised by lesbian, gay, bisexual, or transgender parents would like to be able to make those students feel supported and part of the school community but fear that addressing issues of minority sexuality will put their jobs at risk. LGBTQ parents also face barriers to their participation in schools and are concerned that their children are inadequately protected from harassment (Casper & Schultz, 1999). LGBTQ teachers may be concerned that their identity puts them at risk in their jobs, especially if they are not protected by antidiscrimination laws and policies that cover sexual and gender identity. LGBTQ school leaders face the same pressures, yet research indicates that their experience of their own minority status makes them more concerned with creating a respectful school environment for students and school community members of all identities and backgrounds (Capper, 1999).

Incorporating LGBTQ issues into multicultural education is one way to ensure that schools improve how they address the educational needs of diverse students, families, and communities. Understanding the political and social histories of minority sexualities and gender identities in conversation with more well-known social justice histories can not only help to explain the multicultural aspects of movements for LGBTQ people but also highlight work against biases of all forms that still needs to be done within LGBTQ communities and in other movements and communities. At the same time that LGBTQ and related issues need to be made part of education against bias, the story of bias and limitation is not the only story to be told about sexual-minority people, communities, and cultures. Understanding the long histories and varying experiences of sexuality-based communities and identities can provide a broader and more complex view of how sexuality has been one feature in the organization of social relations and identities. Although examining the story of all differences needs to include looking at the processes of normalization, oppression, and resistance, it is also important to remember that those pressures are not the only experience of difference. That people are resilient, creative, responsible, and innovative is as true for people who have lived lives that do not conform to norms of gender and sexuality as it is for anyone.

Overlapping Histories of Multiculturalism and LGBTQ Movements

The modern gay movement usually dates its beginning to a rebellion of bar patrons at the Stonewall Inn in Greenwich Village, New York, on June 28, 1969. Many of the protesters were young people of color and included lesbian, gay, and transgender people. After years of harassment by police, LGBTQ people decided to fight back, unleashing days of unrest in New York City and providing a center for the political organizing already begun there and elsewhere. However, dating the start of any movement is problematic—the 1966 Compton Cafeteria riots protesting the exclusion of gender-nonconforming people from that establishment predate Stonewall and centralize the link between gender and gay liberation (Stryker, 2008). Other important dates and activities are also associated with the beginning of the LGBTQ civil rights movement. Smaller political advocacy groups or activists starting in the early 20th century challenged the categorization of homosexuality as a psychological disorder. Multiple small sexual- and/or gender-minority communities developed in various racial, ethnic, gendered, and geographic locations before Stonewall. But placing the beginnings of the social movement for sexuality and gender-identity rights in the diverse context of the Stonewall riot underscores the importance of understanding minority sexuality as multicultural and part of the history and future of multicultural education.

Making Stonewall the beginning of the gay liberation movement also centralizes the often unstable and linked struggles for rights for minority sexualities and genders. Patrons of the Stonewall Inn included gay men, lesbians, and transgender, transsexual, and transvestite people, some of whom were gay and some not. As active as transgender people have been in struggles for gay rights, they have also been excluded by those in the gay rights movement seeking rights for only a limited, respectable-appearing segment of the LGBTQ community. Stonewall also stands as a reminder that even radical movements enact exclusions (Frye, 2002).

Indebted to the civil rights movement, the gay liberation movement often modeled itself on activism aimed at improving the lives of people of color. This was so in part because some gay liberation activists were people of color and in part because the civil rights and Black power movements set the standard for activism during the 1960s. Activists in civil rights, Black feminism, women of color feminism, and Black power groups pushed the gay, women's, and lesbian movements to be aware of racism, and leaders in various movements urged their members to be critical of their dislike of gay people (Anzaldúa, 1990; Clarke, 1981, 1983; Combahee River Collective, 1982; Lorde, 1984, 1988; Smith, 1983). This was by no means a simple process or a utopian moment; movements were also energetically split on whether addressing minority sexuality and gender identity would delegitimize their claims or open them to ridicule. For instance, Betty Friedan, leader of the National Organization for Women, characterized lesbian involvement in the women's movement as a "lavender menace" (cited in Brownmiller, 1970, p. 140). Civil rights leaders involved in the 1963 March on Washington wanted Bayard Rustin removed as the lead organizer of the march when his homosexuality became known. Only through the intercession of A. Phillip Randolph was Rustin kept in charge (D'Emilio, 2003), though later he was excluded from prominent roles in the civil rights movement. The tendency to exclude or ignore LGBTQ members of dominant communities is also paralleled in minority communities. It continues today through informal messages about the unacceptability of sexual-minority identities (Duncan, 2005; Kumashiro, 2001, 2002, 2003) as well as through political debate in minority communities about HIV/AIDS (Cohen, 1999). LGBTQ communities are often dominated by Whites and are unwilling to see how Whiteness informs ideas about who is legitimately LGBTQ or who can easily access LGBTQ community resources and social spaces. This White dominance may be expressed through overt racism or through implicit assumptions about what gayness means, leading to an unwillingness to recognize the sexual and gender identities that emerge within racial and ethnic communities.

Even though there may not always be sustained attention to diversity within groups organizing for social justice, by focusing on moments and strands within movements that acknowledge their complicity in forms of bias, we can see that multiculturally influenced politics, a politics attentive to multiple forms of diversity, has been a part of almost every political movement. Indeed, the historian Herbert Apetheker (1992) has asked why so many histories of social movements are framed as interested only in their own issues and represented as if they were made up of relatively homogeneously identified people. He asks us to consider how the expectation that people will work only on their own behalf has limited our contemporary ability to imagine diversely organized politics. Even at the height of what has come to be known as the heyday of identity politics, many groups were calling their own prejudices into question and making connections across struggles and identities. The Black Panther founder Huey Newton (1973), for instance, argued that all movements needed to challenge their biases, including sexism and homophobia, and learn to work together in common cause. He wrote:

> Whatever your personal opinions and your insecurities about homosexuality and the various liberation movements among homosexuals and women (and I speak of the homosexuals and women as oppressed groups), we should try to unite with them in a revolutionary fashion. . . . I do not remember our ever constituting any value that said that a revolutionary must say offensive things towards homosexuals, or that a revolutionary should make sure that women do not speak out about their own particular kind of oppression. As a matter of fact, it is just the opposite: we say that we recognize the women's right to be free. We have not said much about the homosexual at all, but we must relate to the homosexual movement because it is a real thing. And I know through reading, and through my life experience and observations that homosexuals are not given freedom and liberty by anyone in the society. They might be the most oppressed people in the society. (p. 143)

Other groups, such as the Black feminist Combahee River Collective, opposed ranking oppressions. They viewed oppressions as "interlocking," including race, gender, class, and sexuality as part of a critique of unequal social relations (Combahee River Collective, 1982). By taking account of the intersections of categories of identity, it becomes clear that the identities of all people are multiple. By examining the critiques of the various rights and liberation movements, we can further understand that all communities are made up of diverse people, not all of whom are adequately served by community norms or by the political groups that claim to represent them. Furthermore, forms of gender and sexual identity emerge from within different cultural, racial, and ethnic traditions and thus push us to understand the importance of place, context, and relation. Transnational immigration brings diverse understandings of sexual and gender identity into conversation with dominant versions, and racial and ethnic traditions provide particular forms of gender and sexual identities and activities that inform, challenge, and mingle with dominant forms (Manalansan, 2003).

Histories of Gay-Inclusive Multiculturalism and Other Curricular Inclusiveness

Situating the LGBTQ movement squarely within multiculturalism and the struggle for civil rights provides a strategy for understanding the need to bring sexuality more firmly into multicultural education in order to address long-standing exclusions in education. While not common in all approaches to multiculturalism, sexual-minority issues have been incorporated into multicultural curricula and have been strongly challenged. As newer legislation and curricula seek to limit how LGBTQ issues can be addressed in schools, remembering earlier links between sexual- and gender-minority issues and multiculturalism can help remind us of the stakes of such connections. Controversy broke out in New York City in the early 1990s over the multicultural education teachers' guide *Children of the Rainbow* (New York City Board of Education, 1994). The guide included suggestions for lessons on the diversity of family structures—including gay and lesbian families. The goal was to help all students feel comfortable and valued in school. While the earlier outcry over the multicultural New York State social studies standards had mobilized social conservatives to work against inclusion of lessons on racial diversity, the controversy over the *Rainbow* curricula marked a switch in tactics, with social conservatives advocating for the inclusion of so-called legitimate minorities but not minority sexual orientation or families (Mayo, 2004a/2007). *Children of the Rainbow* was not the first time sexual orientation was recognized in New York City's educational policy. The New York City Board of Education had included sexual orientation as a protected class since 1985 (New York City Board of Education, 1994), but *Children of the Rainbow* was the first concerted effort to bring sexual-minority issues into the multicultural curriculum.

A recently passed law in California requires that school districts adopt textbooks on U.S. history that include lessons on the contributions of LGBTQ people. As schools continue to widen the range of inclusiveness in curricula, such laws may encourage textbook publishers as well as educational professionals to widen their understanding of diversity. As LGBTQ families increasingly make their presence and the presence of their children known to schools, schools need to work to accommodate both children and parents. A recent survey of LGBTQ parents indicates that they are more involved in school activities than average parents and that they experience insults from students, other parents, and school personnel (Kosciw & Diaz, 2008). Children of LGBTQ parents also experience a high rate of harassment because of their parents' sexuality or gender identity (Kosciw & Diaz, 2008). In states with gay marriage, gay civil unions, and/or anti-discrimination policies that cover sexual orientation, courts have been supportive of curricular inclusion of LGBTQ-related lessons. These additions to curricula have not been without their critics. In Massachusetts, four parents objected to their inability to receive prior warning about or the right to opt out of lessons that taught respect for a variety of families, including lesbian- and gay-headed households. Courts found that the state had a rational interest in providing students with citizenship education and education promoting the tolerance of diversity, including LGBT people, in part because those are included in the educational standards of the state and also because the state allows gay marriage.

Challenges to Homophobia and Heterosexism

Many of the objections to educating students about LGBTQ, queer, and related issues in multicultural education still remain, arising from the kind of cultural conflicts that sexuality- and gender-related issues often engender. Not everyone thinks that LGBTQ, queer, and gender-nonconforming people should exist or deserve respect. Commonplace derogation of gay people in such phrases as *that's so gay* or epithets such as *faggot* or *dyke* indicate that homosexuality is still a focus of disapproval. A study conducted by students in five Des Moines, Iowa, high schools found that the average student hears words insulting gay people 25 times a day (Ruenzel, 1999). While the rate of hearing those particular insults seems to be dropping, other more severe forms of bullying continue at largely the same rates as ten years ago. Cultural beliefs and religious texts are often interpreted to mean that LGBTQ people are aberrant, sinful, or at the very least unacceptable. Pushing beyond what seem to be determinative statements from a given culture or faith tradition often shows a much more complex picture of the situation in which same-sex affection and partnership have long played an important role in the culture or in which various gender expressions have found support in a tradition. It may, of course, be difficult for adherents of particular religious traditions to see the intensity of same-sex love and commitment in their texts or to even begin to grapple with how those positive representations coexist with prohibitions against similar activities.

Further complicating the issue of sexual orientation and gender identity may be the sense that such forms of diversity and difference come from somewhere else—not from within a particular cultural tradition but imposed from outside. For instance, current dominant forms of homophobia may be directed at people who appear to be simply gay but are, in fact, displaying traditional indigenous identities. Two-spirit people—that is, people who embody American Indian traditional practices that defy dominant definitions of gender and sexuality—often find themselves harassed by those ignorant of the place of third genders and sexualities in indigenous cultures (Wilson, 1996). A commonplace assumption about homosexuality, not unrelated to the former example, is that all gay people are White, a belief partially related to the White dominance in many gay communities and to the inability to see diversity as more than one aspect of identity at a time. Too often discussions of diversity seem to assume that all people have one identity, not that they might live complex lives in which their multiple differences intersect and affect one another.

When we begin to complicate what sexuality means in relation to race, class, gender, disability, region, and religion, it quickly becomes clear that we need to be thinking not only about multiple versions and variations of sexual identity but also how different communities and contexts shape the life possibilities and definitions of sexual and gender identity of LGBTQ, queer, and gender-minority people (Bello, Flynn, Palmer, Rodriguez, & Vente, 2004; Blackburn, 2004, 2005; Irvine, 1994; Johnson & Henderson, 2005; Kumashiro, 2004; Leck, 2000; McCready, 2004; Ross, 2005; Sears, 1995; Sonnie, 2000; Wilson, 1996). Minority sexualities and gender identities—like other differences within communities—are themselves reminders that not all people in a given culture, race, ethnicity, or other seemingly similar coherent group are the same; there are differences within communities and subcultures structured around sexual orientation and gender identity. This may seem an obvious point, but dissent by members of communities from the sexual and/or gender norms of that community can result in a feeling that community norms have been disrupted and perhaps even a sense that the nonconformist person is a traitor to community cohesion. Of course, one can easily reverse the dynamic and wonder why communities and cultures cannot be more accepting of diversity in their midst. Indeed, that is one of the central challenges that multicultural education poses to U.S. public schooling: Can we conceive of educational institutions as welcoming places that recognize difference?

Challenging Assumptions about LGBTQ People

Assumptions about sexual-minority students need to be carefully analyzed. Schools, like the rest of the social world, are structured by heterosexism—the assumption that everyone is heterosexual. Curricula, texts, school policies, and even mundane examples (such as illustrations of magnets showing males attracted to females but repulsed by each other) are most often constructed to reflect heterosexuality as not only the norm but also as the only possible option for students (Friend, 1995). Heterosexism is also reinforced by homophobia—overt expressions of dislike, harassment, and even assaults against sexual-minority people—a practice that members of the school community often ignore or dismiss as typical behavior based on the heterosexist assumption that either there are no gay people present in school communities, or, if there are, those gay people ought to learn to expect a hostile environment. While homophobia may possibly be—at least in some places—less socially acceptable today than it was previously, it is nonetheless the case that schools are not very supportive places for most LGBTQ, queer, questioning, intersex, and ally students (that is, students who are not themselves LGBTQ but who oppose homophobia and heterosexism). The pressure to conform to rigid ideas about proper gender and sexuality is also damaging to heterosexual and gender-conforming students. Many students of all sexual orientations have experienced antigay or gender-identity-related harassment, so teaching all students to be respectful of gender and sexuality diversity helps everyone.

Members of school communities may believe that sexuality is not an appropriate topic for young people. However, there are significant numbers of LGBTQ, queer, and ally students in schools (as well as significant numbers of sexually aware heterosexual students). Ignoring the issue of sexuality means neglecting both to provide LGBTQ students with representations that enable them to understand themselves and to provide examples of ways to counter bias and work toward engendering respect among those who may not initially be willing to respect LGBTQ students. Many LGBTQ students report hearing insulting words on a daily basis. According to the 2009 National School Climate Survey of the Gay, Lesbian, and Straight Educators Network (GLSEN), 72.4 percent of students reported hearing derogatory language such as *faggot* and *dyke* (Kosciw, Greytak, Diaz, & Bartkiewicz, 2010). In the same report, 40.1 percent of students reported physical harassment because of their sexual orientation, while 27.2 percent experienced physical harassment because of their gender orientation. Physical assault on the basis of sexual orientation was reported by 18.8 percent of the students, and 12.5 percent reported physical assault because of their gender identity. Students also reported that they were more likely to hear homophobic comments in the presence of teachers than other forms of biased comments.

In the 2007 National School Climate Survey, Kevin Jennings, then the executive director of GLSEN, expressed his frustration with the lack of improvement since the surveys began in 1999:

> *I quite honestly feel a little depressed by how little things have improved from when we published our first report almost a decade ago. Why is it—when research shows so clearly that there are specific policy and programmatic interventions that will make our schools safer—that so many states and districts do nothing, allowing schools to remain an unsafe space for so many LGBTQ students? (cited in Kosciw, Diaz, & Greytak, 2008, p. viii)*

In the 2009 GLSEN National School Climate Study, researchers found that White, Latina/o, and multiracial LGBT students felt more unsafe at school compared to Black or Asian students. Multiracial students also report higher levels of harassment and assault based on sexual orientation and on gender expression than do other racial groups. Transgender students report feeling more unsafe at school because of gender identity and sexual orientation than do male or female students (Kosciw et al., 2010). This experience of feeling unsafe at schools also extends to young women in general. According to a 2001 study by the American Association of University Women (AAUW), 83 percent of young women experience sexual harassment, and 20 percent of them avoid school or certain classes in order to stay away from their tormentors. Young lesbians, gender-nonconforming young women, and any young person who is deemed by a harasser to be acting in gender-inappropriate ways—including turning down sexual advances—may all be targets for homophobic and sexist harassment.

The relationship among gender bias, homophobia, and harassment is complicated. On the one hand, young women of all sexualities experience harassment, including homophobic harassment if they act in ways that do not fit the norms for women. So the scope of gender- and sexuality-related harassment is quite broad for women. Because young men have a narrower range of acceptable masculine behavior, they, too, are targets for homophobic harassment on the basis of any gender-nonconforming behavior or are apt to have any forms of disagreement devolve into homophobic taunts. The intersections of categories of identity, then, must become central to how educators think and learn before they can begin to teach their students. These complex intersections of identity categories also extend to those of race, ethnicity, gender, and sexuality. As Kosciw and Diaz (2005) put it:

> *It appears that students most often report being targeted for verbal harassment based on multiple characteristics (e.g., being gay and Latino) or perhaps on the intersections of these characteristics (e.g., being a gay Latino). With regard to the more extreme forms of victimization, physical harassment and assault, it appears that sexual orientation alone becomes more salient. For example, the largest number of students of color reported being verbally harassed because of both their sexual orientation and race/ethnicity, followed by sexual orientation only (44.4% and 35.7%, respectively). However, nearly twice as many students of color reported physical assault because of their sexual orientation alone than reported assault because of both race/ethnicity and sexual orientation (11.7% vs. 6.8%). (p. 62)*

While most LGBTQ youth flourish and learn to counter the homophobic challenges they face and while it is important not only to focus on the challenges but also to stress the strength and resiliency of all minority youth, it is also crucial to understand that the costs of homophobia and bias against gender-nonconforming students can be very high. In February 2008, 15-year-old Lawrence King was murdered by a younger White student who had been part of a group bullying him for most of the school year. Out to his friends, Larry endured daily taunting. His 12-year-old friend Erin Mings said, "What he [King] did was really brave—to wear makeup and high-heeled boots." Mings hung out with King at E. O. Green. "Every corner he turned around, people were saying, 'Oh, my God, he's wearing makeup today.'" Mings said Larry stood his ground and was an outgoing and funny boy. "When people came up and started punking him, he just stood up for himself" (quoted in Saillant, 2008a, 2008b). Larry's story underscores the strength of young gender-nonconforming gay people and the very real dangers they can face in public schools. Wearing eye shadow to school and trying to be himself in this hostile context, Larry was continually open to taunting and bullying and tried to keep strong by flirting with his tormentors. Reports indicate that school officials were aware of the potential difficulties between Larry and his attacker but did not intervene (Saillant).

King's story not only demonstrates his energy and commitment to living his life but also stands as a reminder that much homophobia is fueled by bias against gender nonconformity (Gender Public Advocacy Coalition, 2002). The Gender Public Advocacy Coalition (Gender PAC), an organization dedicated to educating about gender identity, also noted in its 2002 annual report not only that gender-nonconforming students were the victims of bullying but also that students who engaged in school violence had experienced such bullying: "[F]ive of eight assailants in recent school shooting incidents were reportedly students who had been repeatedly gender-bashed and gender-baited in school" (p. 8). An AAUW (2001) study reported that more than almost anything else, students do not want to be called gay or lesbian; 74 percent said they would be very upset.

Even students who are not gay report overt homophobic and sexual harassment when they express support for sexual minorities. As one student put it, after experiencing pornographic death threats from other students while teachers did nothing to stop them, "Maybe it's because I have strong views. I've always spoken out for gays and lesbians, for Latinos, for those who get trampled on in our society. Still, I really have no idea why I was treated with such hostility" (quoted in Ruenzel, 1999, p. 24). The pressure on straight allies of LGBTQ individuals not to express their opposition to homophobia may indicate that not supporting gay people is an integral part of indicating one's own heterosexuality. As with Sleeter's (1994) observation that White people perform their race by expressing racist attitudes, people may perform heterosexuality by indicating their dislike of or discomfort around homosexuality.

The pressure on all students to conform to a gendered or heterosexual norm is powerful, especially in the school context, where public knowledge and choices about identity are closely watched (Thorne, 1995). The public context of 15-year-old, Black, gender-nonconforming Sakia Gunn's assertion of her lesbianism when sexually and homophobically harassed on a Newark street was both an important assertion of her claiming space in her community and the occasion of her murder by her harasser ("Lesbian Stabbing," 2003). Her space of assertion was honored by the Newark community's outcry against homophobic violence in a mass vigil commemorating Gunn's death and life (Smothers, 2004). A year after her killing, the school district that refused to have a moment of silence for her immediately after her murder allowed the anniversary to be acknowledged by having "No Name Calling Day" (Smothers, 2004). It is important to understand that homophobic violence and the potential for harassment do structure the lives of sexual minorities. But the understanding of their identities by Gunn and other young people, their knowledge of the places to go to find communities that support their gender and sexual identities, and their ability to express their identities—even in challenging situations—demonstrate that sexual- and gender-minority youth are actively and creatively involved in making their lives and communities.

Despite what sometimes seems to be an overwhelmingly hostile context in schools, the concerted efforts of students, teachers, administrators, and other members of the school community can shift school climates. As the GLSEN 2009 report shows, schools can make a difference in the experiences of LGBTQ youth. Students in schools with gay–straight alliances report hearing fewer homophobic remarks, report seeing staff intervene in bias more often, and were less likely to feel unsafe in their schools (Kosciw et al., 2010). Students in schools with an inclusive curriculum also reported lower levels of harassment, higher attendance rates, and more feelings of connection to their schools (Kosciw et al., 2010). However, progress can be undone without adequate institutional and teacher support. One of the first gay–straight alliances to attain the right to meet in public schools using the federal Equal Access Act disbanded years later because of continuing community hostility and lack of institutional advocacy and support. That group, however, was recently reorganized and supported by a unanimous vote by school officials who were educated about and supportive of antihomophobia projects (American Civil Liberties Union, 2006). There has been much coverage of the role of the Internet in the harassment that led to Rutgers student Tyler Clementi's suicide. The "It Gets Better" (2010–2011) campaign, also Internet-based, provides short videos of LGBT and ally adults reassuring young people that there are adults out there who are supportive or who themselves went through homophobic bullying. Showing young people that there are numerous prominent and caring people who want to see them succeed and provide them with information on bullying hotlines and LGBT advocacy organizations may be one way to help work against the isolation they experience.

Each of these examples points to the need to address homophobia and sexual-minority issues through multilevel approaches. Youths are capable of asserting themselves and finding community with others, but without the institutional support of schools and the interventions of respectful adults, the struggles they may have to face are all the more daunting. Ensuring that sexual- and gender-minority youths have space and time to meet together creates one place in school that addresses their communities. Incorporating LGBTQ and gender-identity issues into curricula, teacher education, school leadership programs, and school antidiscrimination policies is a strategy that reinforces inclusion across the entire institution of education.

Each of these steps requires more than just stopping harassment. It requires thinking critically about the messages in curricula, the way teachers and administrators talk to students, and the way school-based social events are organized. Do representations of historical figures or communities in the curriculum show a diversity of sexual orientation and gender identity? When lessons discuss civil rights movements, do they include ones that advocated gender- and sexual-identity rights? If lessons do include gay liberation and feminism, do those lessons include racial, ethnic, sexual-orientation, and gender-identity diversity? Do lessons on families create openings for even very young children to see a diversity of families represented in children's books and classroom discussions, as well as the diversity of gender identities? Do representations of romance and sexuality—including everything from sex education to advertisements for dances and proms—reflect only heterosexuality? Do teachers reinforce heterosexism by referring only to heterosexual couples, by assuming that everyone has a parent of each gender, by assigning texts that represent only heterosexuality, or by neglecting to address comments such as "that's so gay" with more than a simple prohibition?

Why Homophobia?

Education against homophobia and about sexual-minority issues needs to grapple with cultural and traditional objections to sexual-minority people and communities. Without addressing the deep cultural, political, and historical obstacles to educating LGBTQ people and educating about them, progress toward multicultural education and justice will be only half-hearted at best. While some religious traditions may be the root of some cultural disapproval of homosexuality, most religious traditions do not require their adherents to demand doctrinal discipline from those outside their faith tradition. Given the pervasiveness of homophobia even among people whose discomfort is not grounded in religious traditions, it is clear that other anxieties also motivate discomfort about minority sexualities and gender identities. Many religious denominations are very supportive of sexual and gender minorities. Consequently, the tendency to blame religion for homophobia is an oversimplification. Denominations supportive of sexual and gender minorities include the Metropolitan Community Church, Reform Judaism, the United Church of Christ, the Society of Friends (Quakers), and Unitarianism as well as segments of the Episcopal and Lutheran churches. Individual congregations of many faiths are also supportive of sexual and gender minorities.

As education against homophobia proceeds, then, it is necessary to find ways both to support people who are subjected to homophobia and to ask difficult questions about the cultural, religious, and contemporary roots of or alibis for homophobia. Acknowledging the existence of multiple cultural, local, and global forms of same-sex affection and gender variety may be one starting point. Examining the variety of expressions of tolerance and value of minority identities within minority and majority cultures may provide insights into the differences that make up even seemingly coherent and unified cultures and subcultures. These issues should be familiar to anyone grappling with how to study and educate about any form of identity. But there are particular features to sex and gender identity that make addressing it challenging.

How much of homophobia is a reflection of cultural attitudes about sex in general, and how robust is discrimination when sex and youth are connected (Silin, 1995)? How much of homophobia is bias against gender-nonconforming behavior? Does homophobia reflect a cultural disparagement of femininity, or, as some would put it, is homophobia a weapon of sexism (Pharr, 1997)? We can think here of the use of the word *girls* to insult young men and what that says about the pervasiveness of sexism. Does homophobia indicate anxiety about the fragility of the heterosexual norm? When even slightly gender-nonconforming behavior or friendship with someone of the same sex can start rumors and lead to harassment or when people feel compelled to assert their heterosexuality should doubt arise, we can see the process of normalization working on everyone. The ease with which such anxieties surface despite a climate of heterosexism that generally does not allow discussion of queer possibility indicates the haunting presence of queerness even in the midst of what is generally the unquestioned norm of heterosexuality.

It is important to consider the diverse cultural and political roots of homophobia—to be, in other words, multiculturally aware of different forms of bias against sexual and gender nonconformity. However, there is a danger in letting homophobia define how and why lessons on sexual minorities are included in school. Institutional and legal restrictions have shaped the lives of sexual-minority people, yet it would be a vast oversimplification to say that is the only reality of their lives. Sexuality, as with any other category of meaning, has a long and varied history—indeed, histories of identities and subjectivities that bear little resemblance to the categories by which we currently define sexual identity. As much as their communities and identity formations were related to restrictions on their ability to live, LGBTQ individuals nonetheless formed cultures, associations, and—like other minorities living in a cultural context shaped by bias—reshaped their worlds. Tactically, it may be possible to convince people who do not initially want to include sexual-minority issues in schooling that to do so would help address the risks that LGBTQ students face. However, we also need to be careful that LGBTQ issues are not framed as only risk or deficit. When antihomophobia and multicultural pedagogies—and chapters such as this one—defensively cite statistics on harassment or provide a panel of LGBTQ people to describe their difficulties with homophobia, they miss the opportunity to examine the positive aspects of LGBTQ communities and cultures and the ability of sexual-minority people to live lives beyond institutional constraints.

Uprisings such as those at the Stonewall Inn or the Compton Cafeteria underscore the experience of harassment and exclusion as well as the ability of people to resist. That resistance further points to the fact that communities were already organized and understood themselves to have developed the expectation of respect for one another as members. By focusing on moments of conflict and the particular people injured by bias, do we imply that those groups and identities have meaning only because of their clash with the dominant culture? Is the story of oppression and bias the only way schools are willing to even begin to address sexual and gender minorities? By focusing only on minority sexualities and the experience of bias, schools neglect to examine the relationship between the dominant sexuality's claim to normality and the resultant heterosexism and heteronormativity of the curricula, institutional organizations, and school policies. By thinking of heterosexism and homophobia as evident only in spectacles of bias—such as homophobic injury, assault, or murder—the everyday forms of heterosexism go unremarked upon, as does the everyday presence of people who do not conform to gender and sexual norms. If teachers are unwilling to acknowledge and educate about the positive aspects of sexuality, they also neglect the relationship between sexuality and identity; ignore the place of sexuality in initiating and sustaining personal, cultural, and community relationships; and reinforce the unacceptability of educating about sexuality and pleasure.

Dilemmas of Queer Inclusion

In the 1990s, a group of young queer activists calling themselves Queer Nation coined a new protest chant: "We're here, we're queer, get over it, get used to it." While Queer Nation was immediately challenged for its racism, and groups of people of color such as QueerNAsian split off in protest, the chant is a reminder that queerness is a challenge to critically assess the meanings of gender and sexuality. It is also a reminder that centering gender and sexuality can easily lead to White dominance and the related neglect of the centrality of race and ethnicity to sexuality and gender. The confrontational politics of visibility spawned during this period stressed not the exclusions of heterosexism or the biases of homophobia but simply the presence of non-normative people, bodies, acts, and communities. One of the central claims of the gay liberation and lesbian feminist movements was recentered: People of non-normative gender and sexuality exist; indeed, the presence of non-normativeness defines every sexual and gender identity. Furthermore, the larger conversation about queerness and race was a reminder that the destabilization of one term, such as *sexuality*, without adequate thought and action can simply reinforce Whiteness. But the name "Queer Nation" underscored the tension between a collectivity such as a nation and the destabilizing function of the term *queer*.

To queer something means to challenge its core meaning, and queer politics sought to challenge the claim to normality that structured heterosexuality. Queers of color, continuing to use that "queering" function, queered the Whiteness of the new term. Young people continue to be engaged and to use the potential for critique and reconsideration offered by the term *queer*. By queering social norms and making those critiques into political projects, queer theory and the work that sexual-minority youth and their allies do to improve schools provide a critique of standard attempts at inclusion—attempts that often leave key categories unexamined—and insist, as the transformative approaches to multicultural education do, on critiquing the political structure of schools. But a politics based on visibility can itself be queered: Who is excluded if we privilege visible or legible differences? How does the pressure to be out in a certain way rely on particular culturally specific forms of understanding identity or generationally specific forms of political engagement? Where do other forms of difference appear if the central term is *queer* and implies "White"?

Even in the absence of help and support from adults in school communities, young activists of all sexualities and gender identities now engaged in improving their schools are making it clear that sexuality- and gender-related issues concern everyone. Student-led groups form alliances that include diverse identities and people who find labels restrictive, problematic, or insufficient. These groups work carefully to avoid replicating the same exclusions they have faced. Racial and ethnic exclusions, though, remain a core problem, even as LGBTQ students and allies work to teach their communities that homophobia and heterosexism are everyone's problem.

Gay–straight alliances expand from addressing homophobia to creating an understanding of the place of sexual and gender identity in everyone's life and community. So does the Day of Silence, an annual event in which students who support education about LGBTQ issues remain silent for an entire day in school to dramatize the silencing of sexual- and gender-minority students and the lack of representation of sexual and gender differences in curricula. By focusing on the ties among students of all sexual orientations and gender identities, such groups and events shift the focus from the particularities of student differences to larger coalitional efforts to improve school communities.

Gay–straight alliances provide students a space for critical engagement with media and political issues, a space often not provided by the official curricula. As diverse students meet to queer and question their own self-definitions, they also need to critically engage with the racial, ethnic, gender, and sexual exclusions they may unthinkingly replicate (Mayo, 2004b; Miceli, 2005; Perrotti & Westheimer, 2001). Gay–straight alliances and the Day of Silence, two student-centered projects, underscore the place of youths in defining sexuality-related issues in schools. As youths begin to form new types of sexual and gender identities—such as queer, questioning, gender queer, and curious—they challenge adult understandings and educate all of us about new possibilities (Britzman, 1995, 1997; Leck, 2000; Rasmussen, 2004; Talburt, 2004). These critically important youth-led activities in public schools remind us that queer projects need to work to understand how the intersection of race, ethnicity, and gender must remain central in order for queerness to live up to its potential.

As with any other communities, LGBTQ communities are diversely raced, gendered, classed, and made up of people with complex and intersecting identities. And as with other diverse communities, LGBTQ communities face the challenges of internal and external homophobia, racism, sexism, transphobia, classism, and other forms of bias. Indeed, another way to look at LGBTQ communities is to do so more locally, in which case it becomes clear that LGBTQ people of color find spaces within their racial and ethnic communities because they value these home communities—and find more political and social support there than they would in White-dominated LGBTQ communities. The segregated nature of U.S. public education contributes to the White dominance of LGBTQ organizations in schools and communities (McCready, 2004). LGBTQ youth groups often reflect the racial and ethnic divisions that are crucial forms of support and belonging, but they are also influenced by bias that is exacerbated by how schools are organized and where they are situated. That is, even schools with diverse populations are often structured by internal racial and ethnic segregation. Sexual orientation and gender identity will not only enrich multicultural education but also benefit LGBTQ communities by enabling young people to be educated more vigorously to understand and value differences, whether long-standing or emergent.

Seven Things to Do to Improve Education for Students of All Sexual Orientations and Genders

1. Understand the complexity of sexuality and gender identity: Do not assume heterosexuality or enforce gender conformity. Think about your own coming-out process, whatever your sexual orientation or preference. Think about your own experiences of enforced gender conformity. How can these memories and experiences help you to understand your students' experiences?

2. Think critically about how heterosexism and homophobia have structured all of our understandings of ourselves and of our relationships, communities, and education. Use gender-neutral terms for parents and gender-neutral examples and other techniques that make it clear that you understand that students, parents, school personnel, and other community members are not all heterosexual.

3. Challenge the implicit and explicit heterosexism, homophobia, and gender conformity in the curricula and other school-based practices. Interrupt homophobia, heterosexism, and gender-identity prejudice when you see it, and take the opportunity to educate about it. Do not let harassment continue unchallenged.

4. Understand the intersections among gender, race, sexual orientation, class, and other aspects of identity. Include references to and images of diverse LGBTQ people in your classrooms.

5. Try to queer your own categories of normal; interrogate them for problematic assumptions about sexuality, gender, and youth as well as other categories of diversity and difference.

6. Learn about diverse LGBTQ histories and cultures, and understand how heterosexual allies have been critical to obtaining social justice.

7. Know about community resources for LGBTQ youth, including ally faculty and staff at your own school. If you are unable to provide the kind of support that LGBTQ students, colleagues, or parents need, find out who can.

QUESTIONS AND ACTIVITIES

9.1   In what ways have movements for social justice recognized sexual orientation and gender identity? How have they ignored sexual orientation and gender identity? Why do LGBTQ issues pose a challenge for social justice movements and multicultural education? What do LGBTQ issues bring to social justice movements and multicultural education?

9.2 What can schools do to be more welcoming places for sexual and gender diversity? What assumptions about LGBTQ students need to be challenged in order for their diversity to be recognized?

9.3 What is an intersectional approach? How does it help us to be more aware of the interplay of differences?

9.4 Why is it a problem to think about LGBTQ issues only in terms of harassment and difficulties in school?

9.5 What would it mean to queer the curriculum?

9.6 How could you as a teacher support the LGBTQ and ally activities in which your students might be interested?

REFERENCES

American Association of University Women (AAUW). (2001). *Hostile hallways: Bullying, teasing, and sexual harassment in school.* New York: AAUW Foundation.

American Civil Liberties Union. (2006, February 18). ACLU hails federal court ruling on school trainings aimed at reducing anti-gay harassment. Retrieved January 15, 2009, from http://aclu.org/lgbt/youth/24215prs20060218.html.

Anzaldúa, G. (1990). La conciencia de la mestiza: Towards a new consciousness. In G. Anzaldúa (Ed.), *Haciendo caras: Making face, making soul* (pp. 377–389). San Francisco: Aunt Lute.

Apetheker, H. (1992). *Antiracism in U. S. history: The first two hundred years.* New York: Greenwood.

Bello, N., Flynn, S., Palmer, H., Rodriguez, R., & Vente, A. (2004). *Hear me out: True stories of teens educating and confronting homophobia.* Toronto, ON, Canada: Second Story.

Bennett, L. (1997, Fall). Break the silence. *Teaching Tolerance, 12,* 24–29.

Blackburn, M. V. (2004, Spring). Understanding agency beyond school-sanctioned activities. *Theory into Practice, 43,* 102–110.

Blackburn, M. V. (2005, January). Agency in borderland discourses: Examining language use in a community center with Black queer youth. *Teachers College Record, 107,* 89–113.

Britzman, D. P. (1995). Is there a queer pedagogy? Or, stop reading straight. *Educational Theory, 45,* 151–165.

Britzman, D. P. (1997). What is this thing called love? New discourses for understanding gay and lesbian youth. In S. de Castell & M. Bryson (Eds.), *Radical in(ter)ventions: Identity, politics, and difference/s in educational praxis* (pp. 183–207). Albany: State University of New York Press.

Brownmiller, S. (1970, March 15). "Sisterhood is powerful": A member of the women's liberation movement explains what it's all about. *New York Times Magazine,* p. 140.

Capper, C. A. (1999). (Homo)sexualities, organizations, and administration: Possibilities for inquiry. *Educational Researcher, 28,* 4–11.

Casper, V., & Schultz, S. B. (1999). *Gay parents/straight schools: Building communication and trust.* New York: Teachers College Press.

Clarke, C. L. (1981). Lesbianism: An act of resistance. In C. Moraga & G. Anzaldúa (Eds.), *This bridge called my back: Writings by radical women of color* (pp. 128–137). Watertown, MA: Persephone.

Clarke, C. L. (1983). The failure to transform: Homophobia in the Black community. In B. Smith (Ed.), *Home girls: A Black feminist anthology* (pp. 197–208). New York: Kitchen Table: Woman of Color Press.

Cohen, C. (1999). *Boundaries of Blackness: AIDS and the breakdown of Black politics.* Chicago: University of Chicago Press.

Combahee River Collective. (1982). A Black feminist statement. In B. Smith, P. B. Scott, & G. T. Hull (Eds.), *All the women are White, all the men are Black, but some of us are brave: Black women's studies* (pp. 13–22). Old Westbury, NY: Feminist Press.

D'Emilio, J. (2003). *Lost prophet! The life and times of Bayard Rustin.* New York: Free Press.

Duncan, G. A. (2005). Black youth, identity, and ethics. *Educational Theory, 55,* 3–22.

Friend, R. A. (1995). Choices, not closets: Heterosexism and homophobia in schools. In L. Weis & M. Fine (Eds.), *Beyond silenced voices: Class, race, and gender in United States schools* (pp. 209–235). Albany: State University of New York Press.

Frye, P. R. (2002). Facing discrimination, organizing for freedom: The transgender community. In J. D'Emilio, W. B. Turner, & U. Vaid (Eds.), *Creating change: Sexuality, public policy, and civil rights* (pp. 451–468). New York: Stonewall Inn Editions.

Gender Political Advocacy Coalition (Gender PAC). (2002). *Gender PAC annual report 2002.* Washington, DC: Author.

Humm, A. (1994). Re-building the "Rainbow": The holy war over inclusion in New York City. Unpublished manuscript.

Irvine, J. (Ed.). (1994). *Sexual cultures and the construction of adolescent identities.* Philadelphia: Temple University Press.

It Gets Better Project. (2010–2011). Retrieved September 7, 2011, from www.itsgetsbetter.org.

Johnson, E. P., & Henderson, M. G. (Eds.). (2005). *Black queer studies: A critical anthology.* Durham, NC: Duke University Press.

Kosciw, J. G., & Diaz, E. (2005). *2005 National School Climate Survey.* New York: Gay, Lesbian, and Straight Education Network.

Kosciw, J. G., & Diaz, E. (2008). *Involved, invisible, and ignored: The experiences of lesbian, gay, bisexual, and transgender parents and their children in our nation's K–12 schools.* New York: Gay, Lesbian, and Straight Education Network.

Kosciw, J. G., Diaz, E. M., & Greytak, E. A. (2008). *2007 National School Climate Survey: The experiences of lesbian, gay, bisexual, and transgender youth in our nation's schools.* New York: Gay, Lesbian, and Straight Education Network.

Kosciw, J. G., Greytak, E. A., Diaz, E. M., & Bartkiewicz, M. J. (2010). *2009 National School Climate Survey: The experiences of lesbian, gay, bisexual and transgender youth in our nation's schools.* New York: Gay, Lesbian, and Straight Education Network.

Kumashiro, K. (2001). *Troubling intersections of race and sexuality: Queer students of color and anti-oppressive education.* Lanham, MD: Rowman & Littlefield.

Kumashiro, K. (2002). *Troubling education: Queer activism and anti-oppressive education.* New York: Routledge.

Kumashiro, K. (2003). Queer ideas in education. *Journal of Homosexuality, 45*(2/3/4), 365–367.

Kumashiro, K. (2004). Uncertain beginnings: Learning to teach paradoxically. *Theory into Practice, 43*(2), 111–115.

Leck, G. M. (2000). Heterosexual or homosexual? Reconsidering binary narratives on sexual identities in urban schools. *Education and Urban Society, 32*, 324–348.

Lee, N., Murphy, D., North, L., & Ucelli, J. (2000). Bridging race, class, and sexuality for school reform. In J. D'Emilio, W. B. Turner, & U. Vaid (Eds.), *Creating change: Sexuality, public policy, and civil rights* (pp. 251–260). New York: St. Martin's Press.

Lesbian stabbing coverage draws cries of bias. (2003, August 14). Retrieved September 18, 2008, from planetout.com/news/article-print.html?2003/08/14/4.

Lorde, A. (1984). *Sister/outsider: Essays and speeches.* Trumansburg, NY: Crossing.

Lorde, A. (1988). *A burst of light: Essays by Audre Lorde.* Ithaca, NY: Firebrand.

Manalansan, M. (2003). *Global divas: Filipino men in the diaspora.* Durham, NC: Duke University Press.

Mayo, C. (2004a/2007). *Disputing the subject of sex: Sexuality and public school controversy.* Boulder, CO: Rowman & Littlefield.

Mayo, C. (2004b). The tolerance that dare not speak its name. In M. Boler (Ed.), *Democratic dialogue in education: Disturbing silence, troubling speech* (pp. 33–47). New York: Peter Lang.

Mayo, C. (2006). Pushing the limits of liberalism: Queerness, children, and the future. *Educational Theory, 56*(4), 469–487.

McCready, L. T. (2004). Understanding the marginalization of gay and gender non-conforming Black male students. *Theory into Practice, 43*, 136–143.

Miceli, M. (2005). *Standing out, standing together.* New York: Routledge.

Myers, S. L. (1992, December 1). School board in Queens shuns Fernandez meeting. *New York Times*, p. B4.

Newton, H. (1973). A letter from Huey. In L. Richmond & G. Noguera (Eds.), *The gay liberation book: Writings and photographs on gay (men's) liberation* (pp. 142–145). San Francisco: Ramparts.

New York City Board of Education. (1994). *Comprehensive instructional program first grade teachers' resource guide review draft (Children of the Rainbow).* New York: Board of Education Publications.

Perrotti, J., & Westheimer, K. (2001). *When the drama club is not enough: Lessons from the safe schools program for gay and lesbian students.* Boston: Beacon.

Pharr, S. (1997). *Homophobia: A weapon of sexism.* Hoboken, NJ: Chardon.

Rasmussen, M. L. (2004). The problem of coming out. *Theory into Practice, 43*, 144–150.

Ross, M. B. (2005). Beyond the closet as raceless paradigm. In E. P. Johnson & M. G. Henderson (Eds.), *Black queer studies: A critical anthology* (pp. 161–189). Durham, NC: Duke University Press.

Ruenzel, D. (1999, April). Pride and prejudice. *Teacher Magazine*, pp. 22–27.

Saillant, C. (2008a, February 17). 1,000 march in Oxnard in tribute to slain teen. *Los Angeles Times.* Retrieved June 17, 2008, from http://www.larticles.latimes.com/2008/feb/17/local/me-oxnard17.

Saillant, C. (2008b, May 8). Lawyer blames school in shooting of gay Oxnard student. *Los Angeles Times.* Retrieved June 17, 2008, from http://www.latimes.com/news/printedition/california/la-me-oxnard8-2008may08,0,6901056.story.

Sears, J. T. (1995). Black-gay or gay-black? Choosing identities and identifying choices. In G. Unks (Ed.), *The gay teen* (pp. 135–157). New York: Routledge.

Silin, J. G. (1995). *Sex, death, and the education of children: Our passion for ignorance in the age of AIDS.* New York: Teachers College Press.

Sleeter, C. E. (1994). A multicultural educator views White racism. *Education Digest, 59*(9), 33–36.

Smith, B. (1983). Introduction. In B. Smith (Ed.), *Home girls: A Black feminist anthology* (pp. xix–lvi). New York: Kitchen Table: Woman of Color Press.

Smothers, R. (2004, May 12). Newark preaches tolerance of gays year after killing. *New York Times*, p. B5. Retrieved July 4, 2009 from http://www.nytimes.com/2004/05/12/nyregion/newark-preaches-tolerance-of-gays-year-after-killing.html.

Sonnie, A. (Ed.). (2000). *Revolutionary voices: A multicultural queer youth anthology.* Los Angeles: Alyson.

Stryker, S. (2008). Transgender history, homonormativity, and disciplinarity. *Radical History Review*, 145–157.

Talburt, S. (2004). Constructions of LGBT youth: Opening up subject positions. *Theory into Practice, 43*, 116–121.

Thorne, B. (1995). *Gender play: Girls and boys at school.* New Brunswick, NJ: Rutgers University Press.

Wilson, A. (1996). How we find ourselves: Identity development and two-spirit people. *Harvard Educational Review, 66*, 303–317.

Culturally relevant pedagogy can increase the achievement of ethnically, racially, and linguistically diverse students.

Masterfile Royalty-Free

© jacky chapman/Alamy Limited

Thomas Tolstrup/Taxi/Getty Images, Inc.

Race, Ethnicity, and Language

The drastic increase in the percentage of students of color and of language-minority students in U.S. schools is one of the most significant developments in education in the last two decades. This increase results from several factors, including the wave of immigration that began after 1968 and the aging of the White population. U.S. classrooms are experiencing the largest influx of immigrant students since the beginning of the 20th century. Nearly 14 million new immigrants (legal and undocumented) settled in the United States between 2000 and 2010. Less than 10 percent came from nations in Europe. Most came from Mexico, from nations in Asia, and from nations in Latin America, the Caribbean, and Central America (Camarota, 2011).

Demographers predict that if current trends continue, approximately 46 percent of the nation's school-age youths will be of color by the year 2020. In school year 2009–2010, 45 percent of students in prekindergarten through twelfth grade in public schools were members of a minority group, an increase from 32 percent in 1989 and 39 percent in 1999 (National Center for Education Statistics, 2009). In 2009, students of color exceeded the number of White students in the District of Columbia and in 12 states: Arizona, California, Florida, Georgia, Hawaii, Louisiana, Maryland, Mississippi, New Mexico, Nevada, New York, and Texas (Aud et al., 2011). In 2009, children of undocumented immigrants made up 6.8 percent of students in kindergarten through grade 12 (Perez, 2011). Approximately one of every five students lived in a low-income family in 2011.

While the nation's students are becoming increasingly diverse, most of the nation's teachers remain White (83.5 percent), female (75.6 percent), and middle class. The percentage of teachers of color remains low; in 2007–2008, they made up only 16 percent of teachers in the United States (National Center for Education Statistics, 2008). The growing racial, cultural, and income gap between teachers and students underscores the need for all teachers to develop the knowledge, attitudes, and skills needed to work effectively with students from diverse racial, ethnic, social-class, and language groups. The three chapters in this part of the book present concepts, knowledge, and strategies that all teachers will find helpful in working with students from diverse groups.

REFERENCES

Aud, S., Hussar, W., Kena, G., Bianco, K., Frohlich, L., Kemp, J., & Tahan, K. (2011). *The condition of education 2011* (NCES 2011-033). U.S. Department of Education, National Center for Education Statistics. Washington, DC: U.S. Government Printing Office. Retrieved November 14, 2011, from http://nces.ed.gov/programs/coe/pdf/coe_1er.pdf.

Camarota, S. A. (2011, October). *A record-setting decade of immigration: 2000 to 2010*. Washington, DC: Center for Immigration Studies. Retrieved November 14, 2011, from http://cis.org/2000-2010-record-setting-decade-of-immigration.

National Center for Education Statistics. (2008). *Schools and staffing survey.* Retrieved November 20, 2011, from http://nces.ed.gov/surveys/sass/tables/sass0708_029_t12n.asp.

National Center for Education Statistics. (2009). *The condition of education.* Retrieved November 21, 2011, from http://nces.ed.gov/programs/coe/figures/figure-1er-1.asp.

Perez, W. (2011). *Americans by heart: Undocumented Latino students and the promise of higher education.* New York: Teachers College Press.

Masterfile Royalty-Free

Approaches to Multicultural Curriculum Reform

James A. Banks

The Mainstream-Centric Curriculum

Cultural, ethnic, racial, linguistic, and religious diversity is increasing in the United States as well as in the nation's schools. The U.S. (2009) projects that ethnic minorities will increase from one-third of the nation's population in 2006 to 50 percent in 2042. Despite the deepening ethnic texture in the United States, the U.S. school, college, and university mainstream curriculum is organized around concepts, paradigms, and events that primarily reflect the experiences of mainstream Americans (Banks, 2007, 2008). The dominant, mainstream curriculum has been challenged and fractured in the last four decades, beginning with the civil rights movement of the 1960s and 1970s. Consequently, the mainstream curriculum and textbooks today are much more multicultural than they were when the civil rights movement began. Progress has been made, and it should be acknowledged and appreciated.

An interesting and informative study by Wineburg and Monte-Sano (2008) about who were considered the most famous Americans in history by a national sample of high school students is a significant marker of the changes that have occurred in both the teaching of history and in the "societal" (Cortés, 2000) or "cultural" curriculum (Wineburg & Monte-Sano, 2008) since the late 1960s. Martin Luther King Jr., Rosa Parks, and Harriet Tubman headed the list. The other seven individuals on the list—in descending order—were Susan B. Anthony, Benjamin Franklin, Amelia Earhart, Oprah Winfrey, Marilyn Monroe, Thomas Edison, and Albert Einstein. Wineburg and Monte-Sano found that region had little effect on the students' responses. However, race was a powerful factor. African American students were much more likely than White students to name King, Tubman, Winfrey, and Parks. White students were significantly more likely to name White figures than were African American students.

The curriculum and societal changes suggested by the Wineburg and Monte-Sano study (2008) are encouraging and should be recognized and applauded. However, curricular and societal reforms have been neither as extensive nor as institutionalized as is needed to reflect the complex and increasing diversity in the United States and the world. Consequently, the process of curriculum transformation needs to continue. Curriculum transformation is a process that never ends because of the changes that are continuing within the United States and throughout the world (Banks, 2009a, 2009b).

A curriculum that focuses on the experiences of mainstream Americans and largely ignores the experiences, cultures, and histories of other ethnic, racial, cultural, language, and religious groups has negative consequences for both mainstream students and students of color. A main-stream-centric curriculum is one major way in which racism, ethnocentrism, and pernicious nationalism are reinforced and perpetuated in schools, colleges, universities, and society at large.

A mainstream-centric curriculum has negative consequences for mainstream students because it reinforces their false sense of superiority, gives them a misleading conception of their relationship with other racial and ethnic groups, and denies them the opportunity to benefit from the knowledge, perspectives, and frames of reference that can be gained from studying and experiencing other cultures and groups. A mainstream-centric curriculum also denies mainstream U.S. students the opportunity to view their culture from the perspectives of other cultures and groups. When people view their culture from the point of view of another culture, they are able to understand their own culture more fully, to see how it is unique and distinct from other cultures, and to understand better how it relates to and interacts with other cultures.

A mainstream-centric curriculum negatively influences students of color, such as African Americans, Latinos, and Asian Americans. It marginalizes their experiences and cultures and does not reflect their dreams, hopes, and perspectives. It does not provide them *social equality* within the school, an essential characteristic of democratic institutions (Gutmann, 2004). Students learn best and are more highly motivated when the school curriculum reflects their cultures, experiences, and perspectives. Many students of color are alienated in the school in part because they experience cultural conflict and discontinuities that result from the cultural differences between their school and community (Au, 2011; Lee, 2006). The school can help students of color mediate between their home and school cultures by implementing a curriculum that reflects the culture of their ethnic groups and communities. The school can and should make effective use of the community cultures of students of color when teaching them such subjects as writing, language arts, science, and mathematics (Lee, 2007).

The mainstream-centric curriculum views events, themes, concepts, and issues primarily from the perspective of mainstream Americans and Europeans. Events and cultural developments such as the European explorations in the Americas and the development of American music are viewed from Anglo and European perspectives and are evaluated using mainstream-centric criteria and points of view (Au, 2009).

When the European explorations of the Americas are viewed from a Eurocentric perspective, the Americas are perceived as having been "discovered" by European explorers such as Columbus and Cortés (Loewen, 2010; Zinn, 1999). The view that Native peoples in the Americas were discovered by the Europeans subtly suggests that Indian cultures did not exist until they were "discovered" by the Europeans and that the lands occupied by the American Indians were rightfully owned by the Europeans after they settled on and claimed them.

When the formation and nature of U.S. cultural developments, such as music and dance, are viewed from mainstream-centric perspectives, these art forms become important and significant only when they are recognized or legitimized by mainstream critics and artists. The music of African American musicians such as Chuck Berry and Little Richard was not viewed as significant by the mainstream society until White singers such as the Beatles and Rod Stewart publicly acknowledged the significant ways in which their own music had been heavily influenced by these African American musicians. It often takes White artists to legitimize ethnic cultural forms and innovations created by Asian Americans, African Americans, Latinos, and Native Americans.

Public Sites and Popular History

Anglo-centric history is not only taught in U.S. schools, colleges, and universities but is also perpetuated in popular knowledge in the nation's parks, museums, and other public sites. Loewen (1999) describes the ways in which public history in the nation's historic sites is often distorted in order to present a positive image of Anglo Americans. The title of his book is *Lies across America: What Our Historic Sites Get Wrong.*

I have seen several examples of markers in public sites that perpetuate Anglo-centric views of American history. The first appears on a marker in a federal park on the site where a U.S. Army post once stood in Fort Townsend in the state of Washington. With the choice of words such as *settlers* (instead of *invaders*), *restive,* and *rebelled,* the author justifies the taking of the Indians' lands and depicts their resistance as unreasonable.

Fort Townsend

A U.S. Army Post was established on this site in 1856. In [the] mid-nineteenth century the growth of Port Townsend caused the Indians to become restive. Settlers *started a home guard, campaigned wherever called, and defeated the Indians in the Battle of Seattle. Indians* rebelled *as the government began enforcing the Indian Treaty of 1854, by which the Indians had ceded most of their territory. Port Townsend, a prosperous port of entry on Puget Sound, then asked protection of the U.S. army. (emphasis added)*

The second example is in Marianna, Arkansas, my hometown, which is the city center for Lee County. The site commemorates the lives and achievements of Confederate soldiers from Lee County and the life of Robert E. Lee, a general of the Confederate Army and a southern hero. The marker reads in part, "In loving memory of Lee County's Confederate soldiers. No braver bled for a brighter land. No brighter land had a cause so grand." The final example is from a marker in the Confederate Park in Memphis, Tennessee, which commemorates the life of Jefferson Davis, president of the Confederate States of America. The marker reads, in part: "Before the war between the States, he served with distinction as a United States Congressman and twice as a United States Senator. He also served as Secretary of War of the U.S. He was a true American patriot." Describing Davis as a "true American patriot" is arguable.

Another interesting and revealing book by Loewen (2005) is *Sundown Towns: A Hidden Dimension of American Racism*. In this informative book, Loewen describes communities that kept out groups such as African Americans, Chinese Americans, and Jewish Americans by force, law, or custom. These towns are called "sundown towns" because specific minorities had to be out of the towns before sunset. Loewen found more than 440 of these towns that existed across the United States.

Efforts to Establish a Multicultural Curriculum

Since the civil rights movement of the 1960s, educators have been trying, in various ways, to better integrate the school curriculum with multicultural content and to move away from a mainstream-centric and Eurocentric curriculum (Banks, 2008, 2009a, 2009b). These have proven to be difficult goals for schools to attain for many complex reasons. The strong assimilationist ideology embraced by most U.S. educators is one major reason (Banks, 2006). The assimilationist ideology makes it difficult for educators to think differently about how U.S. society and culture developed and to acquire a commitment to make the curriculum multicultural. Individuals who have a strong assimilationist ideology believe that most important events and developments in U.S. society are related to the nation's British heritage and that the contributions of other ethnic and cultural groups are not very significant by comparison. When educators acquire a multicultural ideology and conception of U.S. culture, they are then able to view the experiences and contributions of a wide range of cultural, ethnic, language, and religious groups as significant to the development of the United States.

Ideological resistance is a major factor that has slowed and is still slowing the development of a multicultural curriculum, but other factors have also affected its growth and development. *Political resistance* to a multicultural curriculum is closely related to ideological resistance. Many people who resist a multicultural curriculum believe that knowledge is power and that a multicultural perspective on U.S. society challenges the existing power structure. They believe that the dominant mainstream-centric curriculum supports, reinforces, and justifies the existing social, economic, and political structure. Multicultural perspectives and points of view, in the opinion of many observers, legitimize and promote social change and social reconstruction.

During the 1980s and 1990s, a heated debate occurred about how much the curriculum should be Western and Eurocentric or should reflect the cultural, ethnic, and racial diversity in the United States. At least three major positions in this debate can be identified. The *Western traditionalists* argue that the West, as defined and conceptualized in the past, should be the focus in school and college curricula because of the major influence of Western civilization and culture in the United States and throughout the world (Ravitch, 1990; Schlesinger, 1998). *Afro-centric* scholars contend that the contributions of Africa and of African peoples should receive major emphasis in the curriculum (Asante, 1998; Asante & Ravitch, 1991). The *multiculturalists* argue that although the West should receive a major emphasis in the curriculum, it should be reconceptualized to reflect the contributions that people of color have made to it (Nieto, 2012). In addition to teaching about Western ideals, the gap between the ideals of the West and its realities of racism, sexism, and discrimination should be taught (Banks, 2009b). Multiculturalists also believe that in addition to learning about the West, students should study other world cultures, such as those in Africa, Asia, the Middle East, and the Americas as they were before the Europeans arrived (Gates, 1999).

Other factors that have slowed the institutionalization of a multicultural curriculum include the focus on high-stakes testing and accountability that has emerged in the last decade, the low level of knowledge about ethnic cultures that most educators have, and the heavy reliance on textbooks for teaching. Many studies have revealed that the textbook is still the main source for teaching, especially in such subjects as the social studies, reading, and language arts (Au, 2012).

Teachers need in-depth knowledge about ethnic cultures and experiences to integrate ethnic content, experiences, and points of view into the curriculum. Many teachers tell their students that Columbus discovered America and that America is a "New World" because they know little about the diverse Native American cultures that existed in the Americas more than 40,000 years before the Europeans began to settle there in significant numbers in the 16th century. As Howard (2006) states in the title of his cogent and informative book, *We Can't Teach What We Don't Know*.

Levels of Integration of Multicultural Content

The Contributions Approach

I have identified four approaches to the integration of multicultural content into the curriculum (see Figure 10.1). The contributions approach to integration (Level 1) is frequently used when a school or district first attempts to integrate multicultural content into the mainstream curriculum. The contributions approach is characterized by the insertion of ethnic heroes/heroines and discrete cultural artifacts into the curriculum, selected using criteria similar to those used to select mainstream heroes/heroines and cultural artifacts. Thus, individuals such as Crispus Attucks, Pocahontas, Martin Luther King Jr., César Chávez, and Barack Obama are added to the curriculum. They are discussed when mainstream American heroes/heroines such as Patrick Henry, George Washington, Thomas Jefferson, Betsy Ross, and Eleanor Roosevelt are studied in the mainstream curriculum. Discrete cultural elements such as the foods, dances, music, and artifacts of ethnic groups are studied, but little attention is given to their meanings and importance within ethnic communities.

An important characteristic of the contributions approach is that the mainstream curriculum remains unchanged in its basic structure, goals, and salient characteristics. Prerequisites for the implementation of this approach are minimal. They include basic knowledge about U.S. society and knowledge about ethnic heroes/heroines and their roles and contributions to U.S. society and culture.

Individuals who challenged the dominant society's ideologies, values, and conceptions and advocated radical social, political, and economic reform are seldom included in the contributions approach. Thus, Booker T. Washington is more likely to be chosen for study than is W.E.B. DuBois or Paul Robeson, and Pocahontas is more likely to be chosen than is Geronimo. The criteria used to select ethnic heroes/heroines for study and to judge them for success are derived from the mainstream society, not from the ethnic community. Consequently, use of the

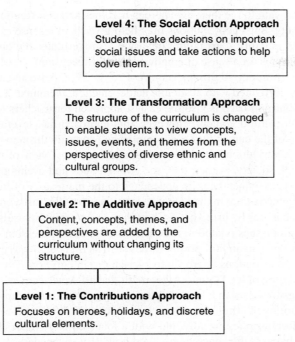

Level 4: The Social Action Approach
Students make decisions on important social issues and take actions to help solve them.

Level 3: The Transformation Approach
The structure of the curriculum is changed to enable students to view concepts, issues, events, and themes from the perspectives of diverse ethnic and cultural groups.

Level 2: The Additive Approach
Content, concepts, themes, and perspectives are added to the curriculum without changing its structure.

Level 1: The Contributions Approach
Focuses on heroes, holidays, and discrete cultural elements.

FIGURE 10.1 Banks's Four Levels of Integration of Ethnic Content

Copyright © 2009 by James A. Banks.

contributions approach usually results in the study of ethnic heroes/heroines who represent only one important perspective within ethnic communities. The more radical and less conformist individuals who are heroes/heroines only to the ethnic community are often invisible in textbooks, teaching materials, and activities used in the contributions approach. Paul Robeson, the singer, actor, and activist—who was a greatly admired hero in the African American community during the 1940s and 1950s—is invisible in most textbooks, in part because he was a Marxist who advocated radical social, economic, and political change (Balaji, 2007).

The heroes/heroines and holidays approach is a variant of the contributions approach. In this approach, ethnic content is limited primarily to special days, weeks, and months related to ethnic events and celebrations. Cinco de Mayo, Martin Luther King Jr.'s birthday, and African American History Week are examples of ethnic days and weeks celebrated in the schools. During these celebrations, teachers involve students in lessons, experiences, and pageants related to the ethnic group being commemorated. When this approach is used, the class studies little or nothing about the ethnic or cultural group before or after the special event or occasion.

The contributions approach (Level 1 in Figure 10.1) provides teachers a way to integrate ethnic content into the curriculum quickly, thus giving some recognition to ethnic contributions to U.S. society and culture. Many teachers who are committed to integrating their curricula with ethnic content have little knowledge about ethnic groups and curriculum revision. Consequently, they use the contributions approach when teaching about ethnic groups. These teachers should be encouraged, supported, and given the opportunity to acquire the knowledge and skills needed to reform their curricula by using one of the more effective approaches described later in this chapter.

There are often strong political demands from ethnic communities for the school to put their heroes/heroines, contributions, and cultures into the school curriculum. These political forces may take the form of demands for heroes and contributions because mainstream heroes, such as Washington, Jefferson, and Lincoln, are highly visible in the school curriculum. Ethnic communities of color want to see their own heroes/heroines and contributions alongside those of the mainstream society. Such contributions may help give them a sense of structural inclusion, validation, and social equality. Curriculum inclusion also facilitates the quests of marginalized ethnic and cultural groups for a sense of empowerment, efficacy, and social equality. The school should help students from ethnic groups acquire a sense of empowerment and efficacy. These factors are positively correlated with academic achievement (Coleman et al., 1966).

The contributions approach is also the easiest approach for teachers to use to integrate the curriculum with multicultural content. However, this approach has several serious limitations. When the integration of the curriculum is accomplished primarily through the infusion of ethnic heroes/heroines and contributions, students do not attain a global view of the role of ethnic and cultural groups in U.S. society. Rather, they see ethnic issues and events primarily as additions to the curriculum and consequently as an appendage to the main story of the development of the nation and to the core curriculum in the language arts, social studies, arts, and other subject areas.

Teaching ethnic issues by using heroes/heroines and contributions also tends to gloss over important concepts and issues related to the victimization and oppression of ethnic groups and their struggles against racism and for power. Issues such as *racism, poverty,* and *oppression* tend to be avoided in the contributions approach to curriculum integration. The focus tends to be on success and the validation of the Horatio Alger myth that all Americans who are willing to work hard can go from rags to riches and "pull themselves up by their bootstraps."

The success stories of ethnic heroes such as Booker T. Washington, George Washington Carver, and Jackie Robinson are usually told with a focus on their success, with little attention to racism and other barriers they encountered and how they succeeded despite the hurdles they faced. Little attention is also devoted to the *process* by which they became heroes/heroines. Students should learn about the process by which people become heroes/heroines as well as about their status and role as heroes/heroines. Only when students learn the process by which individuals become heroes/heroines will they understand fully how individuals, particularly individuals of color, achieve and maintain hero/heroine status and what the process of achieving this status means for their own lives.

When teaching about the historic election of Barack Obama as the 44th president of the United States in 2008, teachers should help students to understand both his struggles and triumphs (Obama, 2004, 2006). His successful presidential election should be discussed within the context of the racism he experienced as a youth, as a presidential candidate, and as president. A number of events during the election had racial overtones and were designed to depict Obama as an "Outsider" who would not be an appropriate president of the United States. These events included falsely claiming that he was a Muslim, highlighting his relationship with the Reverend Jeremiah Wright, attempting to marginalize him by emphasizing that he had been a community organizer, and linking him with William Ayers—whom Sarah Palin, the Republican vice-presidential candidate, called a "domestic terrorist." Michael Massing (2008) concludes about the attacks on Obama, "Amounting to a six-month-long exercise in Swift Boating, these attacks, taken together, constitute perhaps the most vicious smear campaign ever mounted against an American politician" (p. 26). Some of these attacks continued when Obama become president, such as the idea perpetuated by the group that became know as the "birthers." They claimed that Obama was not born in the United States, was not a U. S. citizen, and therefore did not qualify to be president of the United States.

The contributions approach often results in the trivialization of ethnic cultures, the study of their strange and exotic characteristics, and the reinforcement of stereotypes and misconceptions. When the focus is on the contributions and unique aspects of ethnic cultures, students are not helped to view them as complete and dynamic wholes. The contributions approach also tends to focus on the *lifestyles* of ethnic groups rather than on the *institutional structures*, such as racism and discrimination, that significantly affect their life chances and keep them powerless and marginalized.

The contributions approach to content integration may provide students a memorable one-time experience with an ethnic hero/heroine, but it often fails to help them understand the role and influence of the hero/heroine in the total context of U.S. history and society. When ethnic heroes/heroines are studied apart from the social and political context in which they lived and worked, students attain only a partial understanding of their roles and significance in society. When Martin Luther King Jr. and Rosa Parks are studied outside the social and political context of institutionalized racism in the U.S. South in the 1950s and 1960s and without attention to the more subtle forms of institutionalized racism in the North during this period, their full significance as social reformers and activists is neither revealed to nor understood by students.

The Additive Approach

Another important approach to the integration of ethnic content into the curriculum is the addition of content, concepts, themes, and perspectives to the curriculum without changing its basic structure, purposes, and characteristics. The additive approach (Level 2 in Figure 10.1) is often accomplished by the addition of a book, a unit, or a course to the curriculum without substantially changing the curriculum. Examples of this approach include adding a book such as *The Color Purple* (Walker, 1982) to a unit on the 20th century in an English class, using the film *The Autobiography of Miss Jane Pittman* (Korty, 1973) during a unit on the 1960s, and showing a film about the internment of Japanese Americans, such as *Rabbit in the Moon* (Omori, 2004), during a study of World War II in a class on U.S. history.

The additive approach allows the teacher to put ethnic content into the curriculum without restructuring it, a process that would take substantial time, effort, and training as well as a rethinking of the curriculum and its purposes, nature, and goals. The additive approach can be the first phase in a transformative curriculum reform effort designed to restructure the total curriculum and to integrate it with ethnic content, perspectives, and frames of reference.

However, this approach shares several disadvantages with the contributions approach. Its most important shortcoming is that it usually results in viewing ethnic content from the perspectives of *mainstream* historians, writers, artists, and scientists because it does not involve a restructuring of the curriculum. The events, concepts, issues, and problems to be studied are selected using mainstream-centric and Eurocentric criteria and perspectives. When teaching a unit entitled "The Westward Movement" in a fifth-grade U.S. history class, the teacher may integrate the unit by adding content about the Oglala Sioux Indians. However, the unit remains mainstream-centric and focused because of its perspective and point of view.

A unit called "The Westward Movement" is mainstream- and Eurocentric because it focuses on the movement of European Americans from the eastern to the western part of the United States. The Oglala Sioux were already in the West and consequently were not moving westward. The unit might be called "The Invasion from the East" from the point of view of the Oglala Sioux. Black Elk, an Oglala Sioux holy man, lamented the conquering of his people, which culminated in their defeat at Wounded Knee Creek on December 29, 1890. Approximately 200 Sioux men, women, and children were killed by U.S. troops. Black Elk said, "The [Sioux] nation's hoop is broken and scattered. There is no center any longer, and the sacred tree is dead" (Black Elk & Neihardt, 1972, p. 230).

Black Elk did not consider his homeland "the West," but rather the center of the world. He viewed the cardinal directions metaphysically. The Great Spirit sent him the cup of living water and the sacred bow from the west. The daybreak star and the sacred pipe originated from the east. The Sioux nation's sacred hoop and the tree that was to bloom came from the south (Black Elk, 1964). When teaching about the movement of the Europeans across North America, teachers should help students understand that different cultural, racial, and ethnic groups often have varying and conflicting conceptions and points of view about the same historical events, concepts, issues, and developments. The victors and the vanquished, especially, often have conflicting conceptions of the same historical event (Limerick, 1987). However, it is usually the point of view of the victors that becomes institutionalized in the schools and the mainstream society. This happens because history and textbooks are usually written by the people who won the wars and gained control of the society, not by the losers—the victimized and the powerless. The perspectives of both groups are needed to help us fully understand our history, culture, and society.

The people who are conquered and the people who conquered them have histories and cultures that are intricately interwoven and interconnected. They have to learn each other's histories and cultures to understand their own fully. White Americans cannot fully understand their own history in the western United States and in America without understanding the history of the American Indians and the ways their histories and the histories of the Indians are interconnected.

James Baldwin (1985) insightfully pointed out that when White Americans distort African American history, they do not learn the truth about their own history because the histories of African Americans and Whites in the United States are tightly bound together. This is also true for African American history and Indian history. The histories of African Americans and Indians in the United States are closely interconnected, as Katz (1986) documents in *Black Indians: A Hidden Heritage*.

The histories of African Americans and Whites in the United States are tightly connected, both culturally and biologically, as Ball (1998) points out when he describes the African American ancestors in his White family and as Gordon-Reed (1997) reveals when she describes the relationship between Thomas Jefferson and Sally Hemings, his slave mistress. The additive approach fails to help students view society from diverse cultural and ethnic perspectives and to understand the ways in which the histories and cultures of the nation's diverse ethnic, racial, cultural, and religious groups are interconnected.

Multicultural history enables students and teachers to understand America's complexity and the ways in which various groups in the United States are interconnected (Takaki, 2008). Sam Hamod describes the way in which diverse ethnic perspectives enrich our understandings and lead to more accurate versions of U.S. society:

> Our dual vision of "ethnic" and American allows us to see aspects of the United States that mainstream writers often miss; thus, our perspectives often allow us a diversity of visions that, ironically, may lead us to larger truth—it's just that we were raised with different eyes.
>
> (cited in Reed, 1997, p. xxii)

Content, materials, and issues that are added to a curriculum as appendages instead of being integral parts of a unit of instruction can become problematic. Problems might result when a book such as *The Color Purple* or a film like *Miss Jane Pittman* is added to a unit when the students lack the concepts, content background, and emotional maturity to deal with the issues and problems in these materials. The effective use of such emotion-laden and complex materials usually requires that the teacher help students acquire, in a sequential and developmental fashion, the content background and attitudinal maturity to deal with them effectively. The use of both of these materials in different classes and schools has resulted in major problems for the teachers using them. A community controversy arose in each case. The problems developed because the material was used with students who had neither the content background nor the attitudinal sophistication to respond to them appropriately. Adding ethnic content to the curriculum in a sporadic and segmented way can result in pedagogical problems, trouble for the teacher, student confusion, and community controversy.

The Transformation Approach

The transformation approach differs fundamentally from the contributions and additive approaches. In those two approaches, ethnic content is added to the mainstream core curriculum without changing its basic assumptions, nature, and structure. The fundamental goals, structure, and perspectives of the curriculum are changed in the transformation approach.

The transformation approach (Level 3 in Figure 10.1) changes the basic assumptions of the curriculum and enables students to view concepts, issues, themes, and problems from several ethnic perspectives and points of view. The mainstream-centric perspective is one of only several perspectives from which problems, concepts, and issues are viewed. Richard White (1991), a historian of the American West, indicates how viewing it from a transformative perspective can provide new insights into U.S. history. He writes, "The first Europeans to penetrate the West arrived neither as conquerors nor as explorers. Like so many others history has treated as discoverers, they were merely lost" (p. 5).

It is neither possible nor desirable to view every issue, concept, event, or problem from the point of view of each U.S. ethnic and cultural group. Rather, the goal should be to enable students to view concepts and issues from more than one perspective and from the points of view of the cultural, ethnic, and racial groups that were the most active participants in, or were most cogently influenced by, the event, issue, or concept being studied.

The key curriculum issue involved in multicultural curriculum reform is not the addition of a long list of ethnic groups, heroes, and contributions but the infusion of various perspectives, frames of references, and content from different groups that will extend students' understandings of the nature, development, and complexity of U.S. society. When students are studying the revolution in the British colonies, the perspectives of the Anglo revolutionaries, Anglo loyalists, African Americans, Indians, and British are essential for the students to attain a thorough understanding of this significant event in U.S. history (see Figure 10.2). Students must study the various and sometimes divergent meanings of the revolution to these diverse groups to understand it fully (Gay & Banks, 1975).

In the language arts, when students are studying the nature of U.S. English and proper language use, they should be helped to understand the rich linguistic and language diversity in the United States and the ways in which a wide range of regional, cultural, and ethnic groups have influenced the development of U.S. English (Hudley & Mallinson, 2011). Students should also examine how normative language use varies with the social context, region, and situation. The use of Black English is appropriate in some social and cultural contexts and inappropriate in others. This is also true of Standard U.S. English. The United States is rich in languages and dialects. The nation had 50.5 million Latino citizens in 2010; Spanish is the first language for most of them. Most of the nation's approximately 42 million African Americans speak both Standard English and some form of Black English or Ebonics (Alim & Baugh, 2007). The rich language diversity in the United States includes more than 25 European languages; Asian, African, and Middle Eastern languages; and American Indian languages. Since the 1970s, languages from Indochina, spoken by groups such as the Hmong, Vietnamese, Laotians, and Cambodians, have further enriched language diversity in the United States (Ovando, 2012).

When subjects such as music, dance, and literature are studied, the teacher should acquaint students with the ways these art forms as practiced by U.S. ethnic groups have greatly influenced and enriched the nation's artistic and literary traditions. For example, the ways in which African American musicians such as Bessie Smith, W. C. Handy, and Leontyne Price have influenced the nature and development of U.S. music should be examined when the development of U.S. music is studied (Burnim & Maultsby, 2006). African Americans and Puerto Ricans have significantly influenced the development of American dance. Writers of color, such as Langston Hughes, Toni Morrison, N. Scott Momaday, Carlos Bulosan, Maxine Hong Kingston, Rudolfo A. Anaya, and Piri Thomas, have not only significantly influenced the development of American literature but have also provided unique and revealing perspectives on U.S. society and culture.

When studying U.S. history, language, music, arts, science, and mathematics, the emphasis should not be on the ways in which various ethnic and cultural groups have contributed to mainstream U.S. society and culture. *The emphasis should be on how the common U.S. culture and*

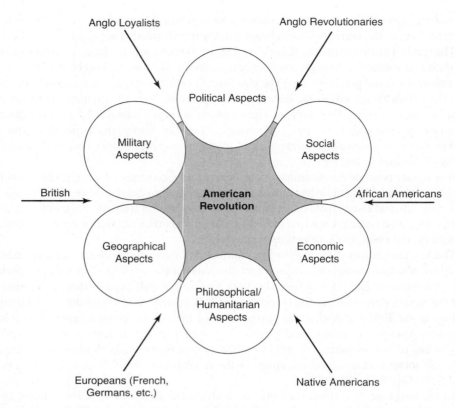

FIGURE 10.2 A Multicultural Interdisciplinary Model for Teaching the American Revolution

Source: James A. Banks and Geneva Gay. "Teaching the American Revolution: A Multiethnic Approach," *Social Education*, November–December 1975, 462. Used with permission of the National Council for the Social Studies.

society emerged from a complex synthesis and interaction of the diverse cultural elements that originated within the various cultural, racial, ethnic, and religious groups that make up U.S. society. I call this process *multiple acculturation* and argue that even though Anglo Americans are the dominant group in the United States—culturally, politically, and economically—it is misleading and inaccurate to describe U.S. culture and society as an Anglo-Saxon Protestant culture (Banks, 2006). Other U.S. ethnic and cultural groups have deeply influenced, shaped, and participated in the development and formation of U.S. society and culture. African Americans, for example, profoundly influenced the development of southern U.S. culture even though they had very little political and economic power. One irony of conquest is that those who are conquered often deeply influence the cultures of the conquerors.

A multiple acculturation conception of U.S. society and culture leads to a perspective that views ethnic events, literature, music, and art as integral parts of the common, shared U.S. culture. Anglo American Protestant culture is viewed as only a part of this larger cultural whole. Thus, to teach American literature without including significant writers of color, such as Maxine Hong Kingston, Carlos Bulosan, and Toni Morrison, gives a partial and incomplete view of U.S. literature, culture, and society.

The Social Action Approach

The social action approach (Level 4 in Figure 10.1) includes all elements of the transformation approach but adds components that require students to make *decisions* and take *actions* related to the concept, issue, or problem studied in the unit (Banks & Banks, 1999). Major instructional goals in this approach are to educate students for social criticism and social change and to teach them decision-making skills. To empower students and help them acquire *political efficacy,* the school must help them become reflective social critics and skilled participants in social change. The traditional goal of schooling has been to socialize students so they would accept unquestioningly the existing ideologies, institutions, and practices in society and the nation-state (Banks, 2004; Arthur, Davies, & Hahn, 2008).

Political education in the United States has traditionally fostered political passivity rather than political action. A major goal of the social action approach is to help students acquire the *knowledge, values,* and *skills* they need to participate in social change so that marginalized and excluded racial, ethnic, and cultural groups can become full participants in U.S. society and the nation will move closer to attaining its democratic ideals (Banks, 2004). To participate effectively in democratic social change, students must be taught social criticism and helped to understand the inconsistency between our ideals and social realities, the work that must be done to close this gap, and how students can, as individuals and groups, influence the social and political systems in U.S. society. In this approach, teachers are agents of social change who promote democratic values and the empowerment of students. Teaching units organized using the social action approach have the following components:

1. *A decision problem or question.* An example of a question is this: What actions should we take to reduce prejudice and discrimination in our school?

2. *An inquiry that provides data related to the decision problem.* The inquiry might consist of questions such as these:

   a. What is prejudice?

   b. What is discrimination?

   c. What causes prejudice?

   d. What causes people to discriminate?

   e. What are examples of prejudice and discrimination in our school, community, nation, and world?

   f. How do prejudice and discrimination affect the groups listed in item *g?* How does each group view prejudice? Discrimination? To what extent is each group a victim or a perpetuator of prejudice and discrimination?

   g. How has each group dealt with prejudice and discrimination? (Groups: White mainstream Americans, African Americans, Asian Americans, Hispanic Americans, Native Americans)

   The inquiry into the nature of prejudice and discrimination would be interdisciplinary and would include readings and data sources in the various social sciences, biography, fiction, poetry, and drama. Scientific and statistical data would be used when students investigate how discrimination affects the income, occupations, frequency of diseases, and health care within these various groups.

3. *Value inquiry and moral analysis.* Students are given opportunities to examine, clarify, and reflect on their values, attitudes, beliefs, and feelings related to racial prejudice and discrimination. The teacher can provide the students with case studies from various sources, such as newspapers and magazines. The case studies can be used to involve the students in discussions and role-playing situations that enable them to express and to examine their attitudes, beliefs, and feelings about prejudice and discrimination. Poetry,

biography, and powerful fiction are excellent sources for case studies that can be used for both discussion and role-playing. The powerful poem "Incident" by Countee Cullen (1993) describes the painful memories of a child who was called "nigger" on a trip to Baltimore. Langston Hughes's (1993) poem "I, too" poignantly tells how the "darker brother" is sent into the kitchen when company comes. The teacher and the students can describe verbally or write about incidents related to prejudice and discrimination they have observed or in which they have participated. The following case, based on a real-life situation, was written by the author for use with his students. After reading the case, the students discuss the questions at the end of it.

Trying to Buy a Home in Lakewood Island

About a year ago, Joan and Henry Green, a young African American couple, moved from the West Coast to a large city in the Midwest. They moved because Henry finished his Ph.D. in chemistry and took a job at a big university in Midwestern City. Since they have been in Midwestern City, the Greens have rented an apartment in the central area of the city. However, they have decided that they want to buy a house. Their apartment has become too small for the many books and other things they have accumulated during the year. In addition to wanting more space, they also want a house so that they can receive breaks on their income tax, which they do not receive living in an apartment. The Greens also think that a house will be a good financial investment.

The Greens have decided to move into a suburban community. They want a new house and most of the houses within the city limits are rather old. They also feel that they can obtain a larger house for their money in the suburbs than in the city. They have looked at several suburban communities and decided that they like Lakewood Island better than any of the others. Lakewood Island is a predominantly White community, which is composed primarily of lower-middle-class and middle-class residents. There are a few wealthy families in Lakewood Island, but they are exceptions rather than the rule.

Joan and Henry Green have become frustrated because of the problems they have experienced trying to buy a home in Lakewood Island. Before they go out to look at a house, they carefully study the newspaper ads. When they arrived at the first house in which they were interested, the owner told them that his house had just been sold. A week later they decided to work with a realtor. When they tried to close the deal on the next house they wanted, the realtor told them that the owner had raised the price $10,000 because he had the house appraised since he put it on the market and had discovered that his selling price was too low. When the Greens tried to buy a third house in Lakewood Island, the owner told them that he had decided not to sell because he had not received the job in another city that he was almost sure he would receive when he had put his house up for sale. He explained that the realtor had not removed the ad about his house from the newspaper even though he had told him that he had decided not to sell a week earlier. The realtor the owner had been working with had left the real estate company a few days ago. Henry is bitter and feels that he and his wife are victims of racism and discrimination. Joan believes that Henry is too sensitive and that they have been the victims of a series of events that could have happened to anyone, regardless of their race.

Questions: What should the Greens do? Why?
   (Reprinted with permission from James A. Banks [2009]. *Teaching Strategies for Ethnic Studies* [8th ed., p. 217]. Boston: Allyn & Bacon.)

4. *Decision-making and social action* (synthesis of knowledge and values). Students acquire knowledge about their decision problem from the activities in item 2. This interdisciplinary knowledge provides them the information they need to make reflective decisions about prejudice and discrimination in their communities and schools. The activities in item 3 enable them to identify, clarify, and analyze their values, feelings, and beliefs about prejudice and discrimination. The decision-making process enables the students to synthesize their knowledge and values to determine what actions, if any, they should take to reduce prejudice and discrimination in their school. They can develop a chart in which they list possible actions to take and their possible consequences. They can then decide on a course of action to take and implement it.

Mixing and Blending Approaches

The four approaches for the integration of multicultural content into the curriculum (see Table 10.1) are often mixed and blended in actual teaching situations. One approach, such as the contributions approach, can be used as a vehicle to move to other, more intellectually challenging approaches, such as the transformation and social action approaches. It is unrealistic to expect a teacher to move directly from a highly mainstream-centric curriculum to one that focuses on decision making and social action. Rather, the move from the first to higher levels of multicultural content integration is likely to be gradual and cumulative. A teacher who has a

Table 10.1 Banks's Approaches for the Integration of Multicultural Content

Approach	Description	Examples	Strengths	Problems
Contributions	Heroes, cultural components, holidays, and other discrete elements related to ethnic groups are added to the curriculum on special days, occasions, and celebrations.	Famous Mexican Americans are studied only during the week of Cinco de Mayo (May 5). African Americans are studied during African American History Month in February but rarely during the rest of the year. Ethnic foods are studied in the first grade with little attention devoted to the cultures in which the foods are embedded.	Provides a quick and relatively easy way to put ethnic content into the curriculum. Gives ethnic heroes visibility in the curriculum alongside mainstream heroes. Is a popular approach among teachers and educators.	Results in a superficial understanding of ethnic cultures. Focuses on the lifestyles and artifacts of ethnic groups and reinforces stereotypes and misconceptions. Mainstream criteria are used to select heroes and cultural elements for inclusion in the curriculum.
Additive	This approach consists of the addition of content, concepts, themes, and perspectives to the curriculum without changing its structure.	Adding the book *The Color Purple* to a literature unit without reconceptualizing the unit or giving the students the background knowledge to understand the book. Adding a unit on the Japanese American internment to a U.S. history course without treating the Japanese in any other unit. Leaving the core curriculum intact but adding an ethnic studies course, as an elective, that focuses on a specific ethnic group.	Makes it possible to add ethnic content to the curriculum without changing its structure, which requires substantial curriculum changes and staff development. Can be implemented within the existing curriculum structure.	Reinforces the idea that ethnic history and culture are not integral parts of U.S. mainstream culture. Students view ethnic groups from Anglocentric and Eurocentric perspectives. Fails to help students understand how the dominant culture and ethnic cultures are interconnected and interrelated.

(continued)

Table 10.1 *(continued)*

Approach	Description	Examples	Strengths	Problems
Transformation	The basic goals, structure, and nature of the curriculum are changed to enable students to view concepts, events, issues, problems, and themes from the perspectives of diverse cultural, ethnic, and racial groups.	A unit on the American Revolution describes the meaning of the revolution to Anglo revolutionaries, Anglo loyalists, African Americans, Indians, and the British. A unit on 20th-century U.S. literature includes works by William Faulkner, Joyce Carol Oates, Langston Hughes, N. Scott Momaday, Saul Bellow, Maxine Hong Kingston, Rudolfo A. Anaya, and Piri Thomas.	Enables students to understand the complex ways in which diverse racial and cultural groups participated in the formation of U.S. society and culture. Helps reduce racial and ethnic encapsulation. Enables diverse ethnic, racial, and religious groups to see their cultures, ethos, and perspectives in the school curriculum. Gives students a balanced view of the nature and development of U.S. culture and society. Helps to empower victimized racial, ethnic, and cultural groups.	The implementation of this approach requires substantial curriculum revision, in-service training, and the identification and development of materials written from the perspectives of various racial and cultural groups. Staff development for the institutionalization of this approach must be continual and ongoing.
Social Action	In this approach, students identify important social problems and issues, gather pertinent data, clarify their values on the issues, make decisions, and take reflective actions to help resolve the issue or problem.	A class studies prejudice and discrimination in their school and decides to take actions to improve race relations in the school. A class studies the treatment of ethnic groups in a local newspaper and writes a letter to the newspaper publisher suggesting ways that the treatment of ethnic groups in the newspaper should be improved.	Enables students to improve their thinking, value analysis, decision-making, and social action skills. Enables students to improve their data-gathering skills. Helps students develop a sense of political efficacy. Helps students improve their skills to work in groups.	Requires a considerable amount of curriculum planning and materials identification. May be longer in duration than more traditional teaching units. May focus on problems and issues considered controversial by some members of the school staff and citizens of the community. Students may be able to take few meaningful actions that contribute to the resolution of the social issue or problem.

mainstream-centric curriculum might use the school's Martin Luther King Jr. birthday celebration as an opportunity to integrate the curriculum with ethnic content about King as well as to think seriously about how content about African Americans and other ethnic groups can be integrated into the curriculum in an ongoing fashion. The teacher could explore with the students questions such as these during the celebration:

1. What were the conditions of other ethnic groups during the time that King was a civil rights leader?

2. How did other ethnic groups participate in and respond to the civil rights movement?

3. How did these groups respond to Martin Luther King Jr.?

4. What can we do today to improve the civil rights of groups of color?

5. What can we do to develop more positive racial and ethnic attitudes?

The students will be unable to answer all of the questions they have raised about ethnic groups during the celebration of Martin Luther King Jr.'s birthday. Rather, the questions will enable the students to integrate content about ethnic groups throughout the year as they study such topics as the family, the school, the neighborhood, and the city. As the students study these topics, they can use the questions they have formulated to investigate ethnic families, the ethnic groups in their school and in schools in other parts of the city, ethnic neighborhoods, and various ethnic institutions in the city such as churches, temples, synagogues, mosques, schools, restaurants, and community centers.

As a culminating activity for the year, the teacher can take the students on a tour of an ethnic institution in the city, such as the Wing Luke Museum of the Asian Pacific Experience (http://wingluke.org/home.htm) or the Northwest African American Museum (http://naamnw.org/) in Seattle, Washington. Similar ethnic museums are located in other major cities, such as Los Angeles, Detroit, and New York. Other ethnic institutions that the students might visit include an African American or Hispanic church, a Jewish temple, or a mosque. However, such a tour should be both preceded and followed by activities that enable the students to develop perceptive and compassionate lenses for seeing ethnic, cultural, and religious differences and for responding to them with sensitivity. A field trip to an ethnic institution might reinforce stereotypes and misconceptions if students lack the knowledge and insights needed to view ethnic and religious cultures in an understanding and caring way. Theory and research indicate that contact with an ethnic group does not necessarily lead to more positive racial and ethnic attitudes (Allport, 1979; Schofield, 2004). Rather, the conditions under which the contact occurs and the quality of the interaction in the contact situation are the important variables.

Guidelines for Teaching Multicultural Content

The following 14 guidelines are designed to help you better integrate content about racial, ethnic, cultural, and language groups into the school curriculum and to teach effectively in multicultural environments.

1. You, the teacher, are an extremely important variable in the teaching of multicultural content. If you have the necessary knowledge, attitudes, and skills, when you encounter racist content in materials or observe racism in the statements and behavior of students, you can use these situations to teach important lessons about the experiences of ethnic, racial, and cultural groups in the United States. An informative source on racism is Gary Howard's (2006) *We Can't Teach What We Don't Know: White Teachers, Multiracial Schools.*

2. Knowledge about ethnic groups is needed to teach ethnic content effectively. Read at least one major book that surveys the histories and cultures of U.S. ethnic groups. One book that includes comprehensive historical overviews of U.S. ethnic groups is James A. Banks (2009b), *Teaching Strategies for Ethnic Studies.*

3. Be sensitive to your own racial attitudes, behaviors, and the statements you make about ethnic groups in the classroom. A statement such as "sit like an Indian" stereotypes Native Americans.

4. Make sure that your classroom conveys positive and complex images of various ethnic groups. You can do this by displaying bulletin boards, posters, and calendars that show the racial, ethnic, and religious diversity in U.S. society.

5. Be sensitive to the racial and ethnic attitudes of your students and do not accept the belief, which has been refuted by research, that "kids do not see colors." Since the pioneering research by Lasker (1929), researchers have known that very young children are aware of racial differences and that they tend to accept the evaluations of various racial groups that are normative in the wider society (Bigler & Hughes, 2009). Do not try to ignore the racial and ethnic differences that you see; try to respond to these differences positively and sensitively. A helpful and informative book is *What if All the Kids Are White? Anti-Bias Multicultural Education with Young Children and Families*, by Louise Derman-Sparks and Patricia G. Ramsey (2011).

6. Be judicious in your choice and use of teaching materials. Some materials contain both subtle and blatant stereotypes of groups. Point out to the students when an ethnic, racial, cultural, or language group is stereotyped, omitted from, or described in materials from Anglocentric and Eurocentric points of view.

7. Use trade books, films, DVDs, CDs, and recordings to supplement the textbook treatment of ethnic, cultural, and language groups and to present the perspectives of these groups to your students. Many of these sources contain rich and powerful images of the experience of being a person of color in the United States. Numerous books and other instructional materials are annotated in James A. Banks (2009b), *Teaching Strategies for Ethnic Studies*.

8. Get in touch with your own cultural and ethnic heritage. Sharing your ethnic and cultural story with your students will create a climate for sharing in the classroom, will help motivate students to dig into their own ethnic and cultural roots, and will result in powerful learning for your students.

9. Be sensitive to the possibly controversial nature of some ethnic studies materials. If you are clear about the teaching objectives you have in mind, you can often use a less controversial book or reading to attain the same objectives. *The Color Purple*, by Alice Walker (1982), for example, can be a controversial book. A teacher, however, who wants his or her students to gain insights about African Americans in the South can use *Roll of Thunder, Hear My Cry*, by Mildred D. Taylor (1976), instead of *The Color Purple*.

10. Be sensitive to the developmental levels of your students when you select concepts, content, and activities related to racial, ethnic, cultural, and language groups. Concepts and learning activities for students in kindergarten and the primary grades should be specific and concrete. Students in these grades should study such concepts as *similarities, differences, prejudice,* and *discrimination* rather than higher-level concepts such as *racism* and *oppression*. Fiction and biographies are excellent vehicles for introducing these concepts to students in kindergarten and the primary grades. As students progress through the grades, they can be introduced to more complex concepts, examples, and activities. (*If you teach in a racially or ethnically integrated classroom or school, you should keep the following guidelines in mind.*)

11. View your students of color as winners. Many students of color have high academic and career goals. They need teachers who believe they can be successful and are willing to help them succeed. Both research and theory indicate that students are more likely to achieve highly when their teachers have high academic expectations for them.

12. Keep in mind that most parents of color are very interested in education and want their children to be successful academically even though the parents may be alienated from the school. Do not equate *education* with *schooling*. Many parents who want their children to succeed have mixed feelings about the schools. Try to gain the support of these parents and enlist them as partners in the education of their children.

13. Use cooperative learning techniques and group work to promote racial and ethnic integration in the school and classroom. Research indicates that when learning groups are racially integrated, students develop more friends from other racial groups and race relations in the school improve. A helpful guide is Elizabeth Cohen's (1994) *Designing Groupwork: Strategies for the Heterogeneous Classroom.*

14. Make sure that school plays, pageants, cheerleading squads, publication staffs, and other formal and informal groups are racially integrated. Also make sure that various ethnic and racial groups have equal status in school performances and presentations. In a multiracial school, if all of the leading roles in a school play are filled by White students, an important message is sent to students and parents of color, whether such a message was intended or not.

Summary

This chapter describes the nature of the mainstream-centric curriculum and the negative consequences it has for both mainstream students and students of color. This curriculum reinforces the false sense of superiority of mainstream students and fails to reflect, validate, and celebrate the cultures of students of color. Many factors have slowed the institutionalization of a multicultural curriculum in the schools, including ideological resistance, lack of teacher knowledge of ethnic groups, heavy reliance of teachers on textbooks, and focus on high-stakes testing and accountability. However, the institutionalization of ethnic content into school, college, and university curricula has made significant progress in the last 40 years. This process needs to continue because curriculum transformation is a development that never ends.

Four approaches to the integration of ethnic content into the curriculum are identified in this chapter. In the *contributions approach,* heroes/heroines, cultural components, holidays, and other discrete elements related to ethnic groups are added to the curriculum without changing its structure. The *additive approach* consists of the addition of content, concepts, themes, and perspectives to the curriculum with its structure remaining unchanged. In the *transformation approach,* the structure, goals, and nature of the curriculum are changed to enable students to view concepts, issues, and problems from diverse ethnic perspectives.

The *social action approach* includes all elements of the transformation approach as well as elements that enable students to identify important social issues, gather data related to them, clarify their values, make reflective decisions, and take actions to implement their decisions. This approach seeks to make students social critics and reflective agents of change. The final part of this chapter presents guidelines to help you teach multicultural content and to function more effectively in multicultural classrooms and schools.

QUESTIONS AND ACTIVITIES

10.1 What is a mainstream-centric curriculum? What are its major assumptions and goals?

10.2 Examine several textbooks and find examples of the mainstream-centric approach. Share these examples with colleagues in your class or workshop.

10.3 How does a mainstream-centric curriculum influence mainstream students and students of color?

10.4 According to the chapter, what factors have slowed the development of a multicultural curriculum in the schools? What is the best way to overcome these factors?

10.5 What are the major characteristics of the following approaches to curriculum reform: the contributions approach, the additive approach, the transformation approach, and the social action approach?

10.6 Why do you think the contributions approach to curriculum reform is so popular and widespread in schools, especially in the primary and elementary grades?

10.7. In what fundamental ways do the transformation and social action approaches differ from the other two approaches identified?

10.8 What are the problems and promises of each of the four approaches?

10.9 What problems might a teacher encounter when trying to implement the transformation and social action approaches? How might these problems be overcome?

10.10 Assume that you are teaching a social studies lesson about the westward movement in U.S. history and a student makes a racist, stereotypic, or misleading statement about Native Americans, such as, "The Indians were hostile to the White settlers." How would you handle this situation? Give reasons to explain why you would handle it in a particular way.

10.11 Since September 11, 2001, and the U.S./British–Iraq War that began in 2003, there has been an increased emphasis on patriotism in U.S. society. Some groups have called for more emphasis on teaching patriotism in the schools. What is patriotism? Describe ways in which multicultural content can be used to teach reflective patriotism. A useful reference for this exercise is *A Patriot's Handbook: Songs, Poems, Stories and Speeches Celebrating the Land We Love,* edited by Caroline Kennedy (2003). It contains selections by authors from diverse racial, ethnic, and cultural groups. Gwendolyn Brooks, Thomas Jefferson, Langston Hughes, Gloria Anzaldúa, E. B. White, and Paul Lawrence Dunbar are among the writers included in this comprehensive and useful collection.

REFERENCES

Alim, H. S., & Baugh, J. (2007). *Talkin Black talk: Language, education, and social change.* New York: Teachers College Press.

Allport, G. W. (1979). *The nature of prejudice* (25th anniversary ed.). Reading, MA: Addison-Wesley.

Arthur, J., Davies, I., & Hahn, C. (Eds.). (2008). *Sage handbook of education for citizenship and democracy.* London & Los Angeles: Sage.

Asante, M. K. (1998). *The Afrocentric idea* (rev. ed.). Philadelphia: Temple University Press.

Asante, M. K., & Ravitch, D. (1991). Multiculturalism: An exchange. *The American Scholar, 60*(2), 267–276.

Au, K. H. (2011). *Literacy achievement and diversity: Keys to success for students, teachers, and schools.* New York: Teachers College Press.

Au, W. (Ed.). (2009). *Rethinking multicultural education: Teaching for racial and cultural justice.* Milwaukee, WI: Rethinking Schools.

Au, W. (2012). *Critical curriculum studies: Education, consciousness, and the politics of knowing.* New York & London: Routledge.

Balaji, M. (2007). *The professor and the pupil: The politics and friendship of W. E. B. Dubois and Paul Robeson.* New York: Nations Books.

Baldwin, J. (1985). *The price of the ticket: Collected nonfiction, 1948–1985.* New York: St. Martin's Press.

Ball, E. (1998). *Slaves in the family.* New York: Farrar, Straus & Giroux.

Banks, J. A. (Ed.). (2004). *Diversity and citizenship education: Global perspectives.* San Francisco: Jossey-Bass.

Banks, J. A. (2006). *Cultural diversity and education: Foundations, curriculum, and teaching* (5th ed.). Boston: Allyn & Bacon.

Banks, J. A. (2007). *Educating citizens in a multicultural society* (2nd ed.). New York: Teachers College Press.

Banks, J. A. (2008). *An introduction to multicultural education* (4th ed.). Boston: Allyn & Bacon.

Banks, J. A. (Ed.). (2009a). *The Routledge international companion to multicultural education.* New York and London: Routledge.

Banks, J. A. (2009b). *Teaching strategies for ethnic studies* (8th ed.). Boston: Allyn & Bacon.

Banks, J. A., & Banks, C. A. M. (with Clegg, A. A., Jr.). (1999). *Teaching strategies for the social studies: Decision-making and citizen action* (5th ed.). New York: Longman.

Bigler, R. S., & Hughes, J. M. (2009). The nature and origins of children's racial attitudes. In J. A. Banks (Ed.), *The Routledge international companion to multicultural education* (pp. 186–198). New York and London: Routledge.

Black Elk (1964). Black Elk's prayer from a mountaintop in the Black Hills, 1931. In J. D. Forbes (Ed.), *The Indian in America's past* (p. 69). Englewood Cliffs, NJ: Prentice Hall.

Black Elk, & Neihardt, J. G. (1972). *Black Elk speaks: Being the life story of a holy man of the Oglala Sioux* (rev. ed.). New York: Pocket Books.

Burnim, M. V., & Maultsby, P. K. (2006). *African American music: An introduction.* New York: Routledge.

Cohen, E. G. (1994). *Designing groupwork: Strategies for the heterogeneous classroom* (2nd ed.). New York: Teachers College Press.

Coleman, J. S., Campbell, E. Q., Hobson, C. J., McPartland, J., Mood, A. M., Weinfeld, F. D., & York, R. L. (1966). *Equality of educational opportunity.* Washington, DC: U.S. Department of Health, Education and Welfare, Office of Education.

Cortés, C. E. (2000). *The children are watching: How the media teach about diversity.* New York: Teachers College Press.

Cullen, C. (1993). Incident. In C. Cullen (Ed.), *Caroling dusk: An anthology of verse by Black poets of the twenties* (p. 187). New York: Citadel.

Derman-Sparks, L., & Ramsey, P. G. (2011). *What if all the kids are White? Anti-bias multicultural education with young children and families* (2nd ed.). New York: Teachers College Press.

Gates, H. L., Jr. (1999). *Wonders of the African world*. New York: Knopf.

Gay, G., & Banks, J. A. (1975). Teaching the American Revolution: A multiethnic approach. *Social Education, 39*(7), 461–466.

Gordon-Reed, A. (1997). *Thomas Jefferson and Sally Hemings: An American controversy*. Charlottesville: University Press of Virginia.

Gutmann, A. (2004). Unity and diversity in democratic multicultural education: Creative and destructive tensions. In J. A. Banks (Ed.), *Diversity and citizenship education: Global perspectives* (pp. 71–96). San Francisco: Jossey-Bass.

Howard, G. R. (2006). *We can't teach what we don't know: White teachers, multiracial schools* (2nd ed.). New York: Teachers College Press.

Hudley, A. H., & Mallinson, C. (2011). *Understanding English language variation in U.S. schools*. New York: Teachers College Press.

Hughes, L. (1993). I, too. In C. Cullen (Ed.), *Caroling dusk: An anthology of verse by Black poets of the twenties* (p. 145). New York: Citadel.

Katz, W. L. (1986). *Black Indians: A hidden heritage*. New York: Atheneum.

Kennedy, C. (Ed.). (2003). *A patriot's handbook: Songs, poems, stories, and speeches celebrating the land we love*. New York: Hyperion.

Korty, J. (Director). (1973). *The autobiography of Miss Jane Pittman* [Motion picture]. Calhoun, GA: Tomorrow Entertainment, Inc.

Lasker, B. (1929). *Race attitudes in children*. New York: Holt.

Lee, C. D. (2007). *Culture, literacy, and learning: Taking bloom in the midst of the whirlwind*. New York: Teachers College Press.

Limerick, P. N. (1987). *The legacy of conquest: The unbroken past of the American West*. New York: Norton.

Loewen, J. W. (2005). *Sundown towns: A hidden dimension of American racism*. New York: The New Press.

Loewen, J. W. (1999). *Lies across America: What our historic sites get wrong*. New York: Touchstone (Simon & Schuster, Inc.).

Loewen, J. W. (2010). *Teaching what really happened: How to avoid the tyranny of textbooks and get students excited about history*. New York: Teachers College Press.

Massing, M. (2008, December 18). Obama: In the divided heartland. *New York Review of Books, 55*(20), 26–30.

Nieto, S. (2012). United States, multicultural education in. In J. A. Banks (Ed.), *Encyclopedia of diversity in education* (vol. 4, pp. 2248-2253). Thousand Oaks, CA: Sage.

Obama, B. (2004). *Dreams from my father: A story of race and inheritance*. New York: Crown.

Obama, B. (2006). *The audacity of hope: Thoughts on reclaiming the American dream*. New York: Vintage.

Omori, E. (Director). (2004). *Rabbit in the moon* [Motion picture]. Hohokus, NJ: New Day Films.

Ovando, C. J. (2012). English language learners. In J. A. Banks (Ed.), *Encyclopedia of diversity in education* (vol. 2, pp. 783-785). Thousand Oaks, CA: Sage.

Ravitch, D. (1990). Diversity and democracy: Multicultural education in America. *American Educator, 14*(1), 16–20, 46–48.

Reed, I. (Ed.). (1997). *MultiAmerica: Essays on cultural wars and cultural peace*. New York: Viking.

Rico, B. R., & Mano, S. (Eds.). (2001). *American mosaic: Multicultural readings in context* (3rd ed.). Boston: Houghton Mifflin.

Schlesinger, A. M., Jr. (1998). *The disuniting of America: Reflections on a multicultural society* (rev. ed.). Knoxville, TN: Whittle Direct.

Schofield, J. W. (2004). Fostering positive intergroup relations in schools. In J. A. Banks & C. A. M. Banks (Eds.), *Handbook of research on multicultural education* (2nd ed., pp. 799–812). San Francisco: Jossey-Bass.

Takaki, R. (2008). *A different mirror: A history of multicultural America* (rev. ed.). Boston: Little, Brown.

Taylor, M. D. (1976). *Roll of thunder, hear my cry*. New York: Puffin.

U.S. Census Bureau. (2009). *2009 national population projections*. Retrieved November 15, 2011, from http://www.census.gov/population/www/projections/2009projections.html.

Walker, A. (1982). *The color purple*. New York: Harcourt Brace.

White, R. (1991). *"It's your misfortune and none of my own": A new history of the American West*. Norman: University of Oklahoma Press.

Wineburg, S., & Monte-Sano, C. (2008). "Famous Americans": The changing pantheon of American heroes. *Journal of American History, 94*, 1186–1202. Retrieved December 27, 2008, from http://www.journalofamericanhistory.org/textbooks/2008/wineburg.html.

Zinn, H. (1999). *A people's history of the United States: 1492–present* (20th anniversary ed.). New York: HarperCollins.

© jacky chapman/Alamy Limited

Backstage Racism: Implications for Teaching

CHAPTER 11

Leslie H. Picca and Ruth Thompson-Miller

Let us start by acknowledging that for most of us, race is an emotionally loaded topic that can conjure up feelings such as anger, guilt, frustration, and many other neutral or negative emotions. Rarely does one walk away from a conversation about race, especially about racism, and say, "I feel really good about that!" We want to challenge that and to empower you, the reader, to examine ordinary or daily interactions with the goal of improving everyday racial occurrences. The intent of the chapter is to empower you with tools to recognize and then to combat the issue of racism in your everyday life. Of course, the *macro* social structures, such as institutional racism in education and the legal system, as well as economic disparities are harder to change. However, each individual has an opportunity, even an obligation, to attempt to make a difference on the *micro* level and bring about change in the racial dynamics of the United States, one person at a time.

Context

Much has been written about the changing forms of racial relations, particularly with the election of the first African American (or biracial) president of the United States. It is popularly believed that we are now in a postracial society where race and ethnicity are no longer important variables for access to resources and opportunities for success (D'Souza, 2011; McWhorter, 2006; Tesler & Sears, 2010). Legal segregation is ancient history for younger Americans (and even for some of their parents); they were raised after the success of *The Cosby Show*, with multicultural programming in schools and diverse images in the media (Bonilla-Silva, 2006; Gallagher, 2003; Jhally & Lewis, 1992). However, many social scientists suggest that racial relations, and specifically racism, are still critically significant issues, even in the post-1960s civil rights era (Coates, 2011; Dawson & Bobo, 2009; Kaplan, 2011).

There is much social science literature on "modern racism" or "color-blind racism": Negative racial attitudes haven't disappeared, they've just gone underground. For example, although there are social pressures to avoid overtly racist statements, subtle measures and tests in psychology and social psychology suggest that a nonracist mask is covering an intact racist core and that Whites regularly underestimate the extent of their prejudice (Feagin, 2009; Kawakami, Dunn, Karmali, & Dovidio, 2009). Specifically, many argue that racism is hidden, subtle, and invisible, even if its consequences are not.

In order to further investigate this underground or subtle racism, the sociologists Leslie H. Picca and Joe Feagin collected the journals or "diaries" of more than a thousand college students of all racial groups from across the United States detailing their everyday racial interactions. The research presented in this chapter is based on data collected for the book *Two-Faced Racism: Whites in the Backstage and Frontstage* (Picca & Feagin, 2007). Using journals collected from 626 White college students, the authors examine Whites' private conversations and conclude that racism is thriving in White-only social networks, even if the White students do not always recognize it themselves. Numerous White college students in the sample said that racism was less of a problem among their generation compared to past generations. Many White students wrote in their journals something like "racism will die when Grandpa dies," indicating their belief that younger people are remarkably different from and more racially accepting than older people. However, analyzing the journals reveals that this is far from true. "Grandpa's racism" is still alive and well—it just looks different for young adults today. Indeed, there is an intergenerational aspect to backstage racism. The White students' interactions were "two-faced," or remarkably different when they were in the company of people of color ("frontstage") compared to when they were with only other Whites ("backstage").

Methodology

In order to better understand "underground" or "hidden" racial attitudes, especially in Whites' everyday racial interactions, data were collected by means of the journal writings of college students across the United States. Undergraduates were asked to keep a regular journal of "everyday" interactions that they participated in or observed via participant observation that revealed racial issues. Students were recruited through personal contacts with instructors who were teaching courses in disciplines where student journal writing might be expected (such as the social sciences and humanities). These instructors were encouraged to invite their colleagues to participate in the study, thus beginning a snowball technique to gather a larger sample size (Warren, 2002).

Faculty members were provided with a five-page handout of journal-writing instructions for each of their students. The instructions were detailed but flexible enough for instructors to adapt them for their individual classes. Each faculty member decided how the journal writing would be used in the class, such as for a course assignment or extra credit. Such decisions influenced how long the students were asked to keep a journal and the length required of each journal entry to merit credit, if any was offered. On average, the students wrote in their journals for a little more than two weeks (15 entries), and each journal entry averaged one full paragraph, or about five sentences.

In the journal instructions, students were advised to document and analyze racial interactions, accounts, events, and comments. A summary of the instructions says, "The goal of this study is to examine what really goes on in our everyday lives with regard to what we think, act, and say about racial matters. You will be asked to keep a journal of your observations of everyday events and conversations that deal with racial issues, images, and understandings." Student were instructed to submit their journals with a cover sheet that asked for their name (to confirm receipt of IRB-approved informed consents) and demographic information; a space was also provided for students to write comments or reflections. Additionally, the instructors were asked to provide feedback by completing an exit interview (for example, attempting to assess why some students opted not to participate in the project).

Although the journal-writing opportunity was open to members of all racial groups who gave consent to share their journals, the book *Two-Faced Racism* examines only the White students. (Picca, Feagin, and Thompson-Miller are currently in the process of writing a book that analyzes the more than 400 journals written by students of color.) Of the 626 White students, 68 percent were women and 32 percent were men. The higher rate of women participants should not be surprising, given that more women tend to take classes in disciplines where journal writing might be expected (such as Sociology or English). The snowball sampling began at a large university in the Southeast, and the majority of the White students (63 percent) were from five universities and colleges in that same region. Of the remaining participants, 19 percent were from the Midwest, 14 percent from the West, and 4 percent from the Northeast.

Analysis and coding of the journals was ongoing throughout the process in order to ensure that insights, data connections, and data categories were constantly being improved.

The accounts of all White students in the sample were read, coded, and analyzed for prevalent themes. We estimate that the 626 White students in the sample provided about 9,000 accounts of racial events. Considering the very large sample size, we paid particular attention to more substantial accounts that provided detailed analysis, narrative linkages, informative stories, and a situated context. (More details regarding the methodology of this project can be found in Picca and Feagin, 2007, pp. 30–41.)

Using student journal writing allows for the collection of rich data; however, there are limitations. For example, journal writing does not provide an opportunity to ask follow-up questions. Bearing in mind the methodology limitations, it is important to note that this qualitative project used a convenient, not representative, sample, and with a very large sample size, the concerns of validity are lessened. Besides checking the data for internal consistency (within one journal, across students in the same class, and comparing students across the country), the details were compared with data from other studies that focus on racial relations among Whites and college students (e.g., Bonilla-Silva & Forman, 2000; Myers, 2005).

Journals by White Students

With this vast data, Picca and Feagin (2007) utilized the dramaturgical theoretical framework most associated with the theorist Erving Goffman (1959). The authors found that White college students have very different interactions when they are in the presence of people of color (the frontstage) compared to when they are in the presence of only Whites or those that are assumed to be White (the backstage). The inclusion of those perceived (or "mistaken") to be White in the backstage illustrates the social construction and fluidity of racial categories. The backstage includes not only White family and friends but also White co-workers, bosses, and strangers.

The authors found conflicting dimensions between the frontstage and backstage, where Whites would even take careful measures to protect the backstage from the intrusion of people of color. For example, Whites would whisper certain words and use vague language, body language, or code language when the backstage was threatened. The following account written by Becky, a White college student, illustrates the conflicting frontstage and backstage dimensions. Becky describes an interaction with some of her former high school friends, who are all White:

> [My friend] Todd asked how school was going and then asked when I was going to let them come down and visit. I said, "I don't know guys, one of my suitemates is Black, you would have to be nice to her." All the guys said, "Black!?!" Like they were shocked that I could actually live with someone of another color. Then David said, "Now why would you go and do that for?" Then they agreed that nothing would be said if they came to visit. . . . The conversation was short lived and I wasn't surprised by their comments or their reactions to Lisa (my suitemate). They are all really nice guys and I think if they came to visit that they would be respectful of Lisa. I know, however, that they would talk and make fun later about me living with a Black girl.
>
> (Becky)

Becky knew there would be a problem with her friends knowing that one of her suitemates was Black. The initial collective shocked response from her friends illustrates the emotions connected with racism. Her White friends appear to negatively sanction Becky and to hold her responsible for the race of her suitemate. Becky's White friends openly admitted that they would be polite to the Black woman to her face in the frontstage, fulfilling the expectations of a nonracist White public identity. However, in the all-White backstage, the men can behave very differently. In a secure all-White setting, the men can mock Becky and give her a hard time. The men clearly possess a level of awareness that their backstage interactions are inappropriate for the frontstage, as they agree not to say anything.

The Frontstage

The frontstage is defined as those social spaces where the White students were in the presence of people of color. It was notably characterized by a nonracist, color-blind perspective (where it does not matter if one is Black, White, green, or polka-dotted as we are all members of the *human* race) (Carr, 1997). There were several broad themes prevalent in the frontstage. First, when around people of color, the White students attempted to prove their tolerance (such as using extreme politeness, confirming they were not a racist by such actions as deliberately saying hello to a person of color, or appropriating racial and cultural characteristics). Second, Whites used avoidance strategies, such as not mentioning racial issues or anything that could be associated with racial issues, or simply avoided people of color. Third, Whites used defensive strategies, such as defending themselves against perceived threats or defending Whiteness (such as debunking the stereotype that Whites cannot dance). Fourth, Whites used confrontational strategies, such as overt racist joking (used in an aggressive and hostile manner as well as a bonding and reciprocal manner). Fifth, Whites described mundane and ordinary interactions; these accounts involved less narrative detail and included some underlying racial messages (such as the frequency of mentioning that a person "happens to be African American" while never mentioning that a person "happens to be White," suggesting a preservation of color-blindness).

In one example of the frontstage, a White student writes in her journal that she is a Resident assistant at her university residence hall and describes a time when her best friend, who is Black, came to visit her in the dorm. As they are walking up the stairs, she notes in her journal:

> *I started noticing how many people were stopping, and even going out of their way, to say hi to her. There are about 20 resident rooms from the side entrance of the building to the stairwell and every person in the hall at that time, along with some standing or sitting in their rooms, greeted my friend. Because I was leading the way, I knew that they were addressing her and not me. And I believe that each greeting given to her was absolutely genuine. . . . When we entered the second floor where I live the same thing happened. . . . [My friend] then commented to me when we got to my room, "People sure are friendly here." When I began to think about it, I realized that this happened every time she came to visit me. The situation leads me to believe that they greeted her the way they did based on her race, because they don't treat each other or other White strangers the way they have treated and continue to treat my friend. It's definitely an interesting twist on interactions and behavior based on race. I also think this situation illustrates that our hall would greatly benefit from having minority residents. If not for any other reason, that people might treat one another more courteously.*
>
> (Elizabeth)

In this journal account, the White residents are overly nice to the resistant assistant's Black friend and their performance is apparent to her Black friend. Elizabeth notes that her mostly White school needs more "minority residents" in order to draw some of the frontstage social pleasantries into apparently less polite backstage realities. She also notes that the residents are sincerely genuine in their interracial performances. As in other journal entries by White students, Elizabeth affirms that her residents are "good people." The White residents should not be viewed as necessarily manipulative because they were probably genuinely interested in expressing an overly positive image to the African American dorm visitor. Other students wrote about feeling the need to prove to people of color that they are not prejudiced, as they felt it was assumed that White skin was equated with a racist identity.

A general rule in frontstage interactions is that it is not appropriate for Whites to express racist sentiments in the frontstage. Most Whites would use a color-blind perspective, where the assumption is that race does not matter. Many Whites expressed a fear of appearing racist in interactions with people of color and would take measures to convey a nonracist ideology. This frontstage concern to appear color-blind almost entirely disappears when students are in the backstage with only other Whites.

The Backstage

The backstage for Whites involves interactions among only those who are White or are perceived to be White. A person whose racial identity is ambiguous or unclear is often asked questions such as, "So what are you?" or "Where are you *really* from?" This ensures that the backstage, where racist comments can be made, is protected. In some instances, the White space is viewed as sacred space where "the other" doesn't belong. There are two general themes in the backstage for Whites: preparing for future frontstage interactions (such as a student who informs her grandmother that the appropriate term is *Asian*, not *Oriental*) and relaxing the frontstage expectation of color-blindness. These frontstage pleasantries could be relaxed and openly contradicted where racial and racist interactions were not only tolerated but often sustained and encouraged. In the White college students' journals, the most frequent theme that emerged was telling or hearing racist jokes in White-only groups. Consider the following journal entry written by Debbie, who was watching a movie with four White friends when one of the men made an aggressively racist joke:

> When we heard the joke, my one roommate Lillian said she thought that joke was "terrible." My other roommate Mike said, "It's true though." We all yelled at him and said he was the worst, etc., etc. However, none of us was really mad or really offended by what he said and we probably should have been. Instances like this make me realize that people have gotten too used of people making jokes about minorities. We are too willing to accept people making inappropriate comments about minorities. I feel like I'm so used to people saying jokes like that, that I don't even take them seriously anymore. The strange thing is that I don't think any of my friends are actually racist, they just sometimes say inconsiderate things that they don't really mean.
>
> (Debbie)

Debbie's comment on how common it is for her friends to tell racist jokes indicates that such jokes appear to be a part of the socialization of many Whites. Many of the jokes date from the era of legal segregation and are repeated in White-only social networks and in private conversations away from people of color. Due to spatial racial segregation (notably in neighborhoods, churches, and schools), most Whites say they largely interact only with other Whites, so they do not worry about "getting caught" telling racist jokes. For many Whites, using racist epithets among themselves is not a problem; it only becomes a problem if they are said in the wrong context, which indicates that there are acceptable contexts for using racist epithets, such as when the target is not around.

Like most Whites in the data sample, Debbie clearly recognizes that such racist humor is wrong, yet no one in her account is offended by the joke. There are no negative consequences for this action; racism is just part of the fun. In the backstage, there is no deeper acknowledgment or questioning of why making fun of people of color is considered normal. There is no consciousness about the meaning or consequences of their fun. The "White-washed education" that children receive has been attributed to the minimal understanding of our racial past and lack of comprehension of how this legacy still has immediate effects today (psychologically, physically, socially, politically, and economically).

Examining the media context that young people are immersed in illustrates the "light-hearted" nature of racism. They listen to comedians who joke about racism. The hip-hop music that Whites listen to regularly features racist epithets (Hurt, 2006). Comedy and music are powerful tools of socialization that can subvert the racial hierarchy; however, with an uninformed audience, it can be a dangerous method of perpetuating the same old stereotypes. For example, comedians like Dave Chappelle often utilize racial stereotypes and racist epithets in order to dismantle their power. However, in their journals, White students would often argue along the lines of "if Dave Chappelle can say the word *nigger*, why can't I?" without recognizing that the social context matters. As an illustration, in 2005 Dave Chappelle walked away from a multimillion-dollar contract because he realized that he was not disempowering, but *contributing to*, the perpetuation of negative stereotypes of people of color.

In this age of technology, everything is immediate, and there is a limited depth of processing in the media world. This lack of reflection translates into racial interactions and stereotypes, where jokes are "just jokes." In the backstage, young people rarely think deeply or critically about why making fun of people of color is normalized in society. Young Whites don't think about the consequences of their actions and how they impact people of color. Some scholars think the responsibility lies with the educational system, specifically the "White-washed education" that children receive in school (Loewen, 1995). The distortion of U.S. history, with its lack of acknowledgment of the contributions made by people of color, is well documented and perpetuates stereotypical notions (Clarke, 2011; Franklin & Higginbotham, 2010). The educational system provides students with a minimal understanding of our racial past and certainly no comprehension of how our racial history still has immediate effects today (Lewis, 2003). However, White students understand "enough," as is evident in their behavior change when they are around people of color.

Debbie claims that her friends who tell racist jokes are not actually racist. Recall that in the earlier journal entry, Becky makes a similar claim—that her White friends are all "really nice guys." Indeed, most Whites in our sample claimed that someone could not be racist if he or she was a really nice person. For young American Whites, a person who is racist is considered to be a bad person, such as a Ku Klux Klan member, a skinhead, or some other radical race fanatic; these White college students are "just having fun." Additionally, for many Whites, a negative comment isn't viewed as a racial slur if it is not said directly to a person of color. Of course, social scientists know that subtle and hidden forms of racism behind the scenes can be just as damaging (some argue more so) as the overt and in-your-face types (see Carter, 2007; Evans-Campbell, Lincoln, & Takeuchi, 2007; Williams & Williams-Morris, 2000; Yamato, 1987). One way in which White society justifies racism is by reducing it to the actions of a few misguided bigots. However, the larger and more insidious aspect of racism is that it is systemic and institutionalized in every social institution in the United States (Feagin, 2009; Grier & Cobbs, 2000). The legacy of racial relations in the United States affects every major decision a person makes (and how he or she is treated), such as where you live, whom you marry, what schools you attend, where you work and shop, the access you have to health care, and interactions with the police (Blank, 2009). A fundamental part of White privilege is the luxury to take the advantageous experiences of whites as the norm and to deny the consequences of current racial injustices (Collins, 2000; Johnson, 2006).

Certainly, White college students are not inventing racial stereotypes or racist jokes. They rely on stereotypes that have been passed down through generations and were created (by Whites) to legitimize slavery, legal segregation, lynchings, rapes, and other atrocities. There is an inter-generational component that has been inherited by young people, even if they claim to celebrate diversity. The "fun" for young Whites in a private backstage has real and serious consequences that reify and perpetuate old racist stereotypes, contributing to and maintaining contemporary racial hierarchies (as evident in higher education, health care, the legal system, housing, etc.) that Whites have the privilege to ignore (Collins, 2000). There never has to be any acknowledgment of how their everyday "micro" interactions sustain the "macro" institutional racism.

On the whole, the accounts from the White college students focused on backstage interactions. In the backstage, expectations of frontstage pleasantries were relaxed and openly racist interactions were tolerated and often encouraged. In the thousands of narratives collected in this research project, "racial joking" in the backstage was the most prevalent theme reported. The backstage is considered a "safe White space" where Whites can relax and temporarily bond with other Whites at the unintentional expense of people of color. Some White students concluded that "it must go both ways," suspecting that students of color sit around telling racist jokes about Whites. A White student, Samuel, made the following entry in his journal after hearing racist jokes in an all-White context:

> *One of my buddies just told us [a joke] with a racial punch line. It was odd to look at such a normal occurrence as a sociologist, but I realized that everyone was laughing. It was then that I realized how much we take our Whiteness for granted. Then I got thinking whether people of color tell White jokes, and concluded that they must, but that they're probably about specific white people, like southerners, etc. When I asked my friends what they thought, one said sarcastically, "I'm sure they do; we did oppress them for 150 years!"*

> (Samuel)

Samuel implies that southerners are considered more racist than residents of other regions based on the history of slavery and legal segregation in the South. However, this misconception has been repeatedly refuted by social researchers (Bowser, 2007; Jaspin, 2007). Additionally, Samuel's friend illustrates either a lack knowledge about racial history or a tendency to minimize it as oppression, since the American slave trade and enforced legal segregation lasted 360 years, not 150 years (Clarke, 2011; Franklin & Higginbotham, 2010).

In addition to collecting the narratives of more than 600 White students, we also collected more than 400 journals written by students of color. The next section describes some of the prevalent themes written about by these students, which are strikingly different from the journals written by their White peers.

Journals by Students of Color

The narratives in the journals of students of color were vastly different from those in the White students' journals. The students of color focused on the differential treatment that they (or their racial-minority friends and family) experienced. These accounts of interactions with White professors, the campus police, and other students (at social gatherings, in the classroom, in restaurants, in public campus spaces) are alarming. This is particularly true for students of color at historically and predominantly White institutions. Unlike White students, who can regularly interact in "safe" White-only spaces, students of color regularly had interactions with people outside of their racial and ethnic identity (Feagin, 1991; Moore, 2007). An African American male wrote about his experiences attending a party during the university's Parents Weekend (which often involves parents socializing and drinking with the college students):

> *I went to a house party with my White roommate to link up with my other White roommate and some friends (all White). We arrived at the party and there were about 100 people of all ages drinking and enjoying each other's company. I didn't feel out of place at all until this somewhat random person, which was talking to our group of parents and friends, stopped mid-conversation and asked "are you the token Black person?" I was shocked and had no clue as to how to positively respond. I thought to myself that I can't be a token Black person because I was there on my own free will. I thought that regardless of me being there, the party would be the same. Even though I was telling myself that I wasn't the token Black person, I jokingly told them that I was because I didn't know what else to say that wouldn't take from or negatively add to the party. I just internalized my feelings and eventually went home.*

> (Len)

Students of color at predominantly and historically White universities often remarked on being *the only* or one of a few racial minorities in their college classes or at parties. Their achievements, such as college admission, scholarships, and selection into prestigious positions, were often minimized and attributed to the fulfillment of a racial quota (Wise, 2005). Instead of being celebrated for their merit and hard work, students of color often had to contend with an added layer of surveillance (Feagin, Vera, & Imani, 1996; McIntosh, 1998). For example, students of color mentioned that their classmates and instructors often expected them to speak on behalf of all members of their racial community. In class, whenever the topic of race was mentioned, their classmates would immediately look at them for their reaction. In comparison, the White students rarely wrote in their journals about being placed in a situation where they were asked to represent all White people.

As noted previously, White students often made racial jokes in private backstage settings, but it was not uncommon for them to "slip" and do so in the company of people of color (see Picca & Feagin, 2007, ch. 5). The students of color do not ask to be placed in an awkward situation, yet their reactions can have serious consequences for future racial interactions. Consider Len's account of being referred to as the "token Black person" above. Len could have reacted by getting angry, laughing it off, educating the White person, or simply walking away. Whatever he did could have had consequences for how White students treat him in the future. Len was "on the spot"; he wrote that he was shocked at the comment and did not pursue the conversation further. The *microaggression* (Sue, 2010)—subtle and often regular racial insults—was unexpected, but Len had to decide within seconds how to react to the comment.

The psychological and consequently physical toll that these microaggressions have on students of color cannot be underestimated. Len's reaction, no matter what it was, might have had negative consequences: Confronting the comment might have made him seem "too sensitive" about racial issues, yet ignoring it or laughing it off might have led to the perception that hurtful comments are "no big deal" (Frye, 1998). Len also noted that he did not want to disrupt the social situation, so he internalized his feelings and left. Many scholars have documented the impact of the additional stress and negative health consequences of dealing with racist interactions (Feagin & McKinney, 2003; Randall, 2006). Racial jokes have real consequences for people of color. Historically, African Americans have swallowed the humiliation, shame, and rage associated with racism. However, research has proven that the internalization of rage associated with racism contributes to high blood pressure, heart attacks and strokes, and other debilitating diseases (Bryant-Davis, 2007; Bryant-Davis & Ocampo, 2005).

While many White college students believe racism is not a significant issue at their campus or nationwide (Feagin et al., 1996), many students of color in our sample wrote painful narratives of hostile racial interactions. Alex, a biracial man, described the frequency with which he is referred to with a racist epithet:

> *This is one of those sad and angry nights for me. Tonight marks the third time since the beginning of the school year that I've been called a nigger by a bunch of White students on a Saturday night, or weekend more in general. At first I used to wonder where they actually take the time in their heads to separate me from everyone else by the color of my skin. I used to just blame alcohol consumption for their obvious ignorance and racist attitudes, but I have since stopped trying to make excuses for them. . . . Sometimes it seems that if I am around all White people, then I become nothing more than a token Black "exhibit" for their amusement. . . . The saddest thing however, is that these people, these COLLEGE STUDENTS are supposed to be the crème de la crème, the future business and political leaders. They are supposed to be the brightest of the brightest, but then again I guess ignorance can't be masked by book smarts.*

(Alex)

The pain and sadness apparent in Alex's narrative is very different from the lighthearted tone of many of the White students' journal entries. In their journals, most Whites reported reserving racial comments for the backstage, away from the presence of people of color. However, Alex reminds us that even in the frontstage, people of color may still be confronted with racist comments, which may increase at certain times of the day or week. Alex notes that the frequency of racist comments increases on evenings and weekends, which are also the times when college students are more likely to consume alcohol excessively. Indeed, in their journal entries, many White students cited alcohol use as an excuse for racist comments and interactions. Alcohol is frequently used as an excuse by Whites to downplay racist activity. In *Two-Faced Racism*, Picca and Feagin (2007) discuss "two-beers racism" (p. 72), where consuming significant amounts of alcohol can relax the social pressures against openly expressing racist ideas. While alcohol can loosen inhibitions, it cannot create racist sentiments that are not already there.

Alex refers to the social construction of racial categories when he wonders why he is separated from his peers based just on his skin color. In the social construction of race and ethnicity, race is not a fixed biological fact but a social agreement. While biology determines our physical phenotypes, it is society that determines the *meanings* we give to arbitrary traits such as skin color, eye shape, and hair texture. Earlier in his journal, Alex notes that he has one Black parent and one White parent. He identifies himself as biracial, even though he writes that he is often identified as just a "token Black exhibit." Alex and Len are both referred to as "tokens" by their White peers. Alex is also referred to as a "nigger," one of the harshest of racist epithets, a term with a long and violent history that is usually reserved for African Americans (Kennedy, 2003). Racial categorizations depend not only on what an individual identifies for him- or herself but also on the identities other people impose. In journal entries we see students of color grappling with their interactions with Whites and giving Whites the benefit of the doubt as a way to cope with microaggressions.

We often think of racist individuals who use the *n*-word as neo-Nazi skinheads or uneducated working-class persons (best characterized by the 1970s Archie Bunker character). Alex emphasizes that the persons making racial insults are educated college students, who constitute the next generation of our nation's leaders. While education is believed to be the great equalizer of racial relations, many scholars suggest that our nation's schools maintain and perpetuate racial inequalities both in structure and in content (Lewis, 2003; Loewen, 1995).

In their journals, students of color indicate that they are often assumed to fit the stereotype of their racial group. Asian students were asked by classmates they did not know to help with math homework. Latinos were asked if they were in the United States legally. Students of Middle Eastern descent were referred to as terrorists. Many Black men wrote about the presumption by other students that they were untrustworthy or their interactions with campus police, where they were assumed to have engaged in violent crimes. For example, Brian wrote about how Whites, especially White women, openly avoided interacting with him:

> This morning I was walking to my 10:30 a.m. class. I was running a few minutes late and I saw another student, a White female, walking toward me. She was about 50 yards down the street from me on [Main Street]. I saw her look up at me, then she crossed the street and walked on the other side. She walked for about another 20 yards then crossed back to the side she was originally on. Now, I don't know if that was really that racist but the implication to me was that she was afraid of me.
>
> (Brian)

Brian gives this woman the benefit of the doubt that she was not behaving in a racially motivated manner, but he senses that she fears him. Other Black males in the sample detailed the hurt they feel when their fellow students do not feel comfortable walking along the street next to them. After detailing a similar experience to Brian's, Todd, another Black man, wrote, "I tried to come up [with] other possible reasons for her actions [crossing the street to avoid him, then crossing back after they passed], but the only logical conclusion I can come up with is that she encountered a Black male, a threat she felt required quick evasive action." Brian and Todd are reminded that they are not equal in the minds of their fellow students but are to be viewed with suspicion and caution.

Students of color wrote that when they confronted their peers about racial stereotypes, they were labeled as being too sensitive about race or as "playing the race card." Jordan wrote in her journal about a recent shopping trip, where a stranger commented on her appearance:

> I was buying windshield wipers at Walmart today and this man told me I reminded him of Lucy Liu. It's been the hundredth time that someone has told me that I look like Lucy Liu. I look nothing like Lucy Liu. [My friend] says I should take it as a compliment because Lucy Liu is hot, but that's not

the damned point. The only reason why they think I look like her is because I'm Asian and have long black hair. . . . How is it a compliment when it has nothing to do with your "self" and everything to do with your race? I'm sick of being told I look like Connie Chung, Zhang Ziyi, Kaity Tong and the latest edition, Lucy Liu. What sucks is that every time I go off on a tirade about it I get pissed on for having a bad attitude. The same question pops up, "why can't you take a compliment?" I try to explain that it is not a compliment but people don't understand why not.

(Jordan)

From the tone of Jordan's narrative, we get a sense of the frustration she feels. Jordan resists the assumption that she should see her comparison with an attractive actress as a compliment. We can speculate that she may be referencing the stereotype of Asian American women as docile and submissive when she says she gets "pissed on for having a bad attitude" and not agreeing with the supposed compliment. Jordan's comparison to the "hot" Lucy Liu references another stereotype of the "exotic, erotic" sexualization of Asian women (Feng Sun, 2003; Shimizu, 2007). She recognizes that the comparison has less to do with her appearance and more to do with her being lumped into the category of "Asian woman," where her individuality is ignored. People of color are often viewed by those not of their race as "all looking alike," referred to as the "other-race effect" in psychology. This homogeneous view of individuals of other races has been attributed to having more experience looking at faces of one own's race (Chiroro & Valentine, 1995). However, studies also suggest that it relates to prejudice, as more prejudiced individuals are focused on racial stereotypes and ignore individual differences (Ferguson, Rhodes, & Lee, 2001).

Comparing the Journals Written by Whites and Students of Color

Comparing the journals written by White students with those written by students of color reveals striking differences, some of which were noted above. Overwhelmingly, the White students wrote about racially hostile comments that could be made "just for fun" in a private backstage setting. The parallel was not true for the students of color. While it is true that there are some accounts of students of color making "anti-White" comments (as Samuel suggested in his narrative), the nature of the comments are vastly different because they are not nearly as common, vicious, or damaging. First, the comments are not nearly as frequent as the anti-Black, anti-Latino, anti-Arab, and anti-Asian comments we see in the White students' journals. Many of the White students reported their surprise at how often they heard racist comments, which often "slip under the radar" of consciousness unless they pay attention. For the students of color, there was no parallel reaction; proportionally, very few of them noted derogatory comments about Whites or other racial group.

Second, the overwhelming majority of anti-White comments were based on a reaction to a specific event. For example, one African American woman reported seeing a White woman leave a public bathroom without washing her hands and commented to her friends that "White people are dirty." Although generalizing negative comments to an entire group is never a good thing, there is a difference between a comment based in direct experiences (as is the case with many students of color) and common stereotypes ungrounded in direct interaction (as is the case with many White students) (Hraba, Brinkman, & Gray-Ray, 1996; Pettigrew, 1985).

Finally, the comments made by students of color lack the institutional support necessary to have any real negative consequences. The pejorative words used against Whites are not equal to the pejorative words used against people of color. The stereotypes of Whites (such as that White people cannot dance or excel at certain sports) do not have nearly as many negative consequences as the stereotypes of people of color (such as that African Americans are criminal and lazy and that Latinos are all illegal Mexicans), which have very real and damaging consequences, such as in the job market or in securing housing and access to health care (Lipsitz, 1995; Mindiola, Flores-Niemann, & Rodriquez, 2002). For example, a number of White students wrote in their journals about instructions they received at work from their White bosses and managers to discriminate against people of color (see Picca & Feagin, 2007, ch. 4), such as not to accept their employment applications or to monitor them for possible shoplifting. In their journals, none of the students of color discussed discrimination against Whites, which is not surprising, as people of color often lack the institutional support to enact it.

Compared to their White peers, many students of color at predominantly White campuses experience added layers of complexity in their everyday interactions. Most White students do not have to contend with negative racial stereotypes. (Notably, even "positive" racial stereotypes, such as the model-minority myth of Asian Americans, carry negative, and sometimes deadly, consequences [Chou & Feagin, 2008].) White students' admission to the university as well as their subsequent successes and failures are not viewed through the lens of their racial identity. When a White student receives a scholarship, it is perceived as based on hard work, effort, and individual accomplishment. The parallel is not true for students of color, who are often presumed to have received preferential treatment at the expense of White students, even when there is no evidence to suggest this is true (see Wise, 2005). Students of color, especially on predominantly White campuses, are all too often reminded that their actions impact, for better or worse, racial stereotypes. White students can be *just* individuals, with their race largely ignored. For these students, using racial stereotypes and racist humor, especially in the backstage, is just fun, without any negative consequences.

Conclusion and Next Actionable Steps

Although we can celebrate the racial progress we have made in the early 21st century, we still have a lot of work to do. We offer four starting points. First, we need to increase the awareness of how racial interactions affect *everyone* and engage in an open dialogue. This can start with something as simple as asking students to pay attention to their interactions. To account for the normalization of racist interactions, many Whites commented in their journals that they never paid attention to it until they were asked to keep a daily journal. Numerous Whites said they were shocked by how often negative comments "slipped under the radar" of consciousness, indicating that part of White racial identity is the privilege to ignore it. Consider the narrative written by Kyle, a White male, who ended his journal on this note:

> As my last entry in this journal, I would like to express what I have gained out of this assignment. I watched my friends and companions with open eyes. I was seeing things that I didn't realize were actually there. By having a reason to pick out of the racial comments and actions I was made aware of what is really out there. Although I noticed that I wasn't partaking in any of the racist actions or comments, I did notice that I wasn't stopping them either. I am now in a position to where I can take a stand and try to intervene in many of the situations
>
> (Kyle)

Kyle discusses how invisible and normal racist actions and comments can seem; he also acknowledges that now that he is able to recognize this, he can now move on to actively resisting the racial hierarchy.

Second, we need to be critical of color-blindness. Color-blindness is often popularly believed to be the solution to racism, yet most race scholars disagree. There are at least four reasons why color-blindness works against those interested in racial justice. (1) Color-blindness ignores the differences among people that should be celebrated (diversity in food, dance, dress, customs, appearances, etc.). (2) Color-blindness can never exist because there are racial meanings attached to other racial markers. There are other ways of categorizing race besides what a person looks like. Race affects every aspect of a person that cannot be ignored: Zip codes, clothing, voice, and even names carry racial meanings. To illustrate this, two economists (Bertrand & Mullainathan, 2004) conducted an experiment in Chicago and Boston using almost 5,000 résumés with either a traditionally White name (like Emily or Greg) or traditionally African American one (like LaToya or Jamal). They found a 50 percent gap in call-back rates favoring the White names, with a White name yielding as many more call-backs as an additional eight years of work experience. Clearly race is simply not just a matter of how people look. (3) Color-blindness is typically code for "White." Numerous scholars have written about how Whiteness is invisible, expected, and the norm (Johnson, 2006; McIntosh, 1998). Whites will often claim, "I don't see color; I just see people." Yet this is true only as long as the person dresses like a White person, talks like a White person, thinks like a White person, studies White subjects, and so on. By the same token, Whiteness is also the standard used for evaluation. For example, most college professors are assessed based on their teaching effectiveness. This is often captured through measures such as student evaluations, which is a seemingly color-blind standard. However, empirical research shows that professors of color regularly receive lower teaching evaluations. Put another way, White professors regularly receive higher teaching evaluations (Messner, 2000). When this is the standard used to evaluate contract renewals, tenure, promotion, and merit pay, Whiteness is rewarded yet never acknowledged in a seemingly color-blind measure. The rewards and privileges are invisible to the dominant group. (4) Color-blindness is often situational. Whites often practice color-blindness only in the frontstage, relaxing these standards in the backstage, as this chapter illustrates.

Third, educators need to be encouraged to become more culturally and racially aware of these issues. In *Racist America: Roots, Current Realities, and Future Reparations*, Feagin (2000) makes important points about how individuals can become culturally and racially aware of antiracist strategies and solutions. This can be done by working on one's own attitudes, stereotypes, and proclivities, which includes understanding the history of racial oppression in the United States:

> Collective forgetting is central to the way in which most Whites have dealt with the history of racism. Most have chosen not to know their history. . . . [L]earning much about the reality of that history, about its brutality and unjust impoverishment for people of color, and its unjust enrichment for Whites, may be critical to increasing the number of Whites who join in antiracist efforts and movements. (p. 254)

With an awareness of the racial social context, educators can provide support systems for students of color. They can listen to their narratives, and although educators may not necessarily have all the answers, listening is a powerful way to be supportive.

Finally, we need to encourage Whites to hold other Whites accountable. Too often, the burden of responsibility rests with people of color to educate Whites about racism. Whites need to recognize that racist comments made in private directly contribute to racial hostilities in the larger society. There are numerous tools Whites can use to diffuse racist comments, such as using humor (sarcastically saying, "Gee, I didn't know you were a racist") or pleading ignorance ("Can you please explain that comment to me? I don't understand what you mean."). Even to the most ignorant person, racist jokes are not funny if you have to explain them.

Substantially improving our cultural racial climate, particularly in educational settings, is critical for many reasons. Taking an other-oriented approach, it is the decent and fair thing to do. Even from a self-interested standpoint, given the competitive global economy that today's students will likely enter and the demographic shifts in the United States, it is critical for students to be prepared to work with people who are not like them. Indeed, one national study indicates that employers' highest priority in hiring college graduates is their ability to collaborate with others in diverse group settings (Peter D. Hart Research Associates, Inc., 2006). Whether students adopt the other-oriented or self-interested position, it is clear that racial issues and racial diversity are critically important and that we still have much work to do.

Journal Exercise

Keep your own racial journal. Below is a modified version of the journal instructions we use in our own classes.

Instructions: Often we take for granted issues of race and ethnicity when talking about social interaction and relationships. These issues are an ever-present factor of our everyday lives, yet we often ignore them, talk around them, or only mention them explicitly in jokes or in private settings. What we say and do in the "backstage" (or private) area is sometimes very different from what we say and do in the public "frontstage." This exercise will require you to think beyond your everyday interactions and to analyze your "everyday world" as a social researcher.

The goal of this assignment is to examine what really goes on in our everyday lives regarding what we think, act, and say about the often taken-for-granted issues of race and ethnicity. You will keep a journal of your observations of everyday events and conversations that deal with the issues we discuss in class—including scenes you encounter, conversations you take part in or observe, images you notice, and understandings you gather. The situations you observe do not need to be negative, derogatory, or discriminatory (i.e., racist) but can occur anytime when race/ethnicity comes up (or does not come up).

How Do I Do This?

Unobtrusive Participant Observation: In your observations, please use unobtrusive research techniques so that the person(s) you write about in your journal will not be aware that they are being studied. In other words, you may *not* interview anyone you observe as a researcher, but you may interact with people as you usually would. Please be detailed in your accounts, yet, to ensure anonymity, it is important that you conceal all identities and disguise all names of persons you write about. Even though there will be no identifying markers in the journal, please keep your journal in a safe, private space so that it is not read by others.

Writing Up Your Observations: *In your journal, you will be asked to emphasize (1) your observations and (2) your reactions to and perceptions of these everyday events.* Please note details, such as whether you are observing a middle-aged White female or a teenage Asian American male. It is helpful to note the approximate age, race, and gender of each person you mention in your journal.

As well as noting *what* happened, be sure to note *where* the observations took place, *when* it took place (such as a Saturday night or your Tuesday lunch break), and *whom* you were with. Often time, place, and the presence or absence of other people critically affect whether people feel comfortable (or not) talking about these issues.

When writing down your observations, be sure to be detailed in your comments on the way in which people interact. For example, if someone makes a comment sarcastically or whispers certain words, be sure to note the sarcasm or volume change. Also, be sure to note the occasions when certain issues are blatantly ignored. For example:

October 27
Monday night I was with a group of girlfriends (4 White, 1 Latina) watching TV. Sue [not her real name] mentioned another girl, Betty, and was trying to describe to the other girls who Betty is. I should mention Betty is from Korea. Sue described her as kinda short, ponytail, and works out

around the same time that we do (which describes just about every girl at our school!!). I don't know why Sue didn't mention she is Asian—it would have made describing her a lot easier.

If you find that you have not noticed any issues to write about, write that down as well! Jot down what you did that day (did you go to the gym, go to class, have lunch with three White friends, then hit the library?). Often even "no data" are data! Be sure to think critically about what you observe.

When Should I Write? If you can, you should jot down your notes as quickly as possible after your observations so the details will be fresh in your mind. You'll be surprised at how quickly you forget key details if you do not jot them down right away. You should make it a point to write in your journal at least once a day, even to note that you did not observe any events.

How Should the Journal Entries Look? Your initial notes to remind yourself of what you saw may certainly be handwritten scribbles on small scraps of paper. (You may find it useful to carry small pads of paper around to jot down notes to yourself.) The journal you submit should be *typed*. The entries should be single-spaced; about a full paragraph to half a page in length is typical. Commit to keeping a journal for two weeks. Be sure to note the date and time when the incidents took place.

Often with these issues, people feel afraid to say or do "the wrong thing." Keep in mind that there are no "right" or "wrong" responses, so there are no "mistakes" that you can make when writing in your journal. You *will not* be graded on your observations or your reactions to your observations. You *will* be graded on your narrative detail and your analysis in the summary essay.

Besides the Journal Accounts, What Else Will I Submit? Summary Essay After you have written in your journal, please reflect back on your experiences: How do your accounts relate to material we've covered in this course? Within the context of this course, were you surprised by your experiences? Does race/ethnicity structure and affect your everyday life?

How Will I Be Graded? To receive the maximum credit, you will write at least ten entries plus a two-page summary essay. The quality of your work counts. Mediocre work (fewer entries, less detailed analysis, spelling/grammatical errors, etc.) will obviously not warrant full credit. Again, you will not be graded on "what" you see; rather, you will be evaluated on the quality and detail of your systematic observations and field notes and, obviously, on your summary essay.

QUESTIONS AND ACTIVITIES

11.1 Consider the chapter in light of other social structures, such as how gender impacts racial interactions. Do you see any gender themes? Do you notice these in your own life?

11.2 How can the overall finding of this chapter, a frontstage/backstage difference in racial interactions, be applied to other social structures? In other words, is there a frontstage/backstage for gender relations? For sexual orientation? For social class? For religion?

11.3 How does the chapter illustrate why color-blindness is not the solution to racism?

11.4 Many Whites claim that comments are not racist if they are not said directly to a person of color. How does the chapter dispute this claim? In other words, why are racist jokes still racist even if they are told to only White people?

11.5 The chapter suggests that race is socially constructed, not biological. What are examples in the chapter that illustrate this? (*Note:* In Chapter 4 of *Two-Faced Racism*, Picca and Feagin [2007] examine the experiences of racially ambiguous individuals, or individuals who "play" with race, who present the frontstage and backstage as more fluid spaces, rather than as discrete and separate.)

11.6 What are steps *you* can take to combat racism on everyday levels? Do you see racism in your own life? How and where?

REFERENCES

Bertrand, M., & Mullainathan, S. (2004). Are Emily and Greg more employable than Lakisha and Jamal? A field experiment on labor market discrimination. *American Economic Review, 94,* 991–1013.

Blank, R. M. (2009). An overview of trends in social and economic well-being, by race. In C. A. Gallagher (Ed.), *Rethinking the color line* (pp. 39–49). New York: McGraw-Hill.

Bonilla-Silva, E. (2006). *Racism without racists: Color-blind racism and the persistence of racial inequality in the United States* (2nd ed.). Landham, MD: Rowman & Littlefield.

Bonilla-Silva, E., & Forman, T. A. (2000). "I am not a racist but . . .": Mapping White college students' racial ideology in the USA. *Discourse and Society, 11*(1), 50–85.

Bowser, B. (2007). *The Black middle class.* Boulder, CO: Lynne Rienner.

Bryant-Davis, T. (2007). Healing requires recognition: The case for race-based traumatic stress. *The Counseling Psychologist, 35*(1), 135–143.

Bryant-Davis, T., & Ocampo, C. (2005). Racist incident-based trauma. *The Counseling Psychologist, 33*(4), 479–500.

Carr, L. G. (1997). *"Colorblind" racism.* Thousand Oaks, CA: Sage.

Carter, R. T. (2007). Racism and psychological and emotional injury: Recognizing and assessing race-based traumatic stress. *The Counseling Psychologist, 35*(1), 13–105.

Chiroro, P., & Valentine, T. (1995). An investigation of the contact hypothesis of the own-race bias in face recognition. *The Quarterly Journal of Experimental Psychology, 48A,* 879–894.

Chou, R. S., & Feagin, J. R. (2008). *The myth of the model minority.* Boulder, CO: Paradigm.

Clarke, J. H. (2011). *Christopher Columbus and the Afrikan holocaust: Slavery and the rise of European capitalism.* Hunlock Creek, PA: EWorld Publishing.

Coates, R. D. (2011). *Covert racism: Theories, institutions, and experiences.* Boston: Brill.

Collins, P. H. (2000). *Black feminist thought: Knowledge, consciousness, and the politics of empowerment* (2nd ed.). New York: Routledge.

Dawson, M. C., & Bobo, L. D. (2009). One year later and the myth of a post-racial society. *DuBois Review: Social Science Research on Race, 6,* 247–249.

D'Souza, D. (2011). *The roots of Obama's rage.* Washington, DC: Regency.

Evans-Campbell, T., Lincoln, K. D., & Takeuchi, D. T. (2007). Race and mental health: Past debates, new opportunities. In W. R. Avison & J. D. McLeod (Eds.), *Mental health, social mirror* (pp. 169–189). New York: Springer.

Feagin, J. R. (1991). The continuing significance of race: Antiblack discrimination in public places. *American Sociological Review, 56,* 101–116.

Feagin, J. R. (2000). *Racist America: Roots, current realities, and future reparations.* New York: Routledge.

Feagin, J. R. (2009). *The White racial frame: Centuries of racial framing and counter-framing.* New York: Routledge.

Feagin, J. R., & McKinney, K. D. (2003). *The many costs of racism.* New York: Rowman & Littlefield.

Feagin, J. R., Vera, H., & Imani, N. (1996). *The agony of education: Black students at White colleges and universities.* New York: Routledge.

Feng Sun, C. (2003). Ling Woo in historical context: The new face of Asian American stereotypes on television. In G. Dines & J. M. Humez (Eds.), *Gender, race, and class in media.* (2nd ed., pp. 656–664). Thousand Oaks, CA: Sage.

Ferguson, D. P., Rhodes, G., & Lee, K. (2001). "They all look alike to me": Prejudice and cross-race face recognition. *British Journal of Psychology, 92,* 567–577.

Franklin, J. H., & Higginbotham, E. (2010). *From slavery to freedom: A history of African Americans* (9th ed.). New York: McGraw-Hill.

Frye, M. (1998). Oppression. In P. S. Rothenberg (Ed.), *Race, class, and gender in the United States: An integrated study* (4th ed., pp. 146–149). New York: St. Martin's Press.

Gallagher, C. A. (2003). Color blind privilege: The social and political functions of erasing the color line in post-race America. *Race, Gender, & Class, 10*(4), 22–37.

Goffman, E. (1959). *The presentation of everyday life.* New York: Anchor.

Grier, W., & Cobbs, P. M. (2000). *Black rage.* New York: Basic Books.

Hraba, J., Brinkman, R., & Gray-Ray, P. (1996). A comparison of Black and White prejudice. *Sociological Spectrum, 16*(2), 129–157.

Hurt, B. (Director and producer). (2006). *Hip-hop: Beyond beats and rhymes.* Plainfield, NJ: Media Education Foundation and God Bless the Child Productions.

Jaspin, E. (2007). *Buried in the bitter waters: The hidden history of racial cleansing in America.* New York: Basic Books.

Jhally, S., & Lewis, J. (1992). *Enlightened racism: The Cosby Show, audiences, and the myth of the American dream.* Boulder, CO: Westview.

Johnson, A. G. (2006). *Privilege, power, and difference* (2nd ed.). New York: McGraw-Hill.

Kaplan, H. R. (2011). *The myth of post-racial America: Searching for equality in the age of materialism.* New York: Rowman & Littlefield.

Kawakami, K., Dunn, E., Karmali, F., & Dovidio, J. F. (2009). Mispredicting affective and behavioral responses to racism. *Science, 323,* 276–278.

Kennedy, R. (2003). *Nigger: The strange career of a troublesome word.* New York: Vintage.

Lewis, A. E. (2003). *Race in the schoolyard: Negotiating the color line in classrooms and communities.* New Brunswick, NJ: Rutgers University Press.

Lipsitz, G. (1995). The possessive investment in Whiteness: Racialized social democracy and the "White" problem in American studies. *American Quarterly, 47*(3), 369–387.

Loewen, J. W. (1995). *Lies my teacher told me: Everything your American history textbook got wrong.* New York: Simon & Schuster.

McIntosh, P. (1998). White privilege and male privilege: A personal account of coming to see correspondences through work in women's studies. In M. L Andersen & P. H. Collins (Eds.), *Race, class, and gender: An anthology* (3rd ed., pp. 94–105). Albany, NY: Wadsworth.

McWhorter, J. (2006). *Winning the race: Beyond the crisis in Black America*. New York: Gotham Books.

Messner, M. A. (2000). White guy habitus in the classroom: Challenging the reproduction of privilege. *Men and Masculinities, 2*(4), 457–469.

Mindiola, T., Flores-Niemann, Y., & Rodriquez, N. (2002). *Black–brown: Relations and stereotypes*. Austin: University of Texas Press.

Moore, W. L. (2007). *Reproducing racism: White space, elite law schools, and racial inequality*. New York: Rowman & Littlefield.

Myers, K. (2005). *Racetalk: Racism hiding in plain sight*. Landham, MD: Rowman & Littlefield.

Peter D. Hart Research Associates, Inc. (2006). *How should colleges prepare students to succeed in today's global economy?* Retrieved October 9, 2009, from http://aacu.org/leap/documents/Re8097abcombined.pdf (retrieved 10/8/09).

Pettigrew, T. F. (1985). New Black–White patterns: How best to conceptualize them? *Annual Review of Sociology, 11,* 329–346.

Picca, L. H., & Feagin, J. R. (2007). *Two-faced racism: Whites in the backstage and frontstage*. New York & London: Routledge.

Randall, V. R. (2006). *Dying while Black*. Dayton, OH: Seven Principles Press.

Shimizu, C. P. (2007). *The hypersexuality of race: Performing Asian/American women on screen and scene*. Durham, NC: Duke University Press.

Sue, D. W. (2010). *Microaggressions in everyday life: Race, gender, and sexual orientation*. Hoboken, NJ: Wiley.

Tesler, M., & Sears, D. O. (2010). *Obama's race: The 2008 election and the dream of a post-racial America*. Chicago: University of Chicago Press.

Warren, C. (2002). Qualitative interviewing. In J. F. Gubrium & J. A. Holstein (Eds.), *Handbook of interview research: Context and method* (pp. 83–102). Thousand Oak, CA: Sage.

Williams, D. R., & Williams-Morris, R. (2000). Racism and mental health: The African American experience. *Ethnicity & Health, 5,* 243–268.

Wise, T. J. (2005). *Affirmative action: Racial preference in Black and White*. New York: Routledge.

Yamato, G. (1987). Something about the subject makes it hard to name. In G. Anzaldúa (Ed.), *Making face, making soul haciendo caras: Creative and critical perspectives by feminists of color* (pp. 20–24). San Francisco: Aunt Lute.

Thomas Tolstrup/Taxi/Getty Images, Inc.

Language Diversity and Schooling CHAPTER 12

Manka M. Varghese and Tom T. Stritikus

The current demographic shift along with the practitioner and scholarly work that has been conducted by teachers, teacher educators, and researchers in the last 30 years have generated the understanding that attending to linguistic diversity among students cannot be relegated to specialists in schools but must be the responsibility of schools as a whole (Echevarria, Vogt, & Short, 2008; Gibbons, 2002; Oláh, 2008). In fact, Enright (2010) proposes that "the new mainstream" in schools consists of culturally and linguistically diverse students (p. 80). This chapter introduces the topic of linguistic diversity with the same assumption—that this is a group of students who are everyone's responsibility. The information here will be helpful to all those who work in and with schools.

Immigrants give rise to the largest part of linguistic diversity among students and are also the fastest-growing group of students in U.S. schools (Oh & Cooc, 2011). In fact, almost all the growth in the child population of the United States in the last two decades can be accounted for by children of immigrants (Cervantes & Hernandez, 2011; Fortuny, Hernandez, & Chaudry, 2010). Children of immigrants are first-generation immigrant children born outside of the United States and second-generation children born in the United States who have at least one foreign-born parent. Many demographers predict that by 2025, approximately 20 to 25 percent of immigrant students enrolled in public schools will have limited proficiency in English (Spellings, 2005). At the same time, as regards language diversity, it is also important to consider cultural and linguistic groups who do not immediately come to mind; these include African Americans and indigenous populations. Many African Americans are "bidialectal"—that is, they speak African American vernacular English (Ebonics) and Standard English—and issues of language diversity have shaped their school experience in important ways (Alim & Baugh, 2007; Smitherman, 2000). Indigenous groups, such as American Indians, Alaskan Natives, and Native Hawaiians, contribute significantly to linguistic diversity, representing speakers of about 175 indigenous languages and numerous varieties of English (Krauss, 1998).

To understand how schools can better meet the needs of linguistically diverse students, we begin this chapter by examining more closely the linguistically diverse population in the United States. Then, to understand the legal obligations of schools in meeting the needs of linguistically diverse students, we examine important events in the legal, policy, and judicial history of linguistically diverse students in the United States. Next, we consider various programmatic responses to linguistic diversity and their efficacy in meeting the needs of linguistically diverse students. We conclude with a discussion of how teachers might better respond to the needs of these students. We now turn to an examination of one of the primary sources of linguistic diversity—immigration—and consider how increased immigration has influenced U.S. schools.

The Immigrant Population in the United States

Immigration continues to be the primary source of linguistic diversity in the United States. The foreign-born population was 34 million in 2000 and made up 12 percent of the population, the largest percentage in 80 years (U.S. Census Bureau, 2004). Because of restrictive immigration laws, most immigrants who came to the United States between 1880 and 1930 were from Europe. Changes to immigration law during the 1960s resulted in a steady increase of immigrants from Latin America, Southeast Asia, the Caribbean, and Africa. While immigration has a tremendous influence on all of American life, nowhere has this impact been more keenly felt than in U.S. public schools.

Historically, immigration to the United States has played a significant role in shaping current perceptions of today's immigrants and, consequently, their reception in schools. The opinions that Americans have about the current wave of immigrants are shaped in part by their views of the earlier waves of immigrants—perceptions influenced by both fact and fiction. Several key differences and similarities exist between the experiences of the immigrants who came at the turn of the 20th century and those who are coming today. Understanding these similarities and differences is an important way for teachers working with linguistically diverse students to fully understand the reality faced by immigrant populations today.

Despite the common perception to the contrary, the immigrants who came at the turn of the last century did not experience universal success in school. In major cities such as Boston, Chicago, and New York, the graduation and school continuation rates of southern Italian, Polish, and Russian Jewish children lagged far behind those of native-born White students (Olneck & Lazerson, 1974). The Italian, Jewish, and Irish immigrants of the early 20th century faced significant social, political, and cultural barriers (Jacobson, 1998). Despite these realities, today's immigration debates are often cast in terms of how the earlier immigrants were more easily absorbed and more beneficial to U.S. society than the Latin American, Asian, and African immigrants today. The concept of *ethnic succession*—which explains that new immigrants are rarely viewed as positively as the groups that came before them—can explain this pattern (Banks, 2005).

Despite the similarities between "earlier" and "new" immigrants, there are important differences as well. The current wave of immigration consists of people from several regions of the world who were not a major part of the last wave of immigration, which occurred in the late 1800s and the early 1900s. In recent years, scholars from various disciplines have claimed that world economies and societies have become increasingly interconnected through advances in technology, media, and mass transit, all of which facilitate the movement of people, goods, services, and ideas. This new phenomenon has been called *globalization, borderless economies,* and the *transnational era* (Castles, 2003). One of the characteristics of globalization is the increased flow of people across the planet. While some people voluntarily migrate in order to improve their lives, others are forced to migrate in order to survive (Suarez-Orozco & Suarez-Orozco, 2003). Social scientists have argued that the role of immigration in providing both cheap unskilled labor and highly technically skilled labor is a key component of the new transnational era that the world's societies have entered (Portes, 1996; Suarez-Orozco, 1997).

The back-and-forth movement of ideas and goods that characterizes the current transitional period also parallels the experience of many immigrant students, which has often been cast in terms of assimilation, whereby immigrants eventually lose contact with their home communities and are slowly absorbed into their new locality. Departing from the traditional model of assimilation, scholars have argued that immigrants negotiate more complex patterns of social interaction in their new countries (Itzigsohn, Dore-Cabral, Hernandez-Medina, & Vazquez, 1999; Rose, 1997; Suarez-Orozco & Suarez-Orozco, 2003), a process currently being defined as *transculturation* (Oh, 2011). In this current transnational era, some immigrant groups continue to have strong ties with their countries of origin once they reside in their receiving community. These ties influence immigrant children's socialization patterns and create social and cultural experiences that span transnational lines (Mahler, 1998; Oh, 2011; Portes, 1999; Smith & Guarnizo, 1998; Stritikus & Nguyen, 2007). Moreover, immigrants are significantly changing the social context of new communities while also shaping the social realities in their home countries.

The immigrant family now enters a country that as a whole is economically, socially, and culturally distinct from the one faced by earlier waves of immigrants. Previous waves of immigrants arrived on the eve of a great expansion of the industrial economy. The manufacturing jobs that were created during the transition to a fully industrialized economy provided a possible entrée for immigrants to the middle class. However, not all immigrants had equal access to the economy and society. Gordon (1964) explains that earlier waves of immigrants who were members of racially diverse groups did not experience the same structural assimilation into U.S. society as did European immigrants.

As Suarez-Orozco and Suarez-Orozco (2003) argue, today's economy—characterized by an hourglass shape—presents unique challenges for immigrant populations. At the top of the hourglass, highly skilled immigrants are moving into well-compensated, knowledge-based industries at an extremely high rate. At the bottom of the hourglass, immigrant workers accept the jobs that many U.S.-born workers are unwilling to take. Immigrants are a large part of the low-skilled, low-paid workers in the service, labor, and agricultural sectors. Unlike the jobs that were available to previous waves of immigrants, these jobs offer limited prospects for upward mobility (Suarez-Orozco & Suarez-Orozco, 2003).

Immigrants today are also more diverse than ever, exhibiting a significant range in educational level, social class, and economic capital. Present immigrants are more likely than native-born populations to have family members who have graduated from college. At the same time, immigrant populations are more likely not to have graduated from high school than are native-born populations (Suárez-Orozco, Suárez-Orozco, & Todorova, 2008). Another important aspect shaping the immigrant experience is outside factors that immigrants come into contact with—the neighborhoods, social networks, and schools—and that are also influenced by the local and national economy, referred to as the *contexts of reception* (Suarez-Orozco & Suarez-Orozco, 2003). The varied pattern of potential outcomes for immigrant students, which is also influenced by their contexts of reception, is further examined in Portes and Rumbaut's (2001) discussion of *segmented assimilation*, which posits three possible outcomes for immigrant families: (1) economic success with integration into the middle class, (2) permanent poverty and integration into the underclass, and (3) economic advancement with the deliberate maintenance of community values and practices. Each outcome is important to consider in the immigrant community today. While a full discussion of the factors contributing to segmented assimilation is beyond the scope of this chapter, it is important for teachers to know that immigrant groups are demonstrating each outcome; they are not just simply assimilated into mainstream society as was once assumed. A further discussion of segmented assimilation and the second generation is found in Zhou (1997).

According to scholars of immigration, another big difference is that the more recent wave of immigrants consists of people of color (Olsen, 1997; Portes, 1996; Suarez-Orozco & Suarez-Orozco, 2003). Today's culturally and ethnically diverse immigrants enter a racialized society that has historically sorted, classified, and excluded people based on the color of their skin (Omi & Winant, 1994). It is not as easy to eventually blend into White America as it was for the mostly European immigrants of the early 1900s. Racial tensions and structural exclusion in the United States make assimilation a problematic process for linguistically and ethnically diverse immigrants; therefore, the racial categorization of different immigrant groups must also be taken into account in terms of the differential outcomes for these groups.

Overall, the social, political, and economic difficulties faced by immigrants make relocation to a new country a very taxing experience. Lucas (1997) describes the experiences of immigrant students in U.S. schools as characterized by a number of critical transitions. She points out that all children experience important transitions in life: childhood to adolescence, home to school, middle to high school. However, as she correctly notes, immigrant students undergo these critical passages while adapting to a new language and culture where the rules of participation and engagement are not always transparent and need to be made so. As an example, consider the following words uttered by Edgar, a 15-year-old immigrant student from Mexico who had been in the United States for five months, in response to a researcher's request to talk about what he hoped to accomplish by attending school here:

> *Cuando eres un inmigrante, muchas puertas están cerradas. Pues, sí, algunas, algunas, están abiertas—pero están escondidas. Sin ayuda, no puedo encontrarlas.*

> *When you are an immigrant, many doors are closed. Well, yes, some, some are open—but they are hidden. Without help, I can't find them.*

(quoted in Stritikus, 2004, p. 1)

Rather than focusing on his career goals or his educational plans after high school, Edgar highlighted the limited educational opportunities he believed characterized his new life in the United States. Although Edgar had been in the country for only a limited time, he had already developed a keen sense of the social, cultural, and linguistic barriers to his success. Unfortunately, Edgar's reality is shared by many immigrant students, for whom the doors of educational opportunity remain obscured and closed. It is critical to help open these doors for these students.

Dramatic Increase in Linguistic Diversity in Schools

State educational statistics reveal the number of immigrants in the United States who are receiving special services to learn English and are classified as English learners (ELs). There has been a dramatic increase in the number of students classified as ELs since the 1970s. Immigrants from most nations in the world can be found in school districts throughout the United States. Although linguistic diversity is a reality throughout the country, the highest populations of EL students are concentrated in a few states such as California, Texas, Florida, New York, Illinois, and Arizona. These states are currently and historically the most common places for immigrants to settle. However, almost all states have been affected by immigration, especially in the last decade (Massey & Capoferro, 2008). Since 1990, the largest increase in percentages of EL students has been in what have been considered unlikely destinations for immigrants: South Carolina, Minnesota, Michigan, and Arkansas (Singer, 2004). Although the exact number is difficult to calculate, in 2006 EL students accounted for about 10.5 percent, or 5.2 million, of the total U.S. public school enrollment (National Clearinghouse for English Acquisition and Language Instruction Educational Programs, 2006). A final important aspect about ELs is that their heterogeneity goes beyond their ethnic heritage and their language to include, among other aspects, their generational status (first or second), their literacy levels in their first language, and their level of schooling. A subgroup that has been a cause of concern for educators is long-term ELs, who have been in U.S. schools for six or more years and have not exited out of English as a Second Language programs (Callahan, 2005).

Additional Sources of Linguistic Diversity: Dialect Variation and Indigenous Languages

Immigration is not the sole contributor to linguistic diversity. Along with multiple languages, dialect variation contributes to our diverse tapestry of language use. A *dialect* is a variation of a language characterized by distinct pronunciation, grammar, and vocabulary. Many linguists have pointed out that the distinction between a *language* and a *dialect* is often more political than linguistic. The famed MIT linguist Noam Chomsky (2000) has often repeated the saying by Max

Weinreich that a language is a dialect with an army and a navy. A common but less than perfect way of distinguishing a language from a dialect is the standard of mutual intelligibility.

Speakers of different dialects are said to be able to understand each other while speakers of different languages are not. However, what are considered dialects of some languages are so distinct that speakers cannot understand each other. Chinese has two major dialects, Cantonese and Mandarin, whose speakers have great difficulty in understanding each other. In contrast, speakers of the Scandinavian languages Danish, Norwegian, and Swedish are capable of understanding a great deal of each other's languages. Thus, it is important to note that the distinction between dialect and language has more to do with political, social, and cultural factors than specific linguistic differences between the two.

Political and social factors surrounding dialect variation play out in language use in U.S. schools, where educational practices emphasize the idea that standard English should be the dominant variety of language used in all written and oral communication. Many linguists dispute the idea that a pure or standard form of a language exists in any form but writing. Thus, *Standard English* often is a term associated with the groups in a society that possess social or political power (Wolfram, Adger, & Christian, 1998). Because dialect variation tends to be associated with race, social class, and geographic region, the dialects of groups with less social power tend to be viewed as inferior or incorrect versions of Standard English. This is the case with Black English (BE)—also referred to as African American vernacular English—and Black Dialect. Most linguists and sociolinguists recognize that no matter how BE is defined, it is a rule-governed language system linked to the identity of a specific community (Alim & Baugh, 2007; Labov, 1972; Smitherman, 2000). As Perry and Delpit (1998) write, "I can be neither for Ebonics nor against Ebonics any more than I can be for or against air. It exists" (p. 17). Speakers of BE are also most likely speakers of other varieties of English, including Standard English. Thus, speakers of BE, as are other speakers of dialects, are often *bidialectal*. The educational experiences of speakers of BE and the Oakland school district case are discussed later in this chapter.

Another major source of linguistic diversity in the United States is indigenous populations. Although a decreasing number of the 175 indigenous languages spoken by more than 550 tribes are spoken by children, the heritage language is still the primary language for a large number of indigenous students (Lomawaima & McCarty, 2006; McCarty, 2002). Indigenous students do not have another homeland from which to garner support for learning and maintaining their language. Krauss (1995) indicates that of 175 American Indian and Alaskan Native languages remaining, 155 are on their way to extinction. Therefore, bilingual/bicultural schooling is critical for indigenous language maintenance, as it is for other linguistic and cultural groups. Most of the efforts in formal language maintenance for indigenous language groups have been directed at Hawaiian dialects and the languages of the Navajo and Pueblo nations in the U.S. Southwest. Attempts to use bilingual education to revitalize these languages have met with modest but important results (McCarty, 2002).

Historical and Legal Overview of Language Policy in the United States

This section describes the legal and historical developments related to linguistic diversity and language education. Understanding the historical evolution of language policy in the United States as well as the legal milestones for language-minority students will help us understand the legal protections for these students and the ambivalent stance that the United States historically has had toward language policy. Language policies and immigration policies are closely connected, and both matter to the outcomes of immigrant and linguistically diverse students, although the latter are beyond the scope of this chapter. Overall, language policy in the United States has leaned toward supporting transition into English rather than supporting other languages and the rights of their speakers. There have been periods in U.S. history that have been more supportive of multilingualism than others.

Implementation of Federal Policy

The goal of the Bilingual Education Act (BEA), Title VII of the Elementary and Secondary Education Act of 1965—signed into law by President Lyndon B. Johnson—was to provide compensatory education for students who were both economically and linguistically disadvantaged in schools. Title VII was also a product of the activist Chicano movement of the Southwest. From 1968 until 2002, Title VII provided funds for different types of programs for ELs throughout the United States, including transitional bilingual education programs and two-way immersion programs; it also provided funding for program evaluators and researchers investigating these different types of programs. There were 30 two-way immersion programs in 1987 and 261 in 1999; most were supported by Title VII monies (Lindholm-Leary, 2001).

A large part of the BEA's inability to move toward a well-defined language policy was that the law did not recommend a particular instructional approach; rather, it provided funding for development, training, and research of innovative approaches to the education of EL students. While native language instruction was originally recommended, the BEA did not specify that it must be used (Wiese & García, 1998). Since its inception, the primary aim of the BEA has been "providing meaningful and equitable access for English-language learners to the curriculum, rather than serving as an instrument of language policy for the nation through the development of their native languages" (August & Hakuta, 1997, p. 16). Echoing this, Wiese and García argue that the BEA has aimed to address equal educational opportunity for language-minority students but has not evolved as a language policy. Therefore, the BEA neither legislated for a particular language policy or instructional approach nor guaranteed the rights of EL students based on language.

As a result, immigrant students and families have frequently turned to the courts for redress. The U.S. Supreme Court's school desegregation decision in *Brown v. Board of Education* (1954), the 1964 Civil Rights Act (Title VI), and the 1974 Equal Educational Opportunity Act (EEOA) have been used as a base to protect these students' rights. This protection has come through a safeguard of these students' other civil rights and their right to equal educational opportunities (Del Valle, 2003). In the prominent case of *Lau v. Nichols* (1974), Kinney Kinmon Lau and 12 Chinese American students, on behalf of about 1,800 Chinese-speaking students, filed a class-action suit against the San Francisco Unified School District, stating that their children were not given equal educational opportunities because of the linguistic barriers they faced. In this landmark case, the San Francisco schools were found to be in violation of the rights of Chinese students under Title VI and the EEOA. While lower courts disagreed with the parents, the Supreme Court supported them in *Lau v. Nichols* (1974) and found that "there is no equality of treatment merely by providing students with the same facilities, textbooks, teachers and curriculum; for students who do not understand English are effectively foreclosed from any meaningful education."

Lau's legacy has created important but vague contributions to the improvement of programs for EL students. Policy guidelines, which were followed by the Office of Civil Rights (OCR), were put together in the *Lau* remedies in 1975 for school districts' compliance with the Title VI requirements upheld in the *Lau* decision. These guidelines have required districts to have a program in place for EL students and for these students to be identified and assessed. While *Lau* did not specify any particular programs or polices for EL students, it created momentum for subsequent federal policies and court rulings to protect the specific rights of linguistically diverse students. Moreover, particulars were fully fleshed out in *Castaneda v. Pickard* (1981), a federal district court case that offers a "test" to determine whether the needs of EL students are being met by policies and programs. This case required that school districts adhere to the following three areas (see Dabach & Callahan, 2011 for an examination of current issues surrounding this case):

1. *Theory.* The school must pursue a program based on an educational theory recognized as sound or at least as a legitimate experimental strategy.

2. *Practice.* The school must actually implement the program with instructional practices, resources, and personnel necessary to transfer theory into reality.

3. *Results.* The school must not persist in a program that fails to produce results.

The Supreme Court ruled in *Plyer v. Doe* (1982) that states cannot deny a free public education to immigrant children because of their immigrant status, whether documented or undocumented. Although this is a federal ruling, states such as Georgia, Indiana, South Carolina, Alabama, and Arizona all currently have state laws that criminalize the participation of undocumented immigrant students in schools (Oh & Cooc, 2011). Although the constitutionality of such laws is being questioned, they are also being passed by state legislatures, often with widespread local support. These state laws have become even more of a "hot button" issue because an estimated 5.5 million children and adolescents have unauthorized parents (Suárez-Orozco, Yoshikawa, Teranishi & Suárez-Orozco, 2011), and many of them are trying to pursue higher education in order to get jobs requiring college degrees. Although the Dream Act, which would make undocumented students eligible for state-funded financial aid for college, did not pass at the federal level, it was recently signed into law in California.

While these requirements may not offer as strong an articulation of EL students' rights as some may have hoped, they do offer some legislative protection for EL students and help in creating effective programs for them. The *Lau* remedies, the BEA, and Title VI have generally provided some protection for equal educational opportunities for linguistically diverse students at the federal level. They also provided federal funding that made possible the inception and growth of a number of bilingual programs in the United States (Hornberger, 2006; Ruiz, 2004; Wiley & Wright, 2004).

Similar to the *Lau* court case, the "Black English case" (1979) (cited in Smitherman, 1981) mandated measures to teach Standard English to children speaking Black English. This 1979 case, *Martin Luther King Junior Elementary School Children v. Ann Arbor School District*, "was as much about educating Black children as about Black English" (Smitherman, 1998, p. 163). The parents of a group of African American children alleged that the school was not enabling their children to succeed in a variety of ways, including preventing them from learning Standard English. The judge ruled that the school had not helped its teachers and personnel to respond to the linguistic needs of its African American children. As a result of the ruling, Black English has also been given legal standing in some districts, such as in Oakland, California.

Language Policy in Recent History

The mandates of bilingual and bidialectal education have been controversial. Critics have adopted different arguments, from the historically prevalent charge that such education promotes social divisiveness to the more recent concerns that students will not learn English if they use their native language or dialect at school. Other critics have argued that bilingual education simply does not work (Porter, 1990). For example, when President Ronald Reagan took office in 1981, he made his views on bilingual education very clear, stating that he understood why teachers who spoke children's native languages were needed but also arguing that "it is absolutely wrong and against American concepts to have a bilingual education program" (cited in Baker, 2001, p. 194).

The proponents of English-only argue that to preserve the unity of the United States, English should become the official language (Crawford, 1992). There have been periods in the nation's history when administrations have leaned more toward a language-as-a-resource orientation, maintaining and supporting the teaching of languages other than English, such as President Bill Clinton's 1994 reauthorization of the BEA. The support or lack of support for a language-as-a resource orientation at the federal level has depended on the particular administration in office (Wiley & Wright, 2004).

As in the preceding 200 years, in the early twenty-first century, the press, politicians, and citizens have been grappling with the ambivalent attitude toward language. In recent years, the debate has escalated to a new level with English-only initiatives, such as the state-level Unz Initiative in California, Proposition 227, spearheaded by the millionaire businessman Ron Unz and passed by California voters in June 1998, outlawing bilingual education in the state. Proposition 227 brought all of the debates on bilingual education under a magnifying lens. The English-only faction stressed that bilingual programs were not working and that students were being ghettoized (although most ELs were not in bilingual programs). Strong proponents of bilingual education, such as Crawford (1999), have argued that the lack of large-scale political support has undermined its potential effectiveness. In bridging these two factions, Cummins (1999) states, "The challenge for opponents and advocates is to create an ideological space to collaborate in planning quality programs for bilingual students" (p. 223). After Proposition 227 was passed in California, similar laws were enacted in Arizona and Massachusetts. In 2008, 26 states had active official English laws.

Many linguists and educators regard the Ebonics debate as being in the same purview as bilingual education. The Oakland school board decision in 1996 to pass the Ebonics resolution, which recognized the legitimacy of Ebonics, was also a way for the school district to receive federal monies reserved for bilingual education and to use them for a Standard English program. The board resolution stated that the district's purpose should be to facilitate the acquisition and mastery of English language skills while respecting and embracing the legitimacy and richness of different language patterns. The rationale for the decision was that students could benefit from instruction that used their cultural and linguistic resources. As in the Ann Arbor case two decades earlier (Smitherman, 1981), a large number of African American parents and students protested the poor academic performance, disproportionate placement in special education, and frequent suspensions of African American students.

Like Proposition 227, the Oakland school board decision resulted in gross misrepresentations by and biases on the part of the media, the public, educators, and academics. One of the most frequently stated misconceptions was that the Oakland school district proposed to replace the teaching of English with Ebonics (Bing & Woodward, 1998).

During the George W. Bush administration in 2002, Title III replaced Title VII (BEA) as part of a larger school reform measure in the United States known as the No Child Left Behind Act. Title III carried with it a new name, "Language Instruction for Limited English Proficient and Immigrant Students." The word *bilingual* was deleted from all government offices and legislation, signaling a shift to the assimilationist, English-first orientation of the 2000–2008 Bush administration. Even though this new law is more supportive of programs that focus on learning English, it does not require English-only programs. Many scholars have argued that there is still space in the new law for the creation of bilingual programs (Freeman, 2004; Hornberger, 2006).

It is important for teachers to have a grasp of the legal and political trends and policies that influence the environments of their linguistically diverse students. Teachers who are aware of such political and social movements can establish historically relevant relationships with their students and influence programmatic decisions at the school and district levels.

Programmatic Responses to Linguistic Diversity

In this section, we summarize different programmatic options for schools. Central to these decisions is the role that English and students' home language will play in instruction. Should students learn to read in their first language (L1) and then learn to read in their second language (L2)? Should recent immigrants be instructed in content-area classes in their L1 so they do not fall behind in the critical areas of math, science, and social studies? Or will culturally and linguistically diverse students benefit from instruction provided solely in English? Across the United States, schools and districts struggle with these questions. Another central question in making decisions about programs has been how English and subject matter should be provided for ELs in terms of both instruction and staffing (Dabach & Callahan, 2011; Gibbons, 2002; Valdés, 2001).

Instructional Programs

Various instructional programs have been devised and implemented over the last several decades to meet the educational needs of linguistically diverse students. We describe the five major program types that districts and schools have designed and implemented that were identified by August and Hakuta's (1997) comprehensive review of the research on linguistic minority students:

- *Submersion.* Students are placed in regular English-only classrooms and are given no special instructional support. This approach is illegal in the United States as a result of the Supreme Court decision in *Lau v. Nichols.* However, many EL students find themselves in submersion-like settings.

- *English as a Second Language (ESL).* No instruction is given in a student's primary language. ESL is either taught through pull-out programs or integrated with academic content throughout the day. Today, many ESL classes, especially at the secondary level, are sheltered English classes where both English and subject matter are taught.

- *Transitional bilingual education (TBE).* Students receive some degree of instruction in their primary language for a period of time. However, the goal of the program is to transition to English-only instruction as rapidly as possible, generally within one to three years.

- *Maintenance bilingual education (MBE).* Students receive instruction in their primary language and in English throughout the elementary school years (K–6) with the goal of developing academic proficiency in both languages.

- *Dual-language programs.* Language-majority and language-minority students are instructed together in the same program with the goal of each group achieving bilingualism and biliteracy.

This list is not exhaustive. However, these programs do not exist in pure forms, and districts mix and blend aspects of various approaches. Various large- and small-scale studies have examined the effectiveness of these programs. The authors of the studies have willingly and unwillingly become a part of the great debate about the effectiveness of bilingual education. It is difficult to determine the exact number of EL students in each of these programs because of the lack of comprehensive national data. However, most EL students are instructed through ESL approaches that use little to no native language instruction (Kindler, 2002).

The Bilingual Debate and the Research Context

As bilingual education continued to evolve throughout the 1960s and 1970s, a major split in public opinion regarding the program occurred. Baker (2001) explains that some citizens viewed bilingual education as failing to foster social integration and as a waste of public funds. Many opponents of bilingual education portrayed Latinos and supporters of bilingual education as using it for their own political gain (Baker, 2001). Critics of bilingual education have drawn from two major reviews of bilingual research (Baker & de Kanter, 1981; Rossel & Baker, 1996) to try to convince schools and districts to move away from bilingual education. Rossel and Baker (1996) reviewed 72 scientifically methodologically acceptable studies. They concluded that bilingual education was not superior to ESL instruction, particularly in reading achievement. This study is widely cited by critics of bilingual education. Several researchers have noted, however, that the review is plagued by many methodological issues. The Rossel and Baker review applied arbitrary and inconsistent criteria to establish methodologically acceptable studies and inaccurate and arbitrary labeling of programs (Cummins, 1999; Stritikus & Manyak, 2000). Baker (2001) points out that the study

> *had a narrow range of expected outcomes for bilingual education in the [research] questions. Only English language and nonlanguage subject areas were considered as the desirable outcome of schooling. Other outcomes such as self-esteem, employment, preservation of minority languages, and the value of different cultures were not considered. (p. 246)*

Critics of bilingual education have drawn heavily from the work of Rossel and Baker (1996) and Baker and de Kanter (1981) to influence educational policy. Advocates of bilingual education have drawn from a body of research that has reached opposite conclusions and supports the use of students' native language in instruction. Willig (1985) conducted a meta-analysis of 23 of the 28 studies reviewed by Baker and de Kanter. *Meta-analysis* is a collection of systematic techniques for resolving apparent contradictions in research findings by translating results from different studies to a common metric and statistically exploring relationships between study characteristics and findings. Employing this technique, Greene (1998) found that an unbiased reading of the scholarly literature indicates that limited-English-proficient students taught using bilingual approaches perform significantly better than do students taught using English-only approaches. In a review of methodologically acceptable research studies, Slavin and Cheung (2003) found that bilingual approaches—particularly those that include reading instruction in the native language—are more effective than English-only approaches.

Program Types That Contribute to Successful Educational Practice

Research examining the success or failure of various program types has not completely addressed the central question of how best to educate culturally and linguistically diverse students. A body of research has reported detailed studies of what has worked in actual classrooms. Rather than focus on program models, this research has concentrated on the characteristics of schools and classrooms that contribute to successful educational practice for culturally and linguistically diverse students. In fact, a controversial observation recently made by scholars researching secondary schools is that most students who are labeled as EL and who are in ESL classes are denied access to higher-level math and science classes (Callahan, Wilkinson, & Muller, 2010). This type of work highlights the need to examine the way schools are organized, the way instruction is delivered, and what opportunities to learn exist in whatever program is ultimately chosen (Dabach & Callahan, 2011).

August and Hakuta (1997) provide a comprehensive review of optimal learning conditions that serve linguistically and culturally diverse student populations and that lead to high academic performance. Their review of 33 studies indicates that there is a set of generally agreed-upon practices that foster academic success. These practices can exist across program types. August and Hakuta found that the following school and classroom characteristics are likely to lead to academic success:

> *A supportive school-wide climate, school leadership, a customized learning environment, articulation and coordination within and between schools, use of native language and culture in instruction, a balanced curriculum that includes both basic and higher-order skills, explicit skill instruction, opportunities for student-directed instruction, use of instructional strategies that enhance understanding, opportunities for practice, systematic student assessment, staff development, and home and parent involvement. (p. 171)*

These findings have been confirmed in other more recent studies, such as those by Corallo and McDonald (2002) and Marzano (2003). Thus, culturally and linguistically diverse students can benefit greatly from cognitively challenging and student-centered instruction that employs their cultural and linguistic resources.

The Lived Reality of Today's Linguistically Diverse Students

Several studies of students' everyday experience provide a powerful but painful picture of how schools meet—or do not meet—the challenge of linguistic diversity. These studies are not meant as simple critique; they provide an understanding of how much further educators need to go in meeting the challenge. Valdés (2001) conducted an important study analyzing the manner in which recent immigrant students are served by schools. Focusing on the way that four Latino students' initial experience with U.S. schooling shaped their future possibilities, Valdés found that the school curriculum for these students focused on English language instruction at the expense of access to a grade-level curriculum in key subject areas such as science, social studies, and math. Valdés describes a significant relationship between the social position of cultural and linguistically diverse students and families in the broader society and the quality of education such students receive. The students in Valdés's research found themselves in "ESL ghettoes," which afforded little possibility for academic advancement.

In a study similar to the Valdés (2001) research, Olsen (1997) examined the experiences of Latino and Asian immigrant students at Madison High School as they attempted to become "American." The teachers at Madison High believed that through hard work and persever-ance, all students—regardless of their linguistic and cultural background—could succeed. The teachers accepted without question the idea of the U.S. meritocracy. Through careful interviews and observations, Olsen revealed the tensions and contradictions of this view. First, linguistically diverse students were segregated in the overall school context. They found themselves in low academic tracks with the most inexperienced teachers. Second, immigrant students felt extreme pressure to forgo defining elements of their own identities—their culture, language, dress, and values. School for recent immigrant students was not a wondrous opportunity but a process in which they found their place in the U.S. racial hierarchy.

Other researchers, such as Toohey (2000) and Valenzuela (1999), have documented how racism, xenophobia, and pro-English attitudes are powerful factors that prevent educators from seeing linguistic diversity as an educational resource. To be sure, there are students who rise above these challenges, but school practices and policies unfortunately make this difficult. The next section of this chapter provides a synopsis of classroom-level issues. It examines what types of knowledge and skills will help teachers who have English language learners in their class-rooms. The purpose of that section is to synthesize some of the important dimensions of second language acquisition for content area and second language (ESL and bilingual) teachers as well as to describe strategies to use in the classroom.

Views on Language Learning and Teaching

This section summarizes what teachers of second language learners need to know about language, language learners, and language learning and teaching. Becoming proficient in a language or dialect can take on different meanings in various social, academic, and personal settings. In attempting to make students learning a second language or dialect successful in schools, scholars have observed that a distinction needs to be made between learning a language *socially* and *academically* (Cummins, 1981; Hakuta, Butler, & Witt, 2000–2001; Valdés, 2001). Therefore, an important goal for teachers should be to enable students to successfully use academic English (Bartolomé, 1998; Gibbons, 2002; Valdés, 2004), as we mentioned in the discussion on program types. In discussing language learning and teaching, we focus most of our discussion on teaching academic English and the language needed for content-area subjects.

Language

Wong Fillmore and Snow (2000) describe the most salient aspects of language that will be helpful for teachers of second languages/dialects to know. Language is a complex system of communication that includes the following major subsystems: *pragmatics* (sociolinguistic rules governing language use, e.g., apologizing in a specific language and culture), *syntax* (rules of word order in a sentence), *semantics* (meanings of words and sentences), *morphology* (rules of word formation), and *phonology* (the sound system of a language). When people are using language, they must manipulate and coordinate all of these subsystems simultaneously, as the following example illustrates: A student in a classroom who asks "What is photosynthesis?" would need to know the social convention of when and how to ask this question. The student would also need to know how to form a *wh-* question and to pronounce the words in a way that is intelligible to the person(s) being asked.

Language Learners

A number of learner characteristics can affect second language learning and success in an English-speaking school setting. Here, we focus on some of the most salient ones, such as age and the learner's first language. Examples of others that can be considered are learning styles and aptitude. Although these tend to be described by researchers as individual learner characteristics, it is important to note that such characteristics are shaped by cultural and social contexts.

Age

There has been a push in the United States and several other countries for early schooling in a second/foreign language because younger children are thought to be better language learners. Research indicates that younger children show advantages in terms of pronunciation and accent. Several researchers (Hyltenstam & Abrahamsson, 2001; Johnson & Newport, 1989; Patowski, 1980) also believe that there is a critical period, a time when the brain is more predisposed to learn all features of a language, not just phonological ones. This belief has been challenged by others who did not find an advantage to being younger. Snow and Hoefnagel-Höhle (1978) found that adolescents and adults learn at a faster rate than do children, especially in the early stages of language development. Even scholars who have found the data on the critical period convincing recommend that programmatic decisions should not be based on the age of learners (Hyltenstam & Abrahamsson, 2001). Rather, the research indicates that more attention should be paid to the quality of the programs and the quantity and quality of exposure to the second/foreign language than to the age of students.

First Language

Research indicates that all second language learners, regardless of their first language, seem to progress through similar developmental stages of language learning in some areas. For example, researchers have found that there is a developmental sequence for learners of English as a second language in question formation, negation, and past tense formation (Lightbown & Spada, 2006). Learners go through preverbal negation ("I no play"); then learn to insert the negative term with auxiliary verbs, although not necessarily correctly ("I can't play," "He don't play"); and finally are able to produce negative sentences correctly ("She doesn't play"). Additionally, there are specific errors that we can attribute to a learner's first language. For example, Spanish-speaking learners will stay in the preverbal negation stage ("I no like") longer because of this structure's similarity to the Spanish language ("No quiero"). This example demonstrates that the popular belief that it is easier to learn a second language the more similar it is to the first language is not necessarily true. Actually, there can be a tendency to revert to the rules of the first language if they share many similarities. Thus, it is useful for teachers to learn about cross-linguistic similarities and differences in terms of different aspects of language, such as phonemes, spelling, writing systems, and sociolinguistic rules (Wong Fillmore & Snow, 2000).

Overall, whatever the learner's first language, students who are literate and have had prior formal schooling in their first language have been found to outperform students who have not had this experience (August & Hakuta, 1997; Collier, 1987; Cummins, 1984).

Language Learning and Teaching

Theories of Second Language Learning

While many theories have been advanced to explain second language learning, four of them have had the most influence on second language students in schools. The four major theories considered here are:

- Input hypothesis

- Interactionist theory

- Basic interpersonal communication skills (BICS) and cognitive academic language proficiency (CALP)

- Sociocultural theories

Input Hypothesis

The set of hypotheses or single theory that has most influenced teachers has been that of Stephen Krashen (1985), the *input hypothesis*. He, with others, has advanced the following hypotheses: (1) Acquisition is the unconscious process of acquiring a language through interaction, while learning is the formal process of memorizing the rules and structures of a language. He contends that language learning is most successful when built on the principle of acquisition through activities that are mostly communicative in nature. (2) Language learning consists of particular sequences and stages, an example of which was given earlier in the way negation develops for language learners. (3) For language acquisition to occur, learners must be offered comprehensible input, language that is just beyond the learner's current level.

This last part of Krashen's theory has been the most influential on classroom teaching. The recommendation for teachers is that input in the classroom can be made comprehensible through strategies such as creating visual cues and establishing background knowledge. Overall, Krashen's proposals suggest that language teaching be conducted in the most natural, communicative situations in which learners are relaxed and teachers are not focusing on error correction.

Interactionist Theory

Interactionist theory (Lightbown & Spada, 2006) has widely influenced and been influenced by research on and teaching in immersion programs in Canada. The basic tenet of this theory is that both input and output are crucial for language learning. Teachers who draw on this theory create tasks for which conversational interactions between speakers are central to the process of language learning. This process has been described as the *negotiation of meaning*, which in many ways is similar to the process between caretakers and children in first language acquisition.

BICS and CALP

The third theory focuses explicitly on language and content learning and pertains to the distinction made between learning a language socially and academically. Learning another language academically is known to be a lengthy process that can take from seven to ten years (Cummins, 1984), as compared to conversational proficiency in a language, which can take from one to five years. Cummins distinguished these language-learning processes with the terms *basic interpersonal conversational skills* (*BICS*) and *cognitive academic language proficiency* (*CALP*). Academic language offers few clues for learners and is therefore much more difficult to learn, while BICS occurs "when there are contextual supports and props for language delivery" (Baker, 2006, p. 174). Many of us might be able to converse with a speaker in our second or third language but have difficulty understanding an academic lecture or writing a technical report in that language. This is especially true for students who start this process in the later grades (Collier, 1987; Cummins & Swain, 1986), students who are not literate or academically skilled in their first language, and many students who come from war-torn countries.

We should also bear in mind the limitations of the BICS and CALP typologies (Wiley, 1996a). First, the strict dichotomy between the two is viewed by some scholars as overly simplistic (Edelsky et al., 1983; Wiley, 1996b). In some cases, as with individuals who can read but not converse in a second language, CALP can be developed before BICS. There is also danger in viewing BICS as inferior to CALP. We know that oral conversation can be equally demanding in certain settings. Second, the notion of academic language is somewhat abstract. In a more recent reworking of this distinction, Cummins (2000) has attempted to define *academic proficiency* in more concrete terms, such as "the extent to which an individual has access to and command of the oral and written academic registers of schooling" (p. 67). Other attempts to make this concept more useful for teachers can be found in the national ESL standards (Teachers of English to Speakers of Other Languages [TESOL], 1997). Even if there is still considerable debate about how academic language should be defined (Valdés, 2004), it has proven to be a significant starting point for those who have advocated for a functional and content-based approach to language learning (Gibbons, 2002; Schleppegrell, Achugar, & Oteíza, 2004).

Sociocultural Theories

A number of sociocultural theories in second language learning have been very influential in the recent past, including one based on Vygotsky's work (Lantolf, 2001), one that highlights the significance of power in language learning (Norton-Peirce, 1995), and one that emphasizes language ecology (Van Lier, 2004) by looking at the multiple interactions that take place as language learning occurs. All of these challenge the notion that language learning goes on solely or even mainly inside one's head, asserting instead that it exists in interaction with the whole world. What has been most influential about all of these theories is that they consider second language learning to exist in a world where ideology and power matter and where the language-learning environment must be extremely rich, scaffolded well, and academically based for students to succeed (Walqui & Van Lier, 2010).

Instructional Methods and Approaches

The input hypothesis, interactionist theory, and sociocultural theories have provided a significant set of guidelines for creating optimal language-learning environments. These theories have influenced teachers and methods in several ways, including encouraging teachers (1) to make verbal input comprehensible at a level that is slightly beyond the learner's level (e.g., using visuals, paraphrasing); (2) to create conversation-based activities (e.g., problem-solving activities) that generate a low anxiety level; (3) to set up tasks so that learners are forced to talk and listen to each other (e.g., through jigsaw activities); and (4) to scaffold language and content instead of merely simplifying tasks. Krashen's work has been associated most closely with the *natural approach*, a method he and Terrell (Krashen & Terrell, 1983) developed that integrates a number of these strategies.

Interactionist theory, as indicated, has been cited mostly in conjunction with immersion programs in Canada. In these programs, researchers have found that the most effective language-learning situation is one that is content-based or communicatively oriented (Lightbown & Spada, 2006). Therefore, as Cummins's work suggests, language and content should be jointly taught to language-minority students. The research and scholarship subsequent to that of Cummins have focused on the importance of learning academic language and content (Bartolomé, 1998; Gibbons, 2002; Valdés, 2004). Much of this research has shown that instruction for students learning a second language must concentrate on their acquiring academic language and subject-specific knowledge in several ways.

Students can attain subject-specific knowledge through instruction in their primary language or through richer and more sustained collaborations between content-area teachers and English language specialists. When these strategies are used, ESL pull-out classes do not focus exclusively on decontextualized skills and language. In many cases, content-area teachers will need to be trained in making language and content more accessible to EL students or to collaborate with EL specialists to do so. Content-based instruction (CBI), in which language is taught in conjunction with academic subject matter, can be used (Snow, Met, & Genesee, 1989). One example of CBI is *specifically designed academic instruction in English (SDAIE)*, often called *sheltered instruction.*

A comprehensive program of sheltered instruction that has gained wide recognition is the *sheltered instruction observation protocol (SIOP)* (Echevarria et al., 2008). Another is the *cognitive academic language learning approach*, which focuses on developing language, content, and learning strategies (Chamot & O'Malley, 1994). A more recent method that is becoming widely adopted is *guided language acquisition design* (Brechtel, 2001). Many of these methods are used in a large number of school districts across the United States. The resource list at the end of this chapter provides more information for mainstream teachers, including additional references for these methods.

Instructional Strategies and Contexts for Learning

The methods that recommend an integration of language and content indicate that teachers should use strategies similar to those described in the effective programs reported by August and Hakuta (1997), Corallo and McDonald (2002), and Marzano (2003). These strategies incorporate a student-centered, meaning-based, context-rich classroom and a cognitively demanding curriculum. Schleppegrell and colleagues (2004) summarize these strategies:

> *Typical recommendations for a CBI approach include a focus on disciplinary vocabulary and use of a variety of learning and teaching strategies, especially visual aids and graphic organizers to make meanings clear. . . . Teachers are encouraged to help students comprehend and use the language structures and discourse features found in different subjects and to facilitate students' practice with academic tasks such as listening to explanations, reading for information, participating in academic discussions, and writing reports. (p. 69)*

A successful class for English language learners is one in which the following features are often present: a high level of noise; students working in groups with hands-on materials; word walls, graphic organizers, and displays of student work; teachers modeling strategies; assessment being used to drive instruction; and high expectations for all students. One example of teacher modeling is to provide students with explicit instruction in different learning strategies for gaining academic competence, such as writing a summary (Chamot & O'Malley, 1994). Teachers cannot assume that students will know how to write a summary; they must either model the necessary steps or collaborate with an English language specialist to accomplish the task. Cooperative learning situations (Johnson, Johnson, & Holubec, 1986) and complex instruction groups (Cohen & Lotan, 1997) in which students are given different roles in completing a project are examples of effective group work. In addition, teachers need to learn tools for authentic assessment (O'Malley & Valdez Peirce, 1996) in order to evaluate students in different ways that facilitate learning.

Although many of the strategies and methods we have described can be very helpful, one should bear in mind that a number of scholars have challenged the assumption that they are sufficient to help second language students succeed, especially students in the higher grades and in gaining language skills equal to their native English-speaking peers. Bartolomé (1998), Gibbons (2002), and Valdés (2004) stress the need to create events in which students have to "address real or imaginary distant audiences with whom they can assume little shared knowledge" (Valdés, 2004, p. 122) in order to enable students to "elaborate linguistic messages explicitly and precisely to minimize audience misinterpretation" (Bartolomé, 1998, p. 66). Schleppegrell and colleagues (2004) discuss the need to delve deeply into discipline-specific linguistic challenges, such as those found in social studies textbooks. In addition, the importance of successful scaffolding cannot be overlooked (Walqui & Van Lier, 2010).

Finally, teachers should always remember that the education of linguistically diverse students is situated in larger issues about immigration, the distribution of wealth and power, and the empowerment of students (Cahnmann & Varghese, 2006; Cummins, 2000; Varghese & Stritikus, 2005). Thus, effective classroom strategies must be situated in a supportive school and societal context. Along with the academic focus, teachers should work toward making the classroom a welcoming place for students and their families. The cultural and linguistic resources that students bring to school, especially with the involvement of parents and community partners, should also be integrated and celebrated in the classroom.

As in other content areas, a question that remains and is currently being asked and studied is who the best teachers are for these students and how they should be trained and assessed (Dabach, 2009; Lucas, 2011). At the same time, what is no longer being questioned as much is whether all school staff are responsible for these students and whether teachers at all grade levels should be gaining such expertise and training or working in collaboration with language specialists—even co-teaching—in order to provide meaningful instruction for these students.

Conclusion

This chapter stresses the social, political, and historical realities that influence schooling for linguistically diverse students. It first examines linguistically diverse populations in the United States and considers how recent trends in immigration have influenced linguistic diversity. To understand the experiences of immigrant students in schools, the political and economic realities that drive and shape immigration must be examined. Immigration has changed the look and feel of schools in every state in the country. The manner in which schools treat linguistically diverse students is directly related to the ways in which they are perceived and treated by society. In the early 21st century, immigrants provide a source of cheap labor as well as workers with highly developed skills that fuel the U.S. economy. Immigrant communities find themselves pinched by social and economic pressures. Thus, it is important for teachers to consider how immigrant populations are viewed and treated by their host country and local communities.

The chapter also considers important legal and political milestones in the evolution of language education policy. Past and recent developments in language policy demonstrate the contradictory position of the United States toward linguistic diversity. While we frequently celebrate our status as a nation of immigrants or as a land of equality, our language policy has continually attempted to suppress and minimize linguistic diversity. Linguistically diverse students have rarely seen their languages and cultures promoted at the federal and state levels. Teacher practice both influences and is influenced by language policy. In order for teachers to support and promote linguistic diversity, they need to understand how language policy shapes education (Varghese & Stritikus, 2005).

Additionally, the chapter reviews the existing research regarding which programs best serve the needs of linguistically diverse students. Research indicates that students learn best in meaning-centered and intellectually rich environments and that linguistically diverse students have the maximum potential to succeed when their language and culture are used and developed in instruction. School practice has not always lived up to this ideal. Finally, the chapter provides the practical knowledge required to meet the needs of linguistically diverse students.

In nearly every classroom, linguistic diversity shapes the nature of teachers' work. Linguistic and cultural diversity is one of the great assets of the United States, yet schooling for linguistically diverse students continues to be plagued by poor programs, limited resources, and lack of commitment from policy makers. The success of the U.S. educational system will be judged, in part, by how well we meet the needs of students from linguistically diverse groups. You and your colleagues can play a significant role in opening the doors of opportunity for linguistically diverse students.

QUESTIONS AND ACTIVITIES

12.1 What did you learn about immigrant students and their schooling in this chapter? Imagine you are asked to provide a 30-minute workshop for grade-level teachers and staff in your school. What concepts and principles would you incorporate into this workshop?

12.2 In what ways are the challenges facing English learners, African American students, and indigenous students in schools similar and different? What types of practices and activities can teachers implement in their classrooms that would help these students?

12.3 What programs and support are provided for English learners in a local school, and how are these decisions made? Interview school staff and document their responses to these questions.

12.4 You are in charge of designing the best possible program in your school for English language learners. What features would be part of this program? Why? What aspects of language and language learning would be useful for mainstream teachers to know? How can they incorporate this knowledge when teaching their subject matter?

12.5 Parents and households as well as their relationships with schools are critical influences on the achievement of immigrant students. Interview one parent and, if possible, one child who has been identified as an EL student. Document their social and educational experiences before and since coming to the United States.

RESOURCES

August, D., & Hakuta, K. (Eds.). (1997). *Improving schooling for language minority students: A research agenda*. Washington, DC: National Academy Press.

Baugh, J. (1999). *Out of the mouth of slaves: African American language educational malpractice*. New York: Oxford University Press.

Davies Samway, K., & McKeon, D. (in press). *Myths and realities: Best practices for language minority students* (2nd ed.). Portsmouth, NH: Heinemann.

Echevarria, J., Vogt, M., & Short, D. J. (2008). *Making content comprehensible for English language learners: The SIOP model* (2nd ed.). Boston: Allyn & Bacon.

Fang, Z., & Schleppegrell, M. J. (2008). *Reading in secondary content areas: A language-based pedagogy*. Ann Arbor: University of Michigan Press.

Gibbons, P. (2002). *Scaffolding language, scaffolding learning: Teaching second language learners in the mainstream classroom*. Portsmouth, NH: Heinemann.

Herrera, S. G., & Murphy, K. G. (2005). *Mastering ESL and bilingual methods: Differentiated instruction for culturally and linguistically diverse (CLD) students*. Boston: Allyn & Bacon.

Lightbown, P., & Spada, N. (2006). *How languages are learned* (3rd ed.). New York: Oxford University Press.

Peregoy, S. F., & Boyle, O. F. (2008). *Reading, writing, and learning in ESL: A resource book for K–12 teachers* (5th ed.). Boston: Pearson Education.

Suarez-Orozco, C. E., & Suarez-Orozco, M. M. (2003). *Children of immigration*. Cambridge, MA: Harvard University Press.

Teachers of English to Speakers of Other Languages. (2006). *Pre K–12 language proficiency standards*. Alexandria, VA: Author.

Walqui, A., & Van Lier (2010). *Scaffolding the academic success of adolescent English language learners: A pedagogy of promise*. San Francisco: WestEd.

Wong Fillmore, L., & Snow, C. (2000). *What teachers need to know about language*. Washington, DC: ERIC Clearinghouse on Languages and Linguistics.

PROFESSIONAL ASSOCIATIONS

National Association for Bilingual Education (NABE)

National Association for Multicultural Education (NAME)

Teachers of English to Speakers of Other Languages (TESOL)

WEBSITES

Center for Applied Linguistics: www.cal.org

National Association for Bilingual Education: www.nabe.org

National Clearinghouse for English Language Acquisition: www.ncela.gwu.edu

Teachers of English to Speakers of Other Languages: www.tesol.org

REFERENCES

Alim, H. S., & Baugh, J. (Eds.). (2007). *Talkin Black talk: Language, education, and social change*. New York: Teachers College Press.

August, D., & Hakuta, K. (Eds.). (1997). *Improving schooling for language minority students: A research agenda*. Washington, DC: National Academy Press.

Baker, C. (2001). *Foundations of bilingual education and bilingualism* (3rd ed.). Clevedon, UK: Multilingual Matters.

Baker, C. (2006). *Foundations of bilingual education and bilingualism* (4th ed.). Clevedon, UK: Multilingual Matters.

Baker, K., & de Kanter, A. (1981). *Effectiveness of bilingual education: A review of the literature*. Washington, DC: U.S. Department of Education.

Banks, C. A. M. (2005). *Improving multicultural education: Lessons from the intergroup education movement*. New York: Teachers College Press.

Bartolomé, L. (1998). *The misteaching of academic discourse: The politics in the language classroom*. Boulder, CO: Westview.

Bing, J. M., & Woodward, W. (1998). Nobody's listening: A frame analysis of the Ebonics debate. *SECOL Review, 22*(1), 1–16.

Brechtel, M. (2001). *Bringing it all together: Language and literacy in the multicultural classroom*. San Diego: Dominic Press.

Brown v. Board of Education, 327 U.S. 483 (1954).

Cahnmann, M., & Varghese, M. (2006). Critical advocacy and bilingual education in the United States. *Linguistics and Education, 16*(1), 59–73.

Callahan, R. M. (2005). Tracking and high school English learners: Limiting opportunity to learn. *American Educational Research Journal, 42*(2), 305-328.

Callahan, R. M., Wilkinson, L., & Muller, C. (2010). Academic achievement and course taking among language minority youth in U.S. schools: Effects of ESL placement. *Educational Evaluation and Policy Analysis, 32*(1), 84–117.

Castaneda v. Pickard, 648 F.2d 989, 1007 5th Cir. (1981).

Castles, S. (2003). Towards a sociology of forced migration and social transformation. *Sociology, 37*(1), 13–34.

Castles, S., & Davidson, A. (2000). *Citizenship and migration: Globalization and the politics of belonging*. New York: Routledge.

Cervantes, W. D., & Hernandez, D. J. (2011, March). Children in immigrant families: Ensuring opportunity for every child in America. *First Focus and Foundation for Child Development*. Retrieved from http://www.firstfocus.net/sites/default/files/FCDImmigration.pdf.

Chamot, A. U., & O'Malley, J. M. (1994). *The CALLA handbook: How to implement the cognitive academic language learning approach*. Reading, MA: Addison-Wesley.

Chomsky, N. (2000). *The architecture of language* (N. Mukherji, B. N. Patnaik, & R. K. Agnihotri, Eds.). Oxford: Oxford University Press.

Cohen, E. G., & Lotan, R. A. (1997). *Working for equity in heterogeneous classrooms: Sociological theory in practice*. New York: Teachers College Press.

Collier, V. P. (1987). Age and rate of acquisition of second language for academic purposes. *TESOL Quarterly, 21*, 617–641.

Corallo, C., & McDonald, D. H. (2002). *What works with low-performing schools: A review of research*. Charleston, WV: AEL, Regional Educational Laboratory, Region IV Comprehensive Center.

Crawford, J. (1992). *Language loyalties: A source book on the official English controversy*. Chicago: University of Chicago Press.

Crawford, J. (1999). *Bilingual education: History, politics, theory, and practice* (4th ed.). Los Angeles: Bilingual Education Services.

Cummins, J. (1981). The role of primary language development in promoting educational success for language minority students. In California State Department of Education (Ed.), *Schooling and language minority students: A theoretical framework* (pp. 3–50). Los Angeles: California State University Evaluation, Dissemination, and Assessment Center.

Cummins, J. (1984). *Bilingualism and special education: Issues in assessment and pedagogy*. Clevedon, UK: Multilingual Matters.

Cummins, J. (1999). Alternative paradigms in bilingual education research: Does theory have a place? *Educational Researcher, 28*, 26–32.

Cummins, J. (2000). *Language, power, and pedagogy*. Clevedon, UK: Multilingual Matters.

Cummins, J., & Swain, M. (1986). *Bilingualism in education*. London: Longman.

Dabach, D. B. (2009). *Teachers as a context for reception for immigrant youth: Adaptations in "sheltered" and "mainstream" classrooms*. Unpublished doctoral dissertation, University of California, Berkeley.

Dabach, D. B., & Callahan, R. (2011, October 7). Rights vs. reality: The gap between civil rights and English learners' high school educational opportunities. *Teachers College Record*. Retrieved from http://www.tcrecord.org/content.asp?contentid=16558.

Del Valle, S. (2003). *Language rights and the law in the United States: Finding our voices*. Clevedon, UK: Multilingual Matters.

Echevarria, J., Vogt, M., & Short, D. J. (2008). *Making content comprehensible for English language learners: The SIOP model* (2nd ed.). Boston: Allyn & Bacon.

Edelsky, C., Hudelson, S., Altwerger, B., Flores, B., Barkin, F., & Jilbert, K. (1983). Semilingualism and language deficit. *Applied Linguistics, 4*(1), 1–22.

Enright, K. A. (2010). Language and literacy for a new mainstream. *American Educational Research Journal, 48*(1), 80–118.

Fortuny, K., Hernandez, D. J., & Chaudry, A. (2010). *Young children of immigrants: The leading edge of America's future*. Washington, DC: Urban Institute.

Freeman, R. D. (2004). *Building on community bilingualism*. Philadelphia: Caslon.

Garcia, E. (1999). *Understanding and meeting the challenge of student cultural diversity*. Boston: Houghton Mifflin.

Gibbons, P. (2002). *Scaffolding language, scaffolding learning: Teaching second language learners in the mainstream classroom*. Portsmouth, NH: Heinemann.

Gordon, M. (1964). *Assimilation in American life*. New York: Oxford University Press.

Greene, J. P. (1998). *A meta-analysis of the effectiveness of bilingual education*. Los Angeles: Tomas Rivera Policy Institute, University of Southern California.

Hakuta, K., Butler, Y. G., & Witt, D. (2000–2001). How long does it take English learners to attain proficiency? Retrieved November 1, 2005, from http://www.stanford.edu/~hakuta.

Hornberger, N. H. (2006). Nichols to NCLB: Local and global perspectives on U.S. language education policy. In O. García,

T. Skutnabb-Kangas, & M. Torres Guzmán (Eds.), *Imagining multilingual schools: Languages in education* (pp. 223-237). Clevedon, UK: Multilingual Matters.

Hyltenstam, H., & Abrahamsson, N. (2001). Age and L2 learning: The hazards of matching practical "implications" with theoretical facts. *TESOL Quarterly, 35*(1), 151–170.

Itzigsohn, J., Dore-Cabral, C. B., Hernandez-Medina, E., & Vazquez, O. (1999). Mapping Dominican transnationalism: Narrow and broad transnational practices. *Ethnic and Racial Studies, 22*(2), 316–339.

Jacobson, M. F. (1998). *Whiteness of a different color: European immigrants and the alchemy of race*. Cambridge, MA: Harvard University Press.

Johnson, J., Johnson, R. T., & Holubec, E. J. (1986). *Circles of learning: Cooperation in the classroom*. Edina, MN: Interaction Books.

Johnson, J., & Newport, E. (1989). Critical period effects in second language learning: The influence of maturational state on the acquisition of English as a second language. *Cognitive Psychology, 21*, 60–99.

Kindler, A. (2002). *Survey of the states' limited English proficient students and available educational programs and services: 1999–2000 summary report*. Washington, DC: National Clearinghouse for English Language Acquisition and Language Instruction Educational Programs.

Krashen, S. (1985). *The input hypothesis: Issues and implications*. New York: Longman.

Krashen, S. D., & Terrell, D. (1983). *The natural approach: Language acquisition in the classroom*. Hayward, CA: Alemany Press.

Krauss, M. (1995, February 3). *Endangered languages: Current issues and future prospects*. Keynote address, Dartmouth College, Hanover, NH.

Krauss, M. (1998). The condition of native North American languages: The need for realistic assessment and action. *International Journal of the Sociology of Language, 132*, 9–21.

Labov, W. (1972). The logic of Standard English. In W. Labov (Ed.), *Language in the inner city: Studies in Black English vernacular* (pp. 201–240). Philadelphia: University of Pennsylvania Press.

Lantolf, J. P. (2001). Sociocultural theory and second language acquisition. In R. Kaplan (Ed.), *Handbook of applied linguistics* (2nd ed., pp. 131-150). Oxford: Oxford University Press.

Lau v. Nichols, 414 U.S. 563 (1974).

Lightbown, P., & Spada, N. (2006). *How languages are learned* (3rd ed.). New York: Oxford University Press.

Lindholm-Leary, K. J. (2001). *Dual language education*. Clevedon, UK: Multilingual Matters.

Lomawaima, K. T., & McCarty, T. L. (2006). *"To remain an Indian": Lessons in democracy from a century of Native American education*. New York: Teachers College Press.

Lucas, T. (1997). *Into, through, and beyond secondary school: Critical transitions for immigrant youths*. New York: National Center for Restructuring Education, Schools, and Teaching, Teachers College, Columbia University.

Lucas, T. (2011) *Teacher preparation for linguistically diverse classrooms: A resource for teacher educators*. New York: Routledge.

Mahler, S. J. (1998). Theoretical and empirical contributions toward a research agenda for transnationalism. In M. P. Smith & L. E. Guarnizo (Eds.), *Transnationalism from below* (pp. 64–102). New Brunswick, NJ: Transaction.

Marzano, R. (2003). *What works in schools: Translating research into action*. Alexandria, VA: Association for Supervision and Curriculum Development.

Massey, D. S., & Capoferro, C. (2008) The geographic diversification of American immigration. In D. S. Massey (Ed.), *New faces in new places: The changing geography of American immigration* (pp. 25–50). New York: Russell Sage Foundation.

McCarty, T. (2002). Comment: Bilingual/bicultural schooling and indigenous students: A response to Eugene Garcia. *International Journal of the Sociology of Language*, 155/156, 161–174.

National Clearinghouse for English Acquisition and Language Instruction Educational Programs. (2006). *The growing numbers of limited English proficient students 1994/95–2004/*. Retrieved November 20, 2008, from http://www.ncela.gwu.edu/policy/states/reports/statedata/2004LEP/GrowingLEP 0405 Nov06.pdf

Norton-Peirce, B. (1995). Social identity, investment and language learning. *TESOL Quarterly, 29*(1), 9–31.

Oh, S. S. (2011, March). *Transculturation: A new theoretical model for understanding dynamic, multidirectional, and synchronous developmental pathways for children of immigrants*. Paper presented at the Immigration and Education Conference: Envisioning Schools, Communities and Policies of Acceptance, City College of New York.

Oh, S. S., & Cooc, N. (2011). Immigration, youth and education: Editors' introduction. *Harvard Educational Review, 81*(3), 396–406.

Oláh, L. N. (2008). *Every teacher a language teacher*. Retrieved from http://www.gse.upenn.edu/node/575.

Olneck, M. R., & Lazerson, M. (1974). The school achievement of immigrant children, 1900–1930. *History of Education Quarterly, 14*, 453–482.

Olsen, L. (1997). *Made in America: Immigrant students in our public schools*. New York: New York Press.

O'Malley, J. M., & Valdez Peirce, L. (1996). *Authentic assessment for English language learners: Practical approaches for teachers*. New York: Addison-Wesley.

Omi, M., & Winant, H. (1994). *Racial formation in the United States: From the 1960s to the 1990s*. New York and London: Routledge.

Patowski, M. (1980). The sensitive period for the acquisition of syntax in a second language. *Language Learning, 30*(2), 449–472.

Perry, T., & Delpit, L. D. (1998). *The real Ebonics debate: Power, language, and the education of African-American children*. Boston: Beacon.

Plyer v. Doe, 457 U.S. 202, 210 (1982).

Porter, R. P. (1990). *Forked tongue: The politics of bilingual education*. New York: Basic Books.

Portes, A. (1996). Global villagers: The rise of transnational communities. *American Prospect, 25*, 74–77.

Portes, A. (1999). Towards a new world: The origins and effects of transnational activities. *Ethnic and Racial Studies, 22*(2), 463–477.

Portes, A., & Rumbaut, R. G. (1996). *Immigrant America: A portrait*. Berkeley: University of California Press.

Portes, A., & Rumbaut, R. G. (2001). *Legacies: The story of the immigrant second generation*. Berkeley: University of California Press.

Rose, P. I. (1997). *They and we: Racial ethnic relations in the United States*. New York: McGraw-Hill.

Rossel, C., & Baker, K. (1996). The effectiveness of bilingual education. *Research in the Teaching of English, 30*, 7–74.

Ruiz, R. (2004, April). *From language as a problem to language as an asset: The promise and limitations of Lau*. Paper presented at the annual conference of the American Educational Research Association, San Diego.

Schleppegrell, M. J., Achugar, M., & Oteíza, T. (2004). The grammar of history: Enhancing content-based instruction through a functional focus on language. *TESOL Quarterly, 38*(1), 67–94.

Singer, A. (2004). *The rise of new immigrant gateways. Living cities census series*. Washington, DC: Center on Urban and Metropolitan Policy, Brookings Institution.

Slavin, R. E., & Cheung, A. (2003). *Effective reading programs for English language learners: A best-evidence synthesis*. Baltimore, MD: Johns Hopkins University Center for Research on the Education of Students Placed at Risk.

Smith, M. P., & Guarnizo, L. E. (Eds.). (1998). *Transnationalism from below: Comparative urban and community research*. New Brunswick, NJ: Transaction.

Smitherman, G. (1981). What go round come round: King in perspective. *Harvard Educational Review, 51*(1), 40–56.

Smitherman, G. (1998). Black English/Ebonics: What it be like? In T. Perry & L. Delpit (Eds.), *The real Ebonics debate: Power, language, and the education of African-American children* (pp. 29–37). Boston: Beacon.

Smitherman, G. (2000). *Talkin that talk: Language, culture and education in African America*. New York: Routledge.

Snow, C., & Hoefnagel-Höhle, M. (1978). The critical period for language acquisition: Evidence from second language learning. *Child Development, 49*(4), 1114–1128.

Snow, M. A., Met, M., & Genesee, F. (1989). A conceptual framework for the integration of language and content in second/foreign language instruction. *TESOL Quarterly, 23*, 201–219.

Spellings, M. (2005). *Academic gains of English language learners prove high standards, accountability paying off*. Retrieved from http://www.ed.gov/news/speeches/2005/12/12012005.html.

Stritikus, T. (2004, April). *Latino immigrant students: Transitions and educational challenges*. Paper presented at the annual meeting of the American Educational Research Association, San Diego, CA.

Stritikus, T., & Manyak, P. (2000). Creating opportunities for the academic success of linguistically diverse students: What does the research say? In T. Bergeson (Ed.), *Educating limited English proficient students in Washington State*. Olympia, WA: Office of Superintendent of Public Instruction.

Stritikus, T., & Nguyen, D. (2007). Strategic transformation: Cultural and gender identity negotiation in first generation Vietnamese youth. *American Educational Research Journal, 44*(4), 853–895.

Suarez-Orozco, C. E., & Suarez-Orozco, M. M. (2003). *Children of immigration.* Cambridge, MA: Harvard University Press.

Suárez-Orozco, C., Suárez-Orozco, M. M., & Todorova, I. (2008). *Learning a new land: Immigrant students in American society.* Cambridge, MA: Belknap Press of Harvard University Press.

Suárez-Orozco, C., Yoshikawa, H., Teranishi, R. T., & Suárez-Orozco, M. M. (2011). Growing up in the shadows: The developmental implications of unauthorized status. *Harvard Educational Review, 81*(3), 438-472.

Suarez-Orozco, M. M. (1997). Globalization, immigration, and education: The research agenda. *Harvard Educational Review, 71*(3), 345–365.

Teachers of English to Speakers of Other Languages (TESOL). (1997). *ESL standards for pre-K–12 students.* Alexandria, VA: Author.

Toohey, K. (2000). *Learning English at school: Identity, social relations and classroom practice.* Clevedon, UK: Multilingual Matters.

U.S. Census Bureau. (2004). *Current population survey, 2004 annual social and economic (ASEC) supplement documentation.* Washington, DC: Author.

Valdés, G. (2001). *Learning and not learning English: Latino students in American schools.* New York: Teachers College Press.

Valdés, G. (2004). Between support and marginalization: The development of academic language in linguistic minority children. In J. Brutt-Griffler & M. Varghese (Eds.), *Bilingualism and language pedagogy* (pp. 102–132). Clevedon, UK: Multilingual Matters.

Valenzuela, A. (1999). *Subtractive schooling: U.S.–Mexican youth and the politics of caring.* New York: State University of New York Press.

Van Lier, L. (2004). *The ecology and semiotics of language learning: A sociocultural perspective.* Boston; Dordrecht, the Netherlands; and Norwell, MA: Kluwer Academic.

Varghese, M., & Stritikus, T. (2005). "Nadie me dijó [Nobody told me]": Language policy negotiation and implications for teacher education. *Journal of Teacher Education, 56*(1).

Walqui, A. & Van Lier (2010). *Scaffolding the academic success of adolescent English language learners: A pedagogy of promise.* San Francisco: WestEd.

Wiese, A., & García, E. E. (1998). The Bilingual Education Act: Language minority students and equal educational opportunity. *Bilingual Research Journal, 22*(1), 1–18.

Wiley, T. G. (1996a). Language planning and policy. In S. L. McKay & N. H. Hornberger (Eds.), *Sociolinguistics and language teaching* (pp. 103–148). New York: Cambridge University Press.

Wiley, T. G. (1996b). *Literacy and language diversity in the United States.* Washington, DC: Center for Applied Linguistics and Delta Systems.

Wiley, T. G., & Lukes, M. (1996). English-only and Standard English ideologies in the US. *TESOL Quarterly, 30*(3), 511–535.

Wiley, T. G., & Wright, W. E. (2004). Against the undertow: Language-minority education policy and politics in the "age of accountability." *Educational Policy, 18*(1), 142–168.

Willig, A. (1985). A meta-analysis of selected studies on the effectiveness of bilingual education. *Review of Educational Research, 55*(3), 269–317.

Wolfram, W., Adger, C. T., & Christian, D. (1998). *Dialects in schools and communities.* Mahwah, NJ: Erlbaum.

Wong Fillmore, L., & Snow, C. (2000). *What teachers need to know about language.* Washington, DC: ERIC Clearinghouse on Languages and Linguistics.

Zhou, M. (1997). Segmented assimilation: Issues, controversies, and recent research on the new second generation. *International Migration Review, 31*(4), 975–1008.

Teachers should be prepared to respond to the special educational needs of students with disabilities and who are intellectually gifted and talented.

Masterfile Royalty-Free

Masterfile Royalty-Free

Realistic Reflections/Getty Images, Inc.

PART V

Exceptionality

The expansion of rights for students with disabilities was one major consequence of the civil rights movement of the 1960s and 1970s. The Supreme Court's *Brown* decision, issued in 1954, established the principle that to segregate students solely because of their race is inherently unequal and unconstitutional. This decision—as well as other legal and social reforms of the 1960s—encouraged advocates for the rights of students with disabilities to push for expanded rights for them. If it was unconstitutional to segregate students because of their race, it was reasoned, segregating students because of their disabilities could also be challenged.

The advocates for the rights of students with disabilities experienced a major victory in 1975 when Congress enacted Public Law 94–142, the Education for All Handicapped Children Act (*Twenty-fifth Annual Report*, 2003). This act is unprecedented and revolutionary in its implications. It requires free public education for all children with disabilities, nondiscriminatory evaluation, and an individualized education program (IEP) for each student with a disability. The act also stipulates that each student with a disability should be educated in the least restricted environment. This last requirement has been one of the most controversial provisions of Public Law 94–142 (Dillon, 2007). Most students who are classified as having disabilities—about 80 percent—have mild disabilities. The landmark law—the Individuals with Disabilities Education Act (IDEA), Public Law 108-446—was reauthorized in 2004 by Congress and focuses on the needs of individual students. IDEA helps students with disabilities attend schools in their own neighborhoods—schools that may not have been open to them previously. More students with disabilities are learning in classes with their peers, instead of studying in separate buildings or classrooms. Moreover, early intervention programs and services are provided to more than 200,000 eligible infants and toddlers and their families, while about 6.5 million children and youths receive special education and related services to meet their individual needs (U.S. Department of Education, 2010). Final directives on modified academic achievement standards were authorized under U.S Department of Education regulations (34 C.F.R. Part 200) in 2007 to develop alternate academic achievement standards for measuring adequate yearly progress (AYP) for students with the most significant cognitive disabilities and to include those students' proficient and advanced scores on alternate assessments (U.S. Department of Education, 2007).

Exceptionality intersects with factors such as race, ethnicity, language, gender, and sexual orientation in interesting and complex ways. Males and students of color are more frequently classified as special education students than are females and White mainstream students. Nearly twice as many males as females are classified as special education students. Consequently, males of color are the most likely group to be classified as mentally retarded or learning disabled (*Demographic and School Characteristics*, 2007). The higher proportion of males and students of color in special education programs is related to the fact that mental retardation is a socially constructed category (see Chapter 1).

Students with disabilities as well as gifted students are considered *exceptional*. Exceptional students are those who have learning or behavioral characteristics that differ substantially from those of most other students and that require special attention in instruction. Concern for U.S. students who are gifted and talented increased after the Soviet Union successfully launched *Sputnik* in 1957. Congress passed the Gifted and Talented Children's Education Act in 1978. However, concern for the gifted is ambivalent and controversial in the United States.

In 1982, special funding for gifted education was consolidated with 29 other educational programs. The Jacob K. Javits Gifted and Talented Students Education Act was passed in 1988 to fund grants, provide leadership, and sponsor a national research center on the education of gifted and talented students. The Javits Act has three primary components: researching effective methods of testing, identification, and programming, which is performed at the National Research Center on the Gifted and Talented; awarding grants to colleges, states, and districts that focus on underrepresented populations of gifted students; and awarding grants to states and districts for program implementation. Critics argue that too much attention is given to the gifted. The controversy over gifted education stems in part from the belief by many people that it is elitist. Others argue that gifted education is a way for powerful mainstream parents to acquire an excellent education for their children in the public schools. The fact that few students of color are classified as gifted is another source of controversy. Despite the controversies that surround programs for gifted and talented youths, schools need to find creative and democratic ways to satisfy these students' needs.

The chapters in Part V describe the major issues, challenges, and promises involved in providing equal educational opportunities for exceptional students—those with disabilities and those who are intellectually gifted and talented.

REFERENCES

Dillon, E. (2007). *The students behind NCLB's "disabilities" designation.* Retrieved October 21, 2008, from http://www.educationsector.org/analysis/analysis_show.htm?doc_id = 509392.

Demographic and school characteristics of students receiving special education in the elementary grades. (2007). Retrieved October 21, 2008, from http://nces.ed.gov/pubs2007/2007005.pdf.

Twenty-fifth annual report to Congress on the implementation of the Individuals with Disabilities Education Act. (2003). Retrieved October 21, 2008, from http://www.ed.gov/about/reports/annual/osep/25th-exec-summ.pdf.

U.S. Department of Education. (2007, May). *Final regulations on modified academic achievement standards*. Retrieved January 22, 2012, from http://www2.ed.gov/policy/speced/guid/modachieve-summary.html.

U.S. Department of Education. (2010). *Thirty years of progress in educating children with disabilities through IDEA*. Retrieved January 22, 2012, from http://www2.ed.gov/policy/speced/leg/idea/history30.html.

Masterfile Royalty-Free

Educational Equality for Students with Disabilities

CHAPTER 13

Sara C. Bicard and William L. Heward

Children differ from one another. Step into any classroom in any school and you will immediately notice differences in children's height, weight, style of dress, hair, skin color, and other physical characteristics. Look a bit closer and you will see some obvious differences in children's language and their academic and social skills. Closely observe the interactions among students, curriculum, and instruction, and you will begin to see how children respond differently to the curriculum content and to the instructional methods.

Children also differ from one another in ways that are not apparent to the casual observer. Differences in the educational opportunities children receive and the benefits they derive from their time in school are two examples. The educational implications of gender, race, social class, religion, ethnicity, and language diversity not only influence how children may respond to curriculum and instruction but also affect the structure and design of educational systems in general.

While diversity in social class, race, culture, and language differences increasingly characterizes U.S. classrooms, every classroom is also characterized by *skill diversity* among students. Some children quickly acquire new knowledge and skills that they have learned in relevant situations. Other children need repeated practice to learn a simple task and the next day may have difficulty successfully performing the same task. Some children begin a lesson with a large store of relevant experience and background knowledge; others come to the same lesson with little or no relevant prerequisite skills or knowledge. Some children are popular and enjoy the company of many friends. Others are ostracized because they have not learned how to be friendly. The skill differences among most children are relatively small, allowing these children to benefit from the general education program offered by their schools. When the physical, social, and academic skills of children differ to such an extent that typical school curricula or teaching methods are neither appropriate nor effective, however, equitable access to and benefits from educational programs are at stake.

Like the others in this book, this chapter is not about surface or educationally irrelevant differences among children. Teachers must have the knowledge and skills to recognize and to be instructionally responsive to the diversity their students represent. This chapter extends the concept of diversity to include children with disabilities, and it lays the foundation for teachers to examine educational equity for learners with diverse skills.

This chapter outlines the history of exclusion and educational inequality experienced by many students with disabilities in U.S. schools. It also examines the progress made during the past three decades, paying particular attention to the Individuals with Disabilities Education Act (IDEA), federal legislation that requires that all children, regardless of the type or severity of their disabilities, be provided a free and appropriate public education. We examine the key features of this landmark law, the outcomes of its implementation, and the major barriers that continue to impede true educational equity for students with disabilities. First, let's take a closer look at the concept of disability and examine when skill diversity necessitates special education.

Identification of Students with Disabilities

Various terms are used to refer to children with special learning needs. When the term *exceptional* is used to describe students, it includes children who have difficulty learning and children whose performance is advanced. The performance of exceptional children differs from the norm (either above or below) to such an extent that individualized programs of special education are necessary to meet their diverse needs. *Exceptional* is an inclusive term that describes not only students with severe disabilities but also those who are gifted and talented. This chapter focuses on children with disabilities—students for whom learning presents a significant challenge.

While the terms *impairment, disability,* and *handicap* are often used interchangeably, they are not synonymous. *Impairment* refers to the loss or reduced function of a certain body part or organ. A *disability* exists when an impairment limits a child's ability to perform certain tasks (e.g., walking, speaking, seeing) in the same way that nondisabled children do. Disability conditions are defined and classified according to body functions and structure, activity domains, and participation in the context of environmental and personal factors (World Health Organization, 2011). *Handicap* refers to the challenges a person with a disability experiences when interacting with the physical or social environment. A disability does not constitute a handicap unless the disability leads to educational, personal, social, vocational, or other difficulties for the individual. For example, a child with one arm who functions successfully in and out of school without special support or accommodations is not considered handicapped. Some disabilities pose a handicap in some environments but not in others. The child with one arm may be handicapped (i.e., disadvantaged) when competing with nondisabled classmates on the playground but experience no handicap in the classroom. Individuals with disabilities also experience handicaps that have nothing to do with their disabilities but instead are the result of the negative attitudes and inappropriate behavior of others who needlessly restrict their access and ability to participate fully in school, work, or community activities.

Children who are not currently identified as handicapped but are considered to have a higher-than-normal chance of developing a disability are referred to as *at risk*. This term is used with infants and preschoolers who, because of difficulties experienced at birth or conditions in the home environment, may be expected to have developmental problems as they grow older. Some educators also use the term to refer to students who are having learning problems in the regular classroom and are therefore "at risk" of being identified as disabled and in need of special education services. Physicians also use the terms *at risk* or *high risk* to identify pregnancies in which there is a higher than usual probability that the babies will be born with a physical or developmental disability.

A physical, behavioral, or cognitive disability is considered a handicap when it adversely affects a student's educational performance. Students with disabilities are entitled to special education because their physical or behavioral attributes conform to one or more of the following categories of disability:

- Intellectual disabilities (formerly referred to as mental retardation and developmental disabilities) (Beirne-Smith, Patton, & Kim, 2006)

- Learning disabilities (Mercer & Pullen, 2009)

- Emotional or behavioral disorders (Kauffman & Landrum, 2009)

- Communication (speech and language) disorders (Anderson & Shames, 2011)

- Hearing impairments (Scheetz, 2012)

- Visual impairments (LaVenture, 2007)

- Physical and health impairments (Heller, Forney, Alberto, Best, & Schwartzman, 2009)

- Autism (Webber & Scheuermann, 2008)

- Traumatic brain injury (Best, Heller, & Bigge, 2010)

- Multiple disabilities (Snell & Brown, 2011)

Regardless of the terms used to refer to students who exhibit diversity in academic, vocational, and social skills, it is incorrect to believe that there are two distinct kinds of students: those who are typical and those with disabilities. All children differ from one another to some extent. Students with disabilities are those whose skill diversity is significant enough to require a specially designed program of instruction in order to achieve educational equality. Students with disabilities are more like other students than they are different from them. All students are alike in that they can benefit from an appropriate education that enables them to do things they were previously unable to do and to do these things with greater independence and enjoyment.

Is Disability a Social Construct?

The proposition that some (perhaps all) disabilities are social constructs merits attention in any discussion of educational equity for exceptional children (Anastasiou & Kauffman, 2010; Forness, Freeman, Paparella, Kauffman, & Walker, in press; Smith, 1999; Smith & Mitchell, 2001; Wiley & Siperstein, 2011). This issue is particularly relevant to a text about multicultural education. The establishment of membership criteria in any group is by definition socially constructed because the criteria have been created by human beings (Banks, 2006). How educational communities respond to the cultural-, ethnic-, gender-, and class-specific attributes children bring to the class-room is more important than how they perceive the establishment of membership criteria for a particular group. Education's response to the diversity that children represent will influence their achievement as well as professional and societal judgments about that achievement. There is evidence that some children's "disabilities" are primarily the result of culture, class, or gender influences that are at odds with the culture, class, or gender that has established a given category of disability and the assessment procedures used to make those determinations (Gollnick & Chinn, 2009). As is discussed later in this chapter, a significant focus of special education litiga-tion and legislation has been directed at these inequities. Deconstructing the traditional socio-political view of exceptionality, changing social-group membership, or passing legislation will not, however, eliminate the real challenges students with disabilities experience in acquiring fundamental academic, self-help, personal-social, and vocational skills. While the criteria for determining the presence or absence of a disability may be hypothetical social constructions, the handicaps created by educational disabilities are not (Fuchs & Fuchs, 1995; Heward, 2013; Kauffman & Hallahan, 2005a; Sugai, 1998).

Be wary of the conception that disabilities are merely socially constructed phenomena. School-age learners with disabilities—those who have pronounced difficulty acquiring and generalizing new knowledge and skills—are real children with real needs in real classrooms. The notion that all children who are identified as disabled would achieve success and behave well if others simply viewed them more positively is romantic ideology seldom promoted by individuals with disabilities themselves or by their parents and families.

Our discussion of students with disabilities and special education's role in addressing their needs assumes that a child's physical, behavioral, or cognitive skill diversity is influenced by, but also transcends, other variables such as ethnicity, gender, and social class. We also assume that the educational challenges students with disabilities experience represent real and signifi-cant barriers to their ability to experience independence and personal satisfaction across a wide range of life experiences and circumstances. Many factors contribute to educational equality for children with disabilities. Among the most important of these factors is carefully planned and systematically delivered instruction with meaningful curricula and future-oriented learning objectives (Heward & Dardig, 2001).

How Many Students with Disabilities Are There?

The most complete and systematic information about the number of students with disabilities in the United States is found in the U.S. Department of Education's child-count data. The most recent information available is for the 2009–2010 school year (U.S. Department of Education, 2011):

- More than 7 million children with disabilities from birth to age 21 received special education services during the 2009–2010 school year.

- Children with disabilities in special education represent approximately 12 percent of the entire school-age population.

- About twice as many males as females receive special education.

- The vast majority—approximately 75 percent—of school-age children receiving special education have mild to moderate disabilities such as learning disabilities (42.3 percent), speech and language impairment (18.8 percent), intellectual disabilities (7.8 percent), and emotional disturbance (6.9 percent) (see Table 13.1).

How Are Students with Disabilities Classified?

The classification and labeling of exceptional students have been widely debated for many years. Some educators believe the classification and labeling of exceptional students serve only to stigmatize and exclude them from the mainstream of educational opportunities (Harry & Klingner, 2007; Kliewer, Biklen, & Kasa-Hendrickson, 2006). Others argue that a workable system of classification is necessary if exceptional students are to obtain the special educational services and programs that are prerequisite to their educational equality (Anastasiou & Kauffman, 2011; Keogh, 2005a, 2005b). Like most complex questions, there are valid perspectives on both sides of the labeling issue, with political, ethical, and emotional concerns competing with educational, scientific, and fiscal considerations (Florian et al., 2006; McLaughlin et al., 2006). Common arguments for labeling students with exceptional learning needs are that labels aid in communication, including visibility and advocacy efforts that are needed to facilitate the structure of funding and resources for research and programs. The most common arguments against labeling students with exceptional learning needs involve the expense of labeling students and the impact of the label, such as the focus on deficits, impact on the child's self-esteem, low expectations held by others, and permanence of the label.

Research conducted to assess the effects of labeling has been of little help; most of the studies contribute inconclusive, often contradictory, evidence. Two important issues are how the use of categorical labels affects a child's access to special education services and the quality of instruction that the child receives as a result of classification.

What Determines Eligibility for Special Education?

Under current law, a student must first be identified as having a disability in order to receive an individualized program of special educational services that meet his or her needs. The student must be labeled and further classified into one of the categories, such as learning disabilities or visual impairment. So, in practice, membership in a given disability category and the corresponding exposure to the potential disadvantages associated with the label is a prerequisite to receiving the special education services necessary to achieve educational equality.

Table 13.1   Number of Students Ages 6–121 Who Received Special Services under the Federal Government's Disability Categories (2009–2010 School Year)

Disability Category	Number	Percent of Total
Specific learning disabilities	2,483,391	42.3
Speech or language impairments	1,107,029	18.8
Other health impairments	678,970	11.6
Intellectual disabilities	460,964	7.8
Emotional disturbance	405,293	6.9
Autism	333,022	5.7
Multiple disabilities	124,380	2.1
Developmental delay	104,432	1.8
Hearing impairments	70,548	1.2
Orthopedic impairments	57,930	1.0
Visual impairments	57,930	1.0
Traumatic brain injury	24,395	0.4
Deaf-blindness	1,359	<0.1
All disabilities	5,877,196	100.0

Source: U.S. Department of Education (2011). *Individuals with Disabilities Education Act (IDEA)* (Table 1-3). Washington, DC: Author. Available at https://www.ideadata.org/PartBReport.asp.

Kauffman (1999) points out the reality of labels as a necessary first step in serving students with important differences in behavior and learning: "Although universal interventions that apply equally to all, regardless of their behavioral characteristics or risks of developing disorders, can be implemented without labels and risk of stigma, no other interventions are possible without labels. Either all students are treated the same or some are treated differently. Any student who is treated differently is inevitably labeled" (p. 452).

How Does Classification Affect Instruction?

The classification of students according to the various categories of exceptionality is made largely under the presumption that students in each category share certain physical, behavioral, and learning characteristics that hold important implications for planning and delivering educational services. It is a mistake, however, to believe that once identified by a certain disability category, a child's educational needs and the manner in which those needs should be met have also been identified. Although it was written four decades ago, this statement by Becker, Engelmann, and Thomas (1971) is still pertinent today: "For the most part the labels are not important. They rarely tell the teacher who can be taught in what way. One could put five or six labels on the same child and still not know what to teach him or how" (p. 436).

History of Educational Equality for Students with Disabilities

If a society can be judged by the way it treats people who are different, the U.S. educational system does not have a distinguished history. Students who are different, whether because of race, culture, language, gender, or disability, have often been denied equal access to educational opportunities. For many years, educational opportunity of any kind did not exist for many students with disabilities. Students with severe disabilities were completely excluded from public schools. Before 1970, many states had laws allowing local school districts to deny access to children whose physical or intellectual disability caused them, in the opinion of school officials, to be unable to benefit from instruction (Murdick, Gartin, & Crabtree, 2006).

Although students with disabilities were enrolled in school, perhaps half of the children with disabilities in the United States were denied an appropriate education through "functional exclusion." They were allowed to come to school but did not participate in an educational program designed to meet their special needs. Students with mild learning and behavior problems remained in the regular classroom but received no special help. If they failed to make satisfactory progress in the curriculum, they were called "slow learners"; if they acted out in class, they were called "disciplinary problems" and were suspended from school (Turnbull, Huerta, & Stowe, 2009).

For students who did receive a program of differentiated curriculum or instruction, special education usually meant a separate education in segregated classrooms and special schools isolated from the mainstream of education. Special education for those students with disabilities often meant a classroom especially reserved for students who could not measure up in the regular classroom. The following passage exemplified what was too often a common occurrence:

> *I accepted my first teaching position in a special education class in a basement room next door to the furnace. Of the fifteen "educable mentally retarded" children assigned to work with me, most were simply nonreaders from poor families. One child had been banished to my room because she posed a behavior problem to her fourth-grade teacher. My class and I were assigned a recess spot on the opposite side of the play yard, far away from the "normal" children. I was the only teacher who did not have a lunch break. I was required to eat with my "retarded" children while the other teachers were permitted to leave their students.*

(Aiello, 1976, p. 14)

As society's concepts of equality, freedom, and justice have expanded, education's response to students with disabilities has changed slowly but considerably over the past several decades. Educational opportunity has gradually shifted from a pattern of exclusion and isolation to one of integration and participation. But change has not come easily, nor has it occurred by chance. Judicial and legislative authority has been necessary to begin to correct educational inequities for children with disabilities. Recent efforts to ensure educational equality for students with disabilities can be viewed as an outgrowth of the civil rights movement. All of the issues and events that helped shape society's attitudes during the 1950s and 1960s affected the development of special education, particularly the 1954 landmark case of *Brown v. Board of Education of Topeka*. This case challenged the common practice at the time of segregating schools according to the race of the children. The U.S. Supreme Court ruled that education must be available to all children on equal terms and that it is unconstitutional to operate segregated schools under the premise that they are separate but equal.

The *Brown* decision that public school education should be provided to African American and White children on equal terms initiated a period of intense questioning by parents of children with disabilities who wondered why the same principles of equal access to education did not also apply to their children. Numerous cases challenging the exclusion and isolation of children with disabilities by the schools were brought to court by parents and advocacy groups. One of the most influential court cases in the development of educational equality for exceptional students was *Pennsylvania Association for Retarded Children [PARC] v. Commonwealth of Pennsylvania* (1972). PARC brought the class-action suit to challenge a state law that enabled public schools to deny education to children they considered unable to benefit from attending public school.

The attorneys and parents who represented PARC argued that it was neither rational nor necessary to assume that the children were uneducable. Because the state could neither prove that the children were uneducable nor demonstrate a rational basis for excluding them from public school programs, the court decided that the children were entitled to a free public education. Other court cases followed with similar rulings: Children with disabilities, like all other people in the United States, are entitled to the same rights and protection under the law as guaranteed in the Fourteenth Amendment, which declares that people may not be deprived of their equality or liberty on the basis of any classification such as race, nationality, or religion (for a summary of these court cases, see Heward, 2013).

The term *progressive integration* (Reynolds, 1989) has been used to describe the history of special education and the gradual but unrelenting progress of ensuring equal educational opportunity for all children. Of the many court cases involving education for children with disabilities, no single case resulted in sweeping educational reform. With each instance of litigation, however, the assembly of what was to become the Individuals with Disabilities Education Act became more complete. Together, all of these developments contributed to the passage of a federal law concerning educational equality for students with disabilities.

The Individuals with Disabilities Act: A Legislative Mandate for Educational Equality for Students with Disabilities

In 1975 Congress passed the Education for All Handicapped Children Act (P.L. 94–142). Since it became law in 1975, Congress has reauthorized and amended P.L. 94–142 five times, most recently in 2004. The 1990 amendments renamed the law the Individuals with Disabilities Education Act—often referred to by its acronym, IDEA.

IDEA is a landmark piece of legislation that has changed the face of education in the United States. It has affected every school in the country and has changed the roles of regular and special educators, school administrators, parents, and many other people involved in the educational process. Its passage marked the culmination of the efforts of a great many educators, parents, and legislators to bring together in one comprehensive bill U.S. laws regarding the education of children with disabilities. The law reflects society's concern for treating people with disabilities as full citizens with the same rights and privileges that all other citizens enjoy. The purpose of IDEA is to ensure the rights of students with disabilities to a free appropriate public education, including early intervention services, and to provide the necessary supports and oversight for states, districts, schools, and educators to improve the educational results for students with disabilities (P.L. 108–466, Sec. 601[d]).

Major Principles of the Individuals with Disabilities Education Act

IDEA is directed primarily at the states, which are responsible for providing education to their residents. The majority of the many rules and regulations defining how IDEA operates are related to six major principles that have remained unchanged since 1975 (Turnbull et al., 2009; Yell, 2012).

Zero Reject

Schools must educate *all* children with disabilities. The zero-reject principle applies regardless of the nature or severity of the disability; no child with disabilities may be excluded from a public education. This requirement of the law is based on the proposition that all children with disabilities can learn and benefit from an appropriate education and that schools, therefore, do not have the right to deny any child access to equal educational opportunity. Each state education agency is responsible for locating, identifying, and evaluating all children, from birth to age 21, residing in the state who have disabilities or are suspected of having disabilities. This requirement is called the *child find system* (P.L. 108–466, Sec. 303.321).

Nondiscriminatory Identification and Evaluation

IDEA requires that students with disabilities be evaluated fairly. The school or parents can request that a child be evaluated for special education. If the school initiates the evaluation, parents must be notified and consent to it, which for special education must be completed within 60 days of receiving parental consent. Assessment must be nondiscriminatory. This requirement is particularly important because of the disproportionate number of children from non-White and non-English-speaking cultural groups who are identified as having disabilities, often solely on the basis of a score from standardized intelligence tests. The intelligence tests that have been used most often in the identification of students with learning problems were developed based on the performance of White, middle-class children. Because of their Anglo-centric nature, the tests are often considered to be unfairly biased against children from diverse cultural groups who have had less opportunity to learn the knowledge sampled by the test items (Venn, 2007). In addition to nondiscriminatory assessment, testing must be multifactored to include as many tests and observational techniques as necessary to fairly and appropriately identify an individual child's strengths and weaknesses. The results of a single test cannot be used as the sole criterion for placement into a special education program.

Free, Appropriate Public Education

All children with disabilities, regardless of the type or severity of their disability, shall receive a free, appropriate public education. This education must be provided at public expense—that is, without cost to the child's parents. An *individualized education program* (IEP) must be developed and implemented for each child with a disability (P.L. 108–466, Sec. 614[d][1][A]). IDEA is specific in identifying the kinds of information an IEP must include and who is to participate in its development. Each IEP must be created by an *IEP team* consisting of (at least) the child's parents (or guardians); at least one regular education teacher of the child; at least one special education teacher; a representative of the local school district who is qualified to provide or supervise specially designed instruction and is knowledgeable of the general curriculum and about the resources of the local education agencies; an individual who can interpret the instructional implications of evaluation results and other individuals who have knowledge of the child (at discretion of the parent or the school); and, whenever appropriate, the child (P.L. 108–466, Sec. 614 [d][1][B]). Many IEP teams also include professionals from various disciplines such as school psychology, physical therapy, and medicine.

The IEP is the foundation of the special education and related services a child with a disability receives. A carefully and collaboratively prepared IEP specifies the skills the child needs to learn in relation to the present levels of performance, the procedures that will be used to bring about that learning, and the means of determining the extent to which learning has taken place (Bateman & Linden, 2006). Essentially, the IEP spells out where the child is, where he or she should be going, how he or she will get there, how long it will take, and how to tell when he or she has arrived. Although the IEP is a written document signed by both school personnel and the child's parents, it is not a legal document in the sense that parents cannot take their child's teachers or school to court if all goals and objectives stated in the IEP are not met. However, schools must be able to document that the services described in the IEP have been provided in a systematic effort to meet those goals (Bartlett, Etscheidt, & Weisentstein, 2007; Wright & Wright, 2006). IEPs must be reviewed by the IEP team at least annually.

Including all of the mandated components in an IEP is no guarantee that the document will guide the student's learning and the teacher's teaching in the classroom as intended by IDEA. Although most educators agree with the idealized concept of the IEP, inspection and evaluation of IEPs often reveal inconsistency between what is written in the document and what students experience in the classroom (e.g., Bateman & Linden, 2006; Grigal, Test, Beattie, & Wood, 1997; Smith & Brownell, 1995).

Least Restrictive Environment

IDEA mandates that students with disabilities be educated in the *least restrictive environment* (LRE). Specifically, the law states that:

> *to the maximum extent appropriate, children with disabilities, including children in public or private institutions or other care facilities, [will be] educated with children who are not disabled, and that special classes, separate schooling or other removal of children with disabilities from the regular educational environment [may occur] only when the nature or severity of the disability is such that education in regular classes with the use of supplementary aids and services cannot be achieved satisfactorily.*

> *(P.L. 108–446, Sec. 612[a][5][A])*

The LRE requirement continues to be one of the most controversial and least understood aspects of IDEA. During the first few years after the passage of IDEA, some professionals and parents erroneously interpreted the law to mean that every child with disabilities, regardless of type or severity, had to be placed in a general education classroom. Instead, the LRE component of IDEA requires that each child with a disability be educated in a setting that most closely resembles a regular class placement in which his or her individual needs can be met. Although some people argue that any decision to place a child with a disability in a special class or school is inappropriate, most educators and parents realize that placement in a regular classroom can be overly restrictive if the child's academic and social needs are not met. LRE is a relative concept; the least restrictive environment for one student with a disability would not necessarily be appropriate for another. Therefore, two students who have the same disability should not necessarily be placed in the same setting.

Children with disabilities need a wide range of special education and related services. Today, most schools provide a *continuum of services*—that is, a range of placement and service options to meet the individual needs of students with disabilities. The continuum can be depicted symbolically as a pyramid, with placements ranging from least restrictive (regular classroom placement without special supports) at the bottom to most restrictive (special schools, residential programs, and hospital or homebound programs) at the top (see Figure 13-1). Typically, the more severe a child's disability, the greater is the need for more intensive and specialized services. As noted, however, the majority of students who receive special education services have mild disabilities; hence, the pyramid's progressively smaller size at the top shows that more restrictive settings are required for fewer students.

Approximately four of five students with disabilities receive at least part of their education in regular classrooms with their nondisabled peers. Many of these students, however, spend part of each school day in a resource room where they receive individualized instruction from a specially trained teacher. Approximately one of every seven students with disabilities is educated in a separate classroom in a regular public school. Special schools and residential facilities

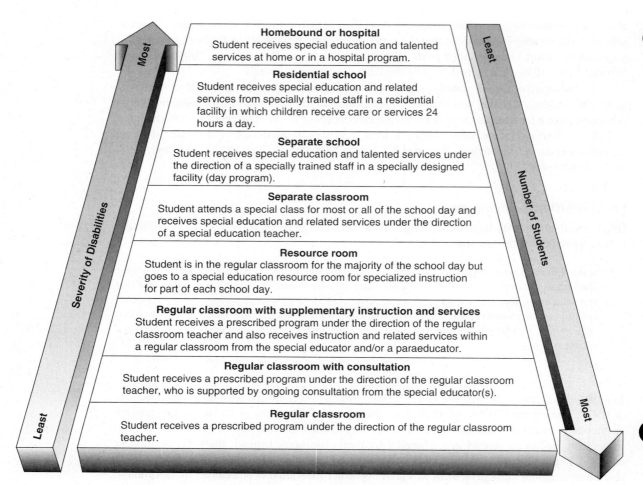

FIGURE 13.1 Continuum of Alternative Placements for Students with Disabilities

Source: W. L. Heward (2013). *Exceptional Children: An Introduction to Special Education* (10th ed., p. 70). Upper Saddle River, NJ: Merrill/Prentice-Hall. Used by permission.

provide the education for less than 4 percent of children with disabilities, usually students with the most severe disabilities (see Table 13.2).

Placement of a student with disabilities should not be viewed as all or nothing at any one level on the continuum or as permanent. IDEA instructs the IEP team to consider the extent to which the student can be integrated effectively in each of three dimensions of school life: the general academic curriculum, extracurricular activities (e.g., clubs), and other school activities (e.g., recess, mealtimes). The LRE is intended to be accommodating so that the IEP team may determine that total integration is appropriate in one dimension and partial integration is better suited for another dimension (Turnbull et al., 2009). The continuum concept is intended to be flexible, with students moving from one placement to another as dictated by their individual educational needs. The IEP team should periodically review the specific goals and objectives for each child—it is required to do so at least annually—and make new placement decisions if warranted.

Neither IDEA nor the regulations that accompany it specify exactly how a school district is to determine LRE. After reviewing the rulings on litigation in four LRE suits that have reached the U.S. courts of appeals, Yell (2012) concluded that the courts have held that IDEA does not

Table 13.2   Percentage of Students Ages 6–21 Served in Six Educational Environments (2009–2010 School Year)

Disability Category	Regular Classroom	Resource Room	Separate Classroom	Separate School	Residential School	Homebound or Hospital
Specific learning disabilities	65.1	25.5	7.3	0.5	0.1	0.1
Speech or language impairments	86.4	5.5	4.7	0.3	<0.1	0.1
Other health impairments	62.4	23.0	10.6	1.6	0.2	0.9
Mental retardation	17.9	26.8	47.6	6.2	0.4	0.5
Emotional disturbance	42.1	18.3	21.3	13.0	2.0	1.1
Autism	38.5	18.1	34.1	7.9	0.5	0.3
Multiple disabilities	13.0	15.9	45.9	19.7	1.8	3.1
Developmental delay	62.4	19.9	16.1	0.9	0.1	0.2
Hearing impairments	56.1	16.7	14.1	8.2	3.4	0.2
Orthopedic impairments	53.3	16.2	22.9	4.9	0.2	1.7
Visual impairments	44.2	13.4	11.8	5.5	3.7	0.6
Traumatic brain injury	47.4	23.6	20.9	5.1	0.5	1.7
Deaf-blindness	23.0	11.9	33.4	18.2	9.6	3.2
All disabilities	60.5	20.1	14.2	3.0	0.4	0.4

Source: U.S. Office of Special Education Programs (2011). *Individuals with Disabilities Education Act (IDEA)* (Table 2-2c). Washington, DC: Author. Available at https://www.ideadata.org/PartBdata.asp.

require the placement of students with disabilities in the regular classroom but fully supports the continuum of services.

Although the continuum-of-services model represents well-established practice in special education, it is not without controversy. A number of specific criticisms have been leveled at this approach to providing services to exceptional students. Some critics have argued that the continuum overly legitimizes the use of restrictive placements, implies that integration of persons with disabilities can take place only in least restrictive settings, and may infringe on the rights of people with disabilities to participate in their communities (e.g., Taylor, 1988).

The relative value of providing special education services to students with disabilities outside the regular classroom—especially in separate classrooms and schools—has been a hotly contested issue for many years (e.g., Giangreco, 2007; Kauffman & Hallahan, 2005b; Mitchell, 2004a, 2004b; Schwartz, 2005; Taylor, 1988; Zigmond, 2006). Virtually all special educators, however, support the responsible inclusion of students with disabilities in which systematic modifications in curriculum and instruction enable meaningful progress toward IEP goals (Fuchs, Fuchs, & Stecker, 2010; Kochhar-Bryant, 2008; McLeskey & Waldron, 2011; Schwartz, 2005).

Due Process Safeguards

IDEA acknowledges that students with disabilities are people with important legal rights. The law makes it clear that school districts do not have absolute authority over exceptional students. Schools may not make decisions about the educational programs of children with disabilities in a unilateral or arbitrary manner.

Due process is a legal concept that is implemented through a series of procedural steps designed to ensure fairness of treatment among school systems, parents, and students. Specific due process safeguards were incorporated into IDEA because of past educational abuses of children with disabilities. In the past, special education placements were often permanent, void of periodic reviews, and made solely on the basis of teacher recommendations. Furthermore, students with severe and profound disabilities were automatically excluded from public school programs and placed in residential programs where the quality of instructional programs often was very poor. The fact that children from minority cultural groups were disproportionately placed in special education programs was another factor in mandating the due process procedures.

Key elements of due process as it relates to special education are the parents' right to the following:

- Be notified in writing before the school takes any action that may alter the child's program (testing, reevaluation, change in placement)

- Give or withhold permission to have their child tested for eligibility for special education services, reevaluated, or placed in a different classroom or program

- See all school records about their child

- Have a hearing before an impartial party (not an employee of the school district) to resolve disagreements with the school system

- Receive a written decision following any hearing

- Appeal the results of a due process hearing to the state department of education (school districts may also appeal)

Parent and Student Participation and Shared Decision Making

IDEA recognizes the benefits of active parent and student participation. Parents not only have a right to be involved in their child's education but also can help professionals select appropriate instructional goals and provide information that will help teachers be more effective in working with their children. As noted, parents (and, whenever appropriate, students) are to take an active role as full members of the IEP team; their input and wishes must be considered in determining IEP goals and objectives, placement decisions, and related services needs (e.g., sign language interpreting, special transportation). Of course, parents cannot be forced to do so and may waive their right to participate.

Section 504 of the Rehabilitation Act of 1973

Another important law that extends civil rights to people with disabilities is Section 504 of the Rehabilitation Act of 1973 (P.L. 93–112). This regulation states, in part, that "no otherwise qualified handicapped individual shall, solely by reason of his handicap, be excluded from the participation in, be denied the benefits of, or be subjected to discrimination in any program or activity receiving federal financial assistance" (U.S.C. § 794[a]). This law, worded almost identically to the Civil Rights Act of 1964 (which prohibited discrimination based on race, color, or national origin), promises to expand opportunities to children and adults with disabilities in education, employment, and various other settings. It calls for the provision of "auxiliary aides for students with impaired sensory, manual, or speaking skills" (e.g., interpreters for students who are deaf) and architectural accessibility (U.S.C. § 794[a]). This requirement does not mean that schools, colleges, and employers must have *all* such aides available at *all* times or a completely barrier-free environment; it simply mandates that no person with disabilities may be excluded from a program because of the lack of an appropriate aide or accessibility to programs.

The Americans with Disabilities Act

The Americans with Disabilities Act (P.L. 101–336) was signed into law on July 26, 1990. Patterned after Section 504 of the Rehabilitation Act of 1973, the Americans with Disabilities Act (ADA) extends civil rights protection to persons with disabilities in private-sector employment, in all public services, and in public accommodations, transportation, and telecommunications. ADA requires that public accommodations, including school buildings, athletic stadiums, and school transportation, be accessible to students with disabilities.

The No Child Left Behind Act

Another landmark piece of federal legislation that affects students with disabilities is the Elementary and Secondary Education Act of 2001, which was later renamed the No Child Left Behind Act (NCLB) (P.L. 107–110). The intended purpose of NCLB is to improve the academic achievement of all children, particularly those from low-income families (Cortiella, 2006). The ultimate goal of NCLB is for all children to be proficient in reading and math by 2014. All children are to be taught by teachers who are highly qualified in their subjects and use curricula and instructional methods validated by rigorous scientific research. The emphasis on scientifically proven curricula and instruction offers the promise of effective instruction in the early grades, which could reduce the number of children who require special education, in particular because of reading problems. In addition, schools that do not make adequate yearly progress toward achieving state goals for test scores, including those scores of students with disabilities, are initially targeted for assistance and then subject to corrective action and ultimately restructuring.

Educational Equality for Students with Disabilities: Progress Made but Challenges Remain

What impact has IDEA had? The most obvious effect is that students with disabilities are receiving special education and related services that before the law's passage were not available. But access to education is what the law requires and is only one aspect of its impact. Since the passage of IDEA, there has been a dramatic increase in the number of both special education teachers and support staff. Perhaps the law has had its most dramatic effect on students with severe disabilities, many of whom had been completely denied the opportunity to benefit from an appropriate education. No longer can schools exclude students with disabilities on the premise that they are uneducable. IDEA is based on the presumption that all students can benefit from an appropriate education, and it states clearly that the local school has the responsibility to modify curriculum content and teaching methods according to the needs of each student. In essence, the law requires schools to adapt themselves to the needs of students rather than allowing schools to deny educational equality to students whose characteristics are inconsistent with traditional school norms and expectations.

　　IDEA has contributed positively to the education of students with disabilities, but significant barriers remain to full educational equality for exceptional students in the United States. We briefly examine five of these issues. If a truly appropriate educational opportunity is to be a reality for students with disabilities, U.S. schools must (1) bridge the research-to-practice gap with regard to effective instruction, (2) improve cooperation and collaboration between special and regular educators, (3) provide more and better early intervention programs for young children with disabilities, (4) increase the success of young adults with disabilities as they make the transition from school to adult life, and (5) ensure relevant, individualized education to students with disabilities from culturally and linguistically diverse backgrounds.

Effective Instruction

IDEA's mandates for multifactored evaluations, IEPs, due process, and placement in the least restrictive environment have enhanced educational equality for students with disabilities. None of these mandated processes, however, teach. True educational equality for children with disabilities can be achieved only through effective instruction (Heward & Dardig, 2001).

Properly implemented, special education is not a slowed-down, watered-down version of general education. Special education is a systematic, purposeful approach to teaching students with disabilities the academic, social, vocational, and personal skills they will need to live independent, satisfying, and productive lives, and to do it more effectively and efficiently than could be accomplished by general education alone. Effective teaching is much more than simply assigning something to be learned. An important responsibility of all teachers, especially special educators, is ensuring that the instruction they deliver is measurably effective in meeting the needs of their students. When this occurs, the education that students with disabilities receive will be truly special (Heward, 2003).

Special education can be nothing more or less than the quality of instruction provided by teachers. Teachers are ultimately responsible for providing effective instruction to exceptional students. With this responsibility come several obligations. Working collaboratively with their regular education colleagues and parents (Heron & Harris, 2001), special educators must (1) target instructional objectives that will improve the quality of students' lives in school, home, community, and workplace; (2) use research-validated methods of instruction (Cook, Tankersley, & Landrum, 2009; Coyne, Kame'enui, & Carnine, 2011; Lewis, Hudson, Richter, & Johnson, 2004); (3) continually evaluate the effectiveness of instruction with direct measures of student performance (Greenwood & Maheady, 1997); and (4) change an instructional program when it does not promote achievement and success (Bushell & Baer, 1994).

Teachers must demand effectiveness from their instructional approaches. For many years, conventional wisdom fostered the belief that it takes unending patience to teach children with disabilities. We believe this view is a disservice to students with special needs and to the educators—both special and general education teachers—whose job it is to teach them. Teachers should not wait patiently for exceptional students to learn, attributing lack of progress to some inherent attribute or faulty process within the child, such as mental retardation, learning disability, attention-deficit disorder, or emotional disturbance. Instead, the teacher should use direct and frequent measures of the student's performance as the primary guide for modifying instruction in order to improve its effectiveness. This is the real work of the educator (Heward, 2013).

To increase the likelihood that instruction is effective, special education must bridge the research-to-practice gap regarding instructional practice in the classroom (Carnine, 1997; Deshler, 2005; Gersten, 2001; Heward & Silvestri, 2005; Vaughn, Klingner, & Hughes, 2000). Contrary to the contentions of some, special education research has produced a significant and reliable knowledge base about effective teaching practices (e.g., Cook et al., 2009; Coyne et al., 2011). While there is a significant gap between what is relatively well understood and what is poorly understood or not understood at all, the more distressing gap may be between what research has discovered about teaching and learning and what is practiced in many classrooms. For example, scientific research has helped us discover a great deal about the features of early reading instruction that can reduce the number of children who later develop reading problems (Simmons, Kame'enui, Coyne, Chard, & Hairrell, 2011), how to enhance the success of students with severe disabilities when learning new skills (Browder, Ahlgrim-Delzell, Spooner, Mims, & Baker, 2009), and the components of secondary special education programs that can increase students' success in making the transition from school to work (Sitlington, Neubert, & Clark, 2010), but the education that many students with disabilities receive does not reflect that knowledge (Heward, 2003; McLesky & Waldron, 2011; Zigmond, 2007).

Regular and Special Education Partnership

Traditionally, regular and special education have been viewed as separate disciplines, each serving a different student population. Today, the concept of "your kids" and "my kids" is gradually being replaced by that of "our kids," and general and special education teachers are becoming partners in meeting the needs of all learners.

Mainstreaming has traditionally been thought of as the process of integrating students with disabilities into regular schools and classes. Today, the term *inclusive education* is changing not only the language of special education reform but also its intent (see Chapter 14). Inclusive education can be successful only with full cooperation of and collaboration among those people responsible for the educational programs of students with disabilities (Smith, Polloway, Patton, & Dowdy, 2012). Although IDEA does not specifically mention mainstreaming or inclusion, it creates a presumption in favor of regular classroom placement by requiring that educational services be provided in the least restrictive environment, which in turn necessitates cooperation between general and special educators.

The effects of IDEA on general education are neither entirely clear nor without controversy. This dissonance is further complicated by the tone and content of many discussions about how special education can or should be reformed while ensuring that the best interests of students with disabilities are appropriately served (Finn, Rotherham, & Hokanson, 2001; Fuchs et al., 2010; Gallagher, Heshusius, Iano, & Skrtic, 2004; McLaughlin, 2010). What is clear, however, is that the entire educational community has the responsibility to do the best job it can in meeting the needs of children with diverse skills. In the final analysis, issues of labeling, classifying, placing, and teaching assignments are secondary to the quality of instruction that takes place in the classroom (Heward & Dardig, 2001).

Improved collaboration between special education and general education is important not only for the 9 to 12 percent of school-age children with disabilities who receive special education but also for the estimated additional 10 to 20 percent of the student population who are struggling learners. An increasingly utilized system of early intervention for students whose performance suggests they are at risk for school failure is *response to intervention* (RTI). The Individuals with Disabilities Education Improvement Act of 2004 (P.L. 108–446) also allows local education agencies to use RTI to identify students with learning disabilities. When implemented properly, RTI embodies scientific, research-based interventions in tiers of intensity and frequent progress monitoring to make instructional decisions and determine whether a student has learning disabilities. Most of this process occurs in general education. The authorization of this new method emphasizes the increasing importance of the collaboration between general education and special education. Both special and regular educators must develop strategies for working together and sharing their skills and resources to prevent these millions of students, who are at risk, from becoming failures of our educational system.

Early Intervention

The years from birth to school age are critical to a child's learning and development. The typical child enters school with a large repertoire of cognitive, language, social, and physical skills on which to build. For many children with disabilities, unfortunately, the preschool years represent a long period of missed opportunities. Without systematic instruction, most young children with disabilities do not acquire many of the skills their nondisabled peers seemingly learn without effort. Parents concerned about their child's inability to reach important developmental milestones have often been told by professionals, "Don't worry. Your child will grow out of it before too long." In truth, without early intervention, many children with disabilities fall further and further behind their nondisabled peers, and minor delays in development often become major delays by the time the child reaches school age.

More than 25 years ago, there were very few early intervention programs for children with disabilities from birth to school age; today, early childhood special education is the fastest-growing area in the field of education. As with special education of school-age exceptional students, federal legislation has played a major role in the development of early intervention programs (Shonkoff & Meisels, 2000). By passing Public Law 99–457, the Education of the Handicapped Act Amendments of 1986, Congress reaffirmed the basic principles of the original P.L. 94–142 and added two major sections concerning early intervention services.

P.L. 99–457 required each state to show evidence of serving all three- to five-year-old children with disabilities in order to receive any preschool funds. The second major change brought about by P.L. 99–457 is the availability of incentive grants to states for developing systems of early identification and intervention for infants and toddlers with disabilities from birth to age two. The services must be planned by a multidisciplinary team that includes the child's parents and must be implemented according to an *individualized family services plan (IFSP)* that is similar in concept to the IEP for school-age students with disabilities (P.L. 108–466, Sec. 636).

Researchers realize the critical importance of early intervention for both children who are at risk and those who have been diagnosed with a disability, and most agree that the earlier intervention is begun, the better (Guralnick, 2005; Sandall, Hemmeter, McLean, & Smith, 2005). Fortunately, many educators are working to develop the programs and services so desperately needed by the increasing numbers of babies and preschoolers who have been or are at risk for developing disabilities (Cook, Klein, Chen, & Tessier, 2012). Early intervention is necessary to give these children a fighting chance to experience educational equality when they enter school.

Transition from School to Adult Life

If the degree of educational equality afforded to students with disabilities is to be judged, as we think it should be, by the extent to which students with disabilities can function independently in everyday environments, then special education still has a long way to go. For example, while data from the National Longitudinal Transition Study-2 (NLTS2) show that 91 percent of youths with disabilities averaged four different jobs during the eight years after completing high school, 59 percent live independently, and 60 percent have participated in postsecondary education (Newman et al., 2011).

Education cannot be held responsible for all of the difficulties adults with disabilities face, but the results of this and other studies make it evident that many young people leave public school special education programs without the skills necessary to function in the community. Many youths with disabilities find all aspects of adult life a challenge (Flexer, Baer, Luft, & Simmons, 2008). Many educators today see the development of special education programs that will effectively prepare exceptional students for adjustment and successful integration into the adult community as the ultimate measure of educational equality for students with disabilities (Ferguson & Ferguson, 2011; Test, Aspel, & Everson, 2006).

Special Education in a Diverse Society

Both special and general educators face major challenges in providing relevant, individualized education to students with disabilities from culturally diverse backgrounds. Many students with disabilities experience discrimination or inadequate educational programs because their race, ethnicity, social class, or gender is different from that of the majority. Students from culturally and linguistically diverse backgrounds are often under- or overrepresented in educational programs for exceptional children (De Valenzuela, Copeland, Qi, & Park, 2006; Kalyanpur, 2008; Waitoller, Artiles, & Cheney, 2010).

The 1997–1998 school year was the first time the federal government required states to report the race and ethnicity of students receiving special education. These data continue to show disparities between the distribution of race/ethnicity within the general population and participation in special education, particularly for African American students, who are more likely to be overrepresented, and Asian American students, who are more likely to be underrepresented (U.S. Department of Education, 2010). For example, although African American students constitute about 15 percent of the general school population, they make up 32 percent of students classified with mental retardation and 28.7 percent of students with severe emotional disturbance (U.S. Department of Education, 2007) (see Table 13.3).

The fact that culturally diverse students are identified as having disabilities is not in itself a problem. All students with a disability that adversely affects their educational performance have the right to special education services. Disproportionate representation is problematic, however, if students have been wrongly placed in special education, are segregated and stigmatized, or are denied access to needed special education because their disabilities are overlooked as a result of their membership in a racial or ethnic minority group. Although a student's ethnicity or language should never be the basis for inclusion in or exclusion from special education programs, the disproportionate numbers of students from culturally and linguistically diverse backgrounds will require that educators attend to three important issues.

Table 13.3 Racial/Ethnic Composition (Percentage) of Students Ages 6–21 Served According to Disability (2006–2007 School Year)

Disability Category	American Indian/ Alaskan	Asian/Pacific Islander	African American (not Hispanic)	Hispanic	White (not Hispanic)
Specific learning disabilities	1.7	1.7	20.1	22.7	53.7
Speech or language impairments	1.3	3.1	15.2	18.7	61.6
Other health impairments	1.2	1.5	17.3	10.5	69.5
Mental retardation	1.25	2.1	32.0	16.0	48.6
Emotional disturbance	1.6	1.1	28.7	11.3	57.3
Autism	0.7	5.4	14.3	12.0	67.6
Multiple disabilities	1.4	2.8	20.7	14.0	61.2
Developmental delay	3.7	2.7	22.5	9.9	61.3
Hearing impairments	1.2	5.0	16.1	23.6	54.1
Orthopedic impairments	1.0	3.6	14.7	21.6	59.2
Visual impairments	1.3	4.2	16.8	20.1	57.6
Traumatic brain injury	1.6	2.5	16.5	13.4	66.0
Deaf-blindness	1.8	4.8	13.3	21.0	59.0
All disabilities	1.5	2.2	20.3	18.5	57.5
Estimated percentage of resident population	1.0	4.2	15.0	18.5	61.3

Sums may not equal 100 percent because of rounding.

Source: U.S. Office of Special Education Programs (2007). *Individuals with Disabilities Education Act (IDEA)* (Tables 1-19 and C-8). Washington, DC: Author. Available at https://www.ideadata.org/PartBdata.asp.

First, the adequacy of assessment and placement procedures must be ensured. Multifactored assessments must be conducted in ways that will be appropriately sensitive to the student's culture and language to ensure that a special education placement is a function of the student's documented needs rather than of biased referral and assessment practices (Utley & Obiakor, 2001).

Second, providing appropriate support services that are responsive to the cultural and linguistic needs of the student may enhance the child's educational program. For example, bilingual aides, in-service training for teachers, and multicultural education for peers may be necessary to ensure that the child's education is meaningful and maximally beneficial.

Third, teachers and other school staff may need to learn about the values and standards of behavior present in the child's home. Because most teachers are White (National Education Association, 2010), learning not only to understand but also to respect and appreciate the child's culture as it is reflected in his or her home will be important for understanding the child's behavior in the classroom and in communicating with parents (Tam & Heng, 2005). Good intentions or token attempts at cultural sensitivity, of course, will do little to provide an appropriate IEP for students with disabilities from culturally diverse backgrounds. The instructional materials that educators use and the methods that they employ while teaching must be responsive to the differing cultural backgrounds of their students.

Does this mean that a teacher with students from four different cultural backgrounds needs four different methods of teaching? The answer is both "no" and "yes." For the first answer, it is our view that systematic instruction benefits children from all cultural backgrounds. When students with disabilities must also adjust to a new or different culture or language, it is especially important for the teacher to plan individualized activities, convey expectations clearly, observe and record behavior precisely, and give the child specific, immediate feedback during instruction. When coupled with a respectful attitude, these procedures will increase the motivation and achievement of most students.

Good teachers must also be responsive to changes (or lack of change) in individual students' performance. It can also be argued that the effective teacher needs as many different ways of teaching as there are students in the classroom. Cultural diversity adds another dimension to the many individual characteristics students present each day. While the basic methods of systematic instruction apply to all learners, teachers who will be most effective in helping children with disabilities from culturally diverse backgrounds achieve success in school will be those who are sensitive to and respectful of their students' heritage and values.

Summary

The task of providing educational equality for students with markedly diverse skills is enormous. By embracing the challenge, U.S. schools have made a promise to exceptional students, to their parents, and to society. Progress has been made, but significant challenges must still be overcome if the promise is to be kept. The views of our society are changing and continue to be changed by people who believe that our past practice of excluding people with disabilities was primitive and unfair. As an institution, education reflects society's changing attitudes.

Common expressions of humanity and fair play dictate that all children are entitled to educational equality, but the history of exclusion and inequality for students with disabilities tells us that humanity and fair play have not driven a great deal of educational policy for children with disabilities in the absence of legislation or litigation. While much progress has been made in achieving educational equality for students with disabilities, much work remains to be done.

Educational equality for children with disabilities in the end must be assessed by the effects of the schooling those children receive. If educational equality means simply having access to curriculum and instruction in schools and classrooms attended by students without disabilities, it has largely been attained. But equal access alone does not guarantee equal outcomes. Special education must ultimately be judged by the degree to which it is effective in helping individuals with disabilities to acquire, maintain, and generalize skills that will appreciably improve their lives. New skills are needed to promote real participation and independence in the changing school, workplace, and community environments of the 21st century.

There is a limit to how much educational equality can be legislated. In many cases, it is possible to meet the letter but not necessarily the spirit of the law. Treating every student with a disability as a student first and as an individual with a disability second may be the most important factor in providing true educational equality. This approach does not diminish the student's exceptionality, but instead it might give us a more objective and positive perspective that allows us to see a disability as a set of special needs. Viewing exceptional students as individuals tells us a great deal about how to help them achieve the educational equality they deserve.

QUESTIONS AND ACTIVITIES

13.1 Why are both children who are learning disabled and those who are gifted considered exceptional?

13.2 In what ways are students with disabilities similar to and different from other students?

13.3 What are the advantages and disadvantages of labeling and classifying students with disabilities?

13.4 How did the civil rights movement influence the movement for educational equality for students with disabilities?

13.5 Analyze a school district/state "report card" to determine (a) how many students in the district/state receive special education services; (b) how many of these students are English language learners, bilingual, males, females, and/or students of color; and (c) how many students with disabilities receive some or all of their education in the regular classroom and the portion of the school day in which they are included in the regular classroom.

13.6 What is an IEP, and how can it benefit students with disabling conditions?

13.7 How does the concept of least restrictive environment influence alternative placements for students with disabilities?

13.8 Do you think all students with disabilities should be educated in regular classrooms? Why or why not?

13.9 Why are collaboration and teaming between special educators and general classroom teachers so critical to the quality of education experienced by children with disabilities?

13.10 In your view, what is the most critical challenge currently facing the education of exceptional students?

REFERENCES

Aiello, B. (1976, April 25). Up from the basement: A teacher's story. *New York Times.* Retrieved December 27, 2008, from http://www.nytimes.com.

Anastasiou, D., & Kauffman, J. M. (2010, September 24). Disability as a cultural difference: Implications for special education. *Remedial and Special Education, 33*(3), 139–149.

Anastasiou, D., & Kauffman, J. M. (2011). A social constructionist approach to disability: Implications for special education. *Exceptional Children, 77*, 367–384.

Anderson, N. B., & Shames, G. H. (2011). *Human communication disorders: An introduction* (8th ed.). Boston: Allyn & Bacon.

Banks, J. A. (2006). *Cultural diversity and education: Foundations, curriculum, and teaching* (5th ed.). Boston: Allyn & Bacon.

Bartlett, L. D., Etscheidt, S., & Weisentstein, G. R. (2007). *Special education law and practice in public schools* (2nd ed.). Upper Saddle River, NJ: Merrill/Prentice Hall.

Bateman, B. D., & Linden, M. L. (2006). *Better IEPs: How to develop legally correct and educationally useful programs* (4th ed.). Verona, WI: Attainment.

Becker, W. C., Engelmann, S., & Thomas, D. R. (1971). *Teaching: A course in applied psychology.* Chicago: Science Research.

Beirne-Smith, M., Patton, J. R., & Kim, S. (2006). *Mental retardation: An introduction to intellectual disability* (7th ed.). Upper Saddle River, NJ: Merrill/Prentice Hall.

Best, S. J., Heller, K. W., & Bigge, J. L., (2010). *Teaching individuals with physical or multiple disabilities* (6th ed.). Upper Saddle River, NJ: Merrill/Prentice Hall.

Browder, D. M., Ahlgrim-Delzell, L., Spooner, F., Mims, P. J., & Baker, J. N. (2009). Using time delay to teach literacy to students with severe developmental disabilities. *Exceptional Children, 75*, 343–364.

Brown v. Board of Education of Topeka. 347 U.S. 483 (1954).

Bushell, D., Jr., & Baer, D. M. (1994). Measurably superior instruction means close, continual contact with the relevant outcome data. Revolutionary! In R. Gardner III, D. M. Sainato, J. O. Cooper, T. E. Heron, W. L. Heward, J. Eshleman, & T. A. Grossi (Eds.), *Behavior analysis in education: Focus on measurably superior instruction* (pp. 3–10). Pacific Grove, CA: Brooks/Cole.

Carnine, D. (1997). Bridging the research to practice gap. *Exceptional Children, 63*, 513–521.

Cook, B. G., Tankersley, M., & Landrum, T. (2009). Determining evidence-based practices in special education. *Exceptional Children, 75*, 365–383.

Cook, R. E., Klein, M. D., Chen, D., & Tessier, A. (2012). *Adapting early childhood curricula for children with special needs* (8th ed.). Boston: Pearson.

Cortiella, C. (2006). *NCLB and IDEA: What parents of students with disabilities need to know and do.* Minneapolis: University of Minnesota National Center on Educational Outcomes.

Coyne, M. D., Kame'enui, E. J., & Carnine, D. W. (Eds.). (2011). *Effective teaching strategies that accommodate diverse learners* (4th ed.). Upper Saddle River, NJ: Merrill/Prentice Hall.

Deshler, D. D. (2005). *Intervention research and bridging the gap between research and practice.* ERIC Clearinghouse on Disabilities and Gifted Education. Retrieved June 25, 2007, from www.ldonline.org/article/5596.

De Valenzuela, J. S., Copeland, S. R., Qi, C. H., & Park, M. (2006). Examining educational equity: Revisiting the disproportionate representation of minority students in special education. *Exceptional Children, 72*, 425–441.

Ferguson, P. M., & Ferguson, D. L. (2011). The promise of adulthood. In M. E. Snell & E. Brown (Eds.), *Instruction of students with severe disabilities* (7th ed., pp. 612–641). Upper Saddle River, NJ: Merrill/Prentice Hall.

Finn, C. E., Rotherham, A. J., & Hokanson, C. R. (2001). *Rethinking special education for a new century.* Washington, DC: Thomas B. Fordham Foundation and the Progressive Policy Institute.

Flexer, R. W., Baer, R. M., Luft, P., & Simmons, T. J. (2008). *Transition planning for secondary students with disabilities* (3rd ed.). Upper Saddle River, NJ: Merrill/Prentice Hall.

Florian, L., Hollenweger, J., Simeonsson, R. J., Wedell, K., Riddell, S., Terzi, L., & Holland, A. (2006). Cross-cultural perspectives on the classification of children with disabilities. Part I: Issues in the classification of children with disabilities. *Journal of Special Education, 40*, 36–45.

Forness, S. R., Freeman, S. F. N., Paparella, T., Kauffman, J. M., & Walker, H. M. (2012). Special education implications of point and cumulative prevalence for children with emotional and behavioral disorders. *Journal of Emotional and Behavioral Disorders, 20*(1), 4–18.

Fuchs, D., & Fuchs, L. S. (1995). What's "special" about special education? *Phi Delta Kappan, 76*(7), 531–540.

Fuchs, D., Fuchs, L. S., & Stecker, P. M. (2010). The "blurring" of special education in a new continuum of general education placements. *Exceptional Children, 76*, 301–323.

Gallagher, D. J., Heshusius, L., Iano, R. P., & Skrtic, T. M. (2004). *Challenging orthodoxy in special education: Dissenting voices.* Denver, CO: Love.

Gersten, R. (2001). Sorting out the roles of research in the improvement of practice. *Learning Disabilities Research and Practice, 16*, 45–50.

Giangreco, M. F. (2007). *Absurdities and realities of special education: The complete digital set.* Minnetonka, MN: Peytral.

Gollnick, D. M., & Chinn, P. G. (2009). *Multicultural education in a pluralistic society* (8th ed.). Upper Saddle River, NJ: Merrill/Prentice Hall.

Greenwood, C. R., & Maheady, L. (1997). Measurable change in student performance: Forgotten standard in teacher preparation? *Teacher Education and Special Education, 20*, 265–275.

Grigal, M., Test, D. W., Beattie, J., & Wood, W. (1997). An evaluation of transition components of individualized education programs. *Exceptional Children, 63*, 357–372.

Guralnick, M. J. (2005). Early intervention for children with intellectual disabilities: Current knowledge and future prospects. *Journal of Applied Research in Intellectual Disabilities, 18*, 313–324.

Harry, B., & Klingner, J. (2007). Discarding the deficit model. *Educational Leadership, 64*(5), 16–21.

Heller, K. W., Forney, P. E., Alberto, P. A., Best, S. J., & Schwartzman, M. N. (2009). *Understanding physical, health, and multiple disabilities* (2nd ed.). Upper Saddle River, NJ: Merrill/Prentice Hall.

Heron, T. E., & Harris, K. C. (2001). *The educational consultant: Helping professionals, parents, and mainstreamed students* (4th ed.). Austin, TX: PRO-ED.

Heward, W. L. (2003). Ten faulty notions about teaching and learning that hinder the effectiveness of special education. *Journal of Special Education, 36*(4), 186–205.

Heward, W. L. (2013). *Exceptional children: An introduction to special education* (10th ed.). Upper Saddle River, NJ: Merrill/Prentice Hall.

Heward, W. L., & Dardig, J. C. (2001, Spring). What matters most in special education. *Education Connection, 41*–44.

Heward, W. L., & Silvestri, S. M. (2005). The neutralization of special education. In J. W. Jacobson, J. A. Mulick, & R. M. Foxx (Eds.), *Fads: Dubious and improbable treatments for developmental disabilities* (pp. 193–214). Hillsdale, NJ: Erlbaum.

Kalyanpur, M. (2008). The paradox of majority of underrepresentation in special education in India. *Journal of Special Education, 42,* 55–64.

Kauffman, J. M. (1999). How we prevent the prevention of emotional and behavioral disorders. *Exceptional Children, 65*, 448–468.

Kauffman, J. M., & Hallahan, D. P. (2005a). *Special education: What it is and why we need it.* Boston: Allyn & Bacon.

Kauffman, J. M., & Hallahan, D. P. (2005b). *The illusion of full inclusion: A comprehensive critique of a current special education bandwagon* (2nd ed.). Austin, TX: PRO-ED.

Kauffman, J. M., & Landrum, T. J. (2009). *Characteristics of emotional and behavioral disorders of children and youth* (9th ed.). Upper Saddle River, NJ: Merrill/Prentice Hall.

Keogh, B. K. (2005a). Revisiting classification and identification. *Learning Disability Quarterly, 28*, 115–118.

Keogh, B. K. (2005b). Revisiting classification and identification: Labeling. *Learning Disability Quarterly, 28*, 100–102.

Kliewer, C., Biklen, D., & Kasa-Hendrickson, C. (2006). Who may be literate? *American Education Research Journal, 43,* 163–192.

Kochhar-Bryant, C. A. (2008). *Collaboration and system coordination for students with special needs: From early childhood to the postsecondary years.* Upper Saddle River, NJ: Merrill/Prentice Hall.

LaVenture, S. (Ed.). (2007). *A parent's guide to special education for children with visual impairments.* New York: American Foundation for the Blind.

Lewis, T. J., Hudson, S., Richter, M., & Johnson, N. (2004). Scientifically supported practices in emotional and behavioral disorders: A proposed approach and brief review of current practices. *Behavioral Disorders, 29*, 247–259.

McLaughlin, M. J. (2010). Evolving interpretations of educational equity and students with disabilities. *Exceptional Children, 76*, 265–278.

McLaughlin, M. J., Dyson, A., Nagle, K., Thurlow, M., Rouse, M., Hardman, M., Norwich, B., Burke, P. J., & Perlin, M. (2006). Cross-cultural perspectives on the classification of children with disabilities. Part II: Implementing classification systems in schools. *Journal of Special Education, 40*, 46–58.

McLeskey, J., & Waldron, N. L. (2011). Educational programs for elementary students with learning disabilities: Can they be both effective and inclusive? *Learning Disabilities Research & Practice, 26*(1), 46–57.

Mercer, C. D., & Pullen, P. C. (2009). *Students with learning disabilities* (7th ed.). Upper Saddle River, NJ: Merrill/Prentice Hall.

Mitchell, D. (Ed.). (2004a). *Special educational needs and inclusive education: Major themes in education.* London and New York: Routledge/Falmer.

Mitchell, D. (Ed.). (2004b). *Contextualizing inclusive education: Evaluating old and new international paradigms.* London and New York: Routledge/Falmer.

Murdick, N., Gartin, B., & Crabtree, T. (2006). *Special education law* (2nd ed.). Upper Saddle River, NJ: Merrill/Prentice Hall.

National Education Association. (2010). *Status of the American public school teacher, 2005–2006.* Washington, DC: Author.

Newman, L., Wagner, M., Knokey, A.-M., Marder, C., Nagle, K., Shaver, D., Wei, X., with Cameto, R., Contreras, E., Ferguson, K., Greene, S., & Schwarting, M. (2011) . *The post-high school outcomes of young adults with disabilities up to 8 years after high school. A report from the National Longitudinal Transition Study-2 (NLTS2)* (NCSER 2011-3005). Menlo Park, CA: SRI International. Available at www.nlts2.org/reports/.

Pennsylvania Association for Retarded Children v. Commonwealth of Pennsylvania, 343 F., Supp. 279 (1972).

Reynolds, M. C. (1989). An historical perspective: The delivery of special education to mildly disabled and at-risk students. *Remedial and Special Education, 10*, 6–11.

Sandall, S., Hemmeter, L., McLean, M. E., & Smith, B. J. (Eds.). (2005). *DEC recommended practices: A comprehensive guide for practical application in early intervention/early childhood special education.* Longmont, CO: Sopris West.

Scheetz, N. A. (2012). *Deaf education in the 21st century: Topics and trends.* Boston: Allyn & Bacon.

Schwartz, I. S. (2005). Inclusion and applied behavior analysis: Mending fences and building bridges. In W. L. Heward, T. E. Heron, N. A. Neef, S. M. Peterson, D. M. Sainato, G. Cartledge, R. Gardner III, L. D. Peterson, S. B. Hersh, & J. C. Dardig (Eds.), *Focus on behavior analysis in education: Achievements, challenges, and opportunities* (pp. 239–251). Upper Saddle River, NJ: Merrill/Prentice Hall.

Shonkoff, J. P., & Meisels, S. J. (Eds.). (2000). *Handbook of early childhood intervention* (2nd ed.). New York: Cambridge University Press.

Simmons, D. C., Kame'enui, E. J., Coyne, M. D., Chard, D. J., & Hairrell, A. (2011). Effective strategies for teaching beginning reading. In M. D. Coyne, E. J. Kame'enui, & D. W. Carnine (Eds.), *Effective teaching strategies that accommodate diverse learners* (4th ed., pp. 51–84). Upper Saddle River, NJ: Pearson.

Sitlington, P. L., Neubert, D. A., & Clark, G. M. (2010). *Comprehensive transition education and services for students with disabilities* (5th ed.). Upper Saddle River, NJ: Pearson.

Smith, J. D., & Mitchell, A. L. (2001). Me? I'm not a drooler. I'm the assistant: Is it time to abandon mental retardation as a classification? *Mental Retardation, 39*(2), 144–46.

Smith, P. (1999). Drawing new maps: A radical cartography of developmental disabilities. *Review of Educational Research, 69*, 117–144.

Smith, S. W., & Brownell, M. T. (1995). Individualized education programs: From intent to acquiescence. *Focus on Exceptional Children, 28*(1), 1–12.

Smith, T. E. C., Polloway, E. A., Patton, J. M., & Dowdy, C. A. (2012). *Teaching students with special needs in inclusive settings* (6th ed.). Upper Saddle River, NJ: Merrill/Prentice Hall.

Snell, M. E., & Brown, F. (Eds.). (2011). *Instruction of students with severe disabilities* (7th ed.). Upper Saddle River, NJ: Merrill/Prentice-Hall.

Sugai, G. (1998). Postmodernism and emotional and behavioral disorders: Distraction or advancement? *Behavioral Disorders, 23*, 171–177.

Tam, K. Y. B., & Heng, M. A. (2005). A case involving culturally and linguistically diverse parents in prereferral intervention. *Intervention in School and Clinic, 40*, 222–230.

Taylor, S. J. (1988). Caught in the continuum: A critical analysis of the principle of least restrictive environment. *Journal of the Association for Persons with Severe Handicaps, 13*, 41–53.

Test, D. W., Aspel, N., & Everson, J. M. (2006). *Transition methods for youth with disabilities.* Upper Saddle River, NJ: Merrill/Prentice Hall.

Turnbull, H. R., Huerta, N. E., & Stowe, M. J., (2009). *What every teacher should know about the Individuals with Disabilities Act as amended in 2004* (2nd ed.). Boston: Pearson.

U.S. Department of Education. (2007). *Individuals with Disabilities Education Act (IDEA)* (Tables 1-19 and C-8). Washington, DC: Author. Available at http://www.ideadata.org/PartBdata.asp.

U.S. Department of Education. (2010). *Twenty-ninth annual report to Congress on the implementation of the Individuals with Disabilities Education Act* (Table 1-13). Washington, DC: Author.

U.S. Department of Education. (2011). *Individuals with Disabilities Education Act (IDEA) Data* (Table 1-3). Washington, DC: Author. Retrieved May 18, 2011, from https://www.ideadata.org/arc_toc11.asp#partbCC.

Utley, C. A., & Obiakor, F. E. (2001). Learning problems or learning disabilities of multicultural learners: Contemporary perspectives. In C. Utley & F. Obiakor (Eds.), *Special education, multicultural education, and school reform: Components of quality education for learners with mild disabilities* (pp. 90–117). Springfield, IL: Thomas.

Vaughn, S., Klingner, J., & Hughes, M. (2000). Sustainability of research-based practices. *Exceptional Children, 66*, 163–171.

Venn, J. J. (2007). *Assessing students with special needs* (4th ed.). Upper Saddle River, NJ: Merrill/Prentice Hall.

Waitoller, F. R., Artiles, A. J., & Cheney, D. A. (2010). The miner's canary: A review of overrepresentation research. *Journal of Special Education, 44*, 29–49.

Webber, J., & Scheuermann, B. (2008). *Educating students with autism: A quick start manual.* Austin, TX: PRO-ED.

Wiley, A., & Siperstein, G. (2011). Seeing red, feeling blue: The impact of state political leaning on state identification rates for emotional disturbance. *Behavioral Disorders, 36*(3), 195–207.

World Health Organization. (2011). *International classification of functioning, disability and health (ICF)*. Geneva, Switzerland: Author. Retrieved July 18, 2011, from http://www.who.int/classifications/icf/en/

Wright, P. W. D., & Wright, P. D. (2006). *Wrightslaw: Special education law* (2nd ed.). Hartfield, VA: Harbor House Law Press.

Yell, M. L. (2012). *The law and special education* (3rd ed.). Upper Saddle River, NJ: Merrill/Prentice-Hall.

Zigmond, N. (2006). Where should students with disabilities receive special education? Is one place better than another? In B. Cook & B. Shermer (Eds.), *What is special about special education?* (pp. 127–136). Austin, TX: PRO-ED.

Zigmond, N. (2007). Delivering special education is a two-person job: A call for unconventional thinking. In J. B. Crockett, M. M. Gerber, & T. J. Landrum (Eds.), *Radical reform of special education: Essays in honor of James M. Kauffman* (pp. 115–138). Mahwah, NJ: Erlbaum.

Masterfile Royalty-Free

School Inclusion and Multicultural Issues in Special Education

CHAPTER 14

Luanna H. Meyer, Jill M. Bevan-Brown, Hyun-Sook Park, and Catherine Savage

Special education emerged alongside the civil rights movement in the United States, representing the value of equality of educational opportunity for students who were being denied access to high-quality schooling to meet their learning needs. Throughout its history, special education has intersected with multicultural education in promoting pedagogical, curricular, and teacher education reforms that address increasingly diverse student school populations. The relationship between special and general education provides one measure of the extent to which public education is preparing students for their future adult roles. Special education represents the state's commitment to meeting diverse needs within the public school system. Yet its very existence has enabled general educators to maintain beliefs in a mythical mainstream, a "one-size-fits-all" approach to schools, classrooms, and pedagogy.

Across the United States, culturally and linguistically diverse (CLD) students drop out of school at high rates, receive disproportionate referrals for special education services, display lower achievement on standardized tests, incur harsh penalties, and experience high rates of exclusion for behavior in comparison to White students who speak English as their first language (Cartledge & Kourea, 2008; Donovan & Cross, 2002). Furthermore, negative beliefs about families of children from certain non-White cultural groups have been found to be pervasive (Harry & Klingner, 2006; Harry, Klingner, & Hart, 2005). Formal inquiries into the quality and quantity of educational services and supports generally afforded to CLD learners have documented extensive inequities in curricula, pedagogy, physical facilities, and resources persisting for more than 40 years (Ferri & Connor, 2005; Kozol, 1967; Rebell, 1999; Sleeter & Grant, 1987). Finally, multiple factors have resulted in there being a limited availability of educators and teachers who are skilled in teaching diverse student populations, including inadequate teacher preparation for diversity and teacher resistance to teaching in schools populated by CLD and low-income students. There is even an absence of teachers who are themselves CLD and might thus serve as positive role models for CLD children (Barton, 2003; Darling-Hammond, 2004; Peske & Haycock, 2006).

This chapter focuses on the intersections between special education, general education, and multicultural education. Despite the positive language about a special education service designed to better meet student needs, special education practices in action often provide a mechanism that enables mainstream educational systems to avoid accommodating diverse learners. Troubling patterns of disproportional identification by ethnicity and failures to engage in culturally responsive educational practices seem intractable, with little improvement evident despite decades of awareness of these issues. We argue that a new conceptualization for educating diverse learners is needed to shift from deficit theorizing applied to individuals (special education) and groups (race and social class). This chapter examines how special education has operated historically and summarizes contemporary visions for shifting from monocultural mainstream practices that no longer reflect reality to acknowledging culturally situated mainstreams. We describe how the relationship between schools and families can reflect culture and power sharing that help to meet children's needs. Next, we discuss how the preparation of teachers can develop cultural competence, skills in effective teaching practices, and care for students as culturally located individuals. Finally, we describe promising practices for inclusive classrooms based on evidence regarding pedagogies and curricula incorporating communal practices and individual supports that recognize interdependencies as well as independence in learning.

Special Education as Exclusion

Special education once occupied "the high ground of many contemporary educational debates" located at "the forefront of pedagogical innovation and judicial reform" (Richardson, 1994, p. 713). Following the passage of federal legislation in the 1970s guaranteeing a free and public education to children with disabilities, special education rose to the challenge of developing diverse instructional strategies and demonstrating meaningful learning even for children who had once been labeled "uneducable" (Horner, Meyer, & Fredericks, 1986). Special educators were the reformers, willing to address the complexities of children as they are rather than as they were supposed to be. This is the generous and idealistic interpretation of the history and purpose of special education.

Special Education and Segregation

Another less benign view of special education has also emerged. Dunn (1968) argued early on that special education had become the new, legally sanctioned segregation for children of color and others who were different at a time when racial segregation was otherwise illegal. His indictment of the disproportionate overrepresentation of African American and other minority groups in special classes included evidence that these classes were not so very special: Children in the special education segregated programs actually did less well academically than similar children who had remained in general education without special services. Dunn questioned whether special education was being manipulated to resegregate the United States through socially acceptable strategies that once again divided children by race.

Dunn focused his critique on the diagnosis of "mild mental retardation," which at the time accounted for the largest percentage of children labeled as having a disability. This diagnosis was always subjective and came under attack for unfairly disadvantaging children who were from non-White cultures, were living in poverty, or spoke English as a second language. These were the students disproportionately represented in this category (Mercer, 1973). The diagnosis of mental retardation became increasingly unpopular; by the 1980s, children with similar characteristics were more likely than in the past to be labeled as having learning disabilities and emotional/behavioral disorders. Nevertheless, the overall pattern of overrepresentation of ethnic and cultural minorities in special education had not changed. Children of color—particularly African Americans—continued to be overrepresented among those receiving services as students with mild to moderate disabilities throughout the 1980s and 1990s (Argulewicz, 1983; Finn, 1982; Oswald, Coutinho, Best, & Singh, 1999; Tucker, 1980; Webb-Johnson, 1999). Yet students who have CLD backgrounds continue to be labeled as having disabilities at significantly higher levels and labeled as gifted and talented at significantly lower levels in comparison to their representation in the general population. Skiba and colleagues (2008) present overwhelming evidence that "the racial disparities in special education service remain one of the key indicators of inequity in our nation's educational system" (p. 264).

Despite overt discussion of what appear to be new forms of discrimination and exclusion, patterns remain unchanged in the 21st century (Artiles, Trent, & Palmer, 2004; Hosp & Reschly, 2004; Skiba, Poloni-Staudinger, Simmons, Feggins-Azziz, & Chung, 2005). Low-income boys who are African American or Native American are those most likely to be diagnosed as having disabilities such as mental retardation and emotional disturbance, and they are least likely to be labeled as gifted and talented (Donovan & Cross, 2002). Artiles, Rueda, Salazar, and Higareda (2005) found that Hispanic and other students whose first language is not English are particularly overrepresented in special education in California districts with diverse school populations. Klingner, Artiles, and Barletta (2006) point out that a large percentage of American students are entering school speaking a language other than English as their first language; this figure is estimated to be 20 percent of the current school population and will increase to 40 percent by 2030. Most children learning English as a second language in the United States are Hispanic, but many speak other first languages, reflecting immigration and refugee status around the world (Klingner et al., 2006).

Furthermore, these disparities in referrals to special education cannot be attributed solely to differences in socioeconomic status—an early hypothesis that would situate the problem outside the responsibility of schools, educators, and the public education system as a whole (MacMillan & Reschly, 1998). This explanation has now largely been laid to rest by large-scale investigations of the interrelationships between race and poverty as factors influencing educational outcomes. Oswald and colleagues (1999) analyzed data from 4,500 U.S. school districts and reported that race contributed independently to placement in special education over and above the impact of socioeconomic status. Skiba and colleagues (2005) investigated this issue in depth in one state and found that poverty made a weak and inconsistent contribution to disproportionality, magnifying existing racial disparities. They concluded that where poverty had an impact, its "primary effect was to magnify existing racial disparity" (Skiba et al., 2008, p. 273). Furthermore, they reported that African American and Native American children were overrepresented in suspensions and expulsions from school.

It has now been more than 25 years since the National Research Council produced its first official report on this issue (Heller, Holtzman, & Messick, 1982) and another decade since its second report (Donovan & Cross, 2002). In 2004, the reauthorization of the Individuals with Disabilities Education Improvement Act (IDEIA) included a number of changes to reinforce the accountability of state and local education agencies for addressing the disproportional representation of CLD students by ethnic/racial groups across disability categories. Significant changes included an emphasis on early identification of at-risk CLD students in order to prevent inappropriate referrals to special education by requiring evidence of culturally responsive teaching and learning in the mainstream.

Strategies to Prevent Misdiagnosis and Disproportionality

Some schools have employed a pre-referral system that was first introduced in the 1970s and has evolved over time into a variety of models for intervening prior to attaching a formal special education label (Ortiz, 2002). The reauthorization of IDEIA in 2004 legitimized the response to intervention (RTI) model for early identification and intervention with at-risk students in general education classrooms prior to referral to special education services (Fuchs & Fuchs, 2006). RTI is a multilevel prevention system designed to maximize student achievement and reduce behavior problems by requiring schools to demonstrate that students are being provided with research-based practices in regular education. At each level of intervention for learning or behavior challenges, the teacher and/or educational team must document the student's responses to evidence-based strategies. Then the intensity and the nature of interventions are adjusted, depending on student responsiveness, before identifying students as having learning and other disabilities (Fuchs & Fuchs, 2006).

The most common model for CLD students is a three-level process. At-risk students are identified by applying a criterion set by the school (e.g., below the 25th percentile), usually through either high-stakes or other assessments identified by the school. Primary prevention, or Level 1, requires culturally responsive quality teaching using evidence-based strategies along with close monitoring of the at-risk students in the general education classroom. Progress monitoring involves evidence-based comparisons of student outcomes for the CLD student and a "true peer" with a similar level of language proficiency and cultural and experiential background, not comparisons with English-speaking students. If several true peers are also struggling, this is regarded as an indication that the instruction provided by the teacher is less than optimal for that group of CLD students (Brown & Doolittle, 2008). Minor instructional adjustments can be made to meet the unique needs of CLD students, and close monitoring is continued for targeted CLD students. Those who do not respond at Level 1 are provided secondary intervention in general education settings at Level 2, such as small-group tutoring after school. Level 2 interventions are supplemental to the general education curriculum and may be provided by either the general education teacher or specialist staff.

Children who do not respond to either primary- or secondary-level interventions are referred to Level 3 for more intensive intervention. Level 3 services include individualized instructional objectives based on student needs that may be delivered within the general education setting by either a special education teacher or related service provider. A three-level RTI model may allow automatic special education services to be provided while further assessments are conducted to determine eligibility for special education (Council for Exceptional Children, 2008; National Joint Committee on Learning Disabilities, 2011). Klingner and Edwards (2006) describe an alternative four-level model that formalizes an assessment process to qualify for additional special education services. These RTI models differ from historical practices in education in requiring evidence that teachers have created meaningful learning environments for CLD students that support them academically and socioemotionally through culturally responsive interventions before referrals to special education can be made (Xu & Drame, 2008).

The RTI is a promising approach to supporting the learning of CLD students in general education classrooms that would, in principle, reduce disproportional representation of CLD students in special education. Fuchs, Fuchs, and Stecker (2010) note that IDEIA as a special education entitlement was not intended to enable schools to abrogate responsibility for implementation of evidence-based interventions shown to be effective with a range of students in the regular classroom. Whenever schools identify at-risk students through high-stakes assessment and particular ethnic and cultural groups are overrepresented as being at risk, Level 1 intervention in the general classroom should focus on strategies that address the needs of overrepresented groups to prevent overreferrals to special education. For example, in a school district in California, the analysis of the state standardized test revealed that a Pacific Islander group consistently scored low. The school formed a study group to find potential explanations for such a prominent pattern and develop an action plan addressing the needs of this particular group in the classroom. Reexamining assessment practices can provide direction for resolving particular equity issues for different groups. Schools must also be sensitive to issues of underrepresentation when some groups may not be noticed due to ethnic stereotypes. For example, Asian American students are sometimes overlooked despite intervention needs because of the prevalent myth of the "Asian model minority" (Chiu & Ring, 1998; Florsheim, 1997; Palmer & Jang, 2005). In contrast to this myth, Asian immigrant youth experience different types of socioemotional and adaptive problems in schools, ranging from minor sociopsychological problems to more serious ones such as juvenile delinquency, gang involvement, and suicide (Chiu & Ring, 1998; Ha, Park, & Lee, 2008; Lee & Zhan, 1998; Yeh & Inose, 2002).

The Monoculture of Mainstream Education

RTI holds promise for refocusing on general education prior to referrals to special education, but this approach still requires that a child be failing prior to intervention and can rest on assumptions that it is the child alone who needs to change. Critics have increasingly called for shifting the focus from assumptions that patterns of disproportionality occur because of deficits in children—whether these are socioeconomic, linguistic, or developmental—and toward a reexamination of the culture of a mainstream public school system that marginalizes differences and reinforces existing disparities. Artiles and Bal (2008) are among those who challenge the present state of affairs and apparent inability or unwillingness to redress imbalances. They note that researchers, policy analysts, and educators continue to acknowledge and debate the issues, yet the imbalances persist. They theorize that the "problem of disproportionate representation" is symptomatic of the inability of public school systems to accommodate *difference.* They note the enduring assumption that the mainstream is somehow *not different,* and they critique the underlying premise that the person (e.g., a mainstream educationalist) "naming a difference does not have a cultural perspective" (Artiles & Bal, 2008, p. 5). They further state:

> *The issue is not that special education is bad for minority (and majority) students. Rather the challenges are greater: How are differences accounted for in systems of educational support for an increasingly diverse student population? . . . Culture indexed in schools' or communities' everyday practices is not considered. (p. 6)*

Unlike those who would argue that one reduces these inequities by fixing and enhancing flawed referrals, assessments, and attitudes, these authors are among those who maintain that it is the so-called mainstream that requires fixing and enhancing.

What is being increasingly emphasized is the failure of mainstream educators and systems to acknowledge that a monocultural perspective underpins and drives teacher education, approaches to pedagogy, curriculum design, classroom organization, school policy, home–school relationships, and even models of discipline in schools. This monocultural perspective is presumed to be so universal as to be invisible without acknowledgment that schools have been designed to suit a dominant culture that no longer represents all children or even most children and their families. This cultural mismatch exists not only in the United States but also in many other nations, such as Australia, New Zealand, Britain, Germany, and Spain (Artiles & Bal, 2008; Bishop & Berryman, 2006; Kozleski et al., 2008; Suárez-Orozco, 2001). The solution requires a major shift in mind-set: Schools are meant to add value to children's lives, not simply reestablish educational definitions for society's shortcomings. If schools cannot function without separating large numbers of children for "nonmainstream" services outside the general education classroom, we need to challenge the culture of the classroom as one that is not reflecting the culture of communities.

Harry and Klingner (2006) have called for increased attention and remediation, to be applied not to individual students or groups of students but to "school-based risk" as a major contributing factor to student failure, exclusion, and rerouting out of general education into special education services that segregate. Skiba and his colleagues (2008) conclude that disparities in special education by race and ethnicity should not be seen as solely a special education problem but be properly attributed to general education sources of inequity, including curriculum, classroom management, teacher quality, and resource distribution. The home–school relationship also contributes to the maintenance of inequities, as will be discussed in the next section.

Parent Participation and Working with Families

Parent participation on behalf of children from CLD groups is widely acknowledged as essential to effective special education services. IDEIA (2004) mandates parent–professional collaboration not only when individualized education plans (IEPs) and individualized family services plans (IFSPs) are being developed but also throughout the entire special education process (Salas, Lopez, Chinn, & Menchaca-Lopez, 2005; Turnbull, Turnbull, Erwin, & Soodak, 2005). The value of parent participation generally was also acknowledged in the Obama administration's Blueprint for Reform proposing increased funding to support programs that involve parents in schooling (Finkel, 2011). Research and practice show that such involvement is a win–win–win situation with positive academic, social, and emotional outcomes for children when parents are involved (Al-Shammari & Yawkey, 2008; Gargiulo, 2006; Howland, Anderson, Smiley, & Abbott, 2006). Parents also benefit through increased confidence, self-esteem, and understanding of the school and their child's education (Gomez & Greenough, 2002; Salas et al., 2005). Benefits for professionals include increased knowledge of the child, culture, and home circumstances; improved parent–professional relationships; and increased parental willingness to participate in school-related activities and to volunteer time (Gomez & Greenough, 2002; Salas et al., 2005).

Nevertheless, the involvement of CLD parents in their child's special education is significantly less than that of their majority-culture counterparts. These parents are reported to withdraw from or be passive in school-based planning and decision making, be less involved in IEP meetings and offer fewer suggestions, have limited knowledge of the special education services entitlements, and be underrepresented in traditional schooling activities (Geenen, Powers, Lopez-Vasquez, & Bersani, 2003; Kim & Morningstar, 2005; Salas et al., 2005). Limited involvement of CLD parents is reported across the age span from early intervention (Zhang & Bennett, 2003) to transition from school (Kim & Morningstar, 2005). Many school initiatives aimed at providing child- and family-centered services and increasing parental participation have resulted in conflict, distrust, confusion, and resentment: Parents find themselves confronting an educational system that purports to seek their involvement but is unyielding and uncompromising when responding to parent and community values (Callicott, 2003).

Causes of Limited Parental Involvement

Reasons for limited parental involvement in special education are multiple, complex, and interrelated. Although CLD parents face many of the same issues and struggles as do majority-group parents of children with special needs, these barriers are often experienced by CLD parents to a greater degree. Additionally, there are obstacles that are specific to members of CLD groups. Some reasons are personal: Parents may feel that they are not valued and respected by professionals, that they are blamed for their child's difficulties, and that their requests for information are ignored (Bevan-Brown, 2009; Zhang & Bennett, 2003; Zionts, Zionts, Harrison, & Bellinger, 2003). Parents also report being discouraged from involvement because of professionals' negative attitudes and treatment of their children:

> The principal at my child's school once stood over the secretary's desk in the front office and told me that my child was lazy, disrespectful, and dumb! And she did it right there in front of all the others who were walking around in the front office and in front of my kid. I can't believe that she is called a "professional" . . . a professional what?
>
> (quoted in Zionts et al., 2003, p. 45)

Mistrust of professionals was frequently reported, as was feeling disheartened by the ever-present focus on their child's weaknesses and labeling accompanied by low expectations (deFur, Todd-Allen, & Getzel, 2001; Geenen et al., 2003; Parette & Petch-Hogan, 2000). Parents were left feeling disenfranchised by ineffective home–school communication methods and a lack of knowledge about rights, entitlements, and special education policies, procedures, and services (deFur et al., 2001; Geenen et al., 2003). Parents also reported being uncomfortable in the school environment due to their own negative schooling experiences (Bevan-Brown, 2009).

There can be culturally based reasons for parental noninvolvement. Parents report being reluctant to engage with professionals because of majority-culture ethnocentrism, negative cultural stereotyping, insensitivity to cultural and religious beliefs and family traditions, a propensity to lump different ethnic groups (e.g., all Polynesians) together, and discriminatory practices. In the study by Zionts and colleagues (2003), for example, several African American parents "believed that their children would not have been judged as severely or held to the same expectations if they had been Caucasian" (p. 47). Cultural deficit thinking can be reflected in undervaluing or ignoring children's ethnicity altogether (Bevan-Brown, 2003, 2009; Bourke et al., 2002; Murtadha-Watts & Stoughton, 2004). It has also been considered justifiable to ignore children's home language and culture based on professional views that these are liabilities in the learning process (Chavez-Reyes, 2010). Salas and colleagues (2005) maintain that the tendency to problematize diversity instead of seeing it as a value contributes to "an eradication of the parent-special education teacher partnership" (p. 52).

Arguably, however, the greatest cause of parental noninvolvement relates to professionals' limited knowledge of diverse cultures and their failure to understand how their own cultural beliefs and attitudes influence their teaching and services. Differing cultural concepts, values, and practices relating to disability provide fertile ground for cultural conflict and misinterpretation. Parents' reluctance to participate in their child's special education is understandable if they do not believe the child has a special need. For example, Harry and Artiles (2007) note that majority-culture perspectives may regard conditions differing significantly from the norm to be signs of pathology to be treated by scientific and educational methods. However, many CLD families "may interpret a physical condition as a sign of a spiritual condition or may disagree that a child's difficulties in learning are important enough to be labeled as a disability" (p. 34). Similarly, Zionts and colleagues (2003) note that culture-based behaviors that vary from teachers' perceptions of what is "normal" can be misinterpreted, resulting in children being mislabeled as possessing behavioral or learning problems. These varying conceptions and interpretations of disability may result in professionals concluding that parents are "in denial" when they question their child's labels or when they choose not to become involved in their education.

Another area of conflict relates to the values that underpin many special education programs, interventions, and professional orientations. In their study of transition, Kim and Morningstar (2005) noted that policies and practices were dominated by Western, middle-class values of independence, autonomy, and physical and emotional separation from parents. These values conflicted with ethnic-minority values of interdependence, family orientation, and extended family support, particularly in many Native American and Hispanic families. Parents from more collectivist cultures will be less likely to support IEP goals and programs that emphasize individualization and independence from the family.

Differing cultural communication styles and expectations about involvement in their child's education can contribute to parent–professional conflict. The nature and extent of parental participation in special education reflects majority-culture norms and ways of operating, which often assume that all parents understand participation requirements and are comfortable interacting as expected by professionals. Some parents believe that intervention activities are the responsibility of teachers and other professionals (Huer, Parette, & Saenz, 2001). This may be related to beliefs that professionals are the "experts" and that it is disrespectful for parents to interfere. Even when they disagree with professionals' opinions and recommendations, parents may refrain from speaking out because it would be culturally inappropriate to question those decisions. Salas and colleagues (2005) write, "Many parents may not believe that their participation is essential and that they should not interfere with professionals such as teachers, and as a result remove themselves from that process" (p. 55).

A final cluster of cultural reasons for parental noninvolvement is evidenced by recently immigrated families and those with limited English proficiency. Parental involvement is severely curtailed when professionals do not speak their language and all documentation, resources, and communications are in English. Hispanic parents, for example, reported that the lack of bilingual communication concerning their child's education was a major barrier to their participation (Kim & Morningstar, 2005). Because of an acute shortage of CLD professionals in special education, parents frequently find themselves the only minority person attending their child's IEP meetings.

Finally, there are contextual reasons for parental noninvolvement relating to poverty and its by-products (Zionts et al., 2003). The costs involved in accessing services and attending meetings is prohibitive for some parents who lack transportation and child-care support. Other barriers include unfriendly or intimidating meeting and service venues; heavy work commitments; fatigue; conflicting family responsibilities; lack of resources; poor health care; and inconvenient, inflexible scheduling of services and meetings (deFur et al., 2001; Geenen et al., 2003; Zionts et al., 2003).

A Mismatch: Special Education and Families

The lack of culturally responsive service models, programs, and processes is a deterrent to parental participation. While there are good intentions behind IDEIA's requirements for parental involvement, its due process model reflects majority-culture values and processes in an IEP process based on Anglo legal traditions. Planning and assessment structures, communication methods, formal IEP meetings that cast parents in a passive role, exclusionary professional jargon and documentation, and the requirements for signatures all contribute to alienating CLD parents. Additionally, as Zionts and colleagues (2003) point out, a legally based system has the potential to turn the people involved into rivals. Assessment is completed and an intervention plan is formulated for many children prior to consultation with their parents, who are then expected to agree with the plan or be considered adversarial (Murtadha-Watts & Stoughton, 2004).

Furthermore, the IEP process is time consuming and work intensive. The sheer volume of paperwork produced can be confusing, overwhelming, and intimidating to parents, particularly those with limited English proficiency. It may also contribute to professional impatience that "can translate to parents as a lack of desire to include them in the process" (Murtadha-Watta & Stoughton, 2004, p. 7). This is further exacerbated by tightly scheduled meetings, in which strict adherence to an agenda leaves little time for the lengthy personal interaction and relationship building that typifies the communication style of some ethnic-minority cultures. When working with ethnic and cultural groups with origins in the Pacific region and with immigrant groups from many other countries, it is essential that professionals take the time to get to know the family before launching into program planning (Bevan-Brown, 2009).

Salas and colleagues (2005) make the point that although U.S. law mandates parental involvement,

> *Most districts have discretion over deciding what role they want parents to play, what programs are offered to parents, and what kind of partnership teachers want to have with parents. Unfortunately, when schools and teachers are the primary decision makers concerning the kinds of partnerships they want to have with parents, parents can never be truly empowered. (p. 53)*

Parents are further disempowered by the medical model that underpins the special education system. This model positions professionals as experts, devalues parental knowledge and cultural capital, and locates learning and behavioral problems within the child and family (Murtadha-Watts & Stoughton, 2004). Such circumstances act as disincentives to parental involvement.

Strategies to Increase Parental Participation

The special education literature contains a variety of strategies and programs aimed at increasing parental participation and improving home–school communication. These range from minor amendments to IEP processes to large-scale home–school–community initiatives. In respect to the former, suggestions include inviting parents to bring extended family, siblings, or community members to support them at IEP meetings; holding meetings in culturally appropriate, family-friendly venues; providing bilingual documentation and translators or asking parents to nominate a suitable person to translate for them; making meetings more informal; allowing time for small talk; including food; providing transportation and child-care facilities; having flexible meeting time schedules; and recording meetings for absent members for later consideration.

Strategies requiring more input and commitment include involving parents from the outset of the IEP process and including them in all decision making; employing CLD paraprofessionals or community-based workers to act as communicators, mediators, and advocates; having translators or cultural advisors work in partnership with professionals; utilizing telephone interpreter services; establishing family/community advisory councils or consultative committees from which both parents and professionals can seek help and advice or present issues; making school culturally relevant and welcoming to parents by celebrating important cultural days and festivals; and utilizing person-centered planning with its emphasis on family input into intervention plans based on parents' priorities and perceptions rather than those of the professionals (Bevan-Brown, 2003; Callicott, 2003).

School-based initiatives in North America that facilitate parental participation include Zigler's Schools for the 21st Century, James Comer's school–community approach, and full-service schools (Pelletier & Corter, 2005). In these models, the school is the hub of community activity and the location of a range of services including medical, recreational, budgeting, child-care, and preschool services; parent support groups; and language and literacy learning centers. The Toronto First Duty (TFD) project integrates early childhood care, education, and community services for CLD families. The model used was thought to be particularly suited to CLD families because it removed the need for them to locate scattered services, a task requiring "sophisticated knowledge of the system and its language" (Pelletier & Corter, 2005, p. 36). Findings from the TFD project revealed that CLD parents' attendance at school events increased significantly and that large numbers of diverse parents who had participated in the project were on various school councils. Corter, Patel, Pelletier, and Bertrand (2008) maintain that the evidence supports the positive impact of service integration on quality of family life as well as parental participation.

Preparation of Professionals for Partnerships with Parents

There is a strong call from both parents and professionals for improved pre-service, graduate, and in-service training to help professionals develop the cultural competence needed to work effectively with CLD parents and families (Bourke et al., 2002; Hains et al., 2005; Lam, 2005; Zionts et al., 2003). Bevan-Brown (2009) recommends that teacher education should include (1) an examination of the teacher's own culture, biases, and underlying assumptions, as well as the influence these have on one's teaching; (2) an investigation of how the majority culture influences a national education system and the effect this has on CLD children; and (3) a study of minority cultures and how cultural knowledge can be incorporated into all aspects of the school curriculum.

Even where there is wide acceptance of the importance of parent–teacher partnerships in enhancing student outcomes, teachers do not receive training in how to work collaboratively with parents (Curran & Murray, 2008). Parents in the Zionts and colleagues (2003) study suggested that professional training should include empathetic communication, advocacy, and input from parents who had "already been through the system" (p. 48). They also recommended that teachers spend time in the neighborhoods and homes of their pupils to increase their understanding of the challenges families face. This recommendation is reflected in the Diverse Urban Interdisciplinary Teams project at the University of Wisconsin. Students are assigned to families of young children with disabilities from cultures different from their own. They spend time with the family at home and accompany them on shopping trips, on visits to the park, or to special events such as family birthday parties three times during a 15-week semester (Hains et al., 2005). Valadez and Moineau (2010) describe a similar program at California State University, San Marcos, in which pre-service teacher education students design and deliver a series of culturally appropriate science activities to parents at an ESL Family Science Workshop. Graduates of this program showed increased confidence in working with Hispanic families and a commitment to involving parents in their child's education.

Preparation of Parents for Partnerships with Educators

Parent-to-parent programs play an important role in connecting parents from similar ethnic backgrounds, emphasizing and valuing strengths of CLD families, and "teaching new ways for parents to use their strengths to overcome obstacles. Parent support programs with these characteristics have been shown to increase self-esteem and provide the skills for dealing with professionals" (Kim & Morningstar, 2005, p. 100). These programs are especially beneficial for new immigrants and others who do not have a wide circle of support. Skills to assist parental participation can also be gained through targeted training sessions. Parents have identified the need for instruction in parenting and advocacy skills, information and strategies specific to their child's disability, special education laws and services available, and ways to find assistance and support and including other family members (Zionts et al., 2003).

The need for ongoing research into effective means of increasing parental participation is critical. Investigation must move beyond measures of parental satisfaction and extent of involvement to focus on significant outcomes. What type of parental involvement leads to improved outcomes for CLD families and children with special needs? Similarly, research is required to determine what types of professional and parental training will be most effective in developing the skills and attitudes needed for these two groups to work in partnership for the benefit of all concerned.

Culturally Competent Teachers and Inclusive Pedagogies

Teachers need to become culturally competent if they are to deliver culturally responsive, evidence-based, high-quality teaching for students with disabilities (Cartledge & Kourea, 2008; Goldenberg, 2008), including (1) creating a nurturing classroom that honors and incorporates the cultural and linguistic heritages of all student members; (2) making connections with students as individuals and understanding how context influences their interactions with others; (3) providing structured communal learning opportunities that enhance and expand the more traditional individualistic and teacher-directed approaches characteristic of mainstream schools; (4) developing learning skills through dynamic teaching utilizing explicit, intensive, and systematic instructional techniques combined with brisk pacing, ample academic responding opportunities, and positive and corrective feedback; (5) utilizing peer-mediated and peer-mentoring activities; (6) monitoring at-risk students frequently while maintaining high expectations and affirming learning for all students; and (7) providing English language and bilingual support services as needed by children for whom English is a second language or one of several languages that may be spoken by immigrant families. A tremendous gap remains between the evidence-based strategies described in the literature and those available and actually being implemented in teacher education and classrooms. Teachers may not have access to evidence-based strategies that are effective for diverse student populations either at pre-service or in-service levels.

Preintervention Culturally Responsive Teaching

Beginning teacher education programs and effective professional development should equip teachers with culturally responsive, evidence-based strategies (Klingner & Edwards, 2006; Trent, Kea, & Oh, 2008). Teachers may need access to ongoing professional development and support to implement such strategies skillfully in their classrooms with diverse learners, who will be different each year. The Te Kotahitanga professional learning program in Aotearoa, New Zealand, is focused on preparing general education teachers to teach Maori students—the indigenous population of New Zealand—who attend mainstream schools. To date, the program has been implemented in dozens of secondary schools across the country to provide professional facilitation support to teachers in the classroom (Bishop, Berryman, Cavanagh, & Teddy, 2007). The facilitators are expert, consultant teachers who carry out systematic observation and feedback sessions with their teacher colleagues. They also organize co-construction meetings with teacher teams working together to set priorities and implement practices that will better meet the educational aspirations of Maori children in mainstream classrooms. This program has been independently evaluated, and the findings support its effectiveness in changing teacher pedagogical practice as well as having a positive impact on students (Sleeter, 2011).

Table 14.1 illustrates key features of the effective teaching profile (ETP) reflected in Te Kotahitanga to prepare secondary teachers to engage in culturally responsive teaching (Bishop & Berryman, 2006). The two underpinning understandings and the six relationships and interactions included in this model do not isolate delivery of culturally responsive pedagogies from good teaching. Instead, the ETP incorporates evidence-based practice for effective teaching and learning with caring for students as culturally situated individuals. Individual teachers can utilize this model to identify their own opportunities to become culturally responsive on a day-to-day basis rather than waiting for their schools or districts to provide them culturally responsive curricula or specific instructions regarding what to do for particular cultural groups.

The ETP is based on two major teacher understandings: (1) rejection of deficit theorizing as an explanation for student failure, and (2) teachers taking agency for enhancing student success. Teachers can use a self-monitoring framework such as the ETP to reflect on their own teaching and alter their practices with CLD students as needed. Other user-friendly tools also support teachers

Table 14.1   The Effective Teaching Profile (ETP)

Relationships and Interactions	Definition	Examples of Teacher Behavior
1. Caring for students as culturally located individuals	The teacher acknowledges students' cultural identities and allows students to "be themselves" through learning interactions that are nurturing and show respect for students' language and culture.	• Incorporates terms in teacher presentations from students' first language/s • Correctly pronounces students' names • References cultural constructs and community activities
2. Caring about student performance	The teacher has high expectations for student learning and participation in classroom learning activities.	• Reinforces that all students can be effective learners • Gives all students positive and corrective feedback on how to improve • Encourages goal setting and praises effective learning behavior, including scaffolding: "You can do this: I'll help"
3. Managing the class to promote learning	The teacher has classroom management and curricular flexibility skills reflecting both individual and collective roles and responsibilities to achieve positive student outcomes.	• Has in place a classwide management system that creates a caring learning community (e.g., Tribes) • Redirects off-task or disruptive behavior in an effective, nonconfrontational way and is a "warm demander"* • After learning activity is introduced, engages personally with individual and small groups of students

(continued)

Table 14.1   *(continued)*

Relationships and Interactions	Definition	Examples of Teacher Behavior
4. Interacting with students discursively and co-constructing knowledge	The teacher promotes student dialogue and debate to share new knowledge and encourage problem solving and higher-order thinking.	• Incorporates co-operative learning principles and practices in group work • Promotes student-to-student problem solving rather than primarily teacher-directed knowledge • Solicits students' local stories, community experiences, and prior knowledge to develop new knowledge
5. Using a range of strategies for teaching and learning activities	The teacher uses different instructional strategies that involve teachers' and students' learning through interactions with one another.	• Facilitates student-led inquiry (e.g., students formulate questions rather than answer teacher questions) • Uses concept maps, think-pair-share, numbered heads together, jigsaw, and role-playing • Links new knowledge and concepts with students' lives.
6. Promoting educational aspirations within culturally responsive contexts	The teacher makes learning objectives and outcomes explicit and empowers students to make educational decisions within culturally meaningful contexts.	• Develops understandings of learning outcomes and engages students in promoting, monitoring, and reflecting on how outcomes lead to future goals • Engages students in critical examination of how knowledge reflects cultural perspectives and values • Encourages students to reflect on strengths and weaknesses as part of the assessment process, including peer assessments that encourage and develop peer support networks

*For a description of "warm demander" pedagogy for diverse learners, see F. Ware (2006). Warm demander pedagogy: Culturally responsive teaching that supports a culture of achievement for African American students. *Urban Education, 41*(4), 427–456.

Source: Adapted from R. Bishop, M. Berryman, T. Cavanagh, & L. Teddy (2007). *Te kotahitanga. Phase 3, Whānaungatanga: Establishing a culturally responsive pedagogy of relations in mainstream secondary school classrooms.* Wellington, New Zealand: Ministry of Education and Waikato University. This illustrates how teachers can ensure that their teaching is culturally responsive to diversity. Note that the ETP is also based on two major teacher understandings: (1) rejection of deficit theorizing as explanation for student failure, and (2) knowledge and commitment to enhance student success.

in this way. One is Bevan-Brown's (2003) *cultural self-review*, a reflective process that enables teachers to evaluate their own practice and compare it to concrete teacher and student behaviors. This comparison will enable them to set priorities for acquiring new skills and understandings.

Culturally Responsive Interventions

Once a student labeled CLD has been referred for special education and other interventions, culturally responsive teaching diminishes further: The myth that "culture doesn't matter" becomes even more prevalent as students' disability identities take precedence. There is also a basic contradiction inherent in special education services that emphasize individualization of instruction at the expense of a child's other identities, including gender, age, language, and culture.

One could argue that key principles in special education are culturally biased; for example, self-determination and independent living have been regarded as ultimate goals in North America for virtually all students with disabilities. These are outcomes of value to Anglo European cultural groups. However, CLD students from Native American, Asian, Polynesian, Hispanic, and other cultural backgrounds may value the harmony of the family and group over self-determination on certain issues, such as favoring interdependence over independence. Instructional practices in special education have similarly favored adult-guided models, including one-to-one teaching with a child as the most intensive form of systematic instruction.

For more than two decades, systematic instruction based on applied behavior analysis principles has been the backbone of successful teaching for students with disabilities. At the same time, multiculturalists in special education have advocated culturally responsive teaching as essential to bridging the gap between home and school cultures for CLD students (Erickson & Mohatt, 1982; Ladson-Billings, 2007). The general education classroom assumes that students can learn in a large group, but this learning is not interdependent as much as it is teacher-led, with relatively inflexible expectations for group compliance, not scaffolding of learning. There have been attempts to incorporate culturally responsive practices into special education intervention, but this literature largely focuses on the home–school relationship rather than illustrating concrete practices for use by teachers (Harry, 2008; for exceptions, see Cartledge & Kourea, 2008; Goldenberg, 2008).

In contrast to both the large-group-focused general education classrooms and the intensive and individualized approaches characterizing special education, a third generation of inclusive communal and collaborative practices could provide an alternative that would empower mainstream classrooms as well as reduce referrals to special education. Clearly, such classrooms would be more responsive in reflecting collectivist cultural values such as belonging and caring for the community rather than only or even primarily individual achievement. Samoan, Maori, other Pacific Island, Asian, African American, and Native American students may be more likely to engage in school activities and enjoy learning in group activities and through peer-to-peer interactions. More work is needed on *systematic* instruction designed for interdependent student groups to guide and support one another. The integration of best practices in special education and in multicultural education is the greatest challenge facing educators.

It will not be a simple matter for teachers to provide culturally responsive assessment and instruction of CLD students. Teachers will need to acquire expanded skills so that they can incorporate visual holistic thinking skills alongside verbal analytic thinking skills for different students. They will need to create opportunities for group rewards rather than continuing to rely exclusively on individual reinforcement and recognition. Because students' learning takes place in sociocultural contexts, educators must learn to collaborate more with families and school communities toward making education more meaningful and relevant to students' cultural identities.

Culturally Situated Schooling and Inclusive Pedagogies

The advancement of quality inclusive schooling began in the 1980s with the integration of students with special needs from segregated special schools into their neighborhood schools and classrooms. Unlike *mainstreaming,* which is a term describing placement in general education classrooms without special education supports, *inclusion* entails providing additional services to students in regular classrooms. Ultimately, all students—regardless of the extent of their educational needs—should be fully included and learn alongside their peers, thus "eliminating exclusionary processes from education that are a consequence of attitudes and responses to diversity in race, social class, ethnicity, religion, gender and attainment" (Vitello & Mithaug, 1998, p. 147). Booth and Ainscow (2000) describe several critical components of inclusion: (1) the presence of all students in the general education classroom without the use of withdrawal classes or other forms of integrated segregation such as ability grouping, (2) student participation in which each student can engage in meaningful educational experiences, (3) acceptance of students with special needs as full members of the classroom by teachers and peers, and (4) achievement within expectations of more academic progress, better social skills, and enhanced emotional adjustment. Descriptions such as these encourage teachers to take an active role to ensure that students are included in the learning and teaching activities of the classroom rather than assuming that inclusion happens through physical proximity alone.

Quality Inclusive Schools

Expecting our schools to accommodate all children in the general education classroom is imperative if we are to create multicultural schools to replace monocultural ones that exclude and separate children into groups of those who belong and those who do not. Inclusion therefore requires emphasis on any learners who are at risk of marginalization, exclusion, or underachievement (Harry, 2008). Inclusion requires a fundamental shift from attributing educational failure to children's characteristics toward analyzing barriers to participation and learning that are blocking student opportunity in school (Ainscow, 2007). Ultimately, the goal is to transform the mainstream in ways that increase the ability to respond to all learners (Meyer, 1997). In inclusive educational settings, special education is reframed as additional services and supports that enhance instruction, not as a different curriculum for learners identified as having disabilities and deficits. In inclusive classrooms, differences are seen as natural and expected, and the purpose of education is not to eliminate differences but to respond to diversity in ways that enhance all students' growth and development.

Inclusive schools actively challenge discrimination, create welcoming communities where everyone belongs, and value diversity (United Nations Educational, Scientific and Cultural Organization, 1994). There is an extensive international literature that describes the essential features of quality inclusive schools, including a shared vision across the school community, teachers who assume responsibility for creating authentic learning communities in the classroom, and ongoing evaluation in order to address problems as they arise (Avramidis, Bayliss, & Burden, 2000; Clarke, Dyson, Millward, & Robson, 1999; Meyer, 1997; Sapon-Shevin, 2004).

Delivery of Special Education in the Context of General Education

Inclusive schools deliver special education services designed to meet the needs of individual students in the classroom context, with meaningful participation being seen as central to learning. Students need interactions with other students and will learn through participation—from their context, their community, and the relationships they develop with others (Meyer, Park, Grenot-Scheyer, Schwartz, & Harry, 1998). Research on teacher professional development reveals that teachers who master culturally responsive pedagogies demonstrate discursive and diverse approaches to teaching and learning associated with high student participation and positive behavior management (Savage et al., 2011; Sleeter, 2011). Furthermore, inclusive strategies and techniques that are effective with students with disabilities have been found to increase the performance of students who are low achievers, average achievers, and gifted (Baker, Gersten, & Scanlon, 2002; Montague & Applegate, 2000; Palincsar, Magnusson, Collins, & Cutter, 2001). Recent syntheses of the research on reading instruction in inclusive settings reveals that techniques such as cooperative learning and peer-mediated instruction can result in substantial gains for students with and without disabilities (Doveston & Keenaghan, 2006; Schmidt, Rozendal, & Greenman, 2002). Strategies such as peer-mediated instruction and classwide peer tutoring require students to switch roles as tutor/student. These strategies individualize instruction and provide opportunities for all students to be actively engaged in mastering new content (Greenwood, Arreaga-Mayer, Utley, Gavin, & Terry, 2001).

These techniques are part of what has been termed *universal design for learning* (*UDL*) in developing strategies that are responsive to a wide range of students in heterogeneous classrooms (Cawley, Foley, & Miller, 2003; King-Sears, 2001; Rose & Meyer, 2000). King-Sears (2008) succinctly summarizes three categories of UDL techniques: (1) *Representation*—new content is demonstrated and presented in auditory, visual, and/or tactile ways. Direct instruction of new and complex material incorporates strategic processes and problem solving. (2) *Engagement*—students practice independently or in cooperative learning groups through a variety of activities and opportunities to acquire proficiency with new content. Feedback to students is delivered in ways that promote student self-evaluation and learning how to learn independently. Teachers monitor performance and make instructional changes based on evidence of learning. (3) *Expression*—students are allowed choices to show what they know about new content, with an emphasis on relevance and real-life examples that are meaningful and motivating. For example, the teacher may allow students to demonstrate mastery of new material through projects that can be done individually, in pairs, or in small groups and that may vary in format, such as giving a presentation or designing a three-dimensional display.

These UDL techniques not only promote social interaction, cooperation, and learning from difference within the classroom but also create a context in which children can develop positive social relationships. Meyer and her colleagues (1998) describe the range of possible social relationships in children's lives that can be influenced by educational practices and the organization of schooling. Their work highlights the importance of attention to the implementation of inclusive schooling, which is much more than the physical presence of students with disabilities in the classroom or even the provision of special education services within the general education environment. They found that when teachers communicated through actions and words that did not fully include children with disabilities, children mirrored those social patterns in their peer interactions. Thus, when teachers emphasized "helping" students with disabilities rather than working together, children without disabilities were most likely to either ignore peers with disabilities or treat them "specially," much as one would interact with very young children or even playthings (Evans, Salisbury, Palombaro, Berryman, & Hollowood, 1992). When classroom practices supported full participation in the range of academic and social activities occurring in school, students with even the most severe disabilities experienced social lives that included both group membership and friendships with classmates (Meyer et al., 1998; Schnorr, 1997).

Inclusive Schools and Teacher Education

In a study examining teachers' attitudes toward including children with special needs, Berry (2008) reported that teachers who are positive about inclusion are less apprehensive about whether they will be seen as fair if they accommodate different student needs than are teachers with negative attitudes about inclusion. Teachers who are positive about inclusion believe that students with disabilities belong in their classrooms; they have confidence in their ability to teach students with disabilities and employ teaching strategies that they believe to be effective. Berry maintained that teacher education programs should have the major responsibility for helping teachers to develop the attitudes and dispositions necessary for teaching in inclusive contexts.

King-Sears (2008) argues that these positive attitudes must also be supported by deliberate instructional actions based on well-developed lesson planning. Spooner, Baker, Harris, Ahlgrim-Delzell, and Browder (2007) found that teachers in graduate courses who received a brief introduction to UDL designed lesson plans accessible to diverse students, whereas the control group of teachers who received no UDL instruction designed lesson plans with fewer modifications, alternatives for communication, and activities that involved students. Clearly, teachers working in inclusive schools must possess the beliefs, attitudes, skills, and dispositions that will enable them to be confident, effective teachers with the skills to design and implement inclusive strategic programs that increase opportunities for all students to learn.

Managing Inclusive Classrooms

As noted earlier, children from nondominant cultures in many Western nations continue to be overrepresented among those diagnosed as having behavior disorders and emotional disturbance. Furthermore, children of color are those most likely to be suspended and expelled for behavior considered unacceptable by schools. Monocultural classroom management practices have evolved over many decades in schools and become embedded as cultural rituals in classrooms (Nuthall, 2005). Furthermore, teachers who may themselves be culturally different from their students make decisions regarding behavior based on their own cultural expectations, interactions, and interpretations (Kyles & Olafson, 2008; Levitt, 2001). If schools are to be inclusive, teachers need to acquire cultural competence and skills for culturally responsive practices that are appropriate for today's diverse student population (Cartledge, Singh, & Gibson, 2008).

Even when teachers adopt culturally responsive practices in their classrooms, the wider school may impose policies and practices that marginalize CLD students because they reflect dominant cultural perspectives on behavior that advantage students from that cultural background and effectively discriminate against others. Weinstein, Curran, and Tomlinson-Clarke (2003) discuss how the structure and practices of schools—such as uneven distribution of resources, culturally biased testing, and ability grouping—continue to privilege select groups while disadvantaging others through low expectations, stigmatization, and even segregation. Wherever certain student groups are overrepresented in statistics for suspensions and expulsions, school leaders need to be challenged to examine the school's norms and values.

The ethos of the school should not represent the institutionalization of societal discrimination patterns but should instead support a context for redressing social inequities and injustice—something public schooling was meant to do. Current behavior management approaches favor systematic implementation of an overall framework that has been agreed upon and is transparent across the school regarding expectations and consequences (Sugai et al., 2005). Internationally, the restorative practices model has been shown to be highly effective as a schoolwide commitment to shifting the emphasis from punishment and retribution to processes for restoration and making amends (Kane et al., 2009). Restorative practices approaches are particularly well suited for responding to the values of diverse cultures, including those of indigenous and other nondominant cultural groups within mainstream settings (Meyer & Evans, 2012).

Diversity and Caring Communities: Outcomes for the Social Good

For more than three decades, a growing number of international scholars have argued for and presented evidence supporting the provision of quality special education services within school communities. With the introduction of IDEIA in 2004 and widespread acceptance of society's responsibility to educate all children, advocacy and research have together progressed toward the development of schools for all children (Ainscow, 2007). Inclusive education is not the sole domain of special education but instead represents a social movement opposing educational exclusion (Slee & Allan, 2005).

The existence and perpetuation of the separation and segregation of students with disabilities inevitably generates (and reflects) several unintended but nonetheless very real negative outcomes.

1. *Efforts to structure general classrooms into homogeneous groups of students with similar learning needs will fail both the children and the educational system.* Systems that allow narrowing of commitment and capacity to serve diverse needs, that expect children to fit curricula rather than adapting schooling to meet children's needs, and that institutionalize identification of differences through tracking and segregation—whether by ability or race—legitimize intolerance of differences and tell children that they do not belong. Such

practices are dysfunctional as proportionately higher numbers of culturally and linguistically diverse students and their families join our school communities. Removing children with special needs from the mainstream turns disabilities into handicaps and drains valuable resources and expertise from general education. As long as the myth persists that general education classrooms cannot accommodate needs outside a hypothetical norm, the inevitable result will be a closed cycle of increasing referrals that continue to exceed the resources of the various special systems, themselves marginalized and devalued by mainstream systems. When children with disabilities are segregated from their nondisabled peers, they lose access to mainstream environments that enhance their teaching and learning. They become increasingly dependent on teacher-directed, highly structured learning and on adults as the source of new knowledge and support. They are also forced to give up their peers and the friendships that should be part of the lives of all children. When natural supports are thwarted and prevented from developing, persons with disabilities are forced to become more and more dependent on costly professional and paid services to fill the void.

2. *When children with and without disabilities grow up in isolation from one another, everyone loses. Children will "do as I do, and not as I say." If we model segregation, rejection, and stereotyping by labels in a social system as central to our democratic institutions as the public schools, we have a great deal to answer for when those exclusionary models play out in the domains of daily living.* More than half a century ago, Adorno, Frenkel-Brunswik, Levinson, and Sanford (1950) advanced their theory that one's attitudes toward persons who are viewed as different are part of a consistent pattern affecting all aspects of an individual's behavior and beliefs. Their studies of racial prejudice were premised on the theory that cultural acceptance is associated with democratic principles and that the promotion of cultural acceptance would thus have broader implications for the greater good of society. The movement to celebrate diversity in education makes this point as well, while also acknowledging the futility of ignoring the diversity that exists in today's schools. Learning to acknowledge and build on individual differences as strengths rather than deficits is consistent with democratic values and caring schools that support children's growth and development (Berman, 1990; Noddings, 2005; Sapon-Shevin, 2005).

The purpose of a public school system goes beyond simply meeting the needs of individual children. While this is important, it should not occur at the expense of the role of the schools in providing a pathway to a democratic community and the betterment of a nation's citizenry—*all, not just some.* Our challenge is, of course, to examine the rhetoric and practices in education with the goal of reaching a better balance between meeting unique needs and building community.

QUESTIONS AND ACTIVITIES

14.1 Why, according to the chapter, are students who are culturally and linguistically diverse overrepresented in special education classes and programs, especially those for learning disabilities, mental retardation, and emotional and behavioral disorders? What kinds of solutions could change this overrepresentation?

14.2 Why is it important for parents of color, low-income parents, and parents of different cultures and linguistic backgrounds to be involved in special education programs for their children? How can teachers and other educators ensure that these parents will be full participants in an educational process that is culturally responsive to their values and contexts?

14.3 What are the characteristics of an effective teacher who is culturally responsive? Give specific examples of how a teacher can demonstrate mastery of the different interactions and relationships needed for culturally effective teaching.

14.4 The chapter maintains that a commitment to the principles and practices of inclusive education will not only benefit special education students but also lead to classrooms and schools that reflect diversity and can thus better serve all students with and without disabilities. How might fully inclusive schools prepare our children for fully inclusive communities?

14.5 How can the incorporation of a schoolwide positive behavior management system and restorative practices assist in ensuring that the school is culturally respectful and responsive? What can individual teachers do in their classrooms to reflect fairness and justice in social and instructional interactions with students?

14.6 What are your own beliefs, skills, and understandings related to the role of culture in special and inclusive education? How can you become a lifelong learner in advancing your own culturally responsive practices?

REFERENCES

Adorno, T. W., Frenkel-Brunswik, E., Levinson, D. J., & Sanford, R. N. (1950). *The authoritarian personality* (Vols. 1 & 2). New York: Harper.

Ainscow, M. (2007). From special education to effective schools for all: A review of progress so far. In L. Florian (Ed.), *The SAGE handbook of special education* (pp. 146–159). London: Sage.

Al-Shammari, Z., & Yawkey, T. D. (2008). Extent of parental involvement in improving the students' levels in special education programs in Kuwait. *Journal of Instructional Psychology, 35*(2), 140–150.

Argulewicz, E. N. (1983). Effects of ethnic membership, socioeconomic status, and home language on LD, EMR, and EH placements. *Learning Disabilities Quarterly, 6*(2), 195–200.

Artiles, A. J., & Bal, A. (2008). The next generation of disproportionality research: Toward a comparative model in the study of equity in ability differences. *Journal of Special Education, 42*(1), 4–14.

Artiles, A. J., Rueda, R., Salazar, J. J., & Higareda, I. (2005). Within-group diversity in minority disproportionate representation: English language learners in urban school districts. *Exceptional Children, 71*(3), 283–300.

Artiles, A. J., Trent, S. C., & Palmer, J. (2004). Culturally diverse students in special education: Legacies and prospects. In J. A. Banks & C. A. M. Banks (Eds.), *Handbook of research on multicultural education* (2nd ed., pp. 716–735). San Francisco: Jossey-Bass.

Avramidis, E., Bayliss, P., & Burden, R. (2000). Student teachers' attitudes towards the inclusion of children with special educational needs in the ordinary school. *Teaching and Teacher Education, 16*(3), 277–293.

Baker, S., Gersten, R., & Scanlon, D. (2002). Procedural facilitators and cognitive strategies: Tools for unraveling the mysteries of comprehension and the writing process, and for providing meaningful access to the general curriculum. *Learning Disabilities Research and Practice, 17*(1), 65–77.

Barton, P. E. (2003). *Parsing the achievement gap: Baselines for tracking progress. Policy information report.* Princeton, NJ: Educational Testing Services.

Berman, S. (1990). The real ropes course: The development of social consciousness. *Educating for Social Responsibility, The ESR Journal, 1*, 1–18.

Berry, R. (2008). Novice teachers' conceptions of fairness in inclusion classrooms. *Teaching and Teacher Education, 24*(5), 1149–1159.

Bevan-Brown, J. (2003). *The cultural self-review: Providing culturally effective, inclusive education for Māori learners.* Wellington, New Zealand: New Zealand Council for Educational Research.

Bevan-Brown, J. (2009). *Culturally appropriate, effective provision for Maori learners with special needs: He waka tino whakarawea.* Saarbrucken, Germany: Lambert Academic Publishing AG & Co.

Bishop, R., & Berryman, M. (2006). *Culture speaks: Cultural relationships and classroom learning.* Wellington, New Zealand: Huia.

Bishop, R., Berryman, M., Cavanagh, T., & Teddy, L. (2007). *Te Kotahitanga. Phase 3, Whānaungatanga: Establishing a culturally responsive pedagogy of relations in mainstream secondary school classrooms.* Wellington, New Zealand: Ministry of Education and Waikato University.

Booth, T., & Ainscow, M. (2000). *Index for inclusion: Developing learning and participation in schools.* Bristol, UK: Centre for Studies on Inclusive Education.

Bourke, R., Bevan-Brown, J., Carroll-Lind, J., Cullen, J., Kearney, A., McAlpine, D., Mentis, M., Poskitt, J., et al. (2002). *Special education 2000: Monitoring and evaluation of the policy. Final report phase three.* Wellington, New Zealand: Ministry of Education.

Brown, J. E., & Doolittle, J. (2008). A cultural, linguistic, and ecological framework for response to intervention with English language learners. *Teaching Exceptional Children, 40*(5), 66–72.

Callicott, K. J. (2003). Culturally sensitive collaboration within person-centered planning. *Focus on Autism and Other Developmental Disabilities, 18*(1), 60–68.

Cartledge, G., & Kourea, L. (2008). Culturally responsive classrooms for culturally diverse students with and at risk for disabilities. *Exceptional Children, 74*(3), 351–371.

Cartledge, G., Singh, A., & Gibson, L. (2008). Practical behavior management techniques to close the accessibility gap for students who are culturally and linguistically diverse. *Preventing School Failure, 52*(3), 29–38.

Cawley, J. F., Foley, T. E., & Miller, J. (2003). Science and students with mild disabilities: Principles of universal design. *Intervention in School and Clinic, 38*(3), 160–171.

Chavez-Reyes, C. (2010). Inclusive approaches to parent engagement for young English language learners and their families. *Yearbook of the National Society for the Study of Education, 109*(2), 474–504.

Chiu, Y.-W., & Ring, J. M. (1998). Chinese and Vietnamese immigrant adolescents under pressure: Identifying stressors and interventions. *Professional Psychology, Research and Practice, 29*(5), 444–449.

Clarke, C., Dyson, A., Millward, A., & Robson, S. (1999). Inclusive education and schools as organizations. *International Journal of Inclusive Education, 3*(1), 37–51.

Corter, C., Patel, S., Pelletier, J., & Bertrand, J. (2008). The early development instrument as an evaluation and improvement tool for school-based, integrated services for young children and parents: The Toronto First Duty project. *Early Education and Development, 19*(5), 773–794.

Council for Exceptional Children. (2008). CEC's position on response to intervention (RTI): The unique role of special education and special educators. *Teaching Exceptional Children, 40*(3), 74–79.

Curran, E., & Murray, M. (2008). Transformative learning in teacher education: Building competencies and changing dispositions. *Journal of the Scholarship of Teaching and Learning, 8*(3), 103–118.

Darling-Hammond, L. (2004). Inequality and the right to learn: Access to qualified teachers in California's public schools. *Teachers College Record, 106*(10), 1936–1966.

deFur, S. H., Todd-Allen, M., & Getzel, E. E. (2001). Parent participation in the transition planning process. *Career Development for Exceptional Individuals, 24*(1), 19–36.

Donovan, S., & Cross, C. (2002). *Minority students in special and gifted education.* Washington, DC: National Academy Press.

Doveston, M., & Keenaghan, M. (2006). Improving classroom dynamics to support students' learning and social inclusion: A collaborative approach. *Support for Learning, 21*(1), 5–11.

Dunn, L. (1968). Special education for the mildly retarded: Is much of it justifiable? *Exceptional Children, 35*(1), 5–22.

Erickson, F., & Mohatt, G. (1982). Cultural organization and participation structures in two classrooms of Indian students. In G. Spindler (Ed.), *Doing the ethnography of schooling: Education anthropology in action* (pp. 131–174). New York: Holt, Rinehart and Winston.

Evans, I. M., Salisbury, C. L., Palombaro, M. M., Berryman, J., & Hollowood, T. M. (1992). Peer interactions and social acceptance of elementary-age children with severe disabilities in an inclusive school. *Journal of the Association for Persons with Severe Handicaps, 17*(4), 205–212.

Ferri, B. A., & Connor, D. J. (2005). In the shadow of *Brown*: Special education and overrepresentation of students of color. *Remedial and Special Education, 26*(2), 93–100.

Finkel, E. (2011). Holding on to parent voices. *District Administration, 46*(1), 62–66.

Finn, J. D. (1982). Patterns in special education placement as revealed by the OCR surveys. In K. A. Heller, W. H. Holtzman, & S. Mesrick (Eds.), *Placing children in special education: A strategy for equity* (pp. 322–381). Washington, DC: National Academy Press.

Florsheim, P. (1997). Chinese adolescent immigrants: Factors related to psychosocial adjustment. *Journal of Youth and Adolescence, 26*(2), 143–163.

Fuchs, D., & Fuchs, L. S. (2006). Introduction to response to intervention: What, why, and how valid is it? *Reading Research Quarterly, 41*(1), 95–99.

Fuchs, D., Fuchs, L. S., & Stecker, P. M. (2010). The "blurring" of special education in a new continuum of general education placements and services. *Exceptional Children, 76,* 301–323.

Gargiulo, R. M. (2006). *Special education in contemporary society: An introduction to exceptionality* (2nd ed.). Belmont, CA: Thomson/Wadsworth.

Geenen, S., Powers, L., Lopez-Vasquez, A., & Bersani, H. (2003). Understanding and promoting the transition of minority adolescents. *Career Development for Exceptional Individuals, 26*(1), 27–46.

Goldenberg, C. (2008). Teaching English language learners: What the research does—and does not—say. *American Educator, 33*(2), 8–44.

Gomez, R., & Greenough, R. (2002). *Parental involvement under the new Title I & Title III: From compliance to effective practice.* Portland, OR: Northwest Regional Educational Laboratory.

Greenwood, C. R., Arreaga-Mayer, C., Utley, C. A., Gavin, K. M., & Terry, B. J. (2001). Class-wide peer tutoring learning management systems: Applications with elementary-level English language learners. *Remedial and Special Education, 22*(1), 34–47.

Ha, Y., Park, H.-S., & Lee, H. (2008, March/April). Social adjustment of Korean immigrant students in secondary schools. *NABE News,* 15–18.

Hains, A. H., Rhyner, P. M., McLean, M. E., Barnekow, K., Johnson, V., & Kennedy, B. (2005). Interdisciplinary teams and diverse families: Practices in early intervention personnel preparation. *Young Exceptional Children, 8*(4), 2–10.

Harry, B. (2008). Collaboration with culturally and linguistically diverse families: Ideal versus reality. *Exceptional Children, 74*(3), 372–388.

Harry, B., & Artiles, A. J. (2007). Considerations about the cultural nature of inclusion, teaching, and learning. In M. Giangreco & M. B. Doyle (Eds.), *Quick-guides to inclusion: Ideas for educating students with disabilities* (2nd ed., pp. 31–44). Baltimore, MD: Brookes.

Harry, B., & Klingner, J. K. (2006). *Why are so many minority students in special education? Understanding race & disability in schools.* New York: Teachers College Press.

Harry, B., Klingner, J. K., & Hart, J. (2005). African American families under fire: Ethnographic views of family strengths. *Remedial and Special Education, 26*(2), 101–112.

Heller, K. A., Holtzman, W. H., & Messick, S. (Eds.). (1982). *Placing children in special education: A strategy for equity.* Washington, DC: National Academy Press.

Horner, R. H., Meyer, L. H., & Fredericks, H. D. B. (Eds.). (1986). *Education of learners with severe handicaps: Exemplary service strategies.* Baltimore, MD: Brookes.

Hosp, J. L., & Reschly, D. J. (2004). Disproportionate representation of minority students in special education: Academic, demographic, and economic predictors. *Exceptional Children, 70*(2), 185–199.

Howland, A., Anderson, J. A., Smiley, A. D., & Abbott, D. (2006). School liaisons: Bridging the gap between home and school. *School Community Journal, 16*(2), 47–68.

Huer, M. B., Parette, H. P., Jr., & Saenz, T. I. (2001). Conversations with Mexican Americans regarding children with disabilities and augmentative and alternative communication. *Communication Disorders Quarterly, 22*(4), 197–206.

Kane, J., Lloyd, G., McCluskey, G., Maguire, R., Riddell, S., Stead, J., & Weeden, E. (2009). Generating an inclusive ethos? Exploring the impact of restorative practices in Scottish schools. *International Journal of Inclusive Education, 13*(3), 231-253.

Kim, K.-H., & Morningstar, M. E. (2005). Transition planning involving culturally and linguistically diverse families. *Career Development for Exceptional Individuals, 28*(2), 92–103.

King-Sears, M. E. (2001). Three steps for gaining access to the general education curriculum for learners with disabilities. *Intervention in School and Clinic, 37*(2), 67–76.

King-Sears, M. E. (2008). Facts and fallacies: Differentiation and the general education curriculum for students with special education needs. *Support for Learning, 23*(2), 55–62.

Klingner, J. K., Artiles, A. J., & Barletta, L. M. (2006). English language learners who struggle with reading: Language acquisition or LD? *Journal of Learning Disabilities, 39*(2), 108–128.

Klingner, J. K., & Edwards, P. A. (2006). Cultural considerations with response to intervention models. *Reading Research Quarterly, 41*(1), 108–117.

Kozleski, E. B., Engelbrecht, P., Hess, R., Swart, E., Eloff, I., Oswald, M., Molina, A., & Swati, J. (2008). Where differences matter: A cross-cultural analysis of family voice in special education. *Journal of Special Education, 42*(1), 26–35.

Kozol, J. (1967). *Death at an early age: The destruction of the hearts and minds of Negro children in the Boston public schools.* Boston: Houghton Mifflin.

Kyles, C., & Olafson, L. (2008). Uncovering preservice teachers' beliefs about diversity through reflective writing. *Urban Education, 43*(5), 500–518.

Ladson-Billings, G. (2007). Culturally responsive teaching: Theory and practice. In J. A. Banks & C. A. M. Banks (Eds.), *Multicultural education: Issues and perspectives* (6th ed., pp. 221–245). Hoboken, NJ: Wiley.

Lam, S. K.-Y. (2005). An interdisciplinary course to prepare school professionals to collaborate with families of exceptional children. *Multicultural Education, 13*(2), 38–42.

Lee, L. C., & Zhan, G. (1998). Psychosocial status of children and youths. In L. C. Lee & N. W. S. Zane (Eds.), *Handbook of Asian American psychology* (pp. 137–163). Thousand Oaks, CA: Sage.

Levitt, K. E. (2001). An analysis of elementary teachers' beliefs regarding the teaching and learning of science. *Science Education, 86*(1), 1–22.

MacMillan, D. L., & Reschly, D. J. (1998). Overrepresentation of minority students: The case for greater specificity or reconsideration of the variables examined. *Journal of Special Education, 32*(1), 15–24.

Mercer, J. R. (1973). *Labeling the mentally retarded: Clinical and social system perspectives on mental retardation.* Berkeley: University of California Press.

Meyer, L. H. (1997). Tinkering around the edges? *Journal of the Association for Persons with Severe Handicaps, 22*(2), 80–82.

Meyer, L. H., & Evans, I. M. (2012). *The school leader's guide to restorative school discipline.* Thousand Oaks, CA: Corwin.

Meyer, L. H., Park, H.-S., Grenot-Scheyer, M., Schwartz, I. S., & Harry, B. (Eds.). (1998). *Making friends: The influences of culture and development.* Baltimore, MD: Brookes.

Montague, M., & Applegate, B. (2000). Middle school students' perceptions, persistence, and performance in mathematical problem solving. *Learning Disability Quarterly, 23*(3), 215–227.

Murtadha-Watts, K., & Stoughton, E. (2004). Critical cultural knowledge in special education: Reshaping the responsiveness of school leaders. *Focus on Exceptional Children, 37*(2), 1–8.

National Joint Committee on Learning Disabilities. (2011). Comprehensive assessment and evaluation of students with learning disabilities. *Learning Disability Quarterly, 34*(1), 3–16.

Noddings, N. (2005). *The challenge to care in schools: An alternative approach to education* (2nd ed.). New York: Teachers College Press.

Nuthall, G. (2005). The cultural myths and realities of classroom teaching and learning: A personal journey. *Teachers College Record, 107*(5), 895–934.

Ortiz, A. A. (2002). Prevention of school failure and early intervention for English language learners. In A. J. Artiles & A. A. Ortiz (Eds.), *English language learners with special education needs: Identification, assessment, and instruction* (pp. 31–48). Washington, DC: Center for Applied Linguistics and Delta.

Oswald, D. P., Coutinho, M. J., Best, A. M., & Singh, N. N. (1999). Ethnic representation in special education: The influence of school-related economic and demographic variables. *Journal of Special Education, 32*(4), 194–206.

Palincsar, A. S., Magnusson, S. J., Collins, K. M., & Cutter, J. (2001). Making science accessible to all: Results of a design experiment in inclusive classrooms. *Learning Disability Quarterly, 24*(1), 15–32.

Palmer, J. D., & Jang, E.-Y. (2005). Korean born, Korean-American high school students' entry into understanding race and racism through social interactions and conversations. *Race, Ethnicity and Education, 8*(3), 297–317.

Parette, H. P., & Petch-Hogan, B. (2000). Approaching families: Facilitating culturally/linguistically diverse family involvement. *Teaching Exceptional Children, 33*(2), 4–10.

Pelletier, J., & Corter, C. (2005). Toronto First Duty: Integrating kindergarten, childcare, and parenting support to help diverse families connect to schools. *Multicultural Education, 13*(2), 30–37.

Peske, H. G., & Haycock, K. (2006). *Teaching inequity: How poor and minority students are shortchanged on teacher quality.* Washington, DC: Education Trust.

Rebell, M. A. (1999). Fiscal equity litigation and the democratic imperative. *Equity & Excellence in Education, 32*(3), 5–18.

Richardson, J. G. (1994). Common, delinquent, and special: On the formalization of common schooling in the American states. *American Educational Research Journal, 31*(4), 695–723.

Rose, D., & Meyer, A. (2000). Universal design for individual differences. *Educational Leadership, 58*(3), 39–43.

Salas, L., Lopez, E. J., Chinn, K., & Menchaca-Lopez, E. (2005). Can special education teachers create parent partnerships with Mexican American families? Si se pueda! *Multicultural Education, 13*(2), 52–55.

Sapon-Shevin, M. (2004). Thinking inclusively about inclusive education. In K. Kesson & E. W. Ross (Eds.), *Defending public schools: Teaching for a democratic society* (Vol. 2, pp. 161–172). Westport, CT: Praeger.

Sapon-Shevin, M. (2005). Teachable moments for social justice. In B. S. Engel & A. C. Martin (Eds.), *Holding values: What we mean by progressive education* (pp. 93–97). Portsmouth, NH: Heinemann.

Savage, C., Hindle, R., Meyer, L.H., Hynds, A., Penetito, W., & Sleeter, C.E. (2011). Culturally responsive pedagogies in the classroom: Indigenous student experiences across the curriculum. *Asia-Pacific Journal of Teacher Education, 39*(3), 183–198.

Schmidt, R. J., Rozendal, M. S., & Greenman, G. G. (2002). Reading instruction in the inclusive classroom: Research-based practices. *Remedial and Special Education, 23*(3), 130–140.

Schnorr, R. F. (1997). From enrollment to membership: "Belonging" in middle and high school classes. *Journal of the Association for Persons with Severe Handicaps, 22*(1), 1–15.

Skiba, R. J., Poloni-Staudinger, L., Simmons, A. B., Feggins-Azziz, L. R., & Chung, C.-G. (2005). Unproven links: Can poverty explain ethnic disproportionality in special education? *Journal of Special Education, 39*(3), 130–144.

Skiba, R. J., Simmons, A. B., Ritter, S., Gibb, A. C., Rausch, M. K., Cuadrado, J., & Chung, C.-G. (2008). Achieving equity in special education: History, status, and current challenges. *Exceptional Children, 74*(3), 264–288.

Slee, R., & Allan, J. (2005). Excluding the included: A reconsideration of inclusive education. In J. Rix, K. Simmons, M. Nind, & K. Sheehy (Eds.), *Policy and power in inclusive education: Values into practice* (pp. 13–24). London: Routledge/Falmer.

Sleeter, C. E. (Ed.). (2011). *Professional development for culturally responsive and relationship-based pedagogy.* New York: Peter Lang.

Sleeter, C. E., & Grant, C. A. (1987). An analysis of multicultural education in the United States. *Harvard Educational Review, 57*(4), 421–444.

Spooner, F., Baker, J. N., Harris, A. A., Ahlgrim-Delzell, L., & Browder, D. M. (2007). Effects of training in universal design for learning on lesson plan development. *Remedial and Special Education, 28*(2), 108–116.

Suárez-Orozco, M. M. (2001). Globalization, immigration, and education: The research agenda. *Harvard Educational Review, 71*(3), 345–365.

Sugai, G., Horner, R., Sailor, W., Dunlap, G., Eber, L., Lewis, T., et al. (2005). *School-wide positive behavior support: Implementers' blueprint and self-assessment.* Washington, DC: Technical Assistance Center on Positive Behavioral Interventions and Supports.

Trent, S. C., Kea, C. D., & Oh, K. (2008). Preparing preservice educators for cultural diversity: How far have we come? *Exceptional Children, 74*(3), 328–350.

Tucker, J. A. (1980). Ethnic proportions in classes for the learning disabled: Issues in nonbiased assessment. *Journal of Special Education, 14*(1), 93–105.

Turnbull, A. P., Turnbull, H. R., Erwin, E. J., & Soodak, L. C. (2005). *Families, professionals and exceptionality: A special partnership* (5th ed.). Upper Saddle River, NJ: Prentice Hall.

United Nations Educational, Scientific and Cultural Organization. (1994). *The Salamanca statement and framework for action on special education needs education: Adopted by the World Conference on Special Needs Education: Access and Quality.* Salamanca, Spain. Paris: Author.

Valadez, G., & Moineau, S. (2010). The ESL family science night: A model for culturally sensitive science education pedagogy. *International Journal of Wholeschooling, 6*(2), 4–18.

Vitello, S. J., & Mithaug, D. E. (Eds.). (1998). *Inclusive schooling: National and international perspectives.* Mahwah, NJ: Erlbaum.

Ware, F. (2006). Warm demander pedagogy: Culturally responsive teaching that supports a culture of achievement for African American students. *Urban Education, 41*(4), 427–456.

Webb-Johnson, G. C. (1999). Cultural contexts: Confronting the overrepresentation of African American learners in special education. In J. R. Scotti & L. H. Meyer (Eds.), *Behavioral intervention: Principles, models, and practices* (pp. 449–464). Baltimore, MD: Brookes.

Weinstein, C.S., Curran, M., & Tomlinson-Clarke, S. (2003). Toward a conception of culturally responsive classroom management. *Journal of Teacher Education, 55*(1), 25–38.

Xu, Y., & Drame, E. (2008). Culturally appropriate context: Unlocking the potential of response to intervention for English language learners. *Early Childhood Education Journal, 35*, 305–311.

Yeh, C., & Inose, M. (2002). Difficulties and coping strategies of Chinese, Japanese, and Korean immigrant students. *Adolescence, 37*(145), 69–82.

Zhang, C., & Bennett, T. (2003). Facilitating the meaningful participation of culturally and linguistically diverse families in the IFSP and IEP process. *Focus on Autism and Other Developmental Disabilities, 18*(1), 51–59.

Zionts, L. T., Zionts, P., Harrison, S., & Bellinger, O. (2003). Urban African American families' perceptions of cultural sensitivity within the special education system. *Focus on Autism and Other Developmental Disabilities, 18*(1), 41–50.

Realistic Reflections/Getty Images, Inc.

Recruiting and Retaining Gifted Students from Different Ethnic, Cultural, and Language Groups

CHAPTER 15

Donna Y. Ford

This chapter focuses on culturally *different* students and their underrepresentation in gifted and Advanced Placement classes. Since the publication of the seventh edition of this book, I have chosen the term *culturally different* to replace *culturally diverse* because I believe *culturally different* is the more accurate term. All groups have a culture, so we are all culturally diverse; however, differences across cultures contribute to misunderstandings, miscommunication, and clashes, as Oberg (1960) noted with his model of cultural shock.

One of the most persistent and pervasive problems in education is the underrepresentation of African American, Hispanic American, and Native American students in gifted education programs (i.e., classes and services) and Advanced Placement (AP) classes. Since at least the 1930s, reports and studies have revealed that culturally different students have always been inadequately represented in gifted education (Artiles, Trent, & Palmer, 2004; Donovan & Cross, 2002; Ford, 1998, 2004, 2010; Ford, Grantham, & Whiting, 2008b; Grantham et al., 2011). Statistics show that these three groups are underrepresented by an average of 50 percent nationally (Office for Civil Rights, 1998, 2000a, 2002, 2004; U.S. Department of Education [USDE], 1993). As of 2006, this percentage means that slightly more than 250,000 Black students had not been identified as gifted and were unlikely to be participating in gifted education. Sufficient data indicate that underidentification is costly; that is, underidentified gifted students are likely to underachieve academically (e.g., grades and rates of high school and college graduation), personally (e.g. self-esteem, self-concept), and socially (e.g., peers, professionally, fiscally) (Ford, 2010).

It is equally important to note that African American students are the most underrepresented ethnic group in AP classes and among AP test takers (College Board, 2008; Ford et al., 2008b). This point is worth highlighting for at least three reasons: (1) the heavy reliance on AP classes to serve gifted students at the high school level, (2) the greater education opportunities afforded students who participate in AP classes; and (3) the eventual social outcomes afforded to students who graduate from institutions of higher education, particularly elite colleges and universities (e.g., income, employment). Likewise, the opposite outcomes need attention: What happens to those students who are denied access, for whatever reason, to gifted and AP classes?

The percentages for gifted education, shown in Table 15.1, support the notion that "a mind is a terrible thing to waste," a statement popularized by the United Negro College Fund. These data also support the reality that a mind is a terrible thing to erase (Ford, 1996, 2010). In other words, many African American, Hispanic American, and Native American students are gifted and can succeed in gifted education, but their gifts frequently go unidentified and undervalued in schools. Consequently, they are neither challenged nor given the opportunity to develop their gifts and talents, which atrophy. The 2002 No Child Left Behind Act recognized that gifted students are unlikely to develop without appropriate services, as evidenced in the following definition:

Table 15.1 Gifted Education Demographics, Biannually 1998–2006

Race/Ethnicity	1998		2000		2002		2004		2006	
	% District	% G&T	% District	% G&T	% District	% G&T	% District	% G&T	% District	% G&T
American Indian/ Alaskan Native	1.1	.87	1.16	.91	1.21	.93	1.23	.97	1.24	.97
African American/Black	17.0	8.40	16.99	8.23	17.16	8.43	16.88	8.99	17.13	9.15
Asian/Pacific Islander	4.0	6.57	4.14	7.0	4.42	7.64	4.50	8.05	4.81	9.40
Hispanic/Latino	14.3	8.63	16.13	9.54	17.8	10.41	19.94	12.33	20.41	12.79
White	63.7	75.53	61.58	74.24	59.42	72.59	58.45	69.67	56.42	67.69
Total	100	100	100	100	100	100	100	100	100	100

Note: At the time of this writing, data for 2009 were available by state and district rather than nationally.
Source: Elementary and Secondary School Civil Rights Survey, 1998, 2000, 2002, 2004, 2006.
Retrieved August 27, 2011, from http://ocrdata.ed.gov/Downloads.aspx.

The term "gifted and talented" . . . means students, children, or youth who give evidence of high achievement capacity in areas such as intellectual, creative, artistic, or leadership capacity, or in specific academic fields, and who need services or activities not ordinarily provided by the school in order to fully develop those capabilities.

(Title IX, Part A, Sec. 9101[22], p. 544, cited in
National Association for Gifted Children [NAGC], 2002)

Assumptions of This Chapter

This chapter explores barriers to and recommendations for recruiting and retaining racially and culturally different students into gifted education programs specifically. Of course, many of the recruitment and retention issues are germane to AP classes. In particular, I present data on the underrepresentation of African American students (rather than other culturally different students) in gifted education for at least two reasons: (1) Between 1998 and 2006, African American students were the only group of color to become *more underrepresented* in gifted education, as noted in Table 15.1, and (2) this group is more often the focus of litigation relative to inequities in gifted education (Office for Civil Rights, 2000b). I recognize that Asian Americans are also racial- and ethnic-minority students. However, I have yet to find a report indicating that Asian American students are underrepresented in gifted education (and AP classes). Furthermore, Asian Americans, unlike African American, Hispanic American, and Native American students, frequently experience positive stereotypes, and many are high achieving. Consequently, they are not discussed in this chapter. By omitting Asian American students, I am not ignoring the social injustices they have experienced and continue to experience in society and in schools (Kitano & DiJosia, 2002; Pang, Kiang, & Pak, 2004).

This chapter is grounded in several assumptions and propositions. First, the majority of past and current efforts to redress the underrepresentation problem have been inadequate and misdirected, resulting in what may be the most segregated programs in our public schools.

Second, gifted education is a need—not a privilege—and ought not be used as a form of de jure segregation. By not being identified as gifted and receiving appropriate services and programming, gifted students who are racial, ethnic, and language minorities are being denied school-based opportunities to develop their gifts and talents—to reach their potential.

Third, no group has a monopoly on "giftedness" or on being intelligent and academically capable and successful. Gifts and talents, however defined and measured, exist in every racial and ethnic group and across all economic strata (USDE, 1993). Consequently, there should be little or no underrepresentation of racial- and ethnic-minority students in gifted education and AP classes.

Fourth, giftedness is a social, cultural, and even political construct; subjectivity along with economic, social, and cultural capital guide definitions, assessments, and perceptions of giftedness (Ford, 2010; Pfeiffer, 2003; Sternberg, 1985). This subjectivity contributes to segregated gifted education programs in numerous and insidious ways. Sapon-Shevon (1996) states that "the ways in which gifted education is defined, constituted, and enacted lead directly to increased segregation, limited educational opportunities for the majority of students, and damage to children's social and political developments" (p. 196). Accordingly, educators must examine and continuously reexamine or interrogate their views about the purposes of gifted education in general and, in particular, their perceptions and misperceptions of students from racially and ethnically different cultures and backgrounds.

Fifth, all decisions made on behalf of students should be made with their best interests in mind. Education should be additive for students, not subtractive. We should be about the business of building on what students have when they enter our schools and are in our classrooms; this helps all students to become bicultural.

Finally, efforts to recruit and retain racial and ethnic minority students in gifted education must be comprehensive, proactive, aggressive, and systematic. Educators, families, and students themselves need to work together to ensure that gifted education is desegregated (Ford, 2010; Harris, Brown, Ford, & Richardson, 2004). Gallagher's (2004) assertion is apropos here:

> In another profession, the physician treating a patient will often start with the weakest treatment available and then progress to stronger treatments once the first attempt has seen little effect. We seem to have been following that approach in educating gifted students by prescribing a minimal treatment (one might even say a non-therapeutic dose) designed hopefully to do some good without upsetting other people. . . . [A]s a profession, we need to come to some consensus that we need stronger treatments. (p. xxviii)

This chapter is divided into three major sections. The first focuses on recruitment issues and barriers, the second focuses on recruitment recommendations, and the third focuses on retention issues and recommendations. The two guiding questions of the chapter are: How can we effectively recruit and retain more racially and ethnically different students in gifted education? How can we ensure that gifted education programs are both excellent and equitable?

Recruitment Issues and Barriers

Most of the scholarship that explains underrepresentation focuses on some aspect of recruitment. Specifically, it is assumed that racial- and ethnic-minority students are underrepresented because of problems associated with screening and identification instruments, specifically tests. Too little attention has been given to retention, which is discussed later in the chapter.

The first step in addressing (or redressing) the underrepresentation of racial- and ethnic-minority students in gifted education is to focus on recruitment. *Recruitment* refers here to screening, identifying, and placing students (or getting them into gifted education). Perceptions about racial- and ethnic-minority students combined with a lack of cultural understanding and competence significantly undermine the ability of educators to recruit culturally different students into gifted education (and AP classes) and to retain them once recruited (i.e., identified and placed). Ford, Harris, Tyson, and Frazier Trotman (2002) argue (Ford, 2010), that a "cultural deficit" perspective pervades decisions made about and on behalf of African American, Hispanic American, and Native American students. This phenomenon remains a barrier and is described next.

Deficit Thinking

The more we retreat from the culture and the people, the less we learn about them. The less we know about them, the more uncomfortable we feel among them. The more uncomfortable we feel among them, the more inclined we are to withdraw. The more we withdraw from the people, the more faults we find with them. The less we know about their culture, the more we seem to dislike it. And the worst of it is that, in the end, we begin to believe the very lies we've invented to console ourselves.

(Storti, 1989, pp. 32–34)

As stated earlier, a major premise of this chapter is that a deficit orientation held by educators hinders access to gifted programs for Black and some other racially different students, as reflected in the preceding quote. This thinking hinders the ability and willingness of educators to recognize the strengths of students from different ethnic, racial, economic, and language groups. Deficit thinking exists when educators interpret differences as deficits, dysfunctions, and/or disadvantages (Valencia, 2010). Consequently, many racially and ethnically different students—those not from the mainstream culture—quickly acquire the "at-risk" label and the focus is on their perceived shortcomings or weaknesses rather than their strengths and potential or possibility. With deficit thinking, differences in someone who is culturally, racially, or ethnically different are misinterpreted or interpreted negatively, as if the individual and/or characteristics are abnormal, substandard, or otherwise inferior. For example, a student who speaks non-Standard or informal English and is making good grades may not be referred to screening and identification if the teacher neither understands nor appreciates non-Standard/informal English (Hudley & Mallinson, 2011). Likewise, a student who has excellent math skills but weak or weaker writing skills may not be perceived by teachers as gifted or intelligent or having potential or being in need of gifted education. Every student has strengths and weaknesses. Gifted students are not perfect. Likewise, educators need to move beyond a deficit orientation in order to recognize the strengths and potential of racial, ethnic, and language minorities, particularly those from low-income backgrounds.

Ideas and preconceived notions about racial- and ethnic-minority students influence the development of definitions, policies, and practices designed to understand and address differences. For instance, Gould (1996), Menchaca (1997), and Valencia (2010) note that deficit thinking contributed to past (and, no doubt, contemporary) beliefs about race, ethnicity, intelligence, and potential. Gould takes readers back two centuries to demonstrate how a priori assumptions and fears associated with different ethnic groups, particularly African Americans, led to conscious fraud: dishonest and prejudicial research methods, deliberate miscalculations, convenient omissions, and data misinterpretation among scientists studying intelligence. These early assumptions and practices gave way to the prevailing belief or misbelief that the human race could be ranked in a linear scale of mental worth, as argued by the fraudulent and/or misguided and quite subjective research of Cyril Burt, Paul Broca, and Samuel Morton on craniometry (see Gould, 1996), to name but a few in the past.

Later, as school districts faced increasing racial and ethnic diversity (often attributable to immigration as well as White flight), educators resorted to increased reliance on biased standardized tests (Armour-Thomas, 1992; Gould, 1996; Helms, 1992; Menchaca, 1997; Naglieri & Ford, 2003). These tests almost guaranteed low test scores for immigrants and racial- and ethnic-minority groups who were unfamiliar with U.S. customs, traditions, values, norms, and language (Ford, 2004). These tests measured familiarity with mainstream American culture and English proficiency, not intelligence. According to Gould, for example, no matter how constructed, intelligence tests provide a snapshot of limited information about racial- and ethnic-minority populations—those who differ from the mainstream or status quo. The results from these tests often limited the educational opportunities of culturally different students, who tend not to score high on them. Menchaca (1997) states:

> Racial differences in intelligence, it was contended, are most validly explained by racial differences in innate, genetically determined abilities. What emerged from these findings regarding schooling were curricular modifications ensuring that the "intellectually inferior" and the social order would best be served by providing these students concrete, low-level, segregated instruction commensurate with their alleged diminished intellectual abilities. (p. 38)

The publication of *The Bell Curve* (Herrnstein & Murray, 1994) revived deficit thinking about racially and ethnically different individuals and groups, specifically African Americans. Seeking to influence public and social policy, Herrnstein and Murray, like researchers of earlier centuries (such as Cyril Burt), interpreted—or misinterpreted and misrepresented—their data to confirm institutionalized prejudices. As Gould (1996) notes, the eugenics/hereditarian theory of IQ is a homegrown American product that persists in current practices of testing, sorting, and discarding. Issues and barriers associated with screening support this assertion.

Screening Issues and Barriers

To be considered for placement in gifted education, students often undergo screening in which they are administered tests and checklists with predetermined criteria (e.g., cutoff scores). If students meet the initial screening requirements, they may be given additional tests and/or instruments, which are used to make final placement decisions. In most schools, entering the screening pool is based on teacher referrals (Colangelo & Davis, 2002; Ford et al., 2008b; Grantham et al., 2011). Despite decades of data showing inequities and the ineffectiveness of this practice, it continues and hinders the equitable screening of racial- and ethnic-minority students because they are seldom referred by teachers for screening (e.g., Ford, 2010; Ford et al., 2008b). For example, an Hispanic American student may meet the school district's criteria for giftedness but be overlooked because she has not been referred for screening. The teacher may not refer her because of biases and stereotypes about Hispanic Americans (deficit thinking), because the student's English skills are not strong or proficient, or because of the teacher's perceptual and attitudinal barriers.

Intuitively, it makes sense that teacher referrals should be used as part of the screening and decision-making process. As the preceding example illustrates, however, this practice often negatively and disproportionately affects racial-, ethnic-, and language-minority students. Furthermore, Ford and colleagues (2008b) report in their review of the literature that every study on teacher referral for gifted education screening and placement revealed that teachers under-refer African American students more than those of any other racial or ethnic group. More recent work by Grantham and colleagues (2011) reinforces this finding.

Similarly, teachers and other adults (e.g., counselors, psychologists, parents/caregivers, administrators, and community members) may be asked or required to complete checklists on the referred students. If the checklists ignore cultural differences—how giftedness manifests itself differently in various cultures—then gifted culturally different students may receive low ratings that do not accurately capture their strengths, abilities, and potential. A framework proposed by Frasier and colleagues (1995) (see also Sternberg, 1985) describes how the core attributes of giftedness vary by culture. They contend that educators should define and assess giftedness with each group's cultural differences in mind. As an illustration, one core characteristic of giftedness is a keen sense of humor. A common verbal game among low-income African Americans is "playing the dozens" or "signifying" (Lee, 1993; Majors & Billson, 1992). African American students exemplify four characteristics of giftedness when playing the dozens—humor, creativity, verbal skills, and interpersonal skills. Teachers may be offended by the students' humor, however, preventing them from seeing these core characteristics of giftedness.

One of the first signs of giftedness is strong verbal skills, such as a large vocabulary. However, if the student does not speak Standard English (e.g., speaks Black English vernacular or Ebonics) or has limited English proficiency, teachers may not recognize the student's strong verbal skills. Another core characteristic of giftedness relates to independence. Racial- and ethnic-minority students who have communal values, such as interdependence and cooperation, may prefer to work in groups rather than individually and competitively (Boykin, 1994; Ramírez & Castañeda, 1974; Shade, Kelly, & Oberg, 1997). Consequently, teachers may not consider such students to be independent workers or thinkers.

Like tests, checklists can be problematic in the recruitment process or phase. In addition to referrals/nomination forms and checklists being "culture-blind," they frequently focus on demonstrated ability and performance. As a result, they often preclude students who are gifted but, due to their limited experiences, lack opportunities to demonstrate their intelligence and achievement. These "potentially gifted" students and gifted underachievers are those who live in poverty and/or are culturally different from mainstream students (Ford, 1996, 2010). An early but still relevant study by Smith, Constantino, and Krashen (1997) sheds light on this issue. These researchers compared the number of books in the homes and classrooms of three California communities. There was an average of 199 books in the homes of Beverly Hills children, 4 in the homes of Watts children, and 2.7 in the homes of Compton children.

In terms of classrooms, there was an average of 392 books in Beverly Hills classrooms, 54 in Watts classrooms, and 47 in Compton classrooms. Essentially, because of their exposure to books and educational opportunities, children from Beverly Hills homes and schools are more likely to demonstrate their giftedness (e.g., have a large vocabulary, be able to read at an early age) than are children from the other homes and schools. Many children in Compton and Watts are gifted but lack essential academic experiences and exposure to develop their abilities and potential. Similar outcomes were found in a six-year longitudinal study by Hart and Risley (1995) and in Barton and Coley's (2009) comprehensive analyses of correlates of the achievement gap.

The U.S. Department of Education has recognized that our schools are filled with potentially gifted students. To help educators improve the recruitment of Black and other underrepresented students into gifted education, the department issued the following definition of giftedness, one that relies heavily on the notion of talent development:

> *Children and youth with outstanding talent perform or show the potential for performing at remarkably high levels of accomplishment when compared with others of their age, experience, or environment. These children and youth exhibit high performance capacity in intellectual, creative, and/or artistic areas, possess an unusual leadership capacity, or excel in specific academic fields. They require services or activities not ordinarily provided by the schools. Outstanding talents are present in children and youth from all cultural groups, across all economic strata, and in all areas of human endeavor.*

(USDE, 1993, p. 3)

The percentage of school districts adopting this definition or some version of it is unknown. The ramification of not adopting the federal definition, or some version of it, is clear: continued underrepresentation of students from racial, ethnic, and language minorities in gifted education (and, by extension, AP classes).

Identification/Assessment Issues and Barriers

Monolithic definitions of *giftedness* pose serious barriers to recruiting diverse students into gifted education. Monolithic definitions ignore human differences in general and cultural differences in particular. They ignore the fact that what is valued as giftedness in one culture may not be valued in another. For example, most European Americans highly value cognitive and academic ability over spatial, musical, interpersonal, and other abilities (Gardner, 1993) and tend to value academic knowledge and skills over tacit or practical knowledge and skills (Sternberg, 2007). Conversely, navigational skills or hunting skills may be prized in another culture. These differences raise this question: If a student is not gifted in the ways that are valued by my culture, is the student gifted? Based on current practice, most culturally different students are not likely to be perceived as gifted.

Perceptions and definitions also influence the instruments or tests selected to assess giftedness. Dozens of intelligence and achievement tests exist. What determines which instrument a school district selects? If we value verbal skills, we will select an instrument that assesses verbal skills. If we value logic and/or problem-solving skills, we will select an instrument that assesses these skills. If we value creativity, the instrument we select will assess creativity. We are not likely to choose an instrument that measures a construct or skill that we do not value.

Many schools use intelligence and achievement tests—more than other types of tests—to identify and label giftedness. Test scores play a dominant role in identification, assessment, placement, and in service decisions and options. For example, a study by VanTassel-Baska, Patton, and Prillaman (1989) revealed that 88.5 percent of states rely primarily on standardized, norm-referenced tests to identify gifted students, including those from economically and culturally diverse groups. More than 90 percent of school districts use scores from these types of tests for labeling and placement (Colangelo & Davis, 2002; Davis & Rimm, 2003). These tests measure verbal skills, abstract thinking, math skills, and other skills considered indicative of giftedness (or intelligence or achievement) by laypersons and educators. Likewise, they ignore skills and abilities that may be valued by other cultures and groups (e.g., creativity, interpersonal skills, group problem-solving skills, navigational skills, and musical skills). Consequently, racial- and ethnic-minority students, Black students in particular, are more likely than others to display characteristics that place them at a disadvantage in testing situations (Ford, 1996, 2010; Frasier et al., 1995; Helms, 1992; Office for Civil Rights, 2000b). Monolithic definitions result in the adoption of one-dimensional, ethnocentric tests that contribute significantly to racially homogeneous or segregated gifted education and AP classes. These tests are more effective at identifying giftedness among middle-class White students than among racial- and ethnic-minority students, particularly if these students are of low socioeconomic status.

An additional concern related to tests is the extensive use of cutoff scores, referred to earlier. The most frequently used cutoff score for placement in gifted education is an IQ of 130 or above, 2 standard deviations above the average IQ of 100 (e.g., Colangelo & Davis, 2002; Ford, 2004). Several decades of data indicate that groups such as African Americans, Hispanic Americans, and Native Americans, even at the highest economic levels, have mean IQ scores lower than those of White students. For the most part, the average IQ of African Americans is 83 to 87, compared to 97 to 100 for White students, on traditional intelligence tests (see Ford, 2004; Helms, 1992; Kaufman, 1994; Naglieri & Ford, 2003, 2005). The same holds for children who live in poverty, regardless of racial background. Their average IQ is about 85. I have consulted with several psychologists who believe that because the average IQ score of African Americans is about 85, giftedness would mean an IQ of 115 or higher among this population. Sadly, those holding racist ideologies will attribute these differences to genetics and argue that giftedness (or intelligence) is primarily inherited. This position implies that the environment is less important than heredity in the development of talents and abilities. Such a view is counterproductive in education, which is supposed to build on and improve the skills and abilities of students.

Conversely, those who recognize the influence of the environment and culture on performance attribute these different scores primarily to social, environmental, and cultural factors. For instance, it has been demonstrated in numerous studies on "environmental racism" that poverty, exposure to lead, malnutrition, and poor educational experiences negatively affect test performance and contribute to the pervasive achievement gap (Barton & Coley, 2009; Baugh,

1991; Bullard, 1993, 1994; Bryant & Mohai, 1992; Ford, 2004, 2010, 2011; Grossman, 1991. Thus, cutoff scores cannot be selected arbitrarily and in a culture-blind or class-blind fashion. If adopted at all, cutoff scores should be used with caution and should take into consideration the different mean scores of the various racial, ethnic, cultural, and language groups.

A final issue related to testing is interpreting results (Gould, 1996; Helms, 1992; Kaufman, 1994). When other information is considered, it is possible to select and use a test that effectively assesses the strengths of racial-, ethnic-, and language-minority students. However, perceptions can prevent a teacher, counselor, or psychologist from interpreting the results in a culturally fair or equitable way. What if a teacher, counselor, and psychologist interpreting the test results hold negative stereotypes about African Americans? What if they hold stereotypes about groups who have limited English proficiency? What if a student from one of these groups receives a very high IQ or achievement test score? How would this affect the psychologist's, teacher's, and counselor's interpretation and use of the results and their work with students? Test interpretation is heavily subjective, and interpretations are influenced by the quantity and quality of training to work with diverse cultural, ethnic, and language groups. Results from a "good" test—one that is valid, reliable, fair, and nonbiased toward Black and other minority students—can be poorly interpreted if the interpreter has little understanding of and appreciation for how culture influences test performance (e.g., Ford, 2004; Whiting & Ford, 2006).

In a collaborative effort, the American Educational Research Association (AERA), the American Psychological Association (APA), and the National Council on Measurement in Education (NCME) (1999) addressed the myriad problems of interpreting test scores. They noted the harmful effects of misinterpreting test results, especially with racial- and ethnic-minority groups: "The ultimate responsibility for appropriate test use and interpretation lies predominantly with the test user. In assuming this responsibility, the user must become knowledgeable about a test's appropriate uses and the populations for which it is appropriate" (p. 112). They advise, as do others, that test users collect extensive data on students to complement test results and use a comprehensive approach in the identification, testing, and assessment process (e.g., Armour-Thomas, 1992; Helms, 1992; NAGC, 1997). Test users must consider the validity of a given instrument or procedure as well as the cultural characteristics of the student when interpreting results (Office of Ethnic Minority Affairs, 1993); extensive information on equity and testing can be found at the National Center for Fair and Open Testing Web site (www.fairtest.org).

In sum, the data collected on all students should be *multidimensional*—a variety of information collected from multiple sources. For example, data are needed from school personnel, family members, and community members. Data on intelligence, achievement, creativity, motivation, interests, and learning styles are essential when making decisions about students. In this era of high-stakes testing, educators should err on the side of having "too much" information rather than too little to make informed, educationally sound, and equity-based decisions. The data collected should also be *multimodal*, that is, gathered in a variety of ways. Information should be collected verbally (e.g., interviews, focus groups, conversations) and nonverbally (e.g., observations, writing, performances), and both subjective and objective information ought to be gathered. Furthermore, if the student speaks a first language other than English, educators should use an interpreter and adopt instruments translated into that student's primary or preferred language. Essentially, assessment should be made with the students' best interests in mind, and the principle of "do no harm" should prevail. As noted by Sandoval, Frisby, Geisinger, Scheuneman, and Grenier (1998): "In any testing situation, but particularly high stakes assessments, examinees must have an opportunity to demonstrate the competencies, knowledge, or attributes being measured" (p. 183). Few equitable opportunities exist when assessments are one-dimensional, unimodal, and ethnocentric (color-blind or culture-blind) (Ford, Moore, & Milner, 2005; Ford & Whiting, 2006; Whiting & Ford, 2006). How can we make proactive, responsible, and defensible decisions about culturally different students when instruments and assessments and the interpretation of test results ignore or trivialize the impact of culture or when they penalize those who are culturally different? After screening, the next step is placement considerations. Like screening, placement considerations are complex and riddled with potential problems, but the challenges can be overcome.

Placement Issues and Barriers

Giftedness is often equated with achievement or productivity. To most educators and laypersons alike, the notion of a "gifted underachiever" may seem paradoxical. However, any educator who has taught students identified as gifted knows that gifted students can and do underachieve; some are unmotivated and uninterested in school, some are procrastinators, and others do not complete assignments or do just enough to get by. In my work with gifted African American students, I have observed about 80 percent of them underachieving (Ford, 1996). Other researchers believe that at least 20 percent of gifted students underachieve, especially gifted females (Reis & Callahan, 1989; Rimm, 2008; Silverman, 1993). Gifted underachievers are understudied; so much is unknown and in need of attention.

One problem associated with placement, therefore, is the belief that gifted students should receive gifted education services *if* they are high achievers, hard workers, and motivated. That is, achievement must be manifested (e.g., high grade point average [GPA] or high achievement test scores). Gifted underachievers are not likely to be referred for or placed in gifted education and AP classes. If placement occurs, it is often provisional, loaded with stipulations, for this group. For example, many school districts will remove students from a gifted program if their GPA falls below a designated level, they fail a course, they display "unacceptable" behavior, or they have poor attendance that is unexcused. This situation of students meeting gifted education criteria (e.g., high test scores) but underachieving often arises when testing has been one-dimensional and unimodal: Educators have focused solely on determining the students' IQ scores and done so with a narrow range of instruments. Conversely, if intelligence *and* achievement data were collected during screening, educators would know whether the student is (1) gifted and achieving, (2) gifted and underachieving, or (3) gifted with weak academic and/or social skills. They could then make placement decisions based on these data. For example, they could place gifted underachievers in gifted education classes and provide them with tutoring in study skills or language skills or with counseling (Ford, 1996, 2010). The objective would be to help gifted underachievers become achievers and experience success in gifted education classrooms.

Many racial-, ethnic-, and language-minority students are likely to be gifted underachievers or potentially gifted students (Ford, 1996, 2010). Some educators do not wish to place these students in gifted education programs and AP classes because they believe that the level and pace of the schoolwork may frustrate these students. In theory, the issue of underachievers being overwhelmed in gifted education programs may be a valid concern, depending on why the students are underachieving. In practice, it has harmed gifted students who are members of racial, ethnic, and language minorities.

Instead of supporting diverse students and helping them to overcome their weaknesses and achievement barriers, educators have often chosen the option of least resistance under the guise of altruism ("I don't want him to be frustrated." "She'll be unhappy." "He'll just fall further behind."). As we seek to prevent students from being frustrated, we should ask: What are we doing to help alleviate their frustration? Tutoring, counseling, and other support systems (academic, vocational, social-emotional) are essential. When placement is combined with support, gifted underachieving students are more likely to be successful in gifted education and AP classes.

As described next, recruiting students from diverse groups into gifted education programs is one thing; retaining them is another. What policies, practices, procedures, philosophies, and supports should be in place for culturally different students to experience success and remain in gifted education, and by extension, AP classes?

Recruitment Recommendations

Recruiting students from nonmainstream groups into gifted education is the first half of resolving their underrepresentation in gifted education. As described here, recruitment should include a talent-development philosophy, changes in standardized tests and assessment practices, culturally sensitive tests, multicultural assessment preparation for professionals, and the development of effective and necessarily equitable policies and procedures.

Talent Development Philosophy

Educators who support a talent development philosophy and culturally sensitive definitions and theories of giftedness are more likely than others to have supports in place to assist students from racially and ethnically different groups. For example, school districts would begin screening and placing students in gifted education at the preschool and primary levels. Currently, most gifted education programs begin in grades 2–4, which may be quite late for potentially gifted students and those beginning to show signs of underachievement, commonly referred to as the *second-grade syndrome*. Abilities or skills—gifts and talents—should be recognized and nurtured early (USDE, 1993), especially among students already at great risk of being unrecognized as gifted.

Changes in Standardized Tests and Assessment Practices

Tests standardized on middle-class White populations are here to stay, despite the reality that they are another form of discrimination that favors the racial, cultural, and economically privileged. However, educators concerned about improving the test performance of Black and other culturally different students on these instruments have several options to consider. First and foremost, they should never select, use, and interpret tests that lack validity for students from racial, ethnic, and language minorities (AERA et al., 1999). Second, they need to mesh the process of assessment with the cultural characteristics of the group being studied while recognizing that assessment is made culturally sensitive through a continuing and open-ended series of substantive and methodological insertions and adaptations (Suzuki & Ponterotto, 2008). In essence, equitable and culturally sensitive assessment necessitates a combination of changed attitudes, accumulation of more knowledge, thoughtful practice, and development of keen insight into the dynamics of human behavior and culture (Helms, 1992; Heubert & Hauser, 1999; Kornhaber, 2004; Sandoval et al., 1998). Tests should never be given so much power that other data are disregarded—tests simply assist educators in making *conditional probability statements* on the basis of the particular test (Kaufman, 1994; Sandoval et al., 1998); the scores and results should not be reified, misused, and abused.

Culturally Sensitive Tests

Tests vary in the amount of language used in the directions and required in the items. When working with linguistically different groups (those for whom English is not the first language and those not yet proficient in formal English), we must use caution when tests have a high linguistic and/or high cultural demand (Flanagan, Ortiz, & Alfonso, 2007). Much data indicate that the results from such tests tend to underestimate what racial-, ethnic-, and language-minority students can do, or they misjudge behaviors as abnormal and in need of intervention when, in reality, they are "normal" in a different cultural context (Boykin, 1994; Dana, 1993; Ford, 2010, 2011; Mercer, 1973; Naglieri & Ford, 2005). To address these issues, educators will need to include more culturally sensitive tests, such as nonverbal tests, in screening and identification procedures (Ford, 2004; Naglieri & Ford, 2003, 2005; Sandoval et al., 1998). To date, the most promising instruments for assessing the strengths of African American students are such nonverbal tests of intelligence as the Naglieri Non-Verbal Abilities Test I and II and Raven's Matrix Analogies Tests, which are considered less culturally loaded than traditional (e.g., language based) tests (Flanagan et al., 2007; Ford, 2004, 2010; Kaufman, 1994; Saccuzzo, Johnson, & Guertin, 1994).

Contrary to popular misconceptions, nonverbal tests do not mean that students are nonverbal. Rather, nonverbal tests measure abilities nonverbally; they rely less on language proficiency. This is an issue of the content of the test. Thus, the intelligence of students with limited English proficiency, bilingual students, and students who speak non-Standard English can be assessed with less reliance on language skills.

Relative to cultural loading, Jensen (1980) distinguishes between culturally loaded and culturally reduced tests. Culturally reduced tests are often performance-based and include abstract figural and nonverbal content; culturally loaded tests have printed instructions, require reading, have verbal content, and require written responses. Essentially, nonverbal tests decrease the confounding effects of language skills on test performance and consequently increase the chances of students from diverse groups being identified as gifted. Other testing accommodations in the best interest of diverse students include using tests that have been translated into different languages, using interpreters and translators when students are not proficient in English, and having educators who are bilingual and bicultural administer the tests.

Multicultural Assessment Preparation

Finally, regarding the issue of testing, multicultural assessment preparation is essential for any educator and professional who administers, interprets, and uses results based on tests with diverse students (AERA et al., 1999). As stated earlier, the test results are only as good—accurate, useful, and equitable—as the test-taking situation, including the qualifications and competencies of the educator administering the test. Comas-Diaz (1996) has developed a list of cultural assessment variables with which educators should be familiar when making comprehensive assessments and interpreting results. These variables include information about the individual's heritage, religion, immigration history, child-rearing practices, language skills, gender roles, and views about assimilation and about authority figures and family structure. The more information there is, the better the assessment. Ford and Whiting (2006) and Whiting and Ford (2006) highlight other specific considerations for applying testing and assessment principles through a cultural lens.

Policies and Procedures

Students should be placed in gifted education based on multiple data, which are then used to create profiles of their strengths and weaknesses. Consequently, recruitment becomes diagnostic and prescriptive—strengths are used to place students in gifted education, and weaknesses are remediated rather than used as an excuse to avoid placement.

If teacher referral is the first step in the screening and placement process, and diverse students are underreferred and underidentified, then teachers are serving as gatekeepers and schools should reevaluate this practice. To qualify as a valid referral source, teachers require preparation in at least three areas: (1) gifted education, (2) urban and multicultural education, and (3) multicultural assessment (Ford & Frazier Trotman, 2001; Ford et al., 2008b). Professional training in these areas prepares educators to be knowledgeable about gifted students from different cultural groups as well as the limitations of testing them.

Retention Recommendations

Half of our efforts to desegregate gifted education should focus on recruitment and half on retention. This section focuses extensively on how multicultural education can be used to retain

Black and other underidentified students in gifted education. At minimum, teachers and school personnel working with gifted students require substantive preparation in multicultural education to ensure that classrooms, programs, and services are culturally responsive and responsible (Ford, 2010, 2011; Ford & Frazier Trotman, 2001; Ford & Harris, 1999).

Multicultural Instruction

Boykin (1994), Saracho and Gerstl (1992), and Shade and colleagues (1997) are just a few of several scholars who have presented convincing research supporting the notion that culture influences learning styles and thinking styles. Due to space limitations, only Boykin's work will be discussed here. Before doing so, I want to add a word of caution. As noted by Irvine and York (2001), we must never adhere so strongly to generalizations or frameworks that they become stereotypes. Irvine and York point out that "negative teacher expectations can be fueled if teachers incorporate generalized and decontextualized observations about children of color without knowledge of the limitations of learning-styles labels" (p. 492). This model is presented with the understanding that although each of us belongs to several groups, we are nonetheless individuals first and foremost.

In his Afro-centric model, Boykin (1994) identifies nine cultural styles commonly found among African Americans: spirituality, harmony, oral tradition, affective orientation, communalism, verve, movement, social time perspective, and expressive individualism. *Movement* and *verve* refer to being tactile and kinesthetic learners who show a preference for being involved in learning experiences. They are active learners who are engaged when they are physically and psychologically involved. Otherwise, they may be easily distracted and go off-task. *Harmony* refers to an ability to read the environment well and to read nonverbal behaviors proficiently. Thus, students who feel unwelcome in their classes may become unmotivated and uninterested in learning. *Communalism* refers to a cooperative, interdependent style of living and learning in which competition—especially with friends—is devalued. Students with this learning preference may be unmotivated in highly individualistic and competitive classrooms, preferring instead to learn in groups.

Harmony, affective orientation, and communalism may explain why an increasing number of African American students—especially middle school and high school students—are choosing not to be in gifted programs. They recognize that such programs are primarily composed of White students and express concerns about alienation and isolation (Ford, 1996; Ford et al., 2008a). Furthermore, communalism may result in some African American students shunning participation in gifted programs and equating high achievement with "acting White" (Fordham, 1988; Fordham & Ogbu, 1986). Educators who take the time to get to know racial-, ethnic-, and language-minority students and their families can avoid what I refer to as "drive-by teaching"— driving into minority communities, teaching students who are strangers, working with families without building relationships and respect, and driving out of the community immediately after school lets out. Drive-by teaching is counterproductive to students and the educational process in general. It does not give educators time to get to know and understand their students and fails to give students opportunities to get to know their teachers in meaningful ways.

Teachers should learn to modify their teaching styles to accommodate different learning styles. For example, to accommodate students' preference for communalism, teachers can use cooperative learning strategies, place students in groups, and allow students to work with and help each other (Cohen & Lotan, 2004). To accommodate the oral tradition as well as verve and movement, teachers can give students opportunities to write and perform skits, to make oral presentations, and to participate in debates. More examples of ways in which teachers can use culturally responsive teaching activities are described by Ford (1998, 2010, 2011), Gay (2000), Lee (1993, 2007), and Shade and colleagues (1997).

Multicultural Gifted Curriculum

In the area of retention, curricular considerations are also critical. How to teach and what to teach gifted students have been discussed extensively by other scholars (Maker & Nielson, 2009; Tomlinson, 2001; VanTassel-Baska & Stambaugh, 2006). These strategies, such as curriculum compacting, independent study, acceleration, and grade skipping, will not be discussed here because of space limitations. While these strategies are certainly appropriate for gifted students from diverse groups, an equally important but overlooked retention recommendation is the need to create culturally responsive and responsible learning environments (Gay, 2000) and to ensure that the curriculum for gifted students is multicultural. Ford and Harris (1999) and Ford (2011) created a framework that uses Bloom's (1956) taxonomy and Banks's (2008) multicultural education model to assist educators in developing learning experiences that are multicultural and challenging. The result is a 24-cell matrix, shown in Table 15.2. Four of the 24 levels in the model are described here (for a more complete discussion of the model, see Ford 2010; Ford & Harris, 1999; Ford & Milner, 2005).

At the *knowledge–contributions* level, students are provided information and facts about cultural heroes, holidays, events, and artifacts. For example, students might be taught about Martin Luther King Jr. and then asked to recall three facts about him on a test. They might be introduced to Cinco de Mayo and be required to name the year when it became a holiday.

At the *comprehension–transformation* level, students are required to explain what they have been taught—but from the perspective of another group or individual. For instance, students might be asked to explain the events that led to slavery in the United States and then to discuss how enslaved persons might have felt about being held captive. They might discuss the Trail of Tears from the perspective of a Native American child living when this tragic event occurred.

At the *analysis–social action* level, students are asked to analyze an event from more than one point of view. Students might be asked to compare and contrast events during slavery with events associated with infractions of child labor laws today. Following these comparisons, students could be asked to develop a social action plan for eliminating illegal child labor.

At the *evaluation–social action* level, students might be asked to conduct a survey about prejudice in their local stores or businesses. This information could be given to store owners along with a plan of action for change, such as developing a diversity-training program.

Multicultural education can engage students and give them opportunities to identify with, connect with, and relate to the curriculum. It consists of deliberate, ongoing, planned, and systematic opportunities to avoid drive-by teaching—to make learning meaningful and relevant to students and to give minority students mirrors in order to see themselves reflected in the curriculum. Multicultural gifted education challenges students culturally, affectively, academically, and cognitively.

Multicultural Counseling

Ford (1998), Fordham (1988), and Fordham and Ogbu (1986) have conducted research examining the concerns that high-achieving, gifted African American students have about being academically successful. A common finding is that many of these students are accused of "acting White" by other African American students because of their academic success (Ford et al., 2008a). Such accusations can be frustrating and overwhelming, leading to diminished motivation. Should an anti-achievement ethic be present in schools, educators must provide students—the accused and the accusers—with social-emotional and psychological supports. The students accused of acting White will need assistance with coping skills, conflict resolution skills, and anger management. The accusers will need assistance in examining the negative implications—the self-defeating thoughts and behaviors—of an anti-achievement ethic. Peer-group counseling is one potentially effective method for addressing these issues (Ford, 2010; Whiting, 2006).

Table 15.2 Ford-Harris Multicultural Gifted Education Framework–Description of Levels

	Knowledge	Comprehension	Application	Analysis	Synthesis	Evaluation
Contributions	Students are taught and know facts about cultural artifacts, events, groups, and other cultural elements.	Students show an understanding of information about cultural artifacts, groups, etc.	Students are asked to and can apply information learned about cultural artifacts, groups, etc.	Students are taught to and can analyze (e.g., compare and contrast) information about cultural artifacts, groups, etc.	Students are required to and can create a new product from the information on cultural artifacts, groups, etc.	Students are taught to and can evaluate facts and information based on cultural artifacts, groups, etc.
Additive	Students are taught and know concepts and themes about cultural groups.	Students are taught and can understand cultural concepts and themes.	Students are required to and can apply information learned about cultural concepts and themes.	Students are taught to and can analyze important cultural concepts and themes.	Students are asked to and can synthesize important information on cultural concepts and themes.	Students are taught to and can critique cultural concepts and themes.
Transformation	Students are given information on important cultural elements, groups, etc., and can understand this information from different perspectives.	Students are taught to understand and can demonstrate an understanding of important cultural concepts and themes from different perspectives.	Students are asked to and can apply their understanding of important concepts and themes from different perspectives.	Students are taught to and can examine important cultural concepts and themes from more than one perspective.	Students are required to and can create a product based on their new perspective or the perspective of another group.	Students are taught to and can evaluate or judge important cultural concepts and themes from different viewpoints (e.g., minority group).
Social action	Based on information about cultural artifacts, etc., students make recommendations for social action.	Based on their understanding of important concepts and themes, students make recommendations for social action.	Students are asked to and can apply their understanding of important social and cultural issues; they make recommendations for and take action on these issues.	Students are required to and can analyze social and cultural issues from different perspectives; they take action on these issues.	Students create a plan of action to address a social and cultural issue; they seek important social change.	Students critique important social and cultural issues, and seek to effect national and/or international change.

Note: Actions taken on the social action level can range from immediate and small scale (e.g., classroom and school level) to moderate scale (e.g., community or regional level) to large scale (state, national, and international levels). Likewise, students can make recommendations for action or actually take social action.

Source: Ford & Harris (1999) and Ford (2011). Adapted from Banks, Chapter 10, this book; Bloom (1956).

Skills-Based Supports

Retention efforts must also address and rectify skill deficits. As stated earlier, many culturally different students are gifted but need support to maintain an acceptable level of achievement. Supportive systems include coaching in test-taking skills, study skills, time-management skills, and organizational skills.

Ongoing Professional Development in Multicultural Education and Counseling

In order to implement the preceding recommendations, educators should participate in ongoing and formal preparation in multicultural education and counseling. Whether in the form of courses or workshops, such preparation should focus on educators becoming culturally competent in the following areas:

1. Understanding cultural diversity and its impact on (a) teaching, (b) learning, and (c) assessment

2. Understanding the impact of biases and stereotypes on (a) teaching, (b) learning, and (c) assessment (e.g., referrals, testing, expectations)

3. Working effectively and proactively with (a) students from racial, ethnic, and language minorities, (b) their families, and (c) their community

4. Creating multicultural (a) curricula and (b) instruction

5. Creating culturally responsive (a) learning and (b) assessment environments

Summary and Conclusions

Gifted students are gifted 24 hours a day, seven days a week. Racial- and ethnic-minority students are culturally different 24 hours a day, seven days a week.

In 1954, the U.S. Supreme Court ruled deliberate (de jure) school segregation unconstitutional. More recently, we have such legislation as No Child Left Behind targeting the pervasive achievement gap, yet de facto segregation persists in schools and in gifted education programs and AP classes. Educators need to focus extensively, consistently, and systematically on the many factors that contribute to and exacerbate the underrepresentation of students from racial, ethnic, and language minorities in gifted education programs as well as AP classes. I have argued that a deficit orientation among educators, based primarily on a lack of understanding of culture, permeates all areas of the recruitment and retention of certain culturally different students in gifted education programs and AP classes.

Deficit thinking has no place in education. Instead, educators should and must acknowledge the realities of cultural differences in the world, in the United States, and in schools, and seek to acquire and use the resources and preparation needed to become culturally responsive and responsible professionals. Culturally competent educators are advocates for students from different racial, ethnic, cultural, and language groups. The multicultural philosophy and preparation of educators will guide their referrals, instrument selection, test interpretation, and placement decisions—all of which are essential for recruiting and retaining diverse students into gifted education programs.

QUESTIONS AND ACTIVITIES

15.1 Why, according to the chapter, are racial- and ethnic-minority students and low-income students underrepresented in school programs for gifted students, including AP classes?

15.2 What does the chapter describe as "deficit thinking," and how might such thinking among educators affect the education of gifted minority students? According to the chapter, how does deficit thinking contribute to the underrepresentation of minority students in programs for gifted students?

15.3 Why are many racial- and ethnic-minority and low-income students likely to be identified as gifted underachievers? Describe some specific actions that teachers can take to

identify these students and to provide them the support they need to achieve at higher levels.

15.4 The chapter describes some ways in which culture influences learning and thinking. How might theories about culture and learning, such as those of Boykin (1994) and Shade and her colleagues (1997), help teachers and other school personnel to better (effectively and equitably) meet the needs of gifted minority students?

15.5 Visit a school in your community and interview teachers and/or administrators in gifted education to determine (a) the criteria used to identify students for gifted classes/ programs, (b) the percentage of students from racial-, ethnic-, and language-minority groups who are in gifted programs in the school, and (c) the steps that are taken by the school to recruit and retain students from low-income

and racially and ethnically different groups into programs for gifted students, including AP classes.

REFERENCES

American Educational Research Association (AERA), American Psychological Association (APA), & National Council on Measurement in Education (NCME). (1999). *Standards for educational and psychological testing.* Washington, DC: Authors.

Armour-Thomas, E. (1992). Intellectual assessment of children from culturally diverse backgrounds. *School Psychology Review, 21*(4), 552–565.

Artiles, A. J., Trent, S. C., & Palmer, J. D. (2004). Culturally diverse students in special education: Legacies and prospects. In J. A. Banks & C. A. M. Banks (Eds.), *Handbook of research on multicultural education* (2nd ed., pp. 716–735). San Francisco: Jossey-Bass.

Banks, J. A. (2008). *An introduction to multicultural education* (4th ed.). Boston: Allyn & Bacon.

Barton, P. E., & Coley, R. J. (2009). *Parsing the achievement gap II.* Princeton. NJ: Educational Testing Service.

Baugh, J. A. (1991). African Americans and the environment: A review essay. *Policy Studies Journal, 19*(2), 182–191.

Bloom, B. S. (Ed.). (1956). *Taxonomy of educational objectives: The classification of educational goals.* New York: McKay.

Boykin, A. W. (1994). Afrocultural expression and its implications for schooling. In E. R. Hollins, J. E. King, & W. C. Hayman (Eds.), *Teaching diverse populations: Formulating a knowledge base* (pp. 243–273). Albany: State University of New York Press.

Bullard, R. D. (Ed.). (1993). *Confronting environmental racism: Voices from the grassroots.* Boston: South End Press.

Bullard, R. D. (1994). Overcoming racism in environmental decision making. *Environment, 36*(4), 10–20, 39–44.

Bryant, B. I., & Mohai, P. (Eds.). (1992). *Race and the incidence of environmental hazards: A time for discourse.* Boulder, CO: Westview.

Cohen, E. G., & Lotan, R. A. (2004). Equity in heterogeneous classrooms. In J. A. Banks & C. A. M. Banks (Eds.), *Handbook of research on multicultural education* (2nd ed., pp. 736–750). San Francisco: Jossey-Bass.

Colangelo, N., & Davis, G. A. (2002). *Handbook of gifted education* (3rd ed.). Boston: Allyn & Bacon.

College Board. (2008). *The 4th annual AP report to the nation.* Washington, DC: Author.

Comas-Diaz, L. (1996). Cultural considerations in diagnosis. In E. W. Kaslow (Ed.), *Handbook on relational diagnosis and dysfunctional family patterns* (pp. 152–168). New York: Guilford.

Dana, R. H. (1993). *Multicultural assessment perspectives for professional psychology.* Boston: Allyn & Bacon.

Davis, G. A., & Rimm, S. B. (2003). *Education of the gifted and talented* (5th ed.). Boston: Allyn & Bacon.

Donovan, M. S., & Cross, C. T. (Eds.). (2002). *Minority students in special and gifted education.* Washington, DC: National Academy Press.

Flanagan, D. P., Ortiz, S. O., & Alfonso, V. C. (2007). *Essentials of cross-battery assessment* (2nd ed.). Boston: Allyn & Bacon.

Ford, D. Y. (1996). *Reversing underachievement among gifted Black students: Promising practices and programs.* New York: Teachers College Press.

Ford, D. Y. (1998). The underrepresentation of minority students in gifted education: Problems and promises in recruitment and retention. *Journal of Special Education, 32*(1), 4–14.

Ford, D. Y. (2004). *Intelligence testing and cultural diversity: Concerns, cautions, and considerations.* Storrs: University of Connecticut National Research Center on the Gifted and Talented.

Ford, D. Y. (2010). *Reversing underachievement among gifted Black students: Theory, research and practice* (2nd ed.). Waco, TX: Prufrock Press.

Ford, D. Y. (2011). *Multicultural gifted education for high-ability learners: Rationale, models, strategies, and resources* (2nd ed.). Waco, TX: Prufrock Press.

Ford, D. Y., & Frazier Trotman, M. (2001). Teachers of gifted students: Suggested multicultural characteristics and competencies. *Roeper Review, 23*(4), 235–239.

Ford, D. Y., Grantham, T. C., & Whiting, G. W. (2008a). Another look at the achievement gap: Learning from the experiences of gifted Black students. *Urban Education, 43*(2), 216–239.

Ford, D. Y., Grantham, T. C., & Whiting, G. W. (2008b). Culturally and linguistically diverse students in gifted education: Recruitment and retention issues. *Exceptional Children, 74*(3), 289–308.

Ford, D. Y., & Harris, J. J., III. (1999). *Multicultural gifted education.* New York: Teachers College Press.

Ford, D. Y., Harris, J. J., III, Tyson, C. A., & Frazier Trotman, M. (2002). Beyond deficit thinking: Providing access for gifted African American students. *Roeper Review, 24*(2), 52–58.

Ford, D. Y., & Milner, H. R. (2005). *Teaching culturally diverse gifted students.* Waco, TX: Prufrock Press.

Ford, D. Y., Moore, J. L., III, & Milner, H. R. (2005). Beyond culture-blindness: A model of culture with implications for gifted education. *Roeper Review, 27*(2), 97–103.

Ford, D. Y., & Whiting, G. W. (2006). Under-representation of diverse students in gifted education: Recommendations for nondiscriminatory assessment (part 1). *Gifted Education Press Quarterly, 20*(2), 2–6.

Fordham, S. (1988). Racelessness as a factor in Black students' school success: Pragmatic strategy or Pyrrhic victory? *Harvard Educational Review, 58*(1), 54–84.

Fordham, S., & Ogbu, J. (1986). Black students' school success: Coping with the "burden of 'acting White.'" *Urban Review, 18*(3), 176–206.

Frasier, M. M., Martin, D., Garcia, J., Finley, V. S., Frank, E., Krisel, S., & King, L. L. (1995). *A new window for looking at gifted children.* Storrs: University of Connecticut National Research Center on the Gifted and Talented.

Gallagher, J. (2004). *Public policy in gifted education.* Thousand Oaks, CA: Corwin Press and National Association for Gifted Children.

Gardner, H. (1993). *Frames of mind: The theory of multiple intelligences* (2nd ed.). New York: Basic Books.

Gay, G. (2000). *Culturally responsive teaching: Theory, research, and practice.* New York: Teachers College Press.

Gould, S. J. (1996). *The mismeasure of man* (rev. and expanded ed.). New York: Norton.

Grantham, T. C., Ford, D. Y., Henfield, M., Trotman Scott, M., Harmon, D., Porchér, S., & Price, C. (2011). *Gifted and advanced Black students in school: An anthology of critical works.* Waco, TX: Prufrock Press.

Grossman, K. (1991). Environmental racism. *Crisis, 98*(4), 14–17, 31–32.

Harris, J. J., III, Brown, E. L., Ford, D. Y., & Richardson, J. W. (2004). African Americans and multicultural education: A proposed remedy for disproportionate special education placement and underinclusion in gifted education. *Education and Urban Society, 36*(3), 304–341.

Hart, B., & Risley, T. R. (1995). *Meaningful differences in the everyday experience of young children.* Baltimore, MD: Brookes Publishing Company.

Helms, J. E. (1992). Why is there no study of cultural equivalence in standardized cognitive ability testing? *American Psychologist, 47*(9), 1083–1101.

Herrnstein, R. J., & Murray, C. (1994). *The bell curve: Intelligence and class structure in American life.* New York: Free Press.

Heubert, J. P., & Hauser, R. M. (Eds.). (1999). *High stakes: Testing for tracking, promotion, and graduation.* Washington, DC: National Academy Press.

Hudley, A. H., & Mallinson, C. (2011). *Understanding English language variation in U.S. schools.* New York: Teachers College Press.

Irvine, J. J., & York, D. E. (2001). Learning styles and culturally diverse students: A literature review. In J. A. Banks & C. A. M. Banks (Eds.), *Handbook of research on multicultural education* (pp. 484–497). San Francisco: Jossey-Bass.

Jensen, A. R. (1980). *Bias in mental testing.* New York: Free Press.

Kaufman, A. S. (1994). *Intelligent testing with the WISC-III.* New York: Wiley.

Kitano, M. K., & DiJosia, M. (2002). Are Asian and Pacific Americans overrepresented in programs for the gifted? *Roeper Review, 24*(2), 76–80.

Kornhaber, M. (2004). Assessment, standards, and equity. In J. A. Banks & C. A. M. Banks (Eds.), *Handbook of research on multicultural education* (2nd ed., pp. 91–109). San Francisco: Jossey-Bass.

Lee, C. D. (1993). *Signifying as a scaffold for literary interpretation: The pedagogical implications of an African American discourse genre.* Urbana, IL: National Council of Teachers of English.

Lee, C. D. (2007). *Culture, literacy, and learning: Taking bloom in the midst of the whirlwind.* New York: Teachers College Press.

Majors, R., & Billson, J. M. (1992). *Cool pose: The dilemmas of Black manhood in America.* New York: Touchstone.

Maker, C. J., & Nielson, A. B. (2009). *Curriculum development and teaching strategies for gifted learners* (3rd ed.). Austin, TX: PRO-ED.

Menchaca, M. (1997). Early racist discourses: The roots of deficit thinking. In R. Valencia (Ed.), *The evolution of deficit thinking: Educational thought and practice* (pp. 13–40). New York: Falmer.

Mercer, J. R. (1973). *Labeling the mentally retarded: Clinical and social system perspectives on mental retardation.* Berkeley: University of California Press.

Naglieri, J. A., & Ford, D. Y. (2003). Addressing underrepresentation of gifted minority children using the Naglieri Nonverbal Ability Test (NNAT). *Gifted Child Quarterly, 47*(2), 155–160.

Naglieri, J. A., & Ford, D. Y. (2005). Increasing minority children's representation in gifted classes using the NNAT: A response to Lohman. *Gifted Child Quarterly, 49*(1), 29–36.

National Association for Gifted Children (NAGC). (1997). *Position paper on testing.* Washington, DC: Author.

National Association for Gifted Children (NAGC). (2002). Does the No Child Left Behind Act "do" anything for gifted students? Retrieved March 2, 2006, from http://www.nagc.org/index.aspx?id=999.

Oberg, K. (1960). Adjustment to new cultural environments. *Practical Anthropology, 7,* 170–179.

Office for Civil Rights. (1998). *Elementary and secondary schools civil rights survey.* Retrieved November 24, 2008, from http://ocrdata. ed.gov/ocr2002rv30/.

Office for Civil Rights. (2000a). *Elementary and secondary schools civil rights survey.* Retrieved November 24, 2008, from http://ocrdata. ed.gov/ocr2002rv30/.

Office for Civil Rights. (2000b). *The use of tests as part of high-stakes decision-making for students: A resource guide for educators and policy-makers.* Washington, DC: Author.

Office for Civil Rights. (2002). *Elementary and secondary schools civil rights survey.* Retrieved November 24, 2008, from http://ocrdata. ed.gov/ocr2002rv30/.

Office for Civil Rights. (2004). *Elementary and secondary schools civil rights survey.* Retrieved November 24, 2008, from http://ocrdata. ed.gov/ocr2002rv30/.

Office for Civil Rights. (2006). *Elementary and secondary school civil rights survey.* Retrieved November 20, 2011 from http://ocrdata. ed.gov/ocr2002rv30/wdsdata.html.

Office of Ethnic Minority Affairs. (1993). Guidelines for providers of psychological services to ethnic, linguistic, and culturally diverse populations. *American Psychologist, 48*(1), 45–48.

Pang, V. O., Kiang, P. N., & Pak, Y. K. (2004). Asian Pacific American students: Challenging a biased educational system. In J. A. Banks & C. A. M. Banks (Eds.), *Handbook of research on multicultural education* (2nd ed., pp. 542–563). San Francisco: Jossey-Bass.

Pfeiffer, S. I. (2003). Challenges and opportunities for students who are gifted: What the experts say. *Gifted Child Quarterly, 47*(2), 161–169.

Ramírez, M., III, & Castañeda, A. (1974). *Cultural democracy, bicognitive development, and education.* New York: Academic Press.

Reis, S. M., & Callahan, C. M. (1989). Gifted females: They've come a long way—or have they? *Journal for the Education of the Gifted, 12*(2), 99–117.

Rimm, S. B. (2008). *Why bright kids get poor grades: And what you can do about it* (2nd ed.). Scottsdale, AZ: Great Potential Press.

Saccuzzo, D. P., Johnson, N. E., & Guertin, T. L. (1994). *Identifying underrepresented disadvantaged gifted and talented children: A multifaceted approach* (Vols. 1 & 2). San Diego, CA: San Diego State University.

Sandoval, J., Frisby, C. L., Geisinger, K. F., Scheuneman, J. D., & Grenier, J. R. (1998). *Test interpretation and diversity: Achieving equity in assessment.* Washington, DC: American Psychological Association.

Sapon-Shevon, M. (1996). Beyond gifted education: Building a shared agenda for school reform. *Journal for the Education of the Gifted, 19*(2), 194–214.

Saracho, O. N., & Gerstl, C. K. (1992). Learning differences among at-risk minority students. In H. C. Waxman, J. Walker de Felix, J. E. Anderson, & H. P. Baptiste (Eds.), *Students at risk in at-risk schools: Improving environments for learning* (pp. 105–135). Newbury Park, CA: Corwin.

Shade, B. J., Kelly, C., & Oberg, M. (1997). *Creating culturally responsive classrooms.* Washington, DC: American Psychological Association.

Silverman, L. K. (1993). *Counseling the gifted and talented.* Denver, CO: Love.

Smith, C., Constantino, R., & Krashen, S. (1997). Differences in print environment for children in Beverly Hills, Compton, and Watts. *Emergency Librarian, 24*(4), 8–9.

Sowell, T. (1993). *Inside American education: The decline, the deception, the dogmas.* New York: Free Press.

Sternberg, R. J. (1985). *Beyond IQ: A triarchic theory of human intelligence.* New York: Cambridge University Press.

Storti, C. (1989). *The art of crossing cultures.* Yarmouth, ME: Intercultural Press.

Suzuki, L. A., & Ponterotto, J. G. (Eds.). (2008). *Handbook of multicultural assessment: Clinical, psychological, and educational applications* (3rd ed.). San Francisco: Jossey-Bass.

Tomlinson, C. A. (2001). *How to differentiate instruction in mixed-ability classrooms* (2nd ed.). Alexandria, VA: Association for Supervision and Curriculum Development.

U.S. Department of Education (USDE). (1993). *National excellence: A case for developing America's talent.* Washington, DC: Author.

Valencia, R. R. (2010). *Dismantling contemporary deficit thinking.* New York & London: Routledge.

VanTassel-Baska, J., Patton, J., & Prillaman, D. (1989). Disadvantaged gifted learners at-risk for educational attention. *Focus on Exceptional Children, 22*(3), 1–16.

VanTassel-Baska, J., & Stambaugh, T. (2006). *Comprehensive curriculum for gifted learners* (3rd ed.). Boston: Allyn & Bacon.

Whiting, G. (2006). Promoting a scholar identity in African American males: Recommendations for gifted education. *Gifted Education Press Quarterly, 20*(3), 1–6.

Whiting, G. W., & Ford, D. Y. (2006). Under-representation of diverse students in gifted education: Recommendations for nondiscriminatory assessment (part 2). *Gifted Education Press Quarterly, 20*(3), 6–10.

Students benefit when their teachers, parents, and community members work together to reform schools.

© Blend Images/SuperStock

Monashee Frantz/Glow Images

Purestock/Getty Images, Inc.

School Reform

Reforming schools so that all students have an equal opportunity to succeed requires a new vision by educators who are willing to advocate for and participate in change. The two chapters in Part VI discuss effective ways to conceptualize and implement school reform within a multicultural framework. In Chapter 16, Nieto and Bode present and analyze five conditions that will promote student achievement within a multicultural perspective. According to Nieto and Bode, schools should (1) be antiracist and antibiased, (2) reflect an understanding and acceptance of all students as having talents and strengths that can enhance their education, (3) be considered within the parameters of critical pedagogy, (4) involve those people most intimately connected with teaching and learning, and (5) be based on high expectations and rigorous standards for all learners.

Cherry A. McGee Banks, in Chapter 17, discusses ways to involve parents in schools. She argues that parent involvement is an important factor in school reform and student achievement and that parents can be a cogent force in school reform. Parents, perhaps more than any other group, can mobilize the community to support school reform. Parents have firsthand knowledge about the school's effectiveness and can be vocal advocates for change. As consumers of educational services, parents can raise questions that are difficult for professional educators and administrators to raise, such as "What is the proportion of males in special education classes?" and "What is the ethnic breakdown of students enrolled in higher-level math and science classes?"

Banks argues that parents are more willing to work for school reform when they are involved in schools. They are more likely to become involved in schools when opportunities for their involvement reflect their varied interests, skills, and motivations. Banks suggests ways to expand traditional ideas about parent involvement and to increase the number and kinds of parents involved in schools.

© Blend Images/SuperStock

School Reform and Student Learning: A Multicultural Perspective

Sonia Nieto and Patty Bode

Learning is at the heart of schooling. If this is the case, then it makes sense that student learning be a major focus of school reform efforts. This means that educational policies and practices need to be viewed in terms of how they affect the learning and academic achievement of students. But some school policies—especially as espoused in the various reform efforts of the past three decades that began with the publication of *A Nation at Risk* (National Commission on Excellence in Education, 1983) and eventually became institutionalized in 2001 through the version of the Elementary and Secondary Education Act (ESEA) called the No Child Left Behind Act (NCLB)—pay scant attention to whether and to what extent students actually learn.

These reform efforts often end up punishing schools, teachers, districts, and ultimately students who have not measured up to norms of success predetermined by politicians, policy makers, and others who know little about schools. These reform efforts were originally enacted to respond to serious issues plaguing our educational system, including the deplorable history of educational inequality in our nation. However, there are many flaws in these policies, including the single-minded focus on standardized tests as the primary criterion for judging academic progress and the dismal results this focus has produced.

While the more recent federal Blueprint for Reform has reprised many of these missteps, it has, in some ways, demonstrated some hopeful turns of policy. For example, the blueprint set forth a plan to eliminate the current accountability system, which in the past has required public schools to make adequate yearly progress (AYP) in raising student achievement as measured by state tests and other indicators. The blueprint aims to replace AYP with a more comprehensive strategy of measuring growth, yet as this book goes to press many questions remain about how that will happen. In the meantime, policymakers continue to implement policies that require longer school days and years, strict retention policies, placement of schools "on probation," state takeovers, privatization, teacher compensation based on student test scores, and more high-stakes testing; less attention to pedagogy and curricula have been the result (Abernathy, 2007; Meier & Wood, 2004; Nichols & Berliner, 2007; Rothstein, 2008).

A number of studies indicate that students who are most at risk of receiving an inadequate education are often the ones most jeopardized by such reform efforts (Darling-Hammond, 2006, 2010). After years of these failed policies, Diane Ravitch (2010)—who, as Assistant Secretary of Education in the administration of George H. W. Bush, touted the benefits and promises of NCLB and its much-lauded goal of 100 percent proficiency of every child by 2014—now sees its detrimental effects and repudiates the overemphasis on testing and the subsequent punishment of schools:

> . . . the most dangerous potential effect of the 2014 goal is that it is a timetable for the demolition of public education in the United States. The goal of 100% proficiency placed thousands of public schools at risk of being privatized, turned into charters, or closed. (p. 104)

Furthermore, Ravitch contends, "There is no substantial body of evidence that low-performing schools can be turned around by any of the remedies prescribed by law" (p. 104).

This chapter rejects decision making based on test scores and asserts that student learning can be positively influenced by changes in school policies and practices that raise academic achievement while affirming students' identities. Two related assumptions undergird this assertion: (1) Students, families, and teachers bring strengths and talents to teaching and learning, and (2) a comprehensive and critical approach to multicultural education can provide an important framework for rethinking school reform.

Given the social nature of schooling, it is impossible to ascribe a fixed causal relationship between student learning and schooling. Many complex forces influence student learning, including personal, psychological, social, cultural, community, and institutional factors (Berliner, 2009; Nieto & Bode, 2012). That is, we cannot simply say that eliminating tracking will help all students succeed or that native language instruction will guarantee success for all language-minority students. Neither can we state unequivocally that culturally responsive pedagogy is always the answer. Although these changes may in fact substantially improve educational outcomes for many more students than are now achieving academic success, taken in isolation, they may fail to reflect the complex nature of student learning.

In what follows, we explore the meaning of school reform with a multicultural perspective and consider implications for student learning. We begin by defining school reform with a multicultural perspective, including how a school's policies and practices implicitly illustrate beliefs about who deserves the benefits of a high-quality education. We do so because certain school policies and practices may exacerbate the pervasive structural inequalities that exist in society. We then describe a set of five interrelated conditions for successful school reform within a multicultural perspective. These conditions are intimately interconnected, but for the purpose of expediency, we explain the five conditions separately along with implications for increasing student achievement.

School Reform with a Multicultural Perspective

Many people assume that multicultural education consists of little more than isolated lessons in sensitivity training or prejudice reduction or separate units about cultural artifacts or ethnic holidays. To some it might mean education geared for urban schools or, more specifically, for African American students. Conceptualizing reform in this limited and misguided way is *not* a multicultural perspective, nor is it multicultural education, and it will have little influence on student learning.

When conceptualized as broad-based school reform, however, multicultural education can have a major influence on how and to what extent students learn. To approach school reform with a multicultural perspective, we need to begin with an understanding of multicultural education within its *sociopolitical context* (Nieto & Bode, 2012). A sociopolitical context underscores that education is part and parcel of larger societal and political forces, such as inequality based on stratification due to race, social class, gender, and other differences. Given this perspective, decisions concerning such practices as ability tracking, high-stakes testing, native language instruction, retention, curriculum reform, and pedagogy are all influenced by broader social policies.

As Freire (1985) made clear, every educational decision, whether made at the classroom, city, state, or national level, is imbedded within a particular ideological framework. Such decisions can be as simple as whether a classroom should be arranged in rows with all students facing the teacher, in tables with groups of students to encourage cooperative work, or in a variety of ways depending on the task at hand. Alternatively, these decisions can be as far-reaching as eliminating tracking in an entire school system, teaching language-minority students by using both their native language and English, or teaching such students by using English only. Embedded within each educational decision are assumptions about the nature of learning, about what particular students are capable of achieving, about whose language has value, and about who should be at the center of the educational process. As stated more extensively elsewhere, Nieto (Nieto & Bode, 2012) defines multicultural education within a sociopolitical context as:

> . . . *a process of comprehensive school reform and basic education for all students. It challenges and rejects racism and other forms of discrimination in schools and society and accepts and affirms the pluralism (ethnic, racial, linguistic, religious, economic, and gender, among others) that students, their communities, and teachers reflect. Multicultural education permeates the schools' curriculum and instructional strategies as well as the interactions among teachers, students, and families, and the very way that schools conceptualize the nature of teaching and learning. Because it uses critical pedagogy as its underlying philosophy and focuses on knowledge, reflection, and action (praxis) as the basis for social change, multicultural education promotes democratic principles of social justice. (p. 42)*

This definition of multicultural education assumes a comprehensive school reform effort rather than superficial additions to the curriculum or one-shot treatments about diversity, such as workshops for teachers or assembly programs for students. As such, we use this definition as a lens through which to view conditions for systemic school reform that can improve the learning of all students.

Conditions for Systemic School Reform with a Multicultural Perspective

Failure to learn does not develop out of thin air; it is scrupulously created through policies, practices, attitudes, and beliefs. In a very concrete sense, the results of educational inequality explain by example what a society believes its young people are capable of achieving and what they deserve. For instance, offering only low-level courses in schools serving culturally diverse and poor youngsters is a clear message that the students are not expected to achieve at high levels; likewise, considering students to be "at risk" simply because of their ethnicity, native language, family characteristics, or social class is another clear sign that some students have been defined by conventional wisdom as uneducable based simply on their identity. Although it is true that conditions such as poverty and attendant hardships such as poor health and nutrition may create obstacles to learning, they should not be viewed as insurmountable obstacles because we have substantive evidence that some students *can* achieve despite such roadblocks. More students achieve to high levels, however, when these obstacles are removed.

As a result, we cannot think about educational reform without taking into account both micro- and macro-level issues that may affect student learning. Micro-level issues include the cultures, languages, and experiences of students and their families and how these are considered in determining school policies and practices (Cummins, 2000; Nieto, 2010). Macro-level issues include the racial stratification that helps maintain inequality and the resources and access to learning that schools provide or deny (Grant-Thomas & Orfield, 2009; Kozol, 2005; Orfield, 2001; Rothstein, 2004; Spring, 2013). Ladson-Billings (2006b) has argued that the focus on school performance gaps is misplaced and that what must be considered are the historical, economic, sociopolitical, and moral components of racial stratification that have accumulated over time, amounting to what she has dubbed "the education debt" (p. 3).

In addition, how students and their families view their status in schools and society must be considered. Recent research focuses on students' perceptions of opportunity structures as well as their personal assertions of identity. Conchas (2006) points out that linking academic rigor with strong collaborative relationships among students and teachers plays a significant, positive role in high achievement for some youths from economically strapped communities. Yet he maintains that transforming students' perceptions of the opportunity structure is tied to the larger social and economic inequality and "its devastating impact on the perceptions of racial minority youth concerning social mobility" (p. 123). Carter (2005) notes the complex ways in which youths take up, express, and border-cross cultural identities in relation to schooling. She calls for teachers, parents, and other adults in the community to become "multicultural navigators" (p. 137), that is, to help demonstrate to students how to use both dominant and nondominant cultural capital and develop adeptness at moving through a range of sociocultural settings. To ensure that all students succeed academically, Carter argues, multicultural navigators are needed to increase students' investment in their education.

Conditions such as inequitable school financing (Johnson, Zhou, & Nakamoto, 2011), unrepresentative school governance (Meier & Stewart, 1991), and large class size (Biddle & Berliner, 2002; Muennig & Woolf, 2007) may play powerful roles in promoting student underachievement. For example, inequities in school financing have remained quite stable since Kozol's (1991) landmark study of more than two decades ago. Yet reform strategies such as longer school days, more rigorous graduation standards, and increased standardized testing often do not take such issues into account. The evidence is growing, for example, that school size and class size make a difference in student learning and that these may also influence students' feelings of belonging and, thus, their engagement with learning (Carter, 2005; Yosso, 2006). In fact, equalizing just two conditions of schooling—funding and class size—would probably result in an immediate and dramatic improvement in learning for students who have not received the benefits of such conditions.

School reform strategies that do not acknowledge such macro-level disparities are bound to be inadequate because they assume that schools provide all students with a level playing field (Berliner, 2009; Grant-Thomas & Orfield, 2009; Rothstein, 2004). The conditions described in this chapter, while acknowledging these disparities, nevertheless provide hope for school systems in which such changes as equitable funding or small class size may not occur in the near future. Rather than wait for these changes to happen, schools and teachers can begin to improve the possibility for successful student learning by attending to a number of conditions. Five such conditions are described here, which, along with changes in funding and resource allocation, would help create schools where all students have a better chance to learn (these conditions are described in greater detail in Nieto, 2010).

School Reform Should Be Antiracist and Antibias

An antiracist and antibias perspective is at the core of multicultural education. This is crucial because too often people believe that multicultural education automatically takes care of racism, but this is far from the reality. In fact, multicultural education without an explicit antiracist focus may perpetuate the worst kinds of stereotypes if it focuses only on superficial aspects of culture and the addition of ethnic tidbits to the curriculum.

Addressing racism is critical, yet if not rooted in theory and in student experience, educators might make erroneous assumptions about students' racial affiliations and other dimensions of multiple identities. We have written elsewhere with colleagues (Nieto, Bode, Kang, & Raible, 2008), drawing from Dolby (2000) and other critical and postmodern perspectives, to address the hybrid nature of contemporary U.S. society. Specifically, we ask how multicultural education might transcend typically essentialist notions of race and other identities to promote a more nuanced, critical understanding of multicultural perspectives. Postmodern frameworks of identity insist that identities and cultures are not static; they shift and evolve according to the context, and so must curriculum and instruction. Yet racism remains a stark reality and needs to be addressed by multicultural education even while contemporary discourse on identities calls into question the notion of race. Put simply, race may no longer exist, but institutionalized racism is alive and well.

Being antiracist means paying attention to all areas in which some students may be favored over others, including the curriculum and pedagogy, sorting policies, and teachers' interactions and relationships with students and their communities. Schools committed to multicultural education with an antiracist perspective need to examine closely both school policies and the attitudes and behaviors of their staff to determine how these might be complicit in causing academic failure. The kind of expectations that teachers and schools have for students (Conchas, 2006; Nieto, 2002–2003; Noguera, 2003, 2008), whether native language use is permitted or punished (Cummins, 2000; Gebhard, Austin, Nieto, & Willett, 2002), how sorting takes place (Oakes, 2005), and how classroom organization, pedagogy, and curriculum may influence student learning (Bennett deMarrais & LeCompte, 1999) all need to be considered.

To become antiracist, schools also need to examine how the curriculum may perpetuate negative, distorted, or incomplete images of some groups while exalting others as the makers of all history. Unfortunately, many textbooks, children's books, software programs, audiovisual media, and web media are still replete with racist and sexist images and with demeaning portrayals of people from low-income communities. Although the situation is improving and the stereotypes that exist are not as blatant as they once were, there are still many inaccuracies and negative portrayals (Botelho & Rudman, 2009; Clawson, 2002; Grever & Stuurman, 2007; Loewen, 2007, 2008).

The images generated by the media and the competing political parties throughout the U.S. presidential campaigns of 2008 and 2012 brought forth multiple examples of how the general public either perpetuated and embraced or refuted and rejected racism and sexism. This makes a compelling case for developing a more critically literate public through multicultural education. Most of the heroes or heroines presented as women and men in the standard curriculum—whether from dominant or nondominant cultures—are "safe"; that is, they do not pose a challenge to the status quo. Other people who have fought for social justice are omitted, presented as bizarre or insane, or made safe by downplaying their contributions. A now-classic article by Kozol (1975) graphically documents how schools bleed the life and soul out of even the most impassioned and courageous heroes, such as Helen Keller and Martin Luther King Jr., in the process making them boring and less-than-believable caricatures. Also, a powerful book by Kohl (2005) demonstrates how Rosa Parks, the mother of the civil rights movement, was made palatable to the mainstream by portraying her not as a staunch civil rights crusader who consciously battled racist segregation but as a tired woman who simply did not want to give up her seat on the bus. These examples are misleading or even racist representations of reality.

Through this kind of "safe" curriculum, many teachers are misled to believe that they are teaching from a multicultural perspective. In such an approach, students from dominant groups learn that they are the norm, and consequently they often assume that anyone different from them is culturally or intellectually disadvantaged. On the other hand, students from subordinated cultures may internalize the message that their cultures, families, languages, and experiences have low status, and they learn to feel inferior. The result may be what Claude Steele (1999) has called "stereotype threat" (p. 44). Steele describes stereotype threat as the impact that devaluation in schools and society may have on African Americans, other people of color, and women, leading them to underperform academically (Aronson & Steele, 2005). All students suffer as a result of these messages, but students from dominated groups are the most negatively affected.

The issue of institutional power is also at play here. The conventional notion of racism is that it is an *individual* bias toward members of other groups. This perception conveniently skirts the issue of how institutions themselves, which are much more powerful than individuals, develop harmful policies and practices that victimize American Indians, African Americans, Asians, Latinos, low-income European Americans, females, gays, lesbians, transgender people, and others from dominated groups. The major difference between *individual racism* and *institutional racism and bias* is the wielding of power because it is primarily through the power of the people who control institutions such as schools that oppressive policies and practices are reinforced and legitimated (Tatum, 2003, 2007; Weinberg, 1996). That is, when racism is understood as a systemic problem, not just as an individual dislike for a particular group of people, we can better understand its negative and destructive effects.

We do not wish to minimize the powerful effect of individual prejudice and discrimination, which can be personally very painful, nor do we suggest that individual discrimination occurs only in one direction, for example, from Whites to African Americans. No group monopolizes prejudice and discrimination; they occur in all directions and even within groups. But interethnic hostility, personal prejudices, and individual biases, while certainly hurtful, do not have the long-range and life-limiting effects on entire groups of people that institutional racism and bias have.

Testing practices, for example, may be institutionally discriminatory because, as a result of their performance on these tests, students from culturally and socially dominated groups may be labeled as inferior (McNeil, 2000; Nichols & Berliner, 2007). Rather than critically examining the tests themselves, the underlying purpose of such tests, or their damaging effects, educational policymakers often blame the students themselves. In addition, the fact that textbook companies and other companies that develop tests earn huge profits from test construction and dissemination is often unmentioned, yet it, too, is a reality (Miner, 2004). Ravitch (2010), once a champion of testing practices, has become a spokesperson for uncovering the multifaceted ways in which the testing craze has damaged the U.S. public school system.

An antiracist perspective is apparent in schools when students are permitted, and even encouraged, to speak about their experiences with racism and other biases. Many White teachers feel great discomfort when racism is discussed in the classroom. They are uncomfortable for several reasons: their lack of experience in confronting such a potentially explosive issue, the conspiracy of silence about racism (as if not speaking about it will make it disappear), the guilt they may feel from being a member of the group that has benefited from racism, the generally accepted assumption that we live in a color-blind society, or a combination of these reasons (Howard, 2006; Sleeter, 1994; Tatum, 2007). According to Pollock (2004), while seemingly color-blind, this discourse is in fact highly racialized because the deletion of race in both classroom practice and policy talk is a deliberate and race-conscious act. Referring to this practice as "colormuteness," Pollock argues that it is an active struggle to mask the perceived or possible relevance of race. She also suggests that true color-blindness is impossible in a nation as racialized as the United States. In her edited compilation *Everyday Antiracism*, Pollock (2008) advances insights from dozens of educators to make the struggle around issues of race and racism more visible and audible.

When students are given time and support for expressing their views, the result can be compelling because their experiences are legitimated and used in the service of their learning. A number of teachers have written eloquently about the impact of addressing issues of racism and discrimination in the classroom (Davis, 2005; Landsman, 2001; Levin, 2001). Van Ausdale and Feagin (2001) provide compelling evidence of preschoolers' racialized views, actions, and language, with a focus on the role of the teacher in antiracist education. Michie (2005) documented how five teachers in Chicago public schools supported students' learning through a rigorous academic program with a social justice focus. These educators found that, rather than shying away from such topics, teachers who directly confront issues of bias can help students become more engaged, critical, and reflective learners.

In our research on students' concerns about their education, they mentioned racism and other examples of discrimination on the part of fellow students and teachers (Nieto & Bode, 2012). Rashaud, an African American high school student in Georgia, said, "Being an African American student, to me, really it's kinda' tense. People are already judging you when you're African American" (p. 96). Nadia, a Syrian student in a midwestern college town told us:

> [A]fter September 11th it was a little shaky, and I didn't want to tell people that I was Arabic because you got the weird looks . . . they said, "Are you . . . you kind of look Afghani?" That's when it's a bit

of a burden, just when you get singled out. People look at you different when they find out you're Arabic, especially now. (p. 322)

Other students also talked about discrimination on the part of teachers. Christina, a recent immigrant from Kenya who was a novice learner of technology, mentioned how teachers expected her to be computer literate and to "get a move on" with her computer assignments. Likewise, she reacted with astonished humor when the track coach in her school assumed she would be a strong runner simply because she was from Kenya, even though she had never been on a track team. Nini, who described herself as racially and ethnically mixed, gave an account of facing competing expectations from peers in segregated White and Black racial groups as well as confronting low expectations from teachers who assume, "Oh she's Black . . . she's not going to achieve well" (p. 272). Eugene, who was adopted by two gay dads, shared the perspective of growing up in a loving, secure family while also feeling the pressure to keep his family "in the closet":

One time in Spanish class we were doing "family words." My teacher was talking to everyone about their mother and their father and I did not want to get called on. . . . [A]nother time we had to do a family tree . . . I only put in one of my parents. (p. 375)

As these examples demonstrate, antiracist and antibias perspectives are essential in schools if all students are to be given equitable environments for learning. An antiracist perspective is a vital lens through which to analyze a school's policies and practices, including the curriculum, pedagogy, testing and tracking, discipline, faculty hiring, student retention, and attitudes about and interactions with families.

School Reform Should Reflect an Understanding and Acceptance of All Students as Having Talents and Strengths That Can Enhance Their Education

Too often educators believe that students from culturally subordinated groups have few experiential or cultural strengths that can benefit their education. A classic example comes from Ryan (1972), who coined the expression "blaming the victim" for the tendency to place responsibility on students and their families for their failure to achieve in school. These students, generally low-income children of all groups and children of color specifically, are often considered deficient or "culturally deprived," a patronizing term popularized in the 1960s (Reissman, 1962). But Ryan (1972) turned the perspective of "cultural deprivation" on its head when he wrote:

We are dealing, it would seem, not so much with culturally deprived children as with culturally depriving schools. And the task to be accomplished is not to revise, amend, and repair deficient children, but to alter and transform the atmosphere and operations of the schools to which we commit these children. (p. 61)

Students might be thought of as culturally deprived simply because they speak a language other than English as their native language or because they have just one parent or live in poverty. Sometimes they are labeled in this way just because of their race or ethnicity. These notions of "the culture of poverty" were developed by Lewis (1965) and Harrington (1971/1997) decades ago. Ladson-Billings (2006a) notes that the way the concept of "culture" is used by some teachers and students in pre-service teacher education can exacerbate the problem and perpetuate stereotypes. They might assume, for example, that certain behaviors are "part of their culture" when students are noisy or parents are absent from open house night. Ladson-Billings points out that a growing number of teachers use "culture" as a catchall concept for all manner of behaviors and characteristics when discussing students who are not White, not English-speaking, or not native-born U.S. citizens. A growing body of research points to the most detrimental results of this deficit view in what has come to be called "the school to prison pipeline" (Edelman, 2007; Noguera, 2003; Vaught, 2011).

Given such dire results, it is urgent to begin with a more positive and, in the end, more realistic and hopeful view of students and their families. School reform measures based on the assumption that children of all families bring cultural and community strengths to their education would go a long way toward providing more powerful learning environments for a greater number of youngsters. The research of Gonzalez, Moll, and Amanti (2005) on incorporating "funds of knowledge" into the curriculum—that is, using the experiences and skills of all families to encourage student learning—is a more promising and productive way of approaching families than is the viewpoint that they have only deficits that must be repaired.

If we begin with the premise that children and their families have substantial talents that can inform student learning, a number of implications for improving schools follow. Instead of placing the blame for failure to learn solely on students, teachers need to become aware of how their own biases can act as barriers to student learning. Teachers also need to consider how their students best learn and how their own pedagogical practices need to change as a result. This implies that teachers need to learn culturally responsive ways of teaching all of their students (Gay, 2004, 2010; Irizarry, 2011; Irvine, 2003; Ladson-Billings, 2001, 2006a).

Teachers also need to consider how the native language of students influences their academic achievement. For this to happen, they need to dispel some of the conventional myths surrounding native language use (Crawford, 2008). For instance, it is common practice in schools to try to convince parents whose native language is other than English that they should speak only English with their children. This recommendation makes little sense for at least three reasons. First, these parents often speak little English themselves, and their children are thus provided with less than adequate models of the language. Second, this practice often results in cutting off, rather than stimulating, communication between parents and children. This kind of communication is essential for learning as well as for family cohesion. Third, if young people are encouraged to learn English at the expense of their native language rather than in conjunction with it, they may lose meaningful ethnic and social connections that help maintain close and loving relations with family members (Beykont, 2000).

A more reasonable recommendation, and one that would honor the contributions parents can make to their children's education, is to encourage rather than discourage them to speak their native language with their children, to speak it often, and to use it consistently. In schools, this means that students would not be punished for speaking their native languages; rather, they would be encouraged to do so, and to do so in the service of their learning (see Zentella, 2005). A rich communicative legacy, both in school and at home, could be the result (for inspiring examples of how children can become biliterate "in spite of the odds," see Reyes, 2011).

Another example of failing to use student and community strengths can be found in the curriculum. A perspective that affirms the talents and experiences of students and their families can expand the people and roles included in the curriculum. We have written elsewhere (Nieto & Bode, 2012) about a curriculum in which the first-grade teachers Susie Secco and Gina Simm endeavor to make *all* families visible by honoring the diversity of their lived experiences through a classroom activity about *Family Responsibilities*. Here we provide a glimpse into the work of these teachers:

> *Each first grader conducts a family survey, by interviewing the adults at home with questions such as: What responsibilities do you have while I am at school? What jobs do you do either at home or away from home? These interview techniques make space for a range of replies to be respected as opposed to a more narrow question that children hear frequently "where do your parents work?" The first graders learn more about what their caregivers are doing, they learn more about the assortment of possibilities of adult responsibilities and the teachers and classmates gain an intimate view into the complex workings of each student's family. The assignment reaps replies from the adults such as: caring for younger children or elders, searching for employment, cleaning or fixing up the home,*

volunteer work, going to school, resting to go to the night shift at work and much more. The students also hear about a variety of places that people call "work": the office, the school, the fire station, the bakery, the construction site, the chemistry lab, the home, the sandwich shop, the docks, the houses that need cleaning, the hospital, grandma's house, the cafeteria, the bus garage, the vending cart, the highway toll booth, the hotel and more. In addition to the academic and research skills gained by six-year-olds, the end result is that each family's contributions are visible and honored in the class-room. This is only one of many activities in the Family Diversity Curriculum designed by Secco and Simm to investigate their four "big ideas" (Wiggins & McTighe, 2005) that include: 1) There are all kinds of families, 2) Families have wants and needs, 3) Family responsibilities, and 4) Experiencing change is common to all families. (pp. 356–360)

A further consideration concerning the talents and strengths of students and their families is what Cummins (1996) has called the "relations of power" in schools. In proposing a shift from "coercive" to "collaborative" relations of power, Cummins argues that traditional teacher-centered transmission models can limit the potential for learning, especially among students from communities whose cultures and languages are devalued by the dominant canon. In a powerful study of urban high school students becoming critical researchers, Morrell (2008) documented how students' experiences, knowledge, and enthusiasm can help engage them in robust learning. He concluded that a significant outcome of the study was students' recognition that youth and urban issues were worthy of serious study and that research can have a social impact. These findings suggest that using students as collaborators in developing the curriculum can help promote learning. By encouraging collaborative relations of power, schools can begin to recognize other sources of legitimate knowledge that have been overlooked.

School Reform Should Be Considered within the Parameters of Critical Pedagogy

According to Banks (2009), the main goal of a multicultural curriculum is to help students develop decision-making and social action skills. Consequently, when students learn to view situations and events from a variety of viewpoints, critical thinking, reflection, and action are promoted. Critical pedagogy is an approach through which students and teachers are encouraged to view what they learn in a critical light, or, in the words of Freire (1970), by learning to read both "the word and the world" (p. 69). According to Freire, the opposite of a critical or empowering approach is "banking education," where students learn to regurgitate and passively accept the knowledge they are given (p. 53). A critical education, on the other hand, expects that students will seek their own answers, be curious, and be questioning.

Shor's (1992) pioneering analysis concerning critical pedagogy is instructive. He begins with the assumption that because no curriculum can be truly neutral, it is the responsibility of schools to present students with the broad range of information they will need to learn to read and write critically and in the service of social justice. Thus, critical pedagogy is not simply the transfer of knowledge from teacher to students even though it may be knowledge that has hereto-fore not been made available to them. A critical perspective does not simply operate on the principle of substituting one truth for another; instead, students are encouraged to reflect on multiple and contradictory perspectives in order to understand reality more fully. This is essential at the K–12 level as well as in teacher education (Shor & Pari, 1999, 2000). For instance, learning about the internment of Americans of Japanese descent and Japanese residents in the United States during World War II is not in itself critical pedagogy; it becomes so only when students learn the rationale for why this was done, explore why most schools gloss over or actually omit this information in the curriculum, analyze different viewpoints concerning the situation, and use them to understand the inconsistencies they uncover. They can then begin to understand the role played by racist hysteria, economic exploitation, and propaganda as catalysts for the internment, and they can judge this incident through the stated ideals of our nation.

Without a critical perspective, reality is often presented to students as if it were static, finished, and flat; underlying conflicts, problems, and inherent contradictions are omitted. As we have seen, textbooks in all subject areas generally exclude information about unpopular perspectives or the perspectives of disempowered groups in society. Few of the books to which students have access present the viewpoints of people who have built our country, from enslaved Africans to immigrant labor to other working-class people, even though they have been the backbone of society (Bigelow, 2008; Takaki, 2008; Zinn, 2010).

Using critical pedagogy as a basis for school reform results in very different policies for schools than do traditional models of school reform. Even more important than just increasing curricular options, critical pedagogy helps to expand teachers' and schools' perspectives about students' knowledge and intellectual capabilities. The use of critical pedagogy helps students become agents of their own learning so they can use what they learn in productive and critical ways. The knowledge they learn can be used to explore the reasons for certain conditions in their lives and to design strategies for changing them.

Examples can be found in a range of approaches to critical pedagogy that adapt curriculum for the multicultural K–12 classroom. (Nieto & Bode, 2012). A summary of a case study of curriculum follows.

A Study of Cambodia and the Cambodian American Experience

A team of seventh-grade teachers were concerned about the academic achievement of their Cambodian and Cambodian American students, so they planned a curriculum that aimed to expand the academic prowess of all students of all backgrounds while affirming the identities of a specific group. The teachers drew from students' questions, curiosities, concerns, and even from their prejudices. They developed "big ideas," learning objectives, assessments, and activities for a curriculum that was engaging and rigorous for students of all learning approaches, ethnicities, languages, and racial identities (Sleeter, 2005; Wiggins & McTighe, 2005). Students engaged in literature research, community action, math and science analysis, artistic production, and more. They enlisted spiritual leaders from the local Buddhist temple, elders from the community, high school students, and veterans of the Vietnam War in their classrooms.

Authentic learning was reported from students of Cambodian and non-Cambodian heritages. After the class attended a dance performance, a seventh-grade boy, Eric, stated, "I wish I was a Cambodian dancer. Those guys can break dance mad-cool and then they know their culture, too. I wish I had something like that." The teachers noted that they had never before heard a European American student express appreciation (and even envy) of Cambodian cultural experiences. One Cambodian student, Prasour, wrote: "I liked this part of school when we studied my own culture. I thought it was awesome. The kids who aren't Cambodian thought it was awesome. It just makes you feel awesome to be Cambodian" (Nieto & Bode, 2012, p. 353).

While feeling "awesome" is a beneficial by-product of critical pedagogy and certainly lends to attachment to and engagement with school, it is not its primary goal. Critical pedagogy listens and responds to students' needs, questions, and knowledge to cultivate critical judgment and decision-making skills they will need if they are to become productive members of a democratic society. Other accounts of critical pedagogy in action are contained in publications by Rethinking Schools (Bigelow, Christensen, Karp, Miner, & Peterson, 1994; Bigelow, Harvey, Karp, & Miller, 2001) and Teaching for Change (Lee, Menkart, & Okazawa-Rey, 2007; Menkart, Murray, & View, 2004). Book-length accounts of critical pedagogy (Cowhey, 2006; Vasquez, 2004) provide compelling examples of the positive and empowering influence that teachers' guidance can have on student learning.

The People Most Intimately Connected with Teaching and Learning (Teachers, Families, and Students) Need to Be Meaningfully Involved in School Reform

Research on the involvement of families, students, and teachers has consistently indicated that democratic participation by people closest to learners can dramatically improve student learning. This is especially true in urban schools and in schools that serve low-income, African American, Latino, and immigrant students (Epstein, 2010; Henderson, Mapp, Johnson, & Davies, 2006; Olsen, 2008), yet these are the people most often excluded from discussions and implementation of school reform measures.

Cummins (1996) reviewed programs that included student empowerment as a goal and concluded that students who are encouraged to develop a positive cultural identity through interactions with their teachers experience a sense of control over their own lives and develop the confidence and motivation to succeed academically. School reform measures that stress the meaningful involvement of teachers, families, and students look quite different from traditional approaches. These measures begin with the assumption that these groups have substantial and insightful perspectives about student learning. Rather than thinking of ways to bypass their ideas, school reformers actively seek the involvement of students, families, and teachers in developing, for instance, disciplinary policies, curriculum development, and decisions concerning tracking and the use of tests. These practices are illustrated in the Boston Teachers Union School, which embraces teacher innovation and fully integrates the participation of parents and families (Nieto & Bode, 2012). Similarly, allowing time in the curriculum for students to engage in critical discussions about issues such as whose language is valued in the school can help to affirm the legitimacy of the discourse of all students.

At the same time, these kinds of discussions also acknowledge the need to learn and become comfortable with the discourse of the larger society (Delpit, 2006; Delpit & Dowdy, 2008). In addition, involving families in curriculum development enriches the curriculum, affirms what families have to offer, and helps students overcome the shame they may feel about their cultures, languages, and values, an all-too-common attitude for students from culturally subordinated groups (Nieto & Bode, 2012; Olsen, 2008).

School Reform Needs to Be Based on High Expectations and Rigorous Standards for All Learners

Many students come to school with experiences and conditions, including speaking a language other than English or simply belonging to a particular racial or ethnic group, that some teachers and schools consider obstacles that place them at risk for learning. But beginning with this deficit perspective leaves teachers and schools with little hope. Rather than viewing language and cultural differences as impediments to learning, they can be viewed as resources that students bring to their education. In this way, instead of using these differences as a rationalization for low expectations of what students are capable of learning, they can be used to promote student learning. In addition, in our society, we have generally expected schools to provide an equal and equitable education for all students, not just for those who have no problems in their lives or who fit the image of successful students due to race, class, or language ability. The promise of an equal education for all students of all backgrounds in the United States has yet to be realized, as is evident from a number of classic critiques of the myth of our schools as "the great equalizer" (Mann, 1848/1903), a claim countered by Bowles and Gintis (1976), Katz (1975), and Spring (1989), among many others. Nevertheless, the ideal of equitable educational opportunity is worth defending and vigorously putting into practice.

Far too many students cope on a daily basis with complex and difficult problems, including poverty, food insecurity, violence, racism, abuse, families in distress, and lack of health care and proper housing (Berliner, 2009). While it is undeniably true that many students face unimaginably difficult problems, the school cannot be expected to solve them all. To address this reality, the Economic Policy Institute convened a task force in 2006 to consider the broader context of the No Child Left Behind Act and how it has informed the nation's approach to education and youth development policy. A group of educational researchers drafted the statement *A Broader, Bolder Approach to Education* to inform legislators and the general public that for "school improvement to be fully effective, [it] must be complemented by a broader definition of schooling and by improvements in the social and economic circumstances of disadvantaged youth" (Ladd, Noguera, & Payzant, 2006, para. 2). This point has been taken up by Geoffrey Canada, president of the Harlem Children's Zone (HCZ), which is "an innovative and unique community-based organization, offering education, social-service and community-building programs to children and families" (HCZ, n.d.). HCZ, which is funded primarily by private donations, has flooded the neighborhood with social, medical, and educational services that are available for free to the 10,000 children and their families who live within 100 blocks of the zone with the specific intent of raising academic achievement for every child. Canada's reluctance to wait for government funding for comprehensive reform led him to integrate private funding with public programs. HCZ's rates of success have been a model to public social service and public school reformers throughout the nation, who point out what the possibilities can be to government officials who have the will and the resources to back such programs (Tough, 2008).

In the absence of the will and the resources to back comprehensive social programs, overwhelming social and economic circumstances cannot be overlooked. At the same time, however, we cannot dismiss the heroic efforts of many teachers and schools that, with limited financial and other material resources, teach students who live in dire circumstances under what can best be described as challenging conditions (Ayers, Ladson-Billings, Michie, & Noguera, 2008). Nevertheless, the difficult conditions in which some students live need not be viewed as insurmountable barriers to their academic achievement. It is too often the case that society's low expectations of students, based on these situations, pose even greater obstacles to their learning.

If we are serious about giving all students more options in life, particularly students from communities denied the necessary resources with which to access these options, then we need to begin with the assumption that these students are academically capable, both individually and as a group. Too many students have been dismissed as uneducable simply because they were not born with the material resources or family conditions considered essential for learning. The conventional attitude that students who do not arrive at school with such benefits are incapable of learning is further promoted by assertions of race-based genetic inferiority, an assumption that is unfortunately still too prevalent (Herrnstein & Murray, 1994; Murray, 2008).

Numerous examples of dramatic success in the face of adversity are powerful reminders that great potential exists in all students. Consider, for example, the historical case of Garfield High School in East Los Angeles, California. There, the mostly Mexican American students taught by Jaime Escalante, the protagonist of the popular film *Stand and Deliver*, were tremendously successful in learning advanced mathematics (Menéndez, 1988). In fact, when they took the Advanced Placement (AP) calculus test, they performed so impressively that the test makers assumed they had cheated. As a result, they had to take it a second time, and this time their performance was even better.

The success of the Algebra Project is another more contemporary example (Moses & Cobb, 2002). This project has expanded throughout the country—from Cambridge, Massachusetts, to Jackson, Mississippi, to New Orleans, Louisiana—to young people who had previously been denied access to algebra because they were thought to be incapable of benefiting from it and yet became high achievers in math. When they went on to high school, 39 percent of the first graduating class of the project were placed in honors geometry or honors algebra classes; in fact, none of the graduates were placed in a low-level math course. The Algebra Project continues to spread to other school systems throughout the United States.

Although students' identities are often perceived to be handicaps to learning by an assimilationist society that encourages cultural and linguistic homogeneity, numerous success stories of students who use their cultural values and traditions as strengths have been reported in the educational research literature (Carter, 2005; Conchas, 2006; Lomawaima, 2004; McCarty, 2002; Nieto & Bode, 2012; Zentella, 2005). This result leads us to the inevitable conclusion that before fixing what they may consider to be problems in students, schools and society need to change their own perceptions of students and view them as capable learners.

Conclusion

There is no simple formula for increasing student learning. A step-by-step blueprint for school reform is both unrealistic and inappropriate because each school differs from all others in its basic structure, goals, and human dimensions. Moreover, conditions such as inequitable school funding and the unequal distribution of resources for learning also help explain why some students are successful but others are not. In spite of these challenges, certain conditions can dramatically improve the learning of many students who are currently marginalized from the center of learning because of school policies and practices based on deficit models. If we begin with the assumptions that students cannot achieve at high levels, that their backgrounds are riddled with deficiencies, and that multicultural education is a frill that cannot help them to learn, we will end up with school reform strategies that have little hope for success.

This chapter presented and analyzed five conditions to promote student achievement within a multicultural perspective:

1. School reform should be antiracist and antibiased.

2. School reform should reflect an understanding and acceptance of all students as having talents and strengths that can enhance their education.

3. School reform should be considered within the parameters of critical pedagogy.

4. The people most intimately connected with teaching and learning (teachers, parents, and students themselves) need to be meaningfully involved in school reform.

5. School reform needs to be based on high expectations and rigorous standards for all learners.

This chapter is based on two related assumptions: (1) Students, families, and teachers bring strengths and talents to teaching and learning, and (2) a comprehensive and critical approach to multicultural education can provide an important framework for rethinking school reform. Given these assumptions, we have a much more promising scenario for effective learning and for the possibility that schools can become places of hope and affirmation for students of all backgrounds and situations.

QUESTIONS AND ACTIVITIES

16.1 What does it mean to say that multicultural education takes place within a sociopolitical context? What social, political, and economic factors must be considered when multicultural education is being implemented? How can a consideration of sociopolitical factors help multicultural school reform be more effective?

16.2 What five conditions does the chapter discuss that are needed to improve students' academic achievement? How are these factors interrelated?

16.3 How does the chapter distinguish between *individual* and *institutional racism?* Why is this distinction important? Give examples of each type of racism from your personal experiences and observations.

16.4 What is an antiracist perspective? Why does the chapter stress that an antiracist perspective is essential for the implementation of multicultural education? Give specific examples of antiracist teaching and educational practices with which you are familiar.

16.5 The chapter briefly describes the concept of incorporating community knowledge into the curriculum advanced by Gonzalez and colleagues (2005). How does this concept help teachers implement multicultural education?

16.6 What is critical pedagogy? How, according to the chapter, can it be used to enrich and strengthen multicultural education?

16.7 What positive contributions can parents and students make to create an effective multicultural school? Give specific examples.

REFERENCES

Abernathy, S. (2007). *No Child Left Behind and the public schools*. Ann Arbor: University of Michigan Press.

Aronson, J., & Steele, C. M. (2005). Stereotypes and the fragility of academic competence, motivation, and self-concept. In A. J. Elliott & C. S. Dweck (Eds.), *Handbook of competence and motivation* (pp. 436–456). New York: Guilford.

Ayers, W., Ladson-Billings, G., Michie, G., & Noguera, P. (Eds.). (2008). *City kids, city schools: More reports from the front row*. New York: The New Press.

Banks, J. A. (2009). *Teaching strategies for ethnic studies* (8th ed.). Boston: Allyn & Bacon.

Bennett deMarrais, K., & LeCompte, M. G. (1999). *The way schools work: A sociological analysis of education* (3rd ed.). New York: Longman.

Berliner, D. C. (2009). Poverty and potential: Out-of-school factors and school success. Boulder, CO, & Tempe, AZ: Education and the Public Interest Center & Educational Policy Research Unit. Retrieved from http://nepc.colorado.edu/publication/poverty-and-potential

Beykont, Z. F. (Ed.). (2000). *Lifting every voice: Pedagogy and politics of bilingual education*. Cambridge, MA: Harvard Educational Publishing Group.

Biddle, B. J., & Berliner, D. C. (2002). What research says about small classes and their effects. San Francisco: WestEd. *Policy Perspectives* [Online]. Retrieved August 15, 2008, from http://www.wested.org/online_pubs/small_classes.pdf.

Bigelow, B. (2008). *A people's history for the classroom*. Milwaukee, WI: Rethinking Schools. Also available at http://www.zinnedproject.org/.

Bigelow, B., Christensen, L., Karp, S., Miner, B., & Peterson, B. (Eds.). (1994). *Rethinking our classrooms: Teaching for equity and justice* (Vol. 1). Milwaukee, WI: Rethinking Schools.

Bigelow, B., Harvey, B., Karp, S., & Miller, L. (Eds.). (2001). *Rethinking our classrooms: Teaching for equity and justice* (Vol. 2). Milwaukee, WI: Rethinking Schools.

Botelho, M. J., & Rudman, M. K. (2009). *Critical multicultural analysis of children's literature: Mirrors, windows, and doors*. New York: Routledge.

Bowles, S., & Gintis, H. (1976). *Schooling in capitalist America: Educational reform and the contradictions of economic life*. New York: Basic Books.

Carter, P. I. (2005). *Keepin' it real: School success beyond Black and White*. New York: Oxford University Press.

Clawson, R. A. (2002). Poor people, Black faces: The portrayal of poverty in economics textbooks. *Journal of Black Studies, 32*(3), 352–362.

Conchas, G. Q. (2006). *The color of success: Race and high-achieving urban youth*. New York: Teachers College Press.

Cowhey, M. (2006). *Black ants and Buddhists: Thinking critically and teaching differently in the primary grades*. Portland, ME: Stenhouse.

Crawford, J. (2008). *Advocating for English learners: Selected essays*. Buffalo, NY: Multilingual Matters.

Cummins, J. (1996). *Negotiating identities: Education for empowerment in a diverse society*. Ontario, CA: California Association for Bilingual Education.

Cummins, J. (2000). *Language, power, and pedagogy: Bilingual children in the crossfire*. Buffalo, NY: Multilingual Matters.

Darling-Hammond, L. (2006). Securing the right to learn: Policy and practice for powerful teaching and learning. *Educational Researcher, 35*(7), 13–24.

Darling-Hammond, L. (2010). *The flat world and education: How America's commitment to equity will determine our future*. New York: Teachers College Press.

Davis, B. M. (2005). *How to teach students who don't look like you: Culturally relevant teaching strategies*. Thousand Oaks, CA: Corwin.

Delpit, L. (2006). *Other people's children: Cultural conflict in the classroom* (2nd ed.). New York: The New Press.

Delpit, L., & Dowdy, J. K. (Eds.). (2008). *The skin that we speak: Thoughts on language and culture in the classroom* (3rd ed.). New York: The New Press.

Dolby, N. (2000). Changing selves: Multicultural education and the challenge of new identities. *Teachers College Record, 102*(5), 898–912.

Edelman, M. W. (2007). The cradle to prison pipeline: An American health crisis. *Preventing Chronic Disease, 4*(3), A43.

Epstein, J. L. (2010). *School, family, and community partnerships: Preparing educators and improving schools* (2nd ed.). Boulder, CO: Westview.

Freire, P. (1970). *Pedagogy of the oppressed*. New York: Seabury.

Freire, P. (1985). *The politics of education: Culture, power, and liberation*. South Hadley, MA: Bergin & Garvey.

Gay, G. (2004). Beyond *Brown*: Promoting equality through multicultural education. *Journal of Curriculum and Supervision, 19*(3), 193–216.

Gay, G. (2010). *Culturally responsive teaching: Theory, research, and practice* (2nd ed.). New York: Teachers College Press.

Gebhard, M., Austin, T., Nieto, S., & Willett, J. (2002). "You can't step on someone else's words": Preparing all teachers to teach language minority students. In Z. F. Beykont (Ed.), *The power of culture: Teaching across language difference* (pp. 219–243). Cambridge, MA: Harvard Educational Publishing Group.

Gonzalez, N., Moll, L. C., & Amanti, C. (Eds.). (2005). *Funds of knowledge: Theorizing practices in households and classrooms*. Mahwah, NJ: Erlbaum.

Grant-Thomas, A., & Orfield, G. (Eds.). (2009). *Twenty-first century color lines: Multiracial change in contemporary America*. Philadelphia: Temple University Press.

Grever, M., & Stuurman, S. (Eds.). (2007). *Beyond the canon: History for the twenty-first century*. New York: Palgrave Macmillan.

Harlem Children's Zone (HCZ). (n.d.). Mission statement. Retrieved September 9, 2008, from http://www.hcz.org/.

Harrington, M. (1997). *The other America: Poverty in the United States*. New York: Scribner. (Original work published 1971)

Henderson, A. T., Mapp, K., Johnson, V., & Davies, D. (2006). *Beyond the bake sale: The essential guide to family-school partnerships*. New York: The New Press.

Herrnstein, R. J., & Murray, C. (1994). *The bell curve: Intelligence and class structure in American life*. New York: Free Press.

Howard, G. (2006). *We can't teach what we don't know: White teachers, multiracial schools* (2nd ed.). New York: Teachers College Press.

Irizarry, J. G. (2011). Culturally responsive pedagogy. In J. M. Cooper (Ed.), *Classroom teaching skills* (9th ed., pp. 188–214). Boston: Houghton Mifflin.

Irvine, J. J. (2003). *Educating teachers for diversity: Seeing with a cultural eye*. New York: Teachers College Press.

Johnson, F., Zhou, L., & Nakamoto, N. (2011). *Revenues and expenditures for public elementary and secondary education: School year 2008–09 (fiscal year 2009)* (NCES 2011-329). Washington, DC: U.S. Department of Education, National Center for Education Statistics. Retrieved September 5, 2011, from http://nces.ed.gov/pubsearch.

Katz, M. B. (1975). *Class, bureaucracy, and the schools: The illusion of educational change in America*. New York: Praeger.

Kohl, H. (2005). *She would not be moved: How we tell the story of Rosa Parks and the Montgomery Bus Boycott*. New York: The New Press.

Kozol, J. (1975). Great men and women (tailored for school use). *Learning Magazine, 4*(4), 16–20.

Kozol, J. (1991). *Savage inequalities: Children in America's schools*. New York: Crown.

Kozol, J. (2005). *The shame of the nation: The restoration of apartheid schooling in America*. New York: Crown.

Ladd, H., Noguera, P., & Payzant, T. (2006). *A broader, bolder approach to education*. Retrieved September 1, 2008, from http://www.boldapproach.org/.

Ladson-Billings, G. (2001). *Crossing over to Canaan: The journey of new teachers in diverse classrooms*. San Francisco: Jossey-Bass.

Ladson-Billings, G. (2006a). It's not the culture of poverty, it's the poverty of culture: The problem with teacher education. *Anthropology and Education Quarterly, 37*(2), 104–109.

Ladson-Billings, G. (2006b). From the achievement gap to the education debt: Understanding achievement in U.S. schools. *Educational Researcher, 35*(7), 3–12.

Landsman, J. (2001). *A White teacher talks about race*. Lanham, MD: Scarecrow.

Lee, E., Menkart, D., & Okazawa-Rey, M. (2007). *Beyond heroes and holidays: A practical guide to K–12 anti-racist, multicultural education and staff development*. Washington, DC: Teaching for Change.

Levin, M. (2001). *Teach me! Kids will learn when oppression is the lesson*. Lanham, MD: Rowman & Littlefield.

Lewis, O. (1965). *La vida: A Puerto Rican family in the culture of poverty—San Juan and New York*. New York: Random House.

Loewen, J. W. (2007). *Lies across America: What our historic sites got wrong*. New York: Touchstone/Simon & Schuster.

Loewen, J. W. (2008). *Lies my teacher told me: Everything your American history textbook got wrong* (rev. ed.). New York: Free Press.

Lomawaima, K. T. (2004). Educating Native Americans. In J. A. Banks & C. A. M. Banks (Eds.), *Handbook of research on multicultural education* (2nd ed., pp. 441–461). San Francisco: Jossey-Bass.

Mann, H. (1903). *Twelfth annual report to the Massachusetts State Board of Education, 1848*. Boston: Directors of the Old South Work. (Original work published 1848.)

McCarty, T. L. (2002). *A place to be Navajo: Rough Rock and the struggle for self-determination in indigenous schooling*. Mahwah, NJ: Erlbaum.

McNeil, L. (2000). *Contradictions of school reform: Educational costs of standardized testing*. New York: Routledge.

Meier, D., & Wood, G. (Eds.). (2004). *Many children left behind: How the No Child Left Behind Act is damaging our children and our schools*. Boston: Beacon.

Meier, K. J., & Stewart, J., Jr. (1991). *The politics of Hispanic education: Un paso pa'lante y dos pátras*. Albany: State University of New York Press.

Menéndez, R. (Writer and Director). (1988). *Stand and deliver* [Motion picture]. Burbank, CA: Warner Bros.

Menkart, D., Murray, A. D., & View, J. (2004). *Putting the movement back into civil rights teaching*. Washington, DC: Teaching for Change and the Poverty and Race Research Action Council (PRRAC).

Michie, G. (2005). *See you when we get there: Teaching for change in urban schools*. New York: Teachers College Press.

Miner, B. (2004). Testing companies mine for gold. *Rethinking Schools, 19*(2), 5–7.

Morrell, E. (2008). *Critical literacy and urban youth: Pedagogies of access, dissent, and liberation*. New York: Routledge.

Moses, R. P., & Cobb, C. E., Jr. (2002). *Radical equations: Math literacy and civil rights*. Boston: Beacon.

Muennig, P., & Woolf, S. H. (2007). Health and economic benefits of reducing the number of students per classroom in US primary schools. *American Journal of Public Health, 97*(11), 2020–2027.

Murray, C. (2008). *Real education: Four simple truths for bringing America's schools back to reality.* New York: Random House/Crown Forum.

National Commission on Excellence in Education. (1983). *A nation at risk: The imperative for educational reform.* Washington, DC: Author.

Nichols, S. L., & Berliner, D. A. (2007). *Collateral damage: How high-stakes testing corrupts America's schools.* Cambridge, MA: Harvard Education Press.

Nieto, S. (2002–2003). Profoundly multicultural questions. *Educational Leadership, 60*(4), 6–10.

Nieto, S. (2010). *The light in their eyes: Creating multicultural learning communities* (10th anniv. ed.). New York: Teachers College Press.

Nieto, S., & Bode, P. (2012). *Affirming diversity: The sociopolitical context of multicultural education* (6th ed.). Boston: Pearson.

Nieto, S., Bode, P., Kang, E., & Raible, J. (2008). Identity, community and diversity: Retheorizing multicultural curriculum for the postmodern era. In F. M. Connelly, M. F. He, & J. Phillion (Eds.), *The Sage handbook of curriculum and instruction* (pp. 176–197). Thousand Oaks, CA: Sage.

Noguera, P. (2003). Schools, prisons, and social implications of punishment: Rethinking disciplinary practices. *Theory into Practice, 42*(4), 341–350.

Noguera, P. (2008). Joaquín's dilemma: Understanding the link between racial identity and school-related behaviors. In P. Noguera (Ed.), *The trouble with Black boys . . . and other reflections on race, equity, and the future of public education* (pp. 1–16). San Francisco: Wiley.

Oakes, J. (2005). *Keeping track: How schools structure inequality* (2nd ed.). New Haven, CT: Yale University Press.

Olsen, L. (2008). *Made in America: Immigrant students in our public schools* (10th anniv. ed.). New York: The New Press.

Orfield, G. (2001). *Schools more separate: Consequences of a decade of resegregation.* Cambridge, MA: Harvard Civil Rights Project.

Pollock, M. (2004). *Colormute: Race talk dilemmas in an American school.* Princeton, NJ: Princeton University Press.

Pollock, M. (Ed.). (2008). *Everyday antiracism: Getting real about race in school.* New York: Basic Books.

Ravitch, D. (2010). *Death and life of the great American school system.* New York: The New Press.

Reissman, F. (1962). *The culturally deprived child.* New York: Harper & Row.

Reyes, M. de la Luz (Ed.). (2011). *Words were all we had: Becoming biliterate against the odds.* New York: Teachers College Press.

Rothstein, R. (2004). *Class and schools: Using social, economic, and educational reform to close the Black–White achievement gap.* New York: Teachers College Press.

Rothstein, R. (2008). Leaving "No Child Left Behind" behind: Our No. 1 education program is incoherent, unworkable, and doomed. But the next president still can have a huge impact on improving American schooling. *American Prospect, 19*(1), 50–54.

Ryan, W. (1972). *Blaming the victim.* New York: Vintage.

Shor, I. (1992). *Empowering education: Critical teaching for social change.* Chicago: University of Chicago Press.

Shor, I., & Pari, C. (Eds.). (1999). *Education is politics: Critical teaching across differences, K–12.* Portsmouth, NH: Boynton/Cook.

Shor, I., & Pari, C. (Eds.). (2000). *Education is politics: Critical teaching across differences, postsecondary.* Portsmouth, NH: Boynton/Cook.

Sleeter, C. E. (1994). White racism. *Multicultural Education, 1*(4), 5–8, 39.

Sleeter, C. E. (2005). *Un-standardizing curriculum: Multicultural education in the standards-based classroom.* New York: Teachers College Press.

Spring, J. H. (1989). *The sorting machine revisited: National educational policy since 1945.* White Plains, NY: Longman.

Spring, J. (2013). *Deculturalization and the struggle for equality: A brief history of the education of dominated cultures in the United States* (8th ed.). New York: McGraw-Hill.

Steele, C. M. (1999). Thin ice: "Stereotype threat" and Black college students. *Atlantic Monthly, 284*(2), 44–54.

Takaki, R. (2008). *A different mirror: A history of multicultural America.* Boston: Back Bay Books.

Tatum, B. D. (2003). *"Why are all the Black kids sitting together in the cafeteria?" and other conversations about race* (rev. ed.). New York: Basic Books.

Tatum, B. D. (2007). *Can we talk about race? And other conversations in an era of school resegregation.* Boston: Beacon.

Tough, P. (2008). *Whatever it takes: Geoffrey Canada's quest to change Harlem and America.* New York: Houghton Mifflin.

Van Ausdale, D., & Feagin, J. R. (2001). *The first r: How children learn race and racism.* New York: Rowman & Littlefield.

Vasquez, V. M. (2004). *Negotiating critical literacies with young children.* Mahwah, NJ: Erlbaum.

Vaught, S. (2011). Juvenile prison schooling, and re-entry: Disciplining young men of Color. In F. Sherman, & F. Jacobs (Eds.), *Juvenile justice: Advancing research, policy, and practice* (pp. 287–310). Hoboken, NJ: John Wiley & Sons.

Weinberg, M. (1996). *Racism in contemporary America.* Westport, CT: Greenwood.

Wiggins, G., & McTighe, J. (2005). *Understanding by design* (2nd ed). Alexandria, VA: Association for Supervision and Curriculum Development.

Yosso, T. (2006). *Critical race counterstories along the Chicana/Chicano pipeline.* New York: Routledge.

Zentella, A. C. (2005). *Building on strengths: Language and literacy in Latino families and communities.* New York: Teachers College Press.

Zinn, H. (2010). *A people's history of the United States.* New York: Harper Perennial Modern Classics.

Monashee Frantz/Glow Images

Communities, Families, and Educators Working Together for School Improvement

CHAPTER 17

Cherry A. McGee Banks

Sally Jenson was sitting at her kitchen table looking somewhat dejected when her husband Ed came home. He immediately knew something was wrong. Sally explained that when she asked their eight-year-old daughter June what she did in school, June said that she got an A on her math test and that it was her turn to help Ms. Douglas, her teacher, with story hour. When Sally asked what story Ms. Douglas read to the class, June eagerly described the book as a nice story about a family with two moms. Sally quickly changed the subject and told June to get ready for her brother's soccer game.

The book Ms. Douglas read to the class was *Heather Has Two Mommies* by Lesléa Newman (2009), a lesbian-themed children's book. The Jensons were concerned about the book because it contained ideas that they did not support. For them, a family has a mother and father, not two mothers. They decided to meet with Ms. Douglas and the school principal so that the teacher could explain why she read *Heather Has Two Mommies* to her class.

At the meeting, the Jensons learned that Ms. Douglas encouraged students to bring their favorite books from home to share during story hour. She reminded the Jensons that June had brought *Little Drummer Boy*, by Katherine Davis (1958), a book based on a popular Christmas song, to class for story hour. Even though the students in June's classroom are religiously diverse, they had enjoyed learning why June loved the book. *Heather Has Two Mommies*, the book the Jensons were concerned about, was brought to class by one of June's classmates, who has two moms. Ms. Douglas explained that two of her goals for story hour were to build community by helping students learn about their classmates and to appreciate the diversity in their classroom.

Ms. Douglas noted that June was one of the first students in the class to share her thoughts after she finished reading the book. June said, "Heather is a nice girl who had fun playing with her dog and cat and mommies." Several other students made similar comments. Ms. Douglas went on to say that she had sent a letter home with June at the beginning of the school year explaining the story hour activity and inviting parents to join the class for story hour whenever they could do so. She encouraged the Jensons to stay in communication with her and extended a sincere invitation to them to visit her classroom.

The Jensons were not completely satisfied with the outcome of the meeting, but they left the meeting knowing that Ms. Douglas was a fair and caring teacher who was open to listening to their concerns. Mrs. Jenson said that she would visit the class on a regular basis and stay in touch with Ms. Douglas about the books she was reading during story hour. Ms. Douglas understood that while it was important for parents and teachers to have open lines of communication, good communication does not necessarily eliminate tensions between the home and school. She made sure that she was following school protocol and she talked with her principal about the books she was planning to use in story hour. As a result, she knew that her principal supported her approach to story hour and was prepared to talk with parents about it should they decide to contact him.

As a result of the Jensons' visit, Ms. Douglas started thinking about invisible barriers, such as values and beliefs, that might limit students' full access to the curriculum. The Jensons' visit helped her to become more sensitive to and aware of the range of student diversity in her classroom. By showing respect and appreciation for the concerns of parents, Ms. Douglas will hopefully have an ally as she learns to work more effectively with her students.

The diversity of parent and community groups, with their different concerns and issues, illustrates one of the important complexities of parent and community involvement in schools (De Carvalho, 2001). This complexity—which may be reflected in different interaction styles, expectations, and concerns—complicates but does not negate the need for parent and community involvement in schools (DeSteno, 2000). Educators lose an important voice for school improvement when parents and community groups are not involved in schools. They can give teachers unique and important views of their students as well as help the school garner resources that are available in the community.

In a comprehensive review of research on parent involvement, Henderson and Berla (2002) found compelling evidence that parent involvement improves student achievement. Parent involvement is also associated with improvements in students' attendance and social behavior. However, to capitalize on the benefits of parent and community involvement, involvement strategies must be broadly conceptualized. Parents should be given an opportunity to contribute to school improvement by working in different settings and at different levels of the educational process (Henderson, Mapp, Johnson, & Davies, 2006; Hidalgo, Sau-Fong, & Epstein, 2004). For example, some parents may want to focus their energies on working with their own children at home. Other parents may want to work on decision-making committees. Still others may be able to provide in-class assistance to teachers. Epstein and her colleagues (2008) have identified six different types of involvement: (1) parenting, (2) communicating, (3) volunteering, (4) learning at home, (5) decision making, and (6) collaborating with the community. Though very different, each type of involvement provides opportunities for parents to have a positive influence on their children's school experience.

Community groups and other family members (in addition to parents) can also work with teachers to reform schools. Many tasks involved in restructuring schools, such as setting goals and allocating resources, are best achieved through a collaborative problem-solving structure that includes educators, parents, other family members, and community members (Ouimette, Feldman, & Tung, 2006). Family and community members can form what Goodlad (1984) calls "the necessary coalition of contributing groups" (p. 293). Educational reform needs their support, influence, and activism. Schools are highly dependent on and vulnerable to citizens, who can support or impede change. Family members and community leaders can validate the need for educational reform and can provide an appropriate forum for exploring the importance of education. They can also extend the discussion on school improvement issues beyond formal educational networks and can help generate support for schools in the community at large. Family members and community leaders can help provide the rationale, motivation, and social action necessary for educational reform.

Reasons That Parent and Family Involvement in Schools Is Important

Parent involvement is important because it acknowledges the importance of parents in the lives of their children, recognizes the diversity of values and perspectives within the community, provides a vehicle for building a collaborative problem-solving structure, and increases the opportunity for all students to learn in school. Parents, however, are not the only adults who support and contribute to the care of children. When parents struggle with poverty, incarceration, substance abuse, mental illness, and other challenges, grandparents and other relatives often become the children's primary caregivers (McCallion, Janicki, & Kolomer, 2004). From 1970 to 2006, there was a 55 percent increase in the number of grandchildren living in grandparent-headed households and a 73 percent increase in cases where neither parent was present in the household (U.S. Census Bureau, 2010C). However, by 2010, even though the trend had slowed, it was still significant. In 2010, 5,396,969 children under 18 lived with their grandparents, and 2,882,224 of them lived in grandparent-headed households. In some cases, the child's mother or father also lived with the grandparent. However, neither a mother nor father was present for 31.9 percent of the 2,882,224 children who lived in grandparent-headed households. These data, shown in Table 17.1, suggest that parent-involvement programs should be conceptualized broadly enough to include grandparents and other family members.

Parent and family involvement in schools benefits not only students and teachers but also the parents and family members themselves (Center for Mental Health in Schools at UCLA, 2007). When parents help their children at home, the children perform better in school (Aikens, 2002). Parent involvement allows parents and teachers to reinforce skills and provides an environment that has consistent learning expectations and standards. Parents benefit because, through their involvement with the school, they become more knowledgeable about their child's school, its policies, and the school staff. Perhaps most importantly, parent involvement provides an opportunity for parents and children to spend time together. During that time, parents can communicate a high value for education, the importance of effort in achievement, and positive regard for their children.

Parents and family members are often children's first and most important teachers. Students come to school with knowledge, values, and beliefs they have learned from their parents and in their communities. Parents directly or indirectly help shape their children's value system,

Table 17.1   Types of Families within which Children Lived in the United States, 1991–2010

1991	4,737,000 children lived with at least one grandparent.
	1,099,000 children lived in a family in which neither parent was present (grandparent was householder).
2001	6,187,000 children lived with at least one grandparent.
	1,341,000 children lived in a family in which neither parent was present (grandparent was householder).
2004	6,471,000 children lived with at least one grandparent.
	1,563,000 children lived in a family in which neither parent was present (grandparent was householder).
2010	5,396,969 children lived with at least one grandparent.
	919,429 children lived in a family in which neither parent was present (grandparent was householder).

Source: Based on data from U.S. Census Bureau (2010C). *America's families and living arrangements: 2010.* Retrieved November 28, 2011, from http://www.census.gov/population/ww/socdemo/jj-fam/cps2010.html.

orientation toward learning, and view of the world (Caspe, Lopez, & Wolos, 2006/2007). Most parents want their children to succeed in school. Schools can capitalize on the high value most parents place on education by working to create a school environment that respects the students' home and community (Hidalgo et al., 2004). When schools are in conflict with their students' home and community, they can alienate students from their families and communities.

To create harmonious relations among the school, home, and community, parents need information about the school. They need to know what the school expects their children to learn, how they will be taught, and the required books and materials their children will use in school. Most important, parents need to know how teachers assess students and how they can support their children's achievement. Teachers need to understand their students' community and home life. Teachers also need to know about their students' parents, homes, and communities. It would be helpful for teachers to have a clear understanding of the educational expectations parents have for their children, the languages spoken at home, the family's values and norms, and how children are taught in their homes and communities. Teachers and principals who know parents treat them with greater respect and show more positive attitudes toward their children (Berger, 2008). Teachers generally see involved parents as concerned individuals who support the school. Parents who are not involved in schools are frequently seen as not valuing education.

Historical Overview

While parent involvement in education is not new, its importance and purpose have varied over time. In the early part of the nation's history, families were often solely responsible for educating children. Children learned values and skills by working with their families in their communities.

When formal systems of education were established, parents continued to influence their children's education. During the colonial period, schools were viewed as an extension of the home. The school reinforced parental and community values and expectations. Teachers generally came from the community and often personally knew their students' parents and shared their values.

At the beginning of the 20th century, when large numbers of immigrants came to the United States, schools became a major vehicle for assimilating immigrant children into U.S. society (Banks, 2008). In general, immigrant parents were not welcomed in the schools. Children of immigrants were taught that their parents' ways of speaking, behaving, and thinking were inferior to those of mainstream Americans. In his study of the sociology of teaching, Waller (1932/1965) concluded that parents and teachers lived in a state of mutual distrust and even hostility. There were, however, some notable exceptions.

One such exception was Benjamin Franklin High School (BFHS) in East Harlem, New York. Leonard Covello, principal at BFHS, instituted a program of intergroup education there in the 1930s. Parents were welcome at Franklin, and teachers encouraged students to appreciate their parents' language, values, and customs. Community groups were also actively involved at BFHS. Covello saw parent and community involvement as a way to promote democratic values, reduce prejudice, and increase cross-cultural understanding and appreciation (Banks, 2005).

As society changed and education became more removed from the direct influence of parents, responsibility for transmitting knowledge from generation to generation was transferred from the home and community to the school. Formal education was seen as a job for trained professionals. Schools became autonomous institutions staffed by people who were often strangers in their students' home communities. Teachers did not necessarily live in their students' neighborhoods, know their students' parents, or share their values. Schools were given more and more duties that traditionally had been the responsibility of the home and community. Schools operated under the assumption that they were *in loco parentis*, and educators were asked to assume the role of both teacher and substitute parent.

In a pluralist society, what the school teaches as well as whom and how the school teaches can create tensions between parents and schools. Issues ranging from what the school teaches about the role of women in our society to mainstreaming students with disabilities point to the need for teachers, parents, and community leaders to work together. However, parents, community leaders, and teachers do not always agree on meaningful ways to cooperate and partner in the educational process (Anderson, 2006).

The Changing Face of the Family

Parent/family diversity mirrors student diversity. As the student population becomes more diverse, parent/family diversity also increases. Involving parents in schools means that teachers have to be prepared to work with a range of parents, including single parents, parents with special needs, low-income parents, parents with disabilities, same-sex parents, and parents who do not speak English as their first language. Working with parents from diverse backgrounds requires sensitivity to and an understanding of their circumstances and worldviews (Amatea, Smith-Adcock, & Villares, 2006; Chavkin & Gonzalez, 1995; Kagan, 1995; Pena, 2000; Schneider & Coleman, 1993).

It is especially important that teachers understand and be sensitive to the changing nature of the ethnic and racial makeup of their students and their students' parents. The ethnic landscape of U.S. schools includes an increasing number of Arab, Jewish, Eastern European, and African students (McFalls, 2007). One of the most significant changes in U.S. immigration in the early 21st century is the increase in the number of immigrants of African descent from African and Caribbean nations. In 2010, African immigrants constituted 4 percent of all the immigrants to the United State (U.S. Census, 2010b). It is important to remember, however, that African immigrants are not all members of the same race. A small percentage of immigrants from East Africa are of Asian origin, and a number of immigrants from South Africa are White (Dodson & Diouf, 2005). In addition, ethnic identity has primacy over racial identity for many African immigrants. For example, some immigrants of African descent would identify themselves as Cubans, Dominicans, Nigerians, Kenyans, Haitians, or Puerto Ricans, not as Blacks or Whites. Their phenotype, however, might conflict with physical characteristics that traditionally are used to identify races in the United States. For example, a Cuban American with brown skin may consider himself White because phenotype is not the only factor that is used to identify race in most Caribbean nations. This can be confusing for Americans, who historically have equated race and phenotype.

However, even in the United States, the lines between racial groups are becoming blurred. A growing number of students and parents are members of more than one racial group. Even though marriage between people from different races is still an exception rather than the rule, more and more people are marrying interracially. Typically, interracial marriages are between a White person and a person from a minority racial group. It does not typically involve two people from different minority racial groups (Lee & Edmonston, 2005). In 2010, more than 9 million people identified with two or more races (U.S. Census Bureau, 2010d). While this is a relatively small percentage of the U.S. population, the percentage of people who are multiracial is more salient when geographic regions and subgroups within the population are examined. For example, children are more likely to be multiracial than adults, and racial groups that have small populations tend to include higher percentages of multiracial people. Additionally, urban areas tend to have higher rates of interracial marriage than rural areas. California, Nevada, Alaska, and Oklahoma have the highest percentage of interracial marriages in the United States. Between 10.0 and 29.3 percent of the married couples in those states are interracial (Lee & Edmonston, 2005). Among all racial groups, Whites and Blacks have the lowest rate of interracial marriage; American Indians, Hawaiians, and multiracial individuals have the highest. With respect to gender, interracial marriage is about equal for all racial groups except African Americans and Asians. African American men are more likely to intermarry than African American women, and Asian women are more likely to intermarry than Asian men (Lee & Edmonston, 2005). The increase in the numbers of interracial children, foreign-born children (usually Asian) who are adopted by American families (usually White), and immigrant children who do not use their phenotype to define their race highlight the importance of teachers not making assumptions about the racial and ethnic background of their students and their parents but allowing them to define their own identity.

Diversity in parent and community groups can be a tremendous asset to the school. However, it can also be a source of potential conflict and tension. Some parents are particularly difficult to involve in their children's education. They resist becoming involved for several reasons (Harry, 1992; Walker, 1996). In a national survey, parents indicated that a lack of time was the primary reason they were not involved in their children's schools (Clark, 1995). The pressures of earning a living and taking care of a home and children can result in a great deal of stress. At the end of the day, some parents just want to rest. Other parents do not believe they have the necessary educational background to be involved in their children's school. They feel intimidated by educators and believe that education should be left to teachers. Still others feel alienated from their children's schools because of negative experiences they had in school or because they believe the school does not support their values (Berger, 2008; Clark, 1995; Rasinski, 1989).

Three groups of parents are frequently underrepresented in school activities: parents with special needs, single parents, and low-income parents. These are not the only groups that are underrepresented in school activities; however, their experiences and needs illustrate particular problem areas. The specific groups of parents discussed below should not be viewed as an indication that only parents from these groups are difficult to involve in schools or that all parents from these groups resist participation in schools. Parents from all groups share many of the concerns discussed next.

Parents with Special Needs

Parents with special needs include a wide range of individuals. They are found in all ethnic, racial, and income groups. Chronically unemployed parents, parents with long-term illnesses, abusive parents, and parents with substance-abuse problems are examples of parents with special needs. As you can see from the list, the concerns are varied, and in some cases they can overlap. Each requires specific responses. For example, abusive parents require special attention from the school. Most schools have policies on how to treat suspected cases of child neglect and abuse. Teachers should be aware of those policies, which should be written down and available to all school personnel. All states require schools to report suspected cases of child abuse.

Although parents with special needs frequently have serious problems that the school cannot address, teachers should not ignore the importance of understanding their students' home environments. Knowing the difficulties students are coping with at home can help teachers create school environments that are supportive (Swadener & Niles, 1991). Schools can help compensate for the difficult circumstances students experience at home. The school, for some students, is the only place during the day where they are nurtured.

Working with special-needs families requires district or building support in identifying places for family referrals and support for students and teachers. Some schools hire outreach community service workers to provide these kinds of services. Although some special-needs parents may resist the school's help, they need to know that their problems can negatively affect their children's success in school. Referring these parents to places where they can receive help can show students who are in difficult home environments that they are not alone. Most parents want to feel that they are valued and adequate human beings and that they can help their children succeed. When they are willing to be involved in school, they do not want to be humiliated (Berger, 2008).

Some parents with special needs will be able to be actively involved in schools, but many will be unable to sustain ongoing involvement. An important goal for working with parents with special needs is to keep lines of communication open. To the extent possible, try to get to know the parents. Do not accept a stereotypical view of them without ever talking to them. Encourage parents to become involved whenever and however they are able to participate. Your goal should be to develop a clear understanding of your students' home environments so that you can provide appropriate intervention at school.

Members of the community who are involved in school may be willing to serve as intermediaries between the school and uninvolved parents and in some cases as surrogate parents. In an ethnography of an inner-city neighborhood, Shariff (1988) found that adults shared goods and services and provided support for each other. Educators can build on the sense of extended family and fictive kinship that may exist in some neighborhoods to connect with community support groups for students whose parents cannot be involved in school. Civic and social community groups, such as The Links, Inc., and the Boys and Girls Clubs, can also provide support for students who do not have the support they need at home.

Working with students whose parents have special needs is complicated and challenging. However, regardless of the circumstances students confront at home, teachers have a responsibility to help them perform at their highest level in school. Schools with large numbers of parents with special needs require experienced and highly qualified teachers who have district and school support to help them meet the additional challenges they will face. Traditionally, however, these schools have many teachers who are relatively new to the field and are not certified in the areas in which they teach (Darling-Hammond, 2004).

Single Parents

One of the most significant social changes in the United States in the last 30 years is the increase in the percentage of children living with one parent. In 2010, 24.2 million children under 18 lived in households headed by a single parent. Women head most single-parent families. Eighty-seven percent of children living with one parent lived with their mother. The number of single-parent families is particularly significant in the African American community. In 2010, about half of Black children lived with a single mother, compared to 10.2 percent of Asian children. Among Hispanic children, 26.3 percent lived with a single mother (U.S. Census, 2010c). Gender is an important factor in single-parent homes because women tend to earn less than men. In 2010, 8.9 percent of children living with a single father lived in households with an income below the poverty level, compared to 56.9 percent of children living with a single mother. Of children in two-parent families, 16.8 percent lived in households with incomes below the poverty level (U.S. Census, 2010e).

Single-parent families have many of the same hopes, joys, and concerns about their children's education as do two-parent families. However, because these parents have a lower rate of attendance at school functions, they are frequently viewed as not supporting their children's education. When teachers respond sensitively to their needs and limitations, they can be enthusiastic partners with teachers. Four suggestions for working with single parents follow. Many of these suggestions apply to other groups of parents as well.

1. Provide flexible times for conferences, such as early mornings, evenings, and weekends.

2. Provide baby-sitting service when activities are held at the school.

3. Work out procedures for acknowledging and communicating with noncustodial parents. For instance, under what circumstances are noncustodial parents informed about their

children's grades, school behavior, or attendance? Problems can occur when information is inappropriately given to or withheld from a noncustodial parent.

4. Use the parent's correct surname. Students will sometimes have different names from their parents.

Low-Income Parents

Nationally, the poverty rate increased from 14.3 percent in 2009 to 15.3 percent in 2010. The number of people in poverty increased from 42.9 million to 46.2 million during the same time period (U.S. Census, 2010a). The poverty level is an official government estimate of the income necessary to maintain a minimally acceptable standard of living. Poverty rates vary by family type. In 2010, households headed by single women had the highest poverty rate at 33.1 percent, compared to a rate of 7.3 percent for married couples (U.S. Census, 2010f).

Even though the number of individuals of color in the highest income brackets has more than doubled since 1980, race continues to be a salient factor in poverty. The poverty rate in 2010 was 10.6 percent for non-Hispanic Whites, 27.1 percent for African Americans, 28.4 percent for American Indians and Native Alaskan Natives, 12.5 percent for Asians, and 18.8 percent for Native Hawaiians and Other Pacific Islanders. Most minorities earn less than Whites. However, Asian Americans earn more than all other groups. In 2010, their median household income was $64,308, compared to $54,620 for non-Hispanic Whites, $37,359 for Hispanics, and $32,068 for African American males. Women in each group earned less than their male counterparts; the female-to-male earnings ratio was 77 percent in 2010 (U.S. Census, 2010e).

Low-income parents are often among the strongest supporters of education because they often see it as a means to a better life for their children. However, their definition and understanding of "support for education" may be different from that of the school staff. Additionally, they are often limited in their ability to buy materials and to make financial commitments that can enable their children to participate in activities such as field trips or extracurricular programs. Schools can provide workbooks and other study materials for use at home as well as transportation for school activities and conferences. The school can also support low-income parents by establishing community service programs. For example, students can help clean up neighborhoods and distribute information on available social services. The school can provide desk space for voter registration and other services.

Perhaps the most important way for schools to work with low-income parents is to recognize that they can contribute a great deal to their children's education. Even though their contributions may not be in the manner traditionally associated with parent involvement, they can be very beneficial to teachers and students. The positive values and attitudes parents communicate to their children and their strong desire for their children to get a good education in order to have a better chance in life than they had are important forms of support for the school.

Teacher Concerns with Parent and Family Involvement

Even though teachers often say they want to involve parents, they may be suspicious of them and not sure what parents expect from them. Some teachers think parents might disrupt their routine, might not have the necessary skills to work with students, might be inconvenient to have in the classroom, and might be interested only in helping their own child, not the whole class. Even teachers who would like to involve parents may not be sure that they have the time, skill, or knowledge to involve parents in the school. Many teachers believe that they already have too much to do and that working with parents would make their already overburdened jobs impossible.

Many of these concerns derive from a limited view of the possibilities for parent involvement. Frequently, when parents and teachers think of parent involvement, they think it means doing something for the school generally at the school or having the school teach parents how to become better parents. In today's ever-changing society, a traditional view of parent involvement inhibits rather than encourages parents and teachers to work together. Traditional ideas about parent involvement have a built-in gender and social-class bias and can be a barrier to many men and low-income parents. Moreover, the ideas tend to focus on parents, not on community groups. With a national focus on education, more and more community groups are interested in working with schools. It is not uncommon for schools to have corporate or community sponsors. While these are generally supportive and cooperative relationships, they are typically linked to the school district or school, not to specific classrooms. Administrators need to think carefully about how to involve classroom teachers with these groups.

When parent involvement is viewed as a means of getting support for the school, parents are encouraged to bake cookies, raise money, or work at the school as unpaid classroom, playground, library, or office helpers. This form of parent involvement is generally directed at mothers who do not work outside the home. However, the number of mothers available for this form of involvement is decreasing. In 2010, 70.8 percent of mothers with children under 18 were either working or looking for work outside the home (U.S. Bureau of Labor Statistics, 2011).

The parent-as-helper idea is geared toward parents who have the skills, time, and resources to become school helpers. While this is a role that many educated, middle-class parents eagerly embrace, not all parents want to or feel they can or should do things for the school. Whether parents are willing to come to school depends largely on their attitudes toward school. These attitudes result in part from the parents' own school experiences.

Cultural perspectives also play an important role in the traditional approach to parent involvement. To be effective, strategies for parent and community involvement should reflect what Bullivant (1993) calls the core of the social group's cultural program, which consists of the knowledge and conceptions embodied in the group's behaviors and artifacts and the values the group subscribes to. When teachers do not understand a group's cultural program, they may conceptualize parent involvement as a means to help deficient parents become better parents (Linn, 1990). This view of parent involvement is often directed toward culturally different and low-income parents (Jennings, 1990). Teachers are presented as more skilled in parenting than parents. Instead of helping parents and teachers work cooperatively, this attitude can create barriers by suggesting that parents are the cause of their children's failure in school. Parents and teachers may even become rivals for the child's affection (Lightfoot, 1978). Involvement efforts based on "the parent in need of parenting skills" assume that there is one appropriate way to parent and that parents want to learn it. Both "the parent as helper" and "the parent in need of parenting skills" are conceptualizations derived from questionable assumptions about the character of contemporary parents and reflect a limited cultural perspective.

Steps to Increase Parent and Family Involvement

Teachers are a key ingredient in parent and family involvement. They play multiple roles, including facilitator, communicator, and resource developer. Their success in implementing an effective parent/community involvement program is linked to their skill in communicating and working with parents and community groups. Teacher attitudes are also very important. Parents are supportive of the teachers they believe like their children and want their children to succeed. Teachers who have a negative attitude toward students will likely have a similar attitude toward the students' parents. Teachers tend to relate to their students as representatives of their parents' perceived status in society. Teachers use such characteristics as class, race, gender, and ethnicity to determine students' prescribed social category. Being aware of this tendency can help teachers guard against it.

You can take five steps to increase parent/community involvement in your classroom: (1) Establish two-way communication, (2) enlist support from staff and students, (3) enlist support from the community, (4) develop resource materials for home use, and (5) broaden the activities included in parent involvement.

Establish Two-Way Communication between the School and the Home

Establishing two-way communication between the school and the home is an important step in involving parents (Decker & Majerczyk, 2000). Most parents are willing to become involved in their children's education if they understand what you are trying to accomplish and how they can help. Teachers should be prepared to engage in outreach to parents, not to wait for them to become involved. Actively solicit information from parents on their thoughts about classroom goals and activities. When you talk with parents and community members, be an active listener. Listen for their feelings as well as for specific information. Listed next are seven ways you can establish and maintain two-way communication with parents and community members:

1. If possible, have an open-door policy in your classroom. Let parents know they are welcome to assist in your classroom. When parents visit, make sure they have something to do.

2. Send home written information about school assignments and goals so that parents are aware of what is going on in the classroom. Encourage parents to send notes to you if they have questions or concerns.

3. Talk to parents by phone. Let them know when they can reach you by phone. Call parents periodically and let them know when things are going well. Have something specific to talk about. Leave some time for the parent to ask questions or make comments.

4. Report problems to parents, such as failing grades and behavior problems, before it is too late for them to take remedial action. Let parents know what improvements you expect from their children and how they can help.

5. Get to know your students' community. Take time to shop in their neighborhoods. Visit community centers and attend religious services. Let parents know when you will be in the community and that you are interested in talking to them.

6. If you teach in an elementary school, try to have at least two in-person conferences a year with parents. When possible, include the student in at least part of the conference. Be prepared to explain your curriculum to parents and have books and materials that students use available for them to examine. Let the parents know in specific terms how their children are doing in class. Find out how parents feel about their children's levels of achievement, and let them know what you think about their children's achievement levels. Give the parents some suggestions on what their children can do to improve and how they can help.

7. Solicit information from parents about their views on education. Identify their educational goals for their children, ways they would like to support their children's education, and their concerns about the school. There are a number of ways to get information from parents, including sending a questionnaire home and asking parents to complete it and return it to you, conducting a telephone survey, and asking your students to interview their parents. Do not forget high-tech solutions for staying in touch with parents. These include school Web pages, homework hotlines, e-mail correspondence, videotaped events, and televised meetings. Be sure to work with local libraries to make sure that parents who do not own computers will be able to use computers in the library to access the information.

Enlist Support from Other Staff Members and Students

Teachers need support from staff, students, the principal, and district-level administrators to design, implement, and enhance their parent-involvement activities (Kirschenbaum, 2001). Teachers generally have some flexibility in their classrooms but are not always able to determine other important factors that influence their ability to have a strong parent-involvement program. For example, when teachers are consulted about the type and amount of supplies purchased for their classroom, they should be able to decide whether they want to have enough supplies to be able to send paper, pencils, and other materials home for parents to use with their children. If the school cannot provide extra supplies for teachers to send home with students, community groups may be able to provide them. Also, if teachers are allowed to modify their schedules, they can find free time to telephone parents, write notes, and hold morning or evening conferences with parents. Additionally, school climate influences parent involvement. Parents will not have positive feelings about schools where they do not believe they are welcome. School climate, however, is not determined by the teacher alone. A broad range of individuals, including students, teachers, the principal, and the school secretary, influence it. The support of all of these individuals is necessary to create a positive school environment.

Your students can help solicit support for parent and community involvement from school staff and other students. Take your class on a tour of the school. Ask the students to think about how their parents would feel if they came to the school. Two obvious questions for students are these: Is there a place for visitors to sit? Are there signs welcoming visitors and inviting them to the school office? Ask your students to list things they could do to make the school a friendlier place for parents.

Invite your principal to come to your classroom and discuss the list with your students. Divide the class into small groups and have them discuss how they would like their parents to become involved in their education. Ask them to talk to their parents and get their views. Have each group write a report on how parents can be involved in their children's education. Each group could make presentations to students in the other classrooms in the building on how they would like to increase parent involvement in their school. They could also publish a newsletter on parent involvement in schools. The newsletter could be sent to the students, parents, and other schools in the district.

If funds or other forms of support are needed from the district office for parent-involvement activities, have the students draw up a petition requesting funding and solicit signatures from teachers, students, and parents. When all of the signatures have been gathered, they can be delivered to an appropriate district administrator. The petition could also be used to inform community groups about school issues and solicit their support.

Building principals and district administrators can give teachers the support they need to do the following:

1. Help create and maintain a climate for positive parent/community involvement. This can include supporting flexible hours for teachers who need to be out of the classroom to develop materials or to work with parents. Teachers can be given time out of the classroom without negatively affecting students. At the secondary school level, time can be carved out of the teacher's schedule by combining homerooms one day a week, by team-teaching a class, or by combining different sections of a class for activities such as chapter tests. At the elementary school level, team-teaching, released time during periods when students are normally out of the classroom for specialized subjects such as music and art, or having the principal substitute in the classroom are ways to provide flexible hours for teachers.

2. Set up a parent room. It could be used for a number of functions, including serving as a community drop-in center where parents could meet other parents for a cup of coffee or as a place for parents to work on school activities without infringing on the teachers' lounge.

It could also be used as a waiting room for parents who need to see a student or a member of the school staff.

3. Host parent nights during which parents can learn more about the school, the curriculum, and the staff.

4. Send a personal note to students and to their parents when students make the honor roll or do something else noteworthy. Some schools give parents bumper stickers for their cars announcing their child's achievements.

5. Develop and distribute a handbook that contains the names and phone numbers of students, PTA or other parent-group contacts, and staff. Be sure to get permission before publishing phone numbers, addresses, and other personal information.

6. Ask the school secretary to make sure visitors are welcomed when they come to the school and that they are given directions as needed.

7. Encourage students to greet visitors and help them find their way around the building.

Enlist Support from the Community

To enlist support from the community, you need to know something about the people, organizations, and issues in it. The following are some questions you should be able to answer:

1. Are there any drama, musical, dance, or art groups in the community?

2. Is there a senior-citizen group, a public library, or a cooperative extension service in the community?

3. Are employment services such as the state employment security department available in the community?

4. Are civil rights organizations such as the Urban League, Anti-Defamation League (ADL), or National Association for the Advancement of Colored People (NAACP) active in the community?

5. What is the procedure for referring people to the Salvation Army, Goodwill, or the state department of public assistance for emergency assistance for housing, food, and clothing?

6. Does the community have a mental health center, family counseling center, or crisis clinic?

7. Are programs and activities for youth—such as Boys and Girls Clubs, Campfire U.S.A., Boy Scouts, Girl Scouts, YMCA, and YWCA—available for your students?

As you learn about the community, you can begin to develop a list of community resources and contacts that can provide support to families, work with your students, and provide locations for students to perform community service projects. Collecting information about your students' community and developing community contacts should be viewed as a long-term project. You can collect information as your schedule permits and organize it in a notebook. This process can be shortened if several teachers work together. Each teacher could concentrate on a different part of the community and share information and contacts.

Community groups can provide support in several ways. They can develop big sister and big brother programs for students, provide quiet places for students to study after school and on weekends, donate educational supplies, help raise funds for field trips, set up mentor programs, and tutor students. Community-based institutions and groups can also provide opportunities for students to participate in community-based learning programs. These learning programs provide an opportunity for students to move beyond the textbook and experience real life. They give students an opportunity to see how knowledge is integrated when it is applied to the real world. They put students in touch with a variety of people and let them see how people cope with their environments. Community-based learning also enhances career development. It can help students learn about themselves, gain confidence, and better understand their strengths and weaknesses. Students can learn to plan, make decisions, negotiate, and evaluate their plans. Here are some examples of community work students can do:

- Paint an apartment for an ill neighbor
- Clean alleys and backyards for the elderly
- Write letters for people who are ill
- Read to people who are unable to read
- Prepare an empty lot as a play area for young children
- Plant a vegetable garden for the needy
- Collect and recycle newspapers
- Serve on a community council

Develop Learning Resources for Parents to Use at Home

At home, parents can use many of the learning materials teachers use with students at school to help students improve their skills. The materials should be in a format suitable for students to take home and should provide clear directions for at-home completion. Parents could let the teacher know how they liked the material by writing a note, giving their child a verbal message for the teacher, or calling the school. Clark (1995) has written a series of math home-involvement activities for kindergarten through eighth grade. The activities are included in booklets and are designed to help students increase their math skills. Teachers can create similar math home-involvement activities that parents can use to reinforce the skills their children learn at school. These kinds of materials are convenient for both parents and teachers to use.

It is important for teachers to have resources available for parents to use. This lets parents know that they can help increase their children's learning and that teachers want their help. Simply telling parents they should work with their children is not sufficient. Parents need specific suggestions. Once parents get an idea of what you want them to do, some will develop their own materials. Other parents will be able to purchase materials or check them out from the library. You can suggest specific books, games, and other materials for parents to purchase and let them know where these learning materials are available. Some parents, however, will not have the financial resources, time, or educational background to develop or purchase learning materials. With help from your principal or from community groups, you can set up a learning center for parents. The learning center could contain paper, pencils, books, games, a computer, and other appropriate resources. The learning center could also have CDs on such topics as instructional techniques, classroom rules, educational goals for the year, and readings from books. Parents and students could check materials out of the learning center for use at home.

Broaden the Conception of Parent and Community Involvement

Many barriers to parent/community involvement can be eliminated by broadly conceptualizing it. Parents can play many roles, depending on their interests, skills, and resources. It is important to have a variety of roles for parents so that more of them will have an opportunity to be involved in the school. It is also important to make sure that some roles can be performed at home as well as at school. Following are four ways parents and community members can be involved in schools. Some of the roles can be implemented by the classroom teacher. Others need support and resources from building principals or central office administrators.

Parents Working with Their Own Children

Working with their own children is one of the most important roles parents can play in the educational process. Parents can help their children develop a positive self-concept and a positive attitude toward school as well as a better understanding of how their effort affects achievement. Most parents want their children to do well in school and are willing to do whatever they can to help them succeed. Teachers can increase the support they receive from their students' homes by giving parents a better understanding of what is going on in the classroom, by letting parents know what is expected in the classroom, and by suggesting ways in which they can support their children's learning. Teachers can work with parents to support the educational process in these three ways:

1. Involve parents in monitoring homework by asking them to sign homework papers.

2. Ask parents to sign a certificate congratulating students for good attendance.

3. Give students extra points if their parents do things such as sign their report card, attend conferences, or read to them.

Some parents want a more active partnership with the school. These parents want to help teach their children. The following are three ways you can help parents work with their children to increase their learning:

1. Encourage parents to share hobbies and games, discuss news and television programs, and talk about school problems and events with their children.

2. Send information home on the importance of reading to children and include a reading list. A one-page sheet could be sent home stating, "One of the best ways to help children become better readers is to read to them. Reading aloud is most helpful when you discuss the stories, learn to identify letters and words, and talk about the meaning of the words. Encourage leisure reading. Reading achievement is related to the amount of reading kids do. It increases vocabulary and reading fluency." Then list several books available from the school library for students to check out and take home.

3. Supply parents with materials they can use to work with their children on skill development. Students can help make math games, crossword puzzles, and other materials that parents can use with them at home. Parents should also be encouraged to take their children to the local library, where they can get their own library card.

Professional Support Person for Instruction

Many parents and community members have skills that can be shared with the school. They are willing to work with students as well as teachers. These people are often ignored in parent- and community-involvement programs. A parent or community member who is a college professor could be asked to talk to teachers about a topic that interests the professor or to participate in an in-service workshop. A bilingual parent or community member could be asked to help tutor foreign language students or to share books or magazines written in the person's language with the class. Parents who enjoy reading or art could be asked to help staff a humanities enrichment course before or after school or to recommend materials for such a course. Parents and community members who perform these kinds of duties could also serve as role models for your students and demonstrate the importance of education in the community. Review this list and think of how you could involve parents and community members in your classroom. Parents and community members can do the following:

- Serve as instructional assistants
- Use carpentry skills to build things for the school
- Tutor during school hours or after school
- Develop or identify student materials or community resources
- Share their expertise with students or staff
- Expand enrichment programs offered before, after, or during school, such as a program on great books or art appreciation
- Sew costumes for school plays
- Videotape or photograph school plays or activities
- Type and edit a newsletter

General Volunteers

Some parents are willing to volunteer their time, but they do not want to do a job that requires specific skills. When thinking of activities for general volunteers, be sure to include activities that can be performed at school as well as ones that can be performed at home. Some possible activities include these:

- Working on the playground as a support person
- Working in the classroom as a support person
- Working at home preparing cutouts and other materials that will be used in class
- Telephoning other parents to schedule conferences

Decision Makers

Some parents are interested in participating in decision making in the school. They want to help set school policy, select curriculum materials, review budgets, or interview prospective staff members. Roles for these parents and community members include school board, committee, and site council members. Serving on a site council is an excellent way for parents to participate in decision making. Site councils are designed to increase parent involvement in schools, empower classroom teachers, and allow decisions to be made at the school level.

The Comer (1995) model is an effective way to involve parents, classroom teachers, and other educators in decision making. Comer (1997) believes schools can be more effective when they are restructured in ways that encourage and support cooperation among parents and educators. Comer did much of his pioneering work on parent involvement and restructuring schools in Prince George's County, Maryland, where he implemented two committees: the School Planning and Management Team (SPMT) and the Student Staff Services Team (SSST).

The SPMT included the school principal, classroom teachers, parents, and support staff. Consensus was used to reach decisions. The committee also had a no-fault policy, which encouraged parents not to blame the school and educators not to blame parents. The SPMT provided a structure for parents and educators to create a common vision for their school, reduce fragmentation, and develop activities, curriculum, and in-service programs. It also developed a comprehensive school plan, designed a schoolwide calendar of events, and monitored and evaluated student progress. The SPMT met at least once a month. Its subcommittees met more frequently.

The second committee that Comer implemented was the SSST, which included the school principal, guidance counselor, classroom teachers, and support staff, including psychologists, health aides, and other appropriate personnel. Teachers and parents were encouraged to join this group if they had concerns they believed should be addressed. The SSST brought school personnel together to discuss individual student concerns. It also brought coherence and order to the services that students received.

Summary

Parent and community involvement is a dynamic process that encourages, supports, and provides opportunities for teachers, parents, and community members to work together to improve student learning. Parent and community involvement is also an important component of school reform and multicultural education. Parents and community groups help provide the rationale, motivation, and social action necessary for educational reform.

Everyone can benefit from parent/community involvement. Students tend to perform better in school and have more people supporting their learning. Parents know more about what is going on at school, have more opportunities to communicate with their children's teachers, and are able to help their children increase their learning. Teachers gain a partner in education. Teachers learn more about their students through their parent and community contacts and are able to use that information to help improve their students' performance.

Even though research has consistently demonstrated that students have an advantage in school when their parents support and encourage educational activities, not all parents know how they can support their children's education or feel they have the time, energy, or other resources to be involved in schools. Some parents have a particularly difficult time supporting their children's education. Three such groups are parents who have low incomes, single parents, and parents with special needs. Parents from these groups are often dismissed as unsupportive of education. However, they want their children to do well in school and are willing to work with the school when the school reaches out to them and responds to their needs.

To establish an effective parent/community involvement program, teachers should establish two-way communication with parents and community groups, enlist support from the community, and have resources available for parents to use in working with their children. Expanding the ways in which parent/community involvement is conceptualized can increase the number of parents and community members able to participate. Parents can play many roles. Ways to involve parents and community members include having parents work with their own children, parents and community members share their professional skills with the school, parents and community groups volunteer in the school, and parents and community members work with educators to make decisions about school reform.

QUESTIONS AND ACTIVITIES

17.1   Compare the role of parents in schools during the colonial period and now. Identify and discuss changes that have occurred and changes you would like to see occur in parent involvement.

17.2   Consider this statement: Regardless of the circumstances students experience at home, teachers have a responsibility to help them perform at their highest level at school. Do you agree? Why or why not?

17.3   Interview a parent of a bilingual, ethnic-minority, religious-minority, or low-income student to learn more about the parent's views on schools and his or her educational goals for the child. This information cannot be generalized to all members of these groups, but it can be an important departure point for learning more about diverse groups within our society.

17.4   Consider this statement: All parents want their children to succeed in school. Do you agree? Why or why not?

17.5   Interview a classroom teacher and an administrator to determine the views each has on parent/community involvement.

17.6 Write a brief paper about your personal views on the benefits and drawbacks of parent/community involvement.

17.7 Form a group with two other members of your class or workshop. One person in the group will be a teacher, the second a parent, and the third an observer. The teacher and the parent will role-play a teacher–parent conference.

Afterward, discuss how it felt to be a parent and a teacher. What can be done to make the parent and teacher feel more comfortable? Was the information shared at the conference helpful? The observer can share his or her view of the parent–teacher interaction. Then change roles and repeat the process.

INTERNET RESOURCES FOR INFORMATION ON PARENT INVOLVEMENT

Center on School, Family, and Community Partnerships: http://www.csos.jhu.edu/P2000/center.htm

National Coalition for Parent Involvement in Education: http://www.ncpie.org/

Parents as Teachers National Center: http://www.parentsasteachers.org/

Partnership for Family Involvement in Education: http://www.ed.gov/pubs/whoweare/index.html

REFERENCES

Aikens, A. M. (2002). Parental involvement: The key to academic success. *Dissertation Abstracts International, 63*(6), 2105. (UMI No. 3056043)

Amatea, E. S., Smith-Adcock, S., & Villares, E. (2006). From family deficit to family strength: Viewing families' contributions to children's learning from a family resilience perspective. *Professional School Counseling, 9*(3), 177–189.

Anderson, J. J. (2006). Bearing olive branches: A case for school-based and home educator dialogue. *Phi Delta Kappan, 87*(6), 468–472.

Banks, C. A. M. (2005). *Improving multicultural education: Lessons from the intergroup education movement*. New York: Teachers College Press.

Banks, J. A. (2008). *Teaching strategies for ethnic studies* (8th ed.). Boston: Allyn & Bacon.

Berger, E. H. (2008). *Parents as partners in education: Families and schools working together* (7th ed.). Upper Saddle River, NJ: Prentice Hall.

Bullivant, B. M. (1993). Culture: Its nature and meaning for educators. In J. A. Banks & C. A. M. Banks (Eds.), *Multicultural education: Issues and perspectives* (2nd ed., pp. 29–47). Boston: Allyn & Bacon.

Caspe, M., Lopez, M. E., & Wolos, C. (2006/2007). Family involvement in elementary school children's education. *Family Involvement Makes a Difference, 2*. Retrieved January 24, 2009, from http://www.hfrp.org/content/download/1182/48686/file/elementary.pdf.

Center for Mental Health in Schools at UCLA. (2007). *Parent and home involvement in schools*. Los Angeles, CA: Author.

Chavkin, N. F., & Gonzalez, D. L. (1995). *Forging partnerships between Mexican American parents and the schools*. Charleston, WV: Clearinghouse on Rural Education and Small Schools. (ERIC Document Reproduction Service No. ED388489)

Clark, C. S. (1995). Parents and schools: Will more parental involvement help students? *CQ Researcher, 5*(3), 51–69.

Comer, J. P. (1995). *School power: Implications of an intervention project*. New York: Free Press.

Comer, J. P. (1997). *Waiting for a miracle: Why schools can't solve our problems—and how we can*. New York: Dutton.

Darling-Hammond, L. (2004). What happens to a dream deferred? The continuing quest for equal educational opportunity. In J. A. Banks & C. A. M. Banks (Eds.), *Handbook of research on multicultural education* (2nd ed., pp. 607–630). San Francisco: Jossey-Bass.

Davis, K. (1958). *Little drummer boy*. London: Bregman, Vocco & Conn.

De Carvalho, M. E. P. (2001). *Rethinking family–school relations: A critique of parental involvement in schooling*. Mahwah, NJ: Erlbaum.

Decker, J., & Majerczyk, D. (2000). *Increasing parent involvement through effective home/school communication*. Chicago: Saint Xavier University. (ERIC Document Reproduction Service No. ED 439790)

DeSteno, N. (2000). Parent involvement in the classroom: The fine line. *Young Children, 55*(3), 13–17.

Dodson, H., & Diouf, S. A. (2005). *In motion: The African-American migration experience*. New York: National Geographic.

Epstein. J. L., Sanders, M. G., Simon, B. S., Salinas, K. C., Jansorn, N. R., & Van Voorhis, F. L. (2008). *School, family, and community partnerships: Your handbook for action* (3rd ed.). Thousand Oaks, CA: Corwin.

Goodlad, J. I. (1984). *A place called school: Prospects for the future*. New York: McGraw-Hill.

Harry, B. (1992). Restructuring the participation of African-American parents in special education. *Exceptional Children, 59*(2), 123–131.

Henderson, A. T., & Berla, N. (Eds.). (2002). *A new wave of evidence: The impact of school, family, and community connections on student achievement*. Austin, TX: National Center for Family & Community Connections with Schools.

Henderson, A. T., Mapp, K. L., Johnson, V. R., & Davies, D. (2006). *Beyond the bake sale: The essential guide to family-school partnerships*. New York: The New Press.

Hidalgo, N. M., Sau-Fong, S., & Epstein, J. L. (2004). Research on families, schools, and communities: A multicultural perspective. In J. A. Banks & C. A. M. Banks (Eds.), *Handbook of research on multicultural education* (2nd ed., pp. 631–655). San Francisco: Jossey-Bass.

Jennings, L. (1990). Parents as partners: Reaching out to families to help students learn. *Education Week, 9*(40), 23–32.

Kagan, S. L. (1995, December). *Meeting family and community needs: The three C's of early childhood education.* Paper presented at the Australia and New Zealand Conference on the First Years of School, Tasmania, Australia.

Kirschenbaum, H. (2001). Educating professionals for school, family, and community partnerships. In D. B. Hiatt-Michael (Ed.), *Promising practices for family involvement in schools* (pp. 185–189). Greenwich, CT: Information Age.

Lee, S. M., & Edmonston, B. (2005). New marriages, new families: U.S. racial and Hispanic intermarriage. *Population Bulletin, 60*(2). Washington, DC: Population Reference Bureau.

Lightfoot, S. L. (1978). *Worlds apart: Relationships between families and schools.* New York: Basic Books.

Linn, E. (1990). Parent involvement programs: A review of selected models. *Equity Coalition, 1*(2), 10–15.

McCallion, P., Janicki, M. P., & Kolomer, S. R. (2004). Controlled evaluation of support groups for grandparent caregivers of children with developmental disabilities and delays. *American Journal on Mental Retardation, 109*(5), 352–361.

McFalls, J. A., Jr. (2007). Population: A lively introduction (5th ed.). *Population Reference Bulletin, 62*(1), 1–33.

Newman, L. (2009). *Heather has two mommies* (20th anniv. ed.). New York: Alyson Books.

Ouimette, M. Y., Feldman, J., & Tung, R. (2006). Collaborating for high school student success: A case study of parent engagement at Boston Arts Academy. *School Community Journal, 16*(2), 91–114.

Pena, D. C. (2000). Parent involvement: Influencing factors and implications. *Journal of Educational Research, 94*(1), 42–54.

Rasinski, T. V. (1989). Reading and the empowerment of parents. *Reading Teacher, 43*(3), 226–231.

Schneider, B. L., & Coleman, J. S. (Eds.). (1993). *Parents, their children, and schools.* Boulder, CO: Westview.

Shariff, J. W. (1988). Free enterprise and the ghetto family. In J. S. Wurzel (Ed.), *Toward multiculturalism: A reader in multicultural education* (pp. 30–54). Yarmouth, ME: Intercultural Press.

Swadener, B. B., & Niles, K. (1991). Children and families "at promise": Making home–school–community connections. *Democracy and Education, 5*(3), 13–18.

U.S. Bureau of Labor Statistics. (2011). Employment characteristics of families summary. Retrieved December 1, 2011, from http://www.bls.gov/news.release/famee.nr0.htm

U.S. Census Bureau. (2010a). *2010 American community survey.* Retrieved November 29, 2011, from http://factfinder2.census.gov/faces/tableservices/jsf/pages/productview.xhtml?pid=ACS_10_1YR_B17006&prodType=table.

U.S. Census Bureau. (2010b). *2010 American community survey.* Retrieved December 5, 2011, from http://factfinder2.census.gov/faces/tableservices/jsf/pages/productview.xhtml?pid=ACS_10_1YR_S0504&prodType=table.

U.S. Census Bureau. (2010c). *America's families and living arrangements: 2010.* Retrieved November 28, 2011, from http://www.census.gov/population/www/socdemo/hh-fam/cps2010.html.

U.S. Census Bureau. (2010d). *An overview: Race and Hispanic origin and the 2010 census.* Retrieved November 29, 2011, from http://2010.census.gov/2010census/.

U.S. Census Bureau. (2010e). *Poverty: 2009 and 2010.* Retrieved November 28, 2011, from http://www.census.gov/prod/2011pubs/acsbr10-01.pdf.

U.S. Census Bureau. (2010f). Selected characteristics of people at specified levels of poverty in the past 12 months. Retrieved November 28, 2011, from http://factfinder2.census.gov/faces/tableservices/jsf/pages/productview.xhtml?pid=ACS_10_1YR_S1703&prodType=table.

U.S. Census Bureau. (2011). *Income, poverty, and health insurance coverage in the United States: 2010.* Retrieved November 20, 2011, from http://www.census.gov/prod/2011pubs/p60-239.pdf.

Walker, V. S. (1996). *Their highest potential: An African American school community in the segregated South.* Chapel Hill: University of North Carolina Press.

Waller, W. (1965). *The sociology of teaching.* New York: Wiley. (Original work published 1932)

ISSUES AND CONCEPTS

Au, W. (Ed.). (2009). *Rethinking multicultural education: Teaching for racial and cultural justice*. Milwaukee, WI: Rethinking Schools.

Banks, C. A. M. (2005). *Improving multicultural education: Lessons from the intergroup education movement*. New York: Teachers College Press.

Banks, J. A. (2006). *Cultural diversity and education: Foundations, curriculum, and teaching* (5th ed.). Boston: Allyn & Bacon.

Banks, J. A. (2006). *Race, culture, and education: The selected works of James A. Banks*. London and New York: Routledge.

Banks, J. A. (2009). *Teaching strategies for ethnic studies* (8th ed.). Boston: Allyn & Bacon.

Banks, J. A. (Ed.). (2009). *The Routledge international companion to multicultural education*. New York and London: Routledge.

Banks, J. A. (Ed.). (2012). *The encyclopedia of diversity in education* (4 vols.). Thousand Oaks, CA: Sage.

Banks, J. A., & Banks, C. A. M. (Eds.). (2004). *Handbook of research on multicultural education* (2nd ed.). San Francisco: Jossey-Bass.

Darling-Hammond, L. (2010). *The flat world and education: How America's commitment to equity will determine our future*. New York: Teachers College Press.

Nieto, S. (2010). *The light in their eyes: Creating multicultural learning communities* (10th anniv. ed.). New York: Teachers College Press.

Sensoy, O., & DiAngelo, R. (2012). *Is everyone really equal? An introduction to key concepts in social justice education*. New York: Teachers College Press.

SOCIAL CLASS

Fiske, S., & Markus, J. (2012). *Facing social class: How societal rank influences interaction*. New York: Russell Sage Foundation.

Gatzambide-Fernandez, R. (2009). *The best of the best: Becoming elite at an American boarding school*. Cambridge, MA: Harvard University Press.

Heath, S. B. (2012). *Words at work and play: Three decades in family and community life*. New York: Cambridge University Press.

Howard, A. (2008). *Learning privilege: Lessons of power and identity in affluent schooling*. New York: Routledge.

Kincheloe, J. L., & Steinberg, S. R. (2007). *Cutting class: Socioeconomic status and education*. Lanham, MD: Rowman & Littlefield.

Lareau, A. (2011). *Unequal childhoods: Race, class, and family life* (2nd ed.). Berkeley: University of California Press.

Lareau, A., & Conley, D. (Eds.). (2008). *Social class: How does it work?* New York: Russell Sage Foundation.

Ornstein, A. C. (2007). *Class counts: Education, inequality, and the shrinking middle class*. Lanham, MD: Rowman & Littlefield.

Sacks, P. (2007). *Tearing down the gates: Confronting the class divide in American education*. Berkeley: University of California Press.

Stevens, M. L. (2007). *Creating a class: College admissions and the education of elites*. Cambridge, MA: Harvard University Press.

Weis, L. (Ed.). (2008). *The way class works: Readings on school, family, and the economy*. New York and London: Routledge.

RELIGION

Alba, R., Raboteau, A., & DeWind, J. (Eds.). (2008). *Immigration and religion in America: Comparative and historical perspectives*. New York: New York University Press.

Cohen, C. L., & Numbers, R. L. (Eds.). (in press). *Religious pluralism in modern America*. New York: Oxford University Press.

Haddad, Y. Y. (2011). *Becoming American? The forging of Arab and Muslim identity in pluralist America*. Waco, TX: Baylor University Press.

Hefner, R. W., & Qasim, M. (2007). *Schooling Islam: The culture and politics of modern Muslim education*. Princeton, NJ: Princeton University Press.

Joshi, K. Y. (2006). *New roots in America's sacred ground: Religion, race, and ehnicity in Indian America.* New Brunswick, NJ: Rutgers University Press.

Kunzan, R. (2006). *Grappling with the good: Talking about religion and morality in public schools.* Albany: State University of New York Press.

Merry, M. S. (2007). *Culture, identity, and Islamic schooling: A philosophical approach.* New York: Palgrave Macmillan.

Neusner, J. (Ed.). (2009). *World religions in America* (4th ed.). Louisville, KY: Westminster John Knox Press.

Prothero, S. R. (2007). *Religious literacy: What every American needs to know—and doesn't.* San Francisco: HarperSanFrancisco.

Salili, F., & Hoosain, R. (2006). *Religion in multicultural education.* Greenwich, CT: Information Age.

Stern, J. (2007). *Schools and religions: Imagining the real.* New York: Continuum.

Thomas, R. M. (2008). *God in the classroom: Religion and America's public schools.* Lanham, MD: Rowman & Littlefield.

Trent, M. A. (2007). *Religion, culture, curriculum, and diversity in 21st century America.* Lanham, MD: University Press of America.

GENDER

Allan, E. J. (2008). *Policy discourses, gender, and education: Constructing women's status.* New York: Routledge.

Dilg, M. (2010). *Our worlds in our words: Exploring race, class, gender and sexual orientation in multicultural classrooms.* New York: Teachers College Press.

Dillabough, J., McLeod, J., & Mills, M. (2009). *Troubling gender in education.* London and New York: Routledge.

Eliot, L. (2010). *Pink brain, blue brain: How small differences grow into troublesome gaps—and what we can do about it.* Boston: Houghton Mifflin.

Jones, L., & Barron, I. (2007). *Research and gender.* London and New York: Continuum.

Kimmel, M. (2008). *Guyland: The perilous world where boys become men.* New York: Harper.

Klein, S. S. (Ed.). (2007). *Handbook for achieving gender equity through education.* Mahwah, NJ: Erlbaum.

Mirza, H. S. (2009). *Race, gender and educational desire: Why Black women succeed and fail.* New York and London: Routledge.

Noguera, P. A. (2008). *The trouble with Black boys: And other reflections on race, equity, and the future of public education.* San Francisco: Jossey-Bass.

Rivers, C., & Barnett, R. C. (2011). *The truth about girls and boys: Challenging toxic stereotypes about our children.* New York: Columbia University. Press.

Sadker, D., Sadker, M., & Zittleman, K. (2009) *Still failing at fairness: How gender bias cheats girls and boys in school and what we can do about it.* New York: Scribners.

Sadker, D. M., & Silber, E. S. (2007). *Gender in the classroom: Foundations, skills, methods, and strategies across the curriculum.* Mahwah, NJ: Erlbaum.

Unterhalter, E. (2007). *Gender, schooling and global social justice.* London and New York: Routledge.

SEXUAL AND GENDER MINORITIES

Blackburn, M. V. (2011). *Interrupting hate: Homophobia in schools and what literacy can do about it.* New York: Teachers College Press.

Blackburn, M. V., Clark, C. T., Kenney, L. M., & Smith, J. M. (2009). *Acting out! Combating homophobia through teacher activism.* New York: Teachers College Press.

Casper, V., & Schultz, S. B. (1999). *Gay parents, straight schools: Building communication and trust.* New York: Teachers College Press.

Driver, S. (Ed.). (2008). *Queer youth cultures.* Albany: State University of New York Press.

Korschoreck, J. W., & Tooms, A. K. (Eds.). (2009). *Sexuality matters: Paradigms and policies for educational leaders.* Lanham, MD: Rowman & Littlefield Education.

Kumashiro, K. (2002). *Troubling education: Queer activism and antioppressive education.* New York: Routledge.

Mayo, C. (2007). *Disputing the subject of sex: Sexuality and public school controversies.* Lanham, MD: Rowman & Littlefield.

McCready, L. T. (2010). *Making space for diverse masculinities: Difference, intersectionality, and engagement in an urban high school.* New York: Peter Lang.

Pasco, C. J. (2007). *Dude, you're a fag: Masculinity and sexuality in high school.* Berkeley: University of California Press.

Rodriguez, N. M., & Pinar, W. F. (Eds.). (2007). *Queering straight teachers: Discourse and identity in education.* New York: Peter Lang.

RACE, ETHNICITY, AND LANGUAGE

Conchas, G. Q. (2012). *Sreetsmart schoolsmart: Urban poverty and the education of adolescent boys.* New York: Teachers College Press.

Gándara, P., & Hopkins, M. (Eds.). (2010). *Forbidden language: English language learners and restrictive language policies.* New York: Teachers College Press.

Gay, G. (2010). *Culturally responsive teaching: Theory, research, and practice* (2nd ed.). New York: Teachers College Press.

Howard, T. C. (2010). *Why race and culture matter in schools: Closing the achievement gap in America's classrooms.* New York: Teachers College Press

Hudley, A. H., & Mallinson, C. (2011). *Understanding language variation in U.S. schools.* New York: Teachers College Press.

Lee, C. D. (2006). *Culture, literacy and learning: Taking bloom in the midst of the whirlwind.* New York: Teachers College Press.

Lee, O., & Buxton, C. A. (2010). *Diversity and equity in science education: Research, policy, and practice.* New York: Teachers College Press.

Nasir, N. S., & Cobb, P. (Eds.). (2007). *Improving access to mathematics: Diversity and equity in the classroom.* New York: Teachers College Press.

Picca, L. H., & Feagin, J. R. (2007). *Two-faced racism: Whites in the backstage and frontstage.* New York and London: Routledge.

Steele, C. (2010). *Whistling Vivaldi and other clues to how stereotypes affect us.* New York: Norton.

Valdés, G., Capitelli, S., & Alvarez, L. (2011). *Latino children learning English: Steps in the journey.* New York: Teachers College Press.

EXCEPTIONALITY

Florian, L. (Ed.). (2007). *The Sage handbook of special education.* Thousand Oaks, CA: Sage.

Friend, M. (2010). *Special education: Contemporary perspectives for school professionals.* Boston: Pearson.

Friend, M., & Bursuck, W. D. (2011). *Including students with special needs: A practical guide for classroom teachers* (5th ed.). Boston: Pearson.

Heward, W. L. (2013). *Exceptional children: An introduction to special education* (10th ed.). Boston: Pearson.

Osgood, R. L. (2008). *The history of special education: A struggle for equality in American public schools.* Westport, CT: Praeger.

Sapon-Shevin, M. (2007). *Widening the circle: The power of inclusive classrooms.* Boston: Beacon.

Turnbull, A., Turnball, H. R., Wehmeyer, M. L., & Shogren, K. A. (2011). *Exceptional lives: Special education in today's schools* (6th ed.). Boston: Pearson.

SPECIAL EDUCATION AND EQUITY

Artiles, A. J., Kozleski, E. B., & Waitoller, F. R. (Eds.). (2011). *Inclusive education: Examining equity on five continents.* Cambridge, MA: Harvard Education Press.

Donovan, S., & Cross, C. T. (2002). *Minority students in special and gifted education.* Washington, DC: National Academy Press.

El-haj, A. (2006). *Elusive justice: Wrestling with difference and educational equity in everyday practice.* New York: Routledge.

Griffin, J. E., Artiles, A. J., & Ortiz, A. (2002). *English language learners with special educational needs: Identification, placement, and instruction.* Washington, DC: Center for Applied Linguistics.

Harry, B., & Klingner, J. K. (2006). *Why are so many minority students in special education? Understanding race and disability in schools.* New York: Teachers College Press.

Harry, B., Klingner, J. K., Cramer, E. P., & Sturges, K. M. (2007). *Case studies of minority student placement in special education.* New York: Teachers College Press.

Heller, K. A., Holtzman, W., & Messick, S. (Eds.). (1982). *Placing children in special education: A strategy of equity.* Washington, DC: National Academy Press.

Losen, D. J., & Orfield, G. (Eds.). (2002). *Racial inequities in special education.* Cambridge, MA: Harvard Education Press.

Wallace, B., & Eriksson, G. I. (2006). *Diversity in gifted education: International perspectives on global issues.* New York: Routledge.

GIFTED EDUCATION AND EQUITY

Cartledge, G., Gardner, R., & Ford, D. Y. (2008). *Diverse learners with exceptionalities: Culturally responsive teaching in the inclusive classroom.* Columbus, OH: Merrill Education.

Castellano, J. A., & Frazier, A. D. (2010). *Special populations in gifted education: Understanding our most able students from diverse backgrounds.* Waco, TX: Prufrock Press.

Davis, J. L. (2010). *Bright, talented, & Black: A guide for families of African American gifted learners.* Scottsdale, AZ: Great Potential Press.

Ford, D. Y. (2010). *Reversing underachievement in gifted Black students* (2nd ed.). Waco, TX: Prufrock Press.

Ford, D. Y. (2011). *Multicultural gifted education* (2nd ed.). Waco, TX: Prufrock Press.

Grantham, T. C., Ford, D. Y., Henfield, M., Trotman Scott, M., Harmon, D., Porchér, S., & Price, C. (2011). *Gifted and advanced Black students in school: An anthology of critical works.* Waco, TX: Prufrock Press.

Tomlinson, C. A., Ford, D. Y., Reis, S. M., Briggs, C. J., & Strickland, C. A. (Eds.). (2009). *In search of the dream: Designing schools and classrooms that work for high potential students from diverse cultural backgrounds* (rev. ed.). Washington, DC: National Association for Gifted Children.

SCHOOL REFORM

Bishop, R., O'Sullivan, D., & Berryman, M. (2010). *Scaling up education reform: Addressing the politics of disparity.* Wellington, New Zealand: New Zealand Council for Educational Research (NZCER) Press.

Bryk, A. S., Sebring, P. B., Allensworth, E., Luppescu, S., & Easton, J. (2010). *Organizing schools for improvement: Lessons from Chicago.* Chicago: University of Chicago Press.

Cuban, L. (2008). *Frogs into princes: Writings on school reform.* New York: Teachers College Press.

Lortie, D. C. (2009). *School principal: Managing in public.* Chicago: University of Chicago Press.

Nitta, K. (2008). *The politics of structural education reform.* New York: Routledge.

Sizemore, B. A. (2008). *Walking in circles: The Black struggle for school reform.* Chicago: Third World Press.

Glossary

African Americans U.S. residents and citizens who have an African biological and cultural heritage and identity. This term is used synonymously and interchangeably with Blacks and Black Americans to describe both a racial and a cultural group. African Americans are projected to increase from 42 million, or 13.6 percent of the population, in 2010 to 65.7 million, or 15 percent in 2050 (U.S. Census Bureau, 2010a). An excellent one-volume encyclopedia on African Americans is *Africana: The Encyclopedia of the African and African American Experience* (Appiah & Gates, 1999).

Afrocentric curriculum A curriculum approach in which concepts, issues, problems, and phenomena are viewed from the perspectives of Africans and African Americans. This curriculum is based on the assumption that students learn best when they view situations and events from their own cultural perspectives (Asante, 1998).

American Indians See *Native Americans and Alaska Natives.*

Anglo Americans Americans whose biological and cultural heritage originated in England or Americans with other biological and cultural heritages who have assimilated into the dominant or mainstream culture in the United States. This term is often used to describe the mainstream U.S. culture or to describe most White Americans. The non-Hispanic, single-race White population is projected to be only slightly larger in 2050 (203.3 million) than in 2010 (196.8 million). In fact, this group is projected to lose population in the 2030s and 2040s and comprise 50 percent of the total population in 2042, down from 63.7 percent in 2010 (U.S. Census Bureau, 2010a).

Antiracist education A term used in the United Kingdom and Canada to describe a process used by teachers and other educators to eliminate institutionalized racism from the schools and society and to help individuals develop nonracist attitudes. When antiracist educational reform is implemented, curriculum materials, grouping practices, hiring policies, teacher attitudes and expectations, and school policy and practices are examined and steps are taken to eliminate racism from these school variables. A related educational reform movement in the United States

that focuses more on individuals than on institutions is known as *prejudice reduction* (Stephan & Vogt, 2004).

Asian Americans Americans who have a biological and cultural heritage that originated on the continent of Asia. The largest groups of Asian Americans in the United States in 2010 were (in descending order) Chinese, Asian Indians, Filipinos, Vietnamese, Koreans, and Japanese. Other groups included Pakistanis, Hmong, Cambodians, Taiwanese, Laotians, Thailanders, and Indonesians. The Asian American population is projected to increase from 17.3 million in 2010 to 40.6 million by 2050. Its share of the nation's population is expected to increase from 5.6 percent to 9.2 percent (U.S. Census Bureau, 2010b).

Cultural assimilation A phenomenon that takes place when one ethnic or cultural group acquires the behavior, values, perspectives, ethos, and characteristics of another ethnic group and sheds its own cultural characteristics. (For a further discussion of assimilation of ethnic groups in the United States since the 1960s, see Alba & Nee, 2003).

Culture The ideations, symbols, behaviors, values, and beliefs that are shared by a human group. Culture can also be defined as a group's program for survival and adaptation to its environment. Pluralistic nation-states such as the United States, Canada, and Australia are made up of an overarching culture, called a *macroculture*, which all individuals and groups in the nation share. These nation-states also have many smaller cultures, called *microcultures*, that differ in many ways from the macroculture or that contain cultural components manifested differently than in the macroculture. (See Chapters 1 and 2 for further discussions of culture.)

Disability The physical or mental characteristics of an individual that prevent or limit that person from performing specific tasks.

Discrimination The differential treatment of individuals or groups based on categories such as race, ethnicity, gender, sexual orientation, social class, or exceptionality.

Ethnic group A microcultural group or collectivity that shares a common history and culture, values, behaviors, and other characteristics that cause members of the group to have a shared identity. A sense of peoplehood is one of the most important characteristics of an ethnic group, which also shares economic and political interests. Cultural characteristics rather than biological traits are the essential attributes of an ethnic group. An ethnic group is not the same as a racial group. Some ethnic groups, such as Puerto Ricans in the United States, are made up of individuals who belong to several different racial groups. White Anglo-Saxon Protestants, Italian Americans, and Irish Americans are examples of ethnic groups. Individual members of an ethnic group vary considerably in the extent to which they identify with the group. Some individuals have a very strong identification with their particular ethnic group, whereas other members of the group have a very weak identification with it.

Ethnic-minority group   An ethnic group with several distinguishing characteristics. An ethnic-minority group has distinguishing cultural characteristics, racial characteristics, or both, which enable members of other groups to identify its members easily. Some ethnic-minority groups, such as Jewish Americans, have unique cultural characteristics. African Americans have unique cultural and physical characteristics. The unique attributes of ethnic-minority groups make them convenient targets of racism and discrimination. Ethnic-minority groups are usually a numerical minority in their societies. However, the Blacks in South Africa, who are a numerical majority in their nation-state, were often considered a sociological minority group by social scientists because they had little political power until the constitution of the Republic of South Africa was established in 1996 (Moodley & Adam, 2004).

Ethnic studies   The scientific and humanistic analysis of behavior influenced by variables related to ethnicity and ethnic group membership. This term is often used to refer to special school, university, and college courses and programs that focus on specific racial and ethnic groups. However, any aspects of a course or program that includes a study of variables related to ethnicity can accurately be referred to as ethnic studies. In other words, ethnic studies can be integrated within the boundaries of mainstream courses and curricula.

Eurocentric curriculum   A curriculum in which concepts, events, and situations are viewed primarily from the perspectives of European nations and cultures and in which Western civilization is emphasized. This approach is based on the assumption that Europeans have made the most important contributions to the development of the United States and the world. Curriculum theorists who endorse this approach are referred to as *Eurocentrists* or *Western traditionalists*.

European Americans   *See Anglo Americans.*

Exceptional   Term used to describe students who have learning or behavioral characteristics that differ substantially from those of most other students and that require special attention in instruction. Students who are intellectually gifted or talented as well as those who have disabilities are considered exceptional.

Gender   A category consisting of behaviors that result from the social, cultural, and psychological factors associated with masculinity and femininity in a society. Appropriate male and female roles result from the socialization of the individual within a group.

Gender identity   An individual's view of the gender to which he or she belongs and his or her shared sense of group attachment to other males or females.

Global education   A curriculum reform movement concerned with issues and problems related to the survival of human beings in the world community. International studies is a part of global education, but the focus of global education is the interdependence of human beings and their common fate regardless of the national boundaries within which they live. Many teachers confuse global education and international studies with ethnic studies, which deal with ethnic groups within a particular national boundary, such as the United States, Canada, or Australia.

Handicapism   The unequal treatment of people who are disabled and the related attitudes and beliefs that reinforce and justify discrimination against people with disabilities. The term *handicapped* is considered negative by some people, who prefer the term *disabled*. "People with disabilities" is considered a more sensitive phrase than "disabled people" because the word *people* is used first and given emphasis.

Hispanic Americans   Americans who share a culture, heritage, and language that originated in Spain. Most of the Hispanics living in the United States have cultural origins in Latin America. Many Hispanics in the United States prefer to use the word *Latino* rather than *Hispanic*, as do the editors of this book. However, the U.S. Census uses the term *Hispanic*. Most Hispanics in the United States speak Spanish and are *mestizos*, persons of mixed biological heritage. Most Hispanics in the United States have an Indian as well as a Spanish heritage, and many also have an African biological and cultural heritage.

More than half the growth in the total population of United States between 2000 and 2010 was due to the increase in the Hispanic population. The Hispanic population is projected to nearly triple, from 50.5 million in 2010 to 132.8 million in 2050. Thus, nearly one in three U.S. residents would be Hispanic (U.S. Census Bureau, 2010a). The largest groups of Hispanics in the United States are Mexican Americans (Chicanos), Puerto Ricans, and Cubans. In 2010, there were 31.8 million Mexican Americans, 4.6 million Puerto Ricans in the mainland United States, 1.8 million Cubans, and 12.2 million Hispanics from other nations, notably Central and South America (U.S. Census Bureau, 2010a).

It is misleading to view Hispanics as one ethnic group. Some Hispanics believe that the word *Hispanics* can help to unify the various Latino groups and thus increase their political power. The primary identity of most Hispanics in the United States, however, is with their particular group, such as Mexican American, Puerto Rican American, or Cuban American.

Mainstream American   A U.S. citizen who shares most of the characteristics of the dominant ethnic and cultural group in the nation. Such individuals are usually White Anglo-Saxon Protestant and belong to the middle class or a higher social class or perceive themselves as having middle-class or higher social-class status.

Mainstream-centric curriculum   A curriculum that presents events, concepts, issues, and problems primarily or exclusively from the points of view and perspectives of the mainstream society and the dominant ethnic and cultural group in the United States: White Anglo-Saxon Protestants. The mainstream-centric curriculum is also usually presented from the perspectives of Anglo males.

Mainstreaming   The process that involves placing students with disabilities into the regular classroom for instruction. They might be integrated into the regular classroom for part or all of the school day. This practice was initiated in response to Public Law 94–142 (passed by Congress in 1975), which requires that students with disabilities be educated in the least restrictive environment.

Multicultural education   A reform movement designed to change the total educational environment so that students from diverse racial and ethnic groups, students of both genders, exceptional students, and students from each social-class group will experience equal educational opportunities in schools, colleges, and universities. A major assumption of multicultural education is that some students—because of their particular racial, ethnic, gender, and cultural characteristics—have a better chance of succeeding in educational institutions as they are currently structured than do students who belong to other groups or who have different cultural and gender characteristics. See the first chapters in the *Handbook of Research on Multicultural Education* (Banks & Banks, 2004) and in *The Routledge International Companion to Multicultural Education* (Banks, 2009) for further discussions of multicultural education.

Multiculturalism   A philosophical position and movement that assumes that the gender, ethnic, racial, and cultural diversity of a pluralistic society should be reflected in all of the institutionalized structures of educational institutions, including the staff, the norms and values, the curriculum, and the student body.

Native Americans and Alaska Natives   U.S. citizens who trace their biological and cultural heritage to the original inhabitants in the land that now makes up the United States. The term *Native American* is sometimes used synonymously with American Indian. In 2010, seven of the ten largest tribes—the Cherokee, Navajo, Choctaw, Chippewa, Sioux, Apache, and Blackfeet—each had a population of more than 100,000 persons. The two largest American Indian tribes were the Cherokee (819,105) and the Navajo (332,129). The Yup'ik (33,889) constituted the largest group of Alaska Natives. Native Americans and Alaska Natives are projected to increase from 5.2 million in 2008 to 8.6 million by 2050—from 1.7 to 2.0 percent of the total population (U.S. Census Bureau, 2010d).

Native Hawaiians and Other Pacific Islanders   U.S. citizens who self-identify as having Native Hawaiian and/or Pacific Islander descent. This group comprises Native Hawaiian (15,146), Samoan (109,637), Tongan (41,219), Guamanian or Chamorro (88,310), Fijian (24,629) and Marshallese (19,814). This population is projected to more than double, from 1.2 million in 2008 to 2.6 million by 2050 (U.S. Census Bureau, 2010c).

People of color   Groups in the United States and other nations who have experienced discrimination historically because of their unique biological characteristics that enabled potential discriminators to identify them easily. African Americans, Asian Americans, and Hispanics in the United States are among the groups referred to as *people of color*. Most members of these groups still experience forms of discrimination today. The U.S. Census Bureau (2010a) projects that ethnic minorities will increase from 36 percent of the nation's population in 2010 to 50 percent in 2042. Ethnic minorities made up 110 million of the total U.S. population of just over 300 million in 2010. By 2023, more than half of all children are projected to be children of color (U.S. Census Bureau, 2010a).

Positionality   An idea that emerged out of feminist scholarship stating that variables such as an individual's gender, class, and race are markers of that individual's relational position within a social and economic context and influence the knowledge that the person produces. Consequently, valid knowledge requires an acknowledgment of the knower's position within a specific context (See Chapter 7).

Prejudice   A set of rigid and unfavorable attitudes toward a particular individual or group that is formed without consideration of facts. Prejudice is a set of attitudes that often leads to *discrimination*, the differential treatment of particular individuals and groups.

Race   A term that refers to the attempt by physical anthropologists to divide human groups according to their physical traits and characteristics. This has proven to be very difficult because human groups in modern societies are highly mixed physically. Consequently, different and often conflicting race typologies exist. An excellent book on the social construction of race that gives a historical perspective on it is *Whiteness of a Different Color: European Immigrants and the Alchemy of Race* (Jacobson, 1999).

Racism   A belief that human groups can be validly grouped according to their biological traits and that these identifiable groups inherit certain mental, personality, and cultural characteristics that determine their behavior. Racism, however, is not merely a set of beliefs but is practiced when a group has the power to enforce laws, institutions, and norms based on its beliefs, which oppress and dehumanize another group. Two informative references on racism are *Racism: A Short History* (Fredrickson, 2002)

and *Two-Faced Racism: Whites in the Backstage and Frontstage* (Picca & Feagin, 2007).

Religion   A set of beliefs and values, especially about explanations that concern the cause and nature of the universe, to which an individual or group has a strong loyalty and attachment. A religion usually has a moral code, rituals, and institutions that reinforce and propagate its beliefs.

Sex   The biological factors that distinguish males and females, such as chromosomal, hormonal, anatomical, and physiological characteristics.

Sexism   Social, political, and economic structures that advantage one sex group over the other. Stereotypes and misconceptions about the biological characteristics of each sex group reinforce and support sex discrimination. In most societies, women have been the major victims of sexism. However, males are also victimized by sexist beliefs and practices.

Social class   A collectivity of people who have a similar socioeconomic status based on such criteria as income, occupation, education, values, behaviors, and life chances. Lower class, working class, middle class, and upper class are common designations of social class in the United States.

REFERENCES

Alba, R. D., & Nee, V. (2003). *Remaking the American mainstream: Assimilation and contemporary immigration.* Cambridge, MA: Harvard University Press.

Appiah, K. A., & Gates, H. L., Jr. (Eds.). (1999). *Africana: The encyclopedia of the African and African American experience.* New York: Perseus.

Asante, M. K. (1998). *The Afrocentric idea* (rev. ed.). Philadelphia: Temple University Press.

Banks, J. A. (Ed.). (2009). *The Routledge international companion to multicultural education.* New York & London: Routleddge.

Banks, J. A., & Banks, C. A. M. (Eds.). (2004). *Handbook of research on multicultural education* (2nd ed.). San Francisco: Jossey-Bass.

Fredrickson, G. M. (2002). *Racism: A short history.* Princeton, NJ: Princeton University Press.

Jacobson, M. F. (1999). *Whiteness of a different color: European immigrants and the alchemy of race.* Cambridge, MA: Harvard University Press.

Moodley, K. A., & Adam, H. (2004). Citizenship education and political literacy in South Africa. In J. A. Banks (Ed.), *Diversity and citizenship education: Global perspectives* (pp. 159–183). San Francisco: Jossey-Bass.

Picca, L. H., & Feagin, J. (2007). *Two-faced racism: Whites in the backstage and frontstage.* New York: Routledge.

Stephan, W., & Vogt, W. P. (Eds.). (2004). *Education programs for improving intergroup relations: Theory, research, and practice.* New York: Teachers College Press.

U.S. Census Bureau. (2010a). *An overview: Race and Hispanic origin and the 2010 census.* Retrieved November 15, 2011, from http://2010.census.gov/2010census/

U.S. Census Bureau. (2010b). *Race reporting for the Asian population by selected categories: 2010.* Retrieved November 16, 2011, from http://factfinder2.census.gov/faces/tableservices/jsf/pages/productview.xhtml?pid=DEC_10_SF1_QTP8&prodType=table

U.S. Census Bureau. (2010c). *Race reporting for the Native Hawaiian and other Pacific Islander population by selected categories: 2010.* Retrieved November 16, 2011, from http://factfinder2.census.gov/faces/tableservices/jsf/pages/productview.xhtml?pid=DEC_10_SF1_QTP9&prodType=table

U.S. Census Bureau. (2010d). *Race reporting for the American Indian and Alaska native population by selected tribes: 2010.* Retrieved January 23, 2011, from http://factfinder2.census.gov/faces/tableservices/jsf/pages/productview.xhtml?pid=DEC_10_SF1_QTP7&prodType=table

Contributors

Cherry A. McGee Banks is professor of education at the University of Washington, Bothell. Her publications include *Improving Multicultural Education: Lessons from the Intergroup Education Movement*. Professor Banks has served on several national committees and boards and is chair of the AERA Books Editorial Board.

James A. Banks holds the Kerry and Linda Killinger Endowed Chair in Diversity Studies and is founding director of the Center for Multicultural Education at the University of Washington, Seattle. His research focuses on multicultural education and diversity and citizenship education in a global context. He is the editor of the *Encyclopedia of Diversity in Education*, published by Sage in four volumes in 2012.

Jill M. Bevan-Brown is an associate professor of inclusive education at Massey University College of Education, New Zealand. Of Maori heritage, she has a particular interest in the special education needs of Maori children and has concentrated her writing and research on their education.

Sara C. Bicard is associate professor of special education at Auburn University, Montgomery, Alabama. Her research interests include reading instruction and materials for students with reading difficulties, active student responding, and inclusive practices.

Patty Bode is visiting associate professor at The Ohio State University. Her research focuses on multicultural education, urban art education, and the role of visual culture in K–12 art rooms.

Christina Convertino is a postdoctoral research associate in educational policy studies at the University of Arizona. Her research and teaching focus on the social, cultural, and organizational contexts of education, with particular attention to spatial justice, community-based pedagogies, and youth identities.

Donna Y. Ford is professor in the Departments of Special Education and Teaching and Learning at Vanderbilt University. She has written numerous articles and several books on multicultural education and gifted education. Her work focuses on recruiting and retaining culturally different students in gifted education and advanced placement classes, creating culturally responsive learning environments, and improving student achievement.

Norma González is a professor in language, reading, and culture in the Department of Teaching, Learning, and Sociocultural Studies at the University of Arizona. Her research includes issues related to anthropology and education and language and language socialization. Her works include *Funds of Knowledge for Teaching: Theorizing Practices in Households, Communities, and Classrooms* (with Luis Moll and Cathy Amanti).

Carl A. Grant is Hoefs-Bascom Professor of Teacher Education in the Department of Curriculum and Instruction at the University of Wisconsin, Madison. His research focuses on multicultural education, teacher preparation, and urban schools in the global context.

William L. Heward is professor emeritus of special education at The Ohio State University. His research focuses on increasing the effectiveness of group instruction, improving the academic success of students with disabilities in general education classrooms, and promoting the generalization and maintenance of newly learned skills.

Bradley A. Levinson is professor of education at Indiana University, Bloomington, where he also has adjunct appointments in anthropology, Latino studies, and Latin American studies. He specializes in the study of youth, secondary education, citizenship education for democracy, and policy. His most recent books include *Beyond Critique: Exploring Critical Social Theories and Education* and *A Companion to the Anthropology of Education* (with Mica Pollock).

Charles H. Lippy is the LeRoy A. Martin Distinguished Professor of Religious Studies Emeritus at the University of Tennessee at Chattanooga. His interests in American religious life range widely, with an emphasis on current issues. He is co-editor of the four-volume *Encyclopedia of Religion in America*.

Cris Mayo is associate professor in gender and women's studies and educational policy studies at the University of Illinois at Urbana, Champaign. Her publications in queer studies and philosophy of education include *Disputing the Subject of Sex: Sexuality and Public School Controversies.*

Luanna H. Meyer is professor of education at Victoria University in Wellington, New Zealand. Her major research interests are inclusive education, student motivation, world-mindedness, culturally responsive educational practices, and restorative practices for challenging behavior. She has also published on higher education and the role of the professoriate.

Sonia Nieto is professor emerita of language, literacy, and culture, University of Massachusetts, Amherst. A Fellow of the American Educational Research Association and a Laureate of Kappa Delta Pi, she has written widely on multicultural education and the education of students of diverse backgrounds. She has received many awards for her research, advocacy, and service.

Hyun-Sook Park is professor of special education in the Connie L. Lurie College of Education at San Jose State University. Her major research interests are social relationships of students with disabilities, transition from school to work, global mindedness, special education for culturally and linguistically diverse students, and research methods.

Leslie H. Picca is associate professor of sociology at the University of Dayton. Her publications in racial relations include (with Joe Feagin) *Two-Faced Racism: Whites in the Backstage and Frontstage.* Her academic interests focus on how everyday interactions maintain structural inequalities.

Diane S. Pollard is professor emerita of educational psychology at the University of Wisconsin–Milwaukee. Her research and writing has focused on intersections of race and gender and factors underlying successful academic achievement in African American children.

David Sadker is professor emeritus at American University and adjunct professor at the University of Arizona. He is the co-author of seven books, including *Teachers, Schools, and Society* and *Still Failing at Fairness.* He invites readers interested in gender issues, scholarships, and teacher awards to visit www.sadker.org.

Catherine Savage (Ngāi Tahu) is the Kaihautū, chief executive, at Te Tapuae o Rehua, a partnership between shareholders of Christchurch Polytechnic Institute of Technology, Lincoln University, Otago Polytechnic, Te Rūnanga o Ngāi Tahu, the University of Canterbury, and the University of Otago, New Zealand.

Christine E. Sleeter is professor emerita of teacher education and multicultural education at California State University–Monterey Bay. Her research and writing focus on multicultural education and antiracist teacher education. Her most recent books include *Professional Development for Culturally-Responsive and Relationship-Based Pedagogy*, and *Teaching with Vision* (with Catherine Cornbleth).

Tom T. Stritikus is dean and professor in the College of Education at the University of Washington, Seattle. His research examines the political, social, and cultural contexts that shape the education of culturally and linguistically diverse students. His work has been published in leading education journals.

Ruth Thompson-Miller is assistant professor of sociology at the University of Dayton. Her research specializations are race and ethnicity, mental illness, and the elderly. She received the American Sociological Association (ASA)–National Institute of Mental Health-Minority Fellowship. She has articles in *Counseling Psychology, Sociology of Racial and Ethnic Relations*, and a chapter in *Globalization and America: Race, Human Rights, and Inequality,* edited by Angela J. Hattery, David Embrick, and Earl Smith.

Mary Kay Thompson Tetreault is provost emerita at Portland State University. Her most recent book (with Frances Maher) is *Privilege and Diversity in the Academy.* She is also the author (with Frances Maher) of *The Feminist Classroom* (2nd ed.).

Manka M. Varghese is associate professor of language, literacy, and culture at the University of Washington, Seattle. Her research specialization is linguistic minority education in the United States, with an emphasis on both teacher education and development and access to higher education for linguistic minorities.

Lois Weis is State University of New York Distinguished Professor of Sociology of Education at the University at Buffalo. Her research focuses on poor and working-class youth and young adults, and the complex role gender and race play in their lives in light of contemporary global dynamics. Her books include *The Way Class Works: Readings on School, Family and the Economy.*

Karen Zittleman has taught in elementary and middle schools and at American University. She is the coauthor of *Teachers, Schools, and Society* and *Still Failing at Fairness.* Her academic interests focus on educational equity, teacher preparation, and contemplative education.

Index